M000035066

Langenscheidt's
Pocket
Merriam-Webster

Rhyming
Dictionary

LANGENSCHEIDT

NEW YORK • BERLIN • MUNICH • VIENNA • ZURICH

Langenscheidt's
Pocket
Merriam-Webster

Rhyming
Dictionary

LANGENSCHEIDT

NEW YORK • BERLIN • MUNICH • VIENNA • ZURICH

PREFACE

Merriam-Webster's Rhyming Dictionary is a listing of words grouped according to the way they rhyme. All of the words are drawn from *Merriam-Webster's Collegiate Dictionary, Tenth Edition*, and decisions about what constitutes a rhyming group are based on pronunciations given in that dictionary. In selecting words for entry, the editors have focused on words that are most likely to be used in poetry; highly technical or otherwise obscure words are generally not included. However, some words that are restricted in their applications (such as slang words and words that carry a stigmatizing usage label or usage note in *Merriam-Webster's Collegiate Dictionary*) as well as words that are likely to be unfamiliar to many users have been included. Thus, not every word listed in this book will be appropriate in every context and *it is essential that the rhyming dictionary be used in conjunction with an adequate dictionary.*

The editors have assigned words to rhyming groups on the basis of pronunciations that are in standard and widespread use. However, many words have more than one standard pronunciation, and these variants often produce alternate rhyming sounds. Thus, some words may appear in more than one list, and not every word on every list will rhyme for every person.

Users of this book who are uncertain about any aspect of meaning, usage status, or pronunciation of any word listed here should consult the entry for that word in *Merriam-Webster's Collegiate Dictionary, Tenth Edition.*

The rhyming sound Words in this book are gathered into entries on the basis of their rhyming sound. The rhyming sound is the terminal part of the word — from the vowel sound in the last stressed syllable to the end of the word. In this book, the rhyming sound may have one, two, or three syllables. One-syllable rhyming sounds are found in one-syllable words and in words in which primary or secondary stress falls on the final syllable. For example, **wide** \\'wīd\\, **appeal** \\ə-'pēl\\, **mongoose** \\'män-ˌgüs\\, and **undergrad** \\'ən-dər-ˌgrad\\ all have one-syllable rhyming sounds. For *wide*, the rhyming sound is \\īd\\, as in *bedside* and *qualified*. For *appeal*, it is \\ēl\\, as in *heal* and *cockatiel*. For *mongoose*, it is \\üs\\, as in *juice* and *introduce*. For *undergrad*, it is \\ad\\, as in *plaid* and *comrade*.

Two-syllable rhyming sounds are found in words in which the last syllable with primary or secondary stress is the next-to-last syllable in the word (often called the penultimate syllable or penult). For example, *cola* \\'kō-lə\\ and *remover* \\rē-'mü-vər\\ have two-syllable rhyming sounds. For *cola*, the rhyming sound is \\ō-lə\\, as in *granola* and *Gorgonzola*. For *remover*, it is \\ü-vər\\, as in *louver* and *maneuver*.

Three-syllable rhyming sounds are found in words in which the syllable before the penult (the antepenultimate syllable or antepenult) carries primary or secondary stress. For example, *mutable* \\'müt-ə-bəl\\ and *frivolity* \\friv-'äl-ət-ē\\ have three-syllable rhyming sounds. For *mutable*, it is \\üt-ə-bəl\\, as in *suitable* and *unscrutable*. For *frivolity*, it is \\äl-ət-ē\\, as in *jollity* and *equality*.

Using this book *Merriam-Webster's Rhyming Dictionary* is designed to be used with a minimum of instruction. In order to use this book successfully, the reader needs to understand the following four points:

1. All of the words in this book are gathered into main entries on the basis of their rhyming sounds.
2. All of the main entries are arranged according to the way the rhyming sound is most often spelled, represented by the boldface form that begins each main entry.
3. Alternate spellings of the rhyming sound are entered as cross-reference entries that direct the user to the appropriate main entry. The alternate spelling is the boldface form that begins each cross-reference entry.
4. All main entries and cross-reference entries, whether for one-, two-, or three-syllable rhyming sounds, are alphabetized by the boldface form in a single sequence.

To find a rhyme for a given word, then, you need to know only the spelling of the word and its rhyming sound. If, for instance, you wanted to find a word to rhyme with *deep*, you would look up *eep*, because that is the way the rhyming sound is spelled. When you look up *eep*, you will find the following entry:

> **eep** \\ēp\\ beep, bleep, cheap, cheep,
> clepe, creep, deep, heap, jeep,
> Jeep, keep, . . .

If the word you wanted to find a rhyme for had been *cheap*, you might have looked up *eap*, because that is how the rhyming sound is spelled in that word. If you had done so, you would have found the following cross-reference entry:

> **eap** \ēp\ see EEP

In some cases (explained in more detail later in this Preface), you may find two entries for the same spelling. If, for instance, you wanted a rhyme for *give*, you would have found the following entries at *ive*:

> **¹ive** \īv\ chive, dive, drive, five,
>   gyve, hive, I've, jive, . . .
> **²ive** \iv\ give, live, sheave, shiv,
>   sieve, spiv, forgive, . . .
> **³ive** \ēv\ see ¹EAVE

In cases like this, you would look at the pronunciation given in the entry. The rhyming sound in *give* is \iv\, and the pronunciation given at *²ive* is \iv\; therefore the entry *²ive* is the appropriate one.

The following sections of this Preface discuss in detail the major features of this book. A careful reading of these sections will ensure that the user gets the maximum benefit from this book.

Main entries   Main entries consist of three principal elements: an entry form, a pronunciation, and a list of words that rhyme:

> **arten** \ärt-ᵊn\ Barton, carton,
>   hearten, marten, martin, Martin,
>   smarten, Spartan, tartan, baum
>   marten, dishearten, Dumbarton,
>   freemartin, Saint Martin, Sint
>   Maarten, kindergarten

The main entry form in this entry is **arten**. It represents the way the rhyming sound is most often spelled. When two or more spellings are used with virtually equal frequency, the editors have chosen one arbitrarily to be the main entry form.

The rhyming sound itself is \ärt-ᵊn\, as shown in pronunciation symbols which appear within reversed virgules following the entry word. These symbols are listed and explained beginning on page xii. The pronunciations include no stress marks; the reader is meant to understand that the first syllable in the pronunciation is the last stressed syllable in the word. The pronunciation is given for identification purposes only; that is, it is meant to help the user confirm that the entry includes words with the desired rhyming sound. Each entry includes only one pronunciation even though there may be more than one way to pronounce the main entry form. Users who wish to find alternate pronunciations of a word in the list can consult the entry for that word in *Merriam-Webster's Collegiate Dictionary, Tenth Edition*. Following the pronunciation is the list of words that share the rhyming sound. The words are arranged by the number of syllables: the words with the fewest syllables are listed first, followed by groups of words with successively more syllables. Groups of words having the same number of syllables are arranged alphabetically. In the list in the sample entry shown above, *Barton, carton, hearten, marten, martin, Martin, smarten, Spartan*, and *tartan*, each with two syllables, come first. They are followed by *baum marten, dishearten, Dumbarton, freemartin, Saint Martin*, and *Sint Maarten*, with three syllables, and *kindergarten*, with four syllables.

Cross-reference entries   Main entries in this book are supplemented by cross-reference entries. Like main entries, cross-reference entries have an entry form and a pronunciation, but in place of a list of rhyming words, cross-reference entries provide a note that directs the user to a main entry where the list of rhyming words can be found. The following cross-reference entries, for instance, send the reader to the entry **arten** shown as a sample earlier:

> **artin** \ärt-ᵊn\ see ARTEN
> **aarten** \ärt-ᵊn\ see ARTEN

The entry form in a cross-reference entry represents an alternate spelling of the rhyming sound. In the sample entries above, the cross-reference entries **artin** and **aarten** have been included because the spellings -*artin* and -*aarten* are represented by the words *freemartin* and *Sint Maarten*, respectively. A cross-reference entry has been included for every alternate spelling of a rhyming sound that is represented by one or more words in the list at the main entry.

The pronunciation in the cross-reference entry matches the pronunciation shown at the main entry. The pronunciation is provided to help the user confirm that the cross-reference leads to the desired main entry, which is shown in small capital letters.

Identification numbers   In some cases, the same spelling has been used to represent more than one rhyme and therefore appears as a main entry form more than once.

> ^{1}**age** \äj\ dodge, lodge, raj, stodge, wodge, barrage, collage, corsage, dislodge, garage, hodgepodge, Karaj, massage, swaraj, camouflage, espionage, counterespionage
>
> ^{2}**age** \äzh\ plage, assuage, barrage, collage, corsage, dressage, frottage, gavage, lavage, massage, ménage, mirage, montage, moulage, . . .
>
> ^{3}**age** \āj\ age, cage, gage, Gage, gauge, mage, page, rage, sage, stage, swage, wage, assuage, backstage, birdcage, broad-gauge, downstage, . . .
>
> ^{4}**age** \āg\ see ^{1}EG
>
> ^{5}**age** \āzh\ see ^{1}EIGE
>
> ^{6}**age** \äg-ə\ see ^{1}AGA

In order to alert users whenever this situation occurs, identification numbers (in the form of small raised numerals that precede the entry form) have been added to all identically spelled entry forms. In order to assist readers in following cross-references, identification numbers also appear as part of the cross-reference when necessary.

> **aj** \äj\ see ^{1}AGE
>
> **itey** \īt-ē\ see ^{2}ITE

Inflected and derived forms   In order to save space, most regular inflected forms of words have not been included in the lists of rhymes. For example, there is no entry **eaks** to cover words such as *beaks, cheeks, cliques,* and *antiques.* In order to find a rhyme for these words, the user needs to go to the entry for the base word (in this case ^{1}**eak** \ēk\) and look for words on the list that will take the inflection that creates the desired rhyming sound.

    In some cases, both inflected and noninflected forms share the same rhyming sounds. For example, the uninflected forms *lox* and *paradox* share the same rhyming sound with the inflected forms *docks* and *socks*. In such cases, all of the uninflected forms are listed at the entry for the rhyming sound. At the end of the list, an italicized note appears telling the user that additional rhymes exist and giving directions to the entry where the base words can be found:

> **ox** \äks\ box, cox, fox, . . . —*also*
> *plurals and possessives of nouns*
> *and third person singular*
> *presents of verbs listed at* ¹OCK

Such notes have been added whenever two or more rhyming words could be created by adding inflections to the base words at the entry. If only one such rhyme could be created, it has simply been added to the list.

The particular inflected forms that are covered by these notes are plurals and possessives of nouns, comparatives and superlatives of adjectives, and past tense and third person singular present tense forms of verbs. In addition, present participles of verbs are covered at entries where the spelling of the entry form (after the *-ing* ending has been removed and any elided *e* or doubled consonant has been taken into account) does not match the spelling of the entry for the base words:

> **aining** \ā-niŋ\veining, complaining,
> sustaining, . . . —*also present*
> *participles of verbs listed at* ¹ANE

The treatment of words derived by adding a suffix to another word is somewhat similar. There is no entry for a rhyming sound if all of the words that would be on the list are regular derived words formed by adding a suffix to words drawn from another list. This treatment applies mostly to adverbs ending in *-ly*, nouns ending in *-ness* or *-ment*, and adjectives ending in *-less*. For instance, there is no entry for **arkly** \ärk-lē\, because the only words on the list would be *darkly* and *starkly*, and they are both formed by adding an *-ly* ending to the adjectives found at the entry **ark** \ärk\. If, however, any of the words on the list are not derived forms, a complete list is entered. There is an entry at ¹**eanly** \ēn-lē\, for instance, because among the adverbs at the entry there is also the adjective *queenly*; and, for the purposes of this book, adjectives ending in *-ly* are not treated as regular derived forms.

Editorial acknowledgements   Like all Merriam-Webster publications, *Merriam-Webster's Rhyming Dictionary* is the product of a collective effort. It draws much of its material from *Webster's Compact Rhyming Dictionary*, and as such, is based on work done by the editors of that book. The updating and expanding of that earlier work was done by Dr. Mary Wood Cornog. Copyediting of the text was the responsibility of Katherine Chapekis Sietsema, Assistant Editor. Cross-reference of the book was done by Adrienne M. Scholz, Editorial Assistant. Data-entry work was accomplished by Florence A. Fowler. Jennifer N. Cislo and Peter D. Haraty, both Assistant Editors, were responsible for proofreading. Robert D. Copeland, Senior Editor, managed the book through its typesetting stages. Overall project coordination was provided by John M. Morse, Vice President and Executive Editor.

PRONUNCIATION SYMBOLS

ə . . . . . . banana, collide, abut

ᵊ . . . . . . immediately preceding \l\ and \n\, as in battle, mitten, and eaten; immediately following \l\, \m\, \r\, as often in French table, prisme, titre

ər . . . . . further, merger, bird

a . . . . . . mat, map, mad, gag, snap, patch

ā . . . . . . day, fade, date, aorta, drape, cape

ä . . . . . bother, cot

aů . . . . . now, loud, out

b . . . . . baby, rib

ch . . . . . chin, nature \'nā-chər\ (actually, this sound is \t\ + \sh\)

d . . . . . did, adder

e . . . . . bet, bed, peck

ē . . . . . fee, easy

f . . . . . fifty, cuff

g . . . . . go, big, gift

h . . . . . hat, ahead

i . . . . . tip, banish, active

ī . . . . . site, side, buy, tripe (actually, this sound is \ä\ + \i\)

j . . . . . job, gem, edge, join, judge (actually, this sound is \d\ + \zh\)

k . . . . . kin, cook, ache

ḵ . . . . . German ich, Buch; one pronunciation of loch

l . . . . . lily, pool

m . . . . . murmur, dim, nymph

n . . . . . no, own

ⁿ . . . . . indicates that a preceding vowel or diphthong is pronounced with the nasal passages open, as in French un bon vin blanc \œⁿ-bōⁿ-vaⁿ-bläⁿ\

ŋ . . . . . sing \'siŋ\, singer \'siŋ-er\, finger \'fiŋ-ger\, ink \'iŋk\

ō . . . . . bone, know, beau

ȯ . . . . . . saw, all, gnaw, caught

ȯi . . . . . . coin, destroy

p . . . . . . pepper, lip

r . . . . . . red, car, rarity

s . . . . . . source, less

sh . . . . . . as in **sh**y, mi**ss**ion, ma**ch**ine, **sp**ecial (actually, this is a single sound, not two); with a hyphen between, two sounds as in *grasshopper* \'gras-ˌhäp-ər\

t . . . . . . tie, attack, late, latter

th . . . . . . as in **th**in, e**th**er (actually, this is a single sound, not two); with a hyphen between, two sounds as in *knighthood* \'nīt-ˌhu̇d\

<u>th</u> . . . . . . **th**en, ei**th**er, **th**is (actually, this is a single sound, not two)

ü . . . . . . rule, youth, union \'yün-yən\, few \'fyü\

u̇ . . . . . . pull, wood, book, curable \'kyu̇r-ə-bəl\, fury \'fyu̇(ə)r-ē\

v . . . . . . vivid, give

w . . . . . . we, away

y . . . . . . yard, young, cue \'kyü\, mute \'myüt\, union \'yün-yən\

z . . . . . . zone, raise

zh . . . . . . as in vi**s**ion, a**z**ure \'azhər\ (actually, this is a single sound, not two); with a hyphen between, two sounds as in *hogshead* \'hȯgz-ˌhed, 'hägz-\

\ . . . . . . slant line used in pairs to mark the beginning and end of a transcription: \'pen\

ˈ . . . . . . mark preceding a syllable with primary (strongest) stress: \'pen-mən-ˌship\

ˌ . . . . . . mark preceding a syllable with secondary (medium) stress: \'pen-mən-ˌship\

- . . . . . . mark of syllable division

a

¹a \ä\ aah, ah, baa, bah, blah, bra, dah, droit, fa, Fra, ha, Jah, Kwa, la, ma, na, nah, pa, pas, qua, Ra, rah, schwa, shah, ska, spa, à bas, aba, Accra, aha, Allah, Armagh, blah-blah, Borgia, bourgeois, brava, Casbah, chamois, Chang-sha, Chita, Degas, Dumas, éclat, fa la, faux pas, fellah, fetah, foie gras, gaga, galah, Galois, grandma, grandpa, ha-ha, halvah, Hama, hoo-ha, hoopla, Hsia, hurrah, huzzah, isba, Issa, Luda, Marat, markka, mudra, Oita, opah, orgeat, Oujda, quinoa, pai-hua, paisa, Para, pasha, patois, pooh-bah, prutah, pya, San'a, sangfroid, selah, Shema, sola, supra, tola, Tonghua, Ufa, Utah, Valois, Vaudois, viva, voilà, whoopla, abaca, Adana, agora, ahimsa, Akita, aloha, assignat, Aymara, baccarat, baklava, Bogotá, brouhaha, cervelat, Chippewa, coup d'état, Cumanà, Delacroix, entrechat, feria, habdalah, haftarah, haniwa, Kashiwa, koruna, Kostroma, la-di-da, Libera, ma-and-pa, Machida, Malinois, Mardi Gras, Modena, moussaka, Omaha, Oshawa, Ottawa, padishah, pakeha, panama, Panama, Paraná, parashah, pas de trois, persona, picara, pietà, podesta, polenta, polynya, port de bras, Quebecois, reseda, rufiyaa, Shangri-la, tempura, ulema, usquebaugh, Ahvenanmaa, Alma-Ata, ayatollah, Baha' Allah, caracara, con anima, coureur de bois, hispanidad, hors de combat, je ne sais quoi, Karaganda, ménage à trois, phenomena, res publica, sursum corda, tamandua, Alto Paraná, Haleakala, Katharevusa, Makhachkala, mousseline de soie, Nishinomiya, Isthmus of Panama, pâté de foie gras, Utsunomiya, Afars and the Isas, exempli gratia, Novaya Zemlya, Tokorozawa

²a \ā\ see ¹AY

³a \ȯ\ see ¹AW

¹aa \a\ see ³AH

²aa \ä\ see ¹A

aachen \ä-kən\ Aachen, lochan

aag \äg\ see ¹OG

¹aal \āl\ see AIL

²aal \ȯl\ see ALL

³aal \äl\ see ¹AL

aam \äm\ see ¹OM

aan \an\ see ⁵AN

¹aans \äns\ see ²ANCE

²aans \änz\ see ONZE

aard \ärd\ see ¹ARD

aari \är-ē\ see ¹ARI

aaron \ar-ən\ see ²ARON

aarten \ärt-ᵊn\ see ARTEN

aas \äs\ see ¹OS

aatz \ätz\ see OTS

¹ab \äb\ see ¹OB

²ab \äv\ see ²OLVE

³ab \ab\ blab, cab, crab, dab, drab, flab, gab, grab, jab, lab, Lab, Mab, nab, scab, slab, stab, tab, Ahab, Moab, baobab, Cantab, confab, prefab, Rajab, rehab, smack-dab, astrolabe, minilab, pedicab, taxicab

aba \äb-ə\ Kaaba, Labe, PABA, Saba, Sabah, casaba, djellaba, indaba, Ali Baba, Orizaba, Sorocaba, jaboticaba, Pico de Orizaba

abah \äb-ə\ see ABA

abala \ab-ə-lə\ cabala, cabbalah, parabola

abalist \ab-ə-ləst\ cabalist, diabolist

abard \ab-ərd\ clapboard, scabbard, tabard—*also pasts of verbs listed at ²ABBER*

abatis \ab-ət-əs\ abatis, habitus

abbalah \ab-ə-lə\ see ABALA

abbard \ab-ərd\ see ABARD

abbas \ab-əs\ see ABBESS

abbat \ab-ət\ see ABIT

¹abbed \ab-əd\ crabbed, rabid

²abbed \abd\ blabbed, stabbed—*also pasts of verbs listed at ³AB*

¹abber \äb-ər\ see OBBER

²abber \ab-ər\ blabber, clabber, crabber, dabber, drabber, gabber, grabber, jabber, slabber, stabber, yabber, rehabber, bonnyclabber

abbess \ab-əs\ abbess, Barabbas

abbet \ab-ət\ see ABIT

abbey \ab-ē\ see ABBY

¹abbie \äb-ē\ see OBBY

²abbie \ab-ē\ see ABBY

abbin \ab-ən\ see ABIN

abbit \ab-ət\ see ABIT

abbitry \ab-ə-trē\ see ABBITTRY

abbitt \ab-ət\ see ABIT

abbittry \ab-ə-trē\ Babbittry, rabbitry

¹abble \äb-əl\ bauble, bobble, cobble, gobble, hobble, Kabul, nobble, obol, squabble, wabble, wobble

²abble \ab-əl\ Babel, babble, brabble, dabble, drabble, gabble, grabble, habile, rabble, scrabble, bedabble, hardscrabble, psychobabble, technobabble

abblement \ab-əl-mənt\ babblement, rabblement

abbler \ab-lər\ babbler, dabbler, gabbler, grabbler, rabbler, scrabbler

abbly \ab-lē\ see ABLY

abbot \ab-ət\ see ABIT

abby \ab-ē\ abbey, Abby, blabby, cabbie, crabby, flabby, gabby, grabby, scabby, shabby, tabby, kohlrabi, Panjabi, Punjabi

¹abe \āb\ babe, mabe, nabe, astrolabe

²abe \ab\ see AB

³abe \ä-bə\ see ABA

abel \ā-bəl\ see ABLE

aben \äb-ən\ see OBIN

¹aber \ā-bər\ see ABOR

²**aber** \äb-ər\ see OBBER

abes \ā-bēz\ see ABIES

¹**abi** \äb-ē\ see OBBY

²**abi** \əb-ē\ see UBBY

³**abi** \ab-ē\ see ABBY

abia \ā-bē-ə\ Arabia, labia, Swabia, Bessarabia, Saudi Arabia

abian \ā-bē-ən\ Fabian, gabion, Arabian, Bessarabian

abid \ab-əd\ see ABBED

abies \ā-bēz\ rabies, scabies, tabes—*also plurals and possessives of nouns listed at* ABY

abile \ab-əl\ see ²ABBLE

abilis \äb-ə-ləs\ obelus, annus mirabilis

abin \ab-ən\ cabin, rabbin

abion \ā-bē-ən\ see ABIAN

abit \ab-ət\ abbot, babbitt, Babbitt, Cabot, habit, rabbet, rabbit, sabbat, cohabit, inhabit, jackrabbit

abitant \ab-ət-ənt\ habitant, cohabitant, inhabitant

abitus \ab-ət-əs\ see ABATIS

able \ā-bəl\ Abel, able, Babel, cable, fable, Froebel, gable, label, Mabel, sable, stable, table, disable, enable, instable, pin-table, retable, round table, timetable, turntable, unable, unstable, worktable

abled \ā-bəld\ fabled, gabled— *also pasts of verbs listed at* ABLE

ablis \ab-lē\ see ABLY

ably \ab-lē\ chablis, drably, scrabbly

abo \ab-ō\ abo, sabot

abola \ab-ə-lə\ see ABALA

abolist \ab-ə-ləst\ see ABALIST

abor \ā-bər\ caber, labor, neighbor, saber, tabor, belabor, von Weber, zeitgeber

aborer \ā-bər-ər\ laborer, taborer

¹**abot** \ab-ō\ see ABO

²**abot** \ab-ət\ see ABIT

abra \äb-rə\ sabra, Sabra, candelabra

abre \äb\ see ¹OB

abul \äb-əl\ see ¹ABBLE

abular \ab-yə-lər\ fabular, tabular, vocabular, acetabular

abulous \ab-yə-ləs\ fabulous, fantabulous

abulum \ab-yə-ləm\ pabulum, acetabulum, incunabulum

aby \ā-bē\ baby, gaby, maybe, crybaby, grandbaby

¹**ac** \ak\ see ²ACK

²**ac** \äk\ see ¹OCK

³**ac** \ȯ\ see ¹AW

¹**aca** \äk-ə\ see ¹AKA

²**aca** \ak-ə\ Dacca, Dhaka, paca, alpaca, malacca, Malacca, sifaka, portulaca, Strait of Malacca

acable \ak-ə-bəl\ see ACKABLE

acao \ō-kō\ see OCO

acas \ak-əs\ Bacchus, fracas, Gracchus, Caracas

¹**acca** \ak-ə\ see ACA

²**acca** \äk-ə\ see ¹AKA

accent \ak-sənt\ accent, relaxant

acchanal \ak-ən-ᵊl\ see ACONAL

acchic \ak-ik\ bacchic, halakic, stomachic, tribrachic, amphibrachic

acchus \ak-əs\ see ACAS

accid \as-əd\ see ACID

accio \ä-chē-ō\ bocaccio, Bocaccio, carpaccio

¹**acco** \ak-ə\ see ACA

²**acco** \ak-ō\ see ²AKO

acculus \ak-yə-ləs\ sacculus, miraculous

¹**ace** \ās\ ace, base, bass, brace, case, chase, dace, face, grace, Grace, lace, mace, Mace, pace, place, plaice, prase, race, res, space, Thrace, trace, vase, abase, airspace, Alsace, ambsace, apace, backspace, best-case, biface, birthplace, blackface, boldface, bookcase, bootlace, braincase, briefcase, crankcase, debase, deface, disgrace, displace, dogface, doughface, efface, embrace, emplace, encase, enchase, cn̄iace, erase, firebase, fireplace, footpace, footrace, foreface, gyrase, half-space, hard case, headspace, Jerez, lightface, manes, millrace, milreis, misplace, notecase, null-space, outface, outpace, outrace, paleface, postface, Quilmes, replace, retrace, scapegrace, shoelace, showcase, showplace, slipcase, smearcase, someplace, staircase, subbase, subspace, suitcase, surbase, tailrace, tenace, typeface, ukase, unbrace, unlace, watchcase, wheelbase, whey-face, whiteface, workplace, worst-case, about-face, aerospace, anyplace, boniface, bouillabaisse, carapace, commonplace, contrabass, double-space, everyplace, interface, interlace, kilobase, lemures, lowercase, marketplace, pillowcase, Samothrace, single-space, steeplechase, thoroughbass, thoroughbrace, triple-space, uppercase, rarae aves, beta-lactamase, in medias res, Aguascalientes, Goya y Lucientes, superoxide dismutase, litterae humaniores

²**ace** \ā-sē\ see ACY

³**ace** \äs\ see ¹OS

⁴**ace** \as\ see ³ASS

⁵**ace** \äch-ē\ see OTCHY

⁶**ace** \äs-ə\ see ¹ASA

aceable \ā-sə-bəl\ placeable, traceable, displaceable, effaceable, embraceable, erasable, persuasible, replaceable, ineffaceable, irreplaceable

acean \ā-shən\ see ¹ATION

aced \āst\ based, baste, chaste, faced, geest, haste, laced, mayest, paste, taste, waist, waste, bald-faced, barefaced, bold-faced, distaste, dough-faced, foretaste, impaste, lambaste, lightfaced, moonfaced, pie-faced, po-faced, posthaste, rad waste, self-paced, shamefaced, shirtwaist, snail-paced, slipcased, stone-faced, straight-faced, straitlaced, toothpaste, two-faced, unchaste, unplaced, white-faced, aftertaste, brazen-faced, double-faced, Janus-faced, hatchet-faced, pantywaist, poker-faced, thorough-paced—*also pasts of verbs listed at* ¹ACE

aceless \ā-sləs\ baseless, faceless, graceless, laceless, placeless, spaceless, traceless

aceman \ā-smən\ baseman, placeman, spaceman

acement \ā-smənt\ basement, casement, placement, abasement, debasement, defacement, displacement, effacement, embracement, emplacement, encasement, enlacement, misplacement, outplacement, replacement, self-effacement

acence \ās-°ns\ see ¹ASCENCE

acency \ās-°n-sē\ adjacency, complacency, subjacency

acent \ās-°nt\ nascent, adjacent, complacent, complaisant, subjacent, circumjacent, superjacent

aceor \ā-sər\ see ¹ACER

aceous \ā-shəs\ see ACIOUS

¹acer \ā-sər\ baser, bracer, chaser, facer, pacer, placer, racer, spacer, tracer, defacer, disgracer, effacer, embraceor, embracer, eraser, replacer, subchaser, steeplechaser

²acer \as-ər\ see ASSER

acery \ās-rē\ tracery, embracery

¹acet \ā-sət\ hic jacet, nonplacet

²acet \as-ət\ asset, facet, tacet, tacit

acewalking \ās-wȯ-kiŋ\ racewalking, spacewalking

acey \ā-sē\ see ACY

¹ach \äk̲\ Bach, saugh, Pesach,

pibroch, Offenbach, Mönchengladbach

²ach \äk\ see ¹OCK

³ach \ak\ see ²ACK

⁴ach \ach\ see ⁴ATCH

acha \äch-ə\ cha-cha, dacha, kwacha, viscacha

achary \ak-ə-r-ē\ see ²ACKERY

¹ache \āk\ see ¹AKE

²ache \ash\ see ³ASH

³ache \äch-ē\ see OTCHY

⁴ache \ach-ē\ see ATCHY

acheal \ā-kē-əl\ brachial, tracheal

ached \acht\ attached, detached, unattached, semidetached—*also pasts of verbs listed at* ⁴ATCH

acher \ā-kər\ see ¹AKER

achet \ach-ət\ see ATCHET

achi \äch-ē\ see OTCHY

achial \ā-kē-əl\ see ACHEAL

achian \ā-shən\ see ¹ATION

achic \ak-ik\ see ACCHIC

aching \ā-kiŋ\ see ¹AKING

¹achio \ash-ō\ mustachio, pistachio

²achio \ash-ē-ō\ mustachio, pistachio

achm \am\ see ²AM

achment \ach-mənt\ see ATCHMENT

achne \ak-nē\ see ACNE

acho \äch-ō\ muchacho, quebracho

achou \a-shü\ see ASHEW

achsen \äk-sən\ see OXEN

acht \ät\ see ¹OT

achtsman \ät-smən\ see OTSMAN

achy \ā-kē\ see AKY

acia \ā-shə\ Dacia, fascia,

geisha, acacia, Croatia,
Dalmatia, ex gratia, Galatia,
prima facie, exempli gratia

acial \ā-shəl\ facial, glacial,
racial, spatial, abbatial,
bifacial, biracial, englacial,
palatial, primatial, subglacial,
interfacial, interglacial,
interracial, multiracial

acian \ā-shən\ see ¹ATION

acias \ā-shəs\ see ACIOUS

acid \as-əd\ acid, Chasid,
flaccid, Hasid, jassid, placid,
Abbasid, antacid

acie \ā-shə\ see ACIA

acient \ā-shənt\ see ATIENT

¹acier \ā-shər\ see ¹ASURE

²acier \ā-zhər\ see AZIER

acile \as-əl\ see ²ASSEL

acing \ā-siŋ\ bracing, casing,
facing, lacing, racing,
spacing, tracing, catfacing,
effacing, all-embracing,
interfacing, letterspacing, self-
effacing

acious \ā-shəs\ gracious,
spacious, audacious,
bodacious, capacious,
ceraceous, cretaceous,
crustaceous, curvaceous,
edacious, fallacious,
flirtatious, fugacious,
herbaceous, Horatius,
Ignatius, loquacious,
mendacious, mordacious,
pomaceous, predaceous,
pugnacious, rapacious,
sagacious, salacious,
sebaceous, sequacious,
setaceous, tenacious,
testaceous, ungracious,
veracious, vexacious,

vinaceous, vivacious,
voracious, alliaceous,
arenaceous, argillaceous,
carbonaceous, contumacious,
coriaceous, disputatious,
efficacious, farinaceous,
foliaceous, ostentatious,
pectinaceous, perspicacious,
pertinacious, saponaceous,
scire facias, stercoraceous,
violaceous, inefficacious, fieri
facias

acis \as-ē\ see ASSY

acist \ā-səst\ see ASSIST

acit \as-ət\ see ²ACET

¹acity \as-tē\ see ²ASTY

²acity \as-ət-ē\ audacity,
capacity, fugacity, loquacity,
mendacity, opacity, rapacity,
sagacity, tenacity, veracity,
vivacity, voracity, efficacity,
incapacity, overcapacity

acive \ā-siv\ see ASIVE

¹ack \äk\ see ¹OCK

²ack \ak\ back, black, clack,
claque, crack, flack, flak,
hack, jack, Jack, knack, lac,
lack, mac, Mac, Mack, pack,
plaque, quack, rack, sac, Sac,
sack, sacque, shack, slack,
smack, snack, stack, tach,
tack, thwack, track, Wac,
whack, wrack, yak, aback,
ack-ack, alack, amtrac, Anzac,
Arak, attack, backpack,
backtrack, Balzac, bareback,
blackjack, blue-black,
bootblack, bootjack,
brushback, bushwhack,
buyback, callback, calpac,
champac, cheapjack,
Coalsack, coatrack, cognac,

come back, comeback, cookshack, cossack, crackback, crookback, cut back, cutback, Dayak, dieback, draw back, drawback, fall back, fallback, fastback, fast-track, fatback, feedback, finback, fireback, flapjack, flareback, flashback, fullback, gimcrack, graywacke, greenback, gripsack, guaiac, halfback, half-track, hardback, hardhack, hardtack, hatchback, hayrack, haystack, hijack, hogback, hold back, holdback, hopsack, horseback, humpback, hunchback, Iraq, jam-pack, jet-black, kayak, Kazak, Kazakh, kickback, knapsack, knickknack, Kodak, kulak, kyack, laid-back, lampblack, leaseback, linac, macaque, man jack, manpack, Micmac, mossback, muntjac, Muzak, notchback, offtrack, outback, packsack, payback, pitch-black, play back, playback, plow back, plowback, Polack, pullback, quillback, racetrack, ransack, rickrack, roll back, rollback, roorback, rucksack, runback, scatback, serac, set back, setback, shellac, shellback, shoeblack, shoepac, sidetrack, six-pack, skewback, skipjack, skyjack, slapjack, slotback, Slovak, smokejack, smokestack, snap back, snapback, snowpack, softback, sumac, swayback,

sweepback, swept-back, switchback, tailback, tarmac, thornback, throw back, throwback, thumbtack, ticktack, tieback, tie tack, tombac, touchback, tow sack, trictrac, tripack, unpack, Welsbach, wetback, whaleback, wingback, wisecrack, woolpack, woolsack, yashmak, Yurak, zwieback, almanac, amberjack, anorak, antiblack, applejack, Arawak, Armagnac, birdyback, bivouac, bric-a-brac, camelback, canvasback, cardiac, carryback, celiac, coeliac, cornerback, Cousin Jack, crackerjack, cul-de-sac, diamondback, fiddleback, fishyback, Frontenac, gunnysack, hackmatack, haversack, high-low-jack, huckaback, hydrocrack, iliac, ipecac, Kodiak, ladder-back, leatherback, lumberjack, maniac, medevac, minitrack, moneyback, nunatak, otomac, paperback, Pasternak, pickaback, piggyback, Pontiac, portapak, quarterback, razorback, retropack, running back, sandarac, Sarawak, Sazerac, silverback, single-track, Skaggerak, snapper-back, solonchak, steeplejack, stickleback, supplejack, Syriac, tamarack, tenure-track, theriac, tokamak, turtleback, umiak, zodiac, Adirondack,

ammoniac, amnesiac,
Aniakchak, biofeedback,
celeriac, counterattack,
demoniac, elegiac, insomniac,
Monterey Jack, paranoiac,
simoniac, tacamahac,
aphrodisiac, coprophiliac,
Dionysiac, dipsomaniac,
egomaniac, hemophiliac,
hypochondriac, intracardiac,
kleptomaniac, melancholiac,
monomaniac, mythomaniac,
necrophiliac, neophiliac,
nymphomaniac, pedophiliac,
pyromaniac, Rhodesian
Ridgeback, sacroiliac, sal
ammoniac, megalomaniac,
Cyrano de Bergerac

ackable \ak-ə-bəl\ packable,
placable, stackable,
implacable

ackage \ak-ij\ package,
trackage, prepackage,
repackage

ackal \ak-əl\ see ACKLE

acked \akt\ see ACT

acken \ak-ən\ blacken, bracken,
flacon, slacken, Arawakan

ackened \ak-ənd\ blackened—
also pasts of verbs listed at
ACKEN

acker \ak-ər\ backer, clacker,
cracker, hacker, jacker,
knacker, lacquer, packer,
sacker, slacker, smacker,
stacker, tacker, tracker,
whacker, attacker,
backpacker, bushwacker,
firecracker, hijacker, kayaker,
linebacker, nutcracker,
racetracker, ransacker,
safecracker, shellcracker,

skyjacker, unpacker,
wisecracker, simulacre,
counterattacker

ackeray \ak-ə-rē\ see ACKERY

ackerel \ak-rəl\ see ACRAL

ackery \ak-ə-rē\ flackery,
quackery, Thackeray,
Zachary, gimcrackery

acket \ak-ət\ bracket, jacket,
packet, placket, racket,
bluejacket, straitjacket,
yellowjacket

ackey \ak-ē\ see ACKY

ackguard \ag-ərd\ see AGGARD

ackie \ak-ē\ see ACKY

acking \ak-iŋ\ backing,
blacking, cracking, packing,
sacking, smacking, tracking,
whacking, bushwacking,
kayaking, linebacking,
meatpacking, nerve-racking,
nerve-wracking, safecracking,
skyjacking

ackish \ak-ish\ blackish,
brackish, quackish

ackle \ak-əl\ cackle, crackle,
grackle, hackle, jackal, macle,
rackle, shackle, spackle,
tackle, debacle, gang-tackle,
ramshackle, unshackle,
tabernacle

ackly \ak-lē\ blackly, crackly,
hackly, abstractly, compactly,
exactly, inexactly

ackman \ak-mən\ hackman,
packman, trackman

ackney \ak-nē\ see ACNE

ackneyed \ak-nēd\ see ACNED

acko \ak-ō\ see ²AKO

acksman \ak-smən\ see AXMAN

ackson \ak-sən\ see AXON

acky \ak-ē\ hackie, Jackie,

Jacky, khaki, lackey, Paki, tacky, wacky, ticky-tacky

¹acle \ik-əl\ see ICKLE

²acle \äk\ see ¹OCK

³acle \äk-əl\ see OCKLE

⁴acle \ak-əl\ see ACKLE

acne \ak-nē\ acne, hackney, Hackney, Arachne

acned \ak-nēd\ acned, hackneyed

aco \äk-ō\ see OCCO

¹acon \ā-kən\ see ¹AKEN

²acon \ak-ən\ see ACKEN

aconal \ak-ən-ᵊl\ bacchanal, diaconal, archidiaconal

¹acque \ak\ see ²ACK

²acque \äk\ see ¹OCK

acquer \ak-ər\ see ACKER

acques \äk\ see ¹OCK

acral \ak-rəl\ mackerel, sacral

¹acre \ā-kər\ see ¹AKER

²acre \ak-ər\ see ACKER

acrum \ak-rəm\ sacrum, simulacrum

act \akt\ act, backed, bract, cracked, fact, packed, pact, stacked, tact, tracked, tract, abstract, attract, coact, compact, contact, contract, crookbacked, detract, didact, diffract, distract, enact, entr'acte, epact, exact, extract, half-tracked, humpbacked, hunchbacked, impact, infract, intact, mossbacked, playact, protract, react, redact, refract, subtract, swaybacked, transact, unbacked, abreact, artifact, cataract, chain-react, counteract, cross-react, inexact, interact, overact, paperbacked, precontact, razor-backed, reenact, subcompact, subcontract, underact, vacuum-packed, ventifact, autodidact, matter-of-fact, overreact, semiabstract, underreact— *also pasts of verbs listed at* ²ACK

actable \ak-tə-bəl\ actable, tractable, abstractable, attractable, compactible, contractible, distractable, extractable, intractable

actance \ak-təns\ attractance, reactance

actant \ak-tənt\ attractant, reactant, surfactant, interactant

¹acte \äkt\ see OCKED

²acte \akt\ see ACT

acted \ak-təd\ fracted, abstracted, impacted—*also pasts of verbs listed at* ACT

acter \ak-tər\ see ACTOR

actery \ak-trē\ see ACTORY

actible \ak-tə-bəl\ see ACTABLE

actic \ak-tik\ lactic, tactic, atactic, climactic, didactic, galactic, syntactic, ataractic, chiropractic, parallactic, paratactic, prophylactic, anaphylactic, anticlimactic, autodidactic, extragalactic, intergalactic, intragalactic, stereotactic

actical \ak-ti-kəl\ practical, tactical, didactical, impractical, syntactical

actice \ak-təs\ cactus, practice, malpractice, cataractous

actics \ak-tiks\ tactics, didactics, syntactics,

phonotactics—*also plurals
and possessives of nouns
listed at* ACTIC

actile \ak-t⁰l\ dactyl, tactile,
contractile, protractile,
refractile, retractile,
polydactyl, pterodactyl

acting \ak-tiŋ\ acting, exacting,
self-acting—*also present
participles of verbs listed at*
ACT

action \ak-shən\ action, faction,
fraction, taction, traction,
abstraction, attraction, bolt-
action, coaction, compaction,
contraction, detraction,
diffraction, distraction,
exaction, extraction,
impaction, inaction,
infraction, olfaction,
protraction, reaction,
redaction, refraction,
retraction, subtraction,
transaction, benefaction,
counteraction, interaction,
liquefaction, malefaction,
overaction, petrifaction,
putrefaction, rarefaction,
retroaction, satisfaction,
single-action, stupefaction,
tumefaction, dissatisfaction,
photoreaction, self-satisfaction

actional \ak-shnəl\ factional,
fractional, tractional,
abstractional, contractional,
redactional, transactional,
interactional, rarefactional

actious \ak-shəs\ factious,
fractious

active \ak-tiv\ active, tractive,
abstractive, attractive,
coactive, contractive,

detractive, distractive,
extractive, impactive,
inactive, proactive, reactive,
refractive, subtractive,
bioactive, counteractive,
hyperactive, interactive,
overactive, psychoactive,
putrefactive, retroactive,
unattractive, radioactive

actly \ak-lē\ see ACKLY

actor \ak-tər\ actor, factor,
tractor, abstractor, attractor,
cofactor, compactor,
contractor, detractor, enactor,
exactor, extractor, g-factor,
impactor, infractor, protractor,
reactor, redactor, refractor,
retractor, subtracter,
transactor, benefactor,
chiropractor, malefactor,
subcontractor, bioreactor,
campylobacter

actory \ak-trē\ factory,
olfactory, phylactery,
refractory, calefactory,
manufactory, satisfactory,
dissatisfactory, unsatisfactory

actous \ak-təs\ see ACTICE

actress \ak-trəs\ actress,
benefactress

actual \ak-chəl\ actual, factual,
tactual, artifactual,
counterfactual

acture \ak-chər\ facture,
fracture, contracture,
manufacture, remanufacture

actus \ak-təs\ see ACTICE

actyl \ak-t⁰l\ see ACTILE

acular \ak-yə-lər\ macular,
oracular, spectacular,
spiracular, tentacular,
vernacular, tabernacular

aculate \ak-yə-lət\ maculate, ejaculate, immaculate

aculous \ak-yə-ləs\ see ACCULUS

acy \ā-sē\ Basie, lacy, pace, précis, racy, spacey, Stacey, Stacy, Tracey, Tracy, O'Casey, prima facie, Sulawesi, Veronese

acyl \as-əl\ see ²ASSEL

¹**ad** \ä\ see ¹A

²**ad** \äd\ see ¹OD

³**ad** \ad\ ad, add, bad, bade, brad, cad, chad, Chad, clad, dad, fad, gad, Gad, glad, grad, had, lad, mad, pad, plaid, rad, sad, scad, shad, tad, Thad, trad, Akkad, aoudad, Baghdad, Belgrade, Carlsbad, caudad, comrade, Conrad, crawdad, doodad, dorsad, dryad, dyad, egad, farad, footpad, forbade, gonad, granddad, heptad, hexad, horn-mad, ironclad, keypad, launchpad, maenad, Mashad, monad, naiad, nicad, nomad, notepad, pentad, pleiad, Sinbad, Sindbad, tetrad, thinclad, triad, triclad, Troad, armor-clad, Ashkhabad, cephalad, chiliad, ennead, Galahad, hebdomad, helipad, Hyderabad, laterad, mediad, oread, overplaid, Pythiad, undergrad, Volgograd, superadd, Trinidad, Allahabad, bromeliad, gesneriad, hamadryad, hispanidad, Kaliningrad, Kirovograd, olympiad, seminomad, Upanishad, Voroshilovgrad

¹**ada** \äd-ä\ Dada, Dhu'l-Qa'dah, aficionada

²**ada** \äd-ə\ nada, sadhe, tsade, Agada, Agade, Aggada, armada, cicada, gelada, Granada, Haggadah, Jumada, Nevada, panada, posada, tostada, autostrada, empanada, enchilada, Ensenada, Theravada, aficionada, Ponta Delgada, Vijayawada, cascara sagrada, Sierra Nevada

³**ada** \ād-ə\ Ada, Veda, armada, cicada, Grenada, alameda, Avellaneda

adable \ād-ə-bəl\ gradable, tradable, wadable, abradable, degradable, evadable, persuadable, biodegradable

a'dah \äd-ä\ see ¹ADA

adah \äd-ə\ see ²ADA

adal \ad-ᵊl\ see ADDLE

adam \ad-əm\ Adam, madam, macadam, tarmacadam

adams \ad-əmz\ Adams—*also possessives and plurals of nouns listed at* ADAM

¹**adan** \ad-n\ see ADDEN

²**adan** \äd-n\ see ODDEN

adant \ād-ᵊnt\ cadent, abradant

add \ad\ see ³AD

adden \ad-ᵊn\ gladden, madden, sadden, Aladdin, Ibadan

adder \ad-ər\ adder, bladder, gadder, ladder, madder, stepladder—*also comparatives of adjectives listed at* ³AD

addie \ad-ē\ see ADDY

addik \äd-ik\ see ODIC

addin \ad-ᵊn\ see ADDEN

adding \ad-iŋ\ cladding, madding, padding

¹addish \äd-ish\ see ODDISH

²addish \ad-ish\ see ADISH

addison \ad-ə-sən\ Addison, Madison

addle \ad-ᵊl\ addle, paddle, raddle, saddle, staddle, straddle, astraddle, foresaddle, gonadal, packsaddle, sidesaddle, skedaddle, unsaddle, fiddle-faddle

¹addler \äd-lər\ see ODDLER

²addler \ad-lər\ saddler, paddler, straddler, skedaddler

addo \ad-ō\ see ADOW

¹addock \ad-ik\ see ²ADIC

²addock \ad-ək\ haddock, paddock, shaddock

¹addy \ad-ē\ baddie, caddie, caddy, daddy, faddy, laddie, paddy, Paddy, forecaddie, granddaddy, finnan haddie

²addy \äd-ē\ see ¹ODY

¹ade \ād\ aid, aide, bade, blade, braid, cade, clade, fade, glade, grade, jade, lade, laid, made, maid, paid, raid, rayed, shade, spade, stade, staid, suede, they'd, trade, wade, Wade, abrade, afraid, aggrade, arcade, Band-Aid, barmaid, Belgrade, blockade, bondmaid, bridesmaid, brigade, brocade, cascade, Cascade, charade, clichéd, cockade, corrade, cross-trade, crusade, decade, degrade, dissuade, downgrade, evade, eyeshade, fair-trade, forebade, gainsaid, glissade, grenade,

handmade, handmaid, homemade, housemaid, inlaid, invade, limeade, low-grade, man-made, mermaid, milkmaid, navaid, nightshade, nursemaid, outlaid, parade, persuade, pervade, plain-laid, pomade, postpaid, repaid, sacheted, scalade, sea-maid, self-made, shroud-laid, souffléed, stockade, sunshade, switchblade, tirade, torsade, twayblade, twice-laid, unbraid, unlade, unmade, unpaid, upbraid, upgrade, waylaid, accolade, Adelaide, ambuscade, aquacade, autocade, balustrade, barricade, bastinade, cable-laid, cannonade, carronade, cavalcade, centigrade, chambermaid, chiffonade, colonnade, countertrade, custom-made, dairymaid, defilade, enfilade, escalade, escapade, esplanade, everglade, fusillade, gallopade, gasconade, grant-in-aid, hawser-laid, intergrade, lemonade, marinade, marmalade, masquerade, medicaid, motorcade, orangeade, orthograde, overtrade, palisade, pasquinade, plantigrade, promenade, ready-made, renegade, retrograde, serenade, stock-in-trade, tailor-made, underlaid, fanfaronade, harlequinade, overpersuade, rodomontade

²ade \äd\ see ¹OD

³**ade** \ad\ see ³AD

⁴**ade** \äd-ə\ see ²ADA

aded \ād-əd\ bladed, arcaded, brocaded, cockaded, colonnaded—*also pasts of verbs listed at* ¹ADE

adeless \ād-ləs\ fadeless, gradeless, shadeless

adely \ad-lē\ see ADLY

¹**aden** \ād-ᵊn\ Aden, laden, maiden, handmaiden, menhaden

²**aden** \äd-ən\ Aden, Wiesbaden

adent \ād-ᵊnt\ see ADANT

ader \ād-ər\ aider, braider, cheder, fader, grader, heder, nadir, raider, seder, shader, spader, trader, wader, blockader, crusader, dissuader, evader, persuader, masquerader, serenader

¹**ades** \ād-ēz\ ladies, Hades, quaker-ladies

²**ades** \ādz\ AIDS, Glades, Cascades, antitrades, Everglades, jack-of-all-trades—*also plurals and possessives of nouns and third singular presents of verbs listed at* ¹ADE

adge \aj\ badge, cadge, Madge, hajj

adger \aj-ər\ badger, cadger

adh \äd\ see ¹OD

¹**adhe** \äd-ə\ see ²ADA

²**adhe** \äd-ē\ see ¹ODY

adia \ād-ē-ə\ stadia, Acadia, arcadia, Arcadia, palladia

adial \ād-ē-əl\ radial, biradial, interstadial

adian \ād-ē-ən\ Acadian, Akkadian, arcadian, Arcadian,

Barbadian, Canadian, circadian, Orcadian, Palladian

adiant \ād-ē-ənt\ gradient, radiant

¹**adic** \ad-ik\ Vedic, tornadic

²**adic** \ad-ik\ Braddock, haddock, paddock, balladic, dyadic, faradic, haggadic, hexadic, maenadic, monadic, nomadic, sporadic, tetradic, tornadic, triadic, Iliadic, seminomadic

adie \ād-ē\ see ADY

adient \ād-ē-ənt\ see ADIANT

adies \ād-ēz\ see ¹ADES

ading \ād-iŋ\ braiding, lading, shading, arcading, degrading, downgrading, unfading

adir \ād-ər\ see ADER

adish \ad-ish\ caddish, faddish, radish, horseradish

adison \ad-ə-sən\ see ADDISON

¹**adist** \òd-əst\ broadest, sawdust, haggadist

²**adist** \äd-əst\ see ODEST

adium \ād-ē-əm\ radium, stadium, caladium, palladium, vanadium

adle \ād-ᵊl\ cradle, dreidel, ladle, wedel

adley \ad-lē\ see ADLY

adly \ad-lē\ badly, Bradley, gladly, madly, sadly, comradely

adness \ad-nəs\ badness, gladness, madness, sadness

¹**ado** \äd-ō\ bravado, camisado, carbonado, cruzado, Manado, mikado, passado, stoccado, strappado, avocado, bastinado, Colorado, Coronado, desperado, El

Dorado, hacendado,
amontillado, zapateado,
aficionado, incommunicado,
Llano Estacado

²**ado** \äd-ō\ dado, credo,
crusado, gambado, strappado,
teredo, tornado, barricado,
bastinado, camisado,
carbonado, desperado, El
Dorado, fettuccine Alfredo

ados \ā-dəs\ see ADUS

adow \ad-ō\ Caddo, shadow,
foreshadow, overshadow

adrate \äd-rət\ see ODERATE

adre \ad-rē\ see ADERY

adrian \ā-drē-ən\ Adrian,
Adrienne, Hadrian

adrienne \ā-drē-ən\ see ADRIAN

adt \ät\ see ¹OT

adual \aj-əl\ see AGILE

adus \ā-dəs\ Padus, Barbados—
*also possessives and plurals
of nouns listed at* ³ADA

ady \ād-ē\ cedi, glady, lady,
Sadie, shady, forelady,
landlady, milady, saleslady

¹**ae** \ā\ see ¹AY

²**ae** \ē\ see ¹EE

³**ae** \ī\ see ¹Y

aea \ē-ə\ see ¹IA

aean \ē-ən\ see ¹EAN

aedal \ēd-ᵊl\ see EEDLE

aedile \ēd-ᵊl\ see EEDLE

aedra \ē-drə\ see EDRA

¹**aegis** \ā-jəs\ see AGEOUS

²**aegis** \ē-jəs\ see EGIS

ael \āl\ see AIL

aeli \ā-lē\ see AILY

¹**aelic** \äl-ik\ see ¹OLIC

²**aelic** \al-ik\ see ALLIC

aemon \ē-mən\ see ¹EMON

aen \ä^n\ see ¹ANT

¹**aena** \ā-nä\ scena, faena

²**aena** \ē-nə\ see ²INA

¹**aenia** \ē-nē-ə\ see ¹ENIA

²**aenia** \ē-nyə\ see ²ENIA

aens \ä^{n}s\ see ¹ANCE

aeon \ē-ən\ see ¹EAN

aera \ir-ə\ see ²ERA

¹**aere** \er-ē\ see ¹ARY

²**aere** \ir-ē\ see EARY

¹**aerial** \er-ē-əl\ see ARIAL

²**aerial** \ir-ē-əl\ see ERIAL

¹**aerie** \ā-rē\ aerie, aery, faerie,
fairy

²**aerie** \er-ē\ see ¹ARY

³**aerie** \ir-ē\ see EARY

¹**aero** \er-ō\ see ²ERO

²**aero** \ar-ō\ see ²ARROW

¹**aeroe** \ar-ō\ see ²ARROW

²**aeroe** \er-ō\ see ²ERO

¹**aery** \ā-rē\ see ¹AERIE

²**aery** \er-ē\ see ¹ARY

aesar \ē-zər\ see ²EASER

aese \ā-zə\ see ²ESA

aestor \ē-stər\ see EASTER

aestus \es-təs\ see ESTIS

aet \āt\ see ¹ATE

aetor \ēt-ər\ see ¹EATER

aeum \ē-əm\ see ¹EUM

aeus \ē-əs\ see ¹EUS

af \af\ see APH

¹**afe** \āf\ chafe, safe, strafe, waif,
fail-safe, vouchsafe,
bathyscaphe

²**afe** \af\ see APH

afel \äf-əl\ offal, waffle, falafel,
pantofle, rijsttafel

afer \ā-fər\ chafer, safer, strafer,
wafer, cockchafer

aff \af\ see APH

affable \af-ə-bəl\ affable,
laughable

affe \af\ see APH

affed \aft\ see ²AFT

¹affer \äf-ər\ see ¹OFFER

²affer \af-ər\ chaffer, gaffer, Kaffir, kafir, Kafir, laugher, staffer, zaffer, paragrapher, polygrapher

affia \af-ē-ə\ raffia, agraphia

affic \af-ik\ see APHIC

affick \af-ik\ see APHIC

affir \af-ər\ see ²AFFER

affish \af-ish\ raffish, giraffish

¹affle \äf-əl\ see AFEL

²affle \af-əl\ baffle, raffle, snaffle

affron \af-rən\ saffron, Biafran

affy \af-ē\ chaffy, daffy, taffy

afic \af-ik\ see APHIC

afir \af-ər\ see ²AFFER

afran \af-rən\ see AFFRON

¹aft \äft\ toft, waft, gemeinschaft, gesellschaft— *also pasts of verbs listed at* ¹OFF

²aft \aft\ aft, craft, daft, draft, graft, haft, kraft, raft, shaft, Taft, waft, abaft, aircraft, campcraft, camshaft, crankshaft, engraft, handcraft, indraft, kingcraft, rockshaft, scoutcraft, seacraft, spacecraft, stagecraft, statecraft, updraft, witchcraft, woodcraft, countershaft, fore-and-aft, handicraft, Hovercraft, overdraft, rotorcraft, turboshaft, understaffed, watercraft, antiaircraft

aftage \af-tij\ graftage, waftage

after \af-tər\ after, dafter, drafter, grafter, laughter, rafter, hereafter, thereafter, fore-and-after, handicrafter, hereinafter, thereinafter

aftness \af-nəs\ daftness, Daphnis, halfness

aftsman \af-smən\ craftsman, draftsman, raftsman, handcraftsman, handicraftsman

afty \af-tē\ crafty, drafty

ag \ag\ bag, brag, crag, dag, drag, fag, flag, gag, hag, jag, lag, mag, nag, quag, rag, sag, scag, scrag, shag, slag, snag, sprag, stag, swag, tag, wag, YAG, zag, beanbag, black-flag, chin-wag, dirtbag, dishrag, fleabag, gasbag, greylag, handbag, hangtag, mailbag, postbag, ragbag, ragtag, ratbag, sandbag, schoolbag, scumbag, seabag, sleazebag, washrag, wigwag, windbag, workbag, zigzag, ballyrag, bullyrag, carpetbag, litterbag, lollygag, saddlebag, scalawag, tucker-bag

¹aga \äg-ə\ quagga, raga, saga, anlage, vorlage's gravenhage

²aga \ā-gə\ Vega, bodega, omega, rutabaga

³aga \eg-ə\ see ¹EGA

⁴aga \ȯ-gə\ see AUGA

agan \ā-gən\ see AGIN

¹agar \ā-gər\ Hagar, jaeger

²agar \äg-ər\ see ¹OGGER

³agar \əg-ər\ see ¹UGGER

agary \ag-ə-rē\ see AGGERY

agate \ag-ət\ see AGGOT

¹age \äj\ dodge, lodge, raj, stodge, wodge, barrage, collage, corsage, dislodge, garage, hodgepodge, Karaj, massage, swaraj, camouflage, espionage, counterespionage

²age \äzh\ plage, assuage, barrage, collage, corsage, dressage, frottage, gavage, lavage, massage, ménage, mirage, montage, moulage, portage, potage, treillage, triage, arbitrage, assemblage, badinage, bon voyage, bricolage, cabotage, camouflage, colportage, curettage, decoupage, empennage, enfleurage, entourage, fuselage, Hermitage, maquillage, persiflage, repechage, sabotage, vernissage, décolletage, espionage, photomontage, rite de passage, counterespionage

³age \āj\ age, cage, gage, Gage, gauge, mage, page, rage, sage, stage, swage, wage, assuage, backstage, birdcage, broad-gauge, downstage, encage, engage, enrage, forestage, front-page, greengage, offstage, onstage, Osage, outrage, presage, rampage, restage, soundstage, space-age, substage, teenage, uncage, upstage, disengage, multistage, ossifrage, overage, saxifrage, underage

⁴age \āg\ see ¹EG

⁵age \āzh\ see ¹EIGE

⁶age \äg-ə\ see ¹AGA

ageable \ā-jə-bəl\ gaugeable, stageable, unassuageable

aged \ājd\ aged, gauged, broad-gauged, engaged, unpaged,

middle-aged—*also pasts of verbs listed at* ³AGE

agel \ā-gəl\ bagel, Hegel, plagal, finagle, inveigle, wallydraigle

ageless \āj-ləs\ ageless, wageless

¹agen \ā-gən\ see AGIN

²agen \ä-gən\ see OGGIN

agenous \aj-ə-nəs\ see AGINOUS

ageous \ā-jəs\ aegis, ambagious, courageous, contagious, outrageous, rampageous, umbrageous, advantageous, disadvantageous

¹ager \ā-jər\ gauger, major, Major, pager, stager, wager, teenager, Canis Major, golden-ager, middle-ager, Ursa Major

²ager \äg-ər\ see ¹OGGER

agey \ā-jē\ see AGY

agga \äg-ə\ see ¹AGA

aggar \äg-ər\ see ¹OGGER

aggard \ag-ərd\ blackguard, haggard, laggard

agged \ag-əd\ cragged, jagged, ragged

agger \ag-ər\ bagger, bragger, dagger, dragger, gagger, jagger, lagger, nagger, sagger, stagger, swagger, wagger, foot dragger, four-bagger, one-bagger, sandbagger, three-bagger, two-bagger, carpetbagger

aggery \ag-ə-rē\ jaggery, staggery, vagary, waggery, carpetbaggery

aggie \ag-ē\ see ²AGGY

agging \ag-iŋ\ bagging,

flagging, lagging, nagging, brown bagging, foot-dragging, unflagging, carpetbagging

aggish \ag-ish\ haggish, waggish

aggle \ag-əl\ draggle, gaggle, haggle, raggle, straggle, waggle, bedraggle, raggle-taggle

aggly \ag-lē\ scraggly, straggly, waggly

aggot \ag-ət\ agate, faggot, fagot, maggot

¹aggy \äg-ē\ see ¹OGGY

²aggy \ag-ē\ aggie, baggy, braggy, craggy, draggy, jaggy, quaggy, ragi, scraggy, shaggy, snaggy, staggy, swaggy

agh \ä\ see ¹A

¹agi \äg-ē\ see ¹OGGY

²agi \ag-ē\ see ²AGGY

agian \ā-jən\ see AJUN

agic \aj-ik\ magic, tragic, choragic, pelagic

agile \aj-əl\ agile, fragile, gradual, vagile

agin \ā-gən\ fagin, pagan, Reagan, Copenhagen

aginal \aj-ən-ᵊl\ paginal, vaginal, imaginal

aging \ā-jiŋ\ aging, raging, staging, unaging

aginous \aj-ə-nəs\ collagenous, farraginous, plumbaginous, viraginous, cartilaginous, mucilaginous, oleaginous

agion \ā-jən\ see AJUN

agious \ā-jəs\ see AGEOUS

¹aglia \äl-yə\ see ¹AHLIA

²aglia \al-yə\ see ALUE

aglio \al-yō\ intaglio, seraglio

agm \am\ see ²AM

agma \ag-mə\ magma, syntagma

agman \ag-mən\ bagman, flagman, swagman

agna \än-yə\ see ¹ANIA

agne \ān\ see ¹ANE

agnes \ag-nəs\ Agnes, Albertas Magnus

agnum \ag-nəm\ magnum, sphagnum

agnus \ag-nəs\ see AGNES

¹ago \äg-ō\ lago, Chicago, farrago, galago, virago, Asiago, Calinago, Santiago, solidago

²ago \ā-gō\ dago, sago, farrago, galago, imago, lumbago, plumbago, sapsago, Tobago, virago, solidago, San Diego, Tierra del Fuego

ago \äŋ-gō\ see ONGO

agon \ag-ən\ dragon, flagon, lagan, wagon, bandwagon, jolt-wagon, Pendragon, snapdragon, battlewagon

agonal \ag-ən-ᵊl\ agonal, diagonal, heptagonal, hexagonal, octagonal, pentagonal, tetragonal

agora \ag-ə-rə\ agora, mandragora

agoras \ag-ə-rəs\ Protagoras, Pythagoras

agot \ag-ət\ see AGGOT

agrance \ā-grəns\ flagrance, fragrance

agrancy \ā-grən-sē\ flagrancy, fragrancy, vagrancy

agrant \ā-grənt\ flagrant, fragrant, vagrant, conflagrant

agster \ag-stər\ dragster,
  gagster
agua \äg-wə\ majagua,
  Managua, piragua,
  Aconcagua, Nicaragua
¹ague \āg\ see ¹EG
²ague \äg\ see ¹OG
aguey \eg-ē\ see EGGY
agus \ā-gəs\ magus, Tagus,
  choragus, Las Vegas, Simon
  Magus
agy \ā-jē\ cagey, Meiji, stagy
¹ah \ä\ see ¹A
²ah \ȯ\ see ¹AW
³ah \a\ baa, nah, pas de chat
aha \ä-hä\ Baja, Naha, Praha
aham \ā-əm\ see AHUM
ahd \äd\ see ¹OD
ahdi \äd-ē\ see ¹ODY
ahdom \äd-əm\ see ODOM
ahib \äb\ see ¹OB
ahl \äl\ see ¹AL
ahler \äl-ər\ see OLLAR
¹ahlia \äl-yə\ dahlia,
  passacaglia
²ahlia \al-yə\ see ALUE
³ahlia \ā-lē-ə\ see ¹ALIA
¹ahma \ä-mə\ see ³AMA
²ahma \äm-ə\ see ²AMA
³ahma \am-ə\ see ⁴AMA
¹ahman \äm-ən\ see OMMON
²ahman \am-ən\ see AMMON
ahn \än\ see ¹ON
ahms \ämz\ see ALMS
ahnda \än-də\ see ONDA
ahr \är\ see ³AR
ahru \ä-rü\ see ARU
aht \ät\ see ¹OT
ahua \ä-wə\ see ¹AWA
ahum \ā-əm\ Graham, mayhem,
  Nahum, Te Deum
ahveh \ä-vā\ see ¹AVE

¹ai \ā\ see ¹AY
²ai \ē\ see ¹EE
³ai \ī\ see ¹Y
⁴ai \ȯi\ see OY
⁵ai \ä-ē\ see AII
a'i \ī\ see ¹Y
¹aia \ā-ə\ Freya, Aglaia,
  cattleya, Hosea, Isaiah,
  Nouméa, Himalaya, Kilauea,
  Mauna Kea, Meghalaya
²aia \ī-ə\ see ¹IAH
¹aiad \ā-əd\ naiad, pleiad
²aiad \ī-əd\ see YAD
aiah \ā-ə\ see AIA
aias \ā-əs\ see ¹AIS
aic \ā-ik\ laic, alcaic, Altaic,
  archaic, Chaldaic, deltaic,
  Hebraic, Incaic, Judaic,
  Mishnaic, Mithraic, mosaic,
  Mosaic, prosaic, Romaic,
  spondaic, stanzaic, trochaic,
  voltaic, algebraic, Aramaic,
  Cyrenaic, faradaic, formulaic,
  pharisaic, Ptolemaic,
  apotropaic, paradisaic,
  photomosaic, Ural-Altaic
aica \ā-ə-k-ə\ Judaica,
  Cyrenaica
aical \ā-ə-kəl\ laical,
  pharisaical, paradisaical
aice \ās\ see ¹ACE
aich \āk̲\ see AIGH
aiche \esh\ see ¹ESH
aicos \ā-kəs\ see ECAS
¹aid \ād\ see ¹ADE
²aid \ed\ see ¹EAD
³aid \ad\ see ³AD
aida \ī-də\ see ²IDA
¹aide \ād\ see ¹ADE
²aide \īd-ē\ see IDAY
aiden \ād-ᵊn\ see ADEN
aider \ād-ər\ see ADER

aiding \ād-iŋ\ see ADING

aido \ī-dō\ see ¹IDO

aids \ādz\ see ²ADES

aiety \ā-ət-ē\ see AITY

aif \āf\ see ¹AFE

aig \āg\ see ¹EG

aiga \ī-gə\ taiga, Auriga

aigh \āk̲\ laigh, quaich

aight \āt\ see ¹ATE

aighten \āt-ᵊn\ see ¹ATEN

aightly \āt-lē\ see ¹ATELY

aign \ān\ see ¹ANE

aigne \ān\ see ¹ANE

aignment \ān-mənt\ see AINMENT

aii \ä-ē\ Hawaii, Tubuai

aiian \ä-yən\ zayin, Hawaiian

aijin \ī-jēn\ gaijin, hygiene

aik \īk\ see ²IKE

aika \ī-kə\ see ¹ICA

ail \āl\ ail, ale, baal, bail, bale, brail, braille, Braille, dale, Dale, drail, fail, flail, frail, Gael, gale, Gale, Gayle, grail, hail, hale, Hale, jail, kale, mail, male, nail, pail, pale, quail, Quayle, rail, sail, sale, scale, shale, snail, stale, swale, tael, tail, taille, tale, they'll, trail, vail, vale, veil, wail, wale, whale, Yale, abseil, airmail, assail, avail, bangtail, bewail, blackmail, blacktail, bobtail, broadscale, broadtail, bucktail, canaille, cattail, Clydesdale, coattail, cocktail, contrail, curtail, derail, detail, doornail, dovetail, downscale, ducktail, E-mail, entail, exhale, fantail, female, fishtail, folktale, foresail, foxtail, full-scale, Glendale, greenmail, guardrail, Hallel, handrail, hangnail, headsail, hightail, hobnail, horntail, horsetail, impale, inhale, Longueuil, lugsail, mainsail, oxtail, passfail, percale, pigtail, pintail, pinwale, portrayal, prevail, rattail, regale, resale, rescale, retail, ringtail, Sangreal, sei whale, shavetail, shirttail, skysail, small-scale, springtail, spritsail, staysail, surveil, swordtail, taffrail, telltale, thumbnail, timescale, toenail, topsail, travail, treenail, trysail, unnail, unveil, upscale, ventail, wagtail, wassail, whitetail, wholesale, abigail, Abigail, aventail, betrayal, bristletail, Chippendale, Corriedale, cottontail, countervail, defrayal, disentail, draggletail, farthingale, fingernail, flickertail, forestaysail, gaff-topsail, galingale, martingale, monorail, montadale, nightingale, Nightingale, overscale, ponytail, romeldale, scissortail, swallowtail, tattletale, tripletail, trundle-tail, yellowtail, self-betrayal, Fort Lauderdale, Oregon Trail, Santa Fe Trail\

ailable \ā-lə-bəl\ bailable, mailable, sailable, salable, scalable, assailable, available, resalable, unassailable

ailand \ī-lənd\ see IGHLAND

ailant \ā-lənt\ see ALANT

aile \ī-lē\ see YLY

ailed \āld\ mailed, nailed, sailed, scaled, tailed, veiled, detailed, engrailed, hobnailed, pigtailed, ring-tailed, unveiled, ponytailed, swallow-tailed—*also pasts of verbs listed at* AIL

ailer \ā-lər\ alar, bailer, bailor, baler, hailer, jailer, mailer, malar, nailer, sailer, sailor, scalar, scaler, tailer, tailor, Taylor, trailer, wailer, waler, whaler, blackmailer, curtailer, derailleur, detailer, entailer, inhaler, loud-hailer, retailer, wassailer, wholesaler, semitrailer—*also comparatives of adjectives listed at* AIL

ailey \ā-lē\ see AILY

ailful \āl-fəl\ see ALEFUL

ailie \ā-lē\ see AILY

ailiff \ā-ləf\ bailiff, caliph

ailing \ā-liŋ\ failing, grayling, mailing, paling, railing, sailing, tailing, veiling, whaling, boardsailing, prevailing, retailing, self-mailing, unfailing, parasailing, unavailing

¹aille \āl\ see AIL

²aille \ī\ see ¹Y

³aille \īl\ see ¹ILE

⁴aille \ä-yə\ see ¹AYA

ailles \ī\ see ¹Y

ailleur \ā-lər\ see AILER

ailment \āl-mənt\ ailment, bailment, curtailment, derailment, entailment, impalement

ailor \ā-lər\ see AILER

ails \ālz\ see ALES

ailsman \ālz-mən\ see ALESMAN

aily \ā-lē\ bailey, Bailey, bailie, daily, gaily, grayly, paly, scaly, shaley, wally, Bareilly, Bareli, Disraeli, Israeli, shillelagh, triticale, ukulele

aim \ām\ see ¹AME

aima \ī-mə\ see YMA

aimable \ā-mə-bəl\ see AMABLE

aiman \ā-mən\ see ¹AMEN

aimant \ā-mənt\ see AYMENT

aiment \ā-mənt\ see AYMENT

aimer \ā-mər\ blamer, claimer, framer, gamer, tamer, declaimer, defamer, disclaimer, exclaimer—*also comparatives of adjectives listed at* ¹AME

aimless \ām-ləs\ see AMELESS

¹ain \ā-ən\ see ¹AYAN

²ain \ān\ see ¹ANE

³ain \en\ see ¹EN

⁴ain \in\ see ¹IN

⁵ain \īn\ see ¹INE

⁶ain \aⁿ\ see ⁴IN

aina \ī-nə\ see ¹INA

ainable \ā-nə-bəl\ stainable, trainable, attainable, containable, explainable, maintainable, restrainable, retrainable, sustainable, inexplainable

ainder \ān-dər\ attainder, remainder

¹aine \ān\ see ¹ANE

²aine \en\ see ¹EN

ained \ānd\ brained, caned, craned, drained, grained, maned, pained, paned, stained, strained, vaned,

veined, birdbrained,
bloodstained, close-grained,
coarse-grained, crackbrained,
cross-grained, edge-grained,
harebrained, ingrained,
lamebrained, mad-brained,
membraned, restrained,
tearstained, unfeigned,
featherbrained, rattlebrained,
scatterbrained, self-contained,
unrestrained—*also pasts of
verbs listed at* ¹ANE

ainer \ā-nər\ caner, drainer,
feigner, gainer, planar, planer,
seiner, stainer, strainer,
trainer, veiner, campaigner,
complainer, container,
coplanar, cordwainer,
detainer, lupanar, maintainer,
ordainer, profaner, restrainer,
retainer, sustainer, Trakehner,
entertainer—*also
comparatives of adjectives
listed at* ¹ANE

ainful \ān-fəl\ baneful, gainful,
painful, disdainful

aininess \ā-nē-nəs\ braininess,
graininess

aining \ā-niŋ\ veining,
complaining, sustaining, self-
sustaining, uncomplaining—
*also present participles of
verbs listed at* ¹ANE

ainish \ā-nish\ brainish, Danish,
swainish

ainless \ān-ləs\ brainless,
painless, stainless

ainly \ān-lē\ mainly, plainly,
thegnly, vainly, humanely,
insanely, profanely, ungainly,
inhumanely

ainment \ān-mənt\ arraignment,

attainment, containment,
detainment, detrainment,
enchainment, entrainment,
ordainment, refrainment,
entertainment, preordainment,
self-containment

aino \ī-nō\ see ¹INO

ains \ānz\ Keynes, reins,
cremains, Great Plains, Mains
Plains, remains—*also plurals
and possessives of nouns and
third person singular presents
of verbs listed at* ¹ANE

ainsman \ānz-mən\ plainsman,
reinsman

aint \ānt\ ain't, faint, feint,
mayn't, paint, plaint, quaint,
saint, taint, 'tain't, acquaint,
attaint, bepaint, complaint,
constraint, distraint,
greasepaint, impaint, restraint,
unconstraint, unrestraint

ain't \ānt\ see AINT

ainting \ān-tiŋ\ underpainting—
*also present participles of
verbs listed at* AINT

aintly \ānt-lē\ faintly, quaintly,
saintly

ainy \ā-nē\ brainy, grainy,
meiny, rainy, veiny, zany,
Allegheny

ainz \īnz\ see ³INES

aipse \āps\ see APES

¹air \er\ see ⁴ARE

²air \ir\ see ¹IRE

aira \ī-rə\ see YRA

aird \erd\ see AIRED

¹aire \er\ see ⁴ARE

²aire \ir\ see ²EER

³aire \ir\ see ¹IRE

aired \ard\ caird, haired, laird,
merde, fair-haired, impaired,

long-haired, misleared, prepared, shorthaired, unpaired, wirehaired, multilayered, underprepared, unimpaired—*also pasts of verbs listed at* ⁴ARE

airer \er-ər\ *see* ³EARER

¹aires \er\ *see* ⁴ARE

²aires \ar-ēs\ *see* ²ARES

¹airess \er-əs\ *see* ERROUS

²airess \ar-əs\ *see* ²ARIS

airie \er-ē\ *see* ¹ARY

airing \ar-iŋ\ *see* ¹ARING

airish \er-ish\ *see* ¹ARISH

airist \er-əst\ *see* ARIST

airly \er-lē\ fairly, ferlie, rarely, squarely

airn \ern\ *see* ¹ERN

airo \ī-rō\ *see* ¹YRO

airs \erz\ theirs, backstairs, downstairs, nowheres, somewheres, upstairs, unawares—*also plurals and possessives of verbs listed at* ⁴ARE

¹airy \er-ē\ *see* ¹ARY

²airy \ā-rē\ *see* ¹AERIE

¹ais \ā-əs\ dais, Laius, Isaias, Menelaus

²ais \ā\ *see* ¹AY

¹aisal \ā-zəl\ *see* ²ASAL

²aisal \ī-səl\ *see* ¹ISAL

aisance \ās-ᵊns\ *see* ¹ASCENCE

aisant \ās-ᵊnt\ *see* ACENT

¹aise \āz\ *see* ¹AZE

²aise \ez\ *see* ¹AYS

aisement \āz-mənt\ *see* AZEMENT

¹aiser \ā-zər\ *see* AZER

²aiser \ī-zər\ *see* IZER

aisian \ā-zhən\ *see* ASION

aisin \āz-ᵊn\ *see* AZON

aising \ā-ziŋ\ braising, glazing, hazing, phrasing, appraising, fund-raising, hair-raising, hell-raising, house-raising, stargazing, trailblazing—*also present participles of verbs listed at* ¹AZE

aisle \īl\ *see* ¹ILE

aisley \āz-lē\ paisley, nasally

aisne \ān\ *see* ¹ANE

aisse \ās\ *see* ¹ACE

aisson \ās-ᵊn\ *see* ¹ASON

¹aist \ā-əst\ *see* AYEST

²aist \āst\ *see* ACED

³aist \äst\ *see* ¹OST

aisy \ā-zē\ *see* AZY

¹ait \ā\ *see* ¹AY

²ait \āt\ *see* ¹ATE

³ait \īt\ *see* ¹ITE

⁴ait \at\ *see* ⁵AT

aite \īt\ *see* ¹ITE

aited \āt-əd\ *see* ATED

aiten \āt-ᵊn\ *see* ATEN

aiter \āt-ər\ *see* ATOR

aith \āth\ eighth, faith, Faith, saithe, scathe, wraith, unfaith, interfaith

aithe \āth\ *see* AITH

aithless \āth-ləs\ faithless, natheless

aiti \āt-ē\ *see* ATY

aitian \ā-shən\ *see* ¹ATION

aiting \āt-iŋ\ *see* ATING

aitly \āt-lē\ *see* ¹ATELY

aitor \āt-ər\ *see* ATOR

aitorous \āt-ə-rəs\ *see* ATERESS

aitour \āt-ər\ *see* ATOR

aitress \ā-trəs\ traitress, waitress, aviatress

aity \ā-ət-ē\ deity, gaiety, laity, corporeity, spontaneity, synchroneity, diaphaneity, contemporaneity, extemporaneity

¹aius \ā-əs\ see ¹AIS

²aius \ī-əs\ see ¹IAS

aiva \ī-və\ see ¹IVA

aive \āv\ see ²AVE

aix \ā\ see ¹AY

aize \āz\ see ¹AZE

aj \äj\ see ¹AGE

¹aja \ä-hä\ see AHA

²aja \ī-ə\ see ¹IAH

ajan \ā-jən\ see AJUN

ajj \aj\ see ADGE

ajor \ā-jər\ see ¹AGER

ajos \ā-əs\ see ¹AIS

ajun \ā-jən\ Cajun, Trajan, contagion, Pelagian, reagin

¹ak \äk\ see ¹OCK

²ak \ak\ see ²ACK

¹aka \äk-ə\ Dacca, Dhaka, kaka, paca, taka, Lusaka, maraca, medaka, Oaxaca, Osaka, pataca, Mbandaka, saltimbocca, Toyonaka, Lake Titicaca, Higashiosaka

²aka \ak-ə\ see ²ACA

akable \ā-kə-bəl\ breakable, makable, shakable, mistakable, unslakable, unmistakable

¹akan \äk-ən\ see ²AKEN

²akan \ak-ən\ see ACKEN

akar \äk-ər\ see OCKER

¹ake \āk\ ache, bake, Blake, brake, break, cake, crake, drake, Drake, fake, flake, hake, jake, Jake, lake, make, quake, rake, sake, shake, sheikh, slake, snake, spake, stake, steak, strake, take, wake, Wake, awake, backache, beefcake, beefsteak, betake, blacksnake, canebrake, caretake, cheesecake, clambake, corncrake, cupcake, daybreak, earache, earthquake, firebreak, firedrake, forsake, friedcake, fruitcake, grubstake, handshake, headache, heartache, heartbreak, hoecake, hotcake, housebreak, intake, jailbreak, keepsake, lapstrake, mandrake, Marsquake, mistake, moonquake, muckrake, namesake, newsbreak, oatcake, opaque, outbreak, outtake, Pan-Cake, pancake, partake, remake, retake, rewake, seaquake, seedcake, sheldrake, shortcake, snowflake, sweepstake, toothache, unmake, uptake, windbreak, youthquake, bellyache, give-and-take, halterbreak, johnnycake, kittiwake, make-or-break, microquake, overtake, pat-a-cake, patty-cake, put-and-take, rattlesnake, stomachache, undertake, wapentake, wideawake, semiopaque

²ake \ak\ see ²ACK

³ake \äk-ē\ see OCKY

aked \ākt\ awaked, half-baked, ringstraked, sunbaked—*also pasts of verbs listed at* ¹AKE

akeless \ā-kləs\ brakeless, wakeless

¹aken \ā-kən\ bacon, Bacon, Macon, waken, shaken, taken, awaken, partaken, retaken, betaken, forsaken, mistaken, rewaken, well-taken, godforsaken, overtaken, undertaken

²**aken** \äk-ən\ kraken, Arawakan

¹**aker** \ā-kər\ acre, baker, breaker, faker, laker, maker, nacre, quaker, Quaker, raker, saker, shaker, taker, waker, backbreaker, bookmaker, caretaker, carmaker, comaker, dressmaker, drugmaker, earthshaker, filmmaker, glassmaker, groundbreaker, grubstaker, hatmaker, haymaker, heartbreaker, homemaker, housebreaker, icebreaker, jawbreaker, kingmaker, lawbreaker, lawmaker, mapmaker, matchmaker, mistaker, muckraker, mythmaker, noisemaker, oddsmaker, pacemaker, peacemaker, phrasemaker, platemaker, playmaker, printmaker, rainmaker, saltshaker, shirtmaker, shoemaker, snowmaker, stavesacre, steelmaker, strikebreaker, tastemaker, tiebreaker, toolmaker, trailbreaker, watchmaker, windbreaker, wiseacre, automaker, bellyacher, boilermaker, merrymaker, moneymaker, moviemaker, papermaker, simulacre, troublemaker, undertaker, cabinetmaker, holidaymaker, policymaker

²**aker** \ak-ər\ see ACKER

akery \ā-krē\ bakery, fakery

akes \āks\ jakes, cornflakes, Great Lakes, sweepstakes— *also plurals and possessives of nouns and third person singular presents of verbs listed at* ¹AKE

ake-up \ā-kəp\ break-up, breakup, make-up, makeup, shake-up, shakeup, take-up, wake-up

akey \ā-kē\ see AKY

¹**akh** \äk\ see ¹OCK

²**akh** \ak\ see ²ACK

¹**aki** \äk-ē\ see OCKY

²**aki** \ak-ē\ see ACKY

akian \äk-ē-ən\ see OCKIAN

akic \ak-ik\ see ACCHIC

¹**aking** \ā-kiŋ\ aching, making, waking, bookmaking, breathtaking, caretaking, dressmaking, earthshaking, filmmaking, glassmaking, groundbreaking, heartbreaking, housebreaking, lawbreaking, lawmaking, leave-taking, lovemaking, mapmaking, matchmaking, mythmaking, noisemaking, pacemaking, painstaking, pathbreaking, peacemaking, phrasemaking, printmaking, rainmaking, snowmaking, stocktaking, strikebreaking, toolmaking, watchmaking, world-shaking, merrymaking, moneymaking, moviemaking, papermaking, undertaking, cabinetmaking, policymaking

²**aking** \ak-iŋ\ see ACKING

¹**ako** \äk-ō\ see OCCO

²**ako** \ak-ō\ shako, wacko, tobacco

aku \äk-ü\ Bunraku, gagaku, nunchaku

akum \ä-kəm\ vade mecum, shalom aleichem

aky \ā-kē\ achy, braky, cakey, flaky, laky, shaky, snaky, headachy

¹al \äl\ Bâle, col, dahl, dal, doll, loll, moll, nal, pol, sol, Sol, Taal, toile, Algol, atoll, austral, Baikal, Bhopal, cabal, Chagall, chorale, grand mal, gun moll, hamal, jacal, mistral, narwhal, Natal, nopal, Pascal, petrol, quetzal, real, rial, riyal, Shawwal, tical, timbale, Transvaal, à cheval, aerosol, Emmenthal, falderal, femme fatale, folderol, Heyerdahl, parasol, pastoral, pastorale, protocol, Provençal, Simmental, urial, Wuppertal, entente cordiale, Neanderthal, procès-verbal, sublittoral, succès de scandale

²al \el\ see ¹EL

³al \ȯl\ see ALL

⁴al \al\ Al, gal, Hal, pal, rale, sal, Val, banal, cabal, canal, Chagall, chorale, copal, corral, decal, fal-lal, grand mal, joual, La Salle, Laval, locale, mescal, moral, morale, nopal, pall-mall, pascal, percale, quetzal, salal, serval, vinal, bacchanal, caracal, chaparral, femme fatale, musicale, pastoral, pastorale, pedocal, rationale, retinal, Seconal, Guadalcanal, kilopascal, sublittoral

¹ala \äl-ä\ à la, Allah, gala

²ala \äl-ə\ Allah, olla, tala, wallah, cabala, cantala, Chapala, chuckwalla, cicala, corolla, Douala, halala, Kampala, koala, Lingala, marsala, nyala, tambala, Tlaxcala, Valhalla, Walhalla, ayotollah, Guatemala, Gujranwala

³ala \ā-lə\ ala, gala, Venezuela, zarzuela

⁴ala \al-ə\ see ALLOW

alaam \ä-ləm\ Balaam, golem, Salem, Winston-Salem

alable \ā-lə-bəl\ see AILABLE

alace \al-əs\ see ²ALIS

alad \al-əd\ see ²ALID

alam \äl-əm\ see OLUMN

alamine \al-ə-mən\ allemande, calamine

alan \al-ən\ see ALLON

alance \al-əns\ balance, valance, imbalance, outbalance, unbalance, counterbalance, overbalance

alant \ā-lənt\ assailant, bivalent, covalent, exhalant, inhalant, multivalent, pentavalent, quadrivalent, surveillant, tetravalent, trivalent, univalent

alap \al-əp\ see ²ALLOP

alar \ā-lər\ see AILER

¹alary \al-rē\ see ALLERY

²alary \al-ə-rē\ calorie, gallery, Mallory, Malory, salary, Valerie, Valery, kilocalorie

alas \al-əs\ see ²ALIS

alate \al-ət\ see ²ALLET

¹alcon \ȯ-kən\ see ¹ALKIN

²alcon \al-kən\ falcon, gyrfalcon, grimalkin

¹ald \ȯld\ bald, scald, skald,

walled, close-hauled, keelhauled, kobold, piebald, ribald, skewbald, so-called, sunscald, Archibald, coveralled, overalled—*also pasts of verbs listed at* ALL

²**ald** \ȯlt\ see ALT

alder \ȯl-dər\ alder, balder, Balder

aldi \ȯl-dē\ Bartholdi, Vivaldi, Garibaldi

aldron \ȯl-drən\ aldron, caldron, cauldron, chaldron

¹**ale** \ā-lē\ see AILY

²**ale** \āl\ see AIL

³**ale** \äl\ see ¹AL

⁴**ale** \al\ see ⁴AL

⁵**ale** \äl-ē\ see ¹OLLY

⁶**ale** \al-ē\ see ⁴ALLY

alea \ā-lē-ə\ see ¹ALIA

¹**aleck** \el-ik\ see ²ELIC

²**aleck** \al-ik\ see ALLIC

aled \āld\ see AILED

aleful \āl-fəl\ baleful, wailful

¹**aleigh** \äl-ē\ see ¹OLLY

²**aleigh** \ȯl-ē\ see AWLY

alem \ā-ləm\ see ALAAM

alement \āl-mənt\ see AILMENT

alen \ä-lən\ see ⁵OLLEN

alence \ā-ləns\ valence, surveillance

alends \al-ənz\ see ALLANS

¹**alent** \al-ənt\ see ALLANT

²**alent** \ā-lənt\ see ALANT

alep \al-əp\ see ²ALLOP

¹**aler** \ā-lər\ see AILER

²**aler** \äl-ər\ see OLLAR

alerie \al-ə-re\ see ²ALARY

alery \al-ə-rē\ see ²ALARY

¹**ales** \ālz\ sales, Wales, entrails, Marseilles, New South Wales, Prince of Wales, cat-o'-nine-tails—*also plurals and possessives of nouns listed at* AIL

²**ales** \äl-əs\ see OLIS

alesman \ālz-mən\ bailsman, dalesman, salesman, talesman

alet \al-ət\ see ²ALLET

alette \al-ət\ see ²ALLET

aley \ā-lē\ see AILY

alf \af\ see APH

alfa \al-fə\ see ALPHA

alfness \af-nəs\ see AFTNESS

algia \al-jə\ neuralgia, nostalgia

¹**ali** \äl-ē\ see ¹OLLY

²**ali** \al-ē\ see ⁴ALLY

³**ali** \ȯ-lē\ see AWLY

⁴**ali** \ā-lē\ see AILY

¹**alia** \ā-lē-ə\ dahlia, Australia, azalea, battalia, realia, regalia, vedalia, Westphalia, bacchanalia, genitalia, glossolalia, inter alia, Lupercalia, marginalia, Orientalia, paraphernalia, penetralia, saturnalia

²**alia** \al-yə\ dahlia, battalia, et alia, passacaglia

¹**alian** \ā-lē-ən\ alien, Australian, Daedalian, Deucalion, Hegelian, mammalian, Pygmalion, Uralian, bacchanalian, Lupercalian, saturnalian, Episcopalian, sesquipedalian, tatterdemalion

²**alian** \al-yən\ see ALLION

alic \al-ik\ see ALLIC

alice \al-əs\ see ²ALIS

¹**alid** \äl-əd\ see OLID

²**alid** \al-əd\ ballad, pallid, salad, valid, invalid

alie \al-yə\ see ¹AHLIA

alien \ā-lē-ən\ see ¹ALIAN
aling \ā-liŋ\ see AILING
alinist \äl-ə-nəst\ see OLONIST
alinn \al-ən\ see ALLON
¹alion \ā-lē-ən\ see ¹ALIAN
²alion \al-yən\ see ALLION
aliph \ā-ləf\ see AILIFF
¹alis \ā-ləs\ AYLESS
²alis \al-əs\ Alice, balas,
  callous, callus, chalice,
  Dallas, gallus, malice, palace,
  Pallas, phallus, talus, thallous,
  thallus, oxalis, digitalis,
  hemerocallis, aurora borealis,
  Corona Borealis
alist \al-əst\ ballast, callused,
  gallused, cabalist, sodalist
¹ality \äl-ət-ē\ jollity, polity,
  quality, equality, frivolity,
  coequality, inequality
²ality \al-ət-ē\ anality, banality,
  brutality, carnality, causality,
  centrality, duality, extrality,
  fatality, feudality, finality,
  formality, frontality, frugality,
  legality, locality, mentality,
  modality, morality, mortality,
  nasality, natality, neutrality,
  nodality, orality, plurality,
  primality, rascality, reality,
  regality, rurality, sodality,
  tonality, totality, venality,
  vitality, vocality, abnormality,
  actuality, amorality,
  animality, atonality, axiality,
  bestiality, bimodality,
  bipedality, cardinality,
  classicality, coevality,
  comicality, commonality,
  communality, conjugality,
  cordiality, corporality,
  criminality, criticality,

ethicality, externality,
factuality, farcicality,
fictionality, functionality,
generality, geniality,
hospitality, ideality, illegality,
immorality, immortality,
informality, integrality,
internality, irreality, lexicality,
liberality, lineality, literality,
logicality, musicality,
mutuality, nationality,
notionality, nuptiality,
optimality, partiality,
personality, physicality,
principality, punctuality,
rationality, seasonality,
sexuality, sociality, spaciality,
speciality, subnormality,
technicality, temporality,
topicality, triviality,
unmorality, unreality,
verticality, virtuality,
whimsicality, asexuality,
atypicality, bisexuality,
collaterality, collegiality,
colloquiality, commerciality,
conceptuality, conditionality,
congeniality, connaturality,
conventionality, conviviality,
corporeality, dimensionality,
directionality, effectuality,
emotionality, ephemerality,
equivocality, essentiality,
ethereality, eventuality,
exceptionality, extensionality,
fantasticality, grammaticality,
illiberality, illogicality,
impersonality, impracticality,
inhospitality, instrumentality,
irrationality, materiality,
microtonality, monumentality,
municipality, originality,

orthogonality, pansexuality,
paranormality, polytonality,
potentiality, provinciality,
self-partiality, sentimentality,
spirituality, substantiality,
theatricality, transexuality,
triaxiality, universality,
veridicality, ambisexuality,
artificiality, circumstantiality,
confidentiality,
consequentiality,
constitutionality,
homosexuality,
hypersexuality, immateriality,
individuality, ineffectuality,
insubstantiality,
intellectuality,
internationality, intersexuality,
paradoxicality,
psychosexuality,
referentiality, superficiality,
supranationality, territoriality,
tridimensionality, two-
dimensionality,
uncongeniality,
unconventionality,
ungrammaticality,
unisexuality, unsubstantiality,
exterritoriality,
heterosexuality,
inconsequentiality,
unconstitutionality,
unidimensionality,
extraterritoriality
alium \al-ē-əm\ see ALLIUM
alius \ā-lē-əs\ alius, Sibelius
alk \ȯk\ auk, balk, calk, caulk,
chalk, gawk, hawk, Koch,
Salk, Sauk, squawk, stalk,
talk, walk, Bartok, Black
Hawk, bemock, boardwalk,
cakewalk, catwalk, chalktalk,

cornstalk, crosswalk,
duckwalk, eyestalk, fast-talk,
goshawk, jaywalk, langue
d'oc, leafstalk, Mohawk,
nighthawk, Norfolk, outtalk,
ropewalk, shoptalk, sidewalk,
skywalk, sleepwalk, Suffolk,
sweet-talk, belle epoque,
catafalque, double-talk,
Swainson's hawk, tomahawk
alkan \ȯl-kən\ see ¹ALKIN
alker \ȯ-kər\ balker, caulker,
gawker, hawker, squawker,
stalker, walker, cakewalker,
deerstalker, floorwalker,
jayhawker, jaywalker,
nightwalker, ropewalker,
sleepwalker, spacewalker,
streetwalker, trackwalker,
double-talker
alkie \ȯ-kē\ balky, chalky,
gawky, gnocchi, pawky,
stalky, talkie, talky,
Milwaukee, Handie-Talkie,
walkie-talkie, Winnipesaukee
¹**alkin** \ȯ-kən\ Balkan, falcon,
malkin, grimalkin, gyrfalcon
²**alkin** \al-kən\ see ²ALCON
alking \ȯ-kiŋ\ caulking,
walking, racewalking,
spacewalking, streetwalking
alkland \ȯk-lənd\ see
AUCKLAND
alky \ȯ-kē\ see ALKIE
¹**all** \ȯl\ all, awl, ball, bawl,
brawl, call, caul, crawl, doll,
drawl, fall, Gall, Gaul, hall,
Hall, haul, kraal, mall, maul,
moll, pall, Paul, pawl, Saul,
scall, scrawl, shawl, small,
Sol, spall, sprawl, squall,
stall, tall, thrall, trawl, wall,

y'all, yauld, yawl, Algol,
ALGOL, appall, argol, air
ball, ashfall, at all, atoll,
AWOL, baseball, Baikal,
beanball, befall, Bengal, best-
ball, birdcall, blackball,
Bokmål, bookstall, boxhaul,
bradawl, broomball, catcall,
catchall, COBOL, cornball,
Cornwall, cure-all, curveball,
deadfall, de Gaulle, dewfall,
dodgeball, downfall,
downhaul, drywall, enthrall,
eyeball, fastball, fireball,
floodwall, football, footfall,
footstall, footwall, forestall,
forkball, four-ball, free-fall,
gadwall, goofball, googol,
grease ball, guildhall, hair
ball, handball, hardball,
headstall, heelball, highball,
holdall, icefall, install,
keelhaul, know-all, landfall,
Landsmål, line-haul, lowball,
meatball, menthol, Metol,
miscall, mothball, naphthol,
Nepal, nightfall, nutgall,
oddball, outfall, outhaul,
pitfall, plimsoll, pratfall, pub-
crawl, puffball, punchball,
pushball, rainfall, rainsquall,
recall, rial, Riksmål, riyal,
rockfall, rorqual, Saint Paul,
save-all, screwball, seawall,
short-haul, shortfall, sidewall,
sleazeball, slimeball,
snowball, snowfall, softball,
speedball, spitball, Stendhal,
stickball, stonewall, stoopball,
T-ball, tell-all, three-ball,
trackball, Tyrol, Walsall,
waterfall, what all, Whitehall,
whitewall, windfall, windgall,
withal, withdrawal, you-all,
aerosol, alcohol, barbital,
basketball, bucky ball,
butterball, buttonball,
cannonball, carryall,
caterwaul, cover-all, coverall,
Demerol, disenthrol, Donegal,
entresol, evenfall, free-for-all,
gasohol, girasole, Grand
Guignol, haute école, know-
it-all, knuckleball, Komsomol,
methanol, minié ball,
Montreal, Nembutal, overall,
overcall, overhaul, paddleball,
parasol, Parsifal, Pentothal,
protocol, racquetball, Seconal,
Senegal, superball, tattersall,
tetherball, therewithal,
timolol, volleyball,
wherewithal, cholesterol,
Costa del Sol, Mariupol,
Massif Central, Neanderthal,
Sevastopol, Transalpine Gaul,
Vincent de Paul, be-all and
end-all

²all \äl\ see ¹AL

³all \al\ see ⁴AL

¹alla \äl-ə\ see ²ALA

²alla \al-ə\ see ⁴ALLOW

allable \ȯ-lə-bəl\ callable,
  spallable

allace \äl-əs\ see OLIS

allacy \al-ə-sē\ fallacy, jalousie

allad \al-əd\ see ²ALID

allage \al-ə-jē\ see ²ALOGY

¹allah \äl-ä\ see ¹ALA

²allah \äl-ə\ see ²ALA

³allah \al-ə\ see ⁴ALLOW

allan \al-ən\ see ALLON

allans \al-ənz\ calends,
  Lallans—*also plurals and*

possessives of nouns listed at
ALLON

allant \al-ənt\ callant, gallant, talent, topgallant, fore-topgallant

allas \al-əs\ see ²ALIS

allasey \äl-ə-sē\ see OLICY

allast \al-əst\ see ALIST

¹alle \al\ see ⁴AL

²alle \al-ē\ see ⁴ALLY

³alle \äl-ē\ see OLLY

alled \old\ see ALD

allee \al-ē\ see ⁴ALLY

allemande \al-ə-mən\ see ALAMINE

¹allen \o-lən\ fallen, stollen, befallen, chapfallen, chopfallen, crestfallen, downfallen, tarpaulin, unfallen

²allen \al-ən\ see ALLON

¹aller \o-lər\ bawler, brawler, caller, drawler, faller, hauler, mauler, scrawler, squaller, trawler, fireballer, footballer, forestaller, installer, stonewaller, knuckleballer

²aller \al-ər\ caller, pallor, valor, high yaller

alles \ī-əs\ see ¹IAS

¹allet \äl-ət\ see OLLET

²allet \al-ət\ ballot, callet, mallet, palate, palette, pallet, sallet, shallot, valet

alley \al-ē\ see ⁴ALLY

alli \al-ē\ see ⁴ALLY

alliard \al-yərd\ galliard, halyard

allic \al-ik\ Gaelic, Gallic, malic, phallic, salic, Salic, thallic, cephalic, italic, mandalic, medallic, metallic, smart aleck, Uralic, Vandalic, vocalic, genitalic, intervallic, ithyphallic, nonmetallic, postvocalic, prevocalic, intervocalic

allid \al-əd\ see ²ALID

allie \al-ē\ see ⁴ALLY

alling \o-liŋ\ balling, calling, drawling, falling, galling, hauling, infalling, mauling, name-calling, Pauling, stalling

alinn \al-ən\ see ALLON

allion \al-yən\ scallion, stallion, battalion, Italian, medallion, rapscallion, tatterdemalion

¹allis \al-əs\ see ²ALIS

²allis \al-ē\ see ⁴ALLY

³allis \äl-əs\ see OLIS

allish \o-lish\ Gaulish, smallish, tallish

allit \ä-lət\ see OLLET

¹allith \äl-əs\ see OLIS

²allith \äl-ət\ see OLLET

allium \al-ē-əm\ allium, gallium, pallium, thallium, Valium

allment \ol-mənt\ enthrallment, forestallment, installment

allo \äl-ō\ see ¹OLLOW

allon \al-ən\ Alan, Allan, Allen, Allyn, gallon, lallan, Talinn, talon

¹allop \äl-əp\ see OLLOP

²allop \al-əp\ gallop, galop, jalap, salep, Salop, scallop, shallop, escallop

allor \al-ər\ see ²ALLER

¹allory \al-re\ see ALLERY

²allory \al-ə-rē\ see ²ALARY

allot \al-ət\ see ²ALLET

allous \al-əs\ see ²ALIS

¹allow \el-ō\ see ELLO

²**allow** \äl-ə\ see ²ALA

³**allow** \äl-ō\ see ¹OLLOW

⁴**allow** \al-ə\ Allah, callow, fallow, gala, Galla, hallow, sallow, shallow, tallow, cavalla, impala, unhallow, Valhalla

⁵**allow** \al-ō\ aloe, callow, fallow, hallow, mallow, sallow, shallow, tallow, unhallow

allowed \al-ōd\ hallowed, unhallowed

allows \al-ōz\ gallows, Allhallows—*also plurals and possessives of nouns listed at* ⁴ALLOW

alls \olz\ Angel Falls, Niagara Falls—*also possessives and plurals of nouns, third person singular presents of verbs listed at* ALL

allsy \ol-zē\ see ALSY

allus \al-əs\ see ²ALIS

allused \al-əst\ see ALIST

¹**ally** \ā-lē\ see AILY

²**ally** \äl-ē\ see ¹OLLY

³**ally** \o-lē\ see AWLY

⁴**ally** \al-ē\ alley, bally, challis, dally, galley, gally, mallee, pally, rally, sallie, sally, Sally, tally, valley, Aunt Sally, bialy, crevalle, Death Valley, finale, Nepali, tomalley, dillydally, Mexicali, shilly-shally, teocalli, Great Rift Valley

allyn \al-ən\ see ALLON

alm \äm\ see ¹OM

alma \al-mə\ Alma, halma

almar \äm-ər\ see ¹OMBER

almer \äm-ər\ see ¹OMBER

almily \äm-ə-lē\ see OMALY

almish \äm-ish\ see ¹AMISH

almist \äm-əst\ palmist, psalmist, Islamist

almody \äm-əd-ē\ see OMEDY

almon \am-ən\ see AMMON

almoner \äm-ə-nər\ see OMMONER

alms \ämz\ alms, Brahms, Psalms—*also plurals and possessives of nouns and third singular presents of verbs listed at* ¹OM

almy \äm-ē\ see ¹AMI

alo \äl-ō\ see ¹OLLOW

aloe \al-ō\ see ⁵ALLOW

¹**alogist** \äl-ə-jəst\ see OLOGIST

²**alogist** \al-ə-jəst\ analogist, dialogist, mammalogist, genealogist

¹**alogy** \äl-ə-jē\ see OLOGY

²**alogy** \al-ə-jē\ analogy, hypallage, mammalogy, tetralogy, mineralogy

alom \äl-əm\ see OLUMN

alon \al-ən\ see ALLON

alop \al-əp\ see ²ALLOP

¹**alor** \äl-ər\ see OLLAR

²**alor** \al-ər\ see ²ALLER

¹**alorie** \al-rē\ see ¹ALLERY

²**alorie** \al-ə-rē\ see ²ALARY

¹**alory** \al-rē\ see ALLERY

²**alory** \al-ə-rē\ see ²ALARY

alousie \al-ə-sē\ see ALLACY

alp \alp\ alp; salp, scalp

alpa \al-pə\ salpa, catalpa, Tegucigalpa

alpal \al-pəl\ palpal, scalpel

alpel \al-pəl\ see ALPAL

alpha \al-fə\ alpha, alfalfa

¹**alque** \ok\ see ALK

²**alque** \alk\ calque, talc, catafalque

als \älz\ see OLS

alsa \ȯl-sə\ balsa, salsa

alse \ȯls\ false, waltz

alsey \ȯl-zē\ see ALSY

alsy \ȯl-zē\ ballsy, Halsey, palsy

alt \ȯlt\ fault, gault, halt, malt, salt, smalt, vault, volt, Walt, asphalt, assault, basalt, cobalt, default, desalt, exalt, footfault, gestalt, Great Salt, Schwarzwald, stringhalt, double-fault, somersault, pepper-and-salt

alta \äl-tə\ Malta, Salta, Volta, Yalta

altar \ȯl-tər\ see ALTER

alter \ȯl-tər\ altar, alter, falter, halter, palter, Psalter, salter, vaulter, Walter, defaulter, desalter, exalter, Gibraltar, pole-vaulter

altery \ȯl-trē\ see ALTRY

¹**alti** \äl-tē\ Balti, difficulty

²**alti** \ȯl-tē\ see ALTY

altic \ȯl-tik\ Baltic, asphaltic, cobaltic, systaltic, peristaltic

alting \ȯl-tiŋ\ halting, salting, vaulting

altless \ȯlt-ləs\ faultless, saltless

alto \al-tō\ alto, contralto, rialto

alton \ȯlt-ᵊn\ Alton, dalton, Dalton, Walton

altry \ȯl-trē\ paltry, psaltery, psaltry

alty \ȯl-tē\ Balti, faulty, malty, salty, vaulty

altz \ȯls\ see ALSE

alu \äl-ü\ Yalu, Tuvalu

alue \al-yü\ value, devalue, disvalue, misvalue, revalue, transvalue, overvalue, undervalue

¹**alus** \ā-ləs\ see AYLESS

²**alus** \al-əs\ see ²ALIS

¹**alve** \äv\ see ²OLVE

²**alve** \alv\ salve, valve, bivalve, univalve, inequivalve

³**alve** \av\ calve, halve, have, salve

alver \al-vər\ salver, salvor, quacksalver

alvin \al-vən\ Alvin, Calvin

alvor \al-vər\ see ALVER

aly \al-ē\ see ⁴ALLY

alyard \al-yərd\ see ALLIARD

alysis \al-ə-səs\ analysis, dialysis, paralysis, cryptanalysis, metanalysis, self-analysis

¹**am** \äm\ see ¹OM

²**am** \am\ am, cam, cham, clam, cram, dam, damn, damned, drachm, dram, DRAM, flam, gam, Graham, gram, ham, Ham, jam, jamb, lam, lamb, Lamb, ma'am, Pam, pram, ram, RAM, Sam, SAM, scam, scram, sham, slam, swam, tam, tram, wham, yam, Annam, ashram, Assam, dirham, Edam, ngram, exam, flimflam, goddamn, grandam, iamb, logjam, madame, mailgram, milldam, nizam, Priam, program, quondam, tam-tam, thiram, trigram, whim-wham, ziram, Abraham, aerogram, Amsterdam, anagram, Birmingham, Boulder Dam, cablegram, centigram,

Christogram, chronogram, cofferdam, cryptogram, decagram, deprogram, diagram, diaphragm, dithyramb, epigram, fluid dram, hexagram, histogram, Hohokam, hologram, Hoover Dam, kilogram, logogram, mammogram, milligram, Minicam, monogram, nomogram, oriflamme, pentagram, phonogram, pictogram, reprogram, Rotterdam, scattergram, skiagram, Smithfield ham, sonogram, subprogram, Surinam, telegram, tetradrachm, thank-you-ma'am, Uncle Sam, ad nauseam, cardiogram, heliogram, ideogram, in personam, microprogram, New Amsterdam, Omar Khayyam, parallelogram

¹**ama** \äm-ə\ Brahma, comma, drama, Kama, lama, llama, mama, momma, squama, Rama, Bahama, pajama, Toyama, Atacama, cyclorama, Dalai Lama, diorama, docudrama, Fujiyama, Fukuyama, Matsuyama, melodrama, monodrama, Mount Mazama, Okayama, panorama, photodrama, psychodrama, Suriname, Wakayama, Yokohama, Fujinoyamia, Puna de Atacama

²**ama** \am-ə\ Brahma, drama, gamma, grama, mamma, da Gama, Manama, Miami,

pajama, Alabama, anadama, cyclorama, diorama, docudrama, melodrama, monodrama, panorama, photodrama, psychodrama

amable \ā-mə-bəl\ blamable, claimable, framable, nameable, tamable, irreclaimable

amah \äm-ä\ see ¹AMA

¹**aman** \ā-mən\ see ¹AMEN

²**aman** \äm-ən\ see OMMON

¹**amant** \ā-mənt\ see AYMENT

²**amant** \am-ənt\ see ²AMENT

amas \am-əs\ see AMICE

amash \äm-ish\ see ¹AMISH

amateur \am-ət-ər\ see AMETER

amatist \am-ət-əst\ dramatist, epigrammatist, melodramatist

amba \äm-bə\ gamba, mamba, samba, Zomba, Cochabamba, viola da gamba

¹**ambar** \äm-bər\ see ²OMBER

²**ambar** \am-bər\ amber, Amber, camber, sambar, timbre, liquidambar

ambe \am-bē\ see AMBY

ambeau \am-bō\ see AMBO

¹**amber** \am-bər\ see ²AMBAR

²**amber** \am-ər\ see AMMER

ambia \am-bē-ə\ Gambia, Zambia

ambit \am-bət\ ambit, gambit

¹**amble** \äm-bəl\ see ¹EMBLE

²**amble** \am-bəl\ amble, bramble, gamble, gambol, ramble, scramble, shamble, preamble, unscramble, skimble-skamble

ambler \am-blər\ ambler, gambler, rambler, scrambler, unscrambler

ambo \am-bō\ crambo,
jambeau, sambo, Ovambo

ambol \am-bəl\ see ²AMBLE

ambray \am-brē\ see AMBRY

ambry \am-brē\ ambry,
chambray

ambulant \am-byə-lənt\
ambulant, somnambulant

amby \am-bē\ crambe,
Dushanbe, namby-pamby

¹**ame** \ām\ aim, blame, came,
claim, dame, fame, flame,
frame, game, hame, kame,
lame, maim, name, same,
shame, tame, wame, A-frame,
acclaim, aflame, airframe,
became, byname, cross-claim,
declaim, defame, disclaim,
endgame, enframe, exclaim,
forename, freeze-frame,
grandame, inflame,
mainframe, misname,
nickname, place-name,
prename, proclaim, quitclaim,
reclaim, selfsame, surname,
counterclaim, overcame,
Niflheim

²**ame** \äm\ see ¹OM

³**ame** \am\ see ²AM

⁴**ame** \äm-ə\ see ¹AMA

ameable \ā-mə-bəl\ see
AMABLE

amed \āmd\ famed, named,
ashamed, forenamed,
unashamed—*also pasts of
verbs listed at* ¹AME

ameful \ām-fəl\ blameful,
shameful

amel \am-əl\ see AMMEL

ameless \ām-ləs\ aimless,
blameless, nameless,
shameless, tameless

amely \ām-lē\ gamely, lamely,
namely, tamely

¹**amen** \ā-mən\ bayman,
Bremen, caiman, Cayman,
Damon, drayman, flamen,
Haman, layman, shaman,
stamen, Yemen, examen,
gravamen, highwayman

²**amen** \äm-ən\ see OMMON

ameness \ām-nəs\ gameness,
lameness, sameness, tameness

¹**ament** \ā-mənt\ see AYMENT

²**ament** \am-ənt\ ament, clamant

amer \ā-mər\ see AIMER

ames \āmz\ James—*also
possessives and plurals of
nouns, third person singular
presents of verbs listed at*
¹AME

ameter \am-ət-ər\ amateur,
decameter, diameter,
heptameter, hexameter,
octameter, parameter,
pentameter, tetrameter

¹**amfer** \am-pər\ see ²AMPER

²**amfer** \am-fər\ camphor,
chamfer

¹**ami** \äm-ē\ balmy, commie,
mommy, palmy, pommy,
qualmy, swami, Tommy,
gourami, pastrami, Sagami,
salami, tatami, tsunami,
origami

²**ami** \am-ə\ see ⁴AMA

³**ami** \am-ē\ see AMMY

amia \ā-mē-ə\ lamia, zamia,
Mesopotamia

¹**amic** \ō-mik\ see ²OMIC

²**amic** \am-ik\ gamic, Adamic,
agamic, balsamic, ceramic,
dynamic, adynamic,
cleistogamic, cryptogrammic,

cycloramic, dioramic, exogamic, panoramic, phonogrammic, polygamic, aerodynamic, biodynamic, hydrodynamic, hypothalamic, ideogramic, thermodynamic, magnetodynamic

amice \am-əs\ amice, camas, chlamys, Lammas

amics \äm-iks\ see OMICS

¹**amie** \ā-mē\ Amy, Jamie, Mamie, ramie, cockamamie, cockamamy

²**amie** \am-ē\ see AMMY

¹**amil** \äm-əl\ see ¹OMMEL

²**amil** \am-əl\ see AMMEL

amily \am-lē\ family, profamily, stepfamily

amin \am-ən\ see AMMON

amina \am-ə-nə\ lamina, stamina

aminal \am-ən-ᵊl\ laminal, foraminal

aminant \am-ə-nənt\ contaminant, examinant

aminar \am-ə-nər\ see ²AMINER

amine \am-ən\ see AMMON

¹**aminer** \äm-ə-nər\ see OMMONER

²**aminer** \am-ə-nər\ laminar, gewurztraminer

aming \ā-miŋ\ flaming, framing, gaming

¹**amish** \äm-ish\ Amish, qualmish, quamash, schoolmarmish

²**amish** \am-ish\ Amish, famish

amist \äm-əst\ see ALMIST

amity \am-ət-ē\ amity, calamity

amlet \am-lət\ camlet, hamlet, Hamlet, samlet

amlets \am-ləts\ Tower

Hamlets—*also possessives and plurals of nouns listed at* AMLET

amma \am-ə\ see ⁴AMA

ammable \am-ə-bəl\ flammable, programmable, diagrammable

ammal \am-əl\ see AMMEL

ammany \am-ə-nē\ see AMMONY

ammar \am-ər\ see AMMER

ammas \am-əs\ see AMICE

ammatist \am-ət-əst\ see AMATIST

amme \am\ see ²AM

ammel \am-əl\ camel, mammal, stammel, Tamil, trammel, enamel

ammer \am-ər\ clamber, clammer, clamor, clamour, crammer, dammar, gammer, glamour, grammar, hammer, jammer, lamber, rammer, shammer, slammer, stammer, yammer, clawhammer, enamor, flimflammer, jackhammer, programmer, sledgehammer, trip-hammer, windjammer, katzenjammer, monogrammer, ninnyhammer, yellowhammer

ammes \äm-əs\ see OMISE

ammie \am-ē\ see AMMY

ammies \am-ēz\ jammies—*also possessives and plurals of nouns listed at* AMMY

amming \am-iŋ\ damning, programming

ammock \am-ək\ drammock, hammock, mammock

ammon \am-ən\ Brahman, famine, gamin, gammon,

mammon, salmon,
backgammon, examine, cross-
examine

ammony \am-ə-nē\ scammony,
Tammany

ammy \am-ē\ chamois,
clammy, gammy, Grammy,
hammy, mammy, ramie,
Sammie, Sammy, shammy,
whammy, Miami

amn \am\ see ²AM

amned \am\ see ²AM

amning \am-iŋ\ see AMMING

amois \am-ē\ see AMMY

¹**amon** \ā-mən\ see ¹AMEN

²**amon** \äm-ən\ see OMMON

amor \am-ər\ see AMMER

amorous \am-rəs\ amorous,
clamorous, glamorous

amos \ā-məs\ see AMOUS

amour \am-ər\ see AMMER

amous \ā-məs\ Amos, famous,
shamus, squamous, biramous,
mandamus, ignoramus,
Nostradamus

¹**amp** \ämp\ see ¹OMP

²**amp** \äⁿ\ see ¹ANT

³**amp** \amp\ amp, camp, champ,
clamp, cramp, damp, gamp,
gramp, guimpe, lamp, ramp,
samp, scamp, stamp, tamp,
tramp, vamp, blackdamp, C-
clamp, chokedamp, decamp,
encamp, firedamp, headlamp,
off-ramp, on-ramp, preamp,
revamp, sunlamp, unclamp,
afterdamp, aide-de-camp,
minicamp

¹**ampean** \äm-pē-ən\ pampean,
tampion

²**ampean** \am-pē-ən\ see
²AMPION

¹**amper** \äm-pər\ see OMPER

²**amper** \am-pər\ camper,
chamfer, damper, hamper,
pamper, scamper, stamper,
tamper

amphor \am-fər\ see ²AMFER

¹**ampi** \äm-pē\ see OMPY

²**ampi** \am-pē\ see AMPY

ampian \am-pē-ən\ see
²AMPION

¹**ampion** \äm-pē-ən\ see
¹AMPEAN

²**ampion** \am-pē-ən\ campion,
champion, Grampian,
pampean, rampion, tampion

ample \am-pəl\ ample, sample,
trample, ensample, example,
subsample, counterexample

ampler \am-plər\ sampler,
trampler

ampo \äm-pō\ see OMPO

ampos \am-pəs\ see AMPUS

ampsia \am(p)-sē-ə\ eclampsia,
preeclampsia

ampton \am-tən\ Hampton,
Easthampton, Northampton,
Southampton,
Wolverhampton

ampus \am-pəs\ Campos,
campus, grampus,
hippocampus

ampy \am-pē\ campy, scampi

ams \amz\ Jams—*also
possessives and plurals of
nouns and third person
singular presents of verbs
listed at* ²AM

amson \am-sən\ damson,
Samson

amster \am-stər\ hamster,
lamster

amsun \äm-sən\ Hamsun,
   Thompson
amulus \am-yə-ləs\ famulus,
   hamulus
¹amus \ā-məs\ see AMOUS
²amus \äm-əs\ see OMISE
amy \ā-mē\ see ¹AMIE
amys \am-əs\ see AMICE
¹an \äⁿ\ see ¹ANT
²an \än\ see ¹ON
³an \ən\ see UN
⁴an \aŋ\ see ²ANG
⁵an \an\ an, Ann, Anne, ban,
   bran, can, clan, crayon, Dan,
   fan, Fan, flan, Jan, Klan, man,
   Mann, nan, Nan, pan, Pan,
   panne, plan, ran, scan, San,
   Shan, span, Stan, tan, van,
   Van, adman, Afghan, aidman,
   ape-man, ashcan, Bataan,
   bedpan, began, Bhutan,
   birdman, boardman, brainpan,
   brogan, caftan, caiman,
   cancan, capstan, captan,
   caveman, Cayman, Cèzanne,
   chessman, Cheyenne,
   chlordan, Chopin, claypan,
   clubman, Cohan, cooncan,
   corban, cowman, Cruzan,
   cyan, deadpan, deskman,
   Dian, Diane, Diann, Dianne,
   dishpan, divan, doorman,
   dustpan, fancy-dan, fan-tan,
   fibranne, flyman, foreran,
   FORTRAN, freedman,
   freeman, frogman, G-man,
   gagman, Georgeann, glucan,
   Gosplan, hardpan, he-man,
   iceman, inspan, Iran, japan,
   Japan, jazzman, Joann,
   Joanne, Kazan, kneepan,
   Koran, Kurgan, leadman,
   Leanne, legman, liftman,
   loran, Luanne, madman,
   Mandan, Marfan, mailman,
   merman, Milan, milkman,
   newsman, oilcan, oilman,
   outran, pavane, pecan,
   plowman, postman, preman,
   pressman, propman, Queen
   Anne, Qur'an, ragman, rattan,
   reedman, reman, rodman,
   Roseanne, routeman,
   Roxanne, Ruthann, Saipan,
   sampan, sandman, Saran,
   saucepan, scalepan,
   schoolman, sedan, sideman,
   snowman, soundman, soutane,
   spaceman, Spokane, stewpan,
   stickman, stockman,
   strongman, stuntman, Sudan,
   suntan, Susanne, Suzanne, T-
   man, TACAN, taipan, Tarzan,
   tisane, toucan, trainman,
   trashman, trepan, Tristan,
   unman, vegan, Walkman,
   wingspan, yardman, yes-man,
   Alcoran, allemande, also-ran,
   Ameslan, anchorman,
   Andaman, astrakhan,
   Astrakhan, ataman, Athelstan,
   attackman, automan,
   balmacaan, Baluchistan,
   Bantustan, bartizan,
   Belmopan, black-and-tan,
   bogeyman, boogeyman,
   businessman, Caliban,
   cameraman, caravan, catalan,
   cattleman, Civitan, colorman,
   cornerman, counterman,
   counterplan, countryman,
   courtesan, dairyman,
   defenseman, everyman,
   exciseman, expressman,

fellowman, funnyman, gamelan, garageman, garbageman, Hamadan, handyman, harmattan, Hindustan, hotelman, Isle of Man, jerrican, Juliann, Julianne, Kazakhstan, Ku Klux Klan, Kurdistan, Kyrgyzstan, man-for-man, man-to-man, Marianne, Maryann, Maryanne, middleman, minuteman, Monaghan, moneyman, Occitan, ombudsman, Omdurman, overman, overran, Pakistan, Parmesan, partisan, pattypan, Peter Pan, pivotman, plainclothesman, Port Sudan, Powhatan, Ramadan, repairman, rewrite man, Ryazan, safetyman, selectman, serviceman, shandrydan, Shantyman, shovelman, signalman, spick-and-span, superman, tallyman, tamarin, Teheran, teleman, teleran, triggerman, trimaran, turbofan, weatherman, workingman, yataghan, Yucatan, Afghanistan, arrière-ban, bipartisan, catamaran, catch-as-catch-can, cavalryman, committeeman, deliveryman, Kalimantan, newspaperman, orangutan, radioman, salary man, Tajikistan, Turkmenistan, Uzbekistan

⁶an \än-yə\ see ¹ANIA

⁷an \äng\ see ¹ONG

⁸an \änt\ see ²ANT

¹ana \än-ə\ ana, anna, Anna, bwana, Dona, donna, Donna, fauna, Ghana, Kana, Lana, Lonna, mana, Botswana, chicana, gymkhana, iguana, jacana, lantana, liana, Madonna, mañana, nagana, nirvana, piranha, Purana, ruana, Tijuana, Tirane, Toscana, zenana, Africana, belladonna, epifauna, French Guiana, Guadiana, Haryana, Hinayana, hiragana, ikebana, Ludhiana, Mahayana, marijuana, parmigiana, pozzolana, prima donna, Rajputana, Rosh Hashanah, Tatiana, Americana, fata morgana, Lincolniana, Ljubljana, nicotiana, Shakespeareana, Victoriana, Ciuda Guyana

²ana \ā-nə\ ana, Dana, Lana, Africana, cantilena, Cartagena, nicotiana, Shakespeareana

³ana \an-ə\ ana, Anna, canna, manna, Ghana, Hannah, Lana, nana, banana, bandanna, cabana, Deanna, Diana, Dianna, Fermanagh, goanna, Guiana, Guyana, gymkhana, Havana, hosanna, Joanna, Johanna, Montana, savanna, Savannah, sultana, Susanna, Susannah, Africana, Indiana, Juliana, Mariana, Marianna, poinciana, Pollyanna, Santa Ana, Americana, fata morgana, Louisiana, nicotiana, Shakespeareana, Victoriana

aña \än-yə\ see ¹ANIA

anacle \an-i-kəl\ see ANICAL

anage \an-ij\ manage, tannage, stage-manage, micro manage

anagh \an-ə\ see ³ANA

¹anah \ō-nə\ see ¹ONA

²anah \än-ə\ see ¹ANA

anal \ān-ᵊl\ anal, banal

analyst \an-ᵊl-əst\ analyst, annalist, panelist, cryptanalyst, psychoanalyst

anan \an-ən\ see ANNON

anape \an-ə-pē\ see ANOPY

¹anary \ān-rē\ see ANERY

²anary \an-rē\ see ²ANNERY

anate \an-ət\ see ANNET

anative \an-ət-iv\ sanative, explanative

anbe \am-bē\ see AMBY

¹anc \aⁿ\ see ¹ANT

²anc \aŋ\ see ²ANG

³anc \aŋk\ see ANK

anca \aŋ-kə\ barranca, Kanka, Casablanca, lingua franca, Salamanca

¹ance \äⁿs\ Reims, nuance, outrance, séance, à outrance, Provence, Saint-Saëns, diligence, Fort-de-France, ordonnance, renaissance, mésalliance, par excellence, concours d'elegance, pièce de résistance

²ance \äns\ Hans, nonce, ponce, sconce, brisance, ensconce, faience, nuance, response, seance, Afrikaans, complaisance, fer-de-lance, nonchalance, provenance, renaissance, pièce de résistance

³ance \ans\ chance, dance, France, glance, lance, Lance, manse, nance, Nantes, prance, stance, trance, trans, Vance, advance, askance, bechance, enhance, entrance, expanse, finance, mischance, perchance, romance, Romance, side-glance, sweatpants, circumstance, complaisance, contredanse, country-dance, fer-de-lance, happenchance, happenstance, Liederkranz, Port-au-Prince, refinance, smarty-pants, underpants—*also plurals and possessives of verbs listed at* ⁵ANT

anceable \an-sə-bəl\ see ANSIBLE

anced \anst\ canst, circumstanced, underfinanced—*also pasts of verbs listed at* ³ANCE

ancel \an-səl\ cancel, chancel, handsel, expansile, precancel

anceler \an-slər\ canceler, chancellor, vice-chancellor

ancellor \an-slər\ see ANCELER

ancement \an-smənt\ advancement, enhancement

ancer \an-sər\ answer, cancer, dancer, glancer, lancer, prancer, advancer, enhancer, free-lancer, merganser, romancer, ropedancer, anticancer, geomancer, necromancer, rhabdomancer

ances \an(t)-səs\ see ANCIS

ancet \an-sət\ lancet, Narragansett

¹anch \änch\ see ¹AUNCH

²anch \önch\ see ²AUNCH

³anch \anch\ blanch, Blanche,

branch, ranch, rebranch,
avalanche

¹anche \äⁿsh\ tranche, carte
blanche, revanche

²anche \anch\ see ³ANCH

³anche \an-chē\ see ANCHY

¹ancher \òn-chər\ see AUNCHER

²ancher \an-chər\ ceinture,
rancher

anchi \an-chē\ see ANCHY

anchion \an-chən\ see ANSION

anchor \aŋ-kər\ see ANKER

anchoress \aŋ-krəs\ see
ANKEROUS

anchy \an-chē\ branchy,
Ranchi, Comanche

ancial \an-chəl\ see ANTIAL

ancis \an(t)-səs\ Frances,
Francis, Aransas—*also third
person singular presents of
verbs and plurals of nouns
listed at* ANCE

anck \änk\ see ¹ONK

anco \äŋ-kō\ see ONCO

ancolin \aŋ-klən\ see ANKLIN

ancor \aŋ-kər\ see ANKER

ancorous \aŋ-krəs\ see
ANKEROUS

ancre \aŋ-kər\ see ANKER

ancrous \aŋ-krəs\ see
ANKEROUS

anct \aŋt\ see ANKED

ancy \an-sē\ chancy, fancy,
Nancy, unchancy,
chiromancy, geomancy,
hydromancy, necromancy,
pyromancy, rhabdomancy,
sycophancy, oneiromancy

¹and \äⁿ\ see ¹ANT

²and \änd\ see ¹OND

³and \and\ and, band, bland,
brand, canned, gland, grand,
hand, land, manned, NAND,
rand, Rand, sand, Sand, stand,
strand, armband, backhand,
backland, badland, bandstand,
benchland, blackland,
broadband, brushland,
bushland, cabstand,
cloudland, coastland,
command, cowhand, crash-
land, cropland, deckhand,
demand, disband, dockhand,
dockland, downland,
dreamland, dryland, duneland,
expand, farmhand, farmland,
fenland, filmland, firebrand,
firsthand, flatland, forehand,
four-hand, free hand,
freehand, gangland, glad-
hand, Gotland, grandstand,
grassland, handstand,
hardstand, hatband, headband,
headstand, heartland,
heathland, homeland, Iceland,
inkstand, inland, Inland,
kickstand, Kokand, Lapland,
left-hand, longhand,
mainland, marshland,
misbrand, newsstand,
nightstand, northland,
noseband, offhand, outland,
outstand, parkland, pineland,
playland, proband,
Queensland, quicksand,
rangeland, remand, repand,
Rheinland, Rhineland,
ribband, right-hand, rimland,
roband, Saarland, scabland,
screenland, scrubland,
seastrand, shorthand,
sideband, softland, southland,
spaceband, stagehand,
summand, swampland,

sweatband, Thailand, thirdhand, tideland, trainband, unhand, unmanned, waistband, washstand, wasteland, watchband, wetland, wildland, withstand, wristband, ampersand, beforehand, behindhand, bellyband, belly-land, borderland, bottomland, confirmand, contraband, countermand, Damavand, Dixieland, fairyland, fatherland, Ferdinand, forestland, four-in-hand, graduand, hand-to-hand, hand to hand, hinterland, Krugerrand, lotusland, meadowland, motherland, Nagaland, narrowband, no-man's-land, operand, ordinand, overhand, overland, pastureland, reprimand, Rio Grande, Samarkand, saraband, secondhand, Swaziland, tableland, Talleyrand, timberland, Togoland, underhand, undermanned, understand, wonderland, Zululand, analysand, Bechuanaland, cloud-cuckoo-land, fantasyland, misunderstand, multiplicand, Prince Rupert's Land, Somaliland, Sudetenland, vacationland, videoland, Witwatersrand, Matabeleland, Alice-in-Wonderland—*also pasts of verbs listed at* ⁵AN

⁴and \än\ see ¹ON

⁵and \änt\ see ²ANT

¹anda \an-də\ Ganda, panda,

Amanda, Luanda, Luganda, Miranda, Uganda, veranda, jacaranda, memoranda, nomina conservanda, propaganda

²anda \än-də\ see ONDA

andable \an-də-bəl\ mandible, commandable, demandable, expandable, understandable

andaed \an-dəd\ see ANDED

andal \an-dᵊl\ see ANDLE

andaled \an-dᵊld\ handled, sandaled, well-handled—*also pasts of verbs listed at* ANDLE

andall \an-dᵊl\ see ANDLE

andalous \an-dləs\ see ²ANDLESS

andam \an-dəm\ see ANDUM

andant \an-dənt\ see ANDENT

andar \ənd-ər\ see UNDER

andarin \an-drən\ mandarin, alexandrine, salamandrine

¹ande \ən\ see UN

²ande \an\ see ⁵AN

³ande \an-dē\ see ANDY

⁴ande \and\ see ³AND

⁵ande \än-də\ see ONDA

anded \an-dəd\ banded, branded, candid, handed, landed, stranded, backhanded, bare-handed, cleanhanded, forehanded, four-handed, freehanded, ham-handed, hardhanded, high-handed, ironhanded, left-handed, light-handed, offhanded, one-handed, red-handed, right-handed, shorthanded, sure-handed, three-handed, two-handed, unbranded, verandaed, empty-handed, evenhanded, heavy-handed,

openhanded, overhanded,
singlehanded, underhanded—
also pasts of verbs listed at
³AND

andel \an-dᵊl\ see ANDLE

andem \an-dəm\ see ANDUM

andent \an-dənt\ candent,
scandent, demandant

¹ander \en-dər\ see ENDER

²ander \än-dər\ see ¹ONDER

³ander \an-dər\ bander, brander,
candor, dander, gander,
grandeur, lander, pander,
sander, slander, strander,
zander, auslander,
backhander, blackhander,
bystander, commander,
demander, expander,
flatlander, germander, glad-
hander, goosander,
grandstander, inlander,
Leander, left-hander,
mainlander, meander,
outlander, philander,
pomander, right-hander,
scrimshander, soft-lander,
Uitlander, Africander,
alexander, Alexander,
calamander, coriander,
gerrymander, oleander,
salamander, single-hander—
*also comparatives of
adjectives listed at* ³AND

anderous \an-drəs\ see
ANDROUS

anders \an-dərz\ Flanders,
Bouvier des Flandres, golden
alexanders—*also plurals and
possessives of verbs listed at*
³ANDER

andery \an-drē\ see ANDRY

andes \an-dēz\ Andes—*also

*possessives and plurals of
nouns and third person
singular presents of verbs
listed at* ANDY

¹andeur \an-dər\ see ³ANDER

²andeur \an-jər\ see ⁴ANGER

andhi \an-dē\ see ANDY

andi \an-dē\ see ANDY

andible \an-də-bəl\ see
ANDABLE

andid \an-dəd\ see ANDED

anding \an-diŋ\ standing,
commanding, crossbanding,
freestanding, hardstanding,
long-standing, outstanding,
upstanding, mind-expanding,
notwithstanding,
understanding

andish \an-dish\ blandish,
brandish, standish, Standish,
outlandish

andist \an-dəst\ contrabandist,
propagandist—*also
superlatives of adjectives
listed at* ³AND

andit \an-dət\ bandit, pandit

andle \an-dᵊl\ candle, dandle,
Handel, handle, Randall,
sandal, scandal, vandal,
footcandle, manhandle,
mishandle, panhandle,
stickhandle, coromandel,
Coromandel

andled \an-dᵊl\ see ANDALED

andler \an-lər\ candler,
chandler, handler, panhandler,
stickhandler

andless \an-ləs\ see ANLESS

andly \an-lē\ see ²ANLY

andment \an-mənt\
commandment, disbandment

ando \an-dō\ Fernando, Orlando

andom \an-dəm\ see ANDUM

andor \an-dər\ see ³ANDER

andra \an-drə\ Sandra, Cassandra, Alexandra, pachysandra

andrea \an-drē-ə\ see ANDRIA

andrel \an-drəl\ mandrel, mandrill, spandrel

andres \an-dərz\ see ANDERS

andria \an-drē-ə\ Andrea, Alexandria

andrill \an-drəl\ see ANDREL

andrine \an-drən\ see ANDARIN

andros \an-drəs\ see ANDROUS

androus \an-drəs\ Andros, slanderous, gynandrous, meandrous, polyandrous

andry \an-drē\ commandery, monandry, polyandry

ands \anz\ Badlands, Lowlands, Canyonlands

andsel \an-səl\ see ANCEL

andsman \anz-mən\ bandsman, clansman, Klansman, landsman

andsome \an-səm\ see ANSOM

andum \an-dəm\ fandom, grandam, random, tandem, memorandum, nomen conservandum, subpoena ad testificandum

andy \an-dē\ Andy, bandy, brandy, Brandy, candy, dandy, handy, Handy, pandy, randy, Randy, sandhi, sandy, Sandy, shandy, jim-dandy, unhandy, Rio Grande, modus operandi

¹ane \ān\ ain, Aisne, ane, bane, blain, Blaine, brain, Cain, cane, chain, crane, Crane, Dane, deign, drain, Duane,

Dwain, Dwayne, fain, fane, feign, gain, grain, Jane, Jayne, lane, Lane, main, Maine, mane, pain, Paine, pane, plain, plane, quean, rain, reign, rein, sain, sane, seine, Seine, skein, slain, Spain, sprain, stain, stane, strain, swain, thane, thegn, train, twain, Twain, vain, vane, vein, wain, wane, Wayne, Zane, abstain, again, airplane, amain, arcane, arraign, attain, Bahrain, Bassein, Beltane, biplane, birdbrain, Biscayne, bloodstain, bugbane, campaign, champagne, champaign, Champlain, checkrein, chicane, chilblain, chow mein, cinquain, cocaine, Cockaigne, coxswain, complain, constrain, contain, cordwain, cowbane, crackbrain, demesne, deplane, destain, detain, detrain, devein, disdain, distain, distrain, dogbane, domain, drivetrain, Duane, dumbcane, edge-grain, Elaine, emplane, enchain, engrain, enplane, entrain, explain, eyestrain, fleabane, floatplane, floodplain, Fort Wayne, Gawain, germane, grosgrain, Helaine, Helene, henbane, house-train, humane, Hussein, Igraine, immane, inane, ingrain, insane, lamebrain, lightplane, lo mein, Loraine, Lorraine, maintain, marchpane, membrane, migraine, Montaigne, montane, moraine, mortmain, Moulmein, mundane, neckrein, obtain, octane, ordain, pertain, plain-Jane, profane, ptomaine, purslane, quatrain, refrain, remain, restrain, retain, retrain, romaine, sailplane, sea-lane, seaplane, seatrain, sustain, tearstain, terrain, terrane, triplane, Touraine, Ukraine, unchain, urbane, vervain, vicereine, villein, volplane, warplane, wolfsbane, aeroplane, appertain, aquaplane, Aquitaine, ascertain, avellane, Bloemfontain, cellophane, Charlemagne, Charles's Wain, chatelain, chatelaine, counterpane, de Montaigne, entertain, featherbrain, foreordain, frangipane, gyroplane, hurricane, hydroplane, hyperplane, inhumane, Kwajalein, La Fontaine, marocain, Mary Jane, mise-en-scène, monoplane, Novocain, neutercane, novocaine, overlain, paravane, papertrain, peneplain, Port of Spain, port-wine stain, preordain, rattlebrain, scatterbrain, shaggymane, Spanish Main, sugarcane, suzerain, Tamburlaine, Tamerlane, terreplein, tramontane, transmontane, windowpane, Alsace-Lorraine, auf Wiedersehen, balletomane, convertiplane, demimondaine, elecampane,

extramundane, intermontane, Lake Pontchartraine, legerdemain, ultramontane, trichalomethane

²ane \an\ see ⁵AN
³ane \än-ə\ see ¹ANA
⁴ane \än\ see ¹ON
anea \ā-nē-ə\ see ²ANIA
anean \ā-nē-ən\ see ²ANIAN
aned \ānd\ see AINED
anee \an-ē\ see ANNY
aneful \ān-fəl\ see AINFUL
anel \an-ºl\ see ANNEL
anelist \an-ºl-əst\ see ANALYST
aneous \ā-nē-əs\ cutaneous, extraneous, spontaneous, coetaneous, consentaneous, instantaneous, miscellaneous, porcelaneous, simultaneous, succedaneous, contemporaneous, extemporaneous
¹aner \ā-nər\ see AINER
²aner \än-ər\ see ¹ONOR
anery \ān-rē\ granary, chicanery
anet \an-ət\ see ANNET
aneum \ā-nē-əm\ see ANIUM
aney \ò-nē\ see ¹AWNY
anford \an-fərd\ Sanford, Stanford
¹ang \äŋ\ see ¹ONG
²ang \aŋ\ bang, bhang, clang, dang, fang, Fang, gang, gangue, hang, pang, prang, rang, sang, slang, spang, sprang, stang, tang, twang, whang, yang, cliff-hang, defang, ginseng, harangue, linsang, meringue, mustang, orang, parang, Pinang, pressgang, probang, shebang, slambang, straphang, trepang,

whizbang, boomerang, charabanc, overhang, parasang, siamang, interrobang, orangutan

³ang \óŋ\ see ²ONG

anga \äŋ-gə\ see ONGA

angar \aŋ-ər\ see ²ANGER

¹ange \äⁿzh\ blancmange, mélange

²ange \ānj\ change, grange, mange, range, strange, arrange, derange, downrange, estrange, exchange, free-range, gearchange, long-range, outrange, short-range, shortchange, counterchange, disarrange, interchange, omnirange, Great Dividing Range

³ange \anj\ flange, phalange

angel \aŋ-gəl\ see ANGLE

angell \aŋ-gəl\ see ANGLE

angement \ānj-mənt\ arrangement, derangement, estrangement, disarrangement

angency \an-jən-sē\ plangency, tangency

angent \an-jənt\ plangent, tangent

¹anger \ān-jər\ changer, danger, granger, manger, ranger, stranger, bushranger, endanger, estranger, exchanger, shortchanger, interchanger

²anger \aŋ-ər\ banger, clanger, clangor, clangour, ganger, hangar, hanger, languor, Sanger, twanger, cliff-hanger, straphanger, haranguer, paperhanger

³anger \aŋ-gər\ anger, clangor

⁴anger \an-jər\ flanger, grandeur, phalanger

angi \aŋ-ē\ see ²ANGY

angible \an-jə-bəl\ frangible, tangible, infrangible, intangible, refrangible

angie \aŋ-ē\ see ²ANGY

¹anging \ān-jiŋ\ bushranging, unchanging, wide-ranging

²anging \aŋ-iŋ\ hanging, cliff-hanging, paperhanging

angle \aŋ-gəl\ angle, bangle, dangle, jangle, mangel, mangle, spangle, strangle, tangle, wangle, wrangle, embrangle, entangle, Mount Wrangell, pentangle, quadrangle, rectangle, triangle, untangle, wide-angle, disentangle

angled \aŋ-gəld\ angled, tangled, newfangled, oldfangled, right-angled, star-spangled—*also pasts of verbs listed at* ANGLE

anglement \aŋ-gəl-mənt\ tanglement, embranglement, entanglement, disentanglement

angler \aŋ-glər\ angler, dangler, jangler, mangler, strangler, wangler, wrangler, entangler

angles \aŋ-gəlz\ Angles, strangles—*also plurals and possessives of nouns and third singular presents of verbs listed at* ANGLE

anglian \aŋ-glē-ən\ Anglian, ganglion

angling \aŋ-gliŋ\ angling, gangling

anglion \aŋ-glē-ən\ see
ANGLIAN

angly \aŋ-glē\ gangly, jangly,
tangly

ango \aŋ-gō\ mango, tango,
Durango, fandango

¹angor \aŋ-ər\ see ²ANGER

²angor \aŋ-gər\ see ³ANGER

angorous \aŋ-ə-rəs\ clangorous,
languorous

angour \aŋ-ər\ see ²ANGER

angster \aŋ-stər\ gangster,
prankster

anguage \aŋ-gwij\ language,
slanguage, metalanguage,
paralanguage, protolanguage

angue \aŋ\ see ²ANG

anguer \aŋ-ər\ see ²ANGER

anguish \aŋ-gwish\ anguish,
languish

anguor \aŋ-ər\ see ²ANGER

anguorous \aŋ-ə-rəs\ see
ANGOROUS

angus \aŋ-gəs\ Angus, Brangus

¹angy \ān-jē\ mangy, rangy

²angy \aŋ-ē\ tangy, twangy,
Ubangi, collieshangie

anha \än-ə\ see ¹ANA

anhope \an-əp\ see ANNUP

¹ani \än-ē\ Bonnie, bonny,
Connie, Donnie, fawny,
johnny, Ronnie, tawny,
afghani, Fulani, chalcedony,
Kisangani, maharani,
Nuristani, quadriphony,
Rajasthani, mulligatawny

²ani \an-ē\ see ANNY

¹ania \än-yə\ Agana, España,
lasagna, Titania, Emilia-
Romagna

²ania \ā-nē-ə\ mania, titania,
Titania, Urania, Acarnania,

Anglomania, Aquitania,
collectanea, dipsomania,
egomania, hypomania,
kleptomania, Lithuania,
Mauretania, Mauritania,
miscellanea, monomania,
mythomania, nymphomania,
Oceania, Pennsylvania,
Pomerania, pyromania,
Transylvania, balletomania,
bibliomania, decalcomania,
megalomania—*see also* ³ANIA

³ania \ān-yə\ Campania,
Catania, Hispania, Titania,
Aquitania, malaguena,
Tripolitania—*also words
listed at* ²ANIA

¹anian \än-ē-ən\ Kiwanian,
Araucanian, Turanian

²anian \ā-nē-ən\ Albanian,
Dardanian, Iranian,
Romanian, Rumanian,
Sassanian, Turanian,
Ukrainian, Uranian,
vulcanian, Lithuanian,
Pennsylvanian, Pomeranian,
Ruritanian, subterranean,
Indo-Iranian, Mediterranean

aniard \an-yərd\ lanyard,
Spaniard

anic \an-ik\ manic, panic,
tannic, Brahmanic, Britannic,
cyanic, firemanic, galvanic,
Germanic, Hispanic, Koranic,
mechanic, melanic, organic,
Romanic, satanic, shamanic,
Sudanic, titanic, tympanic,
volcanic, aldermanic,
Alemannic, councilmanic,
epiphanic, inorganic,
messianic, oceanic, Ossianic,
pre-Hispanic, talismanic,

theophanic, Indo-Germanic, megalomanic, Rhaeto-Romanic, suboceanic, transoceanic

anical \an-i-kəl\ manacle, panicle, sanicle, botanical, mechanical, tyrannical, puritanical

anice \an-əs\ see ANISE

anicle \an-i-kəl\ see ANICAL

anics \an-iks\ annex, mechanics—*also plurals and possessives of nouns listed at* ANIC

¹anid \ā-nəd\ ranid, tabanid

²anid \an-əd\ canid, ranid, Sassanid

aniel \an-əl\ see ANNEL

²aniel \an-yəl\ see ANUAL

anigan \an-i-gən\ see ANNIGAN

anikin \an-i-kən\ see ANNIKIN

animous \an-ə-məs\ animus, magnanimous, unanimous, pusillanimous

animus \an-ə-məs\ see ANIMOUS

¹anion \än-yən\ see ¹ONYON

²anion \an-yən\ banyan, canon, canyon, fanion, companion, Grand Canyon, Hells Canyon

anis \an-əs\ see ANISE

anise \an-əs\ anise, Janice, Janis, stannous, johannes, Johnannes, pandanus, titanous, Scipio Africanus

¹anish \ā-nish\ see AINISH

²anish \an-ish\ banish, clannish, mannish, planish, Spanish, tannish, vanish, Pollyannish, Judeo-Spanish

anist \än-əst\ see ONEST

anister \an-ə-stər\ canister, ganister

anite \an-ət\ see ANNET

anity \an-ət-ē\ sanity, vanity, humanity, inanity, insanity, profanity, urbanity, Christianity, churchianity, inhumanity, superhumanity

anium \ā-nē-əm\ cranium, geranium, uranium, succedaneum

ank \aŋk\ bank, blank, brank, clank, crank, dank, drank, flank, franc, frank, Frank, hank, lank, plank, prank, rank, sank, shank, shrank, spank, stank, swank, tank, thank, yank, Yank, Burbank, claybank, embank, foreshank, gangplank, greenshank, nonbank, outflank, outrank, pickthank, point-blank, redshank, sandbank, sheepshank, snowbank, mountebank, riverbank, clinkety-clank

¹anka \äŋ-kə\ concha, tanka, Sri Lanka

²anka \aŋ-kə\ see ANCA

ankable \aŋ-kə-bəl\ bankable, frankable

anked \aŋt\ shanked, tanked, spindle-shanked, sacrosanct—*also pasts of verbs listed at* ANK

ankee \an-kē\ see ANKY

anken \aŋ-kən\ flanken, Rankine

anker \aŋ-kər\ anchor, banker, canker, chancre, flanker, franker, hanker, rancor, ranker, spanker, tanker,

thanker, co-anchor,
unanchor—*also comparatives
of adjectives listed at* ANK

ankerous \aŋ-krəs\ anchoress,
cankerous, chancrous,
rancorous, cantankerous

ankh \äŋk\ see ¹ONK

ankie \an-kē\ see ANKY

ankine \aŋ-kən\ see ANKEN

ankish \aŋ-kish\ Frankish,
prankish

ankle \aŋ-kəl\ ankle, crankle,
rankle

ankly \aŋ-klē\ blankly, dankly,
frankly

anks \aŋs\ see ANX

ankster \aŋ-stər\ see ANGSTER

anky \aŋ-kē\ cranky, hankie,
lanky, swanky, Yankee,
hanky-panky

anless \an-ləs\ handless,
manless, planless

anley \an-lē\ see ²ANLY

anli \an-lē\ see ²ANLY

¹anly \än-lē\ fondly, thrawnly,
wanly

²anly \an-lē\ blandly, grandly,
manly, Stanley, Osmanli,
unmanly

¹ann \an\ see ⁵AN

²ann \än\ see ¹ON

¹anna \än-ə\ see ¹ANA

²anna \an-ə\ see ³ANA

annage \an-ij\ see ANAGE

annah \an-ə\ see ³ANA

annalist \an-ᵊl-əst\ see
ANALYST

annan \an-ən\ see ANNON

anne \an\ see ⁵AN

anned \and\ see ³AND

annel \an-ᵊl\ channel, Channel,
Daniel, flannel, panel,

scrannel, spaniel, impanel,
English Channel

annequin \an-i-kən\ see
ANNIKIN

anner \an-ər\ banner, canner,
fanner, lanner, manner,
manor, planner, scanner,
spanner, tanner, vanner,
deadpanner, japanner,
caravanner

¹annery \än-rē\ ornery,
swannery

²annery \an-rē\ cannery,
granary, tannery

annes \an-əs\ see ANISE

anness \än-nəs\ fondness,
wanness

annet \an-ət\ gannet, granite,
Janet, planet, pomegranate

annexe \an-iks\ see ANICS

annibal \an-ə-bəl\ cannibal,
Hannibal

annic \an-ik\ see ANIC

annie \an-ē\ see ANNY

annigan \an-i-gən\ brannigan,
shenanigan

annikin \an-i-kən\ cannikin,
manikin, mannequin, pannikin

annin \an-ən\ see ANNON

annish \an-ish\ see ²ANISH

annon \an-ən\ cannon, canon,
Shannon, tannin, Buchanan,
Clackmannan, colcannon

annous \an-əs\ see ANISE

anns \anz\ see ⁴ANS

annual \an-yəl\ see ANUAL

annular \an-yə-lər\ annular,
cannular, granular

annulate \an-yə-lət\ annulate,
annulet, campanulate

annulet \an-yə-lət\ see
ANNULATE

annum \an-əm\ see ²ANUM

annup \an-əp\ sannup, stanhope

anny \an-ē\ Annie, canny, cranny, Danny, fanny, granny, Lanny, nanny, afghani, ca'canny, kokanee, uncanny, frangipani, Hindustani, hootenanny

¹ano \än-ō\ guano, Kano, llano, mano, mono, Chicano, Marrano, Nagano, piano, Romano, Serrano, soprano, altiplano, boliviano, forte-piano, mezzo piano, mezzo-soprano, Città del Vaticano

²ano \ā-nō\ ripieno, volcano

³ano \an-ō\ Hispano, piano, soprano, fortepiano, mezzo-soprano

¹anon \an-ən\ see ANNON

²anon \an-yən\ see ²ANION

anopy \an-ə-pē\ canape, canopy

anor \an-ər\ see ANNER

anous \an-əs\ see ANISE

anqui \än-kē\ see ONKY

¹ans \äns\ see ²ANCE

²ans \änz\ see ONZE

³ans \ans\ see ³ANCE

⁴ans \anz\ banns, Hans, sans, trans, Sextans—*also plurals and possessives of nouns and third singular presents of verbs listed at* ⁵AN

⁵ans \aⁿ\ see ¹ANT

ansard \an-sərd\ see ANSWERED

¹ansas \an(t)-səs\ see ANCIS

²ansas \an-zəs\ Kansas, Arkansas

anse \ans\ see ³ANCE

ansea \än-zē\ see ANZY

anser \an-sər\ see ANCER

anset \an-sət\ see ANCET

ansett \an-sət\ see ANCET

ansible \an-sə-bəl\ danceable, expansible

ansile \an-səl\ see ANCEL

ansing \an-siŋ\ Lansing—*also present participles of verbs listed at* ³ANCE

ansion \an-chən\ mansion, scansion, stanchion, expansion

ansk \änsk\ Bryansk, Gdansk, Murmansk, Saransk

ansman \anz-mən\ see ANDSMAN

ansom \an-səm\ handsome, hansom, ransom, transom, unhandsome

anst \anst\ see ANCED

answer \an-sər\ see ANCER

answered \an-sərd\ answered, mansard, unanswered

ansy \an-zē\ pansy, tansy, chimpanzee

¹ant \äⁿ\ Caen, Gant, arpent, beurre blanc, croissant, en banc, Mont Blanc, riant, roman, Rouen, Tátouan, savant, versant, accouchement, aide-de-camp, au courant, battement, cidevant, contretemps, debridement, denouement, en passant, Maupassant, Mitterand, Orléans, Perpignan, rapprochement, revenant, se tenant, soi-disant, vol-au-vent, arrondissement, chateaubriand, Chateaubriand, Clermont-Ferrand, de Maupassant, idiot savant, ressentiment, sauvignon blanc

²ant \änt\ aunt, can't, daunt,

flaunt, font, fount, gaunt,
taunt, vaunt, want, wont,
avant, avaunt, bacchant,
bacchante, Balante,
Beaumont, bouffant, brisant,
courante, détente, entente,
Fremont, gallant, grandaunt,
piedmont, Piedmont, piquant,
romaunt, Rostand, savant,
sirvente, Vermont, bon vivant,
commandant, complaisant,
confidant, debridement,
debutant, debutante,
dilettante, John of Gaunt,
intrigant, nonchalant, poste
restante, restaurant, symbiont,
dicynodont, subdebutante,
Montcalm de Saint Veran,
sinfonia concertante

³ant \ənt\ see ¹ONT

⁴ant \ȯnt\ see ¹AUNT

⁵ant \ant\ ant, aunt, brant, cant,
can't, chant, grant, Grant,
hant, Kant, pant, plant, rant,
scant, shan't, slant, aslant,
bacchant, bacchante, bezant,
courante, decant, descant,
discant, displant, eggplant,
enceinte, enchant, explant,
extant, formant, gallant,
grandaunt, houseplant,
implant, incant, leadplant,
levant, Levant, pieplant,
pissant, plainchant, pourpoint,
preplant, rampant, recant,
replant, savant, supplant,
transplant, adamant,
commandant, complaisant,
confidant, cormorant,
corposant, Corybant,
covenant, demipointe,
dilettante, disenchant,

gallivant, hierophant,
interplant, sycophant

anta \ant-ə\ anta, manta,
Atlanta, infanta, vedanta,
Atalanta

antage \ant-ij\ vantage,
advantage, coign of vantage,
disadvantage

antain \ant-ᵊn\ see ²ANTON

¹antal \änt-ᵊl\ see ¹ONTAL

²antal \ant-ᵊl\ see ANTLE

antam \ant-əm\ bantam,
phantom

antar \ant-ər\ see ²ANTER

antasist \ant-ə-səst\ see
ANTICIST

¹ante \än-tā\ Brontë, Dante,
andante, Asante, volante, Belo
Horizonte

²ante \änt\ see ²ANT

³ante \ant\ see ⁵ANT

⁴ante \änt-ē\ see ¹ANTI

⁵ante \ant-ē\ ante, canty,
chanteỷ, pantie, scanty,
shanty, slanty, andanti,
Asante, Ashanti, Chianti,
infante, non obstante, penny-
ante, vigilante, pococurante,
status quo ante

antean \ant-ē-ən\ Dantean,
Atlantean, post-Kantian

anteau \an-tō\ see ²ANTO

anted \an-təd\ disenchanted—
also pasts of verbs listed at
⁵ANT

antel \ant-ᵊl\ see ANTLE

antelet \ant-lət\ mantelet,
plantlet

¹anter \änt-ər\ see ¹AUNTER

²anter \ant-ər\ antre, banter,
canter, cantor, chanter,
granter, grantor, plantar,

planter, ranter, scanter, decanter, implanter, instanter, levanter, transplanter, trochanter, covenanter, covenantor, disenchanter

¹**antes** \an-tēz\ Cervantes—*also possessives and plurals of nouns and third person singular presents of verbs listed at* ⁵ANTE

²**antes** \ans\ see ³ANCE

antey \ant-ē\ see ⁵ANTE

anth \anth\ amaranth, coelacanth, perianth, tragacanth

antha \an-thə\ Samantha, polyantha, pyracantha

anthemum \an-thə-məm\ chrysanthemum, mesembryanthemum

anther \an-thər\ anther, panther

anthropy \an-thrə-pē\ lycanthropy, misanthropy, philanthropy

anthus \an-thəs\ acanthus, ailanthus, dianthus, agapanthus, amianthus, polyanthus, Rhadamanthus

¹**anti** \änt-ē\ Brontë, jaunty, monte, Monte, Monty, vaunty, andante, Asante, Ashanti, Chianti

²**anti** \ant-ē\ see ⁵ANTE

antial \an-chəl\ financial, substantial, circumstantial, consubstantial, insubstantial, transsubstantial, unsubstantial, supersubstantial

¹**antian** \änt-ē-ən\ see ONTIAN

²**antian** \ant-ē-ən\ see ANTEAN

¹**antic** \änt-ik\ see ONTIC

²**antic** \ant-ik\ antic, frantic,

mantic, Atlantic, bacchantic, gigantic, pedantic, romantic, semantic, Vedantic, corybantic, geomantic, hierophantic, necromantic, sycophantic, transatlantic

anticist \ant-ə-səst\ fantasist, Atlanticist, romanticist, semanticist

antid \ant-əd\ mantid, Quadrantid—*also pasts of verbs listed at* ⁵ANT

antie \ant-ē\ see ⁵ANTE

antine \ant-ᵊn\ see ²ANTON

¹**anting** \ant-iŋ\ anting, canting, disenchanting

²**anting** \ənt-iŋ\ see UNTING

antis \ant-əs\ cantus, mantis, Santos, Atlantis

antish \ant-ish\ dilettantish, sycophantish

antle \ant-ᵊl\ cantle, mantel, mantle, quintal, dismantle, quadrantal, consonantal, covenantal, overmantel, determinantal

antlet \ant-lət\ see ANTELET

antling \ant-liŋ\ bantling, scantling

¹**anto** \än-tō\ Squanto, Toronto, Esperanto, bel canto

²**anto** \an-tō\ canto, panto, coranto, Otranto, portmanteau, Esperanto, Strait of Otranto

antom \ant-əm\ see ANTAM

¹**anton** \änt-ᵊn\ see ONTON

²**anton** \ant-ᵊn\ Anton, canton, Canton, plantain, Scranton, Stanton, adamantine

antor \ant-ər\ see ²ANTER

¹**antos** \an-təs\ see ANTIS

²**antos** \än-təs\ Santos, Propontis

antra \ən-trə\ tantra, yantra

antre \ant-ər\ see ²ANTER

antry \an-trē\ chantry, gantry, pantry

ants \ans\ see ³ANCE

antua \anch-wə\ mantua, Gargantua

antus \ant-əs\ see ANTIS

anty \ant-ē\ see ⁵ANTE

¹**anual** \an-yəl\ Daniel, spaniel, Nathaniel

²**anual** \an-yə-wəl\ annual, manual, Manuel, biannual, bimanual, Emanuel, Emmanuel, Immanuel, semi-annual, Victor Emmanuel

anuel \an-yəl\ see ²ANUAL

anular \an-yə-lər\ see ANNULAR

anulate \an-yə-lət\ see ANNULATE

¹**anum** \ā-nəm\ paynim, arcanum

²**anum** \an-əm\ per annum, solanum

¹**anus** \ā-nəs\ see AYNESS

²**anus** \an-əs\ see ANISE

anx \aŋs\ Manx, thanks, Grand Banks, phalanx—*also plurals and possessives of nouns and third singular presents of verbs listed at* ANK

¹**any** \ā-nē\ see AINY

²**any** \en-ē\ see ENNY

anyan \an-yən\ see ²ANION

anyard \an-yərd\ see ANIARD

anyon \an-yən\ see ²ANION

anz \ans\ see ³ANCE

¹**anza** \än-zə\ kwanza, Kwanza, Kwanzaa, Sancho Panza

²**anza** \an-zə\ stanza, zanza, bonanza, organza, Sancho Panza, extravaganza

anzaa \än-zə\ see ¹ANZA

anzee \an-zē\ see ANSY

anzer \än-sər\ see ONSOR

anzo \än-zō\ gonzo, garbanzo

anzy \än-zē\ bronzy, Ponzi, Swansea

¹**ao** \ā-ō\ see ¹EO

²**ao** \ō\ see ¹OW

³**ao** \aů\ see ²OW

⁴**ao** \ä-ō\ Caliao, Mindanao

aoedic \ēd-ik\ see ¹EDIC

aoighis \äsh\ see ¹ECHE

aole \aů-lē\ see ²OWLY

aône \ōn\ see ¹ONE

aori \aůr-ē\ see OWERY

¹**aos** \aůs\ see ²OUSE

²**aos** \ā-äs\ chaos, Laos

aotian \ō-shən\ see OTION

aow \aů\ see ²OW

¹**ap** \äp\ see ¹OP

²**ap** \əp\ see UP

³**ap** \ap\ cap, chap, clap, crap, flap, frap, gap, gape, hap, Jap, JAP, knap, lap, Lapp, map, nap, nape, nappe, pap, rap, sap, scrap, slap, snap, strap, tap, trap, wrap, yap, Yap, zap, backslap, backwrap, blackcap, bootstrap, burlap, catnap, claptrap, dewlap, dognap, earflap, entrap, enwrap, firetrap, flatcap, foolscap, giddap, heeltap, hubcap, jockstrap, kidnap, kneecap, lagniappe, livetrap, madcap, mantrap, mayhap, mishap, mobcap, mousetrap, nightcap, pinesap, rattrap, recap, redcap, remap, riprap, satrap, shiplap,

shrink-wrap, skullcap, skycap, snowcap, steel-trap, stopgap, unsnap, unstrap, unwrap, verb sap, whitecap, wiretap, afterclap, gingersnap, handicap, overlap, rattletrap, thunderclap, verbum sap, wentletrap, Venus's-flytrap

¹apa \äp-ə\ grappa, Joppa, papa, poppa, tapa, Jalapa, jipijapa

²apa \ap-ə\ kappa, tapa, Phi Beta Kappa

apable \ā-pə-bəl\ capable, drapable, shapable, escapable, incapable, inescapable

apal \ā-pəl\ see APLE

apas \äp-əs\ Chiapas—*also possessives and plurals of nouns listed at* ¹APA

apboard \ab-ərd\ see ABARD

¹ape \āp\ ape, cape, chape, crape, crepe, drape, gape, grape, jape, nape, rape, scape, scrape, shape, tape, agape, broomrape, cloudscape, duct tape, escape, landscape, moonscape, North Cape, reshape, seascape, shipshape, snowscape, streetscape, townscape, transshape, undrape, waveshape, cityscape, masking tape, waterscape, Xeriscape, audiotape, stereotape, videotape

²ape \ap\ see ³AP

³ape \äp-ē\ see OPPY

⁴ape \ap-ē\ see APPY

aped \āpt\ bell-shaped—*also pasts of verbs listed at* ¹APE

apel \ap-əl\ see APPLE

apelin \ap-lən\ see APLAIN

apen \ā-pən\ capon, shapen, unshapen

aper \ā-pər\ caper, draper, gaper, paper, scraper, shaper, taper, tapir, vapor, vapour, curlpaper, endpaper, flypaper, glasspaper, landscaper, newspaper, notepaper, sandpaper, skyscraper, wallpaper, wastepaper, run-of-paper

aperer \ā-pər-ər\ paperer, taperer, vaporer

apery \ā-prē\ drapery, japery, napery, papery, vapory, sandpapery

apes \āps\ traipse, jackanapes—*also plurals and possessives of nouns and third singular presents of verbs listed at* ¹APE

apey \ā-pē\ crepey, drapy, grapey, grapy, kepi, scrapie

aph \af\ caff, calf, chaff, daff, gaff, gaffe, graph, half, laugh, quaff, raff, sclaff, staff, staph, Waf, waff, agrafe, behalf, carafe, chiffchaff, cowlstaff, digraph, distaff, Falstaff, flagstaff, giraffe, half-staff, horselaugh, kenaf, mooncalf, paraph, pikestaff, riffraff, tipstaff, autograph, barograph, bathyscaphe, cenotaph, chronograph, cryptograph, epigraph, epitaph, half-and-half, hectograph, holograph, homograph, hygrograph, kymograph, lithograph, logograph, micrograph, monograph, pantograph, paragraph, phonograph, photograph, pictograph, polygraph, quarterstaff, seismograph, serigraph, shadowgraph, shandygaff, spectrograph, sphygmograph, telegraph, thermograph, typograph, understaff, cardiograph, choreograph, heliograph, ideograph, mimeograph, oscillograph, pseudepigraph, radiograph, chromolithograph, cinematograph, encephalograph, photomicrograph, radiotelegraph, electrocardiograph, electroencephalograph

aphael \af-ē-əl\ see APHIAL

¹aphe \āf\ see ¹AFE

²aphe \af\ see APH

apher \af-ər\ see ²AFFER

aphia \af-ē-ə\ see AFFIA

aphial \af-ē-əl\ Raphael, epitaphial

aphic \af-ik\ graphic, maffick, sapphic, traffic, digraphic, edaphic, serafic, triaphic, allographic, autographic, barographic, biographic, calligraphic, cartographic, cosmographic, cryptographic, demographic, epigraphic, epitaphic, ethnographic, geographic, hectographic, homographic, hydrographic, lithographic, logographic, mammographic, monographic, orthographic, pantographic, paragraphic, petrographic, phonographic, photographic, pictographic, polygraphic, pornographic, reprographic, stenographic, stratigraphic, telegraphic, tomographic, topographic, typographic, xerographic, bibliographic, choreographic, crystallographic, hagiographic, homolographic, iconographic, ideographic, lexicographic, oceanographic, stereographic, autobiographic, cinematographic, echocardiographic, historiographic, electroencephalographic

aphical \af-i-kəl\ graphical, biographical, cartographical, cosmographical, cryptographical, epigraphical, ethnographical, geographical, orthographical, petrographical, topographical, typographical, bibliographical, choreographical, hagiographical, iconographical, lexicographical, oceanographical, autobiographical, historiographical

aphics \af-iks\ graphics, demographics, micrographics, supergraphics

aphnis \af-nəs\ see AFTNESS

aphora \a-fə-rə\ anaphora, cataphora

api \äp-ē\ see OPPY

apid \ap-əd\ rapid, sapid, vapid

apie \ā-pē\ see APEY

apin \ap-ən\ see APPEN

apine \ap-ən\ see APPEN

apir \ā-pər\ see APER

apis \ā-pəs\ Apis, Priapus, Serapis

apist \ā-pəst\ papist, rapist, escapist, landscapist

aplain \ap-lən\ capelin, chaplain, chaplin, sapling

aple \ā-pəl\ maple, papal, staple

aples \ā-pəlz\ Naples—*also plurals and possessives of nouns and third person singular presents of verbs listed at* APLE

apless \ap-ləs\ hapless, napless, sapless, strapless

aplin \ap-lə-n\ see APLAIN

aply \ap-lē\ see APTLY

apnel \ap-nᵊl\ grapnel, shrapnel

apo \äp-ō\ capo, da capo, gestapo, Mount Apo

apolis \ap-ə-ləs\ Annapolis, Minneapolis, Indianapolis

apon \ā-pən\ see APEN

apor \ā-pər\ see APER

aporer \ā-pər-ər\ see APERER

apory \ā-prē\ see APERY

apour \ā-pər\ see APER

app \ap\ see ³AP

¹appa \äp-ə\ see ¹APA

²appa \ap-ə\ see ²APA

appable \ap-ə-bəl\ flappable, mappable, recappable, unflappable

appalli \äp-ə-lē\ see OPOLY

appe \ap\ see ³AP

apped \apt\ see APT

appen \ap-ən\ happen, lapin, rapine

¹apper \äp-ər\ see OPPER

²apper \ap-ər\ capper, clapper, crapper, dapper, flapper, knapper, rapper, sapper, scrapper, snapper, strapper, tapper, wrapper, zapper, backslapper, catnapper, didapper, kidnapper, knee-slapper, petnapper, wiretapper, handicapper, snippersnapper, understrapper, whippersnapper

appet \ap-ət\ lappet, tappet

apphic \af-ik\ see APHIC

appie \äp-ē\ see OPPY

appily \ap-ə-lē\ happily, scrappily, snappily, unhappily

appiness \ap-ē-nəs\ happiness, sappiness, scrappiness, snappiness, unhappiness

apping \ap-iŋ\ capping, mapping, strapping, trapping, wrapping, kneecapping, petnapping

apple \ap-əl\ apple, chapel, dapple, grapple, scrapple, antechapel, mayapple, pineapple

apps \aps\ see APSE

appy \ap-ē\ crappy, flappy, gappy, happy, nappy, pappy, sappy, scrappy, snappy, zappy, satrapy, serape, slaphappy, unhappy, triggerhappy

aps \aps\ see APSE

apse \aps\ apse, chaps, craps, lapse, schnapps, taps, traps, collapse, elapse, perhaps, prolapse, relapse, synapse, time-lapse—*also plurals and possessives of nouns and third singular presents of verbs listed at* ³AP

apt \apt\ apt, napped, rapt, adapt, black-capped, coapt, dewlapped, enrapt, inapt, snowcapped, unapt, untapped, periapt—*also pasts of verbs listed at* ³AP

apter \ap-tər\ captor, chapter, raptor, adapter

aption \ap-shən\ caption, adaption, contraption

aptive \ap-tiv\ captive, adaptive, maladaptive, preadaptive

aptly \ap-lē\ aptly, haply, raptly, inaptly, unaptly

aptor \ap-tər\ see APTER

apture \ap-chər\ rapture, enrapture, recapture

apular \ap-yə-lər\ papular, scapular

apus \ā-pəs\ see APIS

¹apy \ā-pē\ see APEY

²apy \ap-ē\ see APPY

¹aq \äk\ see ¹OCK

²aq \ak\ see ²ACK

aqi \äk-ē\ see OCKY

¹aque \āk\ see ¹AKE

²aque \ak\ see ²ACK

aqui \äk-ē\ see OCKY

¹ar \er\ see ⁴ARE

²ar \or\ see ¹OR

³ar \är\ ar, are, bar, barre, car, carr, char, charr, czar, far, gar, gnar, guar, jar, Lar, mar, moire, noir, our, par, parr, R, quare, Saar, scar, spar, SPAR, star, tar, tahr, Thar, tsar, tzar, yare, Adar, afar, ajar, all-star, armoire, attar, bazaar, beaux arts, Bihar, bizarre, boudoir, boxcar, boyar, briard, bulbar, Bulgar, bursar, canard, catarrh, Cathar, chukar, cigar, clochard, cougar, couloir, crossbar, crowbar, Dakar,

daystar, debar, decare, devoir, dinar, disbar, drawbar, Dunbar, durbar, earthstar, Elgar, eschar, eyebar, feldspar, five-star, flatcar, four-star, fulmar, gazar, guitar, Gunnar, Hagar, handcar, Hoggar, horsecar, hussar, Invar, Ishtar, Kolar, Loire, Iyar, jack-tar, jowar, Khowar, lahar, Lamar, lekvar, lodestar, Magyar, memoir, Mizar, Mylar, Navarre, nightjar, paillard, peignoir, petard, Pindar, pissoir, planar, plantar, polestar, pourboire, pulsar, qintar, quasar, radar, railcar, rebar, Renoir, Safar, Samar, sandbar, scalar, shikar, shofar, sidebar, sidecar, sirdar, sitar, sofar, solar, sonar, streetcar, Svalbard, tramcar, trocar, unbar, volar, voussoir, Weimar, abattoir, acinar, Ahaggar, Aligarh, aide-memoire, au revoir, avatar, bete noire, beurre noir, bolivar, Bolivar, café noir, caviar, cinnabar, commissar, communard, coplanar, Côte d'Ivoire, cultivar, deciare, deodar, Dreyfusard, escolar, escritoire, exemplar, fluorspar, handlebar, insofar, isobar, Issachar, jacamar, jaguar, Kandahar, Kashgar, kilobar, Krasnodar, Malabar, megabar, megastar, millibar, minicar, montagnard, motorcar, Mudejar, muscle car, Myanmar, Nicobar, objet d'art, pinot noir, Qiqihar,

registrar, rent-a-car,
repertoire, reservoir, ricercar,
samovar, scimitar, seminar,
simular, steak tartare,
subahdar, superstar, tutelar,
turbocar, VCR, Veadar,
zamindar, Zanzibar,
budgerigar, conservatoire,
Gulf of Mannar, Hubli-
Dharwar, kala-azar,
Kathiawar, proseminar

¹**ara** \är-ə\ Kara, Laura, Mara,
Nara, para, vara, Asmara,
Bambara, begorra, Bukhara,
Camorra, Ferrara, Gomorrah,
saguaro, Samara, samsara,
tantara, tiara, capybara,
carbonara, Connemara,
deodara, Gemarara,
Guadalajara, Guanabara,
solfatara, tuatara, Ogasawara,
Sagamihara, Tarahumara,
Timisoara

²**ara** \er-ə\ see ¹ERA

³**ara** \ar-ə\ Clara, jarrah, Kara,
Sara, Sarah, Tara, Bukhara,
cascara, mascara, Sahara,
Samara, Tamara, tantara,
tiara, capybara, caracara,
marinara, Santa Clara

⁴**ara** \ȯr-ə\ see ²ORA

arab \ar-əb\ Arab, Carib, carob,
scarab, shatt-al-Arabk

arable \ar-ə-bəl\ arable,
bearable, parable, shareable,
spareable, wearable,
declarable, unbearable,
inenarrable

aracen \ar-ə-sən\ see ARISON

aracin \ar-ə-sən\ see ARISON

arad \ar-əd\ see ARID

araday \ar-əd-ē\ faraday,
parody

arage \ar-ij\ see ARRIAGE

aragon \ar-ə-gən\ paragon,
tarragon

¹**arah** \er-ə\ see ¹ERA

²**arah** \ar-ə\ see ¹ARROW

¹**aral** \ar-əl\ see ²ARREL

²**aral** \ər-əl\ see ERRAL

¹**aralee** \ar-ə-lē\ Marilee,
Saralee

²**aralee** \er-ə-lē\ see ARILY

¹**aran** \er-ən\ see ¹ARON

²**aran** \ar-ən\ see ²ARON

¹**arant** \er-ənt\ see ¹ARENT

²**arant** \ar-ənt\ see ²ARENT

¹**araoh** \er-ō\ see ²ERO

²**araoh** \ar-ō\ see ²ARROW

araph \ar-əf\ see ARIFF

aras \är-əs\ see ¹ORRIS

arass \ar-əs\ see ²ARIS

arat \ar-ət\ Barrett, carat, caret,
carrot, claret, garret, Garrett,
karat, parrot, disparate

arate \ar-ət\ see ARAT

¹**arative** \er-ət-iv\ declarative,
imperative

²**arative** \ar-ət-iv\ narrative,
comparative, declarative,
preparative, reparative

arator \ar-ət-ər\ barrator,
apparitor, comparator,
preparator

arb \ärb\ barb, barbe, carb,
darb, garb, bicarb, rhubarb

arbel \är-bəl\ see ¹ARBLE

arber \är-bər\ see ARBOR

arbered \är-bərd\ see ARBOARD

arbin \är-bən\ see ARBON

¹**arble** \är-bəl\ barbel, garble,
marble

²**arble** \ȯr-bəl\ see ORBEL

arboard \är-bərd\ barbered,
larboard, starboard,
astarboard, unbarbered

arbon \är-bən\ carbon, Harbin

arbor \är-bər\ arbor, barber,
harbor, Pearl Harbor

¹arc \äk\ see ¹OCK

²arc \ärk\ see ¹ARK

arca \är-kə\ see ¹ARKA

¹arce \ers\ scarce, Nez Percé

²arce \ärs\ see ¹ARSE

arcel \är-səl\ see ARSAL

arcener \ärs-nər\ larcener,
parcener, coparcener

arch \ärch\ arch, larch, march,
March, parch, starch,
cornstarch, frog-march,
countermarch

archal \är-kəl\ darkle, sparkle,
exarchal, monarchal,
hierarchal, matriarchal,
patriarchal

archate \är-kət\ see ARKET

arche \ärsh\ see ARSH

arched \ärcht\ arched,
parched—*also pasts of verbs
listed at* ARCH

archer \är-chər\ archer,
marcher, departure

arches \är-chəz\ Arches,
Marches

archic \är-kik\ anarchic,
autarchic, autarkic,
monarchic, tetrarchic,
hierarchic, oligarchic

archical \är-ki-kəl\ autarchical,
autarkical, monarchical,
oligarchical

archon \är-kən\ see ARKEN

archy \är-kē\ barky, charqui,
darky, larky, snarky, anarchy,
autarchy, autarky, dyarchy,
eparchy, exarchy, heptarchy,
malarkey, menarche,
monarchy, pentarchy,
squirearchy, tetrarchy,
triarchy, trierarchy, hierarchy,
matriarchy, patriarchy,
oligarchy

arck \ärk\ see ¹ARK

arco \är-kō\ arco, narco

arct \ärkt\ see ARKED

¹arctic \ärk-tik\ arctic, Arctic,
antarctic, Antarctic, Holarctic,
Nearctic, subarctic, Palearctic,
subantarctic

²arctic \ärt-ik\ see ¹ARTIC

arcy \är-sē\ farcy, Parsi

¹ard \ärd\ bard, barred, card,
chard, Dard, fard, guard, hard,
lard, nard, pard, sard, shard,
yard, Asgard, backyard,
bankcard, barnyard, Bernard,
blackguard, blowhard,
boatyard, bombard, boneyard,
brassard, brickyard, canard,
churchyard, courtyard,
deeryard, die-hard, diehard,
discard, dockyard, dooryard,
farmyard, filmcard, fireguard,
foreyard, foulard, Gerard,
graveyard, ill-starred,
jacquard, junkyard, lifeguard,
Lombard, mansard, Midgard,
milliard, mudguard,
noseguard, petard, placard,
postcard, poularde, rear guard,
rearguard, regard, retard,
ritard, safeguard, scorecard,
shipyard, spikenard, steelyard,
stockyard, switchyard, tabard,
tanyard, tiltyard, unbarred,
unguard, vanguard, vizard,
avant-garde, Beauregard,

bodyguard, boulevard, disregard, goliard, Hildegard, interlard, Kierkegaard, Langobard, leotard, Longobard, no-holds-barred, lumberyard, Saint Bernard, Savoyard, Scotland Yard, self-regard, undercard, unitard, camelopard—*also pasts of verbs listed at* ³AR

²ard \är\ see ³AR

³ard \ȯrd\ see OARD

ardant \ärd-ᵊnt\ ardent, guardant, regardant, retardant

arde \ärd\ see ¹ARD

¹arded \ärd-əd\ guarded, mansarded, retarded, unguarded—*also pasts of verbs listed at* ¹ARD

²arded \ȯrd-əd\ corded, sordid, swarded, warded—*also pasts of verbs listed at* ²OARD

ardee \ȯrd-ē\ see ¹ORDY

¹arden \ärd-ᵊn\ Arden, Dardan, garden, harden, pardon, bombardon, caseharden, face-harden, Kincardine

²arden \ȯrd-ᵊn\ cordon, Gordon, Jordan, warden, churchwarden

ardener \ärd-nər\ gardener, hardener, pardner, pardoner, partner

ardent \ärd-ᵊnt\ see ARDANT

¹arder \ärd-ər\ ardor, carder, guarder, harder, larder, discarder, green-carder

²arder \ȯrd-ər\ see ORDER

ardi \ärd-ē\ see ARDY

¹ardian \ärd-ē-ən\ guardian, Edwardian, Lombardian

²ardian \ȯrd-ē-ən\ see ORDION

ardic \ärd-ik\ bardic, Dardic, Lombardic, Sephardic, goliardic, Longobardic

ardine \ärd-ᵊn\ see ¹ARDEN

arding \ȯrd-iŋ\ see ¹ORDING

ardingly \ȯrd-iŋ-lē\ see ORDINGLY

ardom \ärd-əm\ czardom, stardom, superstardom

ardon \ärd-ᵊn\ see ¹ARDEN

ardoner \ärd-nər\ see ARDENER

ardor \ärd-ər\ see ¹ARDER

ardy \ärd-ē\ hardy, Hardy, lardy, tardy, foolhardy, Lombardy, Sephardi

¹are \er-ē\ see ¹ARY

²are \är\ see ³AR

³are \är-ē\ see ¹ARI

⁴are \er\ air, Ayr, bare, bear, Blair, blare, chair, chare, Claire, Clare, dare, Dare, e'er, ere, err, eyre, fair, fare, flair, flare, glair, glare, hair, hare, Herr, heir, lair, mare, ne'er, pair, pare, pear, prayer, quare, rare, rear, scare, share, snare, spare, square, stair, stare, swear, tare, tear, their, there, they're, vair, ware, wear, weir, where, yare, affair, aglare, airfare, Ajmer, Altair, armchair, au pair, aware, barware, Basseterre, Baudelaire, beachwear, beware, bricklayer, bugbear, caneware, carfare, clayware, cochair, coheir, compare, compere, confrere, cookware, corsair, courseware, creamware, cudbear, day-care, daymare, decare, declare, delftware, despair, dishware, éclair, elsewhere, enclair, ensnare, eyewear, fanfare, fieldfare, firmware, flatware, Flaubert, footwear, forbear, forebear, forswear, foursquare, funfair, galère, giftware, glassware, Great Bear, Gruyère, hardware, hectare, horsehair, impair, infare, Khmer, Kildare, knitwear, Lake Eyre, life-care, longhair, loungewear, menswear, meunière, midair, mohair, Molière, neckwear, nightmare, outstare, outwear, Pierre, playwear, plein air, plowshare, Poor Clare, portiere, premiere, prepare, pushchair, rainwear, redware, repair, Saint Pierre, Sancerre, shorthair, skiwear, sleepwear, slipware, software, somewhere, spongeware, sportswear, stemware, stoneware, swimwear, threadbare, tinware, torchère, tracklayer, trouvère, tuyere, unfair, unhair, unswear, Voltaire, warfare, welfare, wheelchair, wirehair, workfare, aftercare, air-to-air, antiair, anywhere, bayadere, bêche-de-mer, billionaire, boutonniere, Camembert, chinaware, crackleware, cultivar, debonair, deciare, de la Mare, Delaware, derriere, dinnerware, disrepair, doctrinaire, earthenware, étagère, everywhere, Cape Finisterre, fourragère, Frigidaire, graniteware, hollowware, ironware, jasperware, kitchenware, laissez-faire, Lake Saint Clair, laquerware, legionnaire, luminaire, lusterware, maidenhair, mal de mer, medicare, metalware, millionaire, minaudière, minelayer, Mon-Khmer, Mousquetaire, nom de guerre, otherwhere, outerwear, overbear, overwear, potty-chair, porte cochere, questionnaire, rivière, Robespierre, Santander, savoir faire, self-aware, self-despair, silverware, solitaire, tableware, thoroughfare, unaware, underwear, vaporware, Venushair, vivandière, willowware, woodenware, yellowware, zillionaire, chargé d'affaires, chemin de fer, commissionaire, concessionaire, couturiere, Croix de guerre, devil-may-care, enamelware, memoriter, pied-à-terre, ready-to-wear, son et lumière, vin ordinaire, cordon sanitaire

area \er-ē-ə\ see ARIA

¹areable \er-ə-bəl\ see ¹EARABLE

²areable \ar-ə-bəl\ see ARABLE

areal \er-ē-əl\ see ARIAL

¹arean \er-ē-ən\ see ¹ARIAN

²arean \ar-ē-ən\ see ²ARIAN

ared \erd\ see AIRED

aredness \ar-əd-nəs\ see ARIDNESS

arel \ar-əl\ see ²ARREL

¹arely \er-lē\ see AIRLY

²**arely** \är-lē\ see ARLIE
arem \er-əm\ see ²ARUM
¹**arence** \er-əns\ clarence,
    Clarence, Terence, Terrance,
    Terrence, forbearance,
    transparence
²**arence** \ar-ən(ts)\ see ARENTS
¹**arent** \er-ənt\ daren't, errant,
    parent, aberrant, afferent,
    apparent, declarant, deferent,
    efferent, godparent,
    grandparent, inapparent,
    inerrant, knight-errant,
    sederunt, stepparent,
    transparent, semitransparent
²**arent** \ar-ənt\ arrant, daren't,
    parent, apparent, declarant,
    godparent, grandparent,
    stepparent, transparent,
    inapparent, semitransparent
¹**aren't** \er-ənt\ see ¹ARENT
²**aren't** \ar-ənt\ see ²ARENT
arents \ar-ən(t)s\ Barents,
    Clarence—*also plurals of*
    nouns listed at ²ARENT
¹**arer** \er-ər\ see ¹EARER
²**arer** \ar-ər\ see ³EARER
¹**ares** \erz\ see AIRS
²**ares** \ar-ēz\ Ares, caries, nares,
    Antares, Buenos Aires,
    primus inter pares—*also*
    plurals and possessives of
    nouns and third singular
    presents of verbs listed at
    ³ARRY
³**ares** \är-əs\ see ¹ORRIS
aret \ar-ət\ see ARAT
areve \är-və\ see ARVA
¹**arey** \ar-ē\ see ³ARRY
²**arey** \er-ē\ see ¹ARY
arez \är-əs\ see ¹ORRIS
¹**arf** \ärf\ barf, scarf

²**arf** \òrf\ see ORPH
arfarin \òr-fə-rən\ warfarin,
    hematoporphyrin
argain \är-gən\ bargain, jargon,
    plea-bargain
arge \ärj\ barge, charge, large,
    marge, Marge, parge, sarge,
    sparge, targe, discharge,
    enlarge, litharge, recharge,
    surcharge, take-charge,
    uncharge, by and large,
    hypercharge, overcharge,
    supercharge, undercharge
argent \är-jənt\ argent, margent,
    sargent, sergeant
arger \är-jər\ charger,
    discharger, enlarger,
    recharger, supercharger,
    turbocharger,
    turbosupercharger
arget \är-gət\ argot, garget,
    target, nontarget
argle \är-gəl\ gargle, argle-
    bargle
argo \är-gō\ Argo, argot, cargo,
    Fargo, largo, Margo, Margot,
    embargo, supercargo
argon \är-gən\ see ARGAIN
¹**argot** \är-gət\ see ARGET
²**argot** \är-gō\ see ARGO
arh \är\ see ³AR
¹**ari** \ä-rē\ Bari, gharry, laari,
    sari, scarry, sorry, starry,
    Bihari, curare, Imari, safari,
    scalare, shikari, tamari,
    calamari, cheboksary,
    Kalahari, Stradivari,
    zamindari, certiorari
²**ari** \er-ē\ see ¹ARY
³**ari** \ar-ē\ see ³ARRY
aria \er-ē-ə\ area, Beria, feria,
    kerria, varia, Bavaria,

Bulgaria, hysteria, malaria,
planaria, Samaria, adularia,
Carpentaria, cineraria,
fritillaria, laminaria,
luminaria, militaria,
sanguinaria, calceolaria, opera
seria, acetabularia

arial \er-ē-əl\ aerial, areal,
Ariel, burial, gharial,
glossarial, notarial, subaerial,
vicarial, actuarial, adversarial,
estuarial, secretarial,
prothonotarial

¹arian \er-ē-ən\ Arian, Aryan,
Carian, Marian, Marion,
parian, Parian, agrarian,
Aquarian, barbarian,
Bavarian, Bulgarian,
Cancerian, cesarean,
Caesarian, cnidarian,
frutarian, grammarian,
Hungarian, Khymerian,
librarian, Maid Marian,
ovarian, Pierian, riparian,
rosarian, Rotarian, sectarian,
Sumerian, Tartarean,
Tartarian, Tocharian,
Tractarian, Vulgarian,
Wagnerian, antiquarian,
apiarian, centenarian,
culinarian, Indo-Aryan,
jubilarian, lapidarian,
libertarian, millenarian,
nonsectarian, postlapsarian,
prelapsarian, Presbyterian,
proletarian, Rastafarian,
Ripuarian, Sabbatarian,
Sagittarian, sanitarian,
seminarian, trinitarian,
Trinitarian, unitarian,
Unitarian, vegetarian,
zoantharian, abecedarian,

Austro-Hungarian,
authoritarian, communitarian,
disciplinarian, documentarian,
egalitarian, equalitarian,
futilitarian, hereditarian,
humanitarian, majoritarian,
necessitarian, nonagenarian,
octogenarian, parliamentarian,
postmillinarian,
premillinarian, predestinarian,
radiolarian, Sacramentarian,
sexagenarian, totalitarian,
utilitarian, veterinarian,
establishmentarian,
inegalitarian, latitudinarian,
platitudinarian,
septuagenarian, solitudinarian,
uniformitarian, valetudinarian,
disestablishmentarian

²arian \ar-ē-ən\ Arian, Aryan,
carrion, clarion, Marian,
Marion, parian, Parian,
agrarian, Aquarian, barbarian,
Bavarian, Bulgarian,
caesarean, Caesarian,
cesarean, contrarian,
Hungarian, Megarian,
ovarian, rosarian, Tartarean,
Tartarian, Tocharian,
vulgarian, Indo-Aryan,
Rastafarian, Austro-Hungarian

ariance \ar-ē-əns\ tarriance,
variance, covariance,
vicariance

ariant \ar-ē-ənt\ variant,
vicariant

¹ariat \er-ē-ət\ heriot, lariat,
variate, bivariate, salariat,
vicariate, commissariat,
multivariate, proletariat,
secretariat, undersecretariat

²ariat \är-ē-ət\ see ¹AUREATE

³**ariat** \ar-ē-ət\ chariot, lariat, bivariate, salariat, commissariat, proletariat, Judas Iscariot

ariate \er-ē-ət\ see ¹ARIAT

arib \ar-əb\ see ARAB

aric \ar-ik\ barrack, carrack, Amharic, barbaric, Dinaric, Megaric, Pindaric, isobaric, Balearic

arice \ar-əs\ see ²ARIS

aricide \ar-ə-sīd\ see ARRICIDE

arid \ar-əd\ arid, farad, semiarid

aridin \ar-ə-dᵊn\ see ARRIDAN

aridness \ar-əd-nəs\ aridness, preparedness

¹**aried** \er-ēd\ see ERRIED

²**aried** \ar-ēd\ see ARRIED

ariel \er-ē-əl\ see ARIAL

¹**arier** \er-ē-ər\ see ERRIER

²**arier** \ar-ē-ər\ see ²ARRIER

aries \ar-ēz\ see ²ARES

ariff \ar-əf\ paraph, tariff

aril \ar-əl\ see ²ARREL

¹**arilee** \ar-ə-lē\ see ARALEE

²**arilee** \er-ə-lē\ see ARILY

arily \ar-ə-lē\ Marilee, merrily, Merrily, Saralee, scarily, sterily, verily, contrarily, primarily, arbitrarily, customarily, dietarily, exemplarily, fragmentarily, honorarily, literarily, mercenarily, militarily, momentarily, necessarily, salutarily, sanguinarily, sanitarily, secondarily, temporarily, unitarily, voluntarily, contemporarily, elementarily, extemporarily, extraordinarily, hereditarily, imaginarily, involuntarily, preliminarily, rudimentarily, subsidiarily, unnecessarily, documentarily, evolutionarily, revolutionarily

arin \är-ən\ see ¹ORIN

arinate \ar-ə-nət\ see ARONET

arinet \ar-ə-nət\ see ARONET

¹**aring** \ar-iŋ\ airing, Bering, fairing, flaring, glaring, herring, paring, raring, sparing, tearing, wearing, cheeseparing, childbearing, seafaring, time-sharing, unerring, unsparing, wayfaring

²**aring** \er-ən\ see ¹ARON

ario \er-ē-ō\ stereo, Ontario

¹**arion** \ar-ē-ən\ see ²ARIAN

²**arion** \er-ē-ən\ see ¹ARIAN

ariot \ar-ē-ət\ see ³ARIAT

arious \ar-ē-əs\ Arius, carious, Darious, scarious, various, Aquarius, burglarious, calcareous, contrarious, denarius, gregarious, guarnerius, hilarious, nefarious, precarious, senarius, vagarious, vicarious, multifarious, omnifarious, septenarius, Stradivarius, Sagittarius, temerarious

¹**aris** \är-əs\ see ¹ORRIS

²**aris** \ar-əs\ arras, arris, Clarice, harass, Harris, heiress, Paris, parous, varus, coheiress, embarrass, Polaris, disembarrass, millionairess, Lewis with Harris, plaster of paris

¹**arish** \er-ish\ bearish, cherish,

fairish, garish, perish, squarish, nightmarish

²**arish** \ar-ish\ garish, marish, parish

arison \ar-ə-sən\ characin, garrison, Garrison, Harrison, Saracen, warison, caparison, comparison

arist \er-əst\ Marist, querist, aquarist, pleinairist, scenarist, apiarist—*also superlatives of adjectives listed at* ⁴ARE

aritan \er-ət-ᵊn\ see ERATIN

aritor \ar-ət-ər\ see ARATOR

¹**arity** \er-ət-ē\ see ERITY

²**arity** \ar-ət-ē\ carroty, charity, clarity, parity, rarity, barbarity, disparity, hilarity, imparity, polarity, unclarity, vulgarity, angularity, familiarity, insularity, peculiarity, popularity, regularity, similarity, singularity, solidarity, complementarity, dissimilarity, irregularity, particularity, unfamiliarity, unpopularity

arium \er-ē-əm\ barium, aquarium, herbarium, sacrarium, samarium, solarium, terrarium, velarium, vivarium, cinerarium, columbarium, honorarium, leprosarium, oceanarium, planetarium, sanitarium, syllabarium, termitarium, armamentarium

arius \er-ē-əs\ see ARIOUS

¹**ark** \ärk\ arc, ark, bark, Clark, Clarke, dark, hark, lark, marc, Marc, mark, Mark, marque, narc, nark, park, Park, quark, sark, shark, spark, stark, aardvark, airpark, anarch, ballpark, birchbark, birthmark, Bismarck, bookmark, debark, demark, Denmark, earmark, embark, endarch, exarch, footmark, futhark, Graustark, hallmark, ironbark, landmark, Lake Clark, Lamarck, monarch, ostmark, Ozark, Petrarch, pitch-dark, Plutarch, pockmark, postmark, pressmark, pugmark, reichsmark, remark, remarque, Remarque, ringbark, seamark, shagbark, sitzmark, skylark, soapbark, tanbark, tetrarch, tidemark, titlark, touchmark, trademark, acritarch, cutty sark, deutsche mark, disembark, double-park, hierarch, Joan of Arc, matriarch, meadowlark, metalmark, minipark, oligarch, patriarch, stringybark, telemark, watermark, trierarch, heresiarch, symposiarch

²**ark** \örk\ see ²ORK

³**ark** \ərk\ see ¹ORK

¹**arka** \är-kə\ charka, parka, anasarca, Hamilcar Barca

²**arka** \ər-kə\ see ¹URKA

arke \ärk\ see ¹ARK

arked \ärkt\ marked, chop-marked, infarct, ripple-marked, unremarked—*also pasts of verbs listed at* ¹ARK

arken \är-kən\ darken, hearken

arker \är-kər\ barker, larker,

marker, parker, Parker, sparker, bookmarker, skylarker, nosey parker—*also comparatives of adjectives listed at* ¹ARK

arket \är-kət\ market, downmarket, mass-market, newmarket, test-market, upmarket, aftermarket, hypermarket, matriarchate, patriarchate, supermarket

arkey \är-kē\ see ARCHY

arkian \är-kē-ən\ Graustarkian, Lamarckian, Monarchian

arkic \är-kik\ see ARCHIC

arking \är-kiŋ\ barking, Barking, carking, parking, loan-sharking

arkle \är-kəl\ see ARCHAL

arks \ärks\ Marks, parks—*also plurals of nouns and third person singular presents of verbs listed at* ARK

arky \är-kē\ see ARCHY

arl \ärl\ carl, Carl, farl, gnarl, jarl, Karl, marl, parle, quarrel, snarl, ensnarl, housecarl, unsnarl, Albemarle

arla \är-lə\ Carla, Darla, Karla, Marla

arlan \ä-lən\ see ARLINE

arland \är-lənd\ garland, Garland, Harland

arlatan \är-lət-ᵊn\ charlatan, tarlatan

arlay \är-lē\ see ARLIE

arle \ärl\ see ARL

arlen \är-lən\ see ARLINE

arler \är-lər\ see ARLOR

arless \är-ləs\ Carlos, parlous, scarless, starless

arlet \är-lət\ charlotte,

Charlotte, harlot, scarlet, starlet, varlet

arley \är-lē\ see ARLIE

arlic \är-lik\ garlic, pilgarlic

arlie \är-lē\ barley, charlie, Charlie, gnarly, Harley, marly, parlay, parley, snarly, yarely, bizarrely, Mr. Charlie

arlin \är-lən\ see ARLINE

arline \är-lən\ Arlen, carline, Harlan, marlin, Marlin, marline, Marlyn

arling \är-liŋ\ carling, darling, Darling, starling

arlor \är-lər\ parlor, quarreler, snarler

arlos \är-ləs\ see ARLESS

arlot \är-lət\ see ARLET

arlotte \är-lət\ see ARLET

arlous \är-ləs\ see ARLESS

arlow \är-lō\ Barlow, Harlow

arly \är-lē\ see ARLIE

arlyn \ä-lən\ see ARLINE

¹arm \ärm\ arm, barm, charm, farm, harm, smarm, alarm, disarm, firearm, forearm, gendarme, gisarme, poor farm, rearm, sidearm, stiffarm, straight-arm, strong-arm, tonearm, unarm, yardarm, overarm, underarm

²arm \äm\ see ¹OM

³arm \ȯrm\ see ²ORM

¹arma \är-mə\ dharma, karma, Parma

²arma \ər-mə\ see ERMA

arman \är-mən\ barman, Carmen, carmine, Harmon

armed \ärmd\ armed, charmed, unarmed—*also pasts of verbs listed at* ¹ARM

armen \är-mən\ see ARMAN

arment \är-mənt\ garment, varmint, debarment, disbarment, undergarment, overgarment

¹armer \är-mər\ armor, charmer, farmer, harmer, disarmer

²armer \or-mər\ see ¹ORMER

armic \ər-mik\ see ERMIC

armine \är-mən\ see ARMAN

¹arming \är-miŋ\ charming, farming, alarming, disarming

²arming \or-miŋ\ see ORMING

armint \är-mənt\ see ARMENT

armless \ärm-ləs\ armless, charmless, harmless

armoir \är-mər\ see ¹ARMER

armon \är-mən\ see ARMAN

army \är-mē\ army, barmy, smarmy

¹arn \ärn\ Arne, barn, darn, Marne, tarn, yarn, carbarn, lucarne

²arn \orn\ see ²ORN

arna \ər-nə\ see ERNA

arnal \ärn-°l\ see ARNEL

arnate \är-nət\ Barnet, garnet, discarnate, incarnate

¹arne \ärn\ see ¹ARN

²arne \är-nē\ see ARNY

arnel \ärn-°l\ carnal, charnel, darnel

¹arner \är-nər\ darner, garner, yarner

²arner \or-nər\ see ORNER

arness \är-nəs\ harness, bizarreness

arnet \är-nət\ see ARNATE

arney \är-nē\ see ARNY

arnhem \är-nəm\ see ARNUM

arning \or-niŋ\ see ORNING

arnish \är-nish\ garnish, tarnish, varnish

arnum \är-nəm\ Arnhem, Barnum

arny \är-nē\ Barney, barny, blarney, carny, Killarney, chili con carne

¹aro \er-ō\ see ²ERO

²aro \ar-ō\ see ²ARROW

³aro \är-ə\ see ¹ARA

⁴aro \är-ō\ see ¹ORROW

arob \ar-əb\ see ARAB

arody \ar-əd-ē\ see ARADAY

¹aroe \ar-ō\ see ²ARROW

²aroe \er-ō\ see ²ERO

arol \ar-əl\ see ²ARREL

¹arold \ar-əld\ Darold, Harold

²arold \er-əld\ see ERALD

arole \ar-əl\ see ²ARREL

arom \er-əm\ see ²ARUM

¹aron \er-ən\ Aaron, Charon, Erin, garron, heron, perron, raring, Sharon, Sharron, sierran, rose of Sharon, sub-Saharan

²aron \ar-ən\ Aaron, baron, barren, Charon, garron, Sharon, Sharron, rose of Sharon, sub-Saharan

aronet \ar-ə-nət\ baronet, carinate, clarinet

¹arous \er-əs\ see ERROUS

²arous \ar-əs\ see ²ARIS

¹arp \ärp\ carp, harp, scarp, sharp, tarp, cardsharp, escarp, Jews harp, Autoharp, vibraharp

²arp \orp\ see ORP

arpen \är-pən\ sharpen, tarpon

arper \är-pər\ carper, harper, scarper, sharper, cardsharper

arpie \är-pē\ see ARPY

arpon \är-pən\ see ARPEN

arpy \är-pē\ harpy, sharpie

arque \ärk\ see ¹ARK

arquetry \är-kə-trē\ marquetry, parquetry

arqui \är-kē\ see ARCHY

arrable \ar-ə-bəl\ see ARABLE

¹arrack \ar-ik\ see ARIC

²arrack \ar-ək\ arrack, barrack, carrack

arragon \ar-ə-gən\ see ARAGON

arral \ar-əl\ see ²ARREL

arram \ar-əm\ see ²ARUM

¹arrant \ar-ənt\ see ²ARENT

²arrant \ȯr-ənt\ see ORRENT

arras \ar-əs\ see ²ARIS

arrass \ar-əs\ see ²ARIS

arrative \ar-ət-iv\ see ²ARATIVE

arrator \ar-ət-ər\ see ARATOR

arre \är\ see ³AR

arred \ärd\ see ¹ARD

¹arrel \ȯrl\ see ³ORAL

²arrel \ar-əl\ Aral, aril, barrel, Beryl, carol, Carol, Carole, Caryl, carrel, Carroll, Darrel, Darrell, Darryl, Daryl, Errol, Karol, parol, parral, parrel, apparel, cracker-barrel, double-barrel

arreler \är-lər\ see ARLOR

arrell \ar-əl\ see ²ARREL

arrely \är-lē\ see ARLIE

¹arren \ar-ən\ see ²ARON

²arren \ȯr-ən\ see ²ORIN

³arren \är-ən\ see ¹ORIN

arrener \ȯr-ə-nər\ see ORONER

arreness \är-nəs\ see ARNESS

arret \ar-ət\ see ARAT

arrett \ar-ət\ see ARAT

arrh \är\ see ³AR

arriage \ar-ij\ carriage, marriage, disparage, miscarriage, intermarriage, undercarriage

arriance \ar-ē-əns\ see ARIANCE

arricide \ar-ə-sīd\ parricide, acaricide

arridan \ar-ə-dᵊn\ harridan, cantharidin

arrie \ar-ē\ see ³ARRY

arried \ar-ēd\ harried, married, varied, unmarried

¹arrier \ȯr-ē-ər\ see ARRIOR

²arrier \ar-ē-ər\ barrier, carrier, farrier, harrier, varier, ballcarrier, spear-carrier

arrion \ar-ē-ən\ see ²ARIAN

arrior \ȯr-ē-ər\ quarrier, sorrier, warrior

arris \ar-əs\ see ²ARIS

arrison \ar-ə-sən\ see ARISON

arro \är-ō\ see ¹ORROW

arroll \ar-əl\ see ²ARREL

arron \ar-ən\ see ²ARON

arrot \ar-ət\ see ARAT

arroty \ar-ət-ē\ see ²ARITY

arrow \ar-ō\ aero, arrow, barrow, Darrow, Faeroe, faro, Faroe, farrow, harrow, Harrow, marrow, narrow, pharaoh, sparrow, taro, tarot, yarrow, handbarrow, Point Barrow, wheelbarrow

arrowy \ar-ə-wē\ arrowy, marrowy

¹arry \är-ē\ see ¹ARI

²arry \ȯr-ē\ see ORY

³arry \ar-ē\ Barrie, Barry, Carey, Carrie, carry, Cary, chary, Gary, Garry, gharry, harry, Harry, Larry, marry, nary, parry, Shari, tarry, glengarry, miscarry, safari, shikari, cash-and-carry, hari-

kari, intermarry, Stradivari;
Tom, Dick, and Harry

arryl \ar-əl\ see ²ARREL

ars \ärz\ Lars, Mars, ours—*also
plurals and possessives of
nouns and third person
singular presents of verbs
listed at* ³AR

arsal \är-səl\ parcel, versal,
tarsal, metatarsal

¹arse \ärs\ arse, farce, marse,
parse, sparse

²arse \ärz\ see ARS

arsh \ärsh\ harsh, marsh,
demarche

arshal \är-shəl\ see ARTIAL

arshall \är-shəl\ see ARTIAL

arshen \är-shən\ harshen,
martian

arsi \är-sē\ see ARCY

arsis \är-səs\ see ARSUS

arsle \äs-əl\ see OSSAL

arson \ärs-ᵊn\ arson, Carson,
parson

arsus \är-səs\ arsis, tarsus,
Tarsus, catharsis, metatarsus

¹art \ärt\ art, Art, Bart, cart,
chart, Chartres, dart, hart,
Harte, heart, kart, mart, part,
Sartre, scart, smart, start, tart,
apart, blackheart, compart,
depart, Descartes, dispart,
dogcart, Earhart, flowchart,
forepart, go-cart, greenheart,
handcart, Hobart, impart,
jump-start, Mozart,
mouthpart, outsmart, oxcart,
oxheart, pushcart, rampart,
redstart, restart, street-smart,
Stuttgart, sweetheart, tipcart,
upstart, à la carte, anti-art,
applecart, Bonaparte,

counterpart, heart-to-heart,
purpleheart, underpart,
upperpart

²art \ȯrt\ see ¹ORT

arta \är-tə\ Marta, Sparta,
Djarkarta, Magna Carta, Santa
Marta, Surakarta, yogyakarta

artable \ärt-ə-bəl\ see ARTIBLE

¹artan \ärt-ᵊn\ see ARTEN

²artan \ȯrt-ᵊn\ see ORTEN

artar \ärt-ər\ see ¹ARTER

¹arte \ärt-ē\ see ¹ARTY

²arte \ärt\ see ¹ART

¹arted \ärt-əd\ see EARTED

²arted \ȯrt-əd\ see ORTED

arten \ärt-ᵊn\ Barton, carton,
hearten, marten, martin,
Martin, smarten, Spartan,
tartan, baum marten,
dishearten, Dumbarton,
freemartin, Saint Martin, Sint
Maarten, kindergarten

¹arter \ärt-ər\ barter, carter,
Carter, charter, darter, garter,
martyr, starter, tartar,
nonstarter, self-starter,
protomartyr—*also
comparatives of adjectives
listed at* ¹ART

²arter \ȯt-ər\ see ¹ATER

³arter \ȯrt-ər\ see ORTER

artern \ȯt-ərn\ see AUTERNE

artery \ärt-ə-rē\ artery, martyry

artes \ärt\ see ¹ART

artford \ärt-fərd\ Hartford,
Hertford

arth \ärth\ garth, Garth, hearth,
Hogarth

arti \ärt-ē\ see ¹ARTY

artial \är-shəl\ marshal,
Marshal, Marshall, martial,

Martial, partial, court-martial, impartial

artian \är-shən\ see ARSHEN

artible \ärt-ə-bəl\ partible, startable, impartible, restartable

¹artic \ärt-ik\ arctic, Arctic, antarctic, Antarctic, cathartic, Nearctic, Palearctic

²artic \ort-ik\ quartic, aortic

article \ärt-i-kəl\ article, particle, microparticle

artile \ort-ºl\ see ORTAL

artily \ärt-ºl-ē\ artily, heartily

artin \ärt-ºn\ see ARTEN

arting \ärt-iŋ\ carting, charting, karting, parting, starting, flowcharting, self-starting

artisan \ärt-ə-zən\ artisan, bartizan, partisan, bipartisan, nonpartisan

artist \ärt-əst\ artist, chartist, Chartist, Bonapartist

artizan \ärt-ə-zən\ see ARTISAN

artless \ärt-ləs\ artless, heartless

artlet \ärt-lət\ martlet, partlet, tartlet

¹artly \ärt-lē\ partly, smartly, tartly

²artly \ort-lē\ see ²ORTLY

artment \ärt-mənt\ apartment, compartment, department

artner \ärt-nər\ partner, kindergartner

¹arton \ort-ºn\ see ORTON

²arton \ärt-ºn\ see ARTEN

artre \ärt\ see ¹ART

artres \ärt\ see ¹ART

artridge \är-trij\ cartridge, partridge

¹arts \är\ see ³AR

²arts \ärts\ Hartz—*also plurals*

and possessives of nouns and third person singular presents of verbs listed at ¹ART

arture \är-chər\ see ARCHER

¹arty \ärt-ē\ arty, hearty, party, smarty, tarty, Astarte, ex parte, Havarti, Buonaparte, commedia del l'arte

²arty \ort-ē\ see ORTY

artyr \ärt-ər\ see ¹ARTER

artyry \ärt-ə-rē\ see ARTERY

¹artz \orts\ see ORTS

²artz \ärts\ see ²ARTS

aru \ä-rü\ Bukaru, Johore Bahru, Pakan Baru

¹arum \är-əm\ larum, alarum

²arum \er-əm\ arum, carom, harem, Sarum, Muharram, harum-scarum, arbiter elegantiarum

arus \ar-əs\ see ²ARIS

arva \är-və\ larva, Marva, parve, pareve

arval \är-vəl\ see ARVEL

¹arve \ärv\ carve, starve, varve

²arve \är-və\ see ARVA

arvel \är-vəl\ carvel, larval, marvel

arven \är-vən\ carven, Marvin, Caernarvon

arvin \är-vən\ see ARVEN

arvon \är-vən\ see ARVEN

¹ary \er-ē\ aerie, aery, airy, berry, bury, Carey, Cary, Cherie, cherry, Cherry, chary, clary, dairy, Derry, faerie, fairy, ferry, Gary, Garry, Gerry, glairy, glary, hairy, Jere, Jeri, Jerrie, Jerry, kerry, Kerry, Mary, marry, merry, Merry, nary, perry, Perry, prairie, quaere, query, scary,

serry, Shari, Sheri, Sherrie,
sherry, Sherry, skerry, terry,
Terry, vary, very, wary,
wherry, baneberry, barberry,
bayberry, bearberry, bilberry,
blackberry, blaeberry,
blueberry, Bradbury,
bunchberry, Burberry, canary,
Canary, chokeberry,
chokecherry, cloudberry,
contrary, coralberry,
costmary, cowberry,
cranberry, crowberry,
deerberry, dewberry, equerry,
gooseberry, ground-cherry,
hackberry, hegari, inkberry,
Juneberry, knobkerrie, library,
mulberry, nondairy,
pokeberry, primary, raspberry,
rosemary, Rosemary, scalare,
shadberry, sheepberry,
snowberry, soapberry,
strawberry, summary,
teaberry, tilbury, twinberry,
unwary, vagary, wolfberry,
youngberry, actuary,
adversary, airy-fairy,
ancillary, antiquary, apiary,
arbitrary, aviary, axillary,
beriberi, bestiary, biliary,
boysenberry, breviary,
budgetary, calamari,
calamary, candleberry,
Canterbury, capillary,
cartulary, cassowary,
catenary, cautionary, cavitary,
cemetery, centenary,
certiorari, chartulary,
checkerberry, chinaberry,
ciliary, cinerary, cometary,
commentary, commissary,
condottiere, corollary,

coronary, culinary, customary,
dictionary, dietary, dignitary,
dingleberry, dromedary,
dysentery, elderberry,
emissary, estuary, farkleberry,
February, formicary,
formulary, fragmentary,
fritillary, functionary,
funerary, honorary,
huckleberry, intermarry,
janissary, January, lamasery,
lapidary, lectionary,
legendary, legionary, limitary,
lingonberry, literary,
loganberry, luminary,
mammillary, mandatary,
maxillary, medullary,
mercenary, miliary, military,
millenary, milliary, millinery,
miserere, missionary,
momentary, monastery,
monetary, mortuary,
necessary, ordinary, ossuary,
papillary, parcenary,
partridgeberry, pensionary,
phalanstery, pigmentary,
plagiary, planetary,
Pondicherry, prebendary,
presbytery, pulmonary,
pupillary, quaternary,
questionary, reliquary,
rowanberry, salivary,
salmonberry, salutary,
sanctuary, sanguinary,
sanitary, secondary, secretary,
sedentary, seminary,
serviceberry, silverberry,
solitary, stationary, stationery,
statuary, Stradivari,
subcontrary, sublunary,
sugarberry, sumptuary,
syllabary, temporary,

termitary, tertiary, textuary,
thimbleberry, Tipperary, Tom
and Jerry, topiary, tributary,
tutelary, unitary, urinary,
vestiary, visionary, voluntary,
vulnerary, Waterbury,
whortleberry, winterberry,
ablutionary, accretionary,
antiphonary, apothecary,
bicentenary, bilmillenary,
concessionary, conclusionary,
concretionary, confectionary,
confectionery, consigliere,
constabulary, contemporary,
convulsionary, coparcenary,
depositary, delusionary,
digressionary, disciplinary,
discretionary, distributary,
diversionary, electuary,
epistolary, exclusionary,
expansionary, expeditionary,
extemporary, extortionary,
extraordinary, fiduciary,
hereditary, illusionary,
imaginary, incendiary,
inflationary, insanitary,
intercalary, involuntary,
itinerary, judiciary,
libationary, obituary,
officiary, pecuniary,
petitionary, precautionary,
preliminary, presidiary,
previsionary, probationary,
proprietary, provisionary,
reactionary, recessionary,
reflationary, residuary,
reversionary, revisionary,
stagflationary, stipendiary,
subliterary, subsidiary,
subversionary, tercentenary,
traditionary, tumultuary,
unnecessary, veterinary,
vocabulary, voluptuary,
abolitionary, beneficiary,
consuetudinary, deflationary,
devolutionary, disinflationary,
domiciliary, eleemosynary,
elocutionary, evidentiary,
evolutionary, extraliterary,
intermediary, paramilitary,
penitentiary, quatercentenary,
revolutionary, semicentenary,
semilegendary,
sesquicentenary, superciliary,
supernumerary,
tintinnabulary,
transdisciplinary,
usufructuary, valetudinary,
interdisciplinary,
plenipotentiary,
counterrevolutionary

²**ary** \ar-ē\ see ³ARRY
³**ary** \är-ē\ see ¹ARI
¹**aryan** \er-ē-ən\ see ¹ARIAN
²**aryan** \ar-ē-ən\ see ²ARIAN
aryl \ar-əl\ see ²ARREL
¹**as** \ash\ see ³ASH
²**as** \as\ see ³ASS
³**as** \az\ see AZZ
⁴**as** \ä\ see ¹A
⁵**as** \äsh\ see ¹ASH
⁶**as** \äz\ see ¹OISE
⁷**as** \əz\ see ¹EUSE
⁸**as** \äs\ see ¹OS
⁹**as** \ò\ see ¹AW
¹**asa** \äs-ə\ casa, fossa, glossa,
    Lhasa, Ossa, kielbasa,
    Kinshasa, Landrace,
    Mombasa, tabula rasa
²**asa** \äz-ə\ see ¹AZA
³**asa** \as-ə\ see ASSA
¹**asable** \ā-zə-bəl\ grazeable,
    persuasible, paraphrasable
²**asable** \ā-sə-bəl\ see ACEABLE

¹**asal** \ā-səl\ basal, Basil, stay sail, forestay sail

²**asal** \ā-zəl\ basal, Basil, hazel, Hazel, nasal, phrasal, appraisal, Azazel

asally \āz-lē\ see AISLEY

asca \as-kə\ see ASKA

ascal \as-kəl\ paschal, rascal

ascan \as-kən\ see ASKIN

ascar \as-kər\ see ASKER

¹**ascence** \ās-°ns\ nascence, complacence, complaisance, renascence

²**ascence** \as-°ns\ nascence, renascence

¹**ascent** \as-°nt\ nascent, passant, renascent

²**ascent** \ās-°nt\ see ACENT

¹**asch** \ask\ see ASK

²**asch** \äsh\ see ¹ASH

³**asch** \ȯsh\ see ²ASH

aschal \as-kəl\ see ASCAL

¹**ascia** \ā-shə\ see ACIA

²**ascia** \ash-ə\ see ²ASHA

ascible \as-ə-bəl\ see ASSABLE

ascicle \as-i-kəl\ see ASSICAL

¹**asco** \äs-kō\ see OSCOE

²**asco** \as-kō\ fiasco, Tabasco

ascon \as-kən\ see ASKIN

ascot \as-kət\ see ASKET

ascus \as-kəs\ Damascus, Velazquez

¹**ase** \ās\ see ¹ACE

²**ase** \āz\ see ¹AZE

³**ase** \äz\ see ¹OISE

asel \äz-əl\ see OZZLE

ased \āst\ see ACED

aseless \ā-sləs\ see ACELESS

aseman \ā-smən\ see ACEMAN

asement \ās-mənt\ basement, casement, debasement, bargain-basement

¹**aser** \ā-sər\ see ¹ACER

²**aser** \ā-zər\ see AZER

asey \ā-sē\ see ACY

¹**ash** \äsh\ bosh, cosh, Fosh, frosh, gosh, gouache, josh, Mâche, nosh, posh, quash, slosh, squash, swash, tosh, wash, awash, backwash, blackwash, cohosh, czardas, Dias, Diaz, downwash, eyewash, galosh, ganache, goulash, kibosh, midrash, mishmash, mouthwash, musquash, panache, rainwash, Siwash, whitewash, wish-wash, hamantasch, mackintosh, McIntosh

²**ash** \ȯsh\ Bosch, Foch, gosh, grosz, quash, slosh, squash, swash, wash, awash, backwash, Balkhash, blackwash, brainwash, brioche, Bydgoszcz, downwash, eyewash, hogwash, Iasi, mouthwash, outwash, rainwash, Siwash, whitewash, wish-wash, hamantasch

³**ash** \ash\ ash, bash, brash, cache, cash, clash, crash, dash, fash, flash, gash, gnash, hash, lash, mash, pash, plash, rash, sash, slash, smash, splash, stash, thrash, thresh, trash, abash, backlash, backsplash, Balkhash, calash, Chumash, czardas, encash, eyelash, goulash, mishmash, moustache, mustache, panache, potash, rehash, slapdash, soutache, stramash, tongue-lash, unlash, whiplash,

balderdash, calabash, succotash

¹asha \äsh-ə\ kasha, pasha, quassia, Falasha

²asha \ash-ə\ cassia, fascia, pasha

ashan \ash-ən\ see ASSION

¹ashed \ósht\ sloshed, stonewashed, unwashed—*also pasts of verbs listed at* ²ASH

²ashed \asht\ dashed, Rasht, smashed, unabashed—*also pasts of verbs listed at* ³ASH

ashen \ash-ən\ see ASSION

¹asher \äsh-ər\ josher, nosher, squasher, swasher, washer, dishwasher

²asher \ósh-ər\ swasher, washer, brainwasher, dishwasher, whitewasher

³asher \ash-ər\ Asher, basher, brasher, clasher, crasher, dasher, flasher, masher, rasher, slasher, smasher, splasher, thrasher, gate-crasher, haberdasher

ashew \a-shü\ cachou, cashew

¹ashi \äsh-ē\ see ¹ASHY

²ashi \ash-ē\ see ²ASHY

ashing \ash-iŋ\ crashing, dashing, flashing, mashing, slashing, smashing

ashion \ash-ən\ see ASSION

asht \asht\ see ²ASHED

¹ashy \äsh-ē\ dashi, Iasi, Kashi, squashy, washy, Funabashi, Lubumbashi, Toyohashi, wishy-washy

²ashy \ash-ē\ ashy, flashy, Kashi, splashy, trashy

¹asi \äs-ē\ see ¹OSSY

²asi \äz-ē\ see ¹AZI

³asi \ósh\ see ²ASH

⁴asi \äsh-ē\ see ¹ASHY

asia \ā-zhə\ Asia, aphasia, Eurasia, fantasia, Malaysia, Anastasia, Australasia, euthanasia, antonomasia

¹asian \ā-shən\ see ¹ATION

²asian \ā-zhən\ see ASION

asible \ā-zə-bəl\ see ¹ASABLE

asic \ā-zik\ basic, phasic, biphasic, diphasic, multiphasic, polyphasic

asid \as-əd\ see ACID

asie \ā-sē\ see ACY

¹asil \as-əl\ see ²ASSEL

²asil \az-əl\ see AZZLE

³asil \ās-əl\ see ¹ASAL

⁴asil \āz-əl\ see ²ASAL

⁵asil \äz-əl\ see OZZLE

asin \ās-°n\ see ¹ASON

¹asing \ā-siŋ\ see ACING

²asing \ā-ziŋ\ see AISING

asion \ā-zhən\ Asian, suasion, abrasion, Caucasian, corrasion, dissuasion, equation, Eurasian, evasion, invasion, occasion, persuasion, pervasion, Amerasian, Athanasian, dermabrasion, Rabelaisian, overpersuasion

asional \āzh-nəl\ equational, occasional

¹asis \ā-səs\ basis, stasis, oasis

²asis \as-əs\ see ²ASSIS

asium \ā-zē-əm\ dichasium, gymnasium

asive \ā-siv\ suasive, abrasive, assuasive, corrasive, dissuasive, embracive, evasive, invasive, persuasive, pervasive, noninvasive

ask \ask\ ask, bask, Basque, cask, casque, flask, mask, masque, Pasch, task, unmask, photomask

aska \as-kə\ Alaska, Itasca, Nebraska, Athabaska

askan \as-kən\ see ASKIN

asked \ast\ see ²AST

asker \as-kər\ lascar, masker, masquer, Madagascar

asket \as-kət\ ascot, basket, casket, gasket, breadbasket, handbasket, wastebasket, workbasket

askin \as-kən\ gascon, gaskin, Alaskan, Tarascan, Athapaskan

asking \as-kiŋ\ multitasking—also present participles of verbs listed at ASK

asm \az-əm\ chasm, plasm, spasm, chiasm, orgasm, phantasm, sarcasm, chiliasm, ectoplasm, pleonasm, enthusiasm, blepharospasm, iconoclasm

asma \az-mə\ asthma, plasma, chiasma, miasma, phantasma

asman \az-mən\ see ASMINE

asmine \az-mən\ jasmine, Tasman

asn't \əz-ənt\ doesn't, wasn't

¹aso \as-ō\ see ¹ASSO

²aso \äs-ō\ see ²ASSO

¹ason \ās-ən\ basin, caisson, chasten, hasten, Jason, mason, Mason, Foxe Basin, Freemason, Great Basin, stonemason, washbasin, diapason, Donets Basin

²ason \āz-ən\ see AZON

asp \asp\ asp, clasp, gasp, grasp, hasp, rasp, enclasp, handclasp, last-gasp, unclasp

asper \as-pər\ clasper, jasper, Jasper

asperate \as-prət\ aspirate, exasperate

aspirate \as-prət\ see ASPERATE

asque \ask\ see ASK

asquer \as-kər\ see ASKER

¹ass \ās\ see ¹ACE

²ass \äs\ see ¹OS

³ass \as\ as, bass, Bass, brass, class, crass, frass, gas, glass, grass, has, lass, mass, pass, sass, sauce, strass, tace, tasse, trass, vas, wrasse, admass, alas, Alsace, amass, avgas, bagasse, band-pass, bluegrass, bromegrass, bunchgrass, bypass, cordgrass, crabgrass, crevasse, cuirass, cut-grass, declass, degas, Donbas, Drygas, eelgrass, en masse, eyeglass, first-class, groundmass, harass, high-class, hourglass, impasse, knotgrass, Kuzbass, landmass, Madras, morass, outclass, outgas, palliasse, Petras, plateglass, repass, ribgrass, rubasse, ryegrass, sandglass, shortgrass, spyglass, subclass, sunglass, surpass, switchgrass, tallgrass, teargas, trespass, Troas, wineglass, wiseass, witchgrass, biogas, biomass, demiglace, demitasse, fiberglass, gallowglass, gravitas, Hallowmas, hardinggrass, hippocras, isinglass, Kiribati, lemongrass, lower-class, middle-class, overpass, pampas grass, peppergrass, Plexiglas, sassafras, superclass, underclass, underpass, upper-class, weatherglass

assa \as-ə\ massa, Lake Nyasa, Manasseh

assable \as-ə-bəl\ chasuble, passable, passible, impassable, impassible, irascible

assail \äs-əl\ see OSSAL

assailer \äs-ə-lər\ see OSSULAR

assal \as-əl\ see ²ASSEL

assant \as-ᵊnt\ see ¹ASCENT

assar \as-ər\ see ASSER

¹asse \as\ see ³ASS

²asse \äs\ see ¹OS

assed \ast\ see ²AST

assee \as-ē\ see ASSY

asseh \as-ə\ see ASSA

¹assel \äs-əl\ see OSSAL

²assel \as-əl\ acyl, basil, castle, facile, gracile, hassle, Kassel, passel, tassel, vassal, wrestle, forecastle, Newcastle

asser \as-ər\ crasser, gasser, Nasser, placer, harasser, antimacassar

asset \as-ət\ see ²ACET

¹assia \ash-ə\ see ²ASHA

²assia \äsh-ə\ see ¹ASHA

assian \ash-ən\ see ASSION

assible \as-ə-bəl\ see ASSABLE

assic \as-ik\ classic, Jurassic, Liassic, thalassic, Triassic, neoclassic, pseudoclassic, semiclassic

assical \as-i-kəl\ classical, fascicle, postclassical, unclassical, semiclassical

assid \as-əd\ see ACID

¹assie \as-ē\ see ASSY

²assie \äs-ē\ see ¹OSSY

¹assim \äs-əm\ see OSSUM

²assim \as-əm\ passim, sargassum

assin \as-ᵊn\ see ²ASTEN

assion \ash-ən\ ashen, fashion, passion, ration, Circassian, compassion, dispassion, impassion, refashion, Wakashan

assional \ash-nəl\ see ³ATIONAL

¹assis \as-ē\ see ASSY

²assis \as-əs\ classis, stasis, Parnassus, Halicarnassus

assist \ā-səst\ bassist, racist, contrabassist

assive \as-iv\ massive, passive, impassive

assle \as-əl\ see ²ASSEL

assless \as-ləs\ classless, glassless, massless

assment \as-mənt\ blastment, amassment, harassment

assness \as-nəs\ see ASTNESS

¹asso \as-ō\ basso, lasso, El Paso, Picasso, sargasso, Sargasso, Bobo-Dioulasso

²asso \äs-ō\ Campo Basso, Burkina Faso

assock \as-ək\ cassock, hassock

assum \as-əm\ see ²ASSIM

assus \as-əs\ see ASSIS

assy \as-ē\ brassy, chassis, classy, gassy, glacis, glassie, glassy, grassy, lassie, massy, sassy, saucy, Malagasy, Tallahassee, Haile Salassie

¹ast \əst\ see ¹UST

²ast \ast\ bast, blast, cast, caste, clast, fast, gast, ghast, hast,

last, mast, past, vast, aghast,
avast, bedfast, Belfast,
bombast, broadcast, bypast,
contrast, dicast, dismast,
downcast, dynast, fantast,
flypast, forecast, foremast,
forepassed, gymnast, half-
caste, half-mast, handfast,
holdfast, lightfast, mainmast,
makefast, march-past,
miscast, newscast, oblast,
offcast, outcast, outcaste,
precast, recast, repast,
roughcast, sandblast, sand-
cast, shamefast, soothfast,
sportscast, steadfast, sunfast,
topmast, trade-last, typecast,
unasked, upcast, windblast,
acid-fast, chiliast, cineast,
colorcast, colorfast,
flabbergast, fore-topmast,
hard-and-fast, main-topmast,
mizzenmast, narrowcast,
opencast, overcast, pederast,
rebroadcast, scholiast,
simulcast, telecast,
weathercast, ecdysiast,
encomiast, enthusiast,
iconoclast, radiocast,
symposiast, radiobroadcast—
also pasts of verbs listed at
³ASS

¹**asta** \äs-tə\ *see* OSTA

²**asta** \as-tə\ Rasta, canasta,
Jocasta, Mount Shasta

astable \at-ə-bəl\ *see* ATIBLE

astard \as-tərd\ bastard,
dastard, mastered, plastered

¹**aste** \āst\ *see* ACED

²**aste** \ast\ *see* ²AST

asted \as-təd\ blasted, masted,

plastid—*also pasts of verbs
listed at* ²AST

asteful \āst-fəl\ tasteful,
wasteful, distasteful

¹**asten** \ās-ᵊn\ *see* ¹ASON

²**asten** \as-ᵊn\ fasten, assassin,
unfasten

¹**aster** \ā-stər\ taster, waster

²**aster** \as-tər\ aster, Astor,
caster, castor, Castor, faster,
gaster, master, pastor, plaster,
raster, bandmaster,
bushmaster, cadastre,
choirmaster, disaster,
drillmaster, headmaster,
linecaster, loadmaster,
paymaster, piaster, pilaster,
postmaster, quizmaster,
remaster, ringmaster,
schoolmaster, scoutmaster,
shinplaster, shipmaster,
spymaster, taskmaster, three-
master, toastmaster,
truckmaster, wharfmaster,
whoremaster, yardmaster,
alabaster, burgomaster,
concertmaster, criticaster,
ironmaster, oleaster,
overmaster, poetaster,
quartermaster, rallymaster,
stationmaster, weathercaster,
Zoroaster, cotoneaster

astered \as-tərd\ *see* ASTARD

astering \as-tə-riŋ\
overmastering—*also present
participles of verbs listed at*
ASTER

astes \as-tēz\ cerastes,
Ecclesiastes—*also plurals
and possessives of nouns
listed at* ²ASTY

asthma \az-mə\ *see* ASMA

astian \as-chən\ see ASTION

astic \as-tik\ drastic, mastic, plastic, spastic, bombastic, dynastic, elastic, fantastic, gymnastic, monastic, sarcastic, scholastic, stochastic, anelastic, Hudibrastic, inelastic, onomastic, orgiastic, paraphrastic, pederastic, periphrastic, superplastic, ecclesiastic, enthusiastic, iconoclastic, interscholastic, semimonastic

astics \as-tiks\ gymnastics, slimnastics

astid \as-təd\ see ASTED

astie \as-tē\ see ²ASTY

astiness \ā-stē-nəs\ hastiness, pastiness

¹asting \ā-stiŋ\ basting, wasting—*also present participles of verbs listed at* ACED

²asting \as-tiŋ\ typecasting, everlasting, narrowcasting, overcasting

astion \as-chən\ bastion, Erastian

astle \as-əl\ see ²ASSEL

astly \ast-lē\ ghastly, lastly

astment \as-mənt\ see ASSMENT

astness \as-nəs\ crassness, fastness, gastness, pastness

asto \as-tō\ impasto, antipasto

astor \as-tər\ see ²ASTER

astoral \as-trəl\ see ASTRAL

astral \as-trəl\ astral, gastral, pastoral, plastral, cadastral

astre \as-tər\ see ²ASTER

astric \as-trik\ gastric, nasogastric

astrophe \as-trə-fē\ anastrophe, catastrophe

¹asty \ā-stē\ hasty, pasty, tasty

²asty \as-tē\ blastie, nasty, pasty, vasty, capacity, contrasty, pederasty, angioplasty, bepharoplasty, osteoplasty, overcapacity

asuble \as-ə-bəl\ see ASSABLE

¹asure \ā-shər\ glacier, Glacier, rasure, erasure

²asure \ā-zhər\ see AZIER

asy \as-ē\ see ASSY

¹at \ä\ see ¹A

²at \ät\ see ¹OT

³at \ət\ see ¹UT

⁴at \òt\ see ¹OUGHT

⁵at \at\ bat, batt, blat, brat, cat, Cat, chat, chert, drat, fat, flat, frat, gat, gnat, hat, mat, matt, Matt, matte, pat, Pat, plait, plat, rat, Rat, sat, scat, scatt, skat, slat, spat, splat, sprat, stat, tat, that, vat, all that, at bat, backchat, begat, bobcat, brickbat, bullbat, Cassatt, chitchat, combat, comsat, cowpat, cravat, Croat, defat, dingbat, doormat, expat, fiat, firebrat, format, Hallstatt, hellcat, hepcat, high-hat, jurat, meerkat, muscat, Muscat, muskrat, nonfat, polecat, Sadat, savate, Sno-Cat, stand pat, standpat, stonechat, strawhat, Surat, thereat, tipcat, tomcat, whereat, whinchat, wildcat, wombat, acrobat, apparat, Ararat, assignat, autocrat, Automat, bureaucrat, butterfat, caveat, cervelat, concordat, copycat, democrat,

diplomat, Dixiecrat, Eurocrat,
habitat, Kattegat, Laundromat,
marrowfat, mobocrat,
monocrat, Montserrat,
ochlocrat, pas de quatre,
photostat, pit-a-pat, plutocrat,
pussycat, rat-a-tat, scaredy-
cat, semimatte, technocrat,
theocrat, thermostat, tit for
tat, Uniate, ziggurat,
aristocrat, gerontocrat,
heliostat, Jehoshaphat,
magnificat, meritocrat,
Physiocrat, requiescat,
thalassocrat, proletoriat,
professoriat, secretariat

⁶at \a\ see ³AH

¹ata \ät-ə\ cotta, kata, balata,
cantata, Carlotta, data, errata,
fermata, frittata, La Plata,
Maratha, Niigata, non grata,
pinata, pro rata, reata, riata,
regatta, sonata, Sorata,
toccata, caponata, Hirakata,
Mar del Plata, serenata,
terracotta, Uspallata,
Basilicata, desiderata,
inamorata, medulla oblongata,
missa cantata, persona grata,
res judicata, persona non
grata, res adjudicata, Rio de la
Plata

²ata \āt-ə\ beta, data, eta, strata,
theta, zeta, muleta, peseta,
potato, pro rata, substrata,
tomato, viewdata, corona
radiata

³ata \at-ə\ data, errata, mulatto,
non grata, pro rata, reata,
regatta, riata, viewdata,
paramatta, Paramatta, persona
grata, persona non grata

¹atable \āt-ə-bəl\ datable,
ratable, statable, debatable,
dilatable, inflatable, locatable,
rotatable, translatable,
allocatable, circulatable,
confiscatable, correlatable,
detonatable, undebatable

²atable \at-ə-bəl\ see ATIBLE

atal \āt-ᵊl\ fatal, natal, ratel,
shtetl, hiatal, postnatal,
prenatal, antenatal, neonatal,
perinatal

atalie \at-ᵊl-ē\ see ATTILY

atally \āt-ᵊl-ē\ fatally, natally,
postnatally, prenatally,
antenatally, neonatally,
perinatally

atalyst \at-ᵊl-əst\ catalyst,
philatelist

¹atan \āt-ən\ see ¹ATEN

²atan \at-ᵊn\ see ²ATIN

atancy \āt-ᵊn-sē\ blatancy,
latency, dilatancy

¹atant \āt-ᵊnt\ blatant, latent,
natant, patent, statant

²atant \at-ᵊnt\ patent,
combatant, noncombatant

atany \at-ᵊn-ē\ atony, rhatany

atar \ät-ər\ see OTTER

atary \ät-ə-rē\ see OTTERY

¹atch \ech\ see ETCH

²atch \äch\ see OTCH

³atch \òch\ see ¹AUCH

⁴atch \ach\ bach, batch, catch,
cratch, hatch, klatch, latch,
match, natch, patch, ratch,
scratch, snatch, thatch, attach,
book-match, crosshatch,
crosspatch, despatch, detach,
dispatch, nuthatch, outmatch,
potlatch, rematch, Sasquatch,
throatlatch, unlatch, Wasatch,

coffee klatch, kaffeeklatsch, overmatch

¹atcher \äch-ər\ botcher, watcher, bird-watcher, clock-watcher, debaucher, topnotcher

²atcher \ach-ər\ batcher, catcher, hatcher, matcher, scratcher, stature, thatcher, cowcatcher, dispatcher, dogcatcher, eye-catcher, flycatcher, gnatcatcher, oyster catcher

atchet \ach-ət\ hatchet, latchet, rachet, ratchet

atchily \ach-ə-lē\ patchily, patchouli

atching \ach-iŋ\ back-scratching, cross-hatching, eye-catching, nonmatching

atchman \äch-mən\ see OTCHMAN

atchment \ach-mənt\ catchment, hatchment, attachment, detachment

atchouli \ach-ə-lē\ see ATCHILY

atchy \ach-ē\ catchy, patchy, scratchy, Apache

¹ate \āt\ ait, ate, bait, bate, blate, cate, Cate, crate, date, eight, fate, fete, freight, gait, gate, grate, great, haet, hate, Kate, late, mate, pate, plait, plate, prate, quoit, rate, sate, skate, slate, spate, state, straight, strait, teth, trait, wait, weight, abate, ablate, adnate, aerate, age-mate, agnate, airdate, airfreight, alate, arête, await, backdate, baldpate, bedmate, bedplate, berate, birthrate, bistate, bookplate,

breastplate, casemate, castrate, caudate, cerate, cheapskate, checkmate, chordate, classmate, clavate, cognate, collate, comate, conflate, connate, cordate, create, cremate, crenate, curate, cut-rate, deadweight, debate, deflate, delate, dentate, derate, dictate, dilate, disrate, donate, doorplate, downstate, drawplate, elate, equate, estate, faceplate, falcate, fellate, filtrate, first-rate, fishplate, fixate, flatmate, floodgate, flyweight, formate, frustrate, gelate, gestate, gyrate, hamate, hastate, headgate, helpmate, housemate, hydrate, ice-skate, inflate, ingrate, inmate, innate, instate, irate, jailbait, jugate, khanate, Kuwait, lactate, legate, liftgate, ligate, lightweight, liquate, lobate, locate, lunate, lustrate, lych-gate, lyrate, magnate, makebate, makeweight, mandate, messmate, migrate, misstate, mutate, nameplate, narrate, negate, Newgate, nitrate, notate, nutate, oblate, orate, ornate, ovate, palmate, palpate, peltate, phonate, pinnate, placate, playmate, plicate, portrait, postdate, predate, primate, probate, prolate, prorate, prostate, prostrate, pulsate, punctate, pupate, quadrate, ramate, rebate, red-bait, relate, restate, roommate, rostrate, rotate, saccate, schoolmate, seatmate, sedate, sensate, septate, serrate, shipmate, short weight, soleplate, spectate, spicate, squamate, stagnate, stalemate, stellate, striate, sublate, substrate, sulcate, summate, tailgate, teammate, Tebet, tenth-rate, ternate, terneplate, testate, third-rate, tinplate, toeplate, tollgate, tractate, translate, tristate, truncate, unweight, update, uprate, upstate, V-8, vacate, vallate, valvate, vibrate, virgate, vulgate, whitebait, workmate, zonate, abdicate, abnegate, abrogate, absorbate, acclimate, acerbate, acetate, activate, actuate, acylate, adsorbate, advocate, adulate, adumbrate, aggravate, aggregate, agitate, allocate, altercate, alternate, ambulate, amputate, animate, annotate, annulate, antedate, antiquate, apartheid, apostate, approbate, approximate, arbitrate, arcuate, arrogate, aspirate, automate, aviate, bantamweight, bifurcate, billingsgate, bipinnate, boilerplate, bombinate, brachiate, cachinnate, calculate, calibrate, caliphate, candidate, cantillate, capitate, captivate, carbonate, carbon-date, carinate, castigate, catenate, cavitate, celebrate, cerebrate, circinate, circulate, city-state, cogitate, collimate, collocate, commentate,

commutate, compensate, complicate, concentrate, condensate, confiscate, conglobate, conjugate, consecrate, constellate, consternate, constipate, consummate, contemplate, copperplate, copulate, coronate, correlate, corrugate, coruscate, counterweight, crenulate, crepitate, criminate, cruciate, cucullate, culminate, cultivate, cumulate, cuneate, cupulate, cuspidate, cyclamate, decimate, decollate, decorate, decussate, dedicate, defalcate, defecate, delegate, demarcate, demonstrate, denigrate, deviate, deprecate, depredate, derivate, derogate, desecrate, desiccate, designate, desolate, detonate, devastate, deviate, ' digitate, diplomate, discarnate, dislocate, dissertate, dissipate, distillate, divagate, dominate, duplicate, edentate, educate, elevate, elongate, eluate, emanate, emigrate, emirate, emulate, enervate, ephorate, escalate, estimate, estivate, excavate, exculpate, execrate, expiate, explicate, expurgate, exsiccate, extirpate, extricate, exudate, fabricate, fascinate, featherweight, fecundate, federate, fenestrate, festinate, fibrillate, flabellate, flagellate, flocculate, fluctuate, fluoridate, foliate, formulate, fornicate, fractionate, fragmentate, fulminate, fumigate, fustigate, geminate, generate, germinate, glaciate, Golden Gate, graduate, granulate, gratulate, gravitate, heavyweight, hebetate, herniate, hesitate, hibernate, hundredweight, hyphenate, ideate, illustrate, imamate, imbricate, imitate, immigrate, immolate, impetrate, implicate, imprecate, impregnate, incarnate, increate, incubate, inculcate, inculpate, incurvate, indagate, indicate, indurate, infiltrate, innervate, innovate, insensate, insolate, inspissate, instigate, insulate, interstate, intestate, intimate, intonate, intraplate, inundate, invocate, iodate, irrigate, irritate, isolate, iterate, jubilate, juniorate, lacerate, laminate, Latinate, laureate, legislate, levigate, levitate, liberate, liquidate, litigate, littermate, lubricate, macerate, machinate, magistrate, marginate, margravate, marinate, masticate, masturbate, maturate, mediate, medicate, meditate, meliorate, menstruate, microstate, micturate, middleweight, militate, ministrate, miscreate, mithridate, mitigate, moderate, modulate, motivate, multistate, mutilate, nation-state, nauseate, navigate, neonate, nictitate, niobate, nominate, numerate,

obfuscate, objurgate, obligate, obovate, obviate, operate, opiate, orchestrate, ordinate, oscillate, osculate, out-of-date, overstate, overweight, ovulate, paginate, palliate, palpitate, paperweight, patinate, peculate, penetrate, pennyweight, percolate, perennate, perforate, permeate, perorate, perpetrate, personate, pollinate, populate, postulate, potentate, predicate, procreate, profligate, promulgate, propagate, prorogate, pullulate, pulmonate, punctuate, quantitate, rabbinate, radiate, re-create, reclinate, recreate, regulate, reinstate, relegate, relocate, reluctate, remonstrate, renovate, replicate, reprobate, resonate, retardate, retranslate, roseate, rubricate, ruminate, runagate, rusticate, sagittate, salivate, sanitate, satiate, saturate, scintillate, second-rate, segregate, separate, sequestrate, seriate, sibilate, simulate, sinuate, situate, speculate, spoliate, stablemate, stimulate, stipulate, strangulate, stridulate, stylobate, subjugate, sublimate, subrogate, subulate, suffocate, sultanate, supplicate, surrogate, syncopate, syndicate, tablemate, tabulate, terminate, tessellate, tête-à-tête, thirty-eight, titillate,

titivate, tolerate, transmigrate,
transudate, tribulate, tribunate,
trifurcate, trilobate, tripinnate,
triplicate, tunicate, turbinate,
ulcerate, ululate, umbellate,
uncinate, underrate,
understate, underweight,
undulate, ungulate, urinate,
vaccinate, vacillate, validate,
valuate, variate, vaticinate,
vegetate, venerate, ventilate,
vertebrate, vicarate, vindicate,
violate, vitiate, Watergate,
welterweight, abbreviate,
abominate, accelerate,
accentuate, accommodate,
acculturate, accumulate,
acidulate, adjudicate,
administrate, adulterate,
affiliate, agglomerate,
agglutinate, alienate, alleviate,
alliterate, amalgamate,
ameliorate, annihilate,
annunciate, anticipate,
apostolate, appreciate,
appropriate, articulate,
asphyxiate, assassinate,
asseverate, assimilate,
associate, attenuate,
authenticate, barbiturate,
bicarbonate, calumniate,
campanulate, capacitate,
capitulate, catholicate,
certificate, circumvallate,
coagulate, coelenterate,
collaborate, commemorate,
commiserate, communicate,
compassionate, concatenate,
concelebrate, conciliate,
confabulate, confederate,
conglomerate, congratulate,
consociate, consolidate,

contaminate, cooperate,
coordinate, corroborate, de-
escalate, deaerate, debilitate,
decapitate, decerebrate,
deconcentrate, deconsecrate,
decrepitate, defibrinate,
defribrillate, degenerate,
deliberate, delineate,
demodulate, denominate,
depopulate, depreciate,
deregulate, desegregate,
desiderate, devaluate,
diaconate, dilapidate,
discriminate, disintegrate,
disseminate, dissimilate,
dissimulate, dissociate,
divaricate, domesticate,
edulcorate, effectuate,
ejaculate, elaborate,
electroplate, eliminate,
elucidate, elucubrate, elutriate,
emaciate, emancipate,
emarginate, emasculate,
encapsulate, enumerate,
enunciate, episcopate,
equilibrate, equivocate,
eradicate, etiolate, evacuate,
evaluate, evaporate, eventuate,
eviscerate, exacerbate,
exaggerate, exasperate,
excogitate, excoriate,
excruciate, exfoliate,
exhilarate, exonerate,
expatiate, expatriate,
expectorate, expostulate,
expropriate, extenuate,
exterminate, extrapolate,
extravagate, exuberate,
facilitate, fantasticate,
felicitate, gesticulate,
habilitate, habituate,
hallucinate, homologate,

humiliate, hypothecate,
illuminate, impersonate,
inactivate, inaugurate,
incarcerate, incinerate,
incorporate, incriminate,
indoctrinate, inebriate,
infatuate, infuriate, ingratiate,
ingurgitate, initiate, inoculate,
inosculate, inseminate,
insinuate, instantiate,
intenerate, intercalate,
interpellate, interpolate,
interrelate, interrogate,
intimidate, intoxicate,
invaginate, invalidate,
investigate, invigilate,
invigorate, irradiate,
italianate, itinerate, lanceolate,
legitimate, luxuriate,
machicolate, mandarinate,
manipulate, matriarchate,
matriculate, Merthiolate,
necessitate, negotiate,
noncandidate, obliterate,
obnubilate, officiate, orientate,
originate, oxygenate,
participate, particulate,
patriarchate, patriciate,
penicillate, perambulate,
peregrinate, perpetuate,
pontificate, potentiate,
precipitate, predestinate,
predominate, prefabricate,
premeditate, prenominate,
preponderate, prevaricate,
procrastinate, prognosticate,
proliferate, propitiate,
proportionate, quadruplicate,
quintuplicate, reciprocate,
recriminate, recuperate,
redecorate, redintegrate,
reduplicate, reeducate,

refrigerate, regenerate,
regurgitate, reincarnate,
reintegrate, reiterate,
rejuvenate, remunerate,
renominate, repatriate,
repristinate, repudiate,
resupinate, resuscitate,
retaliate, reticulate, revaluate,
revegetate, reverberate,
scholasticate, self-portrait,
seventy-eight, sextuplicate,
somnambulate, sophisticate,
stereobate, subordinate,
substantiate, syllabicate,
tergiversate, transliterate,
transvaluate, triangulate,
variegate, vituperate,
vociferate, beneficiate,
circumambulate,
circumnavigate,
circumstantiate,
contraindicate, decontaminate,
deteriorate, differentiate,
disaffiliate, disambiguate,
disarticulate, disassociate,
discombobulate, disintoxicate,
disorientate, disproportionate,
domiciliate, excommunicate,
free-associate, hyperventilate,
incapacitate, individuate,
intermediate, interpenetrate,
lithium niobate,
superheavyweight,
microencapsulate,
misappropriate, multivariate,
ratiocinate, recapitulate,
rehabilitate, renegotiate,
superannuate, superelevate,
superordinate, supersaturate,
transilluminate,
transubstantiate,
underestimate,

intercommunicate,
diammonium phosphate,
phosphoenolpyruvate,
peroxyacetyl nitrate

²**ate** \at\ see ⁵AT

³**ate** \ät\ see ¹OT

⁴**ate** \ät-ē\ see ATI

⁵**ate** \ət\ see ¹UT

ated \āt-əd\ gaited, lated, pated,
stated, belated, ill-fated,
outdated, pustulated, related,
striated, three-gaited,
truncated, unbated, X-rated,
aberrated, addlepated,
animated, asteriated,
calculated, capsulated,
carbonated, carburated,
castellated, complicated,
crenellated, disrelated,
elevated, fenestrated,
fimbriated, floriated, foliated,
inspissated, intoxicated,
laminated, marginated,
mentholated, perforated,
pileated, pixilated, saturated,
tessellated, trabeated,
unabated, uncreated,
understated, variegated,
affiliated, configurated,
coordinated, decaffeinated,
domesticated, incorporated,
inebriated, interrelated,
intoxicated, opinionated,
sophisticated, uncalculated,
uncelebrated, uncomplicated,
underinflated, unmediated,
unmitigated, unsaturated,
unsegregated, unadulterated,
unanticipated, unarticulated,
unconsolidated,
undereducated,
underpopulated,
undissociated,
unsophisticated,
polyunsaturated,
underappreciated—*also pasts
of verbs listed at* ¹ATE

ateful \āt-fəl\ fateful, grateful,
hateful, ungrateful

¹**atel** \ət-ᵊl\ see OTTLE

²**atel** \āt-ᵊl\ see ATAL

ateless \āt-ləs\ dateless,
stateless, weightless

atelist \at-ᵊl-əst\ see ATALYST

¹**ately** \āt-lē\ greatly, lately,
stately, straightly, straitly,
innately, irately, ornately, up-
to-dately, Johnny-come-lately

²**ately** \at-ᵊl-ē\ see ATTILY

atem \ät-əm\ see ¹ATUM

atement \āt-mənt\ statement,
abatement, debatement,
misstatement, restatement,
overstatement, reinstatement,
understatement

¹**aten** \āt-ᵊn\ greaten, laten,
Satan, straighten, straiten,
Keewatin

²**aten** \at-ᵊn\ see ²ATIN

³**aten** \ät-ᵊn\ see OTTEN

¹**atent** \āt-ᵊnt\ see ¹ATANT

²**atent** \at-ᵊnt\ see ²ATANT

¹**ater** \ȯt-ər\ daughter, slaughter,
tauter, water, backwater,
bathwater, blackwater,
breakwater, cutwater, dewater,
deepwater, dishwater,
firewater, floodwater,
forequarter, freshwater,
goddaughter, granddaughter,
groundwater, headwater,
hindquarter, jerkwater,
limewater, manslaughter,
meltwater, rainwater,

rosewater, saltwater, seawater,
self-slaughter, shearwater,
springwater, stepdaughter,
tailwater, tidewater,
wastewater, milk-and-water,
polywater, underwater

²ater \āt-ər\ see ATOR

ateral \at-ə-rəl\ lateral,
bilateral, collateral, trilateral,
contralateral, dorsolateral,
equilateral, ipsilateral,
multilateral, quadrilateral,
unilateral, ventrolateral,
posterolateral

aterer \ȯt-ər-ər\ slaughterer,
waterer, dewaterer

ateress \āt-ə-rəs\ cateress,
traitorous

atering \ȯt-ə-riŋ\ mouth-
watering—*also present
participles of verbs listed at*
¹ATER

¹atery \āt-ə-rē\ see OTTERY

²atery \ȯt-ə-rē\ cautery, watery

¹ates \āts\ Yeats, Gulf States,
Papal States, Persian Gulf
States, United States,
Federated Malay States,
United Arab Emirates—*also
plurals and possessives of
nouns and third person
singular presents of verbs
listed at* ATE

²ates \āt-ēz\ Achates, nates,
Euphrates, Penates—*also
plurals and possessives of
nouns listed at* ATY

atest \āt-əst\ latest, statist—*also
superlatives of adjectives
listed at* ¹ATE

atey \āt-ē\ see ATY

¹ath \äth\ see ¹OTH

²ath \ȯth\ see ²OTH

³ath \ath\ bath, hath, lath, math,
path, rathe, snath, strath,
wrath, birdbath, bloodbath,
bypath, footbath, footpath,
sunbath, towpath, warpath,
aftermath, polymath,
psychopath, telepath,
naturopath, osteopath,
sociopath

atha \ät-ə\ see ¹ATA

¹athe \āth\ swathe, enswathe,
unswathe

²athe \āth\ bathe, lathe, rathe,
saithe, scathe, spathe, swathe,
sunbathe, unswathe

³athe \ath\ see ³ATH

atheless \āth-ləs\ see AITHLESS

¹ather \äth-ər\ bother, father,
pother, rather, forefather,
godfather, grandfather,
housefather, stepfather

²ather \əth-ər\ see ¹OTHER

³ather \ath-ər\ blather, Cather,
gather, lather, Mather, rather,
slather, forgather, ingather,
wool-gather

athering \ath-riŋ\ ingathering,
woolgathering

athi \ät-ē\ see ATI

athic \ath-ik\ empathic,
amphipathic, psychopathic,
telepathic, homeopathic,
idiopathic, sociopathic

athlon \ath-lən\ biathlon,
decathlon, pentathlon,
triathlon

athy \ath-ē\ Cathie, Cathy,
Kathie, Kathy, wrathy,
allelopathy

¹ati \ät-ē\ Ate, Dottie, dotty,
Dotty, grotty, knotty, naughty,

plotty, potty, Scottie, Scotty, snotty, spotty, squatty, Amati, basmati, chapati, coati, flokati, karate, Marathi, metate, Scarlatti, Tol'yati, glitterati, Gujarati, Hakodate, literati, manicotti, illuminati

²**ati** \atē\ see ATTY

³**ati** \äts\ see OTS

⁴**ati** \as\ see ³ASS

atia \ā-shə\ see ACIA

atial \ā-shəl\ see ACIAL

atian \ā-shən\ see ¹ATION

atians \ā-shənz\ see ATIONS

atible \at-ə-bəl\ compatible, getatable, incompatible, self-compatible, biocompatible, self-incompatible

¹**atic** \ät-ik\ see ¹OTIC

²**atic** \at-ik\ attic, Attic, batik, phatic, static, vatic, agnatic, aquatic, astatic, asthmatic, chromatic, climatic, comatic, dalmatic, dogmatic, dramatic, ecstatic, emphatic, erratic, fanatic, hepatic, judgmatic, komatik, lymphatic, magmatic, neumatic, phlegmatic, plasmatic, pneumatic, pragmatic, prismatic, protatic, quadratic, rheumatic, schematic, schismatic, sciatic, sematic, Socratic, somatic, spermatic, stigmatic, sylvatic, thematic, traumatic, villatic, achromatic, acrobatic, Adriatic, aerobatic, anabatic, antistatic, aromatic, Asiatic, astigmatic, autocratic, automatic, bureaucratic, charismatic, cinematic, democratic, dilemmatic, diplomatic, Dixiecratic, Eleatic, emblematic, enigmatic, enzymatic, fungistatic, Hanseatic, hieratic, Hippocratic, kerygmatic, leviratic, melismatic, miasmatic, mobocratic, monocratic, morganatic, numismatic, ochlocratic, operatic, phonematic, plutocratic, pre-Socratic, problematic, programmatic, symptomatic, syntagmatic, systematic, technocratic, theocratic, timocratic, undogmatic, undramatic, anagrammatic, apothegmatic, aristocratic, asymptomatic, axiomatic, conglomeratic, diagrammatic, diaphragmatic, epigrammatic, gerontocratic, gynecocratic, homeostatic, idiomatic, logogrammatic, melodramatic, meritocratic, monochromatic, monodramatic, monogrammatic, pantisocratic, paradigmatic, physiocratic, psychodramatic, psychosomatic, semiaquatic, theorematic, undemocratic, undiplomatic, antidemocratic, Austroasiatic, biosystematic, ideogrammatic, semiautomatic

atica \at-i-kə\ Attica, hepatica, sciatica, viatica

atical \at-i-kəl\ statical, dogmatical, erratical, fanatical, grammatical, piratical, pragmatical, sabbatical, schismatical, autocratical, emblematical, enigmatical, magistratical, mathematical, ochlocratical, problematical, systematical, theocratical, timocratical, ungrammatical, anagrammatical, diagrammatical, epigrammatical, pantisocratical

atics \at-iks\ statics, chromatics, dogmatics, dramatics, pneumatics, pragmatics, acrobatics, informatics, mathematics, numismatics, systematics, melodramatics, psychosomatics—*also plurals and possessives of nouns listed at* ²ATIC

atie \āt-ē\ see ATY

atiens \ā-shənz\ see ATIONS

atient \ā-shənt\ patient, impatient, inpatient, outpatient, rubefacient, somnifacient, abortifacient

atik \at-ik\ see ²ATIC

atile \at-ᵊl-ē\ see ATTILY

atim \āt-əm\ see ²ATUM

¹atin \ät-ᵊn\ see OTTEN

²atin \at-ᵊn\ batten, fatten, flatten, gratin, Latin, latten, matin, paten, patten, Patton, platan, platen, ratton, satin, cisplatin, manhattan, Manhattan, Powhatan, lovastatin, Neo-Latin

³atin \āt-ᵊn\ see ¹ATEN

atinate \at-ᵊn-ət\ concatenate, Palatinate, Rhineland-Palatinate

ating \āt-iŋ\ bating, grating, plating, rating, skating, slating, abating, bearbaiting, bullbaiting, frustrating, self-rating, calculating, lancinating, maid-in-waiting, nauseating, operating, titillating, humiliating, lady-in-waiting, nonterminating, self-liquidating, self-regulating, self-replicating, subordinating, uncalculating, undeviating, unhesitating, indiscriminating, self-incriminating

atinous \at-nəs\ see ATNESS

¹ation \ā-shən\ Asian, Haitian, nation, Nation, ration, station, Thracian, ablation, agnation, Alsatian, carnation, castration, causation, cessation, cetacean, chrismation, citation, cognation, collation, conation, conflation, creation, cremation, crenation, Croatian, crustacean, cunctation, dalmatian, damnation, deflation, dictation, dilation, donation, duration, elation, enation, equation, Eurasian, filtration, fixation, flotation, formation, foundation, frustration, furcation, gestation, gradation, gustation, gyration, hydration, illation, inflation, lactation, laudation, lavation, legation, libation, libration, ligation, location, lustration, mentation, migration, mutation, narration, natation, negation, nitration, notation, novation, nutation, oblation, oration, outstation, ovation, phonation, planation, plantation, plication, potation, predation, privation, probation, pronation, proration, prostration, pulsation, purgation, quotation, reflation, relation, rogation, rotation, saltation, salvation, sedation, sensation, serration, slumpflation, squamation, stagflation, stagnation, starvation, striation, stylization, sublation, substation, summation, tarnation, taxation, temptation, translation, truncation, vacation, venation, vexation, vibration, vocation, workstation, zonation, abdication, aberration, abjuration, abnegation, acceptation, acclamation, acclimation, accusation, activation, actuation, adaptation, adjuration, admiration, adoration, adulation, adumbration, advocation, affectation, affirmation, aggravation, aggregation, allegation, allocation, amputation, alteration, altercation, alternation, Amerasian, angulation, animation, annexation, annotation, annulation, antiquation, Appalachian, appellation, application, approbation, arbitration, aspiration, assentation, assignation, attestation, augmentation, Aurignacian, automation, aviation, avocation,

blaxploitation, botheration, brachiation, cachinnation, calculation, calibration, cancellation, capitation, captivation, carbonation, carburation, castigation, celebration, cementation, cerebration, circulation, claudication, cogitation, collocation, coloration, combination, commendation, commination, commutation, compellation, compensation, compilation, complication, compurgation, computation, concentration, condemnation, condensation, condonation, confirmation, confiscation, conflagration, conformation, confrontation, confutation, congelation, congregation, conjugation, conjuration, connotation, consecration, conservation, consolation, conspiration, constellation, consternation, constipation, consultation, consummation, contemplation, contestation, conurbation, conversation, convocation, copulation, coronation, corporation, correlation, corrugation, coruscation, crenellation, culmination, cupellation, cuspidation, cybernation, decimation, declamation, declaration, declination, decoration, dedication, defalcation, defamation, defecation, defloration, deformation, degradation, degustation, dehydration, delectation, delegation, demarcation, demonstration, denegation, denigration, denotation, depilation, deportation, depravation, depredation, deprivation, deputation, derivation, derogation, desecration, desiccation, designation, desolation, desperation, destination, detestation, detonation, devastation, deviation, dilatation, disclamation, disinflation, dislocation, dispensation, disputation, disrelation, dissertation, dissipation, distillation, divination, domination, dubitation, duplication, education, elevation, elongation, emanation, embarkation, embrocation, emendation, emigration, emulation, encrustation, enervation, epilation, equitation, eructation, escalation, estimation, estivation, evocation, exaltation, excavation, excitation, exclamation, exculpation, execration, exhalation, exhortation, expectation, expiation, expiration, explanation, explication, exploitation, exploration, exportation, expurgation, extirpation, extrication, exudation, exultation, fabrication, fascination, federation, fenestration, fermentation, fibrillation,

figuration, filiation, flagellation, fluoridation, fluctuation, foliation, fomentation, formulation, fornication, fragmentation, fulguration, fulmination, fumigation, gemination, generation, germination, glaciation, graduation, granulation, gravitation, habitation, hesitation, hibernation, hyphenation, ideation, illustration, imbrication, imitation, immigration, immolation, implantation, implication, importation, imprecation, imputation, incantation, incarnation, incitation, inclination, incrustation, incubation, inculcation, indentation, indexation, indication, indignation, induration, infestation, infiltration, inflammation, information, inhalation, innovation, insolation, inspiration, installation, instauration, insufflation, insulation, intonation, inundation, invitation, invocation, irrigation, irritation, isolation, iteration, jactitation, jubilation, laceration, lacrimation, lamentation, lamination, legislation, levitation, liberation, limitation, lineation, liquidation, literation, litigation, lubrication, lucubration, maceration, machination, maculation, malformation, malversation, margination, mastication, masturbation, maturation, mediation, medication, meditation, melioration, menstruation, mensuration, metrication, ministration, moderation, modulation, molestation, motivation, navigation, nomination, numeration, obfuscation, objurgation, obligation, observation, obturation, occultation, occupation, operation, orchestration, ordination, oscillation, osculation, ostentation, ovulation, oxidation, ozonation, pagination, palliation, palpitation, patination, penetration, perforation, permeation, permutation, peroration, perpetration, perspiration, perturbation, pigmentation, pixilation, pollination, population, postulation, predication, preformation, prelibation, preparation, presentation, proclamation, procreation, procuration, profanation, prolongation, propagation, prorogation, protestation, provocation, publication, punctuation, radiation, recitation, reclamation, recordation, re-creation, recreation, reformation, refutation, registration, regulation, relaxation, relocation, reparation,

replantation, replication, reprobation, reputation, reservation, resignation, respiration, restoration, retardation, revelation, revocation, ruination, salivation, salutation, sanitation, satiation, saturation, scatteration, scintillation, segmentation, segregation, separation, sequestration, sexploitation, simulation, situation, solmization, speciation, speculation, spoliation, sternutation, stimulation, stipulation, strangulation, structuration, subjugation, sublimation, subrogation, suffocation, suspiration, susurration, sustentation, syncopation, syndication, tabulation, termination, tessellation, titillation, titivation, toleration, transformation, translocation, transmigration, transmutation, transpiration, transplantation, transportation, trepidation, tribulation, trituration, ulceration, ululation, undulation, urination, usurpation, vaccination, vacillation, validation, valuation, variation, vegetation, veneration, ventilation, vindication, violation, visitation, abbreviation, abomination, acceleration, accentuation, accommodation, accreditation, acculturation, accumulation, actualization, adjudication, administration, adulteration, affiliation, afforestation, agglomeration, agglutination, alienation, alleviation, alliteration, amalgamation, amelioration, amortization, amplification, analyzation, anglicization, annihilation, annunciation, anticipation, appreciation, appropriation, approximation, argumentation, articulation, asphyxiation, assassination, asseveration, assimilation, association, attenuation, authorization, autoxidation, barbarization, bastardization, beautification, bowdlerization, brutalization, canalization, canonization, capacitation, capitulation, carbonylation, centralization, certification, cicatrization, civilization, clarification, classification, coagulation, coeducation, cohabitation, colonization, collaboration, columniation, commemoration, commiseration, communication, communization, compartmentation, complementation, concatenation, conciliation, confabulation, confederation, configuration, conglomeration, congratulation, consideration, consociation, consolidation, contamination, continuation, cooperation, coordination,

corroboration, crustification, crystallization, deactivation, debilitation, decapitation, decompensation, defenestration, deforestation, degeneration, deglaciation, deification, deliberation, delineation, denomination, denunciation, depopulation, depreciation, deregulation, desegregation, despoliation, determination, devaluation, dilapidation, diphthongization, disapprobation, discoloration, discrimination, disembarkation, disinclination, disinformation, disintegration, dissemination, dissimilation, dissimulation, dissociation, divarication, documentation, domestication, dramatization, echolocation, edification, ejaculation, elaboration, elicitation, elimination, elucidation, emaciation, emancipation, emasculation, enumeration, enunciation, epoxidation, equalization, equivocation, eradication, evacuation, evagination, evaluation, evaporation, evisceration, exacerbation, exaggeration, examination, exasperation, excoriation, excruciation, exercitation, exhilaration, exoneration, expostulation, expropriation, extenuation, extermination, extrapolation, facilitation, factorization, falsification, fantastication, feminization, fertilization,

Finlandization, formalization,
formulization, fortification,
fossilization, fructification,
gasification, gentrification,
gesticulation, glamorization,
globalization, glorification,
glycosylation, gratification,
habituation, hallucination,
harmonization, haruspication,
hellenization, humanization,
hyperinflation, idolization,
illumination, imagination,
immunization, impersonation,
implementation,
improvisation, inauguration,
incarceration, incardination,
incineration, incorporation,
incrimination, indoctrination,
inebriation, infatuation,
ingratiation, inhabitation,
initiation, inoculation,
insemination, insinuation,
instrumentation,
internalization, interpretation,
interrelation, intimidation,
intoxication, invagination,
investigation, invigoration,
irradiation, itemization,
jollification, justification,
labanotation, laicization,
latinization, legalization,
lionization, localization,
machicolation, magnetization,
magnification, maladaptation,
manifestation,
masculinization,
matriculation, maximization,
mechanization,
miscegenation, mobilization,
modernization, modification,
mollification, mongrelization,
monopolization, moralization,

mortification, multiplication,
mystification, nationalization,
naturalization, necessitation,
negotiation, neutralization,
normalization, notarization,
notification, novelization,
nullification, optimization,
organization, orientation,
ornamentation, ossification,
pacification, paralyzation,
participation, pasteurization,
patronization, penalization,
perambulation, perpetuation,
perseveration, personalization,
plasticization, pluralization,
petrification, polarization,
pontification, preadaptation,
precipitation, predestination,
prefiguration, premeditation,
preoccupation, preregistration,
prettification, procrastination,
prognostication, proliferation,
pronunciation, propitiation,
pulverization, purification,
qualification, quantification,
ramification, randomization,
ratification, ratiocination,
realization, reciprocation,
recombination,
recommendation,
recrimination, recuperation,
redecoration, reduplication,
reforestation, refrigeration,
regeneration, regimentation,
regurgitation, reification,
reincarnation, reintegration,
remediation, remuneration,
renunciation, representation,
republication, repudiation,
reticulation, retrogradation,
reverberation, robotization,
romanization, sanctification,

sanitization, scarification, secularization, sedimentation, sensitization, Serbo-Croatian, signification, simplification, socialization, solemnization, solicitation, solidification, sophistication, specialization, specification, stabilization, standardization, sterilization, stratification, stultification, subalternation, subinfeudation, subordination, subpopulation, subsidization, summarization, supplementation, syllabication, symbolization, synchronization, systemization, teleportation, tergiversation, terrorization, theorization, transfiguration, transliteration, transvaluation, traumatization, triangulation, trivialization, uglification, unification, unionization, urbanization, vandalization, vaporization, variegation, vaticination, velarization, verbalization, verification, versification, victimization, vilification, vinification, vitalization, vituperation, vocalization, vociferation, vulgarization, westernization, x-radiation, acclimatization, allegorization, alphabetization, autocorrelation, automatization, beneficiation, capitalization, characterization, circumnavigation, codetermination, commercialization, conceptualization, consubstantiation, containerization, counterreformation, criminalization, cross-examination, cryopreservation, decarboxylation, decimilization, de-Stalinization, decasualization, decentralization, declassification, decontamination, dehumanization, dehydrogenation, delegitimation, demystification, derealization, derivitization, desulfurization, deterioration, differentiation, disassociation, discombobulation, disorientation, disorganization, disproportionation, disqualification, diversification, dolomitization, electrification, excommunication, exemplification, experimentation, extemporization, externalization, familiarization, federalization, generalization, homogenization, hospitalization, hyperventilation, idealization, identification, immobilization, immortalization, incapacitation, inconsideration,

incoordination,
indemnification,
indetermination,
indiscrimination,
individuation,
institutionalization,
insubordination,
intensification, intermediation,
intermodulation,
intrapopulation, italicization,
legitimization, lexicalization,
maladministration,
mathematization,
megacorporation,
militarization, miniaturization,
misappropriation,
miscommunication,
misinterpretation,
mispronunciation,
misrepresentation,
noncooperation,
nonproliferation,
overcompensation,
overpopulation, palatalization,
periodization, personification,
photoduplication,
photoexcitation,
popularization,
predetermination,
prestidigitation,
proselytization, radicalization,
ratiocination, rationalization,
reafforestation, recapitulation,
reconciliation,
reconsideration, rehabilitation,
reinterpretation, renegotiation,
reorganization, revitalization,
ritualization, Schrödinger
equation, subvocalization,
supererogation,
syllabification,
tintinnabulation,
transubstantiation,
unappreciation,
underestimation,
undervaluation,
unsophistication,
visualization,
Americanization,
automanipulation,
decriminalization,
depersonalization,
electrodesiccation,
intercommunication,
industrialization,
materialization,
oversimplification,
particularization,
pictorialization,
photointerpretation,
pseudosophistication,
recapitalization,
spiritualization,
telecommunication,
universalization,
biodeterioration,
deindustrialization,
intellectualization,
reindustrialization,
internationalization,
deinstitutionalization
²**ation** \ā-zhən\ see ASION
³**ation** \ash-ən\ see ASSION
¹**ational** \ā-shnəl\ stational,
citational, formational,
gestational, gradational,
migrational, narrational,
notational, relational,
sensational, vocational,
aberrational, adaptational,
avocational, compensational,
computational,
conformational,
confrontational,

congregational, conjugational, connotational, conservational, conversational, convocational, derivational, educational, fluctuational, generational, gravitational, ideational, informational, innovational, inspirational, invitational, irrotational, limitational, navigational, observational, operational, orchestrational, postranslational, prevocational, progestational, recreational, reformational, situational, transformational, communicational, coeducational, denominational, improvisational, interpretational, investigational, organizational, representational, nonrepresentational, reorganizational, interdenominational

²ational \āzh-nəl\ see ASIONAL

³ational \ash-nəl\ national, passional, rational, binational, cross-national, irrational, transnational, international, multinational, supranational, suprarational

ationist \ā-shnəst\ salvationist, vacationist, annexationist, confrontationist, conservationist, educationist, integrationist, isolationist, liberationist, operationist, preservationist, recreationist, segregationist, separationist, preservationist, accomodationist, administrationist, assimilationist, associationist, collaborationist, emancipationist

ations \ā-shənz\ Galatians, impatiens, relations, Lamentations, Revelations, United Nations, Rhode Island and Providence Plantations

atious \ā-shəs\ see ACIOUS

¹atis \at-əs\ see ³ATUS

²atis \ät-əs\ see OTTIS

atist \āt-əst\ see ATEST

atitude \at-ə-tüd\ see ATTITUDE

atium \ā-shē-əm\ Latium, pancratium, solatium

atius \ā-shəs\ see ACIOUS

ative \āt-iv\ dative, native, stative, ablative, constative, creative, dilative, mutative, rotative, summative, translative, aggregative, agitative, alterative, applicative, carminative, cogitative, combinative, commutative, connotative, consecrative, consultative, contemplative, copulative, corporative, cumulative, decorative, denotative, dissipative, educative, explicative, facultative, federative, generative, germinative, imitative, implicative, innovative, integrative, irritative, iterative, legislative, limitative, meditative, meliorative, motivative, nominative, nuncupative, operative, palliative, pejorative,

penetrative, procreative,
propagative, qualitative,
quantitative, recreative,
regulative, replicative,
separative, speculative,
terminative, vegetative,
accelerative, accumulative,
administrative, agglutinative,
alliterative, appreciative,
assimilative, associative,
authoritative, collaborative,
commemorative,
commiserative,
communicative,
contaminative, continuative,
cooperative, corroborative,
degenerative, deliberative,
delineative, determinative,
discriminative, evaporative,
exhilarative, exonerative,
illuminative, interpretative,
investigative, justificative,
multiplicative, obliterative,
opinionative, originative,
postoperative, premeditative,
preoperative, proliferative,
reciprocative, recuperative,
regenerative, remunerative,
reverberative, significative,
vituperative,
excommunicative,
incommunicative,
noncooperative, quasi-
legislative, semiquantitative,
uncommunicative

atl \ät-ᵊl\ see OTTLE

atlas \at-ləs\ atlas, Atlas, hatless

atless \at-ləs\ see ATLAS

atli \ät-lē\ see OTLY

atling \at-liŋ\ fatling, flatling,
rattling

atly \at-lē\ flatly, rattly

atnam \ət-nəm\ Machilipatnam,
Vishakhapatnam

atness \at-nəs\ fatness, flatness,
platinous, gelatinous

¹ato \ät-ō\ auto, blotto, grotto,
lotto, motto, otto, Otto, potto,
annatto, castrato, legato,
marcato, mulatto, rabato,
rebato, ridotto, rubato,
sfumato, spiccato, staccato,
agitato, animato, ben trovato,
Guanajuato, moderato,
obbligato, ostinato, pizzicato

²ato \ät-ō\ Cato, Plato, Orvieto,
potato, tomato, Barquisimeto

atomist \at-ə-məst\ atomist,
anatomist

atomy \at-ə-mē\ atomy,
anatomy

aton \at-ᵊn\ see ²ATIN

atony \at-ᵊn-ē\ see ATANY

ator \āt-ər\ baiter, cater, crater,
Crater, dater, faitour,
freighter, gaiter, gator, grater,
hater, krater, later, mater,
plater, rater, satyr, skater,
slater, stater, stator, tater,
traitor, waiter, aerator,
collator, Bay Stater, creator,
curator, debater, Decatur,
dictator, donator, dumbwaiter,
equator, first-rater, glossator,
headwaiter, levator, locator,
mandator, Mercator, narrator,
pronator, pulsator, rotator,
spectator, tailgater, testator,
theater, third-rater, translator,
upstater, vibrator, actuator,
abdicator, activator, adulator,
advocator, agitator, alligator,
allocator, alternator, animator,
annotator, applicator,

arbitrator, aspirator, aviator, buccinator, calculator, captivator, carburetor, celebrator, circulator, commentator, commutator, compensator, compurgator, concentrator, confiscator, congregator, consecrator, consummator, contemplator, corporator, correlator, depredator, desecrater, desecrator, designator, cultivator, decorator, delegator, demonstrator, detonator, deviator, dissipater, dominator, duplicator, dura mater, educator, elevator, emulator, escalator, estimator, excavator, explicator, expurgator, extirpator, fascinator, formulator, fornicator, generator, gladiator, hibernator, illustrator, incubator, indicator, infiltrator, innovator, inhalator, inspirator, insulator, integrator, lacrimator, liquidator, literator, mediator, moderator, motivator, navigator, nomenclator, nominator, numerator, obturator, operator, orchestrator, oscillator, percolator, perpetrator, pia mater, pollinator, postulator, procreator, procurator, propagator, radiator, regulator, resonator, respirator, revelator, second-rater, selling-plater, separator, simulator, subjugator, syndicator, tabulator, terminator, valuator, ventilator, violator, accelerator, accommodator, accumulator, administrator, adulterator, alienator, alleviator, annihilator, annunciator, anticipator, appreciator, appropriator, assassinator, attenuator, continuator, calumniator, collaborator, commemorator, communicator, conciliator, congratulator, consolidator, contaminator, cooperator, coordinator, corroborator, defibrillator, delineator, denominator, depreciator, determinator, discriminator, disseminator, dissimulator, ejaculator, eliminator, emancipator, enumerator, equivocator, eradicator, evaluator, evaporator, exterminator, extrapolator, impersonator, improvisator, incinerator, inseminator, interrogator, intimidator, investigator, negotiator, oxygenator, pacificator, perambulator, predestinator, procrastinator, purificator, redecorator, refrigerator, regenerator, resuscitator, totalizator, subordinator, excommunicator, rehabilitator, turbogenerator, immunomodulator—*also comparatives of adjectives listed at* [1]ATE

atra \ä-trə\ Tatra, Sumatra

¹atre \ätrᵊ\ coup de theatre, pas de quatre

²atre \at\ see ⁵AT

atric \a-trik\ Patrick, sympatric, theatric, allopatric, geriatric, pediatric, podiatric, psychiatric

atrick \a-trik\ see ATRIC

atrics \a-triks\ theatrics, pediatrics

atrist \a-trəst\ geriatrist, physiatrist

atrix \ā-triks\ matrix, cicatrix, testatrix, aviatrix, dominatrix, executrix, mediatrix, administratrix

atron \ā-trən\ matron, natron, patron

¹ats \äts\ see OTS

²ats \ats\ bats, rats, ersatz—*also plurals and possessives of nouns and third singular presents of verbs listed at* ⁵AT

atsa \ät-sə\ see ¹ATZO

atsch \ach\ see ⁴ATCH

atsk \ätsk\ Bratsk, Okhotsk, Petrozavodsk

atsu \ät-sü\ Hamamatsu, shiatsu, shiatzu, Takamatsu

atsy \at-sē\ see ³AZI

¹att \at\ see ⁵AT

²att \ät\ see ¹OT

atta \ät-ə\ see ¹ATA

attage \ät-ij\ see OTTAGE

attan \at-ᵊn\ see ²ATIN

atte \at\ see ⁵AT

atted \a-təd\ superfatted—*also pasts of verbs listed at* ⁵AT

attel \at-ᵊl\ see ATTLE

atten \at-ᵊn\ see ²ATIN

atter \at-ər\ attar, batter, blatter, chatter, clatter, fatter, flatter, hatter, latter, matter, natter, patter, platter, ratter, satyr, scatter, shatter, smatter, spatter, splatter, tatter, backscatter, bespatter, flat-hatter, standpatter, wildcatter, antimatter, pitter-patter

attering \at-ə-riŋ\ nattering, smattering, backscattering, earth-shattering, self-flattering, unflattering, Rayleigh scattering

attern \at-ərn\ pattern, Saturn, slattern

attery \at-ə-rē\ battery, cattery, clattery, flattery, mattery, Cape Flattery, self-flattery

¹atti \ät-ē\ see ¹ATI

²atti \at-ē\ see ATTY

attic \at-ik\ see ²ATIC

attica \at-i-kə\ see ATICA

¹attice \at-əs\ see ³ATUS

²attice \at-ish\ see ATTISH

attie \at-ē\ see ATTY

attily \at-ᵊl-ē\ cattily, chattily, Natalie, Nathalie, nattily, rattly, philately, sal volatile

atting \at-iŋ\ batting, matting, tatting

attish \at-ish\ brattish, fattish, flattish

attitude \at-ə-tüd\ attitude, latitude

attle \at-ᵊl\ battle, brattle, cattle, chattel, prattle, rattle, tattle, embattle, Seattle, tittle-tattle

attler \at-lər\ battler, prattler, rattler, tattler

attling \at-liŋ\ see ATLING

¹attly \at-ᵊl-ē\ see ATTILY

²attly \at-lē\ see ATLY

¹atto \at-ə\ see ³ATA

²**atto** \ät-ō\ see ¹ATO

atton \at-ᵊn\ see ²ATIN

atty \at-ē\ batty, catty, bratty, chatty, fatty, Hattie, natty, Patti, Pattie, patty, Patty, platy, ratty, scatty, tattie, tatty, Cincinnati

¹**atum** \ät-əm\ bottom, datum, satem, erratum, pomatum, desideratum

²**atum** \ät-əm\ datum, pomatum, substratum, verbatim, ageratum, literatim, seriatim, ultimatim, corpus allatum, corpus striatum, desideratum

³**atum** \at-əm\ atom, datum, erratum, substratum, seriatim

atuous \ach-wəs\ fatuous, ignis fatuus

atur \ät-ər\ see ATOR

atural \ach-rəl\ natural, connatural, transnatural, unnatural, preternatural, seminatural, supernatural

¹**ature** \ā-chər\ nature, denature, 4-H'er, magistrature, nomenclature, supernature

²**ature** \ach-ər\ see ²ATCHER

aturn \at-ərn\ see ATTERN

¹**atus** \ät-əs\ flatus, gratis, status, stratus, afflatus, hiatus, meatus, apparatus, coitus reservatus

²**atus** \ät-əs\ see OTTIS

³**atus** \at-əs\ brattice, gratis, lattice, status, stratus, clematis, altostratus, apparatus, cirrostratus, nimbostratus

atute \ach-ət\ see ATCHET

atuus \ach-wəs\ see ATUOUS

aty \āt-ē\ eighty, Haiti, Katie, Katy, Leyte, matey, platy, slaty, weighty, yeti, 1080, Papeete

atyr \āt-ər\ see ATOR

¹**atz** \ats\ see ²ATS

²**atz** \äts\ see OTS

¹**atzo** \ät-sə\ matzo, tazza, Hidatsa, piazza

²**atzo** \ät-sō\ see ¹AZZO

atzu \ät-sü\ see ATSU

¹**au** \ō\ see ¹OW

²**au** \ü\ see ¹EW

³**au** \au̇\ see ²OW

⁴**au** \o̍\ see ¹AW

aub \äb\ see ¹OB

auba \o̍-bə\ carnauba, Catawba

aube \ōb\ see ¹OBE

auber \o̍b-ər\ dauber, Micawber

auble \äb-əl\ see ¹ABBLE

¹**auce** \as\ see ³ASS

²**auce** \o̍s\ see ¹OSS

aucer \o̍-sər\ see OSSER

aucet \äs-ət\ see OSSET

¹**auch** \o̍ch\ nautch, watch, debauch

²**auch** \äch\ see OTCH

auche \ōsh\ see ²OCHE

auchely \ōsh-lē\ see OCIALLY

auckland \o̍k-lənd\ Auckland, Falkland

aucous \o̍-kəs\ caucous, glaucous, raucous

aucus \o̍-kəs\ see AUCOUS

aucy \as-ē\ see ASSY

¹**aud** \o̍d\ awed, baud, bawd, broad, Claud, Claude, clawed, fraud, gaud, god, jawed, laud, Maud, Maude, yod, abroad, applaud, belaud, defraud, dewclawed, maraud, whipsawed, eisteddfod, lantern-jawed, quartersawed—

also pasts of verbs listed at ¹AW

²**aud** \äd\ see ¹OD

audable \ȯd-ə-bəl\ audible, laudable, applaudable, illaudable, inaudible

audal \ȯd-ᵊl\ caudal, caudle, dawdle

audative \ȯd-ət-iv\ see AUDITIVE

¹**aude** \au̇d-ē\ see OWDY

²**aude** \ȯd-ē\ see AWDY

³**aude** \au̇d-ə\ howdah, cum laude, magna cum laude, summa cum laude

⁴**aude** \ȯd\ see ¹AUD

audible \ȯd-ə-bəl\ see AUDABLE

auding \ȯd-iŋ\ auding, applauding, self-applauding

audit \ȯd-ət\ audit, plaudit

auditive \ȯd-ət-iv\ auditive, laudative

audle \ȯd-ᵊl\ see AUDAL

¹**audy** \äd-ē\ see ¹ODY

²**audy** \ȯd-ē\ see AWDY

auer \au̇r\ see ²OWER

auf \au̇f\ see OWFF

auffeur \ō-fər\ see OFER

auga \ȯ-gə\ massasauga, Mississauga, Onondaga

auge \āj\ see ³AGE

augeable \ā-jə-bəl\ see AGEABLE

auged \ājd\ see AGED

¹**auger** \ȯ-gər\ see ²OGGER

²**auger** \ā-jər\ see ¹AGER

¹**augh** \af\ see APH

²**augh** \ä\ see ¹A

³**augh** \äk\ see ¹ACH

⁴**augh** \ȯ\ see ¹AW

aughable \af-ə-bəl\ see AFFABLE

augham \ȯm\ see ¹AUM

¹**aughn** \än\ see ¹ON

²**aughn** \ȯn\ see ³ON

¹**aught** \ät\ see ¹OT

²**aught** \ȯt\ see ²OUGHT

¹**aughter** \af-tər\ see AFTER

²**aughter** \ȯt-ər\ see ¹ATER

aughterer \ȯt-ər-ər\ see ATERER

¹**aughty** \ȯt-ē\ haughty, naughty, zloty, Michelangelo Buonarroti

²**aughty** \ät-ē\ see ATI

augre \ȯg-ər\ see ²OGGER

augur \ȯg-ər\ see ²OGGER

augury \ȯ-gə-rē\ see ²OGGERY

aui \au̇-ē\ see OWIE

auk \ȯk\ see ALK

aukee \ȯ-kē\ see ALKIE

aul \ȯl\ see ALL

aulay \ȯ-lē\ see AWLY

¹**auld** \ȯl\ see ALL

²**auld** \ō\ see ¹OW

auldron \ȯl-drən\ see ALDRON

auled \ȯld\ see ALD

auler \ȯ-lər\ see ¹ALLER

aulin \ȯ-lən\ see ALLEN

auling \ȯ-liŋ\ see ALLING

aulish \ȯ-lish\ see ALLISH

aulk \ȯk\ see ALK

aulker \ȯ-kər\ see ALKER

aulking \ȯ-kiŋ\ see ALKING

aulle \ȯl\ see ¹ALL

aulm \ȯm\ see ¹AUM

¹**ault** \ȯlt\ see ALT

²**ault** \ō\ see ¹OW

aulter \ȯl-tər\ see ALTER

aulting \ȯl-tiŋ\ see ALTING

aultless \ȯlt-ləs\ see ALTLESS

aulty \ȯl-tē\ see ALTY

¹**aum** \ȯm\ gaum, haulm, Maugham, poem, qualm, shawm, meerschaum, Radom

²**aum** \äm\ see ¹OM

¹**aun** \än\ see ¹ON

²**aun** \ən\ see UN

³**aun** \ȯn\ see ³ON

⁴**aun** \aȯn\ see ²OWN

¹**auna** \än-ə\ see ¹ANA

²**auna** \ȯn-ə\ see ¹ONNA

aunce \ȯns\ jaunce, launce

¹**aunch** \änch\ conch, cranch, craunch, paunch, raunch, stanch, Romansh

²**aunch** \ȯnch\ craunch, haunch, launch, paunch, raunch, stanch, staunch

auncher \ȯn-chər\ launcher, stancher, stauncher

aunchy \ȯn-chē\ paunchy, raunchy

aund \ȯnd\ awned, maund— *also pasts of verbs listed at* ³ON

¹**aunder** \ȯn-dər\ launder, maunder

²**aunder** \än-dər\ see ¹ONDER

aunish \än-ish\ see ONISH

¹**aunt** \ȯnt\ daunt, flaunt, gaunt, haunt, jaunt, taunt, vaunt, want, wont, avant, avaunt, keeshond, romaunt, John of Gaunt

²**aunt** \ant\ see ⁵ANT

³**aunt** \änt\ see ²ANT

aunted \ȯnt-əd\ see ONTED

¹**aunter** \änt-ər\ saunter, mishanter, rencontre

²**aunter** \ȯnt-ər\ gaunter, haunter, saunter

¹**aunty** \ȯnt-ē\ flaunty, jaunty, vaunty

²**aunty** \änt-ē\ see ¹ANTI

aunus \än-əs\ see ¹ONUS

aup \ȯp\ gawp, scaup, whaup, yawp

aupe \ōp\ see OPE

auphin \ȯ-fən\ see OFFIN

¹**aur** \aȯr\ see ²OWER

²**aur** \ȯr\ see ¹OR

¹**aura** \ȯr-ə\ see ²ORA

²**aura** \är-ə\ see ¹ARA

aural \ȯr-əl\ see ²ORAL

¹**aure** \ōr\ see ¹ORE

²**aure** \ȯr\ see ¹OR

aurea \ȯr-ē-ə\ see ORIA

aurean \ȯr-ē-ən\ see ORIAN

¹**aureate** \är-ē-ət\ baccalaureate, commisariat

²**aureate** \ȯr-ē-ət\ aureate, laureate, baccalaureate, professoriat

aurel \ȯr-əl\ see ²ORAL

¹**auren** \är-ən\ see ¹ORIN

²**auren** \ȯr-ən\ see ²ORIN

aurence \ȯr-ən(t)s\ see AWRENCE

aureus \ȯr-ē-əs\ see ORIOUS

auri \aȯr-ē\ see OWERY

aurian \ȯr-ē-ən\ see ORIAN

auric \ȯr-ik\ see ORIC

¹**aurice** \är-əs\ see ¹ORRIS

²**aurice** \ȯr-əs\ see AURUS

auricle \ȯr-i-kəl\ see ORICAL

¹**aurie** \ȯr-ē\ see ORY

²**aurie** \är-ē\ see ARI

aurous \ȯr-əs\ see AURUS

aurus \ȯr-əs\ aurous, Boris, chorus, Doris, Flores, Horace, Maurice, morris, Morris, Norris, orris, porous, sorus, Taurus, Torres, torus, canorous, Centaurus, clitoris, decorous, Delores, Dolores, pelorus, phosphorous, sonorous, thesaurus,

allosaurus, brontosaurus,
stegosaurus, apatosaurus,
tyrannosaurus

aury \ȯr-ē\ see ORY

¹**aus** \ā-əs\ see ¹AIS

²**aus** \aus\ see ²OUSE

³**aus** \ȯz\ see ¹AUSE

ausal \ȯ-zəl\ causal, clausal,
menopausal, postmenopausal

¹**ause** \ȯz\ Broz, cause, clause,
gauze, hawse, pause, tawse,
yaws, applause, because,
kolkhoz, sovkhoz, aeropause,
diapause, menopause, Santa
Claus—*also plurals and
possessives of nouns and
third person singular presents
of verbs listed at* ¹AW

²**ause** \əz\ see ¹EUSE

auseous \ȯ-shəs\ see AUTIOUS

auser \ȯ-zər\ causer, hawser

ausey \ȯ-zē\ causey, gauzy

auss \aus\ see ¹OUSE

¹**aussie** \äs-ē\ see ¹OSSY

²**aussie** \ȯ-sē\ see ²OSSY

¹**aust** \aust\ see OUST

²**aust** \ȯst\ see ³OST

austen \ȯs-tən\ see OSTON

austin \ȯs-tən\ see OSTON

austless \ȯst-ləs\ costless,
exhaustless

¹**austral** \äs-trəl\ see OSTREL

²**austral** \ȯs-trəl\ see ¹OSTRAL

¹**aut** \ō\ see ¹OW

²**aut** \aut\ see ³OUT

³**aut** \ät\ see ¹OT

⁴**aut** \ȯt\ see ¹OUGHT

autch \ȯch\ see ¹AUCH

aute \ōt\ see OAT

auten \ȯt-ᵊn\ boughten, tauten

auterne \ȯt-ərn\ quartern,
sauterne, sauternes

auternes \ȯt-ərn\ see AUTERNE

autery \ȯt-ə-rē\ see ATERY

autic \ȯt-ik\ orthotic,
aeronautic, astronautic

autical \ȯt-i-kəl\ nautical,
aeronautical, astronautical

autics \ät-iks\ see OTICS

aution \ȯ-shən\ caution,
groschen, incaution,
precaution

autious \ȯ-shəs\ cautious,
nauseous, incautious

¹**auto** \ȯt-ō\ auto, Giotto, risotto

²**auto** \ät-ō\ see ¹ATO

auve \ōv\ see ²OVE

auze \ȯz\ see ¹AUSE

auzer \au-zər\ see OUSER

auzy \ȯ-zē\ see AUSEY

¹**av** \äv\ see ²OLVE

²**av** \av\ see ²ALVE

¹**ava** \äv-ə\ brava, fava, guava,
java, Java, kava, lava,
baklava, cassava, ottava,
balaclava, Bratislava, Costa
Brava, lavalava, piassava,
Warszawa

²**ava** \av-ə\ java, Ungava,
balaclava

avage \av-ij\ ravage, savage

avan \ā-vən\ see ¹AVEN

avant \av-ənt\ haven't, savant

avarice \av-rəs\ see AVEROUS

¹**ave** \äv-ā\ ave, clave, grave,
Jahveh, soave

²**ave** \āv\ brave, clave, cave,
crave, Dave, fave, gave,
glaive, grave, knave, lave,
nave, pave, rave, save, shave,
slave, stave, they've, trave,
waive, wave, Wave, airwave,
behave, concave, conclave,
deprave, dissave, drawshave,

enclave, engrave, enslave, exclave, forgave, Great Slave, margrave, octave, outbrave, p-wave, palsgrave, shortwave, spokeshave, after-shave, architrave, biconcave, microwave, contraoctave, photoengrave

³**ave** \av\ see ³ALVE

⁴**ave** \äv\ see ²OLVE

aved \āvd\ waved, depraved, unsaved—*also pasts of verbs listed at* ²AVE

avel \av-əl\ cavil, gavel, gravel, ravel, travel, unravel

aveless \āv-ləs\ graveless, waveless

aveling \av-liŋ\ raveling, traveling

avement \āv-mənt\ pavement, depravement, enslavement

¹**aven** \ā-vən\ Avon, Cavan, craven, graven, haven, maven, raven, shaven, New Haven, riboflavin, Stratford-upon-Avon

²**aven** \av-ən\ see AVIN

aven't \av-ənt\ see AVANT

¹**aver** \äv-ər\ slaver, palaver, windhover

²**aver** \ā-vər\ caver, claver, favor, flavor, graver, haver, laver, quaver, raver, saver, savor, shaver, slaver, waiver, waver, disfavor, enslaver, face-saver, flag-waver, lifesaver, semiquaver, demisemiquaver, hemidemisemiquaver—*also comparatives of adjectives listed at* ²AVE

³**aver** \av-ər\ slaver, cadaver, palaver

avern \av-ərn\ cavern, klavern, tavern

averous \av-rəs\ avarice, cadaverous

avery \āv-rē\ bravery, knavery, quavery, savory, slavery, wavery, unsavory

avey \ā-vē\ see AVY

avia \ā-vē-ə\ Moldavia, Moravia, Scandinavia

avial \ā-vē-əl\ gavial, margravial

avian \ā-vē-ən\ avian, Shavian, Moravian, Scandinavian

avid \av-əd\ avid, gravid, pavid

avie \ā-vē\ see AVY

avil \av-əl\ see AVEL

avin \av-ən\ Avon, raven, ravin, savin, spavin

aving \ā-viŋ\ caving, craving, paving, raving, saving, shaving, flagwaving, lifesaving, timesaving, laborsaving

avis \ā-vəs\ Davis, favus, mavis, Mavis, rara avis

¹**avish** \ā-vish\ knavish, slavish

²**avish** \av-ish\ lavish, ravish

avist \äv-əst\ Slavist, suavest, Pan-Slavist

avity \av-ət-ē\ cavity, gravity, concavity, depravity, antigravity, microgravity, supergravity

avl \äv-əl\ see ¹OVEL

¹**avo** \äv-ō\ bravo, Bravo, centavo, octavo

²**avo** \ā-vō\ octavo, relievo, mezzo relievo

¹**avon** \ā-vən\ see ¹AVEN

²avon \a-vən\ see AVIN

avor \ā-vər\ see ²AVER

avored \ā-vərd\ favored, flavored, ill-favored, well-favored—*also pasts of verbs listed at* ²AVER

avory \āv-rē\ see AVERY

avus \ā-vəs\ see AVIS

avvy \av-ē\ navvy, savvy

avy \ā-vē\ cavy, Davey, Davy, gravy, navy, shavie, slavey, wavy

¹aw \ȯ\ aw, awe, blaw, braw, ca, caw, chaw, claw, craw, daw, draw, faugh, flaw, gnaw, haugh, haw, jaw, la, law, maw, pa, paw, pshaw, Ra, rah, raw, saw, shah, shaw, Shaw, slaw, spa, squaw, straw, tau, taw, thaw, yaw, backsaw, bashaw, bedstraw, bucksaw, bylaw, catclaw, cat's-paw, coleslaw, cumshaw, cushaw, Danelaw, declaw, dewclaw, Esau, forepaw, fretsaw, grandma, grandpa, guffaw, hacksaw, handsaw, hawkshaw, hee-haw, hurrah, in-law, jackdaw, jackstraw, jigsaw, kickshaw, lockjaw, macaw, Nassau, old-squaw, outdraw, outlaw, pasha, pooh-bah, ricksha, rickshaw, ringtaw, ripsaw, scofflaw, scrimshaw, seesaw, southpaw, trishaw, tussah, undraw, Utah, vizsla, Warsaw, whipsaw, windflaw, wiredraw, withdraw, Arkansas, Chickasaw, Chippewa, clapperclaw, decree-law, foofaraw, jinrikisha, Kiowa, Mackinac, mackinaw, Omaha, Ottawa, overawe, overdraw, oversaw, overslaugh, padishah, panama, son-in-law, usquebaugh, Wichita, williwaw, windlestraw, Yakima, brother-in-law, daughter-in-law, father-in-law, mother-in-law, pipsissewa, serjeant-at-law, sister-in-law, Straits of Mackinac

²aw \äv\ see ²OLVE

³aw \ȯf\ see ²OFF

⁴aw \äf\ see ¹OFF

¹awa \ä-wə\ Chihuahua, Tarawa, Urawa, Fujisawa, Ichikawa, Kanzawa, Okinawa, Ahashikawa

²awa \ä-və\ see ¹AVA

awain \au̇-ən\ see ²OWAN

awan \au̇-ən\ see ²OWAN

awar \au̇r\ see ²OWER

awba \ȯ-bə\ see AUBA

¹awber \äb-ər\ see OBBER

²awber \ȯb-ər\ see AUBER

awd \ȯd\ see ¹AUD

awddle \äd-ᵊl\ see ODDLE

awdle \ȯd-ᵊl\ see AUDAL

awdry \ȯ-drē\ Audrey, tawdry

awdust \ȯd-əst\ see ¹ADIST

awdy \ȯd-ē\ bawdy, gaudy, summa cum laude

awe \ȯ\ see ¹AW

awed \ȯd\ see ¹AUD

aweless \ȯ-ləs\ see AWLESS

awer \ȯr\ see ¹OR

awers \ōrz\ see OORS

awful \ȯ-fəl\ awful, coffle, lawful, offal, god-awful, unlawful

awfully \óf-ə-lē\ awfully, lawfully, offaly, unlawfully

awing \ó-iŋ\ cloying, drawing, wappenschawing

awk \ók\ see ALK

awker \ó-kər\ see ALKER

awkes \óks\ Fawkes—*also possessives and plurals of nouns, third person singular presents of verbs listed at* ALK

awkish \ó-kish\ gawkish, hawkish, mawkish

awky \ó-kē\ see ALKIE

awl \ól\ see ALL

awler \ó-lər\ see ¹ALLER

awless \ó-ləs\ aweless, flawless, lawless

awling \ó-liŋ\ see ALLING

awly \ó-lē\ brawly, crawly, dolly, drawly, Raleigh, scrawly, squally, Bengali, Macaulay

awm \óm\ see ¹AUM

¹awn \än\ see ¹ON

²awn \ón\ see ³ON

awned \ónd\ see AUND

¹awner \ón-ər\ fawner, goner, pawner, prawner, spawner

²awner \än-ər\ see ¹ONOR

awney \ó-nē\ see ¹AWNY

awning \än-iŋ\ see ¹ONING

awnly \än-lē\ see ¹ANLY

¹awny \ó-nē\ brawny, fawny, lawny, sawney, scrawny, Taney, tawny, mulligatawny

²awny \än-ē\ see ¹ANI

awp \óp\ see AUP

awrence \ór-ən(t)s\ Florence, Laurence, Lawrence, Torrence, abhorrence, Saint Lawrence—*also possessives*

and plurals of nouns listed at ORRENT

awry \ór-ē\ see ORY

aws \óz\ see ¹AUSE

awse \óz\ see ¹AUSE

awser \ó-zər\ see AUSER

awsi \aù-sē\ see ²OUSY

awy \ói\ see OY

awyer \ó-yər\ lawyer, sawyer

¹ax \äks\ see OX

²ax \aks\ ax, fax, flax, lax, max, Max, pax, rax, sax, tax, wax, addax, Ajax, anthrax, banjax, beeswax, borax, broadax, climax, coax, earwax, galax, gravlax, hyrax, meat-ax, panchax, pickax, poleax, pretax, relax, smilax, storax, styrax, surtax, syntax, thorax, toadflax, aftertax, battle-ax, Halifax, minimax, overtax, parallax, supertax, anticlimax, Astyanax—*also plurals and possessives of nouns and third person singular presents of verbs listed at* ²ACK

axant \ak-sənt\ see ACCENT

axen \ak-sən\ see AXON

axi \ak-sē\ see AXY

axic \ak-sik\ ataraxic, stereotaxic

axis \ak-səs\ axis, Naxos, praxis

axman \ak-smən\ axman, cracksman

axon \ak-sən\ flaxen, Jackson, Klaxon, Saxon, waxen, Port Jackson, Anglo-Saxon

axos \ak-səs\ see AXIS

axy \ak-sē\ flaxy, maxi, taxi, waxy

¹ay \ā\ a, ae, aye, bay, bey, blae, brae, bray, chez, clay,

Clay, day, dey, dray, eh, fay,
Fay, Faye, fey, flay, fley, frae,
fray, Frey, gay, Gay, gey,
gley, gray, Gray, greige,
Grey, hae, hay, he, hey, Hue,
j, jay, Jay, Jaye, k, kay, Kay,
Kaye, lay, lei, may, May, nay,
né, née, neigh, pay, pe, play,
pray, prey, qua, quai, quay,
Rae, ray, Ray, re, say, sei,
shay, slay, sleigh, spae, spay,
splay, spray, stay, stray, sway,
they, tray, trey, way, weigh,
whey, yea, abbé, affray,
agley, airplay, airway, all-day,
allay, allée, Angers, Anhui,
Anhwei, archway, array,
ashtray, assay, astray, Augier,
away, aweigh, backstay, ballet, beignet, belay,
beltway, benday, Benet, beret,
betray, bewray, bidet,
bikeway, birthday, Biscay,
Bizet, blasé, bobstay,
Bombay, bombe, bouchée,
bouclé, boule, bouquet,
bourrée, breezeway,
Broadway, buffet, byplay,
byway, cachet, café, cahier,
Cambay, Cape May, Cartier,
Cathay, causeway, chaîné,
chalet, chambray, chassé, ciré,
cliché, cloqué, congé, convey,
corvée, coudé, coupé,
crawlway, crochet, croquet,
crossway, cube, curé, cy pres,
DA, daresay, decay, deejay,
defray, delay, dengue,
dismay, display, distrait, DJ,
donnée, doomsday, doorway,
dossier, downplay, dragée,
driveway, duvet, embay,

entrée, épée, essay, estray,
Ewe, fairway, filé, filet, fillet,
fireclay, fishway, flambé,
floodway, flyway, folkway,
footway, foray, forebay,
foreplay, forestay, formée,
forte, fouetté, four-way,
fourchée, foyer, franglais,
frappé, freeway, frieze, frisé,
fumet, gainsay, Galway,
gamay, gangway, Gaspé,
gateway, gelée, glacé, godet,
gourmet, Green Bay,
greenway, guideway, gunplay,
halfway, hallway, hatchway,
headway, hearsay, Hebei,
Hefei, heyday, highway,
homestay, hooray, horseplay,
Hubei, in re, inlay, inveigh,
issei, jackstay, jeté, keyway,
Kobe, koine, kouprey, lamé,
laneway, leeway, lifeway,
Lomé, Lough Neagh, lwei,
lycée, M-day, maguey,
mainstay, Malay, malgré,
man-day, Mande, Manet,
manqué, margay, Marseilles,
massé, maté, May Day,
Mayday, melee, metier, meze,
midday, Midway, Millay,
Millet, mislay, misplay,
moiré, Monet, moray, nevé,
Niamey, nisei, noonday,
Norway, nosegay, obey, ofay,
OK, olé, ombré, osprey,
outlay, outré, outstay,
outweigh, oyez, PA, parfait,
parkway, parlay, parquet,
partway, passé, pâté, pathway,
pavé, payday, per se, pince-
nez, piqué, piquet, PK, plié,
plissé, pommée, Pompeii,

portray, prepay, projet, pulque, puree, purvey, quale, raceway, railway, rappee, relay, Rene, Renee, repay, replay, risqué, roadway, role-play, ropeway, rosé, rosebay, Roubaix, roué, routeway, runway, sachet, Salé, sansei, sashay, sauté, screenplay, seaway, semé, shar-pei, shipway, short-day, sideway, Skopje, skyway, slideway, slipway, sluiceway, soigné, soiree, someday, someway, soothsay, soufflé, speedway, spillway, stairway, sternway, stingray, straightway, strathspey, subway, survey, swordplay, Taipei, tempeh, thoughtway, three-way, thruway, tideway, Tigré, today, Tokay, tollway, Torbay, touché, toupee, trackway, tramway, unlay, unsay, valet, V-day, veejay, vide, visé, Vouvray, walkway, waylay, weekday, windway, wireway, wordplay, workday, X ray, x-ray, Yaoundé, Adige, A-OK, alleyway, anyway, appliqué, arrivé, atelier, attaché, ballonet, Beaujolais, beurre manié, BHA, botonée, braciole, breakaway, bustier, cabaret, cableway, Camagüey, canapé, cap-a-pie, caraway, carriageway, Cartier, cassoulet, castaway, champlevé, chansonnier, chardonnay, Charolais, chevalier, Chippewa, cloisonné, consommé,

coryphée, croupier, crudités, cutaway, day-to-day, debauchee, déclassé, dégagé, degree-day, démodé, devotee, disarray, disobey, distingué, divorcé, divorcée, DNA, émigré, engagé, entranceway, entremets, entryway, espalier, etoufée, everyday, exposé, expressway, fadeaway, fallaway, faraday, Faraday, faraway, fiancé, fiancée, flageolet, flyaway, foldaway, Galloway, Georgian Bay, getaway, giveaway, gratiné, gratinée, guillemet, Harare, haulageway, Hemingway, hereaway, hideaway, HLA, Hogmanay, holiday, Hugh Capet, IgA, inter se, interplay, intraday, IPA, IRA, Joliet, Kootenay, Kutenai, kyrie, lackaday, latter-day, layaway, lingerie, macramé, Mandalay, Massenet, matinee, MIA, Molise, Monterrey, motorway, muscadet, negligee, overlay, overplay, overstay, overweigh, Paraguay, passageway, patissier, Petare, photoplay, pikake, piolet, pis aller, play-by-play, poly (A), Ponape, popinjay, pourparler, pousse-café, present-day, protégé, protégée, Rabelais, rambouillet, ratiné, recamier, rechauffé, recherché, reconvey, repartee, repoussé, résumé, retroussé, ricochet, right-of-way, rockaway, rondelet, roundelay, RNA, runaway, Saguenay, San Jose, San José, Santa Fe, São Tomé, semplice, sobriquet, sommelier, steerageway, standaway, stowaway, straightaway, Table Bay, taboret, take-away, tarsier, taxiway, tearaway, teleplay, Tempere, Tenebrae, thataway, throwaway, Thunder Bay, Udine, underlay, underpay, underplay, underway, Uruguay, velouté, Venite, vérité, vertebra, virelay, walkaway, waterway, wellaway, Whitsunday, workaday, Yenisey, Zuider Zee, Agnus Dei, areaway, auto-da-fé, bichon frisé, boulevardier, cabriolet, café au lait, cantabile, cDNA, communiqué, costumier, couturier, décolleté, diamanté, Dies Irae, eglomisé, felo-de-se, Fiesole, garde-manger, habitué, Jubilate, laissez-passer, Lavoisier, marrons glacé, mezzo forte, Morgan le Fay, objet trouvé, out-of-the-way, papier collé, papier-mâché, pas de bourrée, photo-essay, Port Philip Bay, pouilly-fuissé, Pouilly-Fumé, prêt-à-porter, roche moutonnée, roman à clef, roturier, sine die, sub judice, superhighway, ukiyo-e, Ulan-Ude, yerba maté, Alto Adige, arrière pensée, Guanabara Bay, lettre de cachet, catalogue raisonné, cinema verité, Dumfries and

Galloway, vers de société, video verité, sinfonia concertante, Trentino-Alto Adige

²**ay** \ē\ see ¹EE

³**ay** \ī\ see ¹Y

¹**aya** \ä-yə\ ayah, maya, taille, Malaya, Koshigaya

²**aya** \ī-ə\ see ¹IAH

³**aya** \ā-ə\ see ¹AIA

ayable \ā-ə-bəl\ payable, playable, sayable, defrayable, displayable, unsayable

ayah \ī-ə\ see ¹IAH

ayal \āl\ see AIL

¹**ayan** \ā-ən\ crayon, Chilean, Malayan, ouabain, papain, Pompeian, Pompeiian, Galilean, Himalayan

²**ayan** \ī-ən\ see ¹ION

¹**aybe** \ā-bē\ see ABY

²**aybe** \eb-ē\ see EBBY

ayday \ā-dā\ Ede, Mayday, May Day

ayden \ī-dᵊn\ see IDEN

¹**aye** \ā\ see ¹AY

²**aye** \ī\ see ¹Y

ayed \ād\ see ¹ADE

¹**ayer** \ā-ər\ brayer, layer, mayor, payer, player, prayer, preyer, sayer, sprayer, stayer, strayer, ballplayer, betrayer, bilayer, bricklayer, cardplayer, conveyer, crocheter, decayer, delayer, doomsayer, doomsdayer, gainsayer, horseplayer, inlayer, essayer, forayer, inveigher, obeyer, manslayer, minelayer, portrayer, purveyor, ratepayer, soothsayer, swordplayer, surveyor, taxpayer, tracklayer,

yea-sayer, disobeyer, holidayer—*also comparatives of adjectives listed at* ¹AY

²ayer \er\ *see* ⁴ARE

ayered \erd\ *see* AIRED

ayest \ā-əst\ mayest, sayest, épéeist, essayist, fideist, Hebraist, Mithraist—*also superlatives of adjectives listed at* ¹AY

¹ayin \ī-ən\ *see* ¹ION

²ayin \īn\ *see* ¹INE

³ayin \ä-yən\ *see* AIIAN

aying \ā-iŋ\ gleying, maying, playing, saying, bricklaying, delaying, long-playing, soothsaying, surveying, taxpaying, tracklaying

ayish \ā-ish\ clayish, grayish

ayist \ā-əst\ *see* AYEST

ayle \āl\ *see* AIL

ayless \ā-ləs\ rayless, talus, wayless, Morelos, aurora australis, Corona Australis

ayling \ā-liŋ\ *see* AILING

aylor \ā-lər\ *see* AILER

ayly \ā-lē\ *see* AILY

ayman \ā-mən\ *see* ¹AMEN

ayment \ā-mənt\ ament, claimant, clamant, payment, raiment, co-payment, embayment, prepayment, underlayment, underpayment

ayne \ān\ *see* ¹ANE

ayness \ā-nəs\ anus, feyness, gayness, grayness, heinous, Janus, manus, awayness, uranous, Uranus, everydayness

aynim \ā-nəm\ *see* ¹ANUM

ayn't \ā-ənt\ *see* EYANT

¹ayo \ā-ō\ *see* ¹EO

²ayo \ī-ō\ *see* ¹IO

¹ayon \an\ *see* ⁵AN

²ayon \ā-ən\ *see* ¹AYAN

ayor \ā-ər\ *see* ¹AYER

¹ayou \ī-ə\ *see* ¹IAH

²ayou \ī-ō\ *see* ¹IO

ayr \er\ *see* ⁴ARE

¹ays \ez\ fez, Fez, Geez, prez, says, Cortez, gainsays, Inez, Suez, unsays, crème anglaise, Louis Seize, Louis Treize, Isthmus of Suez, Vincente López

²ays \āz\ *see* ¹AZE

aysia \ā-zhə\ *see* ASIA

ay-so \ā-sō\ *see* ¹ESO

ayton \āt-ᵊn\ Clayton, Dayton, Layton

¹ayyid \ī-əd\ *see* YAD

²ayyid \ēd-ē\ *see* EEDY

¹az \az\ *see* AZZ

²az \äz\ *see* ¹OISE

³az \äts\ *see* OTS

¹aza \äz-ə\ Gaza, plaza, piazza, tabula rasa

²aza \az-ə\ plaza, piazza

¹azar \äz-ər\ *see* OZZER

²azar \az-ər\ lazar, alcazar, Belshazzar

azard \az-ərd\ hazard, mazard, mazzard, haphazard

¹aze \āz\ baize, blaze, braise, braze, chaise, craze, days, daze, Draize, faze, feaze, fraise, gaze, glaze, graze, Hays, haze, lase, laze, maize, maze, phase, phrase, praise, raise, rase, raze, smaze, vase, ways, ablaze, agaze, amaze, appraise, breadthways, catchphrase, crossways, deglaze, dispraise, edgeways,

emblaze, endways, flatways,
foodways, gainsays,
hereways, leastways,
lengthways, liaise, malaise,
mores, pj's, sideways,
slantways, stargaze, ukase,
upraise, weekdays, anyways,
chrysoprase, cornerways,
crème anglaise, holidays,
Louis Seize, Louis Treize,
lyonnaise, mayonnaise,
metaphrase, multiphase,
nowadays, overglaze,
overgraze, paraphrase,
polonaise, polyphase, single-
phase, underglaze—*also
plurals and possessives of
nouns and third person
singular presents of verbs
listed at* ¹AY

²**aze** \äz\ see ¹OISE

³**aze** \äz-ē\ see ¹AZI

azeable \ā-zə-bəl\ see ¹ASABLE

azed \āzd\ unfazed—*pasts of
verbs listed at* ¹AZE

azel \ā-zəl\ see ²ASAL

azement \āz-mənt\ amazement,
appraisement

azen \āz-ᵊn\ see AZON

azer \ā-zər\ blazer, brazer,
Fraser, gazer, glazer, grazer,
hazer, laser, maser, mazer,
praiser, razer, razor, appraiser,
fund-raiser, hair-raiser, hell-
raiser, stargazer, trailblazer,
paraphraser, free-electron
laser

¹**azi** \äz-ē\ quasi, Swazi,
Benghazi, Anasazi, kamikaze

²**azi** \az-ē\ see AZZY

³**azi** \at-sē\ Nazi, patsy, Patsy,
neo-Nazi

⁴**azi** \ät-sē\ Nazi, neo-Nazi

azier \ā-zhər\ brazier, Frasier,
glacier, glazier, grazier,
leisure, measure, pleasure,
rasure, treasure, admeasure,
embrasure, erasure

azing \ā-zin\ see AISING

azo \az-ō\ diazo, terrazzo

azon \āz-ᵊn\ blazon, brazen,
raisin, emblazon, Marquesan,
diapason, hexenbesen

azor \ā-zər\ see AZER

azquez \as-kəs\ see ASCUS

azy \ā-zē\ crazy, daisy, Daisy,
hazy, lazy, mazy, stir-crazy,
witch of Agnesi

azz \az\ as, has, jazz, razz, spaz,
Hejaz, La Paz, pizzazz, topaz,
whenas, whereas, razzmatazz

¹**azza** \az-ə\ see ²AZA

²**azza** \äz-ə\ see ¹AZA

³**azza** \ät-sə\ see ¹ATZO

azzar \az-ər\ see ²AZAR

azzard \az-ərd\ see AZARD

azzle \az-əl\ basil, Basil, dazzle,
frazzle, bedazzle, razzle-
dazzle

¹**azzo** \ät-sō\ matzo, palazzo,
terrazzo, paparazzo

²**azzo** \az-ō\ see AZO

azzy \az-ē\ jazzy, snazzy,
Ashkenazi

e

¹**e** \ā\ see ¹AY
²**e** \ē\ see ¹EE
³**e** \ə\ see ³U
é \ā\ see ¹AY
¹**ea** \ā\ see ¹AY
²**ea** \ā-ə\ see ¹AIA
³**ea** \ē\ see ¹EE
⁴**ea** \ē-ə\ see ¹IA
eabee \ē-bē\ see ¹EBE
eace \ēs\ see IECE
eaceable \ē-sə-bəl\ see
  ¹EASABLE
each \ēch\ beach, beech, bleach,
  breach, breech, each, fleech,
  leach, leech, peach, pleach,
  preach, reach, screech,
  speech, teach, beseech,
  forereach, impeach, Long
  Beach, outreach, unteach,
  overreach, practice-teach,
  Huntington Beach
eachable \ē-chə-bəl\
  bleachable, leachable,
  reachable, teachable,
  impeachable, unimpeachable
eacher \ē-chər\ bleacher,
  creature, feature, leacher,
  preacher, reacher, screecher,
  teacher, defeature, disfeature,
  schoolteacher
eacherous \ech-rəs\ see
  ECHEROUS
eachery \ech-rē\ see ECHERY
eaching \ē-chiŋ\ see EECHING
eachment \ēch-mənt\
  preachment, impeachment

eachy \ē-chē\ beachy, chichi,
  Nietzsche, peachy, preachy,
  screechy, caliche, Campeche
eacle \ē-kəl\ see ¹ECAL
eacly \ē-klē\ see EEKLY
eacon \ē-kən\ beacon, deacon,
  sleeken, weaken, archdeacon,
  Mohican, subdeacon,
  Neorican
¹**ead** \ed\ bed, bled, bread, bred,
  dead, dread, ed, Ed, fed, fled,
  Fred, head, Jed, lead, led,
  med, Ned, ped, pled, read,
  red, Red, redd, said, shed,
  shred, sled, sped, spread,
  stead, ted, Ted, thread, tread,
  wed, zed, abed, afraid, ahead,
  airhead, baldhead, beachhead,
  bedspread, bedstead,
  beebread, behead, bestead,
  bighead, biped, blackhead,
  blockhead, bloodred,
  bloodshed, bobsled,
  bonehead, bridgehead, brown
  bread, bulkhead, bullhead,
  cathead, childbed, coed,
  cokehead, corn-fed, cowshed,
  crispbread, crossbred,
  crosshead, daybed, deadhead,
  death's-head, deathbed,
  dispread, dogsled, dopehead,
  drophead, drumhead,
  dumbhead, egghead, embed,
  far-red, farmstead, fathead,
  flatbed, forehead, foresaid,
  gainsaid, Gateshead, godhead,

green-head, half-bred,
hardhead, highbred, hogshead,
homebred, homestead,
hophead, hotbed, hothead, ill-
bred, inbred, instead, jarhead,
juicehead, lamed, light bread,
longhead, lowbred, lunkhead,
masthead, meathead, misled,
misread, moped, naled,
nonsked, outsped, outspread,
packthread, phys ed, pinhead,
pithead, pothead, premed,
printhead, purebred, railhead,
re-tread, redhead, retread,
riverbed, roadbed, roadstead,
Roundhead, saphead, seabed, seedbed,
sheep ked, sheepshead,
sheetfed, shewbread,
shortbread, sickbed, skinhead,
snowshed, softhead, sorehead,
spearhead, springhead,
steelhead, straightbred,
streambed, subhead,
sweetbread, swellhead,
thickhead, thunderhead,
toolhead, toolshed, towhead,
trailhead, unbred, undead,
unread, unsaid, unthread,
untread, warhead, webfed,
well-bred, well-read,
wellhead, white-bread,
whitehead, widespread,
wingspread, woodshed,
woolshed, acidhead,
aforesaid, arrowhead,
barrelhead, Birkenhead,
bubblehead, bufflehead,
chowderhead, chucklehead,
colorbred, copperhead,
dragonhead, dunderhead,
featherbed, featherhead,

fiddlehead, figurehead, fire-
engine red, fountainhead,
gingerbread, go-ahead,
hammerhead, infrared,
interbred, knucklehead,
letterhead, loggerhead,
lowlihead, maidenhead,
newlywed, overhead,
overspread, pinniped, pointy-
head, poppyhead, quadruped,
saddlebred, Saint John's
bread, Samoyed, showerhead,
sleepyhead, slugabed,
standardbred, straight-ahead,
timberhead, thoroughbred,
underbred, underfed,
watershed, woodenhead, far-
infrared, near-infrared, West
Quoddy Head, parallelepiped

²**ead** \ēd\ see EED

³**ead** \əd\ see ¹UD

¹**eadable** \ēd-ə-bəl\ kneadable,
pleadable, readable

²**eadable** \ed-ə-bəl\ see EDIBLE

¹**eaded** \ed-əd\ bedded, headed,
bareheaded, bigheaded,
bullheaded, clearheaded,
coolheaded, eggheaded,
embedded, fatheaded,
hardheaded, hotheaded, light-
headed, longheaded,
lunkheaded, pigheaded,
pinheaded, roundheaded,
sapheaded, softheaded,
soreheaded, swelled-headed,
swellheaded, thickheaded,
towheaded, bubbleheaded,
chowderheaded,
chuckleheaded, dunderheaded,
featherheaded, unleaded,
white-headed, empty-headed,
hydra-headed, knuckleheaded,

levelheaded, muddleheaded, pointy-headed, puzzleheaded, woodenheaded, woolly-headed

²**eaded** \ē-dəd\ see EEDED

eaden \ed-ᵊn\ deaden, leaden, redden, steading, Armageddon

¹**eader** \ēd-ər\ cedar, ceder, feeder, kneader, leader, pleader, reader, seeder, speeder, weeder, bandleader, cheerleader, conceder, lip-reader, newsreader, nonreader, proofreader, repleader, ringleader, seceder, stampeder, stockbreeder, succeeder, copyreader, interpleader

²**eader** \ed-ər\ bedder, cheddar, chedar, header, shedder, shredder, sledder, spreader, tedder, threader, wedder, homesteader, doubleheader, triple-header

eadily \ed-ᵊl-ē\ headily, readily, unsteadily

¹**eading** \ed-iŋ\ bedding, heading, Reading, steading, wedding, bobsledding, farmsteading, subheading, wide-spreading

²**eading** \ed-ᵊn\ see EADEN

³**eading** \ēd-ᵊn\ see EDON

⁴**eading** \ēd-iŋ\ see ¹EEDING

¹**eadle** \ed-ᵊl\ see ¹EDAL

²**eadle** \ēd-ᵊl\ see EEDLE

eadly \ed-lē\ see EDLEY

eadow \ed-ə\ see EDDA

¹**eadsman** \edz-mən\ headsman, leadsman

²**eadsman** \ēdz-mən\ see EEDSMAN

¹**eady** \ed-ē\ Eddie, eddy, Eddy, Freddie, heady, leady, ready, steady, Teddie, teddy, Teddy, thready, already, makeready, unsteady, gingerbready, rough-and-ready

²**eady** \ēd-ē\ see EEDY

¹**eaf** \ef\ see ¹EF

²**eaf** \ēf\ see ¹IEF

eafless \ē-fləs\ see IEFLESS

eafy \ē-fē\ see EEFY

eag \ēg\ see IGUE

eagan \ā-gən\ see AGIN

eager \ē-gər\ eager, leaguer, meager, beleaguer, intriguer, Xinjiang Uygur

eagh \ā\ see ¹AY

eagle \ē-gəl\ see EGAL

eague \ēg\ see IGUE

eaguer \ē-gər\ see EAGER

eah \ē-ə\ see ¹IA

¹**eak** \ēk\ beak, bleak, cheek, chic, cleek, clique, creak, creek, Creek, eke, flic, freak, geek, gleek, Greek, keek, leak, leek, meek, peak, peek, peke, pic, pique, reek, screak, seek, sheik, sheikh, shriek, sic, Sikh, sleek, sneak, speak, squeak, steek, streak, streek, teak, tweak, weak, week, wreak, antique, apeak, batik, Belgique, Belleek, bespeak, bezique, boutique, cacique, caique, critique, debeak, forepeak, forespeak, grosbeak, hairstreak, halfbeak, houseleek, misspeak, muzhik, mystique, newspeak, nonpeak, oblique, off-peak, outspeak, perique, physique, Pikes Peak, pip-squeak, pratique, relique,

technic, technique, Tajik,
unique, unspeak, workweek,
biunique, Bolshevik,
Chesapeake, dominique,
doublespeak, ecofreak,
fenugreek, hide-and-seek,
Lassen Peak, Martinique,
Menshevik, Mozambique,
semi-antique, verd antique,
Veronique, electroweak, opéra
comique, realpolitik

²eak \āk\ see ¹AKE

³eak \ek\ see ECK

eakable \ā-kə-bəl\ see AKABLE

eake \ēk\ see ¹EAK

¹eaked \ē-kəd\ peaked, streaked

²eaked \ēkt\ beaked, freaked,
peaked, streaked, apple-
cheeked—*also pasts of verbs
listed at* ¹EAK

³eaked \ik-əd\ see ¹ICKED

eaken \ē-kən\ see EACON

¹eaker \ē-kər\ beaker, leaker,
reeker, seeker, sneaker,
speaker, squeaker,
loudspeaker, self-seeker,
sunseeker, doublespeaker—
*also comparatives of
adjectives listed at* ¹EAK

²eaker \ā-kər\ see ¹AKER

¹eaking \ē-kiŋ\ freaking,
sneaking, speaking, streaking,
heat-seeking, self-seeking

²eaking \ā-kiŋ\ see ¹AKING

eakish \ē-kish\ bleakish,
cliquish, freakish, weakish

eakly \ē-klē\ see EEKLY

eaky \ē-kē\ cheeky, cliquey,
creaky, freaky, leaky, piki,
reeky, sneaky, screaky,
squeaky, streaky, tiki,

daishiki, dashiki, Tajiki, cock-
a-leekie, Kurashiki, Manihiki

¹eal \ē-əl\ empyreal, hymeneal,
laryngeal, apophyseal,
pharmacopeial

²eal \ēl\ ceil, chiel, creel, deal,
deil, eel, feel, heal, heel, he'll,
keel, Kiel, kneel, leal, meal,
Neal, Neil, peal, peel, real,
reel, seal, seel, she'll, shiel,
speel, spiel, squeal, steal,
steel, Steele, Streel, teal,
tuille, veal, weal, we'll,
wheal, wheel, zeal, aiguille,
allheal, anneal, appeal, Arbil,
bastille, Bastille, bonemeal,
bonspiel, Camille, Castile,
cartwheel, Cecile, chainwheel,
chenille, cogwheel, conceal,
congeal, cornmeal, enwheel,
Erbil, flywheel, forefeel, four-
wheel, freewheel, genteel,
handwheel, ideal, inchmeal,
Irbil, irreal, Kuril, Lucille,
misdeal, mobile, Mobile,
newsreel, nosewheel, oatmeal,
O'Neill, ordeal, pastille,
piecemeal, pinwheel, repeal,
reveal, schlemiel, self-heal,
side-wheel, singspiel,
somedeal, stabile, surreal,
tahsil, Tarheel, thumbwheel,
unreal, unreel, unseal, acetyl,
airmobile, Ardabil, bidonville,
beau ideal, blastocoel,
bloodmobile, Bogomil,
bookmobile, campanile,
chamomile, cochineal,
cockatiel, commonweal,
difficile, dishabille, down-at-
heel, glockenspiel, goldenseal,
Guayaquil, manchineel,

megadeal, mercantile,
pimpmobile, skimobile,
snowmobile, thunderpeal,
waterwheel, automobile,
Solomon's seal, varicocele

³**eal** \āl\ see AIL

⁴**eal** \il\ see ILL

ealable \ē-lə-bəl\ peelable,
reelable, stealable, appealable,
concealable, revealable,
repealable, irrepealable,
unappealable

ealand \ē-lənd\ see ELAND

eald \ēld\ see IELD

ealed \ēld\ see IELD

ealer \ē-lər\ dealer, feeler,
healer, heeler, kneeler, peeler,
reeler, sealer, spieler,
squealer, stealer, stelar,
vealer, velar, wheeler,
appealer, concealer, four-
wheeler, freewheeler,
newsdealer, repealer, revealer,
scene-stealer, side-wheeler,
stern-wheeler, three-wheeler,
two-wheeler, double-dealer,
eighteen-wheeler, 18-wheeler,
snowmobiler, wheeler-dealer

ealie \ē-lē\ see EELY

ealing \ē-liŋ\ see EELING

¹**eally** \ē-ə-lē\ leally, ideally,
hymeneally, industrially

²**eally** \il-ē\ see ¹ILLY

³**eally** \ē-lē\ see EELY

ealm \elm\ see ELM

ealment \ēl-mənt\ concealment,
congealment, revealment

ealot \el-ət\ see ELLATE

ealotry \el-ə-trē\ see ELOTRY

ealous \el-əs\ Ellis, Hellas,
jealous, trellis, zealous,
cancellous, ocellus

ealousy \el-ə-sē\ see ELACY

ealth \elth\ health, stealth,
wealth, commonwealth

ealthy \el-thē\ healthy, stealthy,
wealthy, unhealthy

ealty \ēl-tē\ fealty, realty

¹**eam** \ēm\ beam, bream, cream,
deem, deme, dream, gleam,
mime, neem, Nîmes, ream,
scheme, scream, seam, seem,
seme, steam, stream, team,
teem, theme, abeam, agleam,
airstream, berseem, beseem,
bireme, blaspheme,
bloodstream, centime,
daydream, downstream,
esteem, extreme, grapheme,
Gulf Stream, hakim,
headstream, hornbeam, ice
cream, inseam, kilim, lexeme,
mainstream, midstream,
millime, millstream,
moonbeam, morpheme,
onstream, phoneme, redeem,
regime, sememe, sidestream,
slipstream, sunbeam,
supreme, Tarim, taxeme,
toneme, trireme, unseam,
upstream, academe,
disesteem, double-team,
enthymeme, misesteem,
monotreme, self-esteem,
succès d'estime, treponeme

²**eam** \im\ see ¹IM

eaman \ē-mən\ see ¹EMON

¹**eamed** \emt\ see EMPT

²**eamed** \emd\ beamed, steamed,
teamed—*also pasts of verbs
listed at* ¹EAM

eamer \ē-mər\ creamer,
dreamer, femur, lemur,
reamer, schemer, screamer,

seamer, steamer, streamer, blasphemer, daydreamer, redeemer

eaming \ē-miŋ\ see EEMING

eamish \ē-mish\ beamish, squeamish

eamless \ēm-ləs\ dreamless, seamless

eamon \ē-mən\ see ¹EMON

eamster \ēm-stər\ seamster, teamster

eamy \ē-mē\ beamy, creamy, dreamy, gleamy, preemie, seamy, steamy, polysemy

¹ean \ē-ən\ aeon, eon, Ian, Leon, paean, peon, paeon, zein, Achaean, Actaeon, Aegean, Antaean, Archean, Augean, Chaldean, Chilean, Fijian, Korean, Kuchean, Linnaean, Mandaean, Matthean, pampean, plebeian, protean, pygmaean, Tupi-Guaranian, Tupian, apogean, Aramaean, Atlantean, Caribbean, Cerberean, circadian, cyclopean, Clytherean, Damoclean, empyrean, epigean, European, Galilean, Hasmonaean, Herculean, Jacobean, kallikrein, Maccabean, Manichaean, Mycenaean, Odyssean, panacean, perigean, Sadducean, Sisyphean, Typhoean, Tyrolean, antipodean, epicurean, Laodicean, Ponce de Leon, proboscidean, Pythagorean, terpsichorean, un-European, epithalamion, Indo-European

²ean \ēn\ see ³INE

³ean \òn\ see ³ON

⁴ean \ä-ən\ see ¹AYAN

eane \ēn\ see ³INE

eaner \ē-nər\ cleaner, gleaner, keener, meaner, preener, teener, weaner, weiner, wiener, congener, demeanor, fourteener, carabiner, intervenor, misdemeanor, submariner, trampoliner

eanery \ēn-rē\ beanery, deanery, greenery, scenery, machinery, turbomachinery

eanid \ē-ə-nəd\ Leonid, Oceanid

eanie \ē-nē\ see ¹INI

eaning \ē-niŋ\ greening, leaning, meaning, screening, housecleaning, spring-cleaning, sunscreening, unmeaning, well-meaning, overweening—*also present participles of verbs listed at* ³INE

¹eanist \ē-nəst\ see ²INIST

²eanist \ē-ə-nist\ see IANIST

eanliness \en-lē-nəs\ see ENDLINESS

eanling \ēn-liŋ\ greenling, weanling, yeanling

¹eanly \ēn-lē\ cleanly, greenly, leanly, meanly, queenly, pristinely, routinely, serpentinely, uncleanly

²eanly \en-lē\ see ENDLY

eanne \ēn\ see ³INE

eanness \ēn-nəs\ cleanness, greenness, meanness, betweenness, uncleanness

eannie \ē-nē\ see ¹INI

eano \ē-nō\ see ²INO

eanor \ē-nər\ see EANER

eanse \enz\ see ¹ENS

eant \ent\ see ¹ENT

eany \ē-nē\ see ¹INI

eap \ēp\ see EEP

eapen \ē-pən\ see EEPEN

eaper \ē-pər\ see EEPER

eapie \ē-pē\ see EEPY

eapish \ē-pish\ see EEPISH

eapo \ē-pō\ see EPOT

¹ear \er\ see ⁴ARE

²ear \ir\ see ²EER

¹earable \er-ə-bəl\ bearable, shareable, terrible, wearable, unbearable, unwearable

²earable \ar-ə-bəl\ see ARABLE

earage \ir-ij\ see EERAGE

¹earance \ir-əns\ see ¹ERENCE

²earance \er-əns\ see ARENCE

earch \ərch\ see URCH

¹eard \ird\ beard, eared, tiered, weird, afeard, bat-eared, bluebeard, crop-eared, dog-eared, graybeard, lop-eared, misleared, whitebeard, chandeliered, engineered, pre-engineered—*also pasts of verbs listed at* ²EER

²eard \ərd\ see IRD

eare \ir\ see ²EER

earean \ir-ē-ən\ see ¹ERIAN

¹eared \erd\ see AIRED

²eared \ird\ see ¹EARD

¹earer \er-ər\ airer, bearer, carer, error, sharer, terror, casebearer, crossbearer, cupbearer, declarer, furbearer, pallbearer, seafarer, talebearer, torchbearer, trainbearer, wayfarer, color-bearer, standard-bearer, stretcher-bearer—*also*

comparatives of adjectives listed at ⁴ARE

²earer \ir-ər\ cheerer, clearer, fearer, hearer, mirror, shearer, smearer, coherer, sheepshearer, veneerer, electioneerer—*also comparatives of adjectives listed at* ²EER

³earer \ar-ər\ airer, bearer, casebearer, crossbearer, cupbearer, declarer, furbearer, live-bearer, pallbearer, seafarer, talebearer, torchbearer, trainbearer, wayfarer, color-bearer, standard-bearer, stretcher-bearer

earful \ir-fəl\ cheerful, earful, fearful, tearful

earies \ir-ēz\ see ERIES

¹earing \ir-iŋ\ clearing, earing, earring, gearing, God-fearing, sheepshearing, fictioneering, hard-of-hearing, orienteering—*also present participles of verbs listed at* ²EER

²earing \er-iŋ\ see ¹ARING

earish \er-ish\ see ¹ARISH

earl \ərl\ see ¹IRL

earle \irl\ see ¹IRL

earler \ər-lər\ see IRLER

earless \ir-ləs\ cheerless, fearless, gearless, peerless, tearless

¹earling \ir-liŋ\ shearling, yearling

²earling \ər-lən\ ERLIN

¹early \ir-lē\ clearly, dearly, merely, nearly, queerly, yearly, austerely, biyearly, severely, sincerely, cavalierly, semiyearly, insincerely

²**early** \ər-lē\ see URLY

earn \ərn\ see URN

earned \ərnd\ see URNED

earner \ər-nər\ see URNER

earnist \ər-nəst\ see ERNIST

earnt \ərnt\ burnt, learnt, weren't

earring \ir-iŋ\ see ¹EARING

earsal \ər-səl\ see ¹ERSAL

earse \ərs\ see ERSE

earser \ər-sər\ see URSOR

earst \ərst\ see URST

eart \ärt\ see ¹ART

earted \ärt-əd\ hearted, parted, bighearted, coldhearted, downhearted, fainthearted, freehearted, good-hearted, greathearted, halfhearted, hard-hearted, kindhearted, largehearted, lighthearted, proudhearted, softhearted, stouthearted, truehearted, uncharted, warmhearted, weakhearted, wholehearted, brokenhearted, chickenhearted, heavyhearted, ironhearted, lionhearted, openhearted, single-hearted, stonyhearted, tenderhearted— *also pasts of verbs listed at* ¹ART

¹**earth** \ärth\ see ARTH

²**earth** \ərth\ see IRTH

eartha \ər-thə\ see ERTHA

earthen \ər-thən\ see URTHEN

earthy \ər-thē\ see ORTHY

eartily \ärt-ᵊl-ē\ see ARTILY

eartless \ärt-ləs\ see ARTLESS

earty \ärt-ē\ see ¹ARTY

eary \ir-ē\ aerie, beery, bleary, cheery, dreary, eerie, Erie, leery, Peary, peri, quaere, query, smeary, sphery, teary, veery, weary, aweary, Kashmiri, Lake Erie, Valkyrie, world-weary, hara-kiri, miserere, overweary, whigmaleerie, Mount Dhaulagiri

eas \ē-əs\ see ¹EUS

¹**easable** \ē-sə-bəl\ peaceable, increasable

²**easable** \ē-zə-bəl\ see EASIBLE

¹**easand** \iz-ᵊn\ see ²ISON

²**easand** \ēz-ᵊnd\ see EASONED

¹**ease** \ēs\ see IECE

²**ease** \ēz\ see EZE

¹**eased** \ēzd\ pleased, diseased— *also pasts of verbs listed at* EZE

²**eased** \ēst\ see ¹EAST

easel \ē-zəl\ bezel, deasil, diesel, easel, measle, teasel, weasel

easeless \ē-sləs\ ceaseless, creaseless, greaseless

easelly \ē-zlē\ see EASLY

easement \ēz-mənt\ easement, appeasement

¹**easer** \ē-sər\ creaser, greaser, piecer, increaser, one-piecer, releaser, two-piecer

²**easer** \ē-zər\ Caesar, freezer, geezer, greaser, pleaser, sneezer, squeezer, teaser, tweezer, appeaser, brainteaser, crowd-pleaser, misfeasor, stripteaser, timepleaser

eash \ēsh\ see ²ICHE

easible \ē-zə-bəl\ feasible, squeezable, appeasable, defeasible, infeasible, inappeasable, indefeasible, unappeasable

easil \ē-zəl\ see EASEL

easily \ēz-lē\ see EASLY

¹easing \ē-siŋ\ leasing, unceasing—*also present participles of verbs listed at* IECE

²easing \ē-ziŋ\ pleasing, subfreezing—*also present participles of verbs listed at* EZE

easingly \ē-siŋ-lē\ decreasingly, increasingly, unceasingly

easle \ē-zəl\ see EASEL

easly \ēz-ə-lē\ easily, measly, weaselly

eason \ēz-ᵊn\ reason, season, seisin, treason, disseisin, off-season, unreason, diocesan

easonable \ēz-nə-bəl\ reasonable, seasonable, treasonable, unreasonable, unseasonable

easoned \ēz-ᵊnd\ weasand, unreasoned—*also pasts of verbs listed at* EASON

easoning \ēz-niŋ\ seasoning, unreasoning

easonless \ēz-ᵊn-ləs\ reasonless, seasonless

easor \ē-zər\ see ²EASER

¹east \ēst\ beast, east, East, feast, fleeced, geest, least, piste, priest, reest, triste, yeast, archpriest, artiste, batiste, deceased, Far East, hartebeest, modiste, Near East, northeast, southeast, tachiste, arriviste, dirigiste, hartebeest, Middle East, north-northeast, pointillist,

wildebeest—*also pasts of verbs listed at* IECE

²east \est\ see EST

easted \es-təd\ see ESTED

easter \ē-stər\ Dniester, Easter, keister, leister, quaestor, down-easter, northeaster, southeaster

eastie \ē-stē\ see EASTY

eastly \ēst-lē\ beastly, Priestley, priestly

easty \ē-stē\ beastie, yeasty

easurable \ezh-rə-bəl\ pleasurable, treasurable, immeasurable

¹easure \ezh-ər\ leisure, measure, pleasure, treasure, admeasure, displeasure, countermeasure

²easure \ā-zhər\ see AZIER

easurer \ezh-ər-ər\ measurer, treasurer

¹easy \ē-zē\ breezy, cheesy, easy, greasy, queasy, sleazy, sneezy, wheezy, pachisi, Parcheesi, speakeasy, uneasy, Zambezi

²easy \ē-sē\ see EECY

¹eat \ēt\ beat, beet, bleat, cheat, cleat, Crete, deet, eat, feat, fleet, Geat, gleet, greet, heat, keet, lied, meat, meet, mete, neat, peat, Pete, pleat, seat, sheet, skeet, sleet, street, suite, sweet, teat, treat, tweet, weet, wheat, accrete, aesthete, afreet, athlete, backbeat, backseat, backstreet, bedsheet, bolete, Bradstreet, broadsheet, browbeat, buckwheat, bystreet, clipsheet, compete, compleat, complete, conceit, concrete, crabmeat, deadbeat, deceit, defeat, delete, deplete, discreet, discrete, disseat, downbeat, drumbeat, effete, elite, en suite, entreat, escheat, esthete, excrete, facete, forcemeat, foresheet, groundsheet, heartbeat, heat-treat, helpmeet, hoofbeat, ill-treat, mainsheet, maltreat, mesquite, mincemeat, mistreat, offbeat, petite, preheat, receipt, recheat, regreet, repeat, replete, retreat, secrete, slip-sheet, sweetmeat, terete, unmeet, unseat, upbeat, vegete, volkslied, zizith, aquavit, biathlete, bittersweet, cellulite, corps d'elite, countryseat, decathlete, exegete, incomplete, indiscreet, indiscrete, lorikeet, marguerite, Marguerite, Masorete, meadowsweet, Nayarit, obsolete, overeat, overheat, Paraclete, parakeet, pentathlete, plebiscite, polychaete, progamete, self-conceit, semisweet, tête-à-tête, superheat, triathlete, winding-sheet

²**eat** \āt\ see ¹ATE

³**eat** \et\ see ¹ET

⁴**eat** \it\ see ¹IT

eatable \ēt-ə-bəl\ eatable, heatable, treatable, depletable, escheatable, repeatable, unbeatable

¹**eated** \ēt-əd\ heated, pleated, conceited, deep-seated, repeated, overheated, superheated—*also pasts of verbs listed at* ¹EAT

²**eated** \et-əd\ see ETID

³**eated** \it-əd\ see ITTED

¹**eaten** \ēt-ᵊn\ eaten, beaten, Cretan, cretin, Eaton, Eton, neaten, sweeten, wheaten, browbeaten, moth-eaten, secretin, unbeaten, worm-eaten, overeaten, weather-beaten

²**eaten** \āt-ᵊn\ see ¹ATEN

¹**eater** \ēt-ər\ beater, bleater, cheater, eater, fetor, greeter, heater, liter, meter, peter, Peter, pleater, praetor, rhetor, seater, sheeter, skeeter, teeter, treater, tweeter, anteater, beefeater, blue peter, Demeter, drumbeater, eggbeater, excreter, fire-eater, flowmeter, man-eater, Main Streeter, maltreater, preheater, propraetor, repeater, saltpeter, secretor, seedeater, toadeater, Wall Streeter, windcheater, world-beater, altimeter, centiliter, centimeter, deciliter, decimeter, drunkometer, lotus-eater, milliliter, millimeter, overeater, taximeter—*also comparatives of adjectives listed at* ¹EAT

²**eater** \et-ər\ see ETTER

eatery \ēt-ə-rē\ see ETORY

¹**eath** \ēth\ eath, heath, Keith, Meath, neath, sheath, wreath, beneath, bequeath, hadith, monteith, underneath

²**eath** \ēth\ see EATHE

eathe \ēth\ breathe, Meath, seethe, sheathe, teethe,

wreathe, bequeath, ensheathe, enwreathe, inbreathe, unsheathe, unwreathe, Westmeath

eathean \ē-thē-ən\ lethean, Promethean

¹eather \eth-ər\ see ¹ETHER

²eather \ē-thər\ see EITHER

eathern \eth-ərn\ see ETHERN

eathery \eth-rē\ feathery, heathery, leathery

eathing \ē-thiŋ\ breathing, sheathing, teething, firebreathing

eathless \eth-ləs\ breathless, deathless

eathy \ē-thē\ heathy, lethe, wreathy

eating \ēt-iŋ\ beating, eating, meeting, seating, sheeting, sweeting, breast-beating, drumbeating, fire-eating, man-eating, unweeting, Sunday-go-to-meeting

eatise \ēt-əs\ see ETUS

¹eatly \āt-lē\ see ¹ATELY

²eatly \ēt-lē\ see EETLY

eaton \ēt-ᵊn\ see ¹EATEN

¹eats \ēts\ Keats—*also possessives and plurals of nouns and third person singular presents of verbs listed at* EAT

²eats \āts\ see ¹ATES

eature \ē-chər\ see EACHER

eaty \ēt-ē\ meaty, peaty, sleety, sweetie, treaty, ziti, entreaty, Tahiti, Dolomiti, spermaceti

eau \ō\ see ¹OW

eaucracy \äk-rə-sē\ see OCRACY

eauteous \üt-ē-əs\ see UTEOUS

eautiful \üt-i-fəl\ see UTIFUL

eauty \üt-ē\ see ¹OOTY

eaux \ō\ see ¹OW

eavable \ē-və-bəl\ see EIVABLE

eaval \ē-vəl\ see IEVAL

¹eave \ēv\ breve, cleave, eve, Eve, greave, grieve, heave, leave, lief, peeve, reave, reeve, reive, scrieve, sheave, shrieve, sleave, sleeve, steeve, Steve, thieve, weave, weve, Abib, achieve, aggrieve, believe, bereave, conceive, deceive, inweave, khedive, Maldive, motive, naive, perceive, qui vive, receive, relieve, reprieve, retrieve, shirtsleeve, unreeve, unweave, upheave, apperceive, by-your-leave, disbelieve, Genevieve, interleave, interweave, Laccadive, make-believe, misbelieve, misconceive, preconceive, semibreve, Tel Aviv, undeceive, adam-and-eve, recitative, ticket-of-leave, underachieve, Saint Agnes' Eve

²eave \iv\ see ²IVE

eaved \ēvd\ leaved, sleeved, aggrieved, bereaved, relieved—*also pasts of verbs listed at* ¹EAVE

eavement \ēv-mənt\ see EVEMENT

eaven \ev-ən\ devon, Devon, Evan, heaven, Kevin, leaven, levin, Nevin, seven, Sevin, sweven, eleven, replevin, South Devon

eaver \ē-vər\ see IEVER

eavers \ē-vərz\ cleavers, vivers

eaves \ēvz\ eaves, Treves, shirtsleeves

eavey \ē-vē\ peavey, divi-divi

eaward \ē-wərd\ see EEWARD

¹eaze \ēz\ see EZE

²eaze \āz\ see ¹AZE

eazo \ē-zō\ see ¹IZO

eazy \ē-zē\ see ¹EASY

eb \eb\ bleb, deb, ebb, neb, pleb, reb, Reb, web, ardeb, celeb, cobweb, cubeb, Deneb, Horeb, subdeb, Zagreb, zineb, cause célèbre, Johnny Reb, spiderweb

eba \ē-bə\ Chiba, Reba, Sheba, amoeba, zareba, copaiba, Curitiba

ebate \ab-ət\ see ABIT

ebb \eb\ see EB

ebbie \eb-ē\ see EBBY

ebble \eb-əl\ pebble, rebel, treble

ebbuck \eb-ək\ kebbuck, rebec

ebby \eb-ē\ blebby, Debbie, Debby, maybe, webby, cobwebby

¹ebe \ē-bē\ BB, freebie, Hebe, phoebe, Phoebe, Seabee, caribe, Galibi

²ebe \ēb\ glebe, grebe, hebe, plebe, ephebe, sahib

ebec \eb-ək\ see EBBUCK

ebel \eb-əl\ see EBBLE

eber \ā-bər\ see ABOR

ebes \ēbz\ Thebes—*also possessives and plurals of nouns listed at* EBE

eble \eb-əl\ see EBBLE

ebo \ē-bō\ see IBO

ebral \ē-brəl\ cerebral, palpebral, vertebral

ebrity \eb-rət-ē\ celebrity, muliebrity

¹ebs \eps\ see EPS

²ebs \ebz\ Debs—*also possessives and plurals of nouns, third person singular presents of verbs listed at* EB

ebt \et\ see ¹ET

ebted \et-əd\ see ETID

ebtor \et-ər\ see ETTER

ebus \ē-bəs\ Phoebus, rebus, ephebus

¹ec \ek\ see ECK

²ec \ets\ see ETS

eca \ē-kə\ see ¹IKA

ecal \ē-kəl\ cecal, fecal, meikle, treacle, intrathecal, bibliothecal

ecan \ek-ən\ see ECKON

ecant \ē-kənt\ piquant, secant

ecas \ä-kəs\ Turksand Caicos, Zacatecas

ecca \ek-ə\ Decca, mecca, Mecca, weka, Rebecca, Rebekah, Rijeka

eccable \ek-ə-bəl\ see ECKABLE

eccan \ek-ən\ see ECKON

ecce \ek-ē\ see ECKY

ecco \ek-ō\ see ECHO

ecency \ēs-ᵊn-sē\ decency, recency, indecency

ecent \ēs-ᵊnt\ decent, recent, indecent, obeisant

eces \ē-sēz\ see ECIES

¹ech \ek\ see ECK

²ech \ək\ see UCK

³ech \esh\ see ¹ESH

¹eche \āsh\ crèche, flèche, Laoighis, Leix, resh, seiche, bobeche, Bangladesh, tête-bêche, Andhra Pradesh, Madhya Pradesh, Uttar

Pradesh, Himadral Pradesh, Arunachal Pradesh

²**eche** \esh\ see ¹ESH

eche \ē-chē\ see EACHY

êche \esh\ see ¹ESH

èche \esh\ see ¹ESH

eched \echt\ see ETCHED

echerous \ech-rəs\ lecherous, treacherous

echery \ech-rē\ lechery, treachery

echie \ek-ē\ see ECKY

echin \ek-ən\ see ECKON

echo \ek-ō\ deco, echo, gecko, secco, el Greco, reecho

echnical \ek-ni-kəl\ technical, biotechnical, geotechnical

echt \ekt\ see ECT

ecia \ē-shə\ see ¹ESIA

ecially \esh-lē\ see ESHLY

ecian \ē-shən\ see ¹ETION

ecibel \es-ə-bəl\ see ESSIBLE

¹**ecie** \ē-sē\ see EECY

²**ecie** \ē-shē\ see ISHI

ecies \ē-sēz\ feces, species, theses, prostheses, subspecies, exegeses

¹**ecil** \ē-səl\ Cecil, diesel

²**ecil** \es-əl\ see ¹ESTLE

ecile \es-əl\ see ¹ESTLE

ecily \es-ə-lē\ see ESSALY

ecimal \es-ə-məl\ see ESIMAL

eciman \es-mən\ see ESSMAN

ecious \ē-shəs\ specious, capricious, facetious, Lucretius

ecium \ē-shē-əm\ aecium, lutecium, technetium, zoecium, androecium, apothecium, gynoecium, paramecium, perithecium

eck \ek\ beck, check, cheque, Czech, deck, dreck, fleck, heck, lek, neck, pec, peck, reck, sec, sneck, spec, speck, trek, wreak, wreck, Aztec, Baalbek, backcheck, bedeck, breakneck, Capek, cromlech, crookneck, cross-check, cusec, ewe-neck, exec, flyspeck, fore-check, foredeck, gooseneck, haček, hatcheck, henpeck, high tech, kopeck, limbeck, low-tech, Lubeck, Mixtec, paycheck, pinchbeck, Quebec, rebec, redneck, ringneck, roll-neck, roughneck, samekh, shipwreck, spot-check, Steinbeck, tenrec, Toltec, Uzbek, wryneck, xebec, afterdeck, à la grecque, Aquidneck, biotech, bodycheck, bottleneck, Chiang Kai-shek, countercheck, demi-sec, discotheque, double-check, double-deck, hunt-and-peck, leatherneck, littleneck, Pont l'évêque, quarterdeck, rubberneck, triple sec, turtleneck, Yucatec, Zapotec, cinematheque, Melchizedek, de Toulouse-Lautrec

eckable \ek-ə-bəl\ checkable, impeccable

ecked \ekt\ see ECT

ecker \ek-ər\ checker, chequer, decker, pecker, trekker, wrecker, exchequer, three-decker, woodpecker, dominicker, double-decker, rubbernecker, triple-decker

ecking \ek-iŋ\ decking, necking

ecklace \ek-ləs\ see ECKLESS

eckle \ek-əl\ deckle, freckle, heckle, shekel, speckle, kenspeckle

eckless \ek-ləs\ feckless, checkless, necklace, reckless, affectless

ecko \ek-ō\ see ECHO

eckon \ek-ən\ beckon, Brecon, Deccan, reckon, zechin, Aztecan, misreckon, Toltecan, Yucatecan

ecks \ecks\ eks\ see EX

ecky \ek-ē\ Becky, recce, techie, shimonoseki

econ \ek-ən\ see ECKON

¹econd \ek-ənd\ see ECUND

²econd \ek-ənt\ see ECCANT

ecque \ek\ see ECK

ecs \eks\ see EX

ect \ekt\ necked, sect, specked, abject, affect, aspect, bisect, cathect, collect, confect, connect, convect, correct, defect, deflect, deject, detect, direct, dissect, effect, eject, elect, erect, ewe-necked, expect, goosenecked, infect, inflect, inject, insect, inspect, neglect, object, pandect, perfect, porrect, prefect, prelect, project, prospect, protect, rednecked, refect, reflect, reject, resect, respect, ring-necked, select, stiff-necked, subject, suspect, traject, transect, trisect, Utrecht, V-necked, acrolect, architect, circumspect, deselect, dialect, disaffect, disconnect, disinfect, disrespect, double-decked,

genuflect, grapholect, incorrect, indirect, intellect, interject, intersect, introject, introspect, misdirect, preselect, re-collect, recollect, redirect, reelect, resurrect, retrospect, self-respect, turtlenecked, vivisect, aftereffect, hypercorrect, idiolect, interconnect, megaproject, semierect, semi-indirect—*also pasts of verbs listed at* ECK

ecta \ek-tə\ dejecta, ejecta, perfecta, trifecta

ectable \ek-tə-bəl\ affectable, collectible, correctable, deflectable, delectable, detectable, ejectable, erectable, expectable, inflectable, injectable, electable, indefectible, perfectible, projectable, respectable, disrespectable, indefectible

ectacle \ek-ti-kəl\ see ECTICAL

ectal \ek-t³l\ see ECTILE

ectance \ek-təns\ expectance, reflectance

ectant \ek-tənt\ expectant, humectant, injectant, protectant, disinfectant

ectar \ek-tər\ see ECTOR

ectarous \ek-trəs\ see ECTRESS

ectary \ek-tə-rē\ sectary, insectary

ected \ek-təd\ affected, collected, complected, dejected, recollected, self-affected, self-collected, self-elected, self-selected, unaffected, undirected, unexpected, unselected, inner-directed, other-directed—*also pasts of verbs listed at* ECT

ecten \ek-tən\ nekton, pecten, pectin, fibronectin, ivermectin

ecter \ek-tər\ see ECTOR

ectible \ek-tə-bəl\ see ECTABLE

ectic \ek-tik\ hectic, pectic, cathectic, eclectic, synectic, anorectic, apoplectic, catalectic, dialectic

ectical \ek-ti-kəl\ spectacle, dialectical

ectile \ek-tᵊl\ sectile, erectile, insectile, projectile, colorectal, dialectal

ectin \ek-tən\ see ECTEN

ecting \ek-tiŋ\ affecting, self-respecting, self-correcting

ection \ek-shən\ flexion, lection, section, abjection, advection, affection, bisection, collection, complexion, confection, connection, connexion, convection, correction, C-section, defection, deflection, dejection, detection, direction, dissection, ejection, election, erection, evection, infection, inflection, injection, inspection, midsection, objection, perfection, prelection, projection, protection, refection, reflection, rejection, resection, selection, subjection, subsection, trajection, transection, trisection, by-election, circumspection, disaffection, disconnection, disinfection, genuflection, imperfection, indirection, introjection, introspection, insurrection, intellection, interjection, intersection, misdirection, predilection, preselection, recollection, redirection, reelection, reinfection, resurrection, retroflexion, retrospection, vivisection, antirejection, hypercorrection, interconnection, Cesarean section

ectional \ek-shnəl\ sectional, affectional, bisectional, complexional, connectional, convectional, correctional, cross-sectional, directional, inflectional, projectional, reflectional, bidirectional, introspectional, interjectional, resurrectional, vivisectional, omnidirectional, unidirectional

ectionist \ek-shə-nəst\ perfectionist, projectionist, protectionist, selectionist, introspectionist, resurrectionist, vivisectionist

ective \ek-tiv\ advective, affective, adjective, bijective, collective, connective, convective, corrective, defective, deflective, detective, directive, effective, elective, ejective, infective, inflective, injective, invective, objective, perfective, perspective, projective, prospective, reflective, respective, selective, subjective, cost-effective,

imperfective, ineffective,
intellective, introspective,
nondirective, nonobjective,
retrospective, cryoprotective,
intersubjective

ectless \ek-ləs\ see ECKLESS

ectly \ekt-lē\ abjectly, correctly,
directly, erectly, incorrectly,
indirectly

ectness \ekt-nəs\ abjectness,
correctness, directness,
erectness, selectness,
incorrectness, indirectness,
hypercorrectness

ecto \ek-tō\ recto, perfecto

ectomy \ek-tə-mē\ mastectomy,
vasectomy, appendectomy,
hysterectomy, tonsillectomy,
clitoridectomy

ector \ek-tər\ hector, Hector,
lector, nectar, rector, sector,
specter, vector, bisector,
collector, convector, corrector,
defector, deflector, detector,
director, dissector, effector,
ejector, elector, erector,
infector, injector, inspector,
neglecter, objector, perfecter,
projector, prospector,
protector, reflector, selector,
trisector, vivisector

ectoral \ek-trəl\ spectral,
pectoral, electoral, protectoral,
multispectral

ectorate \ek-tə-rət\ rectorate,
directorate, electorate,
inspectorate, protectorate

ectory \ek-tə-rē\ rectory,
directory, protectory,
refectory, trajectory,
ex-directory

ectral \ek-trəl\ see ECTORAL

ectress \ek-trəs\ nectarous,
directress, electress,
protectress

ectrix \ek-triks\ rectrix,
directrix

ectrum \ek-trəm\ plectrum,
spectrum, electrum

¹**ectual** \ek-chə-wəl\ effectual,
ineffectual, intellectual, anti-
intellectual

²**ectual** \eksh-wəl\ see EXUAL

ectually \ek-chə-lē\ effectually,
ineffectually, intellectually

¹**ectural** \ek-chə-rəl\
conjectural, prefectural,
architectural

²**ectural** \ek-shrəl\ flexural,
conjectural, architectural

ecture \ek-chər\ lecture,
conjecture, prefecture,
architecture

ectus \ek-təs\ conspectus,
prospectus

ecular \ek-yə-lər\ secular,
specular, molecular

ecum \ē-kəm\ vade mecum,
subpoena duces tecum

ecund \ek-ənd\ fecund, second,
femtosecond, microsecond,
millisecond, nanosecond—
also pasts of verbs listed at
ECKON

ecutive \ek-ət-iv\ consecutive,
executive, inconsecutive

ed \ed\ see ¹EAD

e'd \ēd\ see EED

¹**eda** \ēd-ə\ Freda, Frieda, Leda,
Vida, Machida, alameda, olla
podrida

²**eda** \äd-ə\ see ³ADA

¹**edal** \ed-ᵊl\ heddle, medal,
meddle, pedal, peddle,

treadle, backpedal, bipedal, soft-pedal, intermeddle

²**edal** \ēd-ᵊl\ see EEDLE

edance \ēd-ns\ see EDENCE

¹**edar** \ed-ər\ see ²EADER

²**edar** \ēd-ər\ see ¹EADER

edator \ed-ət-ər\ see EDITOR

edd \ed\ see ¹EAD

edda \ed-ə\ Jedda, Vedda

eddar \ed-ər\ see ²EADER

edded \ed-əd\ see EADED

edden \ed-ᵊn\ see EADEN

edder \ed-ər\ see ²EADER

eddie \ed-ē\ see ¹EADY

edding \ed-iŋ\ see ¹EADING

eddle \ed-ᵊl\ see ¹EDAL

eddler \ed-lər\ meddler, medlar, peddler

eddon \ed-ᵊn\ see EADEN

eddy \ed-ē\ see ¹EADY

¹**ede** \ād\ see ¹ADE

²**ede** \ēd\ see EED

³**ede** \ā-dā\ see AYDAY

edeas \ēd-ē-əs\ see ¹EDIOUS

eded \ē-dəd\ see EEDED

edel \ād-əl\ see ADLE

eden \ēd-ᵊn\ Eden, Sweden, Dunedin

edence \ēd-ns\ credence, impedance, precedence, antecedence

edent \ēd-ᵊnt\ credent, needn't, decedent, precedent, succedent, antecedent

¹**eder** \ād-ər\ see ADER

²**eder** \ēd-ər\ see ¹EADER

edes \ē-dēz\ Diomedes, Archimedes

edge \ej\ dredge, edge, fledge, hedge, kedge, ledge, pledge, sedge, sledge, veg, wedge, allege, frankpledge, gilt-edge,

two-edged, hard-edge, knife-edge, nutsedge, straightedge, featheredge, sortilege

edged \ejd\ edged, wedged, alleged, full-fledged, gilt-edged, two-edged, unfledged, deckle-edged, double-edged— *also pasts of verbs listed at* EDGE

edger \ej-ər\ dredger, edger, hedger, ledger, leger, pledger

edgie \ej-ē\ see EDGY

edgy \ej-ē\ edgy, ledgy, Reggie, sedgy, veggie, wedgie, wedgy, Himeji

edi \ād-ē\ see ADY

edia \ēd-ē-ə\ media, Media, acedia, cyclopedia, via media, encyclopedia

edial \ēd-ē-əl\ medial, predial, remedial

edian \ēd-ē-ən\ median, comedian, tragedian

ediant \ēd-ē-ənt\ see EDIENT

edible \ed-ə-bəl\ credible, edible, spreadable, incredible, inedible

¹**edic** \ēd-ik\ comedic, cyclopedic, logaoedic, orthopedic, encyclopedic

²**edic** \ed-ik\ Eddic, medic, comedic, paramedic, samoyedic

³**edic** \ād-ik\ see ¹ADIC

edicable \ed-i-kə-bəl\ medicable, predicable, immedicable

edical \ed-i-kəl\ medical, pedicle, premedical, biomedical, paramedical

edicate \ed-i-kət\ dedicate, predicate

edicle \ed-i-kəl\ see EDICAL

edience \ēd-ē-əns\ expedience, obedience, disobedience, inexpedience

edient \ēd-ē-ənt\ mediant, expedient, ingredient, obedient, submediant, disobedient, inespedient

ediment \ed-ə-mənt\ pediment, sediment, impediment

edin \ed-ᵊn\ see EDEN

eding \ēd-iŋ\ see ¹EEDING

¹edious \ēd-ē-əs\ tedious, supersedeas

²edious \ē-jəs\ see EGIS

edist \ēd-əst\ orthopedist, encyclopedist

edit \ed-ət\ credit, edit, accredit, coedit, discredit, noncredit, reedit, subedit, copyedit

editor \ed-ət-ər\ creditor, editor, predator, coeditor, subeditor

edium \ēd-ē-əm\ medium, tedium, cypripedium

edlar \ed-lər\ see EDDLER

edley \ed-lē\ deadly, medley, redly, chance-medley

edly \ed-lē\ see EDLEY

¹edo \ēd-ō\ credo, lido, Lido, speedo, aikido, libido, Toledo, torpedo, tuxedo

²edo \äd-ō\ see ²ADO

³edo \ēd-ə\ see ¹EDA

⁴edo \e-dō\ Edo, meadow, Yedo

edom \ēd-əm\ see EDUM

edon \ēd-ᵊn\ bleeding, Eden, steading, Sarpedon, boustrophedon

edouin \ed-wən\ see EDWIN

edra \ē-drə\ Phaedra, cathedra

edral \ē-drəl\ cathedral, dihedral, trihedral, hemihedral, holohedral, octahedral, pentahedral, polyhedral, procathedral, tetrahedral, dodecahedral, icosahedral, tetartohedral

edro \ā-drō\ Pedro, Murviedro

edulous \ej-ə-ləs\ credulous, sedulous, incredulous

edum \ēd-əm\ Edam, Edom, freedom, sedum

edure \ē-jər\ besieger, procedure, supersedure

edwin \ed-wən\ Edwin, bedouin

¹ee \ē\ b, be, bee, Brie, c, cay, cee, Cree, d, dee, Dee, dree, e, fee, flea, flee, free, g, gee, ghee, gie, glee, gree, he, key, Key, Klee, knee, lea, lee, Lee, Leigh, li, me, mi, p, pea, plea, pree, quay, re, scree, sea, see, she, shri, si, ski, spree, sri, t, tea, tee, the, thee, three, ti, tree, Tshi, twee, Twi, v, vee, we, wee, whee, ye, z, zee, agley, aiguille, agree, alee, ani, Bacchae, bailee, Bangui, banshee, bargee, bawbee, Belgae, Black Sea, bohea, bootee, bougie, buckshee, bungee, burgee, Bt, Capri, carefree, Castries, CB, CD, Chablis, Chaldee, chick-pea, Chi-li, chili, confit, cowpea, croquis, curie, Curie, Dead Sea, debris, decree, deep-sea, degree, Denis, donee, DP, draftee, drawee, Dundee, emcee, ennui, esprit, etui, farci, feoffee, foresee, fusee, GB, germfree, glacis, goatee, grand prix, grandee, grantee, GT, heart-free, he/she, HIV,

Horae, IC, IV, Jaycee, jaygee, jayvee, knock-knee, KP, latchkey, lessee, look-see, low-key, LP, mame, maquis, Marie, marquee, MC, métis, Midi, mille-feuille, muggee, must-see, Nancy, ngwee, OD, off-key, ogee, Osee, Parcae, pardie, passkey, Pawnee, payee, PC, perdie, per se, PG, pledgee, pongee, post-free, précis, puree, puttee, qt, raki, rani, razee, rooftree, rupee, rushee, RV, sati, scotfree, settee, Shaanxi, Shanxi, Shawnee, s/he, sightsee, signee, sirree, spadille, spahi, spondee, squeegee, squilgee, standee, strophe, suttee, sycee, T_3, T-3, TB, testee, 3-D, titi, to-be, topee, towhee, townee, trainee, trustee, trusty, Tupi, turfski, turnkey, tutee, Tutsi, tutti, TV, unbe, vendee, vestee, Volsci, vouchee, whangee, whoopee, would-be, Yang-Tze, yen-shee, abatis, ABC, ABD, absentee, addressee, adoptee, advisee, alienee, allottee, ambergris, AMP, amputee, appellee, appointee, après-ski, arrestee, assignee, attendee, B.V.D., Bahai, barley-bree, batterie, billi-bi, bonhomie, booboisie, bourgeoisie, brasserie, brusquerie, bumblebee, camporee, cap-a-pie, causerie, CCD, chickaree, chimpanzee, coati, Coligny, committee, conferee, consignee, counselee, context-free, counterplea, Danae, DDD, Debussy, departee, DDT, debauchee, DDE, deportee, dernier cri, deshabille, designee, detainee, devisee, devotee, diploe, disagree, discharge, dishabille, divorce, divorcee, DME, DMT, dungaree, duty-free, eau-de-vie, employee, endorsee, enlistee, enrollee, epopee, escadrille, escapee, ESP, evictee, expellee, FAD, fancy-free, fantasie, fantasy, fedayee, filigree, fleur-de-lis, formulae, franchisee, fricassee, galilee, Galilee, garnishee, gaucherie, Gemini, GTP, guarani, guarantee, Hawaii, honeybee, honoree, humble-bee, hydro-ski, IgE, IgG, inductee, internee, invitee, IUD, jacquerie, jamboree, Jiangxi, jus soli, Kayseri, kidnappee, LCD, LED, legatee, libelee, licensee, LSD, maître d', manatee, Medici, millidegree, murderee, NAD, nominee, obligee, oversea, oversee, parolee, parti pris, patentee, pedigree, peppertree, picotee, piroshki, point d'appui, potpourri, praecipe, presentee, promisee, rapparee, referee, refugee, rejectee, renminbi, repartee, retiree, retrainee, returnee, Rosemarie, RPV, saddletree, Sadducee, San Luis, sangaree, Savaii, selectee, Semele, shivaree, snickersnee, SOB, SST, STD,

Tenebrae, Tennessee, thirty-three, TNT, toile de Jouy, torii, transferee, undersea, Urümqi, vaccinee, value-free, verdigris, VIP, vis-à-vis, warrantee, Adar Sheni, Agri Dagi, alienee, biographee, bouquet garni, casus belli, charcuterie, charivari, chincherinchee, chinoiserie, covenantee, DBCP, dedicatee, de Medici, delegatee, distributee, ESOP, evacuee, examinee, exuviae, facetiae, fait accompli, felo-de-se, fortunately, Galilei, HTLV, interrogee, interviewee, jaborandi, Jiamusi, minutiae, Omega-3, Pasiphae, patisserie, prima facie, reliquiae, relocatee, Sargasso Sea, Simon Legree, Sault Sainte Marie, Southend on Sea, communicatee, HTLV-III, taedium vitae, Tupi-Guarani, ignoratio elenchi, petitio principii

²ee \ā\ see ¹AY

ée \ā\ see ¹AY

eeable \ē-ə-bəl\ seeable, skiable, agreeable, foreseeable, disagreeable

eebie \ē-bē\ see ¹EBE

eece \ēs\ see IECE

eeced \ēst\ see ¹EAST

eech \ēch\ see EACH

eecher \ē-chər\ see EACHER

eeches \ich-əz\ see ITCHES

eeching \ē-chiŋ\ breeching, far-reaching—*also present participles of verbs listed at* EACH

eechy \ē-chē\ see EACHY

eecy \ē-sē\ fleecy, greasy, specie, Tbilisi, AC/DC

eed \ēd\ bead, Bede, bleed, brede, breed, cede, creed, deed, feed, Gide, glede, gleed, greed, he'd, heed, keyed, knead, kneed, lead, mead, Mead, Mede, meed, need, plead, read, rede, reed, Reed, Reid, screed, seed, she'd, speed, steed, swede, Swede, treed, tweed, Tweed, we'd, weed, accede, airspeed, allseed, bindweed, birdseed, blueweed, bourride, breast-feed, bugseed, burweed, cheerlead, chickweed, concede, crossbreed, cudweed, debride, degreed, duckweed, exceed, fairlead, fireweed, flaxseed, Godspeed, gulfweed, half-breed, hand-feed, hawkweed, hayseed, high-speed, horseweed, impede, implead, inbreed, indeed, ironweed, Jamshid, jetbead, knapweed, knotweed, Lake Mead, linseed, lip-read, milkweed, misdeed, mislead, misread, moonseed, nosebleed, off-speed, oilseed, pigweed, pinweed, pokeweed, pondweed, Port Said, precede, proceed, proofread, ragweed, rapeseed, recede, reseed, rockweed, seaweed, secede, self-feed, Siegfried, sight-read, silkweed, smartweed, snakeweed, sneezeweed, speed-read, spoon-feed, stall-feed, stampede, stickseed, stickweed, stinkweed, succeed, ten-speed, tickseed, weak-kneed, witchweed, wormseed, aniseed, antecede, beggarweed, bitterweed, bottle-feed, bugleweed, butterweed, carpetweed, centipede, copyread, cottonseed, cottonweed, crazyweed, Ganymede, interbreed, intercede, interplead, jewelweed, jimsonweed, locoweed, millipede, overfeed, pedigreed, pickerelweed, pumpkinseed, retrocede, riverweed, rosinweed, Runnymede, silverweed, supersede, thimbleweed, tumbleweed, underfeed, waterweed, velocipede

eedal \ēd-ᵊl\ see EEDLE

eeded \ē-dəd\ beaded, deeded, kneaded, receded—*also pasts of verbs listed at* EED

eeder \ēd-ər\ see ¹EADER

eedful \ēd-fəl\ heedful, needful

¹eeding \ēd-iŋ\ bleeding, breeding, leading, reading, reeding, inbreeding, linebreeding, lipreading, outbreeding, preceding, speed-reading

²eeding \ēd-ᵊn\ see EDON

eedle \ēd-ᵊl\ aedile, beadle, credal, creedal, daedal, needle, wheedle

eedless \ēd-ləs\ deedless, heedless, needless, seedless

eedn't \ēd-ᵊnt\ see EDENT

eedo \ēd-ō\ see ¹EDO

eedom \ēd-əm\ see EDUM

eeds \ēdz\ Leeds, needs, Beskids, proceeds—*also plurals and possessives of nouns and third person singular presents of verbs listed at* EED

eedsman \ēdz-mən\ beadsman, seedsman

eedy \ēd-ē\ beady, deedy, greedy, needy, reedy, seedy, speedy, tweedy, weedy

eef \ēf\ see ¹IEF

eefe \ēf\ see ¹IEF

eefy \ē-fē\ beefy, leafy, reefy

eegee \ē-jē\ see IJI

eeing \ē-iŋ\ seeing, skiing, farseeing, ill-being, sight-seeing, turfskiing, well-being, heli-skiing, waterskiing

¹eek \ik\ see ICK

²eek \ēk\ see ¹EAK

eeked \ēkt\ see ²EAKED

eeken \ē-kən\ see EACON

eeker \ē-kər\ see ¹EAKER

eekie \ē-kē\ see EAKY

eeking \ē-kiŋ\ see ¹EAKING

eekly \ē-klē\ bleakly, chicly, sleekly, weakly, weekly, treacly, biweekly, midweekly, newsweekly, triweekly, semiweekly

eeks \ēks\ see ¹IXE

eeky \ē-kē\ see EAKY

eel \ēl\ see ²EAL

eelable \ē-lə-bəl\ see EALABLE

eele \ēl\ see ²EAL

eeled \ēld\ see IELD

eeler \ē-lər\ see EALER

eeley \ē-lē\ see EELY

eelie \ē-lē\ see EELY

eelin \ē-lən\ see ELIN

eeling \ē-liŋ\ ceiling, dealing,

Ealing, feeling, peeling, shieling, wheeling, appealing, Darjeeling, freewheeling, self-dealing, self-feeling, self-sealing, unfeeling, double-dealing, self-revealing, snowmobiling, unappealing—*also present participles of verbs listed at* ²EAL

eelson \el-sən\ see ELSON

eely \ē-lē\ Chi-li, dele, eely, Ely, freely, Greeley, mealie, mealy, really, seely, steelie, steely, stele, surreally, syli, vealy, wheelie, scungilli, Swahili, campanile, contumely, Isle of Ely, monostele, touchy-feely

eem \ēm\ see ¹EAM

eeman \ē-mən\ see ¹EMON

eemer \ē-mər\ see EAMER

eemie \ē-mē\ see EAMY

eeming \ē-miŋ\ seeming, streaming, redeeming, unbeseeming—*also present participles of verbs listed at* ¹EAM

eemly \ēm-lē\ seemly, supremely, unseemly

¹een \in\ see ¹IN

²een \ēn\ see ³INE

e'en \ēn\ see ³INE

eena \ē-nə\ see ²INA

eene \ēn\ see ³INE

eener \ē-nər\ see EANER

eenery \ēn-rē\ see EANERY

eening \ē-niŋ\ see EANING

eenling \ēn-liŋ\ see EANLING

eenly \ēn-lē\ see ¹EANLY

eenness \ēn-nəs\ see EANNESS

eens \ēnz\ Queens, teens, Grenadines, Philippines, smithereens

eenwich \in-ich\ see INACH

eeny \ē-nē\ see ¹INI

eep \ēp\ beep, bleep, cheap, cheep, clepe, creep, deep, heap, jeep, Jeep, keep, leap, neap, neep, peep, reap, seep, sheep, sleep, sneap, steep, sweep, threap, veep, weep, asleep, barkeep, bopeep, dustheap, housekeep, knee-deep, skin-deep, upkeep, upsweep, overleap, oversleep, Lakshadweep, Louis Philippe

eepage \ē-pij\ creepage, seepage

eepen \ē-pən\ cheapen, deepen, steepen

eepence \əp-əns\ see UPPANCE

eepenny \əp-nē\ see OPENNY

eeper \ē-pər\ beeper, creeper, keeper, leaper, Dnieper, peeper, reaper, sleeper, sweeper, weeper, barkeeper, beekeeper, bookkeeper, crowkeeper, doorkeeper, gamekeeper, gatekeeper, goalkeeper, greenkeeper, groundskeeper, housekeeper, innkeeper, lockkeeper, minesweeper, peacekeeper, scorekeeper, shopkeeper, stockkeeper, storekeeper, timekeeper, zookeeper, honeycreeper—*also comparatives of adjectives listed at* EEP

eepie \ē-pē\ see EEPY

eeping \ē-piŋ\ creeping, keeping, weeping, beekeeping, bookkeeping, gatekeeping, housekeeping,

minesweeping, peacekeeping,
safekeeping, timekeeping

eepish \ē-pish\ cheapish,
sheepish

eeple \ē-pəl\ see EOPLE

eepy \ē-pē\ cheapie, creepy,
seepy, sleepy, sweepy, tepee,
tipi, weepie, weepy

¹**eer** \ē-ər\ freer, seer, skier,
we're, CBer, decreer,
foreseer, sightseer, overseer,
water-skier

²**eer** \ir\ beer, bier, blear, cere,
cheer, clear, dear, deer, drear,
ear, fear, fere, fleer, gear,
hear, here, jeer, Lear, leer,
mere, mir, near, peer, pier,
Pierre, queer, rear, schmear,
sear, seer, sere, shear, sheer,
skirr, smear, sneer, spear,
speer, sphere, spier, steer,
tear, tier, Trier, Tyr, veer,
were, year, adhere, Aesir,
Ajmer, ambeer, appear, arrear,
Asir, austere, Ayrshire,
Berkshire, besmear, brassiere,
Cape Fear, career, cashier,
cashmere, Cheshire, chimere,
clavier, cohere, compeer,
destrier, dog-ear, Ellesmere,
emir, Empire, endear,
ensphere, eyrir, Fafnir,
Fifeshire, Flintshire, footgear,
frontier, gambier, Goodyear,
haltere, Hampshire, headgear,
inhere, Izmir, Kashmir, kefir,
killdeer, laveer, light-year,
man-year, menhir, mishear,
monsieur, mouse-ear, nadir,
Nairnshire, out-year, Pamir,
Perthshire, pickeer, portiere,
premier, premiere, redear,

rehear, reindeer, revere,
Revere, Robespierre, revers,
Saint Pierre, santir, severe,
Shakespeare, Shropshire,
sincere, slick-ear, tapir,
uprear, Vanir, veneer, vizier,
voir dire, wheatear, Wiltshire,
Ymir, Yorkshire, zaire, Zaire,
atmosphere, auctioneer,
balladeer, bandolier, bayadere,
Bedfordshire, Bedivere,
belvedere, biosphere, black-
tailed deer, bombardier,
boutonniere, brigadier,
buccaneer, budgeteer,
Cambridgeshire, cameleer,
cannoneer, cassimere,
cavalier, chandelier,
chanticleer, chevalier,
chiffonier, chocolatier,
commandeer, corsetiere,
cuirassier, Denbighshire,
Derbyshire, diapir, disappear,
domineer, Dumfriesshire,
ecosphere, Elzevir, engineer,
fictioneer, financier,
fourdrinier, fusilier, gadgeteer,
gasolier, gazetteer,
Gloucestershire, gondolier,
grenadier, Guinevere,
halberdier, hemisphere,
Herefordshire, Hertfordshire,
IJsselmere, insincere,
interfere, jardiniere, junketeer,
kerseymere, Lanarkshire,
Lancashire, lavaliere,
leafleteer, marketeer,
Meyerbeer, missileer,
Monmouthshire, Morayshire,
mountaineer, Mount Ranier,
muleteer, musketeer,
mutineer, Oxfordshire,

overhear, overseer, oversteer, pamphleteer, Pembrokeshire, persevere, pioneer, pistoleer, pontonier, privateer, profiteer, puppeteer, racketeer, Radnorshire, rocketeer, Rutlandshire, scrutineer, Selkirkshire, sloganeer, sonneteer, souvenir, Staffordshire, stratosphere, summiteer, Tyne and Wear, understeer, volunteer, Warwickshire, white-tailed deer, Windermere, Worcestershire, yesteryear, acyclovir, animalier, black marketeer, Buckinghamshire, Clackmannanshire, carabineer, Caernarvonshire, Cardiganshire, Carmarthenshire, charioteer, conventioneer, Dunbartonshire, electioneer, Eskisehir, Glamorganshire, free-marketeer, harquebusier, Huntingdonshire, Invernessshire, Kincardineshire, Montgomeryshire, Northamptonshire, Nottinghamshire, Merionethshire

e'er \er\ see ⁴ARE

eerage \ir-ij\ peerage, steerage, arrearage

eered \ird\ see ¹EARD

eerer \ir-ər\ see ²EARER

eeress \ir-əs\ see EROUS

eerful \ir-fəl\ see EARFUL

¹eerie \ir-ē\ see EARY

²eerie \ē-rē\ see EIRIE

eering \ir-iŋ\ see ¹EARING

eerist \ir-əst\ see ¹ERIST

eerless \ir-ləs\ see EARLESS

eerly \ir-lē\ see ¹EARLY

eersman \irz-mən\ steersman, frontiersman

eerut \ir-ət\ see IRIT

eery \ir-ē\ see EARY

ees \ēz\ see EZE

eese \ēz\ see EZE

eesh \ēsh\ see ²ICHE

eesi \ē-zē\ see ¹EASY

eesia \ē-zhə\ see ²ESIA

eesome \ē-səm\ gleesome, threesome

¹eest \āst\ see ACED

²eest \ēst\ see ¹EAST

eesy \ē-zē\ see ¹EASY

eet \ēt\ see ¹EAT

eetah \ēt-ə\ see ²ITA

eete \āt-ē\ see ATY

eeten \ēt-ᵊn\ see ¹EATEN

eeter \ēt-ər\ see ¹EATER

eethe \ēth\ see EATHE

eether \ē-thər\ see EITHER

eething \ē-thiŋ\ see EATHING

eetie \ēt-ē\ see EATY

eeting \ēt-iŋ\ see EATING

eetle \ēt-ᵊl\ see ETAL

eetly \ēt-lē\ featly, fleetly, neatly, sweetly, completely, concretely, discreetly, discretely, effetely, bittersweetly, incompletely, indiscreetly

eety \ēt-ē\ see EATY

ee-um \ē-əm\ see ¹EUM

eeve \ēv\ see ¹EAVE

eeved \ēvd\ see EAVED

eeves \ēvz\ see EAVES

eevil \ē-vəl\ see IEVAL

eevish \ē-vish\ peevish, thievish

eeward \ē-wərd\ leeward, Leeward, seaward

eewee \ē-wē\ kiwi, peewee, pewee

eewit \ü-ət\ see UET

eez \ēz\ see EZE

eezable \ē-zə-bəl\ see EASIBLE

eeze \ēz\ see EZE

eezer \ē-zər\ see ²EASER

eezing \ē-ziŋ\ see ²EASING

eezy \ē-zē\ see ¹EASY

¹ef \ef\ chef, clef, deaf, ef, f, lev, ref, teff, aleph, Brezhnev, enfeoff, H-F, Kiev, Lwiw, stone-deaf, tone-deaf, emf, Kishinev

²ef \ā\ see ¹AY

³ef \ēf\ see ¹IEF

efanie \ef-ə-nē\ see EPHONY

efany \ef-ə-nē\ see EPHONY

efe \ef-ē\ see EFFIE

eferable \ef-rə-bəl\ preferable, referable

eference \ef-rəns\ deference, preference, reference, cross-reference

eferent \ef-rənt\ deferent, referent

eff \ef\ see ¹EF

effer \ef-ər\ see EPHOR

efic \ef-ik\ Efik, benefic, malefic

eficence \ef-ə-səns\ beneficence, maleficence

efik \e-fik\ see EFIC

efsk \efsk\ Izhefsk, Profopyevsk

eft \eft\ cleft, deft, eft, heft, klepht, left, theft, weft, bereft

efty \ef-tē\ hefty, lefty

¹eg \āg\ Craig, plague, vague, stravage, The Hague

²eg \eg\ beg, Craig, dreg, egg, gleg, Greg, Gregg, keg, leg, peg, reg, skeg, squeg, yegg, blackleg, bootleg, bowleg, dogleg, foreleg, jackleg, jake leg, muskeg, nutmeg, redleg, renege, roughleg, Tuareg, unpeg, Winnipeg, mumblety-peg

³eg \ej\ see EDGE

¹ega \eg-ə\ omega, rutabaga

²ega \ā-gə\ see ²AGA

³ega \ē-gə\ see ¹IGA

egal \ē-gəl\ beagle, eagle, egal, legal, regal, illegal, porbeagle, spread-eagle, viceregal, extralegal, paralegal, medicolegal

egan \ē-gən\ Megan, vegan, Mohegan

egas \ā-gəs\ see AGUS

¹ege \ezh\ barege, cortege, Liège, manege, solfege

²ege \eg\ see ²EG

³ege \ej\ see EDGE

⁴ege \ēg\ see IGUE

⁵ege \ig\ see IG

eged \ejd\ see EDGED

egel \āgəl\ see AGEL

egent \ē-jənt\ regent, sejant, allegiant, vice-regent

eger \ej-ər\ see EDGER

egg \eg\ see ²EG

eggar \eg-ər\ see EGGER

eggary \eg-ə-rē\ beggary, Gregory

egger \eg-ər\ beggar, bootlegger, Heidegger, thousand-legger

eggie \ej-ē\ see EDGY

eggio \ej-ē-ō\ Reggio, arpeggio, solfeggio

eggs \egz\ see EGS

eggy \eg-ē\ dreggy, eggy, leggy, Peggy, plaguey, Carnegie

egia \ē-jə\ Ouija, aqua regia, aquilegia, paraplegia, quadriplegia

egian \ē-jən\ see EGION

egiant \ē-jənt\ see EGENT

egiate \ē-jət\ collegiate, elegit, intercollegiate

egic \ē-jik\ strategic, paraplegic, quadriplegic

egie \eg-ē\ see EGGY

egion \ē-jən\ legion, region, Norwegian, subregion, collegian

egious \ē-jəs\ see EGIS

egis \ē-jəs\ aegis, egis, Regis, tedious, egregious

egit \ē-jət\ see EGIATE

egm \em\ see ¹EM

egn \ān\ see ¹ANE

egnant \eg-nənt\ pregnant, regnant, impregnant, unpregnant

egnly \ān-lē\ see AINLY

egno \ān-yō\ see ¹ENO

¹ego \ē-gō\ chigoe, ego, Vigo, amigo, alter ego, impetigo, superego

²ego \ā-gō\ see ²AGO

egory \eg-ə-rē\ see EGGARY

egro \ē-grō\ Negro, Montenegro

egs \egz\ sheerlegs, yellowlegs, butter-and-eggs, daddy longlegs—*also plurals and possessives of nouns and third person singular presents of verbs listed at* ²EG

egular \eg-lər\ see EGLER

¹eh \ā\ see ¹AY

²eh \a\ see ³AH

ehen \ān\ see ¹ANE

ehner \ā-nər\ see AINER

¹ei \ēk\ dreich, skeigh

²ei \ā\ see ¹AY

³ei \ī\ see ¹Y

¹eia \ē-ə\ see ¹IA

²eia \ī-ə\ see ¹IAH

eial \ē-əl\ see ¹EAL

¹eian \ē-ən\ see ¹EAN

²eian \ā-ən\ see ¹AYAN

eic \ē-ik\ oleic, epigeic, logorrheic, mythopoeic, onomatopoeic

eich \ēk\ see ¹EI

eiche \āsh\ see ¹ECHE

eickel \ī-kəl\ see YCLE

¹eid \āt\ see ¹ATE

²eid \īt\ see ¹ITE

³eid \ēd\ see EED

¹eidel \ād-əl\ see ADLE

²eidel \īd-ᵊl\ see IDAL

eidi \īd-ē\ see IDAY

eidon \īd-ᵊn\ see IDEN

eier \īr\ see ¹IRE

eifer \ef-ər\ see EPHOR

¹eige \āzh\ beige, assuage

²eige \ā\ see ¹AY

eiger \ī-gər\ see IGER

¹eigh \ā\ see ¹AY

²eigh \ē\ see ¹EE

eighbor \ā-bər\ see ABOR

¹eight \āt\ see ¹ATE

²eight \īt\ see ¹ITE

eighter \āt-ər\ see ATOR

eightless \āt-ləs\ see ATELESS

eights \īts\ see IGHTS

eighty \āt-ē\ see ATY

eign \ān\ see ¹ANE

eigner \ā-nər\ see AINER

eii \ā\ see ¹AY

eiian \ā-ən\ see ¹AYAN

eiji \ā-jē\ see AGY

eik \ēk\ see ¹EAK

eikh \ēk\ see ¹EAK

eikle \ē-kəl\ see ECAL

¹eil \āl\ see AIL

²eil \el\ see ¹EL

³eil \ēl\ see ²EAL

⁴eil \īl\ see ¹ILE

eila \ē-lə\ see ¹ELA

eiled \āld\ see AILED

eiler \ī-lər\ see ILAR

¹eiling \ā-liŋ\ see AILING

²eiling \ē-liŋ\ see EELING

eill \ēl\ see ²EAL

eillance \ā-ləns\ see ALENCE

eillant \ā-lənt\ see ALANT

¹eilles \ā\ see ¹AY

²eilles \ālz\ see ALES

eilly \ā-lē\ see AILY

¹eim \ām\ see ¹AME

²eim \īm\ see ¹IME

eimer \ī-mər\ see ¹IMER

¹eims \äⁿs\ see ¹ANCE

²eims \ēmz\ Reims, Rheims—
  *also possessives and plurals
  of nouns and third person
  singular presents of verbs
  listed at* ¹EAM

¹ein \ān\ see ¹ANE

²ein \ē-ən\ see ¹EAN

³ein \ēn\ see ³INE

⁴ein \īn\ see ¹INE

¹eine \ān\ see ¹ANE

²eine \ēn\ see ³INE

³eine \ī-nə\ see ¹INA

⁴eine \en\ see ¹EN

eined \ānd\ see AINED

¹einer \ā-nər\ see AINER

²einer \ē-nər\ see EANER

eing \ē-iŋ\ see EEING

einie \ī-nē\ see ¹INY

eining \ā-niŋ\ see AINING

einous \ā-nəs\ see AYNESS

eins \ānz\ see AINS

einsman \ānz-mən\ see
  AINSMAN

eint \ānt\ see AINT

einte \ant\ see ⁵ANT

einture \an-chər\ see ²ANCHER

einy \ā-nē\ see AINY

eipt \ēt\ see ¹EAT

eir \er\ see ⁴ARE

eira \ir-ə\ see ²ERA

eird \ird\ see ¹EARD

eiress \ar-əs\ see ²ARIS

eiric \ī-rik\ see YRIC

eiro \er-ō\ see ²ERO

eirs \erz\ see AIRS

¹eis \ās\ see ¹ACE

²eis \ē-əs\ see ¹EUS

³eis \īs\ see ¹ICE

eisant \ēs-ᵊnt\ see ECENT

eise \ēz\ see EZE

eisel \ī-zəl\ see ²ISAL

eisen \īz-ᵊn\ see ¹IZEN

¹eiser \ī-sər\ see ICER

²eiser \ī-zər\ see IZER

¹eisha \ā-shə\ see ACIA

²eisha \ē-shə\ see ¹ESIA

eisin \ēz-ᵊn\ see EASON

eiss \īs\ see ¹ICE

eissen \īs-ᵊn\ see ¹ISON

¹eist \ā-əst\ see AYEST

²eist \īst\ see ¹IST

¹eister \ī-stər\ shyster,
  concertmeister, kapellmeister

²eister \ē-stər\ see EASTER

eisure \ē-zhər\ see EIZURE

¹eit \ē-ət\ fiat, albeit, howbeit

²eit \it\ see ¹IT

³eit \ēt\ see ¹EAT

⁴eit \īt\ see ¹ITE

eited \ēt-əd\ see ¹EATED

¹eiter \it-ər\ see ITTER

²eiter \ī-tər\ see ¹ITER

eith \ēth\ see ¹EATH

either \ē-_th_ər\ breather, either, neither, teether

eitus \īt-əs\ see ITIS

eity \ē-ət-ē\ deity, velleity, corporeity, spontaneity, synchroneity, diaphaneity, homogeneity, incorporeity, instantaneity, contemporaneity, extemporaneity, heterogeneity, inhomogeneity

eivable \ē-və-bəl\ cleavable, achievable, believable, conceivable, deceivable, perceivable, receivable, relievable, retrievable, imperceivable, inconceivable, irretrievable, unbelievable, unconceivable

eive \ēv\ see ¹EAVE

eiver \ē-vər\ see IEVER

eix \āsh\ see ¹ECHE

¹eize \āz\ see ¹AZE

²eize \ēz\ see EZE

eizure \ē-zhər\ leisure, seizure

ejant \ē-jənt\ see EGENT

eji \ej-ē\ see EDGY

ejo \ā-ō\ see ¹EO

ek \ek\ see ECK

¹eka \ek-ə\ see ECCA

²eka \ē-kə\ see ¹IKA

ekah \ek-ə\ see ECCA

eke \ēk\ see ¹EAK

ekel \ek-əl\ see ECKLE

ekh \ek\ see ECK

eki \ek-ē\ see ECKY

ekker \ek-ər\ see ECKER

ekoe \ē-kō\ see ICOT

ekton \ek-tən\ see ECTEN

¹el \el\ bel, bell, Bell, belle, cel, cell, dell, dwell, el, ell, fell, gel, Hel, hell, jell, knell, l, mell, quell, sel, sell, shell, smell, snell, spell, swell, tell, they'll, well, yell, Adele, Ardell, artel, barbell, befell, Blackwell, bluebell, boatel, bombshell, Boswell, botel, bridewell, cadelle, cartel, carvel, chandelle, clamshell, compel, cormel, cornel, corral, cowbell, Cromwell, cupel, Danielle, diel, dispel, doorbell, dumbbell, duxelles, echelle, eggshell, Estelle, excel, expel, farewell, fjeld, foretell, gabelle, gazelle, Giselle, gromwell, handbell, hard-shell, harebell, hotel, impel, indwell, inkwell, jurel, lampshell, lapel, marcel, maxwell, Maxwell, micelle, Michele, Michelle, misspell, morel, Moselle, motel, nacelle, Nobel, noel, nouvelle, nutshell, oat-cell, Orel, Orwell, outsell, pall-mall, Parnell, pastel, pell-mell, pixel, pointelle, presell, propel, quenelle, rakehell, rappel, Ravel, rebel, refel, repel, respell, retell, riel, Rochelle, rondel, saurel, scalpel, seashell, sequel, Seychelles, soft-shell, solgel, speedwell, spinel, stairwell, unsell, unwell, upwell, Weddell, wind-bell, Annabelle, APL, aquarelle, asphodel, Azazel, bagatelle, BAL, barbicel, bechamel, brocatelle, Camberwell, caramel, caravel, carousel, cascabel, chanterelle, chaparral, Charles Martel, citadel, clientele, cockleshell, Cozumel, damozel, decibel, demoiselle, fare-thee-well, fontanel, immortelle, Isabel, Isabelle, Jezebel, kiss-and-tell, lenticel, mangonel, muscatel, ne'er-do-well, Neufchatel, nonpareil, organelle, oversell, parallel, pedicel, pennoncel, personnel, petronel, Philomel, pimpernel, show-and-tell, tortoiseshell, undersell, T4 cell, villanelle, William Tell, zinfandel, Aix-la-Chapelle, au naturel, crème caramel, mademoiselle, maître d'hôtel, matériel, Mont-Saint-Michel, spirituel, T-helper cell, Thompson's gazelle, VLDL, antiparallel, antipersonnel, AWOL

²**el** \āl\ see AIL

¹**ela** \ē-lə\ Gila, Leila, Lela, selah, sheila, Sheila, stela, Vila, Braila, candela, tequila, weigela, sheila, Coahuila, Philomela, sinsemilla, Tutuila

²**ela** \ā-lə\ see ³ALA

³**ela** \el-ə\ see ELLA

elable \el-ə-bəl\ see ELLABLE

elacy \el-ə-sē\ jealousy, prelacy

elagh \ā-lē\ see AILY

elah \ē-lə\ see ¹ELA

eland \ē-lənd\ eland, Leland, Zealand, New Zealand

elanie \el-ə-nē\ see ELONY

elar \ē-lər\ see EALER

elate \el-ət\ see ELLATE

elatin \el-ət-ᵊn\ see ELETON

elative \el-ət-iv\ relative,

appellative, correlative, irrelative

elba \el-bə\ Elba, Elbe, Melba

elbe \el-bə\ see ELBA

elbert \el-bərt\ Delbert, Elbert, Mount Elbert

elch \elch\ belch, squelch, welch, Welch, Welsh

¹**eld** \eld\ eld, geld, held, meld, shelled, weld, beheld, danegeld, handheld, hard-shelled, upheld, withheld, jet-propelled, self-propelled, unparalleled—*also pasts of verbs listed at* ¹EL

²**eld** \el\ see ¹EL

³**eld** \elt\ see ELT

elda \el-də\ Zelda, Dar el Belda

eldam \el-dəm\ see ELDOM

elder \el-dər\ elder, welder

eldom \el-dəm\ beldam, seldom, hoteldom

eldon \el-dən\ Sheldon, Weldon

eldt \elt\ see ELT

¹**ele** \ā-lē\ see AILY

²**ele** \el\ see ¹EL

³**ele** \el-ē\ see ELLY

⁴**ele** \ē-lē\ see EELY

¹**eled** \eld\ see ¹ELD

²**eled** \ēld\ see IELD

elen \el-ən\ see ELON

elena \el-ə-nə\ Elena, Helena

elens \el-ənz\ Saint Helens, Mount Saint Helens—*also plurals and possessives of nouns at* ELON

eleon \ēl-yən\ see ²ELIAN

eletal \el-ət-ᵊl\ pelletal, skeletal

eleton \el-ət-ᵊn\ gelatin, skeleton

eleus \ē-lē-əs\ see ELIOUS

elf \elf\ elf, Guelf, pelf, self,

shelf, bookshelf, herself, hisself, himself, itself, meself, myself, nonself, oneself, ourself, top-shelf, thyself, yourself, mantelshelf, do-it-yourself

elfer \el-fər\ telpher, do-it-yourselfer

elfish \el-fish\ elfish, selfish, unselfish

elhi \el-ē\ see ELLY

eli \el-ē\ see ELLY

¹elia \ēl-yə\ Delia, Lelia, Shelia, Amelia, camellia, Camellia, Cecilia, Cornelia, Karelia, lobelia, obelia, Ophelia, Rumelia, sedilia, stapelia, psychedelia, seguidilla

²elia \il-ē-ə\ see ¹ILIA

elial \ē-lē-əl\ Belial, epithelial

¹elian \ē-lē-ən\ Melian, Pelion, abelian, Karelian, Mendelian

²elian \ēl-yən\ anthelion, aphelion, carnelian, chameleon, cornelian, Mendelian, parhelion, perihelion, Aristotelian, Mephistophelian

³elian \el-ē-ən\ see ELLIAN

elible \el-ə-bəl\ see ELLABLE

¹elic \ē-lik\ parhelic, autotelic

²elic \el-ik\ melic, relic, telic, angelic, Goidelic, smart aleck, archangelic, autotelic, philatelic, psychedelic

elical \el-i-kəl\ helical, pellicle, angelical, double-helical, evangelical

elier \el-yer\ see ELURE

elin \ē-lən\ shieling, theelin

¹elion \el-ē-ən\ see ELLIAN

²elion \ēl-yən\ see ²ELIAN

³elion \ēl-ē-ən\ see ¹ELIAN

elios \ē-lē-əs\ see ELIOUS

elious \ē-lē-əs\ Helios, Peleus, Cornelius, contumelious

elish \el-ish\ see ELLISH

elist \el-əst\ trellised, cellist, Nobelist, pastelist

¹elius \ā-lē-əs\ see ALIUS

²elius \ē-lē-əs\ see ELIOUS

elix \ē-liks\ Felix, helix, double helix

¹elk \elk\ elk, whelk

²elk \ilk\ see ILK

ell \el\ see ¹EL

e'll \ēl\ see ²EAL

ella \el-ə\ Celle, Della, Ella, fella, fellah, stella, Stella, Benguela, candela, Capella, Estella, favela, Gisela, glabella, lamella, Luella, Marcella, Mandela, novella, paella, patella, prunella, quiniela, rubella, sequela, umbrella, vanilla, a cappella, Cinderella, citronella, columella, fraxinella, Isabella, mortadella, mozzarella, panatela, salmonella, sarsaparilla, subumbrella, tarantella, villanella, valpolicella

ellable \el-ə-bəl\ fellable, gelable, compellable, expellable, indelible

ellah \el-ə\ see ELLA

ellan \el-ən\ see ELON

ellant \el-ənt\ gellant, appellant, flagellant, propellant, repellent, water-repellent

ellar \el-ər\ see ELLER

ellas \el-əs\ see EALOUS

ellate \el-ət\ helot, pellet,

prelate, zealot, appellate, flagellate, haustellate, lamellate, scutellate

ellative \el-ət-iv\ see ELATIVE

¹elle \el\ see ¹EL

²elle \el-ə\ see ELLA

ellean \el-ē-ən\ see ELLIAN

elled \eld\ see ¹ELD

ellen \el-ən\ see ELON

ellent \el-ənt\ see ELLANT

eller \el-ər\ cellar, dweller, feller, heller, Keller, seller, sheller, smeller, speller, stellar, teller, yeller, bestseller, bookseller, compeller, expeller, foreteller, glabellar, impeller, indweller, lamellar, ocellar, patellar, propeller, rathskeller, repeller, rostellar, saltcellar, tale-teller, cereballar, circumstellar, columellar, fortune-teller, interstellar, Rockefeller, storyteller

¹elles \el\ see ¹EL

²elles \elz\ see ELLS

ellet \el-ət\ see ELLATE

elletal \el-ət-ᵊl\ see ELETAL

elley \el-ē\ see ELLY

elli \el-ē\ see ELLY

ellia \ēl-yə\ see ELIA

ellian \el-ē-ən\ Chellean, Boswellian, pre-Chellean, Sabellian, triskelion, Pantagruelian, Machiavellian

ellicle \el-i-kəl\ see ELICAL

ellie \el-ē\ see ELLY

elline \el-ən\ see ELON

elling \el-iŋ\ belling, selling, spelling, swelling, telling, bookselling, compelling, indwelling, misspelling, tale-

telling, upwelling, fortune-telling, self-propelling—*also present participles of verbs listed at* ¹EL

ellington \el-iŋ-tən\ Ellington, Wellington, beef Wellington

ellion \el-yən\ hellion, rebellion

ellis \el-əs\ see EALOUS

ellised \el-əst\ see ELIST

ellish \el-ish\ hellish, relish, disrelish, embellish

ellist \el-əst\ see ELIST

ello \el-ō\ bellow, Bellow, cello, fellow, Jell-O, mellow, yellow, Yellow, bargello, bedfellow, bordello, duello, hail-fellow, Longfellow, marshmallow, morello, niello, Othello, playfellow, schoolfellow, yokefellow, Pirandello, punchinello, ritornello, saltarello, Robin Goodfellow, violoncello

ell-o \el-ō\ see ELLO

ellous \el-əs\ see EALOUS

¹ellow \el-ə\ see ELLA

²ellow \el-ō\ see ELLO

ells \elz\ Welles, Dardanelles—*also plurals and possessives of nouns and third person singular presents of verbs listed at*¹EL

ellum \el-əm\ blellum, skellum, vellum, postbellum, rostellum, antebellum, cerebellum

ellus \el-əs\ see EALOUS

elly \el-ē\ belly, Delhi, deli, felly, jelly, Kellie, Kelly, Nellie, shelly, Shelley, Shelly, smelly, tele, telly, wellie, New Delhi, nice-nelly, potbelly, rakehelly, sowbelly,

Boticelli, nervous Nellie, underbelly, vermicelli, Machiavelli, Dadra and Nagar Haveli

ellyn \el-ən\ see ELON

elm \elm\ elm, helm, realm, whelm, overwhelm, underwhelm

elma \el-mə\ Selma, Velma

elmar \el-mər\ see ELMER

elmer \el-mər\ Delmar, Delmer, Elmer

elmet \el-mət\ helmet, Helmut, pelmet

elmut \el-mət\ see ELMET

elo \ē-lō\ see ²ILO

elon \el-ən\ Ellen, Ellyn, felon, Helen, melon, avellan, Magellan, McClellan, muskmelon, Snellen, vitelline, Mary Ellen, watermelon, Strait of Magellan

elony \el-ə-nē\ felony, Melanie

elop \el-əp\ develop, envelop, redevelop, overdevelop

elopment \el-əp-mənt\ development, envelopment, redevelopment, overdevelopment

elos \ā-ləs\ see AYLESS

elot \el-ət\ see ELLATE

elotry \el-ə-trē\ helotry, zealotry

elp \elp\ help, kelp, skelp, whelp, yelp

elpher \el-fər\ see ELFER

elsea \el-sē\ see ELSIE

elsh \elch\ see ELCH

elsie \el-sē\ Chelsea, Elsie, Kensington and Chelsea

elson \el-sən\ keelson, nelson, Nelson

elt \elt\ belt, celt, Celt, dealt, delt, dwelt, felt, gelt, melt, pelt, Scheldt, smelt, spelt, svelte, veld, welt, black belt, flybelt, forefelt, greenbelt, heartfelt, hot-melt, jacksmelt, Krefeld, self-belt, snowbelt, snowmelt, Sunbelt, Bielefeld, Roosevelt, shelterbelt

elte \elt\ see ELT

elted \el-təd\ bias-belted—*also pasts of verbs listed at* ELT

elter \el-tər\ melter, pelter, shelter, skelter, smelter, spelter, swelter, welter, helter-skelter

eltered \el-tərd\ earth-sheltered—*also pasts of verbs listed at* ELTER

elting \el-tiŋ\ belting, felting, melting, pelting

elure \el-yər\ velure, hotelier

elve \elv\ delve, helve, shelve, twelve

elves \elvz\ elves, ourselves, theirselves, themselves, yourselves—*also plurals and possessives of nouns and third person singular present of verbs at* ELVE

elvin \el-vən\ Elvin, Kelvin, Melvin, Melvyn

elvyn \el-vən\ see ELVIN

ely \ē-lē\ see EELY

¹em \em\ Clem, crème, em, femme, gem, hem, m, mem, phlegm, REM, Shem, stem, them, ad rem, ahem, AM, Arnhem, Belem, bluestem, condemn, contemn, FM, idem, in rem, item, mayhem, millieme, modem, poem, problem, pro tem, proem, Shechem, ABM, anadem, apothegm, apothem, Bethlehem, diadem, exanthem, ibidem, IgM, meristem, OEM, SAM, stratagem, ad hominem, carpe diem, crème de la crème, ICBM, post meridiem, star-of-Bethlehem, terminus ad quem

²em \əm\ see ¹UM

ema \ē-mə\ bema, Lima, Pima, schema, Colima, eczema, edema, diastema, emphysema, Hiroshima, Iwo Jima, Kagoshima, Matsushima, terza rima, Tokushima, ottava rima

emacist \em-ə-səst\ see EMICIST

¹eman \em-ən\ see ²EMON

²eman \ē-mən\ see ¹EMON

emane \em-ə-nē\ see EMONY

emanence \em-ə-nəns\ see EMINENCE

emanent \em-ə-nənt\ see EMINENT

ematis \em-ət-əs\ see EMITUS

ematist \em-ət-əst\ see EMITIST

ematous \em-ət-əs\ see EMITUS

ember \em-bər\ ember, member, December, dismember, November, remember, September, disremember

¹emble \äm-bəl\ wamble, ensemble

²emble \em-bəl\ tremble, assemble, atremble, dissemble, resemble, disassemble

embler \em-blər\ temblor, trembler, assembler, dissembler

emblor \em-blər\ see EMBLER

embly \em-blē\ trembly, assembly, disassembly, self-assembly, subassembly

¹eme \em\ see ¹EM

²eme \ēm\ see ¹EAM

emel \ā-məl\ see EMILE

emely \ēm-lē\ see EEMLY

¹emen \ē-mən\ see ¹EMON

²emen \em-ən\ see ²EMON

³emen \ā-mən\ see ¹AMEN

emer \ē-mər\ see EAMER

emeral \em-rəl\ femoral, ephemeral

emery \em-rē\ emery, Emery, Emory, memory

emesis \em-ə-səs\ emesis, nemesis

emi \em-ē\ see EMMY

emia \ē-mē-ə\ anemia, bohemia, Bohemia, leukemia, toxemia, academia, septicemia, thalassemia, hypoglycemia, hypokalemia, beta-thalassemia

emian \ē-mē-ən\ anthemion, Bohemian

¹emic \ē-mik\ emic, anemic, graphemic, morphemic, lexemic, phonemic, taxemic, tonemic, epistemic

²emic \em-ik\ chemic, alchemic, endemic, pandemic, polemic, sachemic, systemic, totemic, academic, epidemic, epistemic

emical \em-i-kəl\ chemical, alchemical, polemical, academical, biochemical, epidemical, petrochemical, biogeochemical

emicist \em-ə-səst\ polemicist, supremacist

emics \ē-miks\ graphemics, morphemics, phonemics, proxemics

emile \ā-məl\ Emile, Memel

eminal \em-ən-ᵊl\ geminal, seminal

eminate \em-ə-nət\ geminate, effeminate

eminence \em-ə-nəns\ eminence, remanence, preeminence

eminent \em-ə-nənt\ eminent, remanent, preeminent

eming \em-iŋ\ Fleming, Heminge, lemming

eminge \em-iŋ\ see EMING

emini \em-ə-nē\ see EMONY

eminy \em-ə-nē\ see EMONY

emion \ē-mē-ən\ see EMIAN

emis \ē-məs\ see EMUS

emish \em-ish\ blemish, Flemish

emist \em-əst\ chemist, polemist, biochemist

emitist \em-ət-əst\ Semitist, systematist

emitus \em-ət-əs\ clematis, fremitus, edematous

emlin \em-lən\ gremlin, kremlin

emma \em-ə\ Emma, gemma, lemma, stemma, dilemma

emme \em\ see ¹EM

emmer \em-ər\ emmer, hemmer, stemmer, tremor, condemner, contemner

emming \em-iŋ\ see EMING

emmy \em-ē\ Emmy, gemmy, jemmy, phlegmy, semi, stemmy

emn \em\ see ¹EM

emner \em-ər\ see EMMER

emnity \em-nət-ē\ indemnity, solemnity

emo \em-ō\ demo, memo

¹emon \ē-mən\ demon, freeman, Freeman, gleeman, Piman, seaman, semen, Lake Leman, pentstemon, Philemon, cacodemon, Lacedaemon

²emon \em-ən\ Bremen, leman, lemon, Yemen

emone \em-ə-nē\ see EMONY

emony \em-ə-nē\ Gemini, lemony, anemone, bigeminy, Gethsemane, hegemony

emor \em-ər\ see EMMER

emoral \em-rəl\ see EMERAL

emory \em-rē\ see EMERY

emous \ē-məs\ see EMUS

emp \emp\ hemp, kemp, temp

emperer \em-pər-ər\ emperor, temperer

emperor \em-pər-ər\ see EMPERER

emplar \em-plər\ Templar, exemplar

emple \em-pəl\ semple, temple

emps \äⁿ\ see ¹ANT

empt \emt\ dreamt, kempt, tempt, attempt, contempt, exempt, preempt, undreamed, unkempt, tax-exempt

emptable \em-tə-bəl\ attemptable, contemptible

emptible \em-tə-bəl\ see EMPTABLE

emption \em-shən\ exemption, preemption, redemption

emptive \em-tiv\ preemptive, redemptive

emptor \em-tər\ tempter, preemptor, caveat emptor

emptory \em-trē\ peremptory, redemptory

emulous \em-yə-ləs\ emulous, tremulous

emur \ē-mər\ see EAMER

emus \ē-məs\ Remus, in extremis, Polyphemus, polysemous

emy \ē-mē\ see EAMY

¹en \en\ ben, Ben, den, en, fen, gen, glen, Glen, Glenn, Gwen, hen, ken, Ken, Len, men, n, pen, Penn, Rennes, Seine, sen, Sten, ten, then, wen, when, wren, Wren, yen, Zen, again, amen, Ardennes, Big Ben, Cayenne, Cevennes, Cheyenne, Chosen, Dairen, doyen, doyenne, Duchenne, Fulcien, hapten, hymen, Karen, La Tène, moorhen, peahen, pigpen, Phnom Penh, playpen, RN, Touraine, Tynmen, somewhen, Adrienne, Debrecen, DPN, five-and-ten, FMN, julienne, Kerguelen, La Fontaine, LPN, madrilene, mise-en-scène, samisen, Sun Yat-sen, TPN, carcinogen, comedienne, equestrienne, tamoxifen, tragedienne, Valenciennes

²en \ēn\ see ³INE

³en \aⁿ\ see ⁴IN

⁴en \ən\ see UN

⁵en \äⁿ\ see ¹ANT

¹ena \ā-nä\ see ¹AENA

²ena \ā-nə\ see ²ANA

³ena \än-yə\ see ³ANIA

⁴ena \ē-nə\ see ²INA

enable \en-ə-bəl\ tenable, amenable, untenable

enace \en-əs\ see ¹ENIS

enacle \en-i-kəl\ see ENICAL

enae \e-nē\ see ¹INI

enal \ēn-ᵊl\ penal, renal, venal, adrenal, vaccinal, duodenal

enancy \en-ən-sē\ tenancy, lieutenancy, subtenancy

enant \en-ənt\ pennant, tenant, lieutenant, se tenant, subtenant, sublieutenant, undertenant

enary \en-ə-rē\ hennery, plenary, senary, venery, centenary, millenary, bicentenary, bimillenary, quincentenary, tercentenary, quatercentenary, semicentenary, sesquicentenary

enas \ē-nəs\ see ¹ENUS

enate \en-ət\ see ENNET

enator \en-ət-ər\ see ENITOR

ençal \en-səl\ see ENCIL

¹ence \ens\ see ENSE

²ence \äⁿs\ see ¹ANCE

³ence \äns\ see ²ANCE

encel \en-səl\ see ENCIL

enceless \en-sləs\ see ENSELESS

encer \en-sər\ see ENSOR

ench \ench\ bench, blench, clench, drench, french, French, mensch, quench, stench, tench, trench, wench, wrench, entrench, luftmensch, retrench, unclench, workbench, Anglo-French, Mariana Trench

enchant \en-chənt\ see ENTIENT

enched \encht\ trenched, unblenched—*also pasts of verbs listed at* ENCH

encher \en-chər\ see ENTURE

enchman \ench-mən\
Frenchman, henchman

encia \en-chə\ see ENTIA

encil \en-səl\ mensal, pencel,
pencil, stencil, tensile, blue-
pencil, commensal, extensile,
Provençal, prehensile, red-
pencil, utensil, intercensal

ençon \en-sən\ see ENSIGN

ency \en-sē\ Montmorency,
residency, nonresidency

end \end\ bend, blend, blende,
end, fend, friend, lend, mend,
rend, scend, send, shend,
spend, tend, trend, vend,
wend, Wend, addend, amend,
append, ascend, attend,
augend, befriend, Big Bend,
bookend, boyfriend, closed-
end, commend, compend,
contend, dead end, dead-end,
defend, depend, descend,
distend, downtrend, emend,
expend, extend, forfend,
girlfriend, godsend,
hornblende, impend, intend,
Land's End, low-end,
missend, misspend, offend,
outspend, perpend,
pitchblende, portend, pretend,
propend, protend, rear-end,
resend, South Bend, stipend,
subtend, suspend, transcend,
unbend, unkenned, upend,
uptrend, weekend, year-end,
adherend, apprehend, bitter
end, comprehend,
condescend, Damavend,
discommend, dividend,
minuend, overspend,
recommend, repetend,
reprehend, subtrahend,

vilipend, hyperextend,
misapprehend, overextend,
superintend—*also pasts of
verbs listed at* ¹EN

enda \en-də\ Brenda, Glenda,
Venda, agenda, hacienda—
also plurals of nouns listed at
ENDUM

endable \en-də-bəl\ lendable,
mendable, spendable,
vendible, amendable,
ascendable, commendable,
defendable, dependable,
descendible, expendable,
extendable, unbendable,
comprehendable,
recommendable

endal \en-dᵊl\ Grendel, Kendall,
Mendel, Wendell, prebendal,
pudendal

endall \en-dᵊl\ see ENDAL

endance \en-dəns\ see ENDENCE

endancy \en-dən-sē\ see
ENDENCY

endant \en-dənt\ see ENDENT

¹ende \end\ see END

²ende \en-dē\ see ENDI

ended \en-dəd\ ended, splendid,
befriended, unfriended,
double-ended, open-ended,
undescended—*also pasts of
verbs listed at* END

endel \en-dᵊl\ see ENDAL

endell \en-dᵊl\ see ENDAL

endence \en-dəns\ tendance,
ascendance, attendance,
intendance, resplendence,
transcendence,
condescendence,
independence, Independence,
superintendence

endency \en-dən-sē\ pendency,

tendency, ascendancy, dependency, resplendency, transcendency, superintendency, independency

endent \en-dənt\ pendant, pendent, splendent, appendant, ascendant, attendant, defendant, dependent, descendant, impendent, intendant, respendent, transcendent, independent, superintendant, semi-independent

ender \en-dər\ bender, blender, fender, gender, lender, render, mender, slender, spender, sender, splendor, tender, vendor, amender, ascender, attender, auslander, bartender, commender, contender, defender, descender, emender, engender, expender, extender, fork-tender, goaltender, hellbender, intender, offender, pretender, surrender, suspender, tailender, weekender, double-ender, moneylender, over-spender, self-surrender

endi \en-dē\ bendy, Mende, trendy, Wendy, effendi, modus vivendi

endible \en-də-bəl\ see ENDABLE

endid \en-dəd\ see ENDED

ending \en-diŋ\ bending, ending, pending, sending, ascending, attending, fence-mending, goaltending, heartrending, mind-bending, unbending, unending,

uncomprehending, unpretending, uncomprehending—*also present participles of verbs listed at* END

endium \en-dē-əm\ compendium, antependium

endless \end-ləs\ endless, friendless

endliness \en-lē-nəs\ cleanliness, friendliness, uncleanliness, unfriendliness

endly \en-lē\ cleanly, friendly, loop of Henle, uncleanly, unfriendly

endment \en-mənt\ amendment, intendment

endo \en-dō\ kendo, crescendo, stringendo, decrescendo, innuendo, diminuendo

endor \en-dər\ see ENDER

endous \en-dəs\ horrendous, stupendous, tremendous

endron \en-drən\ philodendron, rhododendron

ends \enz\ see ¹ENS

endum \en-dəm\ addendum, agendum, pudendum, corrigendum, referendum, definiendum

endy \en-dē\ see ENDI

¹**ene** \ā-nā\ nene, sene

²**ene** \en\ see ¹EN

³**ene** \en-ē\ see ENNY

⁴**ene** \ē-nē\ see ¹INI

⁵**ene** \ēn\ see ³INE

⁶**ene** \ān\ see ¹ANE

enel \en-ᵊl\ see ENNEL

eneous \ē-nē-əs\ genius, homogeneous, heterogeneous

ener \ē-nər\ see EANER

enerable \en-rə-bəl\ generable,
venerable, regenerable

eneracy \en-rə-sē\ degeneracy,
regeneracy

enerate \en-rət\ degenerate,
regenerate, unregenerate

enerative \en-rət-iv\ generative,
degenerative, regenerative,
neurodegenerative

eneris \en-ə-rəs\ mons veneris,
sui generis

¹**enery** \en-ə-rē\ see ²ENARY

²**enery** \ēn-rē\ see EANERY

¹**enet** \en-ət\ see ENNET

²**enet** \ē-nət\ see EANUT

¹**eng** \aŋ\ see ²ANG

²**eng** \əŋ\ see ¹UNG

enge \enj\ venge, avenge,
revenge, Stonehenge

engi \eŋ-gē\ dengue, sengi

english \iŋ-glish\ English,
Yinglish

engo \eŋ-gō\ marengo,
camerlengo

¹**ength** \eŋth\ length, strength,
full-length, half-length,
wavelength, understrength,
industrial-strength

²**ength** \enth\ see ENTH

engthen \eŋ-thən\ lengthen,
strengthen

engue \eŋ-gē\ see ENGI

enh \en\ see ¹EN

¹**enia** \ē-nē-ə\ taenia, Slovenia,
sarracenia, schizophrenia

²**enia** \ē-nyə\ Armenia,
Encaenia, Eugenia, gardenia,
Ruthenia, Tigrinya

enial \ē-nē-əl\ genial, menial,
venial, congenial

enian \ē-nē-ən\ Fenian,
Armenian, Essenian, Icenian,
sirenian, Slovenian,
Tyrrhenian, Achaemenian,
Magdalenian

¹**enic** \ēn-ik\ genic, scenic

²**enic** \en-ik\ fennec, pfennig,
phrenic, splenic, sthenic,
arsenic, asthenic, Edenic,
Essenic, eugenic, Hellenic,
hygienic, irenic, transgenic,
allergenic, androgenic,
autogenic, calisthenic,
chromogenic, cryogenic,
cryptogenic, hygienic,
mutagenic, Panhellenic,
pathogenic, photogenic,
Saracenic, schizophrenic,
telegenic, carcinogenic,
cariogenic, hallucinogenic,
hypoallergenic

enical \en-i-kəl\ cenacle,
arsenical, galenical,
ecumenical

enice \en-əs\ see ¹ENIS

enicist \en-ə-səst\ eugenicist,
ecumenicist

enics \en-iks\ eugenics,
euphenics, euthenics,
hygienics, calisthenics,
cryogenics—*also plurals and
possessives of nouns listed at*
²ENIC

¹**enie** \en-ē\ see ENNY

²**enie** \ē-nē\ see ¹INI

enience \ē-nyəns\ lenience,
convenience, provenience,
inconvenience

enient \ēn-yənt\ convenient,
prevenient

enim \en-əm\ see ENOM

enin \en-ən\ see ENNON

enior \ē-nyər\ senior,
monsignor

¹**enis** \en-əs\ Denis, Dennis, Denys, genus, menace, tenace, tennis, Venice, frontenis, summum genus

²**enis** \ē-nəs\ see ¹ENUS

¹**enison** \en-ə-sən\ benison, Tennyson, venison

²**enison** \en-ə-zən\ benison, denizen, venison

enist \en-əst\ tennist, euthenist

enitive \en-ət-iv\ genitive, lenitive, philoprogenitive, polyphiloprogenitive

enitor \en-ət-ər\ senator, progenitor, primogenitor

enity \en-ət-ē\ see ENTITY

enium \ē-nē-əm\ hymenium, proscenium

enius \ē-nē-əs\ see ENEOUS

enizen \en-ə-zən\ see ²ENISON

enn \en\ see ¹EN

enna \en-ə\ Glenna, henna, senna, antenna, duenna, Gehenna, sienna, Vienna

ennae \en-ē\ see ENNY

ennant \en-ənt\ see ENANT

¹**enne** \en\ see ¹EN

²**enne** \en-ē\ see ENNY

³**enne** \an\ see ⁵AN

ennec \en-ik\ see ²ENIC

enned \end\ see END

ennel \en-ᵊl\ crenel, fennel, kennel, unkennel

enner \en-ər\ see ¹ENOR

ennery \en-ə-rē\ see ²ENARY

ennes \en\ see ¹EN

ennet \en-ət\ Bennett, genet, jennet, rennet, senate, sennet, sennit, tenet

ennett \en-ət\ see ENNET

enney \en-ē\ see ENNY

enni \en-ē\ see ENNY

ennial \en-ē-əl\ biennial, centennial, decennial, millennial, perennial, quadrennial, quinquennial, septennial, triennial, vicennial, bicentennial, bimillennial, postmillennial, premillennial, quincentennial, tercentennial, semicentennial, sesquicentennial, quadricentennial

ennies \en-ēz\ tennies—*also possessives and plurals of nouns listed at* ENNY

ennig \en-ik\ see ²ENIC

ennin \en-ən\ see ENNON

ennis \en-əs\ see ¹ENIS

ennist \en-əst\ see ENIST

ennit \en-ət\ see ENNET

ennium \en-ē-əm\ biennium, decennium, millennium, quadrennium, quinquennium, triennium

ennon \en-ən\ Lenin, pennon, rennin, tenon, antivenin

enny \en-ē\ any, benne, benny, Benny, blenney, Dene, Denny, fenny, genie, Jennie, jenny, Jenny, many, penni, penny, Penny, antennae, catchpenny, halfpenny, Kilkenny, Na-dene, pinchpenny, sixpenny, tenpenny, threepenny, truepenny, twopenny, lilangeni, spinning jenny

ennyson \en-ə-sən\ see ¹ENISON

¹**eno** \än-yō\ segno, dal segno, jalapeño

²**eno** \en-ō\ steno, ripieno

³**eno** \ā-nō\ see ²ANO

enoch \ē-nik\ see ¹INIC

enom \en-əm\ denim, plenum, venom, envenom

enon \en-ən\ see ENNON

¹enor \en-ər\ Brenner, Jenner, tenner, tenor, tenour, countertenor, heldentenor

²enor \ē-nər\ see EANER

enour \en-ər\ see ¹ENOR

enous \ē-nəs\ see ¹ENUS

¹ens \enz\ cleanse, gens, lens, amends, beam-ends, weekends, sapiens, definiens, locum tenens—*also plurals and possessives of nouns and third person singular presents of verbs listed at ¹EN*

²ens \ens\ see ENSE

ensable \en-sə-bəl\ see ENSIBLE

ensal \en-səl\ see ENCIL

ensary \ens-rē\ see ENSORY

ensch \ench\ see ENCH

ense \ens\ cense, dense, fence, flense, gens, hence, mense, pence, sense, spence, tense, thence, whence, commence, condense, defense, dispense, expense, immense, incense, intense, missense, nonsense, offense, prepense, pretense, propense, sequence, sixpence, subsequence, suspense, twopence, accidence, antisense, commonsense, confidence, consequence, diffidence, evidence, frankincense, multisense, nondefense, providence, Providence, recompense, residence, self-defense, subsequence, coincidence, ego-defense, inconsequence, New Providence,

nonresidence, self-confidence, self-evidence

enseful \ens-fəl\ menseful, senseful, suspenseful

enseless \en-sləs\ fenceless, senseless, defenseless, offenseless

ensem \en-səm\ see ENSUM

enser \en-sər\ see ENSOR

ensian \en-chən\ see ENSION

ensible \en-sə-bəl\ sensible, compensable, condensable, defensible, dispensable, distensible, extensible, insensible, ostensible, apprehensible, commonsensible, comprehensible, incondensable, indefensible, indispensable, reprehensible, supersensible, incomprehensible

ensign \en-sən\ ensign, alençon

ensil \en-səl\ see ENCIL

ensile \en-səl\ see ENCIL

ension \en-chən\ gentian, mention, pension, tension, abstention, ascension, attention, contention, convention, declension, descension, detention, dimension, dissension, distension, extension, indention, intension, intention, invention, Laurentian, low-tension, posttension, prehension, pretension, prevention, recension, retention, subvention, suspension, sustention, Vincentian, Waldensian, Albigensian, apprehension,

circumvention,
comprehension,
condescension, contravention,
hypertension, hypotension,
inattention, reinvention,
reprehension, salientian,
incomprehension,
misapprehension,
nonintervention,
overextension,
Premonstratensian

ensional \ench-nəl\ tensional,
ascensional, attentional,
conventional, declensional,
dimensional, extensional,
intensional, intentional,
unconventional,
tridimensional,
unidimensional

ensioner \ench-nər\ see
ENTIONER

ensis \en-səs\ see ENSUS

ensitive \en-sət-iv\ sensitive,
insensitive, photosensitive,
hypersensitive, oversensitive,
photosensitive, supersensitive

ensity \en-sət-ē\ density,
tensity, extensity, immensity,
intensity, propensity

ensive \en-siv\ pensive, tensive,
ascensive, defensive,
expensive, extensive,
intensive, offensive,
ostensive, protensive,
suspensive, apprehensive,
coextensive, comprehensive,
hypertensive, hypotensive,
inexpensive, inoffensive,
reprehensive, self-defensive,
counteroffensive, labor-
intensive

ensor \en-sər\ censer, censor,
fencer, sensor, spencer,
Spencer, Spenser, tensor,
commencer, condenser,
dispenser, extensor,
precensor, sequencer,
suspensor, biosensor—*also
comparatives of adjectives
listed at* ENSE

ensory \ens-rē\ sensory,
dispensary, suspensory,
extrasensory, multisensory,
supersensory

¹**ensual** \en-chəl\ see ENTIAL

²**ensual** \ench-wəl\ see ¹ENTUAL

ensum \en-səm\ sensum, per
mensem

ensurable \ens-rə-bəl\
censurable, mensurable,
commensurable,
immensurable,
incommensurable

ensure \en-chər\ see ENTURE

ensus \en-səs\ census,
consensus, dissensus,
amanuensis

¹**ent** \ent\ bent, Brent, cent,
dent, gent, Ghent, Gwent,
hent, Kent, leant, lent, Lent,
meant, pent, rent, scent, sent,
sklent, spent, sprent, tent,
Trent, vent, went, absent,
accent, Advent, anent, ascent,
assent, augment, besprent,
cement, chimkent, comment,
concent, consent, content,
convent, descent, detent,
dissent, docent, event, extent,
ferment, foment, forewent,
forspent, fragment, frequent,
hell-bent, indent, intent,
invent, lament, loment, low-
rent, mordent, outspent,

outwent, percent, pigment, portent, present, prevent, quitrent, relent, repent, resent, segment, Tashkent, torment, unbent, well-meant, wisent, accident, aliment, argument, circumvent, compartment, complement, compliment, confident, devilment, diffident, discontent, document, evident, heaven-sent, implement, instrument, Jack-a-Lent, malcontent, nonevent, Occident, ornament, orient, president, provident, regiment, reinvent, represent, re-present, resident, sediment, self-content, Stoke on Trent, subsequent, underwent, supplement, coincident, disorient, experiment, ferro-cement, inconsequent, misrepresent, nonresident, privatdocent, self-evident

²ent \änt\ see ²ANT

³ent \ä^n\ see ¹ANT

enta \ent-ə\ menta, yenta, magenta, momenta, placenta, polenta, tegmenta, tomenta, irredenta, impedimenta

entable \ent-ə-bəl\ presentable, documentable, fermentable, preventable, representable, sedimentable

entacle \ent-i-kəl\ see ENTICAL

entage \ent-ij\ tentage, ventage, percentage

ental \ent-°l\ cental, dental, dentil, gentle, lentil, mental, rental, cliental, fragmental, judgmental, parental, placental, segmental, accidental, adjustmental, apartmental, biparental, compartmental, complemental, condimental, continental, departmental, deterimental, developmental, documental, excremental, elemental, environmental, firmamental, fundamental, governmental, grandparental, incidental, incremental, instrumental, managemental, monumental, nonjudgmental, occidental, oriental, ornamental, regimental, rudimental, sacramental, sentimental, supplemental, temperamental, transcendental, vestamental, coincidental, developmental, experimental, presentimental, subcontinental, transcontinental, uniparental, intercontinental, interdepartmental, intergovernmental, semigovernmental

entalist \ent-°l-əst\ gentlest, mentalist, documentalist, fundamentalist, governmentalist, incrementalist, instrumentalist, orientalist, sacramentalist, sentimentalist, transcendentalist, environmentalist, experimentalist

entalness \ent-°l-nəs\ see ENTLENESS

entance \ent-°ns\ see ENTENCE

entary \en-trē\ gentry, sentry,

passementerie, reentry, subentry, alimentary, complementary, complimentary, documentary, elementary, filamentary, integumentary, parliamentary, rudimentary, sedimentary, supplementary, tenementary, testamentary, uncomplimentary, unparliamentary, semidocumentary

entative \ent-ət-iv\ tentative, augmentative, fermentative, frequentative, presentative, preventative, argumentative, representative, misrepresentative

¹ente \en-tā\ al dente, lentamente

²ente \ent-ē\ see ENTY

³ente \änt\ see ²ANT

ented \ent-əd\ tented, augmented, contented, demented, lamented, segmented, untented, battlemented, malcontented, oriented, self-contented, unfrequented, unprecedented, overrepresented, underrepresented—*also pasts of verbs listed at* ¹ENT

enten \ent-ᵊn\ Benton, dentin, Denton, Kenton, Lenten, Quentin, Trenton

entence \ent-ᵊns\ sentence, repentance

enter \ent-ər\ center, enter, mentor, renter, stentor, tenter, venter, assenter, augmentor, cementer, concenter, consentor, dissenter, incenter,

indenter, fermenter, frequenter, inventor, precentor, preventer, rackrenter, reenter, repenter, subcenter, tormentor, documenter, epicenter, representer, supplementer, hypocenter, metacenter, experimenter, hundredpercenter

entered \en-tərd\ centered, facecentered, self-centered, bodycentered—*also pasts of verbs listed at* ENTER

enterie \en-trē\ see ENTARY

entful \ent-fəl\ eventful, resentful, uneventful

enth \enth\ nth, strength, tenth, crème de menthe

enthe \enth\ see ENTH

enthesis \en-thə-səs\ epenthesis, parenthesis

enti \ent-ē\ see ENTY

entia \en-chə\ dementia, Florentia, sententia, Valencia, differentia, in absentia

ential \en-chəl\ cadential, consensual, credential, demential, essential, eventual, potential, prudential, sciential, sentential, sequential, tangential, torrential, componential, conferential, confidential, consequential, deferential, differential, evidential, existential, expediential, exponential, inessential, inferential, influential, nonessential, penitential, pestilential, preferential, presidential, providential, referential, residential, reverential, transferential, unessential, circumferential, equipotential, experiential, inconsequential, intelligential, interferential, jurisprudential, multipotential, reminiscential

entialist \en-chə-ləst\ essentialist, existentialist

entian \en-chən\ see ENSION

entiary \ench-rē\ century, penitentiary, plenipotentiary

entic \ent-ik\ lentic, argentic, authentic, crescentic, identic, inauthentic

entical \ent-i-kəl\ denticle, pentacle, tentacle, conventicle, identical, nonidentical, self-identical

entice \ent-əs\ see ENTOUS

enticle \ent-i-kəl\ see ENTICAL

entient \en-chənt\ penchant, sentient, trenchant, dissentient, insentient, presentient

entil \ent-ᵊl\ see ENTAL

entin \ent-ᵊn\ see ENTEN

enting \ent-iŋ\ dissenting, unrelenting

ention \en-chən\ see ENSION

entionable \ench-nə-bəl\ mentionable, pensionable, unmentionable

entional \ench- nəl\ see ENSIONAL

entioned \en-chənd\ aforementioned, well-intentioned—*also pasts of verbs listed at* ENSION

entioner \ench-nər\ mentioner, pensioner, tensioner

entious \en-chəs\ abstentious, contentious, dissentious, licentious, pretentious, sententious, tendentious, conscientious, unpretentious

entis \ent-əs\ see ENTOUS

entist \ent-əst\ dentist, cinquecentist, irredentist

entity \en-ət-ē\ entity, lenity, amenity, identity, nonentity, obscenity, serenity, coidentity, self-identity

entium \ent-ē-əm\ jus gentium, unnilpentium

entive \ent-iv\ adventive, attentive, incentive, inventive, pendentive, preventive, retentive, argumentive, disincentive, inattentive

entle \ent-ᵊl\ see ENTAL

entleness \ent-ᵊl-nəs\ gentleness, accidentalness

entment \ent-mənt\ contentment, presentment, resentment, discontentment, self-contentment

ento \en-tō\ cento, lento, Trento, memento, pimento, pimiento, seicento, trecento, cinquecento, papiamento, portamento, quatrocento, Sacramento, aggiornamento, divertimento, pronunciamento, risorgimento

enton \ent-ᵊn\ see ENTEN

entor \ent-ər\ see ENTER

entous \ent-əs\ prentice, apprentice, argentous, momentous, portentous, compos mentis, filamentous, ligamentous, non compos mentis, in loco parentis

entral \en-trəl\ central, ventral, subcentral, dorsiventral

entress \en-trəs\ gentrice, inventress

entric \en-trik\ centric, acentric, concentric, dicentric, eccentric, acrocentric, androcentric, Christocentric, egocentric, ethnocentric, Eurocentric, geocentric, phallocentric, polycentric, theocentric, topocentric, anthropocentric, areocentric, Europocentric, heliocentric, selenocentric

entrice \en-trəs\ see ENTRESS

entry \en-trē\ see ENTARY

ents \ents\ gents, events, dollars-and-cents—*also plurals of nouns listed at* [1]ENT

[1]entual \en-chə-wəl\ sensual, accentual, consensual, conventual, eventual

[2]entual \en-chəl\ see ENTIAL

entum \ent-əm\ centum, mentum, cementum, momentum, per centum, tegmentum, tomentum, argumentum

enture \en-chər\ bencher, censure, denture, drencher, trencher, venture, wencher, adventure, backbencher, debenture, front-bencher, indenture, misventure, misadventure, peradventure

enturer \ench-rər\ venturer, adventurer

enturess \ench-rəs\ see ENTUROUS

enturous \ench-rəs\ venturous, adventuress, adventurous

entury \ench-rē\ see ENTIARY

enty \ent-ē\ plenty, sente, senti, tenty, twenty, aplenty, licente, cognoscente, twenty-twenty, Deo volente, dolce far niente

enuis \en-yə-wəs\ see ENUOUS

enum \en-əm\ see ENOM

enuous \en-yə-wəs\ strenuous, tenuis, tenuous, ingenuous, disingenuous

[1]enus \ē-nəs\ genus, lenis, penis, venous, Venus, Campinas, Delphinus, Maecenas, Quirinus, silenus, intravenous

[2]enus \en-əs\ see [1]ENIS

eny \ā-nē\ see AINY

enys \en-əs\ see [1]ENIS

[1]enza \en-zə\ Penza, cadenza, credenza, influenza

[2]enza \en-sə\ Polenza, Vicenza, Piacenza

[1]eo \ā-ō\ mayo, Mayo, cacao, paseo, rodeo, aparejo, Bulawayo, cicisbeo, zapateo, Montevideo

[2]eo \ē-ō\ see [2]IO

[1]eoff \ef\ see [1]EF

[2]eoff \ēf\ see [1]IEF

eoffor \ef-ər\ see EPHOR

eolate \ē-ə-lət\ triolet, alveolate, areolate, urceolate

eoman \ō-mən\ see OMAN

[1]eon \ē-ən\ see [1]EAN

[2]eon \ē-än\ eon, freon, neon, prion

eonid \ē-ə-nəd\ see EANID

eopard \ep-ərd\ jeopard, leopard, peppered, shepard, shepherd

eopardess \ep-ərd-əs\ shepherdess, leopardess

eople \ē-pəl\ people, pipal, steeple, craftspeople, dispeople, laypeople, newspeople, salespeople, spokespeople, townspeople, tradespeople, tribespeople, unpeople, workpeople, anchorpeople, businesspeople, congresspeople

eopled \ē-pəld\ unpeopled— *also pasts of verbs listed at* EOPLE

eordie \órd-ē\ see ¹ORDY

eorem \ir-əm\ see ERUM

eorge \órj\ see ORGE

eorgian \ór-jən\ see ORGIAN

eorist \ir-əst\ see ¹ERIST

eoul \ōl\ see ¹OLE

eous \ē-əs\ see ¹EUS

ep \ep\ hep, pep, prep, rep, schlepp, skep, step, steppe, strep, yep, Alep, crowstep, doorstep, footstep, goose-step, instep, lockstep, misstep, one-step, quickstep, salep, sidestep, two-step, unstep, corbiestep, demirep, overstep, step-by-step, Gaziantep

eparable \ep-rə-bəl\ reparable, separable, inseparable, irreparable

epard \ep-ərd\ see EOPARD

epe \āp\ see ¹APE

epee \ē-pē\ see EEPY

eper \ep-ər\ see EPPER

eperous \ep-rəs\ leprous, obstreperous

epey \ā-pē\ see APEY

eph \ef\ see ¹EF

epha \ē-fə\ ephah, Recife, synalepha, synaloepha

ephalin \ef-ə-lən\ cephalin, encephalon, enkephalin, acanthocephalan

ephaly \ef-ə-lē\ anencephaly, brachycephaly, microcephaly

ephen \ē-vən\ see EVEN

epherd \ep-ərd\ see EOPARD

epherdess \ep-ərd-əs\ see EOPARDESS

ephone \ef-ə-nē\ see EPHONY

ephony \ef-ə-nē\ Stefanie, Stefany, Persephone, telephony

ephor \ef-ər\ deafer, ephor, feoffor, heifer, zephyr, hasenpfeffer

ephrine \ef-rən\ epinephrine, norepinephrine

epht \eft\ see EFT

ephyr \ef-ər\ see EPHOR

epi \ā-pē\ see APEY

epid \ep-əd\ tepid, trepid, intrepid

epo \ēp-ō\ see EPOT

epot \ēp-ō\ depot, Ipo, pepo, el cheapo

epp \ep\ see EP

eppe \ep\ see EP

epped \ept\ see EPT

epper \ep-ər\ hepper, leper, pepper, stepper, Colepeper, Culpeper, sidestepper

eppy \ep-ē\ peppy, preppy, orthoepy

eprous \ep-rəs\ see EPEROUS

eps \eps\ biceps, forceps, triceps, quadriceps, editio princeps—*also plurals and possessives of nouns and third person singular presents of verbs listed at* EP

epsis \ep-səs\ skepsis, prolepsis, syllepsis, omphaloskepsis epsy \ep-sē\ catalepsy, epilepsy, narcolepsy, nympholepsy

ept \ept\ crept, kept, sept, slept, stepped, swept, wept, accept, adept, backswept, concept, except, incept, inept, percept, precept, transept, upswept, windswept, yclept, high-concept, intercept, nympholept, overslept, self-concept—*also pasts of verbs listed at* EP

eptable \ep-tə-bəl\ see EPTIBLE

eptacle \ep-ti-kəl\ skeptical, conceptacle, receptacle

epter \ep-tər\ see EPTOR

eptible \ep-tə-bəl\ acceptable, perceptible, susceptible, imperceptible, insusceptible, unacceptable

eptic \ep-tik\ peptic, septic, skeptic, aseptic, dyspeptic, eupeptic, proleptic, sylleptic, antiseptic, cataleptic, epileptic, narcoleptic, nympholeptic

eptical \ep-ti-kəl\ see EPTACLE

eptile \ep-t°l\ see EPTAL

eption \ep-shən\ conception, deception, exception, inception, perception, reception, subreption, apperception, contraception, interception, misconception, preconception, self-conception, self-perception

eptional \ep-shnəl\ conceptional, deceptional, exceptional, unexceptional

eptive \ep-tiv\ acceptive, conceptive, deceptive, exceptive, inceptive, perceptive, preceptive, receptive, susceptive, apperceptive, contraceptive, imperceptive

eptor \ep-tər\ scepter, accepter, acceptor, inceptor, preceptor, receptor, intercepter, interceptor

eptual \ep-chəl\ conceptual, perceptual

eptus \ep-təs\ conceptus, textus receptus

epy \ep-ē\ see EPPY

epys \ēps\ Pepys—*also possessives and plurals of nouns and third person singular presents of verbs listed at* EEP

equal \ē-kwəl\ equal, prequel, sequel, coequal, unequal

eque \ek\ see ECK

equel \ē-kwəl\ see EQUAL

equence \ē-kwəns\ frequence, sequence, infrequence, subsequence

equency \ē-kwən-sē\ frequency, sequency, infrequency

equent \ē-kwənt\ frequent, sequent, infrequent

equer \ek-ər\ see ECKER

¹er \ā\ see ¹AY

²er \er\ see ⁴ARE

³er \ər\ see ¹EUR

⁴er \ir\ see ²EER

¹era \er-ə\ era, Sara, Sarah, sclera, terra, caldera, Rivera, sierra, tiara, aloe vera, ciguatera, cordillera, guayabera, habanera, Halmahera, riviera, Riviera, Santa Clara

²era \ir-ə\ era, gerah, Hera, lira,

Pyrrha, sera, sirrah, Vera,
wirra, chimaera, chimera,
hetaera, lempira, Madeira,
mbira, Altamira

erable \ər-ə-bəl\ thurible,
conferrable, deferrable,
deterrable, inferable,
preferable, transferable

erah \ir-ə\ see ²ERA

¹**eral** \ir-əl\ Cyril, feral, seral,
spheral, virile

²**eral** \er-əl\ see ERIL

³**eral** \ər-əl\ see ERRAL

erald \er-əld\ Gerald, Harold,
herald, Jerald, Jerold, Jerrold,
Fitzgerald, FitzGerald

eraph \er-əf\ see ERIF

erapy \er-əld\ therapy,
chemotherapy, chronotherapy,
aromatherapy

eratin \er-ət-ᵊn\ keratin,
Sheraton, Samaritan

erative \er-ət-iv\ see ¹ARATIVE

eraton \er-ət-ᵊn\ see ERATIN

erb \ərb\ blurb, curb, herb,
kerb, Serb, verb, acerb,
adverb, disturb, exurb,
perturb, potherb, pro-verb,
proverb, reverb, suburb,
superb

erbal \ər-bəl\ burble, gerbil,
herbal, verbal, deverbal,
nonverbal, preverbal

erbalist \ər-bə-ləst\ herbalist,
verbalist, hyperbolist

erbally \ər-bə-lē\ verbally,
hyperbole, nonverbally

erber \ər-bər\ see URBER

erberis \ər-bər-əs\ berberis,
Cerberus

erberus \ər-bər-əs\ see
ERBERIS

erbet \ər-bət\ see URBIT

erbia \ər-bē-ə\ see URBIA

erbial \ər-bē-əl\ adverbial,
proverbial

erbid \ər-bəd\ see URBID

erbil \ər-bəl\ see ERBAL

erbium \ər-bē-əm\ erbium,
terbium, ytterbium

erbole \ər-bə-lē\ see ERBALLY

erbolist \ər-bə-ləst\ see
ERBALIST

erby \ər-bē\ derby, Derby,
herby, Kirby

ercal \ər-kəl\ see IRCLE

erce \ərs\ see ERSE

ercé \ers\ see ¹ARCE

ercel \ər-səl\ see ¹ERSAL

ercement \ər-smənt\
amercement, disbursement,
reimbursement

ercer \ər-sər\ see URSOR

ercery \ərs-rē\ see URSARY

erch \ərch\ see URCH

ercia \ər-shə\ see ERTIA

ercial \ər-shəl\ Herschel,
Hershel, commercial, inertial,
controversial, uncommercial,
semicommercial

ercian \ər-shən\ see ERTIAN

ercible \ər-sə-bəl\ see ERSIBLE

ercion \ər-zhən\ see ¹ERSION

ercis \ər-səs\ see ERSUS

ercive \ər-siv\ see ERSIVE

ercular \ər-kyə-lər\ see
IRCULAR

ercy \ər-sē\ Circe, mercy,
Percy, pursy, gramercy,
controversy

erd \ərd\ see IRD

¹**erde** \erd\ see AIRED

²**erde** \ərd\ see IRD

³**erde** \ərd-ē\ see URDY

erder \ərd-ər\ birder, girder, herder, murder, self-murder, sheepherder

erderer \ərd-ər-ər\ see URDERER

¹erdi \ər-dē\ see URDY

²erdi \er-dē\ Verdi, Monteverdi

erdin \ərd-ᵊn\ see URDEN

erding \ərd-iŋ\ wording, sheepherding

erdu \ər-dü\ perdu, perdue, Urdu

erdue \ər-dü\ see ERDU

erdure \ər-jər\ see ERGER

¹ere \er\ see ⁴ARE

²ere \er-ē\ see ¹ARY

³ere \ir\ see ²EER

⁴ere \ir-ē\ see EARY

⁵ere \ər\ see ¹EUR

e're \ē-ər\ see ¹EER

ère \er\ see ⁴ARE

ereal \ir-ē-əl\ see ERIAL

ereid \ir-ē-əd\ see ERIOD

erek \erik\ see ¹ERIC

erely \ir-lē\ see ¹EARLY

erement \er-ə-mənt\ see ERIMENT

¹erence \ir-əns\ clearance, adherence, appearance, coherence, inherence, incoherence, interference, perseverance

²erence \ər-əns\ see URRENCE

³erence \er-ᵊns\ see ARENCE

¹erency \ir-ən-sē\ coherency, vicegerency

²erency \er-ən-sē\ see ERRANCY

¹erent \ir-ənt\ gerent, adherent, coherent, inherent, sederunt, vicegerent, incoherent

²erent \er-ənt\ see ¹ARENT

¹eren't \ərnt\ see EARNT

²eren't \ər-ənt\ see URRENT

ereo \er-ē-ō\ see ARIO

ereous \ir-ē-əs\ see ERIOUS

erer \ir-ər\ see ²EARER

¹eres \erz\ see AIRS

²eres \ir-ēz\ see ERIES

³eres \ərs\ see ERS

eresy \er-ə-sē\ clerisy, heresy

ereth \er-ət\ see ERIT

ereus \ir-ē-əs\ see ERIOUS

erf \ərf\ see URF

erg \ərg\ berg, burg, erg, Augsburg, Boksburg, exergue, hamburg, Hamburg, Hapsburg, homburg, iceberg, Lemberg, Limburg, Lindbergh, Newburg, Pittsburgh, Salzburg, Sandburg, Strasbourg, svedberg, Tilburg, Drakensberg, Gutenberg, Harrisburg, Inselberg, Königsberg, Luxembourg, Magdeburg, Nuremberg, Toggenburg, Venusberg, Wallenberg, Würtemberg, Rube Goldberg, Johannesburg, St. Petersburg, von Hindenberg, Baden-Wurtenberg, Pietermaritzburg, Yekaterinburg, Roodepoort-Maraisburg

ergative \ər-gə-tir\ ergative, purgative

erge \ərj\ see URGE

ergeant \är-jənt\ see ARGENT

ergen \ər-gən\ Bergen, Spitzbergen

ergence \ər-jəns\ convergence, divergence, emergence, immergence, insurgence, resurgence, submergence

ergency \ər-jən-sē\ urgency,
convergency, detergency,
divergency, emergency,
insurgency, counterinsurgency

ergent \ər-jənt\ see URGENT

ergeon \ər-jin\ see URGEON

erger \ər-jər\ merger, perjure,
purger, scourger, urger,
verdure, verger, deterger

ergh \ərg\ see ERG

ergic \ər-jik\ allergic, synergic,
theurgic, demiurgic,
dramaturgic, thaumaturgic,
alpha-adrenergic, beta-
adrenergic

ergid \ər-jid\ see URGID

¹ergne \ərn\ see URN

²ergne \ern\ see ¹ERN

ergo \ər-gō\ ergo, Virgo

ergue \ərg\ see ERG

ergy \ər-jē\ see URGY

¹eri \er-ē\ see ¹ARY

²eri \ir-ē\ see EARY

¹eria \ir-ē-ə\ feria, Styria, Syria,
Algeria, Assyria, asteria,
bacteria, collyria, criteria,
diphtheria, Egeria, franseria,
Illyria, Liberia, Nigeria,
plumeria, porphyria, Siberia,
wisteria, cafeteria,
cryptomeria, latimeria,
sansevieria, washateria, opera
seria

²eria \er-ē-ə\ see ARIA

erial \ir-ē-əl\ aerial, cereal,
ferial, serial, arterial,
bacterial, empyreal, ethereal,
funereal, imperial, material,
sidereal, venereal, vizierial,
immaterial, magisterial,
managerial, ministerial,
presbyterial

¹erian \ir-ē-ən\ Adlerian,
Assyrian, Aterian,
Cimmerian, criterion,
Hesperian, Hutterian,
Hyperion, Iberian, Illyrian,
Mousterian, Mullerian,
Pierian, Shakespearean,
Spencerian, Spenglerian,
Sumerian, valerian, Valerian,
Wagnerian, Hanoverian,
Presbyterian, Thraco-Illyrian

²erian \er-ē-ən\ see ¹ARIAN

¹eric \er-ik\ Berwick, cleric,
Derek, derrick, Eric, Erich,
Erik, ferric, Herrick, xeric,
aspheric, chimeric, choleric,
cholesteric, entheric, generic,
Homeric, mesmeric, numeric,
alphanumeric, atmospheric,
climacteric, congeneric,
dysenteric, esoteric

²eric \ir-ik\ lyric, pyric, pyrrhic,
spheric, xeric, aspheric,
chimeric, empiric, satiric,
satyric, atmospheric,
hemispheric, stratospheric,
panegyric

erica \er-i-kə\ erica, Erica,
Erika, America, esoterica,
North America, South
America, Latin America

¹erical \er-i-kəl\ clerical,
chimerical, numerical,
anticlerical

²erical \ir-i-kəl\ lyrical, miracle,
spherical, spiracle, empirical,
hemispherical

erich \erik\ see ¹ERIC

erics \er-iks\ sferics, hysterics—
*also plurals and possessives
of nouns listed at* ¹ERIC

eried \ir-ē-əd\ see ERIOD

eries \ir-ēz\ Ceres, series, dundrearies, miniseries—*also plurals and possessives of nouns and third person singular presents of verbs listed at* EARY

erif \er-əf\ seraph, serif, sheriff, teraph, sans serif

eriff \er-əf\ see ERIF

erik \erik\ see ¹ERIC

erika \er-i-kə\ see ERICA

eril \er-əl\ beryl, Beryl, Cheryl, Errol, feral, ferrule, ferule, Merrill, peril, Sherrill, Sheryl, sterile, Terrell, Terrill, imperil, chrysoberyl

erilant \er-ə-lənt\ see ERULENT

erile \er-əl\ see ERIL

erilous \er-ə-ləs\ perilous, querulous, glomerulus

eriment \er-ə-mənt\ cerement, experiment, gedankenexperiment

erin \er-ən\ see ¹ARON

ering \ar-iŋ\ see ¹ARING

eriod \ir-ē-əd\ myriad, nereid, Nereid, period, photoperiod

erion \ir-ē-ən\ see ¹ERIAN

erior \ir-ē-ər\ anterior, exterior, inferior, interior, posterior, superior, ulterior, Lake Superior—*also comparatives of adjectives listed at* EARY

eriot \er-ē-ət\ see ¹ARIAT

erious \ir-ē-əs\ cereus, Nereus, serious, Sirius, cinereous, delirious, Guarnerius, imperious, mysterious, Tiberius, deleterious

¹eris \ir-əs\ see EROUS

²eris \er-əs\ see ERROUS

¹erist \ir-əst\ querist, theorist, verist, careerist, panegyrist—*also superlatives of adjectives listed at* ²EER

²erist \er-əst\ see ARIST

erisy \er-ə-sē\ see ERESY

erit \er-ət\ ferret, merit, terret, demerit, inherit, disinherit, Shemini Atzereth

eritable \er-ət-ə-bəl\ heritable, veritable, inheritable

eritor \er-ət-ər\ ferreter, heritor, inheritor

erity \er-ət-ē\ ferity, ferrety, rarity, verity, asperity, celerity, dexterity, legerity, posterity, prosperity, severity, sincerity, temerity, insincerity, ambidexterity, subsidiarity

erium \ir-ē-əm\ Miriam, criterium, bacterium, collyrium, delirium, imperium, psalterium, atmospherium, magisterium, archaeobacterium

¹erius \er-ē-əs\ see ARIOUS

²erius \ir-ē-əs\ see ERIOUS

erjure \ər-jər\ see ERGER

erjury \ərj-rē\ perjury, surgery, microsurgery, neurosurgery

erk \ərk\ see ¹ORK

erker \ər-kər\ see ¹ORKER

erkin \ər-kən\ see IRKIN

erking \ər-kiŋ\ see ORKING

erkly \ər-klē\ clerkly, berserkly

erky \ər-kē\ birkie, jerky, murky, perky, smirky, turkey, Turkey, Turki, Albuquerque, herky-jerky

erle \ərl\ see ¹IRL

erlie \er-lē\ see AIRLY

erlin \ər-lən\ merlin, Merlin,

merlon, Merlyn, purlin,
yearling

erling \ər-liŋ\ see URLING

erlon \ər-lən\ see ERLIN

erlyn \ər-lən\ see ERLIN

erm \ərm\ see ¹ORM

erma \ər-mə\ dharma, Erma,
herma, Irma, scleroderma,
terra firma

ermal \ər-məl\ dermal, thermal,
nonthermal, subdermal,
transdermal, ectodermal,
endothermal, epidermal,
exothermal, hydrothermal,
hypodermal, hypothermal

erman \ər-mən\ ermine,
german, German, germen,
Herman, Hermann, merman,
sermon, Sherman, Thurman,
vermin, determine, extermine,
Mount Hermon, predetermine,
cousin-german, Tibeto-
Burman

ermanent \ər-mə-nənt\
permanent, determinant,
impermanent, semipermanent

ermann \ər-mən\ see ERMAN

ermary \ərm-rē\ see IRMARY

erment \ər-mənt\ averment,
conferment, deferment,
determent, interment,
preferment, disinterment

ermer \ər-mər\ see URMUR

ermes \ər-mēz\ Hermes, kermes

ermi \ər-mē\ see ERMY

ermic \ər-mik\ dharmic,
thermic, geothermic,
hypodermic, taxidermic,
electrothermic

ermin \ər-mən\ see ERMAN

erminable \ərm-nə-bəl\

terminable, determinable,
interminable, indeterminable

erminal \ərm-nəl\ germinal,
terminal, preterminal,
subterminal

erminant \ər-mə-nənt\ see
ERMANENT

ermine \ər-mən\ see ERMAN

ermined \ər-mənd\ ermined,
determined, self-determined,
overdetermined

erminous \ər-mə-nəs\ terminus,
verminous, conterminous,
coterminous

erminus \ər-mə-nəs\ see
ERMINOUS

ermis \ər-məs\ dermis, kermis,
kirmess, thermos, endodermis,
epidermis, exodermis

ermit \ər-mət\ hermit, Kermit,
Thermit

ermon \ər-mən\ see ERMAN

ermos \ər-məs\ see ERMIS

ermy \ər-mē\ fermi, germy,
squirmy, wormy, diathermy,
endothermy, taxidermy

¹ern \ern\ bairn, Bern, cairn,
hern, Nairn, Auvergne,
moderne, Pitcairn, Sauternes,
Ygerne, art moderne

²ern \ərn\ see URN

erna \ər-nə\ dharna, Myrna,
sterna, Verna, cisterna

ernal \ərn-ᵊl\ colonel, journal,
kernel, sternal, vernal,
diurnal, eternal, external,
fraternal, hibernal, infernal,
internal, maternal, nocturnal,
paternal, supernal, coeternal,
sempiternal, semidiurnal

ernary \ər-nə-rē\ fernery,
ternary, turnery, quaternary

¹erne \ern\ see ¹ERN

²erne \ərn\ see URN

erned \ərnd\ see URNED

ernel \ərn-ᵊl\ see ERNAL

erner \ər-nər\ see URNER

¹ernes \ern\ see ¹ERN

²ernes \ərn\ see URN

ernest \ər-nəst\ see ERNIST

ernia \ər-ne-ə\ hernia, Ibernia

ernian \ər-nē-ən\ Hibernian, quaternion, Saturnian

ernible \ər-nə-bəl\ see URNABLE

ernie \ər-nē\ see ¹OURNEY

ernier \ər-nē-ər\ see OURNEYER

ernion \ər-nē-ən\ see ERNIAN

ernist \ər-nəst\ earnest, Earnest, Ernest, internist

ernity \ər-nət-ē\ eternity, fraternity, maternity, modernity, paternity, quaternity, coeternity, confraternity, sempiternity

ernment \ərn-mənt\ adjournment, attornment, concernment, discernment, internment

ernum \ər-nəm\ see URNUM

erny \ər-nē\ see ¹OURNEY

¹ero \ē-rō\ giro, gyro, hero, Hero, Nero, zero, subzero, antihero, superhero

²ero \er-ō\ aero, cero, Duero, Faeroe, faro, Faroe, pharaoh, taro, tarot, bolero, bracero, cruzeiro, Guerrero, Herero, Madero, montero, pampero, primero, ranchero, sombrero, torero, vaquero, burladero, caballero, Mescalero, novillero, banderillero, carabinero, embarcadero, Rio de Janeiro

³ero \ir-ō\ giro, guiro, gyro, hero, zero, primero

erod \er-əd\ Herod, out-Herod, viverrid

erold \er-əld\ see ERALD

eron \er-ən\ see ¹ARON

erous \ir-əs\ cerous, cirrous, cirrus, Eris, peeress, Pyrrhus, scirrhous, scirrhus, seeress, serous

erp \ərp\ see URP

erpe \ər-pē\ see IRPY

erque \ər-kē\ see ERKY

¹err \er\ see ⁴ARE

²err \ər\ see ¹EUR

erra \er-ə\ see ¹ERA

errable \ər-ə-bəl\ see ERABLE

errace \er-əs\ see ERROUS

erral \ər-əl\ bharal, scurrile, squirrel, conferral, deferral, demurral, referral, transferal

errance \er-əns\ see ARENCE

errancy \er-ən-sē\ errancy, aberrancy, coherency, inerrancy

errand \er-ənd\ errand, gerund

errant \er-ənt\ see ¹ARENT

erre \er\ see ⁴ARE

errell \er-əl\ see ERIL

¹errence \ər-əns\ see URRENCE

²errence \er-əns\ see ARENCE

errent \ər-ənt\ see URRENT

errer \ər-ər\ burrer, stirrer, conferrer, deferrer, demurer, demurrer, deterrer, inferrer, preferrer, referrer, transferrer

erret \er-ət\ see ERIT

erreter \er-ət-ər\ see ERITOR

erria \er-ē-ə\ see ARIA

errible \er-ə-bəl\ see ¹EARABLE

erric \er-ik\ see ¹ERIC

errick \er-ik\ see ¹ERIC

errid \er-əd\ see EROD

errie \er-ē\ see ¹ARY

erried \er-ēd\ berried, serried, varied—*also pasts of verbs listed at* ¹ARY

errier \er-ē-ər\ burier, terrier, varier, bullterrier—*also comparatives of adjectives listed at* ¹ARY

errill \er-əl\ see ERIL

errily \er-ə-lē\ see ARILY

¹erring \ar-iŋ\ see ¹ARING

²erring \ər-iŋ\ see URRING

erris \er-əs\ see ERROUS

errol \er-əl\ see ERIL

errold \er-əld\ see ERALD

erron \er-ən\ see ¹ARON

error \er-ər\ see ¹EARER

errous \er-əs\ derris, Eris, ferrous, parous, terrace, nonferrous, millionairess

errule \er-əl\ see ERIL

erry \er-ē\ see ¹ARY

¹ers \ərz\ furze, hers, somewheres, Voyageurs—*also plurals and possessives of nouns and third person singular presents of verbs listed at* ¹EUR

²ers \ā\ see ¹AY

ersa \ər-sə\ bursa, Bursa, vice versa

ersable \ər-sə-bəl\ see ERSIBLE

¹ersal \ər-səl\ bursal, tercel, versal, dispersal, rehearsal, reversal, transversal, traversal, universal

²ersal \är-səl\ see ARSAL

ersant \ərs-ᵊnt\ versant, conversant

ersary \ərs-rē\ see URSARY

erse \ərs\ birse, burse, curse, Erse, hearse, nurse, perse, purse, terce, terse, thyrse, verse, worse, adverse, amerce, asperse, averse, coerce, commerce, converse, cutpurse, disburse, disperse, diverse, immerse, inverse, Nez Perce, obverse, perverse, rehearse, reverse, sesterce, stress-verse, submerse, transverse, traverse, intersperse, reimburse, universe

ersed \ərst\ see URST

erser \ər-sər\ see URSOR

ersey \ər-zē\ furzy, jersey, Jersey, kersey, Mersey, New Jersey

erschel \ər-shəl\ see ERCIAL

ershel \ər-shəl\ see ERCIAL

ersial \ər-shəl\ see ERCIAL

ersian \ər-zhən\ see ¹ERSION

ersible \ər-sə-bəl\ coercible, conversable, dispersible, eversible, immersible, reversible, submersible, traversable, incoercible, irreversible, semisubmersible

¹ersion \ər-zhən\ Persian, version, aspersion, aversion, coercion, conversion, dispersion, diversion, emersion, eversion, excursion, immersion, incursion, inversion, perversion, recursion, reversion, submersion, subversion, ambiversion, extroversion, interspersion, introversion, reconversion, retroversion,

animadversion,
seroconversion

²**ersion** \ər-shən\ see ERTIAN

ersional \ər-zhə-nəl\ versional,
conversional, reversional

ersionist \ər-zhə-nəst\
diversionist, excursionist

¹**ersity** \ər-sət-ē\ adversity,
diversity, multiversity,
university, biodiversity

²**ersity** \ər-stē\ see IRSTY

ersive \ər-siv\ cursive,
ambersive, aversive, coercive,
detersive, discursive,
dispersive, excursive,
inversive, perversive,
recursive, subversive,
extroversive, introversive

erson \ərs-ᵊn\ person, worsen,
chairperson, craftsperson,
draftsperson, houseperson,
MacPherson, newsperson,
nonperson, salesperson,
spokesperson, unperson,
anchorperson, businessperson,
gentleperson, weatherperson

erst \ərst\ see URST

ersted \ər-stəd\ oersted,
worsted, kilooersted

ersus \ər-səs\ cercis, thyrsus,
versus, excursus

ersy \ər-sē\ see ERCY

¹**ert** \ərt\ Bert, blurt, Burt, chert,
curt, dirt, flirt, girt, hurt, Kurt,
pert, quirt, shirt, skirt, spurt,
squirt, sturt, vert, wert, wort,
advert, alert, assert, avert,
bellwort, birthwort,
Blackshirt, brownshirt, Cape
Vert, colewort, concert,
convert, covert, desert,
dessert, dissert, divert, evert,

exert, expert, exsert, figwort,
fleawort, frankfurt, glasswort,
hoopskirt, hornwort, inert,
insert, invert, lousewort,
lungwort, madwort, milkwort,
nightshirt, outskirt, overt,
pervert, pilewort, ragwort,
redshirt, revert, ribwort,
saltwort, sandwort, seagirt,
Shubert, soapwort, spearwort,
spleenwort, stitchwort,
stonewort, subvert, sweatshirt,
toothwort, T-shirt, ungirt,
ambivert, bladderwort,
butterwort, controvert,
disconcert, extrovert,
feverwort, inexpert, introvert,
liverwort, malapert, miniskirt,
mitrewort, moneywort,
overshirt, overskirt,
pennywort, pettiskirt,
preconcert, reconvert, Saint-
John's-wort, spiderwort,
swallowwort, thoroughwort,
undershirt, underskirt,
animadvert, interconvert

²**ert** \er\ see ⁴ARE

³**ert** \at\ see ⁵AT

erta \ərt-ə\ Gerta, Alberta,
Roberta

ertain \ərt-ᵊn\ burton, Burton,
certain, curtain, Merton,
uncertain

ertant \ərt-ᵊnt\ see ERTENT

erted \ərt-əd\ skirted,
concerted, perverted,
T-shirted, extroverted,
miniskirted, undershirted—
also pasts of verbs listed at
¹ERT

ertedly \ərt-əd-lē\ assertedly,
concertedly, pervertedly

ertence \ərt-ᵊns\ advertence, inadvertence

ertent \ərt-ᵊnt\ advertent, revertant, inadvertent

erter \ərt-ər\ blurter, skirter, squirter, stertor, converter, inverter, subverter, controverter—*also comparatives of adjectives listed at* ¹ERT

¹**ertes** \ərt-ēz\ certes, Laertes

²**ertes** \ərts\ SEE ERTS

ertford \ärt-fərd\ SEE ARTFORD

erth \ərth\ SEE IRTH

ertha \ər-thə\ Bertha, Eartha

ertia \ər-shə\ Mercia, Murcia, inertia

ertial \ər-shəl\ SEE ERCIAL

ertian \ər-shən\ tertian, assertion, Cistercian, desertion, exertion, insertion, Mercian, self-assertion

ertible \ərt-ə-bəl\ convertible, invertible, controvertible, inconvertible, incontrovertible, interconvertible

ertile \ərt-ᵊl\ curtal, fertile, hurtle, kirtle, myrtle, Myrtle, spurtle, turtle, cross-fertile, exsertile, infertile, interfertile

ertinence \ərt-ᵊn-əns\ pertinence, purtenance, appurtenance, impertinence

¹**ertinent** \ərt-ᵊn-ənt\ pertinent, appurtentant, impertinent

²**ertinent** \ərt-nənt\ SEE IRTINENT

erting \ərt-iŋ\ shirting, skirting, disconcerting, self-asserting—*also present participles of verbs listed at* ¹ERT

ertion \ər-shən\ SEE ERTIAN

ertisement \ərt-əs-mənt\ advertisement, divertisement

ertium \ər-shəm\ SEE URTIUM

ertive \ərt-iv\ furtive, assertive, self-assertive, unassertive

erton \ərt-n\ SEE ERTAIN

ertor \ərt-ər\ SEE ERTER

erts \ərts\ certes, hertz, nerts, weltschmerz, gigahertz, kilohertz, megahertz—*also plurals and possessives of nouns and third person singular presents of verbs listed at* ¹ERT

erty \ər-tē\ SEE IRTY

ertz \ərts\ SEE ERTS

erule \er-əl\ SEE ERIL

erulent \er-ə-lənt\ sterilant, puberulent, pulverulent

erulous \er-ə-ləs\ SEE ERILOUS

erum \ir-əm\ theorem, serum

erund \er-ənd\ SEE ERRAND

erunt \er-ənt\ SEE ¹ARENT

erval \ər-vəl\ SEE ERVIL

ervancy \ər-vən-sē\ SEE ERVENCY

ervant \ər-vənt\ fervent, servant, maidservant, manservant, observant

ervative \ər-vət-iv\ conservative, preservative, archconservative, neoconservative, semiconservative

ervator \ər-vət-ər\ SEE ERVITOR

erve \ərv\ curve, MIRV, nerve, serve, swerve, verve, conserve, deserve, disserve, hors d'oeuvre, incurve, innerve, observe, preserve,

reserve, self-serve, subserve, unnerve, unreserve

erved \ərvd\ nerved, decurved, deserved, recurved, reserved, underserved, unreserved— *also pasts of verbs listed at* ERVE

ervency \ər-vən-sē\ fervency, conservancy

ervent \ər-vənt\ see ERVANT

erver \ər-vər\ fervor, server, deserver, observer, timeserver

ervice \ər-vəs\ nervous, service, disservice, full-service, in-service, self-service, interservice

ervil \ər-vəl\ chervil, serval, servile

ervile \ər-vəl\ ERVIL

erviness \ər-vē-nəs\ nerviness, topsy-turviness

erving \ər-viŋ\ Irving, serving, deserving, self-serving, timeserving, unswerving

ervitor \ər-vət-ər\ servitor, conservator

ervor \ər-vər\ see ERVER

ervous \ər-vəs\ see ERVICE

ervy \ər-vē\ see URVY

erwick \er-ik\ see ¹ERIC

erwin \ər-wən\ Irwin, Sherwin

¹ery \er-ē\ see ¹ARY

²ery \ir-ē\ see EARY

eryl \er-əl\ see ERIL

erz \erts\ see ¹ERTZ

¹es \ā\ see ¹AY

²es \ās\ see ¹ACE

³es \āz\ see ¹AZE

⁴es \es\ see ESS

⁵es \ēz\ see EZE

e's \ēz\ see EZE

¹esa \ā-sə\ mesa, Mesa, presa, omasa, Teresa, Theresa

²esa \ā-zə\ presa, impresa, marchesa, Bel Paese, Maria Theresa

esage \es-ij\ see ESSAGE

¹esan \āz-ᵊn\ see AZON

²esan \ēz-ᵊn\ see EASON

esant \ez-ᵊnt\ bezant, peasant, pheasant, pleasant, present, unpleasant, omnipresent

esas \ā-zəs\ Marquesas—*also plurals and possessives of nouns listed at* ²ESA

esce \es\ see ESS

escence \es-ᵊns\ essence, candescence, concrescence, excrescence, florescence, fluorescence, pearlescence, pubescence, putrescence, quiescence, quintessence, senescence, tumescence, turgescence, virescence, acquiescence, adolescence, arborescence, coalescence, convalescence, decalescence, defervescence, deliquescence, detumescence, effervescence, efflorescence, evanescence, incandescence, inflorescence, iridescence, juvenescence, luminescence, obsolescence, opalescence, prepubescence, preadolescence

escency \es-ᵊn-sē\ excrescency, incessancy

escent \es-ᵊnt\ crescent, Crescent, candescent, canescent, concrescent, decrescent, depressant, excrescent, fluorescent, frutescent, incessant,

increscent, liquescent,
pearlescent, pubescent,
putrescent, quiescent,
rufescent, senescent,
suppressant, tumescent,
turgescent, virescent,
acaulescent, acquiescent,
adolescent, coalescent,
convalescent, detumescent,
effervescent, efflorescent,
arborescent, evanescent,
incandescent, inflorescent,
intumescent, irridescent,
juvenescent, luminescent,
opalescent, phosphorescent,
prepubescent, recrudescent,
viridescent, antidepressant,
preadolescent

escible \es-ə-bəl\ see ESSIBLE

escience \ēsh-əns\ nescience,
prescience

escive \es-iv\ see ESSIVE

esco \es-kō\ alfresco, barbaresco

escue \es-kyü\ fescue, rescue

¹ese \ēs\ see IECE

²ese \ēz\ see EZE

³ese \ā-sē\ see ACY

esence \ez-ᵊns\ pleasance,
presence, omnipresence

eseus \ē-sē-əs\ Theseus,
Tiresias

¹esh \esh\ crèche, flèche, flesh,
fresh, mesh, thresh, afresh,
bobeche, calèche, crème
fraîche, enmesh, gooseflesh,
horseflesh, immesh, parfleche,
refresh, tête-bêche,
Bangladesh, Gilgamesh,
intermesh, Marrakech, Andhra
Pradesh, Madhya Pradesh,
Uttar Pradesh, Himachral
Pradesh, Arunachal Pradesh

²esh \āsh\ see ¹ECHE

³esh \ash\ see ³ASH

eshed \esht\ fleshed, meshed—
also pasts of verbs listed at
¹ESH

eshen \esh-ən\ see ESSION

eshener \esh-ə-nər\ see
ESSIONER

esher \esh-ər\ see ESSURE

eshly \esh-lē\ fleshly, freshly,
specially, especially

eshment \esh-mənt\ fleshment,
enmeshment, refreshment

¹esi \ā-zē\ see AZY

²esi \ā-sē\ see ACY

¹esia \ē-shə\ geisha, Moesia,
Letitia, Lucretia, Magnesia,
Phoenicia, alpoecia

²esia \ē-zhə\ freesia, amnesia,
esthesia, frambesia, magnesia,
rafflesia, Silesia, Tunisia,
analgesia, anesthesia,
Austronesia, Indonesia,
Melanesia, Micronesia,
Polynesia, synesthesia

esial \ē-zē-əl\ mesial, ecclesial

¹esian \ē-zhən\ Friesian,
Frisian, lesion, adhesion,
Cartesian, cohesion, etesian,
Salesian, Austronesian,
holstein-friesian, Indonesian,
Melanesian, Micronesian,
Polynesian

²esian \ē-shən\ see ¹ETION

esias \ē-sē-əs\ see ESEUS

esicant \es-i-kənt\ see ESICCANT

esiccant \es-i-kənt\ desiccant,
vesicant

esidency \ez-əd-ən-sē\
presidency, residency,
nonresidency, vice-presidency

esident \ez-əd-ənt\ president,

resident, nonresident, vice-
president

esima \es-ə-mə\
Quinquagesima, Sexagesima,
Septuagesima

esimal \es-ə-məl\ centesimal,
millesimal, vigesimal,
duodecimal, planetesimal,
sexagesimal, infinitesimal

esin \ez-ᵊn\ resin, muezzin,
oleoresin

esion \ē-zhən\ see ¹ESIAN

esis \ē-səs\ Croesus, thesis,
tmesis, ascesis, askesis,
esthesis, mimesis, prosthesis,
anamnesis, catachresis,
catechesis, Dionysus,
exegesis, hyperkinesis,
Peloponnesus, psychokinesis,
telekinesis, amniocentesis

esium \ē-zē-əm\ see EZIUM

esive \ē-siv\ adhesive, cohesive,
self-adhesive

esk \esk\ see ESQUE

esley \es-lē\ see ESSLY

eslie \es-lē\ see ESSLY

esne \ēn\ see ³INE

¹eso \ā-sō\ peso, say-so

²eso \es-ō\ see ESSO

espass \es-pəs\ Thespis,
trespass

espis \es-pəs\ see ESPASS

espite \es-pət\ see ESPOT

espot \es-pət\ despot, respite

esque \esk\ desk, burlesque,
grotesque, moresque,
arabesque, Bunyanesque,
copydesk, gigantesque,
humoresque, Junoesque,
Kafkaesque, picaresque,
picturesque, plateresque,
Rubenesque, Romanesque,

sculpturesque, statuesque,
churrigueresque

ess \es\ bless, cess, chess, cress,
dress, ess, fess, guess, Hesse,
jess, less, loess, mess, ness,
press, s, stress, tress, yes,
abscess, access, address,
aggress, assess, caress,
clothespress, coatdress,
compress, confess, CS,
depress, digress, distress,
duress, egress, excess,
express, finesse, handpress,
headdress, housedress,
impress, ingress, largess,
Meknes, nightdress, noblesse,
obsess, oppress, outguess,
pantdress, possess, precess,
prestress, princess, process,
profess, progress, re-press,
recess, redress, regress,
repress, shirtdress, sidedress,
SS, success, sundress,
suppress, top-dress,
transgress, undress, unless,
winepress, ABS, acquiesce,
baroness, coalesce,
convalesce, DES, decompress,
deliquesce, derepress,
dispossess, effervesce,
effloresce, evanesce,
gentilesse, GR-S, IHS, in-
process, incandesce,
intumesce, inverness,
Inverness, letterpress,
luminesce, Lyonnesse,
minidress, nonetheless,
obsolesce, otherguess,
overdress, pennycress,
phosphoresce, politesse,
prepossess, preprocess,
recrudesce, repossess,

reprocess, retrogress, second-guess, SOS, sweaterdress, unsuccess, watercress, window-dress, another-guess, nevertheless

essa \es-ə\ see ³ESSE

essable \es-ə-bəl\ see ESSIBLE

essage \es-ij\ message, presage, expressage

essaly \es-ə-lē\ Cecily, Thessaly

essamine \es-mən\ see ESSMAN

essan \es-ᵊn\ see ESSEN

essancy \es-ᵊn-sē\ see ESCENCY

essant \es-ᵊnt\ see ESCENT

¹esse \es\ see ESS

²esse \es-ē\ see ESSY

³esse \es-ə\ Hesse, Odessa, Vanessa

essed \est\ see EST

essedly \es-əd-lē\ blessedly, confessedly, professedly, possessedly, self-possessedly

essel \es-əl\ see ¹ESTLE

essen \es-ᵊn\ Essen, lessen, lesson, messan, delicatessen

essence \es-ᵊns\ see ESCENCE

esser \es-ər\ see ESSOR

essex \es-iks\ Essex, Wessex

essful \es-fəl\ stressful, distressful, successful, unsuccessful

essian \esh-ən\ see ESSION

essible \es-ə-bəl\ decibel, accessible, addressable, compressible, confessable, depressible, expressible, impressible, processible, putrescible, suppressible, inaccessible, incompressible, inexpressible, insuppressible, irrepressible

essie \es-ē\ see ESSY

essile \es-əl\ see ¹ESTLE

ession \esh-ən\ cession, freshen, hessian, session, accession, aggression, compression, concession, confession, depression, digression, discretion, egression, expression, impression, ingression, obsession, oppression, possession, precession, procession, profession, progression, recession, refreshen, regression, repression, secession, succession, suppression, transgression, decompression, dispossession, indiscretion, intercession, intersession, introgression, misimpression, prepossession, reimpression, repossession, retrogression, self-confession, self-expression, self-possession, supersession

essional \esh-ə-nəl\ sessional, acessional, concessional, congressional, diagressional, expressional, obsessional, possessional, precessional, processional, professional, progressional, recessional, successional, paraprofessional, preprofessional, subprofessional, paraprofessional, semiprofessional

essioner \esh-ə-nər\ freshener, concessioner

essionist \esh-ə-nəst\ expressionist, repressionist, impressionist, secessionist

essity \es-tē\ see ESTY
essive \es-iv\ crescive,
aggressive, caressive,
compressive, concessive,
degressive, depressive,
digressive, excessive,
expressive, impressive,
ingressive, obsessive,
oppressive, possessive,
progressive, recessive,
regressive, successive,
suppressive, transgressive,
inexpressive, retrogressive,
unexpressive, manic-
depressive
essly \es-lē\ Leslie, Lesley,
Wesley, expressly
essman \es-mən\ chessman,
pressman, expressman,
jessamine, specimen
essment \es-mənt\ see ESTMENT
esso \es-ō\ gesso, espresso
esson \es-ᵊn\ see ESSEN
essor \es-ər\ dresser, guesser,
lesser, pressor, stressor,
addresser, aggressor, assessor,
caresser, compressor,
confessor, depressor,
expressor, hairdresser,
oppressor, processor,
professor, regressor, repressor,
successor, suppresssor,
transgressor, vinedresser,
antecessor, dispossessor,
intercessor, predecessor,
repossessor, second-guesser,
microprocessor,
multiprocessor
essory \es-ə-rē\ pessary,
accessory, possessory,
intercessory
essure \esh-ər\ pressure,

impressure, low-pressure,
refresher, acupressure,
overpressure
essy \es-ē\ Bessie, dressy, Jesse,
Jessie, messy
est \est\ best, breast, Brest,
chest, crest, gest, geste, guest,
hest, jessed, jest, lest, nest,
pest, prest, quest, rest, test,
tressed, vest, west, West,
wrest, zest, abreast, appressed,
armrest, arrest, attest,
backrest, beau geste, behest,
bequest, bird's-nest, celeste,
Celeste, compressed, congest,
conquest, contest, detest,
devest, digest, divest, egest,
field-test, flight-test, footrest,
gabfest, hard-pressed,
headrest, hillcrest, houseguest,
imprest, incest, infest, ingest,
inquest, interest, invest, low-
test, Mae West, Midwest,
molest, northwest, posttest,
pretest, professed, protest,
redbreast, repressed, request,
retest, revest, slugfest,
southwest, suggest, trapnest,
Trieste, t-test, unblessed,
undressed, unrest, unstressed,
almagest, anapest, Bucharest,
Budapest, decongest,
disinfest, disinvest, empty-
nest, galley-west, manifest,
north-northwest, palimpsest,
predigest, reinvest, rinderpest,
second-best, self-addressed,
self-confessed, self-interest,
self-possessed, supraprotest,
sweatervest, uninterest,
unprofessed, autosuggest,
disinterest, robin redbreast,

underinvest, thirty-second
rest—*also pasts of verbs
listed at* ESS

esta \es-tə\ cesta, cuesta, testa,
vesta, Vesta, Avesta, celesta,
egesta, fiesta, ingesta, siesta,
Zend-Avesta

estable \es-tə-bəl\ see ESTIBLE

estae \es-tē\ see ESTY

estal \es-t°l\ crestal, pestle,
vestal

estan \es-tən\ see ESTINE

estant \es-tənt\ arrestant,
contestant, infestant,
protestant, Protestant,
decongestant, disinfestant,
manifestant

este \est\ see EST

ested \es-təd\ bested, crested,
nested, tested, vested, time-
tested, barrel-chested, double-
breasted, hairy-chested,
indigested, single-breasted—
also pasts of verbs listed at
EST

ester \es-tər\ Chester, ester,
Esther, fester, Hester, jester,
Leicester, Lester, nester,
Nestor, pester, quaestor,
quester, questor, nester, tester,
wester, yester, zester,
ancestor, arrester, contester,
detester, digester, infester,
investor, Manchester,
molester, northwester,
Rochester, semester,
sequester, southwester,
sou'wester, suggester,
Sylvester, trimester,
Winchester, arbalester, empty-
nester, monoester, polyester

esti \es-tē\ see ESTY

estial \es-tē-əl\ celestial,
forestial

estible \es-tə-bəl\ testable,
comestible, detestable,
digestible, ingestible,
investable, suggestible,
incontestable, indigestible

estic \es-tik\ gestic, domestic,
majestic, anapestic,
catachrestic

estical \es-ti-kəl\ see ESTICLE

esticle \es-ti-kəl\ testicle,
catachrestical

estimate \es-tə-mət\ estimate,
guesstimate

estinate \es-tə-nət\ festinate,
predestinate

estine \es-tən\ destine, Preston,
Avestan, clandestine,
intestine, predestine

esting \es-tiŋ\ cresting, vesting,
westing, arresting

estion \es-chən\ question,
congestion, cross-question,
digestion, egestion, ingestion,
self-question, suggestion,
decongestion, indigestion,
self-suggestion,
autosuggestion

estis \es-təs\ cestus, testis,
Alcestis, asbestos, Hephaestus

estival \es-tə-vəl\ estival,
festival

estive \es-tiv\ festive, restive,
congestive, digestive,
egestive, ingestive,
suggestive, decongestive

¹**estle** \es-əl\ Bessel, Cecil,
decile, nestle, pestle, sessile,
trestle, vessel, wrestle, Indian-
wrestle

²**estle** \as-əl\ see ²ASSEL

³**estle** \əs-əl\ see USTLE

estless \est-ləs\ crestless,
restless

estment \es-mənt\ vestment,
arrestment, assessment,
divestment, impressment,
investment, disinvestment,
reinvestment

esto \es-tō\ pesto, presto,
manifesto

eston \es-tən\ see ESTINE

estor \es-tər\ see ESTER

estos \es-təs\ see ESTIS

estra \es-trə\ fenestra, orchestra,
palaestra, Clytemnestra

estral \es-trəl\ estral, kestrel,
ancestral, campestral,
fenestral, semestral, orchestral

estrel \es-trəl\ see ESTRAL

estress \es-trəs\ see ESTRUS

estrial \es-trē-əl\ semestrial,
terrestrial, extraterrestrial

estrian \es-trē-ən\ equestrian,
pedestrian

estrous \es-trəs\ see ESTRUS

estrum \es-trəm\ estrum,
sequestrum

estrus \es-trəs\ estrous, estrus,
ancestress

estry \es-trē\ vestry, ancestry

estuous \es-chə-wəs\
incestuous, tempestuous

esture \es-chər\ gesture, vesture

estus \es-təs\ see ESTIS

esty \es-tē\ chesty, testae, testy,
pesty, zesty, res gestae,
necessity, Tibesti

esus \ē-səs\ see ESIS

¹**et** \et\ bet, Bret, Brett, debt, et,
fret, get, jet, let, Lett, met,
net, pet, ret, set, stet, sweat,
Tet, threat, vet, wet, whet,

yet, abet, aigrette, Annette,
asset, Babette, backset,
baguette, banquette, barbette,
Barnet, Barnett, barquette,
barrette, beget, beset,
blanquette, boneset, brevet,
briquette, brochette, brunet,
burette, burnet, cadet,
cassette, cermet, Claudette,
Colette, coquet, coquette,
cornet, corselet, corvette,
coset, courgette, croquette,
curette, curvet, cuvette,
daleth, dinette, diskette,
dragnet, duet, egret, fan-jet,
fishnet, flechette, forget,
frisette, gazette, georgette,
Georgette, gillnet, godet,
grisette, handset, hard-set,
headset, ink-jet, inlet, inset,
Janette, Jeanette, Jeannette,
Juliet, kismet, layette,
lorgnette, lunette, Lynette,
maquette, Marquette, mind-
set, moonset, moquette,
motet, musette, Nanette,
Nannette, noisette, nonet,
nymphet, octet, offset, onset,
Osset, outlet, outset, paillette,
palet, pallette, palmette,
Paulette, pipette, piquet,
planchette, poussette, preset,
quartet, quickset, quintet,
raclette, ramet, regret, reset,
revet, rocket, roomette,
rosette, roulette, saw-whet,
septet, sestet, sextet, sharp-
set, soubrette, spinet, stylet,
sublet, subset, sunset, Syrette,
tacet, thickset, Tibet, toilette,
tonette, trijet, twinset, typeset,
unset, upset, vedette, vignette,

well-set, Yvette, aiguillette, alphabet, anchoret, andouilette, anisette, Antoinette, avocet, banneret, basinet, bassinet, bayonet, Bernadette, bobbinet, briolette, burgonet, calumet, canzonet, castanet, cellarette, chemisette, cigarette, clarinet, consolette, coronet, corselet, crepe suzette, dragonet, electret, en brochette, epaulet, epithet, etiquette, falconet, farmerette, featurette, flageolet, flannelette, guillemet, heavyset, jaconet, Juliett, kitchenette, Lafayette, landaulet, lanneret, launderette, Leatherette, luncheonette, maisonette, majorette, marmoset, marquisette, martinet, mignonette, minaret, minuet, miquelet, novelette, Olivet, oubliette, parapet, paupiette, photoset, pirouette, quodlibet, rondelet, Samoset, satinet, scilicet, sermonette, serviette, silhouette, sobriquet, solleret, somerset, Somerset, soviet, spinneret, statuette, stockinette, suffragette, superjet, swimmeret, taboret, thermoset, towelette, trebuchet, tricolette, underlet, usherette, vinaigrette, wagonette, analphabet, bachelorette, drum majorette, electrojet, Hospitalet, marionette, microcassette, micropipette, musique concrète, photo-offset, videlicet, audiocassette, caulifloweret, hail-fellow-well-met, Marie Antoinette, videocassette

²et \ā\ see ¹AY
³et \āt\ see ¹ATE
⁴et \es\ see ESS
¹eta \ät-ə\ see ²ATA
²eta \et-ə\ see ETTA
³eta \ēt-ə\ see ²ITA
¹etable \et-ə-bəl\ see ETTABLE
²etable \ēt-ə-bəl\ see EATABLE
¹etal \ēt-ᵊl\ beetle, betel, fetal, decretal, excretal
²etal \et-ᵊl\ see ETTLE
¹etan \et-ᵊn\ Breton, threaten, Cape Breton, Tibetan
²etan \ēt-ᵊn\ see ¹EATEN
etch \ech\ catch, etch, fetch, fletch, ketch, kvetch, lech, letch, retch, sketch, stretch, vetch, wretch, backstretch, homestretch, outstretch
etched \echt\ teched, farfetched—*also pasts of verbs listed at* ETCH
etcher \ech-ər\ etcher, catcher, fetcher, fletcher, Fletcher, lecher, sketcher, stretcher, cowcatcher, dogcatcher, eye-catcher, flycatcher, gnatcatcher
etching \ech-iŋ\ etching, fletching—*also present participles of verbs listed at* ETCH
etchy \ech-ē\ sketchy, stretchy, tetchy
¹ete \āt\ see ¹ATE
²ete \et\ see ¹ET
³ete \ēt\ see ¹EAT
⁴ete \ät-ē\ see ATY

ête \āt\ see ¹ATE

eted \ād\ see ¹ADE

etel \ēt-ᵊl\ see ETAL

etely \ēt-lē\ see EETLY

eteor \ēt-ē-ər\ meteor, confiteor—*also comparatives of adjectives listed at* EATY

eter \ēt-ər\ see ¹EATER

etera \e-trə\ see ETRA

eterate \et-ə-rət\ see ETERIT

eterit \et-ə-rət\ preterit, inveterate

etes \ēt-əs\ see ETUS

¹eth \eth\ Beth, breath, breadth, death, saith, Seth, snath, daleth, handbreadth, hairbreadth, Macbeth, Ashtoreth, isopleth, megadeath, shibboleth, Elisabeth, Elizabeth

²eth \ās\ see ¹ACE

³eth \āt\ see ¹ATE

⁴eth \et\ see ¹ET

etha \ē-thə\ Aretha, Ibiza

ethane \e-thān\ ethane, methane, nitromethane, dichloroethane

ethe \ē-thē\ see EATHY

¹ether \eth-ər\ blether, feather, heather, Heather, leather, nether, tether, weather, wether, whether, aweather, bellwether, pinfeather, together, untether, altogether, get-together

²ether \əth-ər\ see ¹OTHER

ethic \eth-ik\ ethic, erethic

ethral \ē-thrəl\ urethral, bulbourethral

ethyl \eth-əl\ bethel, Ethel, ethyl, methyl, triethyl

¹eti \ēt-ē\ see EATY

²eti \āt-ē\ see ATY

etia \ē-shə\ see ¹ESIA

etian \ē-shən\ see ¹ETION

¹etic \ēt-ik\ thetic, acetic, docetic

etic \et-ik\ etic, thetic, aesthetic, ascetic, athletic, balletic, bathetic, cosmetic, docetic, eidetic, emetic, frenetic, gametic, genetic, hermetic, kinetic, limnetic, magnetic, mimetic, noetic, Ossetic, paretic, pathetic, phenetic, phonetic, phrenetic, phyletic, poetic, prophetic, prosthetic, pyretic, splenetic, syncretic, syndetic, synthetic, tonetic, Venetic, alphabetic, analgetic, anesthetic, antithetic, apathetic, asyndetic, copacetic, cybernetic, diabetic, dietetic, digenetic, diphyletic, diuretic, empathetic, energetic, epithetic, geodetic, homiletic, Masoretic, nomothetic, parenthetic, sympathetic, synergetic, synesthetic, aeromagnetic, antimagnetic, antipathetic, antipoetic, antipyretic, apologetic, epexigetic, epigenetic, ferrimagnetic, ferromagnetic, geomagnetic, gyromagnetic, homogametic, hydrokinetic, hydromagnetic, hyperkinetic, isomagnetic, monophyletic, morphogenetic, ontogenetic, optokinetic, palingenetic, paramagnetic, pathogenetic, peripatetic, phylogenetic, polyphyletic, psychokinetic, telekinetic, thermomagnetic, aposiopetic, cyanogenetic, electrokinetic, electromagnetic, heterogametic, parasympathetic, parthenogenetic, psychotomimetic, unapologetic, onomatopoetic

etical \et-i-kəl\ metical, reticle, aesthetical, genetical, heretical, phonetical, antithetical, arithmetical, catechetical, cybernetical, epithetical, exegetical, geodetical, hypothetical, parenthetical, theoretical, atheoretical, epexegetical

eticist \et-ə-səst\ geneticist, kineticist, cyberneticist

etics \et-iks\ aesthetics, athletics, genetics, homiletics, kinetics, phonetics, poetics, tonetics, cybernetics, dietetics, apologetics, cytogenetics, immunogenetics—*also plurals and possessives of nouns listed at* ETIC

etid \et-əd\ fetid, fretted, sweated, indebted, parapeted—*also pasts of verbs listed at* ¹ET

etin \ēt-ᵊn\ see ¹EATEN

¹etion \ē-shən\ Grecian, accretion, Capetian, completion, concretion, deletion, depletion, excretion, Ossetian, Phoenician, repletion, secretion, suppletion, Tahitian, Austronesian, Diocletian,

Melanesian, Polynesian, Taracahitian

²etion \esh-ən\ see ESSION

etious \ē-shəs\ see ECIOUS

¹etis \ēt-əs\ see ETUS

²etis \et-əs\ see ETTUCE

etist \et-əst\ cornetist, librettist, vignettist, clarinetist, exegetist, operettist—*also superlatives of adjectives listed at* ¹ET

etitive \et-ət-iv\ competitive, repetitive, uncompetitive, anticompetitive

etium \ē-shē-əm\ see ECIUM

etius \ē-shəs\ see ECIOUS

etive \ēt-iv\ accretive, completive, decretive, depletive, secretive, suppletive

¹etl \ät-ᵊl\ see ATAL

²etl \et-ᵊl\ see ETTLE

etland \et-lənd\ Shetland, wetland

etment \et-mənt\ abetment, besetment, curettement, revetment

¹eto \āt-ō\ see ²ATO

²eto \ēt-ō\ see ¹ITO

eton \ēt-ᵊn\ see ¹EATEN

¹etor \et-ər\ see ETTER

²etor \ēt-ər\ see ¹EATER

etory \ēt-ə-rē\ eatery, decretory, secretory, suppletory

etous \ēt-əs\ see ETUS

¹etra \e-trə\ Petra, tetra, etcetera

²etra \ē-trə\ Petra, Kenitra

¹etral \ē-trəl\ petrel, retral

²etral \e-trəl\ see ¹ETREL

être \etrᵊ\ fête champêtre, raison d'être

¹etrel \e-trəl\ petrel, petrol, retral

²etrel \ē-trəl\ see ¹ETRAL

etric \e-trik\ metric, obstetric, symmetric, asymmetric, barometric, decametric, dekametric, diametric, dissymmetric, geometric, hypsometric, isometric, optometric, psychometric, telemetric, volumetric, acidometric, amperometric, sociometric

etrical \e-tri-kəl\ metrical, obstetrical, symmetrical, asymmetrical, barometrical, diametrical, geometrical, unsymmetrical

etrics \e-triks\ obstetrics, geometrics, isometrics, sabermetrics

etrist \e-trəst\ metrist, belletrist

etrol \e-trəl\ see ¹ETREL

ets \ets\ let's, Donets, rillettes, Steinmetz, pantalets, solonetz, Sosnowiec—*also plurals and possessives of nouns and third person singular presents of verbs listed at* ¹ET

etsk \etsk\ Donetsk, Kuznetsk, Lipetsk, Novokuznetsk

ett \et\ see ¹ET

etta \et-ə\ betta, Etta, feta, geta, Greta, Quetta, biretta, cabretta, galleta, Loretta, mozzetta, pancetta, poinsettia, Rosetta, Valletta, vendetta, anchoveta, arietta, cabaletta, Henrietta, Marietta, operetta, sinfonietta

ettable \et-ə-bəl\ retable, wettable, forgettable, regrettable, unforgettable

ette \et\ see ¹ET

etter \et-ər\ better, bettor, debtor, fetter, getter, letter, netter, rhetor, setter, sweater, tetter, wetter, whetter, abettor, begetter, bonesetter, enfetter, gill-netter, go-getter, jet-setter, newsletter, pacesetter, pinsetter, red-letter, regretter, trendsetter, typesetter, unfetter, vignetter, carburetter—*also comparatives of adjectives listed at* ¹ET

ettered \et-ərd\ fettered, lettered, unfettered, unlettered

ettes \ets\ see ETS

ettia \et-ə\ see ETTA

ettie \et-ē\ see ¹ETTY

ettier \it-ē-ər\ see ITTIER

ettiness \it-ē-nəs\ see ITTINESS

etting \et-iŋ\ netting, setting, bed-wetting, bloodletting, go-getting, onsetting, typesetting, thermosetting, phototypesetting

ettish \et-ish\ fetish, Lettish, pettish, wettish, coquettish, novelettish

ettle \et-ᵊl\ fettle, kettle, metal, mettle, nettle, petal, settle, shtetl, bimetal, gunmetal, nonmetal, teakettle, unsettle, Citlaltepetl, Popocatepetl

ettlesome \et-ᵊl-səm\ mettlesome, nettlesome

ettling \et-liŋ\ fettling, settling, unsettling

etto \et-ō\ ghetto, stretto, cavetto, falsetto, in petto,

larghetto, libretto, palmetto,
stiletto, zucchetto, allegretto,
amaretto, amoretto, fianchetto,
Kazan Retto, lazaretto,
Tintoretto, vaporetto

ettor \et-ər\ see ETTER

ettuce \et-əs\ lettuce, Thetis,
Hymettus

ettus \et-əs\ see ETTUCE

¹etty \et-ē\ Betty, jetty, Nettie,
netty, petit, petty, sweaty,
yeti, brown Betty, cavetti,
confetti, libretti, machete,
Rossetti, spaghetti, amoretti,
Donizetti, Serengeti,
spermacetti, cappelletti,
cavalletti, vaporetti

²etty \it-ē\ see ITTY

etum \ēt-əm\ pinetum,
arboretum, equisetum

etus \ēt-əs\ Cetus, fetus, Thetis,
treatise, acetous, Admetus,
boletus, coitus, quietus,
diabetes

etzsche \ē-chē\ see EACHY

euben \ü-bən\ Cuban, Reuben,
Ruben, von Steuben

euce \üs\ see ¹USE

euced \ü-səd\ see UCID

eucey \ü-sē\ see UICY

euch \ük\ see UKE

euchre \ü-kər\ see UCRE

eucid \ü-səd\ see UCID

¹eud \üd\ see UDE

²eud \öid\ see ¹OID

eudal \üd-ᵊl\ see OODLE

eudist \üd-əst\ see ¹UDIST

eudo \üd-ō\ see UDO

eue \ü\ see ¹EW

euer \ü-ər\ see ¹EWER

euil \āl\ see AIL

euille \ē\ see ¹EE

euk \ük\ see UKE

eukin \ü-kən\ see UCAN

¹eul \əl\ see ¹ULL

²eul \ərl\ see ¹IRL

eulah \ü-lə\ see ULA

eulean \ü-lē-ən\ see ULEAN

¹eum \ē-əm\ geum, lyceum,
museum, no-see-um, odeum,
per diem, Te Deum,
athenaeum, coliseum,
colosseum, hypogeum,
mausoleum

²eum \ā-əm\ see AHUM

³eum \üm\ see ¹OOM

euma \ü-mə\ see UMA

eume \üm\ see ¹OOM

eumon \ü-mən\ see UMAN

eumy \ü-mē\ see OOMY

eunice \ü-nəs\ see EWNESS

eunt \ùnt\ see ¹UNT

eunuch \ü-nik\ see UNIC

¹eur \ər\ birr, blur, buhr, burr,
Burr, chirr, churr, cur, curr,
err, fir, for, fur, her, knur,
murre, myrrh, per, purr, shirr,
sir, skirr, slur, spur, stir, thir,
'twere, were, whir, your,
you're, à deux, as per, astir,
auteur, aver, bestir, chasseur,
chauffeur, claqueur, coiffeur,
concur, confer, danseur, defer,
demur, deter, douceur, du
jour, farceur, flaneur, friseur,
frondeur, hauteur, him/her,
his/her, incur, infer, inter,
jongleur, larkspur, liqueur,
longspur, masseur, Malmö,
millefleur, occur, Pasteur,
poseur, prefer, recur, refer,
sandbur, sandspur, seigneur,
transfer, voyeur, accoucheur,
amateur, cocklebur,

colporteur, connoisseur, cri de coeur, cross-refer, cubature, curvature, de rigueur, disinter, force majeure, franc-tireur, monseigneur, nonconcur, pasticheur, prosateur, raconteur, rapporteur, regisseur, saboteur, secateur, underfur, voyageur, arbitrageur, carillonneur, conglomerateur, entrepreneur, litterateur, provocateur, restaurateur, agent provocateur

²eur \úr\ see ¹URE

eure \ər\ see ¹EUR

eurial \úr-ē-əl\ see ¹URIAL

eurish \ər-ish\ see OURISH

eurs \ərz\ see ¹ERS

eury \úr-ē\ see ¹URY

¹eus \ē-əs\ Aeneas, Aggeus, Alpheus, Arius, Chryseis, Linnaeus, Micheas, Piraeus, uraeus, coryphaeus, epigeous, scarabaeus, prelate nullius, Duque de Caxias, Judas Maccabaeus

²eus \üs\ see ¹USE

¹euse \əz\ buzz, 'cause, coz, does, fuzz, 'twas, was, abuzz, because, outdoes, undoes, overdoes

²euse \üs\ see ¹USE

³euse \üz\ see ²USE

¹eusel \ü-səl\ see ¹USAL

²eusel \ü-zəl\ see ²USAL

eut \üt\ see UTE

euter \üt-ər\ see UTER

euth \üth\ see ²OOTH

eutian \ü-shən\ see UTION

eutic \üt-ik\ see UTIC

eutical \üt-i-kəl\ see UTICAL

eutics \üt-iks\ toreutics, hermeneutics, therapeutics

eutist \üt-əst\ see UTIST

euton \üt-ᵊn\ see UTAN

eutonist \üt-ᵊn-əst\ see UTENIST

euve \əv\ see ¹OVE

euver \ü-vər\ see ³OVER

¹eux \ü\ see ¹EW

²eux \ər\ see ¹EUR

¹ev \ef\ see ¹EF

²ev \óf\ see ²OFF

eva \ē-və\ see ²IVA

eval \ē-vəl\ see IEVAL

evalent \ev-ə-lənt\ see EVOLENT

¹evan \ē-vən\ see EVEN

²evan \ev-ən\ see EAVEN

¹eve \ev\ breve, rev, Sevres, Negev, alla breve

²eve \ēv\ see ¹EAVE

evel \ev-əl\ bevel, devil, level, Neville, revel, baselevel, bedevil, bi-level, daredevil, dishevel, go-devil, split-level, entry-level

eveler \ev-lər\ leveler, reveler

evelly \ev-ə-lē\ heavily, levelly, reveille

evement \ēv-mənt\ achievement, aggrievement, bereavement, underachievement

even \ē-vən\ even, Stephen, Steven, breakeven, break-even, Genevan, Kesteven, uneven

eventh \ev-ənth\ seventh, eleventh

¹ever \ev-ər\ clever, ever, lever, never, sever, Trevor, dissever, endeavor, forever, however, soever, whatever, whenever, wherever, whichever,

whoever, whomever,
cantilever, howsoever, live-
forever, whatsoever,
whencesoever, whensoever,
wheresoever, whichsoever,
whomsoever, whosesoever,
whosoever, whithersoever

²**ever** \ē-vər\ see IEVER

everage \ev-rij\ beverage,
leverage

everence \ev-rəns\ reverence,
severance, disseverance,
irreverence

every \ev-rē\ every, reverie

eves \ēvz\ see EAVES

eviate \ē-vē-ət\ deviate, qiviut

evice \ev-əs\ clevis, crevice,
Ben Nevis

evil \ē-vəl\ see IEVAL

eville \ē-vəl\ see EVEL

evilry \ev-əl-rē\ devilry, revelry

evin \ev-ən\ see EAVEN

evious \ē-vē-əs\ devious,
previous

¹**evis** \ev-əs\ see EVICE

²**evis** \ē-vəs\ see EVUS

evity \ev-ət-ē\ brevity, levity,
longevity

evo \ē-vō\ in vivo, relievo, ring-
a-lievo, alto-relievo, basso-
relievo, mezzo-relievo,
recitativo, Antananavivo

evocable \ev-ə-kə-bəl\
evocable, revocable,
irrevocable

evolence \ev-ə-ləns\ prevalence,
benevolence, malevolence

evolent \ev-ə-lənt\ prevalent,
benevolent, malevolent

evor \ev-ər\ see ¹EVER

evous \ē-vəs\ grievous, Nevis,

nevus, longevous, redivivus,
Saint Kitts and Nevis

evsk \efsk\ see EFSK

evus \ē-vəs\ see EVOUS

evy \ev-ē\ bevy, heavy, levee,
levy, replevy, top-heavy

¹**ew** \ü\ blue, boo, brew, chew,
clew, clue, coo, coup, crew,
cue, dew, do, doux, drew,
due, ewe, few, flew, flu, flue,
fou, glue, gnu, goo, hew, hue,
Hugh, Jew, knew, lieu, loo,
Lou, mew, moo, moue, mu,
new, nu, ooh, pew, phew, piu,
pooh, prau, q, queue, roux,
rue, screw, shoe, shoo, shrew,
Sioux, skew, slew, slough,
slue, smew, sou, sous, spew,
sprue, stew, strew, sue, Sue,
thew, threw, thro, through, to,
too, true, two, u, view, whew,
who, woo, Wu, xu, yew, you,
zoo, accrue, adieu, ado,
aircrew, airscrew, anew,
Anjou, askew, au jus, Baku,
bamboo, battu, battue, bedew,
beshrew, bestrew, bijou,
boubou, brand-new,
breakthrough, burgoo, cachou,
can-do, canoe, caoutchouc,
Cebu, Cheng-du, Chongju,
Chonju, construe, Corfu,
corkscrew, coypu, CQ, debut,
ecu, endue, ensue, eschew,
floor-through, fondue, fordo,
foreknew, Gansu, Gentoo,
Gifu, gansun, gumshoe, guru,
hairdo, hereto, Honshu,
horseshoe, how-to, HQ, Hutu,
imbrue, imbue, IQ, jackscrew,
K2, Kansu, karoo, Karoo,
kazoo, Khufu, kung fu,

Kwangju, leadscrew, lean-to,
make-do, Matthew, me-too,
mildew, milieu, miscue,
misdo, misknew, muumuu,
Nehru, non-U, old-shoe, one-
two, outdo, outgrew, perdu,
Peru, poilu, preview, pursue,
purview, ragout, redo, renew,
Ren Crew, review, revue,
rough-hew, run-through,
sandshoe, see-through, set-to,
setscrew, shampoo, Shih Tzu,
skiddoo, snafu, snowshoe,
soft-shoe, span-new, subdue,
surtout, taboo, Taegu, tattoo,
thank-you, thereto,
thumbscrew, to-do, too-too,
undo, undue, unglue,
unscrew, untrue, vatu,
vendue, venue, vertu, virtu,
wahoo, walk-through,
wherethrough, whereto, who's
who, withdrew, worldview,
aperçu, avenue, babassu,
ballyhoo, barbecue, barley-
broo, billet-doux, black-and-
blue, buckaroo, bugaboo,
callaloo, caribou, catechu,
clerihew, cockapoo, cockatoo,
Cotonou, counterview, déjà
vu, derring-do, detinue,
feverfew, follow-through,
gardyloo, hitherto, honeydew,
Ignaçu, ingenue, interview,
IOU, jabiru, Jiangsu,
kangaroo, Kathmandu,
kinkajou, loup-garou, Makalu,
manitou, marabou, Masaru,
Montague, Montesquieu,
ormolu, overdo, overdue,
overflew, overgrew, overshoe,
overstrew, overthrough,
overview, parvenu, parvenue,
pas de deux, passe-partout,
PDQ, peekaboo, Port Salut,
rendezvous, residue, retinue,
revenue, Richelieu, Ryukyu,
seppuku, Shikoku, succès fou,
switcheroo, talking-to,
teleview, Telugu, thereunto,
thirty-two, thitherto,
Timbuktu, tinamou, trou-de-
loup, twenty-two, view
halloo, vindaloo, wallaroo,
waterloo, well-to-do, whoop-
de-do, Xanadu, Aracaju,
Brian Boru, didgeridoo,
hullabaloo, Kota Bharu, Nova
Iguaçu, Ouagadougou,
pirarucu, Port du Salut, tu-
whit tu-whoo, Vanuatu,
Daman and Diu, Guangxi
Zhuangzu, Ningxia Huizu,
Havant and Waterloo
²ew \ō\ see ¹OW
¹ewable \ō-ə-bəl\ see ¹OWABLE
²ewable \ü-ə-bəl\ see UABLE
ewage \ü-ij\ brewage, sewage
ewal \ü-əl\ see ¹UEL
ewar \ü-ər\ see ¹EWER
¹eward \ùrd\ see ¹URED
²eward \ü-ərd\ Seward, steward
ewd \üd\ see UDE
ewdness \üd-nəs\ see UDINOUS
¹ewe \ō\ see ¹OW
²ewe \ü\ see ¹EW
ewed \üd\ see UDE
ewee \ē-wē\ see EEWEE
ewel \ü-əl\ see ¹UEL
eweled \üld\ see OOLED
ewell \ü-əl\ see ¹UEL
¹ewer \ü-ər\ brewer, chewer,
dewar, doer, ewer, fewer,
hewer, queuer, screwer,

sewer, skewer, spewer, suer, viewer, wooer, you're, horseshoer, me-tooer, misdoer, previewer, renewer, reviewer, shampooer, snowshoer, tattooer, undoer, wrongdoer, barbecuer, evildoer, interviewer, revenuer, televiewer—*also comparatives of adjectives listed at* ¹EW

²**ewer** \ùr\ see ¹URE

³**ewer** \ō-ər\ see ⁴OER

ewerage \ùr-ij\ see ¹OORAGE

ewery \ùr-ē\ see ¹URY

ewess \ü-əs\ Jewess, lewis, Lewis, Louis, Luis, Port Louis, Saint Louis

ewey \ü-ē\ see EWY

ewie \ü-ē\ see EWY

¹**ewing** \ō-iŋ\ see ¹OING

²**ewing** \ù-iŋ\ see ²OING

ewis \ü-əs\ see EWESS

ewish \ü-ish\ bluish, Jewish, newish, shrewish, aguish

ewl \ül\ see ¹OOL

ewless \ü-ləs\ clueless, crewless, dewless, shoeless, viewless

ewly \ü-lē\ see ULY

ewman \ü-mən\ see UMAN

ewment \ü-mənt\ strewment, accruement

ewn \ün\ see ¹OON

ewness \ü-nəs\ blueness, dueness, Eunice, newness, skewness, Tunis, askewness

ewpie \ü-pē\ see OOPY

ewry \ùr-ē\ see ¹URY

ews \üz\ see ²USE

ewsman \üz-mən\ bluesman, newsman

ewsy \ü-zē\ see OOZY

ewt \üt\ see UTE

ewter \üt-ər\ see UTER

ewterer \üt-ər-ər\ see UITERER

ewton \üt-ᵊn\ see UTAN

ewy \ü-ē\ bluey, buoy, chewy, Dewey, dewy, flooey, gluey, gooey, hooey, Louie, Louis, newie, phooey, rouille, screwy, sloughy, viewy, chop suey, mildewy, Port Louis, ratatouille, waterzooi

ex \eks\ dex, ex, flex, hex, lex, rex, Rex, sex, specs, vex, x, annex, apex, carex, codex, complex, convex, cortex, culex, desex, duplex, DX, fourplex, ibex, ilex, index, Kleenex, Lastex, latex, mirex, murex, MX, narthex, perplex, Perspex, pollex, Pyrex, reflex, remex, Rx, scolex, silex, silvex, simplex, spandex, telex, Tex-Mex, triplex, unsex, vertex, videotex, vortex, analects, belowdecks, biconvex, circumflex, cross-index, googolplex, haruspex, intersex, Malcolm X, Middlesex, multiplex, PBX, pontifex, retroflex, spinifex, subindex, unisex—*also plurals and possessives of nouns and third person singular presents of verbs listed at* ECK

exas \ek-səs\ see EXUS

exed \ekst\ see EXT

exedly \ek-səd-lē\ vexedly, perplexedly

exer \ek-sər\ flexor, hexer,

duplexer, indexer,
multiplexer, demultiplexer

exia \ek-sē-ə\ dyslexia, anorexia

exic \ek-sik\ dyslexic, anorexic

exical \ek-si-kəl\ lexical,
indexical, nonlexical

exion \ek-shən\ see ECTION

exis \ek-səs\ see EXUS

exity \ek-sət-ē\ complexity,
convexity, perplexity

exor \ek-sər\ see EXER

ext \ekst\ next, sexed, sext, text,
vexed, context, deflexed,
inflexed, perplexed, plaintext,
pretext, reflexed, subtext,
urtext, ciphertext, oversexed,
teletext, undersexed—*also
pasts of verbs listed at* EX

extant \ek-stənt\ extant, sextant

exterous \ek-strəs\ dexterous,
ambidextrous

extrous \ek-strəs\ see
EXTEROUS

extual \eks-chəl\ textual,
contextual, subtextual

exual \eksh-wəl\ sexual,
asexual, bisexual, effectual,
pansexual, transsexual,
ambisexual, homosexual,
hypersexual, intersexual,
parasexual, psychosexual,
unisexual, heterosexual,
sociosexual, anti-intellectual

exural \ek-shrəl\ see [2]ECTURAL

exus \ek-səs\ lexis, nexus,
plexus, texas, Texas, Alexis

exy \ek-sē\ prexy, sexy,
apoplexy

[1]**ey** \ā\ see [1]AY

[2]**ey** \ē\ see [1]EE

[3]**ey** \ī\ see [1]Y

[1]**eya** \ā-ə\ see [1]AIA

[2]**eya** \ē-ə\ see [1]IA

eyance \ā-əns\ abeyance,
conveyance, purveyance,
surveillance, reconveyance

eyant \ā-ənt\ mayn't, abeyant,
surveillant

eyas \ī-əs\ see IAS

ey'd \ād\ see [1]ADE

eye \ī\ see [1]Y

[1]**eyed** \ēd\ see EED

[2]**eyed** \īd\ see [1]IDE

eyedness \īd-nəs\ eyedness,
snideness, cockeyedness

eyeless \ī-ləs\ see ILUS

eyelet \ī-lət\ see ILOT

eyen \īn\ see [1]INE

[1]**eyer** \ā-ər\ see [1]AYER

[2]**eyer** \īr\ see [1]IRE

eyes \īz\ see IZE

eying \ā-iŋ\ see AYING

[1]**ey'll** \āl\ see AIL

[2]**ey'll** \el\ see [1]EL

eyn \in\ see [1]IN

eynes \ānz\ see AINS

eyness \ā-nəs\ see AYNESS

eyor \ā-ər\ see [1]AYER

ey're \er\ see [4]ARE

eyre \er\ see [4]ARE

eyrie \īr-ē\ see [1]IRY

eys \ēz\ see EZE

eyser \ī-zər\ see IZER

eyte \ā-tē\ see ATY

ey've \āv\ see [2]AVE

[1]**ez** \ez\ see [1]AYS

[2]**ez** \ā\ see [1]AY

[3]**ez** \ās\ see [1]ACE

eza \ē-zə\ Giza, Lisa, Pisa, visa,
mestiza, lespedeza

eze \ēz\ bise, breeze, cheese,
ease, feaze, feeze, freeze,
frieze, he's, jeez, lees, please,
res, seize, she's, sleaze,

sneeze, squeeze, tease, tweeze, wheeze, Andes, appease, Aries, Belize, betise, Burmese, camise, Castries, cerise, chemise, Chinese, deep-freeze, Deep-freeze, degrease, Denise, disease, displease, disseise, d.t.'s, Elise, fasces, fauces, Ganges, headcheese, heartsease, Hermes, Kirghiz, Louise, Maltese, marquise, menses, nates, Pisces, quick-freeze, Ramses, reprise, sharp-freeze, soubise, striptease, Tabriz, Thales, trapeze, unease, unfreeze, Xerxes, Amboinese, Androcles, Annamese, antifreeze, Assamese, Balinese, Brooklynese, Cantonese, Cervantes, Chersonese, Congolese, Cyclades. Damocles, diocese, Eloise, Erinyes, expertise, Faeroese, federalese, genovese, gourmandise, Hebrides, Heracles, Hercules, Hunanese, Hyades, Japanese, Javanese, Johnsonese, journalese, Kanarese, Lake Louise, legalese, litotes, manganese, Nipponese, overseas, Pekinese, Pekingese, Pericles, Pleiades, Portuguese, Pyrenees, Siamese, Silures, Sinhalese, Socrates, Sophocles, Sporades, Albigenses, antipodes, Aragonese, archdiocese, Averroës, bona fides, bureaucratese, cheval-de-frise, computerese, Diogenes, Dodecanese, Eumenides, Euripides, Florida Keys, Gaucher's disease, governmentese, Great Pyrenees, Hesperides, Hippocrates, Hippomenes, Hodgkin's disease, Indo-Chinese, nephritides, officialese, pentagonese, Philoctetes, Sammarinese, superficies, telegraphese, Themistocles, Thucydides, Vietnamese, Alcibiades, Aristophanes, educationese, ferromanganese, Lou Gehrig's disease, Mephistopheles, sociologese, sword of Damocles, muscae volitantes, Pillars of Hercules—*also plurals and possessives of nouns and third person singular presents of verbs listed at* ¹EE

ezel \ē-zəl\ see EASEL

ezi \ē-zē\ see ¹EASY

ezium \ē-zē-əm\ cesium, magnesium, trapezium

ezzle \ez-əl\ bezel, embezzle

i

¹i \ē\ see ¹EE

²i \ī\ see ¹Y

³i \ā\ see ¹AY

¹ia \ē-ə\ Gaea, kea, Leah, Mia, rhea, Rhea, rya, via, Achaea, Crimea, althaea, Apia, Bahia, buddleia, cabrilla, cattleya, Chaldea, Euboea, Hygeia, idea, Judea, Kaffiyeh, Korea, mantilla, Maria, Medea, mens rea, Morea, Nicaea, ohia, Omiya, Oriya, ouguiya, rupiah, sangria, Sofia, Sophia, spirea, tortilla, Baile Atha Cliath, Banranquilla, barathea, bougainvillea, camarilla, Caesarea, cascarilla, Cytherea, dulcinea, Eritrea, fantasia, Galatea, gonorrhea, granadilla, hamartia, Hialeah, Idumea, Ikaria, Jicarilla, Kampuchea, latakia, Latakia, logorrhea, Manzanilla, mausolea, mythopoeia, Nabatea, Nicosia, panacea, Parousia, pizzeria, ratafia, sabadilla, Santeria, sapodilla, seguidilla, sinfonia, Tanzania, trattoria, alfilaria, Andalucia, Andalusia, Ave Maria, Cassiopeia, Diego Garcia, echeveria, Ismailia, peripeteia, pharmacopoeia, prosopopoeia, onomatopoeia, Joseph of Arimathea

²ia \ī-ə\ see ¹IAH

³ia \ä\ see ¹A

¹iable \ī-ə-bəl\ dryable, dyeable, flyable, friable, liable, pliable, triable, viable, deniable, inviable, reliable, certifiable, classifiable, justifiable, liquefiable, notifiable, pacifiable, qualifiable, quantifiable, rectifiable, satisfiable, specifiable, undeniable, unifiable, verifiable, emulsifiable, identifiable, unfalsifiable

²iable \ē-ə-bəl\ see EEABLE

iacal \ī-ə-kəl\ dandiacal, heliacal, maniacal, theriacal, zodiacal, ammoniacal, elegiacal, simoniacal, dipsomaniacal, egomaniacal, hypochondriacal, monomaniacal, nympomaniacal, pyromaniacal, paradisiacal, bibliomaniacal, megalomaniacal

iad \ī-əd\ see YAD

¹iah \ī-ə\ ayah, maya, Maya, playa, Praia, stria, via, Aglaia, Mariah, messiah, papaya, pariah, Thalia, Hezekiah, jambalaya, Jeremiah, Nehemiah, Obadiah, Surabaja, Zechariah, Zephaniah, Atchafalaya, Iphigenia, peripeteia

²iah \ē-ə\ see ¹IA

¹ial \ī-əl\ dial, diel, pial, redial

²ial \īl\ see ¹ILE

ialer \ī-lər\ see ILAR

ially \ē-ə-lē\ see ¹EALLY

iam \ī-əm\ Priam, per diem

¹ian \ē-ən\ see ¹EAN

²ian \ī-ən\ see ¹ION

iance \ī-əns\ science, affiance, alliance, appliance, compliance, defiance, nonscience, reliance, mesalliance, misalliance

iancy \ī-ən-sē\ pliancy, compliancy

ianist \ē-t-nist\ pianist, Indo-Europeanist

iant \ī-ənt\ Bryant, client, giant, pliant, riant, affiant, compliant, defiant, reliant, incompliant, self-reliant, supergiant

iao \aù\ see ²OW

iaour \aùr\ see ²OWER

iaper \ī-pər\ see IPER

iar \īr\ see ¹IRE

¹iary \ī-ə-rē\ diary, fiery, miry, priory

²iary \īr-ē\ see ¹IRY

¹ias \ī-əs\ Aias, bias, dais, eyas, Laius, Lias, pious, Pius, Abdias, Elias, Messias, Nehemias, Tobias, Ananias, Jeremias, Malachias, Roncesvalles, Sophonias, Zacharias, Mount Saint Elias

²ias \ē-əs\ see ¹EUS

³ias \äsh\ see ¹ASH

iasis \ī-ə-səs\ diesis, diocese, archdiocese, psoriasis, acariasis, amebiasis, ascariasis, bilharziasis, helminthiasis, leishmaniasis, satyriasis, elephantiasis, hypochondriasis, schistosomiasis

¹iat \ē-ət\ see ¹EIT

²iat \ī-ət\ see IET

iate \ī-ət\ see IET

¹iath \ī-əth\ Wyeth, Goliath

²iath \ē-ə\ see ¹IA

iatry \ī-ə-trē\ podiatry, psychiatry

iaus \aùs\ see ²OUSE

iaz \äsh\ see ¹ASH

¹ib \ib\ bib, bibb, crib, drib, fib, gib, glib, jib, lib, nib, rib, sib, squib, ad-lib, corncrib, midrib, sahib, memsahib

²ib \ēb\ see ²EBE

³ib \ēv\ see ²EAVE

iba \ē-bə\ see EBA

ibable \ī-bə-bəl\ bribable, ascribable, describable, indescribable

ibal \ī-bəl\ bible, Bible, libel, scribal, tribal

ibb \ib\ see ¹IB

ibband \ib-ən\ see IBBON

ibbed \ibd\ bibbed, rock-ribbed—*also pasts of verbs listed at* ¹IB

ibber \ib-ər\ bibber, cribber, dibber, fibber, gibber, glibber, jibber, libber, ribber

ibbet \ib-ət\ gibbet, exhibit, inhibit, prohibit, flibbertigibbet

ibbing \ib-iŋ\ cribbing, ribbing

ibble \ib-əl\ dibble, dribble, fribble, gribble, kibble, nibble, quibble, scribble, sibyl, Sibyl

ibbler \ib-lər\ dribbler, nibbler, quibbler, scribbler

ibbly \ib-lē\ dribbly, ghibli, glibly

ibbon \ib-ən\ gibbon, Gibbon, ribbon, inhibin

ibby \ib-ē\ Libby, ribby

¹ibe \īb\ bribe, gibe, gybe, jibe, kibe, scribe, tribe, vibe, ascribe, conscribe, describe, imbibe, inscribe, prescribe, proscribe, subscribe, transcribe, circumscribe, diatribe, redescribe, superscribe, oversubscribe

²ibe \ē-bē\ see ¹EBE

ibel \ī-bəl\ see IBAL

iber \ī-bər\ briber, fiber, giber, Khyber, scriber, Tiber, describer, inscriber, prescriber, proscriber, subscriber, transcriber

ibi \ē-bē\ see ¹EBE

ibia \i-bē-ə\ Lybia, tibia, Namibia

ibin \ib-ən\ see IBBON

ibit \ib-ət\ see IBBET

ibitive \ib-ət-iv\ exhibitive, prohibitive

ibitor \ib-ət-ər\ exhibitor, inhibitor, ACE inhibitor

ible \ī-bəl\ see IBAL

iblet \ib-lət\ driblet, giblet, riblet

ibli \ib-lē\ see IBBLY

ibly \ib-lē\ see IBBLY

ibo \ē-bō\ Ibo, Kibo, gazebo

iboly \i-ə-lē\ see YBELE

ibrous \ī-brəs\ fibrous, hybris

ibs \ibz\ dibs, nibs, spareribs—
also plurals and possessives of nouns and third person singular presents of verbs listed at ¹IB

ibular \ib-yə-lər\ fibular, mandibular, vestibular, infundibular

¹ibute \ib-yət\ tribute, attribute, contribute, distribute, redistribute

²ibute \ib-ət\ see IBBET

ibutive \ib-yət-iv\ attributive, contributive, distributive, retributive, redistributive

ibutor \ib-ət-ər\ see IBITOR

ibyl \ib-əl\ see IBBLE

¹ic \ik\ see ICK

²ic \ēk\ see ¹EAK

¹ica \ī-kə\ mica, Micah, pica, pika, plica, spica, Spica, Formica, lorica, balalaika

²ica \ē-kə\ see ¹IKA

icable \ik-ə-bəl\ despicable, explicable, extricable, inexplicable, inextricable

icah \ī-kə\ see ¹ICA

ical \ik-əl\ see ICKLE

icament \ik-ə-mənt\ medicament, predicament

ican \ē-kən\ see EACON

icar \ik-ər\ see ¹ICKER

icative \ik-ət-iv\ fricative, siccative, affricative, explicative, indicative, vindicative, multiplicative

iccative \ik-ət-iv\ see ICATIVE

iccio \ē-chō\ capriccio, pasticcio

¹ice \īs\ Bryce, dice, fice, fyce, gneiss, ice, lice, lyse, mice, nice, pice, price, rice, rise, slice, spice, splice, syce, thrice, trice, twice, vice, vise, advice, allspice, Brandeis, bride-price, concise, cut-price, deice, device, entice, excise, precise, suffice, beggars-lice, cockatrice, edelweiss, imprecise, merchandise, overprice, paradise, point-device, sacrifice, underprice, imparadise, self-sacrifice

²ice \ē-chä\ see ¹ICHE

³ice \ēs\ see IECE

⁴ice \ī-sē\ see ICY

⁵ice \īz\ see IZE

⁶ice \ēt-zə\ see ¹ITZA

iceless \ī-sləs\ iceless, priceless

icely \is-lē\ see ISTLY

iceous \ish-əs\ see ¹ICIOUS

icer \ī-sər\ dicer, Dreiser, nicer, pricer, ricer, slicer, splicer, deicer, sufficer, sacrificer, self-sacrificer

ices \ī-sēz\ Pisces, Anchises, Polynices, Coma Berenices

icety \ī-stē\ see EISTY

icey \ī-sē\ see ICY

¹ich \ich\ see ITCH

²ich \ik\ see ICK

ichael \ī-kəl\ see ¹YCLE

¹iche \ē-chä\ ceviche, seviche, Beatrice, cantatrice

²iche \ēsh\ fiche, leash, quiche, sneesh, baksheesh, corniche, hashish, maxixe, pastiche, schottische, unleash, microfiche, nouveau riche

³iche \ish\ see ¹ISH

⁴iche \ich\ see ITCH

⁵iche \ē-chē\ see EACHY

¹ichen \ī-kən\ lichen, liken, proteoglycan

²ichen \ich-ən\ see ITCHEN

ichener \ich-nər\ see ITCHENER

icher \ich-ər\ see ITCHER

iches \ich-əz\ see ITCHES

¹ichi \ē-chē\ see EACHY

²ichi \ē-shē\ see ISHI

ichment \ich-mənt\ see ITCHMENT

ichore \ik-rē\ see ICKERY

ichu \ish-ü\ see ¹ISSUE

¹icia \ish-ə\ see ITIA

²icia \ēsh-ə\ see ¹ESIA

icial \ish-əl\ altricial, comitial, initial, judicial, official, simplicial, solstitial, surficial, artificial, beneficial, cicatricial, interstitial, prejudicial, sacrificial, superficial

ician \ē-shən\ see ¹ETION

icience \ish-əns\ omniscience, insufficience

iciency \ish-ən-sē\ deficiency, efficiency, proficiency, sufficiency, inefficiency, immunodeficiency

icient \ish-ənt\ deficient, efficient, omniscient, proficient, sufficient, coefficient, cost-efficient, inefficient, insufficient, self-sufficient

icinable \is-nə-bəl\ see ISTENABLE

icinal \is-ᵊn-əl\ vicinal, medicinal, officinal, vaticinal

¹icing \ī-siŋ\ icing, splicing, self-sufficing

²icing \ī-ziŋ\ see IZING

¹icious \ish-əs\ vicious, ambitious, auspicious, capricious, delicious, factitious, fictitious, flagitious, judicious, lubricious, malicious, Mauritius, nutritious, officious, pernicious, propitious, pumiceous, seditious,

sericeous, suspicious,
adscititious, adventitious,
avaricious, expeditious,
inauspicious, injudicious,
meretricious, prejudicious,
subreptitious, superstitious,
suppositious, surreptitious,
excrementitious, supposititious

²icious \ē-shəs\ see ECIOUS

icipal \is-ə-bəl\ see ISSIBLE

icipant \is-ə-pənt\ anticipant,
participant

icit \is-ət\ licit, complicit, elicit,
explicit, illicit, implicit,
solicit, inexplicit

¹icitor \is-ət-ər\ elicitor,
solicitor

²icitor \is-tər\ see ISTER

icitous \is-ət-əs\ complicitous,
duplicitous, felicitous,
solicitous, infelicitous

¹icity \is-ət-ē\ basicity,
causticity, centricity,
chronicity, complicity,
conicity, cyclicity, duplicity,
ethnicity, felicity, lubricity,
mendicity, plasticity,
publicity, rhythmicity,
seismicity, simplicity,
spasticity, sphericity, tonicity,
toxicity, triplicity, atomicity,
authenticity, canonicity,
catholicity, concentricity,
domesticity, eccentricity,
elasticity, electricity,
ellipticity, endemicity,
ergodicity, historicity,
iconicity, impudicity,
infelicity, multiplicity,
organicity, pneumaticity,
quadruplicity, specificity,
synchronicity, volcanicity,

aperiodicity, aromaticity,
automaticity, ecumenicity,
egocentricity, epidemicity,
ethnocentricity,
hydrophilicity,
hydrophobicity,
inauthenticity, inelasticity,
pathogenicity, periodicity,
theocentricity, aeroelasticity,
anthropocentricity,
carcinogenicity,
homoscedasticity,
quasiperiodicity

²icity \is-tē\ christie, Christie,
misty, twisty, wristy, Corpus
Christi, sacahuiste

ick \ik\ brick, chick, click,
crick, creek, Dick, flick, hick,
kick, KWIC, lick, mick, nick,
Nick, pic, pick, prick, quick,
rick, shtick, sic, sick, slick,
snick, spick, stick, strick,
thick, tic, tick, trick, wick,
airsick, alsike, bluetick,
bootlick, boychick, brainsick,
broomstick, carsick,
chopstick, cowlick, crabstick,
dabchick, dead-stick, detick,
dik-dik, dipstick, drop-kick,
drumstick, firebrick, flagstick,
goldbrick, greensick,
handpick, hayrick, heartsick,
homesick, joystick, lipstick,
lovesick, matchstick, moujik,
muzhik, nightstick, nitpick,
nonstick, nutpick, outslick,
peacenik, pigstick, pinprick,
placekick, redbrick, rubric,
seasick, self-stick, shashlik,
sidekick, slapstick, slipstick,
Tajik, toothpick, topkick,
unpick, unstick, uptick,

yardstick, bailiwick, biopic,
Bolshevik, candlestick,
candlewick, Dominic,
dominick, Dominick, double-
quick, EBCDIC, fiddlestick,
hemistich, heretic, lunatic,
Menshevik, meterstick,
overtrick, politic, politick,
polyptych, Reykjavik,
singlestick, taperstick,
undertrick, Watson-Crick,
arithmetic, carrot-and-stick,
computernik, impolitic,
kinnikinnick

icka \ē-kə\ see ¹IKA

¹**icked** \ik-əd\ picked, wicked

²**icked** \ikt\ see ¹ICT

ickel \ik-əl\ see ICKLE

icken \ik-ən\ chicken, quicken,
sicken, stricken, thicken,
awestricken, panic-stricken,
planet-stricken, poverty-
stricken

ickens \ik-ənz\ dickens,
Dickens, pickings—*also
plurals and possessives of
nouns and third person
singular presents of verbs
listed at* ICKEN

¹**icker** \ik-ər\ bicker, dicker,
flicker, icker, licker, liquor,
nicker, picker, pricker, sicker,
slicker, snicker, sticker, ticker,
tricker, vicar, whicker,
wicker, billsticker, bootlicker,
dropkicker, flea-flicker,
nitpicker, pigsticker,
placekicker, pot likker,
ragpicker, dominicker,
politicker—*also comparatives
of adjectives listed at* ICK

²**icker** \ek-ər\ see ECKER

ickery \ik-rē\ chicory, flickery,
hickory, snickery, trickery,
Terpsichore

icket \ik-ət\ cricket, picket,
Pickett, pricket, spigot,
stickit, thicket, ticket,
wicket, Big Thicket, big-
ticket

ickett \ik-ət\ see ICKET

ickety \ik-ət-ē\ rickety,
thickety, pernickety,
persnickety

ickey \ik-ē\ see ICKY

icki \ik-ē\ see ICKY

ickie \ik-ē\ see ICKY

icking \ik-iŋ\ ticking, wicking,
brain-picking, flat-picking,
high-sticking, nit-picking,
cotton-picking, finger-picking

ickings \ik-ənz\ see ICKENS

ickish \ik-ish\ hickish, sickish,
trickish

ickit \ik-ət\ see ICKET

ickle \ik-əl\ brickle, chicle,
fickle, mickle, nickel, pickle,
picul, prickle, sickle, stickle,
strickle, tical, tickle, trickle,
bicycle, icicle, obstacle,
Popsicle, spectacle, tricycle,
vehicle, pumpernickel

ickler \ik-lər\ stickler, tickler,
bicycler, particular

ickly \ik-lē\ fickly, prickly,
quickly, sickly, slickly,
impoliticly

ickness \ik-nəs\ lychnis,
quickness, sickness, slickness,
thickness, airsickness,
heartsickness, homesickness,
lovesickness, seasickness

icksy \ik-sē\ see IXIE

icky \ik-ē\ dickey, hickey, icky,

kicky, Mickey, picky, quickie, rickey, sickie, sticky, tricky, Vicki, Vickie, Vicky, doohickey

icle \ik-əl\ see ICKLE

¹icly \ik-lē\ see ICKLY

²icly \ē-klē\ see EEKLY

ico \ē-kō\ see ICOT

icope \ik-ə-pē\ see ICOPY

icopy \ik-ə-pē\ wicopy, pericope

icory \ik-rē\ see ICKERY

icot \ē-kō\ fico, pekoe, picot, tricot, Tampico, Puerto Rico

ics \iks\ see ¹IX

¹ict \ikt\ picked, Pict, strict, ticked, addict, afflict, conflict, constrict, convict, delict, depict, edict, evict, inflict, lipsticked, predict, restrict, unlicked, benedict, Benedict, contradict, derelict, interdict, maledict, retrodict, eggs Benedict—*also pasts of verbs listed at* ICK

²ict \īt\ see ¹ITE

ictable \īt-ə-bəl\ see ¹ITABLE

ictal \ik-tᵊl\ fictile, rictal, edictal

icted \ik-təd\ conflicted, evicted, restricted—*also pasts of verbs listed at* ICT

icter \ik-tər\ see ICTOR

ictic \ik-tik\ deictic, panmictic, amphimictic, apodictic

ictile \ik-tᵊl\ see ICTAL

ictim \ik-təm\ see ICTUM

iction \ik-shən\ diction, fiction, friction, stiction, addiction, affliction, confliction, constriction, conviction, depiction, eviction, indiction, inflection,

nonfiction, prediction, reliction, restriction, transfixion, benediction, contradiction, crucifixion, dereliction, jurisdiction, malediction, metafiction, valediction

ictional \ik-shnəl\ fictional, frictional, nonfictional, jurisdictional

ictionist \ik-shnəst\ fictionist, restrictionist

ictive \ik-tiv\ fictive, addictive, afflictive, conflictive, constrictive, inflictive, restrictive, vindictive, nonrestrictive

ictment \īt-mənt\ see ITEMENT

ictor \ik-tər\ lictor, stricter, victor, constrictor, depicter, evictor, inflicter, contradictor, vasoconstrictor

ictory \ik-tə-rē\ victory, benedictory, contradictory, maledictory, valedictory

ictual \it-ᵊl\ see ITTLE

ictualler \it-ᵊl-ər\ see ITALER

ictum \ik-təm\ dictum, victim, obiter dictum

icture \ik-chər\ picture, stricture

icul \ik-əl\ see ICKLE

icula \ik-yə-lə\ auricula, Canicula

iculant \ik-yə-lənt\ gesticulant, matriculant

¹icular \ik-yə-lər\ spicular, acicular, articular, auricular, canicular, clavicular, curricular, cuticular, fascicular, follicular, funicular, lenticular,

navicular, orbicular, ossicular,
particular, radicular, reticular,
testicular, vehicular,
ventricular, vermicular,
versicular, vesicular,
appendicular, perpendicular,
extracurricular, extravehicular,
intra-articular,
supraventricular

²**icular** \ik-lər\ see ICKLER

icularly \ik-lē\ see ICKLY

iculate \ik-yə-lət\ articulate,
denticulate, geniculate,
particulate, reticulate,
straticulate, vermiculate,
inarticulate

iculous \ik-yə-ləs\ meticulous,
pediculous, ridiculous

iculum \ik-yə-ləm\ curriculum,
reticulum, diverticulum

icuous \ik-yə-wəs\ conspicuous,
perspicuous, transpicuous,
inconspicuous

icy \ī-sē\ dicey, icy, pricey,
spicy

¹**id** \id\ bid, chid, Cid, did, fid,
gid, grid, hid, id, kid, Kidd,
lid, mid, quid, rid, skid, slid,
squid, SQUID, whid, Yid,
amid, backslid, bifid, El Cid,
equid, eyelid, forbid,
grandkid, Madrid, nonskid,
outdid, resid, schoolkid, trifid,
undid, katydid, ootid, overbid,
overdid, pyramid, underbid,
tertium quid, Valadolid

²**id** \ēd\ see EED

I'd \īd\ see ¹IDE

¹**ida** \ēd-ə\ see ¹EDA

²**ida** \ī-də\ Haida, Ida, Vida

¹**idable** \īd-ə-bəl\ guidable,

decidable, dividable,
subdividable

²**idable** \id-ə-bəl\ see IDDABLE

idal \īd-ᵊl\ bridal, bridle, idle,
idol, idyll, seidel, sidle, tidal,
unbridle, Barmecidal,
fratricidal, fungicidal,
genocidal, germicidal,
herbicidal, homicidal,
intertidal, lunitidal, matricidal,
parricidal, patricidal,
septicidal, spermicidal,
suicidal, viricidal, virucidal,
bactericidal, infanticidal,
insecticidal

idance \īd-ᵊns\ guidance,
stridence, abidance,
misguidance

idas \īd-əs\ Midas, nidus

iday \īd-ē\ Friday, Heidi, tidy,
vide, alcaide, man Friday,
untidy, mala fide

idays \īd-ēz\ see ¹IDES

idd \id\ see ¹ID

iddable \id-ə-bəl\ biddable,
formidable

iddance \id-ᵊns\ riddance,
forbiddance

idden \id-ᵊn\ bidden, chiden,
hidden, midden, ridden,
stridden, swidden,
backslidden, bedridden,
bestridden, forbidden,
outbidden, unbidden,
overridden

idder \id-ər\ bidder, gridder,
kidder, siddur, skidder,
consider, forbidder,
reconsider, underbidder

iddie \id-ē\ see IDDY

iddish \id-ish\ kiddish, Yiddish

iddity \id-ət-ē\ see IDITY

iddle \id-ᵊl\ diddle, fiddle, griddle, middle, piddle, riddle, twiddle, unriddle, paradiddle, taradiddle

iddler \id-lər\ diddler, fiddler, middler, riddler, tiddler,

iddling \id-liŋ\ fiddling, middling, piddling, riddling

iddly \id-le\ diddly, ridley, tiddly

iddock \id-ik\ see IDIC

iddur \id-ər\ see IDDER

iddy \id-ē\ biddy, giddy, kiddie, middy, midi, skiddy, widdy

¹ide \īd\ bide, bride, chide, Clyde, eyed, fried, glide, guide, hide, I'd, pied, plied, pride, ride, side, slide, snide, stride, thighed, tide, tried, wide, abide, allied, applied, aside, astride, backside, backslide, bankside, beachside, bedside, beside, bestride, betide, blear-eyed, blindside, blowdried, blue-eyed, broadside, bromide, bug-eyed, Burnside, clear-eyed, cockeyed, cold-eyed, collide, confide, courtside, cowhide, cross-eyed, curbside, dayside, decide, deride, divide, dockside, doe-eyed, downside, dry-eyed, elide, fireside, foreside, four-eyed, freeze-dried, glass-eyed, graveside, green-eyed, hagride, hawkeyed, hayride, hillside, horsehide, inside, ironside, joyride, kingside, lakeside, landslide, lynx-eyed, misguide, moon-eyed, nearside, nightside, noontide,

offside, onside, outride, outside, pie-eyed, poolside, pop-eyed, preside, provide, quayside, queenside, rawhide, reside, ringside, riptide, roadside, seaside, sharp-eyed, shipside, shoreside, Shrovetide, sloe-eyed, snowslide, springtide, squint-eyed, stateside, statewide, storewide, Strathclyde, streamside, subside, tailslide, Tayside, tongue-tied, topside, trackside, trailside, untried, upside, vat-dyed, walleyed, waveguide, wayside, wide-eyed, wild-eyed, worldwide, yuletide, alkoxide, almond-eyed, alongside, Argus-eyed, Barmecide, bleary-eyed, bona fide, chicken-fried, Christmastide, citified, citywide, classified, coincide, countrified, countryside, countrywide, cut-and-dried, cyanide, deicide, demand-side, dewy-eyed, dignified, double-wide, downslide, Eastertide, eventide, feticide, fluoride, formamide, fratricide, fungicide, genocide, germicide, gimlet-eyed, glassy-eyed, goggle-eyed, googly-eyed, harbor-side, herbicide, homicide, Humberside, humified, matricide, Merseyside, misty-eyed, miticide, monoxide, mountainside, nationwide, Naugahyde, open-eyed, override, overstride, parricide,

Passiontide, patricide, pesticide, planetwide, qualified, rarefied, raticide, regicide, riverside, Riverside, set-aside, silverside, sissified, slickenside, spermicide, starry-eyed, subdivide, suicide, supply-side, trisulfide, underside, verbicide, vermicide, viricide, waterside, Whitsuntide, wintertide, acrylamide, antimonide, borohydride, dissatisfied, formaldehyde, infanticide, insecticide, interallied, Jekyll and Hyde, preoccupied, rodenticide, self-satisfied, thalidomide, Trinitytide, tyrannicide, uxoricide, monoglyceride, overqualified, parasiticide—*also pasts of verbs listed at* ¹Y

²ide \ēd\ *see* EED

idean \id-ē-ən\ *see* IDIAN

ided \īd-əd\ sided, lopsided, misguided, one-sided, slab-sided, two-sided, many-sided, sobersided—*also pasts of verbs listed at* ¹IDE

ideless \īd-ləs\ idlesse, tideless

iden \īd-ᵊn\ guidon, Hayden, widen, Poseidon

idence \īd-ᵊns\ *see* IDANCE

ideness \īd-nəs\ *see* EYEDNESS

ident \īd-ᵊnt\ strident, trident

ideon \id-ē-ən\ *see* IDIAN

ideous \id-ē-əs\ *see* IDIOUS

¹ider \īd-ər\ bider, cider, eider, glider, guider, hider, rider, slider, spider, strider, stridor, abider, backslider, confider, decider, derider, divider, insider, joyrider, misguider, outrider, outsider, presider, provider, resider, rough rider, Top-Sider, subdivider, supply-sider, supercollider—*also comparatives of adjectives listed at* ¹IDE

²ider \id-ər\ *see* IDDER

¹ides \īd-ēz\ Fridays, Aristides—*also plurals and possessives of nouns and third person singular presents of verbs listed at* IDAY

²ides \īdz\ ides, besides, burnsides, silversides, sobersides—*also plurals and possessives of nouns and third person singular presents of verbs listed at* ¹IDE

idge \ij\ bridge, fidge, fridge, midge, ridge, abridge, Blue Ridge, browridge, drawbridge, footbridge, Oxbridge, teethridge

idged \ijd\ ridged, unabridged—*also pasts of verbs listed at* IDGE

idgen \ij-ən\ *see* YGIAN

idget \ij-ət\ Brigitte, digit, fidget, midget, widget, double-digit

idgin \ij-ən\ *see* YGIAN

idi \id-ē\ *see* IDDY

idia \i-dē-ə\ Lydia, basidia, chlamydia, clostridia, coccidia, conidia, glochidia, nephridia, Numidia, oidia, peridia, Pisidia, presidia, pycnidia, pygidia, antheridia, enchiridia, hesperidia, miricidia, ommatidia

idian \id-ē-ən\ Gideon, Lydian, Midian, ascidian, Dravidian, euclidean, Floridian, meridian, obsidian, ophidian, quotidian, viridian, enchiridion, non-euclidean

idic \id-ik\ piddock, acidic, bromidic, Davidic, druidic, fatidic, fluidic, Hasidic, nuclidic

idical \id-i-kəl\ druidical, fatidical, juridical, veridical, pyramidical

idice \id-ə-sē\ Chalcidice, Eurydice

idiem \id-ē-əm\ idiom, iridium, presidium, rubidium, post meridiem, ante meridiem

iding \īd-iŋ\ riding, Riding, siding, tiding, abiding, confiding, East Riding, joyriding, West Riding, law-abiding, nondividing

idiom \id-ē-əm\ see IDIEM

idious \id-ē-əs\ hideous, fastidious, insidious, invidious, perfidious

idity \id-ət-ē\ quiddity, acidity, aridity, avidity, cupidity, fluidity, flaccidity, floridity, frigidity, gelidity, gravity, hispidity, humidity, hybridity, limpidity, liquidity, lividity, lucidity, morbidity, rabidity, rapidity, rigidity, sapidity, solidity, stupidity, tepidity, timidity, torridity, turbidity, turgidity, validity, vapidity, viridity, viscidity, illiquidity, insipidity, intrepidity, invalidity

idium \id-ē-əm\ see IDIEM

idle \īd-ᵊl\ see IDAL

idlesse \īd-ləs\ see IDELESS

idley \id-lē\ see IDDLY

idney \id-nē\ kidney, Sidney, Sydney

¹**ido** \īd-ō\ dido, Dido, fido, Hokkaido

²**ido** \ēd-ō\ see ¹EDO

idol \īd-ᵊl\ see IDAL

¹**idz** \idz\ Beskids, rapids, Grand Rapids—*also plurals of nouns listed at* ¹ID

²**ids** \ēdz\ see EEDS

idst \idst\ didst, midst, amidst

¹**idual** \ij-wəl\ residual, individual

²**idual** \ij-əl\ see IGIL

idulent \ij-ə-lənt\ see IGILANT

idulous \ij-ə-ləs\ stridulous, acidulous

idus \īd-əs\ see IDAS

iduum \ij-ə-wəm\ triduum, residuum

idy \īd-ē\ see IDAY

idyll \īd-ᵊl\ see IDAL

¹**ie** \ā\ see ¹AY

²**ie** \ē\ see ¹EE

³**ie** \ī\ see ¹Y

iece \ēs\ cease, crease, fleece, grease, Greece, kris, lease, Nice, niece, peace, piece, apiece, Bernice, Burmese, camise, caprice, cassis, cerise, chemise, Chinese, Clarice, Cochise, codpiece, coulisse, crosspiece, decease, decrease, degrease, Denise, Dumfries, earpiece, Elise, eyepiece, Felice, fieldpiece, grandniece, hairpiece, headpiece, heelpiece, increase, Janice, lend-lease, Matisse, Maurice, mouthpiece, nosepiece, obese, patsis, pelisse, police, release, release, seapiece, shankpiece, showpiece, sidepiece, stringpiece, sublease, surcease, tailpiece, Therese, timepiece, toepiece, two-piece, valise, workpiece, afterpiece, altarpiece, Amboinese, Annamese, Assamese, Balinese, Brooklynese, Cantonese, centerpiece, Chersonese, chimneypiece, diocese, directrice, ex libris, expertise, Faeroese, frontispiece, mantelpiece, masterpiece, Nipponese, Pekinese, Pekingese, Portugese, predecease, rerelease, São Luis, Siamese, Sinhalese, timed-release, verdigris, archdiocese, computerese, Dodecanese, officialese, telegraphese, Vietnamese, educationese

iecer \ē-sər\ see ¹EASER
¹ied \ēd\ see EED
²ied \ēt\ see ¹EAT
³ied \īd\ see ¹IDE
ieda \ēd-ə\ see ¹EDA
¹ief \ēf\ beef, brief, chief, fief, grief, kef, leaf, lief, reef, sheaf, thief, belief, debrief, endleaf, enfeoff, flyleaf, loose-leaf, massif, motif, naif, O'Keefe, relief, sharif, sherif, shinleaf, bas-relief, cloverleaf, disbelief, handkerchief, leatherleaf, neckerchief, leitmotiv, misbelief, overleaf, unbelief, waterleaf, aperitif,

Capitol Reef, Vinson Massif, Great Berrier Reef, Santa Cruz de Tenerife

²ief \ēv\ see ¹EAVE
iefless \ē-fləs\ briefless, leafless
iefly \ē-flē\ briefly, chiefly
¹ieg \ēg\ see IGUE
²ieg \ig\ see IG
¹iege \ēj\ liege, siege, besiege, prestige
²iege \ēzh\ see ¹IGE
ieger \ē-jər\ see EDURE
iek \ēk\ see ¹EAK
¹iel \ēl\ see ²EAL
²iel \ī-əl\ see ¹IAL
iela \el-ə\ see ELLA
ield \ēld\ bield, field, keeled, shield, weald, wheeled, wield, yield, afield, airfield, backfield, brickfield, coalfield, cornfield, downfield, Enfield, four-wheeled, Garfield, goldfield, grainfield, infield, Masefield, midfield, minefield, outfield, playfield, Sheffield, Smithfield, snowfield, Springfield, subfield, unsealed, upfield, well-heeled, windshield, Winfield, battlefield, brokenfield, chesterfield, Chesterfield, color-field, Huddersfield, track-and-field, unaneled—*also pasts of verbs listed at* ²EAL
ielder \ēl-dər\ fielder, shielder, wielder, yielder, infielder, outfielder
ields \ēldz\ South Shields—*also possessives and plurals of nouns and third person*

*singular presents of verbs
listed at* IELD

ieler \ē-lər\ see EALER
ieless \ī-ləs\ see ILUS
¹ieling \ē-lən\ see ELIN
²ieling \ē-liŋ\ see EELING
¹iem \ē-əm\ see ¹EUM
²iem \ī-əm\ see IAM
ien \ēn\ see ³INE
ience \ī-əns\ see IANCE
iend \end\ see END
iendless \en-ləs\ see ENDLESS
iendliness \en-lē-nəs\ see
  ENDLINESS
iendly \en-lē\ see ENDLY
iene \ēn\ see ³INE
¹iener \ē-nər\ see EANER
²iener \ē-nē\ see ¹INI
ienic \en-ik\ see ²ENIC
ienics \en-iks\ see ENICS
ienie \ē-nē\ see ¹INI
ienist \ē-nəst\ see ²INIST
iennes \en\ see ¹EN
ient \ī-ənt\ see IANT
ieper \ē-pər\ see EEPER
¹ier \ir\ see ²EER
²ier \ē-ər\ see ¹EER
³ier \īr\ see ¹IRE
ierate \ir-ət\ see IRIT
ierce \irs\ Bierce, birse, fierce,
  pierce, Pierce, tierce,
  transpierce
¹iere \er\ see ⁴ARE
²iere \ir\ see ²EER
iered \ird\ see ¹EARD
ieria \ir-ē-ə\ see ¹ERIA
ierial \ir-ē-əl\ see ERIAL
ierian \ir-ē-ən\ see ¹ERIAN
ierly \ir-lē\ see ¹EARLY
¹ierre \ir\ see ²EER
²ierre \er\ see ⁴ARE
iers \irz\ Algiers, Pamirs—*also*

*plurals and possessives of
nouns and third person
singular presents of verbs
listed at* EER

iersman \irz-mən\ see EERSMAN
iery \ī-rē\ see ¹IARY
¹ies \ēz\ see EZE
²ies \ē\ see ¹EE
³ies \ēs\ see IECE
¹iesel \ē-zəl\ see EASEL
²iesel \ē-sᵊl\ see ¹ECIL
ieseling \ēz-liŋ\ see ESLING
iesian \ē-zhən\ see ¹ESIAN
iesis \ī-ə-səs\ see IASIS
iesling \ēz-liŋ\ see ESLING
iest \ēst\ see ¹EAST
iester \ē-stər\ see EASTER
iestley \ēst-lē\ see EASTLY
iestly \ēst-lē\ see EASTLY
iet \ī-ət\ diet, fiat, quiet, riot,
  striate, Wyatt, disquiet,
  unquiet
ietal \ī-ət-ᵊl\ parietal, societal,
  varietal
ieter \ī-ət-ər\ dieter, quieter,
  rioter, proprietor
ietor \ī-ət-ər\ see IETER
ietzsche \ē-chē\ see EACHY
iety \ī-ət-ē\ piety, anxiety,
  dubiety, impiety, nimiety,
  propriety, satiety, sobriety,
  society, Society, variety,
  contrariety, impropriety,
  inebriety, insobriety, notoriety
ieu \ü\ see ¹EW
ieur \ir\ see ²EER
iev \ef\ see ¹EF
ievable \ē-və-bəl\ see EIVABLE
ieval \ē-vəl\ evil, shrieval,
  weevil, coeval, khedival,
  medieval, primeval, reprieval,
  retrieval, upheaval

¹ieve \iv\ see ²IVE

²ieve \ēv\ see ¹EAVE

ieved \ēvd\ see EAVED

ievement \ēv-mənt\ see EVEMENT

iever \ē-vər\ beaver, cleaver, fever, griever, leaver, reaver, reiver, weaver, achiever, believer, conceiver, deceiver, enfever, perceiver, receiver, reliever, retriever, upheaver, school-leaver, transceiver, cantilever, disbeliever, misbeliever, misconceiver, unbeliever, overachiever, underachiever

ievish \ē-vish\ see EEVISH

ievo \ē-vō\ see EVO

ievous \ē-vəs\ see EVOUS

ieze \ēz\ see EZE

¹if \if\ see IFF

²if \ēf\ see ¹IEF

¹ife \īf\ fife, Fife, knife, life, rife, strife, wife, alewife, drawknife, fishwife, flick-knife, goodwife, half-life, housewife, jackknife, loosestrife, lowlife, mid-life, nightlife, oldwife, penknife, pro-life, true-life, wakerife, whole-life, wildlife, afterlife, antilife, Duncan Phyfe, nurse-midwife, pocketknife, Yellowknife, right-to-life

²ife \ē-fə\ see EPHA

³ife \ēf\ see ¹IEF

ifeless \ī-fləs\ lifeless, strifeless, wifeless

ifer \ī-fər\ see IPHER

iferous \if-ər-əs\ coniferous, floriferous, lactiferous, luciferous, pestiferous, somniferous, splendiferous, vociferous, carboniferous, luminiferous, odoriferous, salutiferous, seminiferous, soporiferous, sudoriferous

iff \if\ biff, cliff, glyph, if, iff, jiff, kif, miff, quiff, riff, Riff, skiff, sniff, spiff, spliff, stiff, syph, tiff, whiff, Er Rif, midriff, Plovdiv, triglyph, what-if, Wycliffe, anaglyph, bindle stiff, hieroglyph, hippogriff, logogriph, petroglyph

iffany \if-ə-nē\ see IPHONY

iffe \if\ see IFF

iffed \ift\ see IFT

iffen \if-ən\ see IFFIN

iffey \if-ē\ see IFFY

iffian \if-ē-ən\ Riffian, Pecksniffian

iffin \if-ən\ griffin, griffon, stiffen, tiffin

iffish \if-ish\ sniffish, stiffish

iffle \if-əl\ piffle, riffle, skiffle, sniffle, whiffle, Wiffle

iffler \if-lər\ riffler, sniffler, whiffler

iffness \if-nəs\ stiffness, swiftness

iffon \if-ən\ see IFFIN

iffy \if-ē\ iffy, cliffy, jiffy, Liffey, sniffy, spiffy

ific \if-ik\ glyphic, calcific, febrific, horrific, magnific, pacific, Pacific, prolific, salvific, specific, terrific, vivific, anaglyphic, beatific, calorific, colorific, felicific, frigorific, hieroglyphic, honorific, scientific, soporific, sudorific, tenebrific, prescientific

ifical \if-i-kəl\ magnifical, pontifical

ificate \if-i-kət\ certificate, pontificate

ificent \if-ə-sənt\ magnificent, omnificent

ifle \ī-fəl\ rifle, stifle, trifle

ifling \ī-fliŋ\ rifling, stifling, trifling

ift \ift\ drift, gift, grift, lift, rift, shift, shrift, sift, squiffed, swift, Swift, thrift, adrift, airlift, blueshift, downshift, face-lift, festschrift, forklift, frameshift, gearshift, Great Rift, makeshift, redshift, shoplift, snowdrift, spendthrift, spindrift, spoondrift, unshift, uplift, upshift—*also pasts of verbs listed at* IFF

ifter \if-tər\ drifter, snifter, swifter, sceneshifter, shapeshifter, shoplifter

ifth \ith\ see ²ITH

iftness \if-nəs\ see IFFNESS

ifty \if-tē\ drifty, fifty, nifty, shifty, thrifty, wifty, fiftyfifty, LD50

ig \ig\ big, brig, dig, fig, frig, gig, Grieg, grig, jig, pig, prig, rig, sprig, swig, trig, twig, vig, Whig, wig, zig, bagwig, bigwig, bushpig, earwig, hedgepig, lime-twig, renege, shindig, unrig, caprifig, infra dig, jury-rig, periwig, thimblerig, whirligig, WYSIWYG, Zagazig, thingamajig

¹iga \ē-gə\ Riga, Vega, viga, Antigua, omega, quadriga

²iga \ī-gə\ see AIGA

igamous \ig-ə-məs\ bigamous, polygamous

igamy \ig-ə-mē\ bigamy, digamy, polygamy

¹igan \ī-gən\ ligan, tigon

²igan \ig-ən\ see IGGIN

igand \ig-ənd\ brigand, ligand

igas \ī-gəs\ see YGOUS

igate \ig-ət\ see ¹IGOT

¹ige \ēzh\ siege, prestige, noblesse oblige

²ige \ēj\ see ¹IEGE

igel \ij-əl\ see IGIL

igenous \ij-ə-nəs\ see IGINOUS

igeon \ij-ən\ see YGIAN

iger \ī-gər\ tiger, braunschweiger

igerent \ij-rənt\ belligerent, refrigerant, cobelligerent

iggan \ig-ən\ see IGGIN

iggard \ig-ərd\ niggard, triggered—*also pasts of verbs listed at* IGGER

igged \igd\ twigged, wigged, bewigged, cat-rigged, squarerigged, periwigged—*also pasts of verbs listed at* IG

igger \ig-ər\ bigger, chigger, digger, jigger, nigger, rigger, rigor, snigger, swigger, trigger, vigor, vigour, ditchdigger, outrigger, rejigger, reneger, squarerigger, thimblerigger

iggered \ig-ərd\ see IGGARD

iggery \ig-ə-rē\ piggery, priggery, Whiggery

iggie \ig-ē\ see IGGY

iggin \ig-ən\ biggin, piggin, wigan, balbriggan

iggish \ig-ish\ biggish, piggish, priggish, Whiggish

iggle \ig-əl\ giggle, higgle, jiggle, niggle, sniggle, squiggle, wiggle, wriggle

iggler \ig-lər\ giggler, higgler, niggler, wiggler, wriggler

iggy \ig-ē\ biggie, piggy, twiggy

igh \ī\ see ¹Y

ighed \īd\ see ¹IDE

ighland \ī-lənd\ highland, Highland, island, Thailand, Long Island, Rhode Island, Staten Island, Prince Edward Island

ighlander \ī-lən-dər\ highlander, islander

ighlands \ī-lənz\ Highlands, Virgin Islands

ighly \ī-lē\ see YLY

ighness \ī-nəs\ see ¹INUS

ight \īt\ see ¹ITE

ightable \īt-ə-bəl\ see ¹ITABLE

ighted \īt-əd\ blighted, sighted, whited, attrited, benighted, clear-sighted, farsighted, foresighted, longsighted, nearsighted, sharp-sighted, shortsighted, skylighted, united, unrequited—*also pasts of verbs listed at* ¹ITE

ighten \īt-ᵊn\ brighten, Brighton, chitin, chiton, frighten, heighten, lighten, tighten, titan, Titan, triton, Triton, whiten, enlighten

ightener \īt-nər\ brightener, lightener, tightener, whitener

ightening \īt-niŋ\ see IGHTNING

ighter \īt-ər\ see ¹ITER

ightful \īt-fəl\ frightful, rightful, spiteful, sprightful, delightful, despiteful, foresightful, insightful

ightie \īt-ē\ see ²ITE

ightily \īt-ᵊl-ē\ flightily, mightily

ightiness \īt-ē-nəs\ flightiness, mightiness, almightiness

ighting \īt-iŋ\ see ITING

ightless \īt-ləs\ flightless, lightless, sightless

ightly \īt-lē\ knightly, lightly, nightly, rightly, sightly, sprightly, whitely, fortnightly, midnightly, unsightly—*also adverbs formed by adding* -ly *to adjectives listed at* ¹ITE

ightment \īt-mənt\ see ITEMENT

ightning \īt-niŋ\ lightning, tightening, belt-tightening

ightn't \īt-ᵊnt\ see ITANT

ighton \īt-ən\ see IGHTEN

ights \īts\ lights, nights, tights, footlights, houselights, weeknights, Dolomites, Golan Heights—*also plurals and possessives of nouns and third person singular presents of verbs listed at* ¹ITE

ightsome \īt-səm\ lightsome, delightsome

ighty \īt-ē\ see ²ITE

igian \ij-ən\ see YGIAN

igid \ij-əd\ Brigid, frigid, rigid

igil \ij-əl\ Rigel, sigil, strigil, vigil, residual

igilant \ij-ə-lənt\ vigilant, acidulent

igine \ij-ə-nē\ polygyny, aborigine

iginous \ij-ə-nəs\ caliginous, fuliginous, indigenous, polygynous, vertiginous

igion \ij-ən\ see YGIAN

igious \ij-əs\ litigious, prestigious, prodigious, religious, irreligious

igit \ij-ət\ see IDGET

igitte \ij-ət\ see IDGET

iglet \ig-lət\ piglet, wiglet

¹igm \im\ see ¹IM

²igm \īm\ see ¹IME

igma \ig-mə\ sigma, stigma, enigma, kerygma

igment \ig-mənt\ figment, pigment

ign \īn\ see ¹INE

ignable \ī-nə-bəl\ see INABLE

ignancy \ig-nən-sē\ benignancy, malignancy

ignant \ig-nənt\ benignant, indignant, malignant

igned \īnd\ see ¹IND

igneous \ig-nē-əs\ igneous, ligneous

igner \ī-nər\ see ¹INER

igness \ig-nəs\ bigness, Cygnus

ignet \ig-nət\ see YGNET

igning \ī-niŋ\ see INING

ignity \ig-nət-ē\ dignity, indignity, malignity

ignly \īn-lē\ see ¹INELY

ignment \īn-mənt\ alignment, assignment, confinement, consignment, enshrinement, refinement, nonalignment, realignment

ignon \in-yən\ see INION

ignor \ē-nyər\ see ENIOR

¹igo \ī-gō\ Sligo, prurigo, vitiligo

²igo \ē-gō\ see EGO

igoe \ē-gō\ see EGO

igon \ī-gən\ see ¹IGAN

igor \ig-ər\ see IGGER

igorous \ig-rəs\ rigorous, vigorous

¹igot \ig-ət\ bigot, frigate, gigot, spigot

²igot \ik-ət\ see ICKET

igour \ig-ər\ see IGGER

igrapher \ig-rə-fər\ calligrapher, epigrapher, polygrapher, serigrapher

igraphist \ig-rə-fəst\ calligraphist, epigraphist, polygraphist

igraphy \ig-rə-fē\ calligraphy, epigraphy, pseudepigraphy

igua \ē-gə\ see ¹IGA

igue \ēg\ gigue, Grieg, league, blitzkrieg, colleague, fatigue, garigue, intrigue, sitzkrieg, squeteague, wampumpeag

iguer \ē-gər\ see EAGER

iguous \ig-yə-wəs\ ambiguous, contiguous, exiguous, unambiguous

igured \ig-ərd\ see IGGARD

ii \ī\ see ¹Y

iing \ē-iŋ\ see EEING

ija \ē-jə\ see EGIA

ijah \ī-jə\ Elijah, steatopygia

iji \ē-jē\ Fiji, squeegee

ijl \īl\ see ¹ILE

ijn \īn\ see ¹INE

ijssel \ī-sə\ see ISAL

¹ik \ik\ see ICK

²ik \ēk\ see ¹EAK

¹ika \ē-kə\ pika, theca, areca, eureka, Frederica, Fredericka, paprika, Costa Rica, Dominica, oiticica, Topeka, Tanganyika, bibliotheca

²**ika** \ī-kə\ see ¹ICA

¹**ike** \ī-kē\ Nike, Psyche, crikey, spiky

²**ike** \īk\ bike, caique, dike, dyke, fyke, haik, hike, kike, like, mike, Mike, pike, psych, shrike, sike, spike, strike, trike, tyke, alike, belike, catlike, childlike, clocklike, dislike, fly-strike, garpike, godlike, handspike, hitchhike, homelike, Klondike, lifelike, mislike, pealike, prooflike, push-bike, rampike, restrike, scalelike, sheaflike, shunpike, suchlike, ten-strike, turnpike, unlike, Updike, Vandyke, warlike, wifelike, winglike, berrylike, businesslike, fatherlike, ladylike, look-alike, machinelike, marlinespike, marlinspike, minibike, motorbike, rubberlike, Scafell Pike, soundalike, thunderstrike, womanlike, workmanlike, unsportsmanlike

³**ike** \ik\ see ICK

¹**iked** \īkt\ liked, piked, spiked, vandyked—*also pasts of verbs listed at* ²IKE

²**iked** \ī-kəd\ see YCAD

iken \ī-kən\ see ¹ICHEN

iker \ī-kər\ biker, diker, duiker, hiker, piker, spiker, striker, disliker, hitchhiker, shunpiker, minibiker

ikes \īks\ yikes—*also possessives and plurals of nouns and third person singular presents of verbs listed at* IKE

ikey \ī-kē\ see ¹IKE

ikh \ēk\ see ¹EAK

¹**iki** \ik-ē\ see ICKY

²**iki** \ē-kē\ see EAKY

iking \ī-kiŋ\ liking, striking, Viking, shunpiking

ikker \ik-ər\ see ¹ICKER

iky \ī-kē\ see ¹IKE

¹**il** \il\ see ILL

²**il** \ēl\ see ²EAL

¹**ila** \il-ə\ see ²ILLA

²**ila** \ē-lə\ see ¹ELA

³**ila** \ī-lə\ Lila, Delilah

ilae \ī-lē\ see YLY

ilage \ī-lij\ mileage, silage

ilah \ī-lə\ see ³ILA

ilament \il-ə-mənt\ filament, habiliment, monofilament

ilar \ī-lər\ dialer, filar, flier, hilar, miler, smiler, stylar, styler, tiler, Tyler, beguiler, bifilar, compiler, defiler, freestyler, profiler, rottweiler, stockpiler, unifilar

ilary \il-ə-rē\ see ILLARY

ilate \ī-lət\ see ILOT

ilbe \il-be\ see ILBY

ilbert \il-bərt\ filbert, gilbert, Gilbert

ilby \il-bē\ trilby, astilbe

¹**ilch** \ilk\ see ILK

²**ilch** \ilch\ filch, milch, zilch

¹**ild** \īld\ mild, piled, wild, Wilde, brainchild, godchild, grandchild, hog-wild, man-child, pantiled, Rothschild, schoolchild, self-styled, stepchild—*also pasts of verbs listed at* ¹ILE

²**ild** \il\ see ILL

³**ild** \ilt\ see ILT

⁴**ild** \ild\ see ILLED

ilda \il-də\ Hilda, tilde, Wilda
¹ilde \il-də\ see ILDA
²ilde \īld\ see ¹ILD
¹lder \il-dər\ builder, gilder, guilder, wilder, bewilder, boatbuilder, shipbuilder, upbuilder, bodybuilder, jerry-builder
²ilder \īl-dər\ milder, wilder, Wilder
ilding \il-diŋ\ building, gilding, hilding, abuilding, outbuilding, shipbuilding, bodybuilding—*also present participles of verbs listed at* ILLED
ildish \īl-dish\ childish, wildish
ildly \īld-lē\ childly, mildly, wildly
¹ile \īl\ aisle, bile, dial, faille, file, guile, I'll, isle, Kyle, lisle, Lyle, mile, Nile, phial, pile, rile, roil, smile, spile, stile, style, tile, trial, vial, vile, viol, while, wile, abseil, aedile, agile, anile, argyle, Argyll, audile, awhile, axile, beguile, Blue Nile, Carlyle, compile, condyle, cross-file, de Stijl, decile, defile, denial, docile, ductile, enisle, ensile, erewhile, erstwhile, espial, exile, febrile, fictile, fissile, flexile, fragile, freestyle, futile, genial, gentile, gracile, habile, hairstyle, Kabyle, labile, life-style, meanwhile, mistrial, mobile, motile, nubile, pantile, penile, pensile, profile, puerile, quartile, quintile, redial, reptile, resile, retrial, revile,

sandpile, scissile, sectile, senile, servile, sessile, stabile, stockpile, sundial, tactile, tensile, textile, turnstile, typestyle, unpile, utile, vagile, virile, woodpile, worthwhile, afebrile, airmobile, Anglophile, chamomile, contractile, crocodile, discophile, domicile, endostyle, epistyle, erectile, extensile, Francophile, Gallophile, halophile, homophile, hypostyle, infantile, interfile, juvenile, low-profile, mercantile, negrophile, oenophile, otherwhile, pedophile, percentile, peristyle, prehensile, projectile, protractile, pulsatile, reconcile, refractile, retractile, self-denial, Slavophile, spermophile, technopile, thermopile, turophile, urostyle, versatile, vibratile, xenophile, ailurophile, amphiprostyle, audiophile, bibliophile, electrophile, fluviatile, Germanophile, heterophile, Italophile, nucleophile
²ile \il\ see ILL
³ile \ē-lē\ see EELY
⁴ile \ēl\ see ²EAL
⁵ile \il-ē\ see ¹ILLY
ilead \il-ē-əd\ see ILIAD
ileage \ī-lij\ see ILAGE
ileal \il-ē-əl\ see ¹ILIAL
ileless \īl-ləs\ guileless, pileless, smileless
¹iler \ē-lər\ see EALER

²iler \ī-lər\ see ILAR

iles \īlz\ Giles, Miles, Niles, Wade-Giles, British Isles, Western Isles

ileum \il-ē-əm\ see ILIUM

iley \ī-lē\ see YLY

ilford \il-fərd\ Milford, Wilford

¹ili \il-ē\ see ¹ILLY

²ili \ē-lē\ see EELY

¹ilia \il-ē-ə\ Celia, cilia, Cecelia, Cecilia, Massilia, Anglophilia, basophilia, coprophilia, hemophilia, juvenilia, necrophilia, neophilia, pedophilia, sensibilia, memorabilia

²ilia \il-yə\ Brasilia, sedilia, bougainvillea, sensibilia, memorabilia

³ilia \ēl-yə\ see ELIA

iliad \il-ē-əd\ Gilead, Iliad, balm of Gilead

ilial \il-ē-əl\ filial, ileal, familial, unfilial

¹ilian \il-ē-ən\ Gillian, Ilian, Lillian, Basilian, reptilian, Abbevillian, crocodilian, preexilian, vespertilian

²ilian \il-yən\ see ILLION

ilias \il-ē-əs\ see ¹ILIOUS

iliate \il-ē-ət\ ciliate, affiliate

ilic \il-ik\ killick, acrylic, allylic, Cyrillic, dactylic, exilic, idyllic, sibylic, amphiphilic, Anglophilic, hemophilic, necrophilic, pedophilic, postexilic, zoophilic, bibliophilic

ilica \il-i-kə\ silica, basilica

ilican \il-i-kən\ see ILICON

ilicon \il-i-kən\ Millikan, silicon, spillikin, basilican, ferrosilicon

ilience \il-yəns\ see ILLIANCE

iliency \il-yən-sē\ see ILLIANCY

ilient \il-yənt\ brilliant, resilient

iliment \il-ə-mənt\ see ILAMENT

¹iling \ī-liŋ\ filing, piling, spiling, styling, tiling, hairstyling

²iling \ē-liŋ\ see EELING

¹ilion \il-yən\ see ILLION

²ilion \il-ē-ən\ see ¹ILIAN

¹ilious \il-ē-əs\ punctilious, supercilious, materfamilias, paterfamilias

²ilious \il-yəs\ bilious, atrabilious, supercilious

ilip \il-əp\ see ILLIP

ilitant \il-ə-tənt\ militant, rehabilitant

ility \il-ət-ē\ ability, agility, anility, civility, debility, docility, ductility, facility, fertility, fragility, futility, gentility, gracility, hostility, humility, lability, mobility, motility, nobility, nubility, scurrility, sectility, senility, stability, sterility, suability, tactility, tranquility, utility, vagility, virility, actability, affability, arability, audibility, bearability, biddability, breathability, brushability, capability, changeability, coilability, contractility, countability, credibility, crossability, culpability, curability, cutability, disability, disutility, drapability, drillability, drinkability, durability,

dyeability, edibility,
equability, erectility,
fallibility, feasibility,
fishability, flammability,
flexibility, forgeability,
formability, frangibility,
friability, gullibility,
imbecility, immobility,
inability, incivility, indocility,
infantility, infertility,
instability, inutility,
juvenility, laudability,
leachability, legibility,
liability, likability, livability,
mailability, meltability,
miscibility, movability,
mutability, notability,
packability, placability,
plausibility, playability,
portability, possibility,
potability, pregnability,
prehensility, printability,
probability, puerility,
readability, risibility,
roadability, salability,
sensibility, sewability,
shareability, sociability,
solubility, solvability,
spreadability, squeezability,
stainability, stretchability,
tenability, testability,
traceability, treatability,
tunability, usability,
vendability, versatility,
viability, visibility, volatility,
washability, wearability,
wettability, workability,
absorbability, acceptability,
accessibility, accountability,
adaptability, adjustability,
admirability, admissibility,
adoptability, adorability,

advisability, affectability,
agreeability, alterability,
amenability, amiability,
amicability, appealability,
applicability, approachability,
assumability, attainability,
automobility, availability,
believability, collapsibility,
combustability, comparability,
compatibility, compensability,
compressability,
computability, conceivability,
conductability, confirmability,
contemptibility,
contractibility, controllability,
convertibility, corrigibility,
corruptibility, cultivability,
damageability, decidability,
deductibility, defeasibility,
defensibility, delectability,
demonstrability, deniability,
dependability, desirability,
destructibility, detachability,
detectability, deterrability,
detonability, digestibility,
dilatability, dispensability,
disposability, dissociability,
dissolubility, distensibility,
distractibility, divisibility,
educability, electability,
eligibility, employability,
enforceability, equitability,
erasability, erodability,
exchangeability, excitability,
excludability, exhaustibility,
expansibility, expendability,
explosibility, exportability,
extensibility, extractibility,
extrudability, fashionability,
fatigability, filterability,
fissionability, formidability,
habitability, heritability,

illegibility, immiscibility,
immovability, immutability,
impalpability, impassability,
impassibility, impeccability,
implacability, implausibility,
impossibility, impregnability,
impressibility, improbability,
improvability, inaudibility,
incapability, incredibility,
indelibility, inductibility,
ineffability, infallibility,
infeasibility, inflammability,
inflexibility, infrangibility,
infusibility, insensibility,
insolubility, insurability,
intangibility, invincibility,
invisibility, irascibility,
irritability, knowledgeability,
machinability, maintainability,
manageability, marketability,
merchantability,
measurability, modulability,
navigability, negligibility,
nonflammability, openability,
operability, opposability,
palatability, penetrability,
perceptibility, perdurability,
perfectibility, performability,
perishability, permeability,
permissibility, pleasurability,
practicability, preferability,
presentability, preservability,
preventability, processibility,
programmability,
punishability, reasonability,
refundability, reliability,
renewability, repeatability,
reputability, resistibility,
respectability, responsibility,
retrievability, reusability,
reversability, salvageability,
separability, severability,

serviceability, suggestability,
supportability, suppressibility,
survivability, susceptibility,
sustainability, tolerability,
trafficability, transferability,
translatability,
transmissibility,
transplantability,
transportability,
unflappability, unthinkability,
untouchability, variability,
violability, vulnerability,
weatherability, alienability,
analyzability, assimilability,
codifiability,
commensurability,
communicability,
comprehensibility,
decomposability,
deliverability,
discriminability,
disrespectability,
distinguishability,
enumerability,
exceptionability,
hypnotizability, illimitability,
impenetrability,
imperishability,
impermeability,
impermissibility,
imponderability,
impracticability,
impressionability,
inaccessibility,
inadmissibility, inadvisability,
inalterability, inapplicability,
incalculability,
incombustibility,
incomparability,
incompatibility,
incompressibility,
inconceivability,

incontestability,
inconvertibility,
incorrigibility,
incorruptibility,
indefeasibility, indefensibility,
indefinability,
indestructibility,
indigestibility,
indispensability,
indissolubility, indivisibility,
indomitability, indubitability,
ineducability, ineffaceability,
ineligibility, ineluctability,
inevitability, inexhaustibility,
inexplicability,
inexpressibility,
inextricability, inheritability,
insatiability, inseparability,
insociability, insusceptibility,
intelligibility,
interchangeability,
intolerability, invariability,
invulnerability, irreducibility,
irreformability, irrefutability,
irremovability, irrepealability,
irreplaceability,
irrepressibility,
irreproachability,
irresistibility, irresponsibility,
irretrievability, irreversibility,
irrevocability,
maneuverability,
manipulability, negotiability,
polarizability, recognizability,
recoverability, rectifiability,
reprehensibility,
reproducibility,
substitutability,
unacceptability,
unaccountability,
understandability,
undesirability, verifiability,

biocompatability,
biodegradability,
differentiability, inalienability,
incommensurability,
incommunicability,
incomprehensibility,
indefatigability,
indistinguishability,
ineradicability,
incontrovertibility,
irreconcilability,
irreproducibility,
interoperability

ilium \il-ē-əm\ cilium, ileum,
ilium, Ilium, milium, trillium,
beryllium, penicillium

ilk \ilk\ bilk, ilk, milch, milk,
silk, buttermilk, liebfraumilch

ilker \il-kər\ bilker, milker

ilky \il-kē\ milky, silky

ill \il\ bill, Bill, brill, chill, dill,
drill, fill, frill, gill, grill,
grille, hill, ill, Jill, kill, krill,
mil, mill, mille, Milne, nil,
nill, Phil, pill, prill, quill, rill,
shill, shrill, sild, sill, skill,
spill, squill, still, swill, thill,
thrill, til, till, trill, twill, vill,
will, Will, anthill, backfill,
bluegill, Brazil, Catskill,
Churchill, cranesbill,
crossbill, de Mille, dentil,
deskill, distill, doorsill,
downhill, duckbill, dullsville,
dunghill, fiberfill, foothill,
freewill, fulfill, goodwill,
Granville, gristmill, handbill,
hawksbill, hornbill,
Huntsville, instill, Knoxville,
lambkill, landfill, limekiln,
manille, Melville, molehill,
mudsill, Nashville, no-till,

playbill, quadrille, refill, roadkill, sawmill, self-will, Seville, sheathbill, shoebill, sidehill, sigil, spadille, spoonbill, stabile, standstill, stockstill, storksbill, T-bill, treadmill, unreal, until, uphill, vaudeville, waxbill, waybill, windchill, windmill, Brazzaville, chlorophyll, daffodil, deshabille, de Toqueville, dishabille, escadrille, espadrille, Evansville, Francophil, Hooverville, Jacksonville, Libreville, Louisville, minimill, overfill, overkill, overspill, razorbill, rototill, tormentil, verticil, windowsill, whippoorwill, winter-kill, Yggdrasil, acidophil, ivorybill, minoxydil, Nizhni Togil, run-of-the-mill

I'll \īl\ see ¹ILE

¹**illa** \ē-yə\ barilla, cuadrilla, banderilla, quesadilla

²**illa** \il-ə\ scilla, Scylla, squilla, villa, Willa, ancilla, Aquila, Attila, axilla, Camilla, cedilla, chinchilla, flotilla, gorilla, guerrilla, manila, Manila, megillah, papilla, perilla, Priscilla, scintilla, vanilla, camarilla, cascarilla, granadilla, potentilla, sabadilla, sapodilla, sarsaparilla

³**illa** \ē-ə\ see ¹IA

⁴**illa** \ēl-yə\ see ELIA

⁵**illa** \ē-lə\ see ¹ELA

illable \il-ə-bəl\ billable, drillable, fillable, spillable, syllable, tillable, disyllable, refillable, trisyllable, decasyllable, monosyllable, octosyllable, polysyllable, hendecasyllable

illage \il-ij\ grillage, millage, pillage, spillage, tillage, village, no-tillage, permillage, Greenwich Village

illah \il-ə\ see ²ILLA

illain \il-ən\ see ILLON

illar \il-ər\ see ILLER

illary \il-ə-rē\ Hilary, Hillary, phyllary, codicillary

illate \il-ət\ see ILLET

¹**ille** \il\ see ILL

²**ille** \ē\ see ¹EE

³**ille** \ēl\ see ²EAL

illea \il-yə\ see ²ILIA

illed \ild\ build, dilled, drilled, gild, gilled, guild, skilled, twilled, willed, Brynhild, engild, gold-filled, goodwilled, rebuild, self-willed, spoonbilled, unbuild, unskilled, upbuild, wergild, jerry-build, overbuild, semiskilled—*also pasts of verbs listed at* ILL

illedness \il-nəs\ see ILLNESS

illein \il-ən\ see ILLON

iller \il-ər\ biller, chiller, driller, filler, giller, griller, hiller, killer, miller, Miller, pillar, schiller, spiller, swiller, thriller, tiller, triller, axillar, distiller, fulfiller, painkiller, pralltriller, von Schiller, caterpillar, lady-killer, Rototiller—*also comparatives of adjectives listed at* ILL

illery \il-rē\ pillory, artillery, distillery

illes \il-ēz\ see ILLIES

illet \il-ət\ billet, fillet, millet, rillet, skillet, willet, distillate

illful \il-fəl\ skillful, willful, unskillful

¹**illi** \il-ē\ see ¹ILLY

²**illi** \ē-lē\ see EELY

¹**illian** \il-ē-ən\ see ¹ILIAN

²**illian** \il-yən\ see ILLION

illiance \il-yəns\ brilliance, resilience

illiancy \il-yən-sē\ brilliancy, resiliency

illiant \il-yənt\ see ILIENT

illick \il-ik\ see ILIC

illie \il-ē\ see ¹ILLY

illies \il-ēz\ willies, Achilles, Antilles, Greater Antilles, Lesser Antilles, Netherlands Antilles—*also plurals and possessives of nouns listed at* ¹ILLY

illikan \il-i-kən\ see ILICON

illikin \il-i-kən\ see ILICON

¹**illin** \il-əm\ see ILLUM

²**illin** \il-ən\ see ILLON

illing \il-iŋ\ billing, drilling, filling, killing, milling, schilling, shilling, skilling, twilling, willing, fulfilling, spine-chilling, unwilling

illion \il-yən\ billion, jillion, Lillian, million, pillion, trillion, zillion, caecilian, Castilian, centillion, civilian, cotillion, decillion, modillion, nonillion, octillion, pavilion, postilion, quadrillion, Quintilian, quintillion, reptilian, septillion, sextillion, toubillion, vaudevillian, vermilion, crocodilian, Maximilian, preexilian, quindecillion, sexdecillion, tredecillion, undecillion, vespertilian, vigintillion, duodecillion, novemdecillion, octodecillion, septendecillion, quattuordecillion

illip \il-əp\ fillip, Philip

illis \il-əs\ see ILLUS

illium \il-ē-əm\ see ILIUM

illness \il-nəs\ chillness, illness, shrillness, stillness

¹**illo** \il-ō\ billow, pillow, willow, Negrillo, tornillo, Amarillo, armadillo, cigarillo, coyotillo, peccadillo, tamarillo

²**illo** \ē-ō\ see ²IO

illon \il-ən\ billon, Dylan, Uilleann, villain, villein, tefillin, penicillin, amoxycillin

illory \il-rē\ see ILLERY

illous \il-əs\ see ILLUS

¹**illow** \il-ə\ see ²ILLA

²**illow** \il-ō\ see ¹ILLO

illowy \il-ə-wē\ billowy, pillowy, willowy

ills \ilz\ Black Hills, no-frills, Alban Hills—*also plurals and possessives of nouns, third person singular presents of verbs at* ILL

illum \il-əm\ chillum, vexillum

illus \il-əs\ Phyllis, villous, Willis, bacillus, lapillus, amaryllis, toga virilis

¹**illy** \il-ē\ Billie, billy, Chile, chili, chilly, dilly, filly, frilly, gillie, hilly, illy, Lillie, lily, Lily, Millie, really, Scilly,

silly, stilly, Willie, Willy,
bacilli, Caerphilly, daylily,
fusilli, guidwillie, hillbilly,
piccalilli, rockabilly, willy-
nilly

²illy \il-lē\ shrilly, stilly

¹iln \il\ see ILL

²iln \iln\ kiln, Milne

¹ilne \iln\ see ²ILN

²ilne \il\ see ILL

¹ilo \ī-lō\ milo, Milo, phyllo,
silo

²ilo \ē-lō\ helo, kilo, phyllo,
Iloilo

ilom \ī-ləm\ see ILUM

iloquence \il-ə-kwəns\
grandiloquence,
magniloquence

iloquent \il-ə-kwənt\
grandiloquent, magniloquent

iloquist \il-ə-kwəst\ soliloquist,
ventriloquist

iloquy \il-ə-kwē\ soliloquy,
ventriloquy

ilot \ī-lət\ eyelet, islet, Pilate,
pilot, stylet, copilot, autopilot,
Pontius Pilate

ils \ils\ fils, grilse, Nils

ilse \ils\ see ILS

ilt \ilt\ built, gilt, guilt, hilt, jilt,
kilt, lilt, milt, quilt, silt, stilt,
tilt, wilt, atilt, bloodguilt,
Brunhild, homebuilt, inbuilt,
rebuilt, unbuilt, uptilt, carvel-
built, clinker-built, custom-
built, purpose-built

ilter \il-tər\ filter, kilter, milter,
philter, off-kilter

ilth \ilth\ filth, spilth, tilth

iltie \il-tē\ see ILTY

ilton \ilt-ᵊn\ Hilton, Milton,
Stilton, Wilton

ilty \il-tē\ guilty, kiltie, milty,
silty, bloodguilty

ilum \ī-ləm\ filum, hilum,
phylum, whilom, xylem,
asylum

ilus \ī-ləs\ eyeless, pilus, stylus,
tieless

¹ily \ī-lē\ see YLY

²ily \il-ē\ see ¹ILLY

¹im \im\ bream, brim, dim,
glim, grim, Grimm, gym,
him, hymn, Jim, Kim, limb,
limn, mim, nim, prim, rim,
scrim, shim, skim, slim,
swim, Tim, trim, vim, whim,
bedim, dislimn, forelimb,
passim, prelim, Purim,
Sikkim, slim-jim, snap-brim,
acronym, anonym, antonym,
eponym, homonym,
metonym, paradigm,
paronym, pseudonym,
seraphim, synonym,
tautonym, toponym,
underbrim, ad interim,
heteronym

²im \ēm\ see ¹EAM

I'm \īm\ see ¹IME

ima \ē-mə\ see EMA

imable \ī-mə-bəl\ climable,
sublimable, unclimbable

imace \im-əs\ grimace, tzimmes

image \im-ij\ image,
scrimmage, self-image,
afterimage

iman \ē-mən\ see ¹EMON

imate \ī-mət\ climate, primate,
acclimate

¹imb \im\ see ¹IM

²imb \īm\ see ¹IME

imba \im-bə\ limba, kalimba,
marimba

imbable \ī-mə-bəl\ see IMABLE
imbal \im-bəl\ see IMBLE
imbale \im-bəl\ see IMBLE
imbed \imd\ limbed, rimmed, clean-limbed—*also pasts of verbs listed at* ¹IM
¹**imber** \im-bər\ limber, timber, sawtimber, unlimber
²**imber** \ī-mər\ see ¹IMER
imble \im-bəl\ cymbal, gimbal, nimble, symbol, thimble, timbal, timbale, wimble
imbo \im-bō\ bimbo, limbo, akimbo, gumbo-limbo
imbral \am-brəl\ see AMBREL
imbre \am-bər\ see ²AMBAR
imbrel \im-brəl\ timbrel, whimbrel
imbus \im-bəs\ limbus, nimbus
¹**ime** \īm\ chime, climb, clime, crime, dime, disme, grime, I'm, lime, mime, prime, rhyme, rime, slime, stime, thyme, time, airtime, all-time, bedtime, begrime, big time, birdlime, daytime, downtime, dreamtime, enzyme, flextime, foretime, halftime, lifetime, longtime, lunchtime, Mannheim, Maytime, mealtime, meantime, nighttime, noontime, old-time, onetime, part-time, pastime, peacetime, playtime, quicklime, ragtime, schooltime, seedtime, small-time, sometime, space-time, springtime, sublime, teatime, two-time, uptime, wartime, aftertime, Anaheim, anytime, beforetime, Christmastime, dinnertime, double-time,

harvesttime, Jotunheim, lysozyme, maritime, monorhyme, overtime, pantomime, paradigm, summertime, wintertime, nickel-and-dime
²**ime** \ēm\ see ¹EAM
imel \im-əl\ gimel, gimmal, kümmel
imeless \īm-ləs\ rhymeless, timeless
imely \īm-lē\ primely, timely, untimely
imen \ī-mən\ flyman, hymen, Hymen, limen, Lyman, Simon
imeon \im-ē-ən\ see IMIAN
imeous \ī-məs\ see IMIS
¹**imer** \ī-mər\ chimer, climber, dimer, mimer, primer, rhymer, timer, trimer, full-timer, old-timer, small-timer, sublimer, two-timer, wisenheimer
²**imer** \im-ər\ see IMMER
imerick \im-rik\ see YMRIC
¹**imes** \īmz\ times, betimes, daytimes, sometimes, betweentimes, oftentimes—*also plurals and possessives of nouns and third person singular presents of verbs listed at* ¹IME
²**imes** \ēm\ see ¹EAM
imeter \im-ət-ər\ dimeter, limiter, scimitar, trimeter, altimeter, delimiter, perimeter, tachymeter
imetry \im-ə-trē\ symmetry, gravimetry, polarimetry, sypersymmetry
imian \im-ē-ən\ Simeon, simian, Endymion, prosimian

imic \im-ik\ see ²YMIC

imical \im-i-kəl\ inimical, metonymical, synonymical, toponymical

imicry \im-i-krē\ gimmickry, mimicry

imilar \im-ə-lər\ similar, dissimilar

imile \im-ə-lē\ simile, swimmily, facsimile

¹iminal \im-ən-ᵊl\ criminal, liminal, subliminal, supraliminal

²iminal \im-nəl\ see YMNAL

iminy \im-ə-nē\ see IMONY

imis \ī-məs\ primus, thymus, timeous, imprimis, untimeous

imitable \im-ət-ə-bəl\ imitable, illimitable, inimitable

imitar \im-ət-ər\ see IMETER

imiter \im-ət-ər\ see IMETER

imits \im-its\ limits, Nimitz

imity \im-ət-ē\ dimity, proximity, sublimity, anonymity, equanimity, longanimity, magnanimity, pseudonymity, synonymity, unanimity, pusillanimity

imitz \im-its\ see IMITS

imm \im\ see ¹IM

immable \im-ə-bəl\ dimmable, swimmable

immage \im-ij\ see IMAGE

immal \im-əl\ see IMEL

imme \i-mē\ see IMMY

immed \imd\ see IMBED

immer \im-ər\ brimmer, dimmer, glimmer, krimmer, limmer, limner, primer, shimmer, simmer, skimmer, slimmer, swimmer, trimmer—

also comparatives of adjectives listed at ¹IM

immes \im-əs\ see IMACE

immick \im-ik\ see ²YMIC

immickry \im-i-krē\ see IMICRY

immily \im-ə-lē\ see IMILE

immy \im-ē\ gimme, jimmy, limby, shimmy, swimmy

imn \im\ see ¹IM

imner \im-ər\ see IMMER

imo \ē-mō\ primo, sentimo

imon \ī-mən\ see IMEN

imony \im-ə-nē\ simony, niminy-piminy

imothy \im-ə-thē\ timothy, Timothy, polymathy

imp \imp\ blimp, chimp, crimp, gimp, guimpe, imp, limp, pimp, primp, scrimp, shrimp, simp, skimp, wimp, comsymp

impe \imp\ see IMP

imper \im-pər\ limper, shrimper, simper, whimper

imping \im-pən\ see YMPAN

impish \im-pish\ blimpish, impish

imple \im-pəl\ dimple, pimple, simple, wimple, oversimple

imply \im-plē\ dimply, limply, pimply, simply

impy \im-pē\ crimpy, gimpy, scrimpy, shrimpy, skimpy, wimpy

imsy \im-zē\ flimsy, slimsy, whimsy

imulus \im-yə-ləs\ limulus, stimulus

imus \ī-məs\ see IMIS

imy \ī-mē\ grimy, limey, limy, rimy, slimy, stymie, thymy, old-timey

¹in \in\ been, bin, blin, chin,

din, fin, Finn, gin, grin,
Gwyn, hin, in, inn, kin, linn,
Lynn, Lynne, pin, shin, Shin,
sin, skin, spin, thin, tin, twin,
whin, win, wyn, yin, zin,
again, agin, akin, all-in,
backspin, bearskin, begin,
Benin, Berlin, Boleyn,
bowfin, break-in, buckskin,
built-in, burn-in, calfskin,
capeskin, cave-in, chagrin,
check-in, Chongjin, close-in,
clothespin, coonskin, Corinne,
crankpin, cut-in, deerskin,
doeskin, drive-in, drop-in,
duckpin, dustbin, fade-in, fill-
in, foreskin, goatskin, Guilin,
hairpin, Harbin, has-been,
headpin, herein, Jilin, Kerin,
kidskin, kingpin, lambskin,
lead-in, lie-in, linchpin, live-
in, lived-in, lobe-fin, locked-
in, look-in, love-in, moleskin,
munchkin, Nankin, ninepin,
no-win, oilskin, Pekin, phone-
in, pigskin, pinyin, plug-in,
pushpin, redskin, ruin, run-in,
saimin, scarfpin, scarfskin,
sealskin, set-in, sharkskin,
sheepskin, shoo-in, shut-in,
sidespin, sit-in, sleep-in,
snakeskin, stand-in, step-in,
stickpin, swanskin, tailspin,
take-in, tap-in, teach-in,
tenpin, therein, tholepin,
threadfin, throw-in, tie-in,
tiepin, tip-in, toe-in, trade-in,
tuned-in, turn-in, unpin, walk-
in, weigh-in, wherein,
wineskin, within, woolskin,
write-in, candlepin, catechin,
Ha-erh-pin, Ho Chi Minh,
Lohengrin, lying-in,
mandolin, maximin, Mickey
Finn, onionskin, palanquin,
Tianjin, underpin, underspin,
Vietminh, violin, whipper-in,
canthaxanthin

²**in** \ēn\ see ³INE

³**in** \an\ see ⁵AN

⁴**in** \aⁿ\ Chopin, doyen,
Gauguin, moulin, Petain,
Rodin, serin, coq au vin, coup
de main, fleur de coin,
Mazarin

⁵**in** \ən\ see ¹UN

¹**ina** \ī-nə\ china, China, Dina,
Dinah, Heine, Ina, mina,
mynah, Aegina, angina,
Lucina, nandina, piscina,
Regina, salina, shechinah,
vagina, Cochin China,
Carolina, Indochina,
kamaaina, Poland China,
North Carolina, South
Carolina

²**ina** \ē-nə\ Deena, Dena, kina,
Lena, Nina, plena, Shina,
Tina, vena, vina, arena,
Athena, cantina, catena,
Christina, coquina, corbina,
corvina, czarina, Edwina,
euglena, farina, fontina,
Georgina, hyena, kachina,
Kristina, marina, Marina,
medina, Medina, Messina,
nandina, novena, patina,
piscina, platina, Regina,
retsina, Rowena, salina,
sestina, Shechinah, subpoena,
verbena, Agrippina, amberina,
Angelina, Argentina,
ballerina, casuarina, Carolina,
Catalina, catilena, cavatina,

Chianina, concertina, Filipina, javelina, Katerina, ocarina, Palestrina, palomino, Pasadena, Saint Helena, semolina, signorina, sonatina, Taormina, Teresina, Wilhelminia, Herzegovina, Pallas Athena, Strait of Messina

inable \ī-nə-bəl\ minable, consignable, declinable, definable, inclinable, indeclinable, indefinable

inach \in-ich\ Greenwich, spinach

¹inah \ē-nə\ see ²INA

²inah \ī-nə\ see ¹INA

¹inal \īn-ᵊl\ clinal, final, rhinal, spinal, trinal, vinyl, matutinal, officinal, quarterfinal, semifinal, serotinal

²inal \ēn-ᵊl\ see ENAL

inally \īn-ᵊl-ē\ clinally, finally, spinally, matutinally

inary \ī-nə-rē\ binary, trinary

¹inas \ī-nəs\ see ¹INUS

²inas \ē-nəs\ see ¹ENUS

inative \in-ət-iv\ see INITIVE

inc \iŋk\ see INK

inca \iŋ-kə\ Dinka, Inca, vinca, Mandinka

incal \iŋ-kəl\ see INKLE

incan \iŋ-kən\ Incan, Lincoln

¹ince \ins\ blintz, chintz, mince, prince, quince, rinse, since, wince, convince, evince, shinsplints, Port-au-Prince

²ince \ans\ see ³ANCE

incely \in-slē\ princely, tinselly

incer \in-chər\ see INCHER

inch \inch\ chinch, cinch, clinch, finch, flinch, grinch,

inch, lynch, pinch, squinch, winch, bullfinch, goldfinch, greenfinch, hawfinch, unclinch

incher \in-chər\ clincher, flincher, lyncher, pincer, pincher, wincher, affenpinscher, penny-pincher, Doberman pinscher

inching \in-chiŋ\ unflinching, penny-pinching

incible \in-sə-bəl\ principal, principle, vincible, evincible, invincible, inconvincible

incing \in-siŋ\ ginseng, mincing, convincing, unconvincing

incipal \in-sə-bəl\ see INCIBLE

inciple \in-sə-bəl\ see INCIBLE

inck \iŋk\ see INK

incky \iŋ-kē\ see INKY

incoln \iŋ-kən\ see INCAN

inct \iŋt\ linked, kinked, tinct, distinct, extinct, instinct, precinct, succinct, unlinked, indistinct

inction \iŋ-shən\ distinction, extinction, contradistinction

inctive \iŋ-tiv\ distinctive, extinctive, instinctive, indistinctive

incture \iŋ-chər\ cincture, tincture

¹ind \īnd\ bind, blind, find, grind, hind, kind, mind, rind, signed, spined, tined, wind, wynd, affined, behind, confined, inclined, in-kind, night-blind, purblind, refined, remind, rewind, sand-blind, snow-blind, spellbind, stone-blind, streamlined, unbind, unkind, unwind, color-blind, double-blind, gavelkind, gravel-blind, hoodman-blind, humankind, mastermind, nonaligned, single-blind, unaligned, undersigned, well-defined, womankind—*also pasts of verbs listed at* ¹INE

²**ind** \ind\ finned, Ind, Sind, skinned, wind, buckskinned, crosswind, downwind, exscind, prescind, rescind, soft-finned, thick-skinned, thin-skinned, upwind, whirlwind, woodwind, Amerind, spiny-finned, tamarind—*also pasts of verbs listed at* ¹IN

³**ind** \int\ see INT

inda \in-də\ Linda, Lucinda, Melinda, Samarinda

indar \in-dər\ see ²INDER

¹**inded** \īn-dəd\ minded, rinded, broad-minded, fair-minded, high-minded, large-minded, like-minded, low-minded, right-minded, small-minded, strong-minded, tough-minded, weak-minded, absentminded, bloody-minded, civic-minded, evil-minded, feebleminded, narrow-minded, open-minded, simpleminded, single-minded, social-minded, tender-minded—*also regular pasts of verbs listed at* ¹IND

²**inded** \in-dəd\ brinded, long-winded, short-winded, broken-winded—*also pasts of verbs listed at* ²IND

¹**inder** \īn-dər\ binder, blinder, finder, grinder, hinder, minder, winder, bookbinder, faultfinder, highbinder, netminder, pathfinder, ring binder, self-binder, sidewinder, spellbinder, stem-winder, viewfinder, organ-grinder—*also comparatives of adjectives listed at* ¹IND

²**inder** \in-dər\ cinder, hinder, Pindar, tinder

indful \īn-fəl\ mindful, remindful, unmindful

indhi \in-dē\ see INDY

indi \in-dē\ see INDY

indic \in-dik\ Indic, syndic

indie \in-dē\ see INDY

inding \īn-diŋ\ binding, finding, winding, bookbinding, fact-finding, faultfinding, pathfinding, self-winding, spellbinding, stem-winding

indlass \in-ləs\ see INLESS

indle \in-dᵊl\ brindle, dwindle, kindle, spindle, swindle, enkindle

indless \īn-ləs\ kindless, mindless, spineless

¹**indling** \in-lən\ pindling, spindling

²**indling** \ind-liŋ\ dwindling, kindling, pindling, spindling

¹**indly** \in-lē\ see INLY

²**indly** \īn-lē\ see ¹INELY

indness \īn-nəs\ blindness, fineness, kindness, purblindness, unkindness, loving-kindness

indowed \in-dəd\ see ²INDED

indus \in-dəs\ Indus, Pindus

indy \in-dē\ Cindy, Hindi, indie, lindy, shindy, Sindhi, windy, Rawalpindi

¹**ine** \īn\ bine, brine, chine,

cline, dine, dyne, eyen, fine,
Jain, kine, line, Line, Main,
mine, nine, pine, Rhein,
Rhine, rind, shine, shrine,
sign, spine, spline, stein,
Stein, swine, syne, thine, tine,
trine, twine, vine, whine,
wine, A-line, affine, airline,
align, alkyne, alpine, assign,
balkline, baseline, beeline,
benign, Bernstein, bloodline,
bovine, bowline, branchline,
breadline, buntline, bustline,
byline, canine, caprine,
carbine, carmine, cervine,
clothesline, coastline,
combine, compline, condign,
confine, consign, corvine,
cutline, dateline, deadline,
decline, define, design, divine,
dragline, driveline, earthshine,
Einstein, eiswein, enshrine,
ensign, entwine, equine,
ethyne, feline, ferine, fraulein,
frontline, gantline, grapevine,
guideline, hairline, hard-line,
headline, hemline, hipline,
Holbein, Holstein, incline,
indign, in-line, jawline,
landline, lang syne, lifeline,
longline, lupine, mainline,
malign, midline, moline,
moonshine, off-line, old-line,
opine, outline, outshine,
ovine, Pauline, Pennine,
Petrine, pipeline, piscine,
plotline, pontine, Pontine,
porcine, potline, propine,
quinine, rapine, recline,
redline, refine, reline, repine,
resign, ridgeline, roofline,
Sabine, saline, setline,

shoreline, sideline, Sixtine,
skyline, soft-line, straight-
line, strandline, streamline,
strychnine, subline, sunshine,
supine, syncline, taurine, tie-
line, time-line, topline,
touchline, towline, tramline,
trapline, trephine, trotline,
truckline, tumpline, turbine,
untwine, ursine, vespine,
vulpine, waistline, woodbine,
zayin, zebrine, aerodyne,
alkaline, androgyne,
Angeline, anodyne, anserine,
anticline, aquiline, argentine,
asinine, auld lang syne,
borderline, bottom-line,
Byzantine, calamine,
calcimine, Caroline,
catarrhine, Catiline, celandine,
centerline, cisalpine,
Cisalpine, clandestine,
colubrine, columbine,
Columbine, concubine,
Constantine, countermine,
countersign, crystalline,
cytokine, disincline, eglantine,
endocrine, exocrine,
falconine, fescennine,
Frankenstein, gregarine,
infantine, interline, intertwine,
iodine, Johannine, leonine,
Liechtenstein, monkeyshine,
muscadine, opaline, palatine,
Palestine, passerine,
porcupine, psittacine, realign,
redefine, redesign, riverine,
Rubenstein, saccharine,
sapphirine, saturnine,
serpentine, sibylline, sixty-
nine, subalpine, Theatine,
timberline, turnverein,

turpentine, underline, undermine, Ursuline, uterine, valentine, vespertine, viperine, vulturine, waterline, zibeline, accipitrine, adamantine, adulterine, alexandrine, amaranthine, Capitoline, elephantine, Evangeline, Frankfurt am Main, Rembrandt van Rijn, Scheswig-Holstein, nonoxynol-9, Newcastle-upon Tyne

²ine \ē-nā\ fine, wahine

³ine \ēn\ bean, clean, dean, Dean, Deane, dene, e'en, gene, Gene, glean, green, Green, greene, jean, Jean, Jeanne, keen, lean, lien, mean, mesne, mien, peen, preen, quean, queen, scene, screen, seen, sheen, shin, sin, skean, skene, spean, spleen, teen, tween, wean, ween, wheen, yean, Aileen, Arlene, baleen, beguine, Beguine, Benin, Bernstein, between, boreen, bovine, buckbean, caffeine, canteen, carbine, careen, Carlene, Cathleen, Charlene, chlorine, chopine, chorine, Christine, citrine, Claudine, codeine, colleen, Colleen, convene, Coreen, cotquean, cuisine, Darlene, dasheen, dauphine, demean, demesne, dentine, Doreen, dry-clean, dudeen, eighteen, Eileen, Essene, Eugene, fanzine, fascine, fifteen, fourteen, Francine, gamine, gangrene, glassine, gyrene,

Helene, Hellene, Hermine, hoatzin, holstein, Holstein, horsebean, houseclean, hygiene, Ilene, Irene, Jacqueline, Jeanine, Jeannine, Jolene, Justine, Kathleen, khamsin, Kristine, Ladin, lateen, latrine, Lorene, Lublin, machine, malines, marine, Marlene, Maureen, Maxine, moline, moreen, morphine, Nadine, nankeen, naphthene, Nicene, nineteen, nongreen, Noreen, obscene, offscreen, on-screen, patine, Pauline, piscine, Pontine, poteen, praline, preteen, pristine, propine, protein, quinine, Rabin, Racine, ratteen, ravine, routine, saline, saltine, Salween, sardine, sateen, scalene, serene, shagreen, Sharlene, shebeen, siren, Sistine, sixteen, Slovene, soybean, spalpeen, strychnine, subteen, sunscreen, Szczecin, takin, taurine, terrene, terrine, thirteen, Tolkien, tontine, tureen, umpteen, unclean, undine, unseen, vaccine, vitrine, windscreen, yestreen, Yibin, zechin, Aberdeen, almandine, Angeline, argentine, Argentine, Augustine, barkentine, bengaline, Bernadine, bombazine, Borodin, brigandine, brigantine, brilliantine, Byzantine, carotene, carrageen, celandine, clandestine, columbine, Constantine, contravene, crepe de chine, crystalline, damascene, Dexedrine, Dramamine, duvetyn, eglantine, endocrine, Eocene, epicene, Ernestine, estaurine, evergreen, fescennine, figurine, Florentine, fluorine, fukerene, gabardine, gaberdine, gadarene, galantine, gasoline, Geraldine, Ghibelline, go-between, grenadine, Gretna Green, guillotine, Halloween, haute cuisine, Hippocrene, histamine, Holocene, Imogene, in-between, indigene, intervene, Jeraldine, Josephine, Kalinin, kerosene, langoustine, legatine, libertine, limousine, M16, magazine, mangosteen, margravine, Medellìn, melamine, messaline, Methedrine, mezzanine, Miocene, mousseline, Nazarene, nectarine, nicotine, overseen, opaline, organzine, palanquin, palatine, pelerine, percaline, peregrine, philhellene, Philistine, plasticene, plasticine, Pleistocene, Pliocene, riverine, quarantine, reserpine, saccharine, Sakhalin, Saladin, San Joaquin, San Martin, sapphirine, schizophrene, serpentine, seventeen, silkaline, Stelazine, submarine, subroutine, supervene, tambourine, tangerine, Theatine, tourmaline, trampoline, transmarine, travertine, Tridentine, Vaseline, velveteen, wintergreen, wolverine, Ursuline, adamantine, alexandrine, amphetamine, aquamarine, Benedictine, bromocriptine, carbon 13, doxycycline, elephantine, Evangeline, internecine, leukotirene, methylxanthene, mujahideen, niphedipine, nouvelle cuisine, Oligocene, Paleocene, pentamedine, tricothecene, ultramarine, antihistamine, benzoapyrene, diphenhydramine, Mary Magdalene, NC-17, polybutadiene, alpha-fetaprotein, apolipoprotein, buckminsterfullerene, General San Martin, oleomargarine

⁴ine \in-ē\ see INNY

⁵ine \ē-nē\ see ¹INI

⁶ine \ən\ see UN

inea \in-ē\ see INNY

ineal \in-ē-əl\ finial, lineal, matrilineal, patrilineal, unilineal

ined \īnd\ see ¹IND

inee \ī-nē\ see ¹INY

ineless \īn-ləs\ see INDLESS

¹inely \īn-lē\ blindly, finely, kindly, affinely, condignly, equinely, felinely, purblindly, unkindly

²inely \ēn-lē\ see ¹EANLY

inement \īn-mənt\ see IGNMENT

ineness \īn-nəs\ see INDNESS

ineous \in-ē-əs\ gramineous, sanguineous, consanguineous, ignominious

¹**iner** \ī-nər\ briner, diner, finer, liner, miner, minor, shiner, Shriner, signer, twiner, whiner, airliner, aligner, baseliner, byliner, combiner, confiner, cosigner, definer, designer, diviner, eyeliner, hardliner, headliner, incliner, jetliner, long-liner, moonshiner, one-liner, recliner, refiner, repiner, sideliner, soft-liner, streamliner, Asia Minor, Canis Minor, forty-niner, party-liner, Ursa Minor, superliner

²**iner** \ē-nər\ see EANER

¹**inery** \īn-rē\ finery, pinery, vinery, winery, refinery

²**inery** \ēn-rē\ see EANERY

¹**ines** \ēn\ see ³INE

²**ines** \ēnz\ see EENS

³**ines** \īnz\ Mainz, Appenines—*also plurals and possessives of nouns and third person singular presents of verbs listed at* ¹INE

inest \ī-nəst\ see ¹INIST

inet \in-ət\ see INNET

inew \in-yü\ see INUE

infield \in-fēld\ infield, Winfield

ing \iŋ\ bring, Ching, cling, ding, fling, king, King, ling, Ming, ping, ring, sing, sling, spring, sting, string, swing, thing, wing, wring, zing, backswing, Baoding, bedspring, Beijing, bi-swing, bitewing, bowstring, bullring, Chongqing, clearwing, downswing, drawstring, D ring, earring, first-string, forewing, G-string, greenwing, hairspring, hamstring, handspring, headspring, heartstring, Kunming, lacewing, lapwing, latchstring, mainspring, Nanjing, Nanning, O-ring, offspring, Paoting, plaything, redwing, shoestring, showring, unsling, unstring, upspring, upswing, wellspring, whitewing, windwing, wingding, Xining, à la king, anything, buck-and-wing, ding-a-ling, double-ring, everything, innerspring, Liaoning, pigeonwing, superstring, underwing

inga \iŋ-gə\ anhinga, syringa

inge \inj\ binge, cringe, dinge, fringe, hinge, singe, springe, swinge, tinge, twinge, whinge, impinge, infringe, syringe, unhinge

inged \iŋd\ ringed, stringed, winged, net-winged—*also regular pasts of verbs listed at* ING

ingement \inj-mənt\ impingement, infringement

ingency \in-jən-sē\ stringency, astringency, contingency

ingent \in-jənt\ stringent, astringent, constringent, contingent, refringent

¹**inger** \iŋ-ər\ bringer, clinger, dinger, flinger, pinger, ringer, singer, springer, stinger, stringer, swinger, winger, wringer, zinger, folksinger, gunslinger, humdinger, left-winger, mudslinger, right-

winger, mastersinger,
Meistersinger, minnesinger

²**inger** \iŋ-gər\ finger, linger,
five-finger, forefinger,
malinger, ladyfinger

³**inger** \in-jər\ ginger, Ginger,
injure, singer, swinger

ingery \inj-rē\ gingery, injury

inghy \iŋ-ē\ see ¹INGY

ingi \iŋ-ē\ see ¹INGY

ingian \in-jən\ Thuringian,
Carlovingian, Carolingian,
Merovingian

inging \iŋ-iŋ\ ringing,
springing, stringing, swinging,
folksinging, free-swinging,
gunslinging, handwringing,
mudslinging, upbringing

ingit \iŋ-kət\ see INKET

ingle \iŋ-gəl\ cringle, dingle,
jingle, mingle, shingle, single,
tingle, atingle, commingle,
immingle, Kriss Kringle,
surcingle, intermingle

ingler \iŋ-glər\ jingler, shingler

inglet \iŋ-lət\ kinglet, ringlet,
winglet

ingletree \iŋ-gəl-trē\ singletree,
swingletree

ingli \ing-lē\ see INGLY

inglish \iŋ-glish\ see ENGLISH

ingly \iŋ-glē\ jingly, shingly,
singly, tingly, Zwingli

ingo \iŋ-gō\ bingo, dingo,
gringo, jingo, lingo, pingo,
flamingo, Mandingo, Santo
Domingo

ings \iŋz\ Kings, springs,
eyestrings, Hot Springs,
Colorado Springs—*also
plurals and possessives of
nouns and third person
singular presents of verbs
listed at* ING

ingue \aŋ\ see ²ANG

inguish \iŋ-wish\ distinguish,
extinguish

¹**ingy** \iŋ-ē\ clingy, dinghy,
springy, stringy, swingy,
zingy, shilingi

²**ingy** \in-jē\ dingy, mingy,
stingy

inh \in\ see ¹IN

¹**ini** \ē-nē\ beanie, djinni, genie,
greeny, Jeanie, Jeannie,
meanie, meany, jinni, Meany,
sheeny, spleeny, teeny,
weanie, weeny, wienie,
Alcmene, Athene, Bellini,
Bernini, bikini, Bikini,
Cabrini, Cellini, Eugenie,
linguine, martini, Mazzini,
Mbini, Mycenae, Puccini,
rappini, Rossini, Selene,
tahini, wahine, zucchini,
fantoccini, fettucine,
kundalini, malihini,
Mussolini, Mytilene, nota
bene, scaloppine, spaghettini,
teeny-weeny, tetrazzini,
tortellini

²**ini** \in-ē\ see INNY

inia \in-ē-ə\ zinnia, Bithynia,
Gdynia, gloxinia, Lavinia,
Sardinia, Virginia, Abyssinia,
West Virginia

inial \in-ē-əl\ see INEAL

¹**inian** \in-ē-ən\ dynein,
Arminian, Darwinian,
Latinian, Sardinian, Socinian,
Apollinian, Argentinian,
Augustinian, Carolinian

²**inian** \in-yən\ see INION

¹**inic** \ē-nik\ Enoch, nicotinic

²**inic** \in-ik\ clinic, cynic, Finnic, platinic, rabbinic, Jacobinic, mandarinic, misogynic, muscarinic, nicotinic, parafinic

inical \in-i-kəl\ binnacle, clinical, cynical, finical, pinnacle, dominical, Jacobinical

inican \in-i-kən\ see INIKIN

inikin \in-i-kən\ minikin, Dominican

inim \in-əm\ minim, Houyhnhnm

ining \ī-niŋ\ lining, mining, shining, declining, designing, inclining, long-lining, interlining, undesigning

inion \in-yən\ minion, minyan, pinion, piñon, champignon, dominion, Justinian, opinion, Sardinian, Abyssinian

¹**inis** \in-əs\ finis, pinnace, Erinys

²**inis** \ī-nəs\ see ¹INUS

inish \in-ish\ finish, Finnish, thinnish, diminish, refinish

¹**inist** \ī-nəst\ dynast, finest

²**inist** \ē-nəst\ hygienist, machinist, Orleanist, Byzantinist, magazinist, trampolinist

initive \in-ət-iv\ carminative, definitive, infinitive

inity \in-ət-ē\ trinity, Trinity, affinity, bovinity, concinnity, divinity, felinity, feminity, infinity, latinity, salinity, sanguinity, vicinity, virginity, alkalinity, aquitinity, clandestinity, consanguinity, crystallinity, femininity,

inconcinnity, masculinity, saccharinity

inium \in-ē-əm\ delphinium, triclinium, condominium

injure \in-jər\ see ³INGER

injury \inj-rē\ see INGERY

ink \iŋk\ blink, brink, chink, Chink, clink, dink, drink, fink, gink, ink, jink, kink, link, mink, pink, plink, prink, rink, shrink, sink, skink, slink, stink, swink, sync, think, wink, zinc, bethink, chewink, cross-link, eyewink, groupthink, hoodwink, iceblink, lip-synch, misthink, outthink, preshrink, rethink, snowblink, unkink, bobolink, countersink, distelfink, doublethink, interlink, kitchen-sink, Maeterlinck, rinky-dink

inka \iŋ-kə\ see INCA

inkable \iŋ-kə-bəl\ drinkable, sinkable, thinkable, undrinkable, unsinkable, unthinkable

inkage \iŋ-kij\ linkage, shrinkage, sinkage

inke \iŋ-kē\ see INKY

inked \iŋt\ see INCT

inker \iŋ-kər\ blinker, clinker, drinker, pinker, sinker, skinker, stinker, tinker, winker, diesinker, freethinker, headshrinker

inket \iŋ-kət\ Tlingit, trinket

inkey \iŋ-kē\ see INKY

inkgo \iŋ-kō\ see INKO

inki \iŋ-kē\ see INKY

inkie \iŋ-kē\ see INKY

inking \iŋ-kiŋ\ freethinking, unblinking, unthinking

inkle \iŋ-kəl\ crinkle, inkle, sprinkle, tinkle, twinkle, winkle, wrinkle, besprinkle, periwinkle, Rip van Winkle

inkling \iŋ-kliŋ\ inkling, sprinkling, twinkling

inkly \iŋ-klē\ crinkly, pinkly, tinkly, twinkly, wrinkly

inko \iŋ-kō\ ginkgo, pinko

inks \iŋs\ see INX

inky \iŋ-kē\ dinkey, dinky, inky, kinky, pinkie, pinky, slinky, stinky, zincky, Helsinki, Malinke

inland \in-lənd\ Finland, inland, Vinland

inless \in-ləs\ chinless, sinless, skinless, spinless, windlass

inley \in-lē\ see INLY

inly \in-lē\ inly, spindly, thinly, McKinley, Mount McKinley

inn \in\ see ¹IN

innace \in-əs\ see ¹INIS

innacle \in-i-kəl\ see INICAL

inned \ind\ see ²IND

inner \in-ər\ dinner, ginner, grinner, inner, pinner, sinner, skinner, spinner, spinor, thinner, tinner, winner, beginner, breadwinner, prizewinner, money-spinner

innet \in-ət\ linnet, minute, spinet

inney \in-ē\ see INNY

inni \ē-nē\ see ¹INI

innia \in-ē-ə\ see INIA

innic \in-ik\ see ²INIC

innie \in-ē\ see INNY

inning \in-iŋ\ ginning, inning, spinning, winning, beginning,

breadwinning, prizewinning, underpinning

innish \in-ish\ see INISH

innity \in-ət-ē\ see INITY

innow \in-ō\ minnow, winnow, topminnow

inny \in-ē\ cine, finny, ginny, guinea, Guinea, hinny, mini, Minnie, ninny, pinny, Pliny, shinny, skinny, spinney, squinny, tinny, whinny, Winnie, ignominy, micromini, pickaninny, Papua New Guinea, Equatorial Guinea

¹ino \ī-nō\ lino, rhino, Taino, wino, albino

²ino \ē-nō\ beano, chino, fino, keno, leno, Pinot, vino, Zeno, bambino, casino, cioppino, ladino, merino, sordino, zecchino, andantino, Angeleno, Bardolino, campesino, cappuccino, concertino, Filipino, maraschino, palomino, Philipino, San Marino, pecorino, sopranino, Cape Mendocino, San Bernardino

³ino \ē-nə\ see ²INA

iñon \in-yən\ see INION

¹inor \in-ər\ see INNER

²inor \ī-nər\ see ¹INER

inos \ī-nəs\ see INNS

inot \ē-nō\ see ²INO

inous \ī-nəs\ see ¹INUS

inscher \in-chər\ see INCHER

inse \ins\ see INCE

inselly \in-slē\ see INCELY

inseng \in-siŋ\ see INCING

insk \insk\ Minsk, Dzerzhinsk, Semipalatinsk

insky \in-skē\ buttinsky, kolinsky, Nijinsky, Stravinsky

inster \in-stər\ minster, spinster, Axminster, Westminster, Kidderminster

int \int\ bint, Clint, dint, flint, Flint, glint, hint, lint, mint, print, quint, skint, splint, sprint, squint, stint, suint, tint, blueprint, catmint, footprint, forint, gunflint, handprint, hoofprint, horsemint, imprint, in-print, large-print, newsprint, offprint, preprint, remint, reprint, skinflint, spearmint, thumbprint, voiceprint, aquatint, calamint, cuckoopint, fingerprint, mezzotint, monotint, overprint, peppermint, photoprint, wunderkind, Septuagint

intage \int-ij\ mintage, vintage

intager \int-i-jər\ see INTEGER

intain \int-ᵊn\ see INTON

¹intal \int-ᵊl\ lintel, pintle, quintal, Septuagintal

²intal \ant-ᵊl\ see ANTLE

integer \int-i-jər\ integer, vintager

intel \int-ᵊl\ see ¹INTAL

inter \int-ər\ hinter, linter, minter, printer, sinter, splinter, sprinter, squinter, tinter, winter, imprinter, midwinter, reprinter, overwinter, teleprinter

intery \int-ə-rē\ printery, splintery

inth \inth\ plinth, synth, helminth, colocynth, labyrinth, terebinth

inthia \in-thē-ə\ Cynthia, Carinthia

inthian \in-thē-ən\ Corinthian, labyrinthian

inthine \in-thən\ hyacinthine, labyrinthine

inting \int-iŋ\ imprinting, unstinting—*also present participles of verbs listed at* INT

intle \int-ᵊl\ see ¹INTAL

¹into \in-tō\ pinto, Shinto, spinto

²into \in-tü\ thereinto, whereinto

inton \int-ᵊn\ Clinton, quintain, Winton, badminton

ints \ins\ see INCE

inty \int-ē\ flinty, linty, minty, squinty, pepperminty

intz \ins\ see INCE

inue \in-yü\ sinew, continue, discontinue

inuous \in-yə-wəs\ sinuous, continuous, discontinuous

¹inus \ī-nəs\ dryness, finis, highness, Minas, Minos, minus, shyness, sinus, slyness, spinous, vinous, wryness, Aquinas, Delphinus, echinus, Quirinus, Antoninus, Pontus Euxinus

²inus \ē-nəs\ see ¹ENUS

inute \in-ət\ see INNET

inx \iŋs\ jinx, links, lynx, minx, sphinx, hijinks, methinks, tiddledywinks

¹iny \ī-nē\ briny, heinie, liny, piny, shiny, spiny, tiny, twiny, viny, whiny, winy, enshrinee, sunshiny

²iny \in-ē\ see INNY

inya \ē-nyə\ see ²ENIA

inyan \in-yən\ see INION

inyl \īn-ᵊl\ see ¹INAL

inys \in-əs\ see ¹INIS

¹**io** \ī-ō\ bayou, bio, Clio, Io, Lucayo, Ohio

²**io** \ē-ō\ brio, Cleo, clio, guyot, Krio, Leo, Rio, trio, caudillo, con brio, Negrillo, tornillo, Trujillo, cigarillo, Hermosillo, Manzanillo, ocotillo

iocese \ī-ə-səs\ see IASIS

iolate \ī-ə-lət\ see ¹IOLET

¹**iolet** \ī-ə-lət\ triolet, violate, violet, Violet, inviolate, ultraviolet, near-ultraviolet

²**iolet** \ē-ə-lət\ see EOLATE

¹**ion** \ī-ən\ ayin, Brian, Bryan, cyan, ion, lion, Lyon, Mayan, Ryan, scion, Sion, Zion, Amphion, anion, Bisayan, Ixion, Orion, Visayan, counterion, dandelion, zwitterion

²**ion** \ē-ən\ see ¹EAN

³**ion** \ē-än\ see ²EON

ior \īr\ see ¹IRE

iory \ī-rē\ see ¹IARY

iot \ī-ət\ see IET

ioter \ī-ət-ər\ see IETER

iouan \ü-ən\ see UAN

ious \ī-əs\ see IAS

ioux \ü\ see ¹EW

ip \ip\ blip, chip, clip, dip, drip, flip, grip, grippe, gyp, hip, kip, lip, nip, pip, quip, rip, scrip, ship, sip, skip, slip, snip, strip, tip, trip, whip, yip, zip, airship, airstrip, atrip, bullwhip, catnip, chiefship, clerkship, courtship, cowslip, deanship, equip, fieldstrip, filmstrip, flagship, friendship, guildship, gunship, half-slip, handgrip, hardship, harelip, headship, horsewhip, inclip, judgeship, kingship, kinship, landslip, lightship, lordship, nonslip, outstrip, oxlip, pip-pip, princeship, Q-ship, queenship, reship, round-trip, saintship, sheep-dip, sideslip, spaceship, steamship, thaneship, township, transship, troopship, unship, unzip, wardship, warship, airmanship, authorship, battleship, biochip, brinkmanship, censorship, chairmanship, chaplainship, chieftainship, churchmanship, coverslip, dealership, draftsmanship, ego-trip, externship, fellowship, fingertip, gamesmanship, Gaza Strip, grantsmanship, helmsmanship, horsemanship, internship, ladyship, leadership, lectureship, listenership, marksmanship, membership, microchip, oarsmanship, overslip, ownership, partnership, penmanship, pogonip, premiership, readership, ridership, rulership, salesmanship, scholarship, seamanship, showmanship, skinny-dip, speakership, sponsorship, sportsmanship, statesmanship, stewardship, studentship, swordsmanship, trusteeship, underlip, upmanship, viewership, workmanship, assistantship, attorneyship, championship, chancellorship, citizenship, companionship, containership, cross-ownership, dictatorship, directorship, good-fellowship, guardianship, instructorship, landownership, laureateship, governorship, musicianship, one-upmanship, outdoorsmanship, professorship, protectorship, receivership, relationship, survivorship, treasurership, ambassadorship, associateship, bipartisanship, entrepreneurship, librarianship, nonpartisanship, proprietorship, secretaryship, solicitorship, interrelationship

ipal \ē-pəl\ see EOPLE

ipari \ip-rē\ see IPPERY

ipatus \ip-ət-əs\ see IPITOUS

ipe \īp\ Cuyp, gripe, hype, pipe, ripe, slype, snipe, stipe, stripe, swipe, tripe, type, wipe, bagpipe, blowpipe, downpipe, drainpipe, hornpipe, hosepipe, lead-pipe, n-type, p-type, panpipe, pinstripe, rareripe, sideswipe, standpipe, stovepipe, tintype, touch-type, unripe, windpipe, archetype, calotype, Dutchman's-pipe, guttersnipe, haplotype, Linotype, liripipe, logotype, monotype, overripe, prototype, stenotype, Teletype, electrotype, stereotype, daguerreotype, anti-idiotype

¹iped \ī-ped\ biped, parallelepiped

²iped \īpt\ stiped, striped, pin-striped—*also pasts of verbs listed at* IPE

ipend \ī-pənd\ ripened, stipend

iper \ī-pər\ diaper, griper, hyper, piper, riper, sniper, striper, viper, wiper, bagpiper, sandpiper, candy-striper, stereotyper

iperous \ī-prəs\ see YPRESS

ipetal \ip-ət-ᵊl\ basipetal, bicipital, centripetal, occipital

ipety \ip-ət-ē\ snippety, peripety, serendipity

iph \if\ see IFF

iphany \if-ə-nē\ see IPHONY

ipher \ī-fər\ cipher, lifer, rifer, decipher, encipher, pro-lifer, right-to-lifer

iphery \if-rē\ see IFERY

iphon \ī-fən\ see YPHEN

iphony \if-ə-nē\ tiffany, Tiffany, antiphony, epiphany, polyphony

ipi \ē-pē\ see EEPY

ipid \ip-əd\ lipid, insipid

ipience \ip-ē-əns\ incipience, percipience, impercipience

ipient \ip-ē-ənt\ excipient, incipient, percipient, recipient, impercipient

iping \ī-piŋ\ piping, striping, blood-typing

ipit \ip-ət\ see IPPET

ipital \ip-ət-əl\ see IPETAL

ipitance \ip-ət-əns\ see IPOTENCE

ipitant \ip-ət-ənt\ see IPOTENT

ipitous \ip-ət-əs\ peripatus, precipitous, serendipitous

ipity \ip-ət-ē\ see IPETY

¹**iple** \ip-əl\ see IPPLE

²**iple** \ī-pəl\ see YPAL

ipless \ip-ləs\ dripless, lipless, zipless

ipling \ip-liŋ\ Kipling, stripling

ipment \ip-mənt\ shipment, equipment, transshipment

ipo \ēp-ō\ see EPOT

ipoli \ip-ə-lē\ see IPPILY

ipotence \ip-ət-əns\ omnipotence, precipitance

ipotent \ip-ət-ənt\ omnipotent, plenipotent, pluripotent, precipitant

¹**ippe** \ip\ see IP

²**ippe** \ip-ē\ see IPPY

³**ippe** \ēp\ see EEP

ipped \ipt\ see IPT

ippee \ip-ē\ see IPPY

ippen \ip-ən\ lippen, pippin

ipper \ip-ər\ chipper, clipper, dipper, dripper, flipper, gripper, hipper, kipper, nipper, ripper, shipper, sipper, skipper, slipper, snipper, stripper, tipper, tripper, whipper, zipper, blue-chipper, day-tripper, mudskipper, Yom-Kippur, double-dipper, gallinipper, lady's slipper, skinny-dipper

ippery \ip-rē\ frippery, Lipari, slippery

ippet \ip-ət\ pipit, sippet, snippet, tippet, trippet, whippet

ippety \ip-ət-ē\ see IPETY

ippi \ip-ē\ see IPPY

ippie \ip-ē\ see IPPY

ippily \ip-ə-lē\ nippily, tripoli, Tripoli, Gallipoli

ippin \ip-ən\ see IPPEN

ipping \ip-iŋ\ chipping, clipping, dripping, lipping, nipping, ripping, shipping, double-dipping, skinny-dipping

ippingly \ip-iŋ-lē\ grippingly, nippingly, trippingly

ipple \ip-əl\ cripple, nipple, ripple, stipple, tipple, triple, participle

ippur \ip-ər\ see IPPER

ippy \ip-ē\ chippy, dippy, drippy, flippy, grippy, hippie, hippy, Lippi, lippy, nippy, slippy, snippy, tippy, trippy, whippy, yippee, yippie, zippy, Xanthippe, Mississippi

ips \ips\ snips, thrips, yips, eclipse, ellipse, midships, amidships, athwartships, fish-and-chips, tidytips, apocalypse—*also plurals and possessives of nouns and third person singular presents of verbs listed at* IP

ipse \ips\ see IPS

ipso \ip-sō\ dipso, calypso, Calypso

ipster \ip-stər\ hipster, quipster, tipster

ipsy \ip-sē\ see YPSY

ipt \ipt\ crypt, hipped, lipped, ripped, script, tipped, conscript, decrypt, encrypt, harelipped, postscript, prescript, rescript, subscript, tight-lipped, transcript, typescript, eucalypt, filter-tipped, manuscript, nondescript, superscript, swivel-hipped—*also pasts of verbs listed at* IP

ipter \ip-tər\ scripter, lithotripter

iptic \ip-tik\ see YPTIC

iption \ip-shən\ ascription, conniption, conscription, decryption, description, Egyptian, encryption, inscription, prescription, proscription, subscription, transcription, circumscription, nonprescription

iptive \ip-tiv\ ascriptive, descriptive, inscriptive, prescriptive, proscriptive

iptych \ip-tik\ see YPTIC

ipular \ip-yə-lər\ stipular, manipular

ipy \ī-pē\ stripy, typey, stenotypy, daguerrotypy, stereotypy

iquant \ē-kənt\ see ECANT

ique \ēk\ see ¹EAK

iquey \ē-kē\ see EAKY

iquish \ē-kish\ see EAKISH

iquitous \ik-wət-əs\ iniquitous, ubiquitous

iquity \ik-wət-ē\ antiquity, iniquity, obliquity, ubiquity

iquor \ik-ər\ see ¹ICKER

¹ir \ir\ see ²EER

²ir \ər\ see ¹EUR

¹ira \ir-ə\ see ²ERA

²ira \ī-rə\ see YRA

irable \ī-rə-bəl\ wirable, acquirable, desirable, respirable, undesirable

iracle \ir-i-kəl\ see ²ERICAL

irae \īr-ē\ see ¹IRY

iral \ī-rəl\ chiral, gyral, spiral, viral

irant \ī-rənt\ spirant, tyrant, aspirant, retirant

irate \ir-ət\ see IRIT

irby \ər-bē\ see ERBY

irca \ər-kə\ see ¹URKA

irce \ər-sē\ see ERCY

irch \ərch\ see URCH

¹irchen \ər-chən\ see URCHIN

²irchen \ər-kən\ see IRKIN

ircher \ər-chər\ Bircher, lurcher, nurture

irchist \ər-chəst\ Birchist, researchist

ircon \ər-kən\ see IRKIN

ircuit \ər-kət\ circuit, trifurcate, microcircuit

ircular \ər-kyə-lər\ circular, opercular, tubercular, semicircular

ird \ərd\ bird, burred, curd, furred, gird, heard, herd, nerd, spurred, surd, third, turd, word, absurd, begird, bellbird, blackbird, bluebird, buzzword, byword, Cape Verde, catbird, catchword, cowbird, cowherd, crossword, cussword, engird, goatherd, headword, jailbird, jaybird, kingbird, loanword, lovebird, lyrebird, oilbird, password, potsherd, railbird, rainbird, redbird, reword, ricebird, seabird, Sigurd, shorebird, snakebird, snowbird, songbird, sunbird, surfbird, swearword, swineherd, textured, ungird, unheard, watchword, yardbird, afterword, bowerbird, butcher-bird, cedarbird, dollybird, hummingbird,

ladybird, mockingbird,
ovenbird, overheard,
riflebird, tailorbird,
thunderbird, undergird,
wattlebird, weaverbird,
wirlybird—*also pasts of verbs
listed at* [1]EUR

irder \ərd-ər\ see ERDER

irdie \ərd-ē\ see URDY

irdle \ərd-ᵊl\ see URDLE

irdum \ərd-əm\ dirdum,
reductio ad absurdum

[1]**ire** \īr\ briar, brier, byre, choir,
dire, drier, fire, flier, friar,
fryer, gyre, hire, ire, liar, lyre,
mire, prier, prior, pyre, quire,
shire, sire, Speyer, spier,
spire, squire, tier, tire, trier,
tyer, Tyre, wire, zaire,
acquire, admire, afire, Altair,
aspire, attire, backfire,
balefire, barbed wire,
barbwire, bemire, Blantyre,
blow-dryer, bonfire, brushfire,
bushfire, catbrier, cease-fire,
complier, conspire, defier,
denier, desire, drumfire,
empire, Empire, entire,
esquire, expire, flytier,
grandsire, greenbrier, gunfire,
haywire, hellfire, highflier,
hot-wire, inquire, inspire,
misfire, outlier, perspire,
pismire, prior, quagmire,
require, respire, retire, rimfire,
samphire, sapphire, satire,
Shropshire, spitfire, surefire,
suspire, sweetbrier, tightwire,
transpire, umpire, vampire,
wildfire, amplifier,
Biedermeier, butterflyer,
classifier, fly-by-wire,

fortifier, lammergeier,
magnifier, modifier,
multiplier, nitrifier, nullifier,
pacifier, qualifier, quantifier,
rapid-fire, rectifier, retrofire,
sanctifier, signifier, testifier,
versifier, identifier, intensifier,
Second Empire, down-to-the-
wire—*also nouns formed by
adding* -er *to verbs listed at*
[1]Y

[2]**ire** \ir\ see [2]EER

[3]**ire** \ī-rē\ see [1]IARY

[4]**ire** \īr-ē\ see [1]IRY

[5]**ire** \ər\ see EUR

ired \īrd\ fired, spired, tired,
wired, hardwired, retired—
also pasts of verbs listed at
[1]IRE

ireless \īr-ləs\ tireless, wireless

ireman \īr-mən\ fireman,
wireman

irement \īr-mənt\ environment,
requirement, retirement

iren \ī-rən\ Byron, gyron,
Myron, siren, environ,
ribavirin

irge \ərj\ see URGE

irgin \ər-jən\ see URGEON

irgo \ər-gō\ see ERGO

iri \ir-ē\ see EARY

iriam \ir-ē-əm\ see ERIUM

iric \ir-ik\ see [2]ERIC

irin \i-rən\ see IREN

irine \ī-rən\ see IREN

iring \īr-iŋ\ firing, wiring,
retiring

irious \ir-ē-əs\ see ERIOUS

iris \ī-rəs\ see IRUS

irish \īr-ish\ Irish, squirish

irit \ir-ət\ Meerut, spirit,

dispirit, emirate, inspirit, vizierate

irium \ir-ē-əm\ see ERIUM

irius \ir-ē-əs\ see ERIOUS

¹irk \irk\ birk, dirk, Dirk, kirk

²irk \ərk\ see ¹ORK

irker \ər-kər\ see ¹ORKER

irkie \ər-kē\ see ERKY

irkin \ər-kən\ firkin, gherkin, jerkin, zircon, Gelsenkirchen

irky \ər-kē\ see ERKY

¹irl \ərl\ birl, burl, churl, curl, dirl, earl, Earl, Earle, furl, girl, hurl, knurl, merle, Merle, pearl, Pearl, purl, skirl, squirrel, swirl, thirl, thurl, tirl, twirl, virl, whirl, whorl, aswirl, awhirl, cowgirl, impearl, pas seul, playgirl, salesgirl, schoolgirl, showgirl, uncurl, unfurl, mother-of-pearl

²irl \irl\ dirl, skirl

irler \ər-lər\ birler, curler, pearler, twirler, whirler

irley \ər-lē\ see URLY

irlie \ər-lē\ see URLY

irling \ər-liŋ\ see URLING

irlish \ər-lish\ see URLISH

irly \ər-lē\ see URLY

irm \ərm\ see ¹ORM

irma \ər-mə\ see ERMA

irmary \ərm-rē\ spermary, infirmary

irmess \ər-məs\ see ERMIS

irmity \ər-mət-ē\ furmity, infirmity

irmy \ər-mē\ see ERMY

¹irn \irn\ firn, girn, pirn

²irn \ərn\ see URN

¹iro \ir-ō\ see ³ERO

²iro \ē-rō\ see ¹ERO

³iro \ī-rō\ see ¹YRO

¹iron \īrn\ iron, andiron, environ, flatiron, gridiron

²iron \ī-rən\ see IREN

ironment \īr-mənt\ see IREMENT

irp \ərp\ see URP

irps \ərps\ stirps, turps—*also plurals and possessives of nouns and third person singular presents of verbs listed at* URP

irpy \ər-pē\ chirpy, Euterpe

irque \ərk\ see ¹ORK

¹irr \ir\ see ²EER

²irr \ər\ see ¹EUR

irra \ir-ə\ see ²ERA

irrah \ir-ə\ see ²ERA

¹irrel \ərl\ see ¹IRL

²irrel \ər-əl\ see ERRAL

irrely \ər-lē\ see URLY

irrer \ər-ər\ see ERRER

irrhous \ir-əs\ see EROUS

irrhus \ir-əs\ see EROUS

irring \ər-iŋ\ see URRING

irror \ir-ər\ see ²EARER

irrous \ir-əs\ see EROUS

irrup \ər-əp\ chirrup, stirrup, syrup

irrupy \ər-ə-pē\ chirrupy, syrupy

irrus \ir-əs\ see EROUS

irry \ər-ē\ see URRY

irs \irz\ see IERS

irsch \irsh\ see IRSH

¹irse \irs\ see IERCE

²irse \ərs\ see ERSE

irsh \irsh\ girsh, kirsch

irst \ərst\ see URST

irsty \ər-stē\ thirsty, bloodthirsty

irt \ərt\ see ¹ERT

irted \ərt-əd\ see ERTED

irter \ərt-ər\ see ERTER

irth \ərth\ berth, birth, dearth, earth, firth, girth, mirth, Perth, worth, childbirth, Fort Worth, rebirth, self-worth, stillbirth, unearth, Wordsworth, afterbirth, down-to-earth, pennyworth

irthful \ərth-fəl\ mirthful, worthful

irthless \ərth-ləs\ mirthless, worthless

irtinent \ərt-nənt\ pertinent, appurtenant, impertinent

irting \ərt-iŋ\ see ERTING

irtle \ərt-ᵊl\ see ERTILE

irtually \ərch-lē\ see URCHLY

irtue \ər-chə\ see ERCHA

irty \ərt-ē\ dirty, QWERTY, shirty, thirty

irus \ī-rəs\ Cyrus, iris, Iris, Skyros, virus, desirous, Epirus, Osiris, papyrus, lentivirus, parvovirus, rotavirus, papillomavirus

irv \ərv\ see ERVE

irving \ər-viŋ\ see ERVING

irwin \ər-wən\ see ERWIN

¹iry \īr-ē\ eyrie, friary, miry, spiry, wiry, expiry, inquiry, venire, praemunire, anno hegirae

²iry \ī-rē\ see ¹IARY

i's \īz\ see IZE

¹is \is\ see ¹ISS

²is \iz\ see ¹IZ

³is \ē\ see ¹EE

⁴is \ēs\ see IECE

⁵is \ish\ see ¹ISH

¹isa \ē-zə\ see EZA

²isa \ī-zə\ Lisa, Liza, Elisa, Eliza

isabeth \iz-ə-bəth\ see IZABETH

isable \ī-zə-bəl\ see IZABLE

¹isal \ī-səl\ Faisal, Ijssel, sisal, skysail, trysail, radisal

²isal \ī-zəl\ Geisel, incisal, reprisal, revisal, surprisal, paradisal

isan \is-ᵊn\ see ISTEN

isbane \iz-bən\ see ISBON

isbe \iz-bē\ Frisbee, Thisbe

isbee \iz-bē\ see ISBE

isbon \iz-bən\ Brisbane, Lisbon

isc \isk\ see ISK

iscable \is-kə-bəl\ confiscable, episcopal

iscan \is-kən\ see ISKIN

iscate \is-kət\ see ISKET

isce \is\ see ¹ISS

¹iscean \ī-sē-ən\ Piscean, Dionysian

²iscean \is-kē-ən\ Piscean, saurischian, ornithischian

³iscean \is-ē-ən\ see ¹YSIAN

iscence \is-ᵊns\ puissance, dehiscence, impuissance, indehiscence, reminiscence, reviviscence

iscent \is-ᵊnt\ puissant, dehiscent, impuissant, indehiscent, reminiscent, reviviscent

isces \ī-sēz\ see ICES

ische \ēsh\ see ²ICHE

ischian \is-kē-ən\ see ²ISCEAN

iscia \ish-ə\ see ITIA

iscible \is-ə-bəl\ see ISSIBLE

iscience \ish-əns\ see ICIENCE

iscient \ish-ənt\ see ICIENT

isco \is-kō\ cisco, disco,

Francisco, Jalisco, Morisco, San Francisco

iscopal \is-kə-bəl\ see ISCABLE

iscous \is-kəs\ see ISCUS

iscuit \is-kət\ see ISKET

iscus \is-kəs\ discus, viscous, viscus, hibiscus, meniscus

¹ise \ēs\ see IECE

²ise \ēz\ see EZE

³ise \īs\ see ¹ICE

⁴ise \īz\ see IZE

¹ised \īst\ see ¹IST

²ised \īzd\ see IZED

isel \iz-əl\ see IZZLE

iseled \iz-əld\ see IZZLED

iseler \iz-lər\ see IZZLER

isement \īz-mənt\ advisement, chastisement, despisement, disguisement, advertisement, disfranchisement, enfranchisement, disenfranchisement

iser \ī-zər\ see IZER

ises \ī-sēz\ see ICES

¹ish \ish\ dish, fiche, fish, flysch, Nis, pish, squish, swish, whish, wish, blackfish, blowfish, bluefish, bonefish, catfish, codfish, crawfish, crayfish, dogfish, filefish, finfish, flatfish, garfish, globefish, goldfish, goosefish, Irtysh, kingfish, knish, lungfish, lumpfish, monkfish, pigfish, pipefish, ratfish, redfish, rockfish, sailfish, sawfish, shellfish, spearfish, starfish, stonefish, sunfish, swordfish, tilefish, unwish, weakfish, whitefish, angelfish, anglerfish, archerfish, butterfish, candlefish, cuttlefish, damselfish, devilfish, jellyfish, John Bullish, ladyfish, lionfish, microfiche, muttonfish, needlefish, overfish, paddlefish, ribbonfish, silverfish, surgeonfish, triggerfish

²ish \ēsh\ see ²ICHE

isha \ish-ə\ see ITIA

ishable \ish-ə-bəl\ fishable, justiciable

ished \isht\ dished, whisht—*also pasts of verbs listed at* ¹ISH

isher \ish-ər\ fisher, fissure, swisher, ill-wisher, kingfisher, well-wisher

ishery \ish-rē\ fishery, Tishri, shellfishery

ishi \ē-shē\ chichi, specie, maharishi

ishing \ish-iŋ\ bonefishing, fly-fishing, sportfishing, well-wishing

ishioner \ish-nər\ see ITIONER

ishna \ish-nə\ Krishna, Mishnah

ishnah \ish-nə\ see ISHNA

isht \isht\ see ISHED

ishu \ish-ü\ see ¹ISSUE

ishy \ish-ē\ dishy, fishy, squishy, swishy

¹isi \ē-zē\ see ¹EASY

²isi \ē-sē\ see EECY

¹isia \izh-ə\ baptisia, Dionysia, artemisia

²isia \ē-zhə\ see ²ESIA

¹isian \izh-ən\ see ISION

²isian \ē-zhən\ see ¹ESIAN

isible \iz-ə-bəl\ risible, visible, divisible, invisible, indivisible

isin \i-zən\ see ²ISON

ising \ī-ziŋ\ see IZING

ision \izh-ən\ fission, Frisian, scission, vision, abscission, collision, concision, decision, derision, division, elision, elysian, envision, excision, incision, misprision, precisian, precision, prevision, provision, recision, rescission, revision, circumcision, Dionysian, imprecision, indecision, subdivision, supervision, television

isional \izh-ə-nəl\ visional, collisional, decisional, divisional, excisional, previsional, provisional

isis \ī-səs\ crisis, Isis, lysis, nisus, Dionysus, stare decisis

isit \iz-ət\ visit, exquisite, revisit

isite \iz-ət\ see ISIT

isitive \iz-ət-iv\ acquisitive, inquisitive

isitor \iz-ət-ər\ visitor, acquisitor, inquisitor

¹isive \ī-siv\ visive, decisive, derisive, divisive, incisive, indecisive

²isive \iz-iv\ visive, derisive, divisive

isk \isk\ bisque, brisk, disc, disk, fisc, frisk, risk, whisk, lutefisk, asterisk, basilisk, blastodisc, compact disc, laserdisc, obelisk, odalisque, tamarisk, videodisc

isker \is-kər\ brisker, frisker, risker, whisker

isket \is-kət\ biscuit, brisket, frisket

iskey \is-kē\ see ISKY

iskie \is-kē\ see ISKY

iskin \is-kən\ siskin, Franciscan

isky \is-kē\ frisky, pliskie, risky, whiskey

island \ī-lənd\ see IGHLAND

islander \ī-lən-dər\ see IGHLANDER

islands \ī-lənz\ see IGHLANDS

isle \īl\ see ¹ILE

isles \īlz\ see ILES

islet \ī-lət\ see ILOT

isling \iz-liŋ\ brisling, quisling

isly \iz-lē\ see IZZLY

ism \iz-əm\ chrism, chrisom, ism, prism, schism, abysm, autism, baalism, baptism, Birchism, bossism, Buddhism, casteism, centrism, charism, Chartism, chemism, classism, cubism, cultism, czarism, deism, dwarfism, faddism, fascism, fauvism, Gaullism, Grecism, Hobbism, holism, Jainism, Klanism, leftism, lyrism, Mahdism, Maoism, Marxism, monism, mutism, Nazism, nudism, Orphism, priggism, purism, racism, Ramism, rightism, sadism, Saivism, sapphism, Scotism, sexism, Shaktism, Shiism, Sikhism, simplism, snobbism, sophism, statism, Sufism, tachism, Tantrism, Taoism, theism, Thomism, tourism, tropism, truism, Turkism, verism, Whiggism, Yahwism, absurdism, activism, Adventism, alarmism, albinism, alpinism, altruism, amorphism, anarchism, aneurysm, anglicism, animism, aphorism, Arabism, archaism, asterism, atavism, atheism, atomism, atticism, Bahaism, barbarism, Benthamism, biblicism, blackguardism, bolshevism, boosterism, botulism, bourbonism, Brahmanism, Briticism, Byronism, cabalism, Caesarism, Calvinism, careerism, Castroism, cataclysm, catechism, Catharism, centralism, chauvinism, chimerism, classicism, colorism, communism, concretism, conformism, cretinism, criticism, cronyism, cynicism, dadaism, dandyism, Darwinism, defeatism, de Gaullism, despotism, die-hardism, dimorphism, dirigisme, Docetism, do-goodism, dogmatism, Donatism, Don Juanism, druidism, dualism, dynamism, egoism, egotism, elitism, embolism, endemism, erethism, ergotism, erotism, escapism, Essenism, etatism, eunuchism, euphemism, euphuism, exorcism, expertism, extremism, fairyism, familism, fatalism, feminism, feudalism, fideism, Fidelism, fogyism, foreignism, formalism, futurism, Galenism, gallicism, galvanism, gangsterism, genteelism, Germanism,

giantism, gigantism, globalism, gnosticism, Gongorism, Gothicism, gourmandism, gradualism, grangerism, greenbackism, Hasidism, heathenism, Hebraism, hedonism, Hellenism, helotism, hermetism, hermitism, heroism, highbrowism, Hinduism, hipsterism, hirsutism, hispanism, Hitlerism, hoodlumism, hoodooism, hucksterism, humanism, Hussitism, hybridism, hypnotism, Ibsenism, idealism, imagism, Irishism, Islamism, Jansenism, jingoism, journalism, John Bullism, Judaism, Junkerism, kaiserism, Krishnaism, Ku Kluxism, laconism, laicism, Lamaism, Lamarckism, landlordism, Latinism, legalism, Leninism, lobbyism, localism, locoism, Lollardism, luminism, lyricism, magnetism, mammonism, mannerism, Marcionism, masochism, mechanism, melanism, meliorism, Menshevism, Mendelism, mentalism, mesmerism, methodism, me-tooism, modernism, Mohockism, monachism, monadism, monarchism, mongolism, Montanism, moralism, Mormonism, morphinism, mullahism, mysticism, narcissism, nationalism,

nativism, nepotism,
neutralism, new dealism,
nihilism, nomadism,
occultism, onanism,
optimism, oralism,
Orangeism, organism,
ostracism, pacifism,
paganism, Pan-Slavism,
pantheism, paroxysm,
Parsiism, passivism,
pauperism, pessimism,
phallicism, pianism, pietism,
plagiarism, Platonism,
pleinairism, Plotinism,
pluralism, pointillism,
populism, pragmatism,
presentism, privatism,
prosaism, Prussianism,
puerilism, pugilism,
Puseyism, Pyrrhonism,
Quakerism, quietism,
rabbinism, racialism,
rationalism, realism,
reformism, rheumatism,
rigorism, robotism,
Romanism, Rousseauism,
rowdyism, royalism, satanism,
savagism, scapegoatism,
schematism, scientism,
sciolism, Scotticism,
Semitism, Shakerism,
Shamanism, Shintoism,
skepticism, socialism,
solecism, solipsism,
Southernism, specialism,
speciesism, Spartanism,
Spinozism, spiritism,
spoonerism, Stalinism,
standpattism, stoicism,
syllogism, symbolism,
synchronism, syncretism,
synergism, talmudism,

tarantism, tectonism,
tenebrism, terrorism,
Teutonism, titanism, Titoism,
tokenism, Toryism, totalism,
totemism, transvestism,
traumatism, tribalism,
tritheism, Trotskyism,
ultraism, unionism, urbanism,
utopism, Vaishnavism,
vampirism, vandalism,
vanguardism, Vedantism,
veganism, verbalism, virilism,
vitalism, vocalism, volcanism,
voodooism, vorticism,
voyeurism, vulcanism,
vulgarism, Wahhabism,
warlordism, welfarism,
Wellerism, witticism,
yahooism, Yankeeism,
Yiddishism, Zionism,
zombiism, absenteeism,
absolutism, abstractionism,
adoptionism, adventurism,
aestheticism, Africanism,
agnosticism, alcoholism,
alienism, amateurism,
amoralism, anabaptism,
anachronism, Anglicanism,
animalism, antagonism,
Arianism, astigmatism,
athleticism, asynchronism,
Atlanticism, atonalism,
Australianism, automatism,
avant-gardism, behaviorism,
Big Brotherism, bilingualism,
biologism, bipedalism,
biracialism, Bonapartism,
bureaucratism, cannibalism,
capitalism, Cartesianism,
catastrophism, Catholicism,
cavalierism, charlatanism,
clericalism, collectivism,

Colonel Blimpism,
commensalism,
commercialism,
communalism, Confucianism,
conservatism, constructivism,
consumerism, corporatism,
creationism, credentialism,
determinism, diabolism,
didacticism, diffusionism,
dilettantism, doctrinairism,
do-nothingism, eclecticism,
ecumenism, egocentrism,
Eleatism, empiricism,
epicenism, epicurism,
epigonism, eremitism,
eroticism, erraticism,
essentialism, ethnocentrism,
eudaemonism, euhemerism,
evangelism, exceptionalism,
exclusivism, exoticism,
expansionism, expressionism,
externalism, Fabianism,
factionalism, factualism,
fanaticism, favoritism,
federalism, Fenianism,
feuilletonism, fifth
columnism, flagellantism,
Fourierism, fraternalism,
freneticism, Freudianism,
funambulism, functionalism,
gallicanism, gutturalism,
henotheism, hermeticism,
Hispanicism, historicism,
hooliganism, Hugenotism,
hypocorism, idiotism,
illiberalism, illuminism,
illusionism, immanentism,
immobilism, impressionism,
indifferentism, Indianism,
infantilism, inflationism,
initialism, insularism,
invalidism, iotacism,

irredentism, Ishmaelitism,
Italianism, Jacobinism,
Jacobitism, jesuitism,
Keynesianism, know-
nothingism, legitimism,
lesbianism, liberalism,
libertinism, literalism,
Lutheranism, Lysenkoism,
Magianism, malapropism,
mandarinism, McCarthyism,
medievalism, mercantilism,
messianism, metabolism,
metamorphism, militarism,
minimalism, misoneism,
monasticism, monetarism,
monotheism, mosaicism,
mutualism, naturalism,
Naziritism, necrophilism,
negativism, neologism, neo-
Nazism, neuroticism, nice-
nellyism, nominalism,
nonconformism, objectivism,
obscurantism, obstructionism,
officialism, opportunism,
organicism, pacificism,
Pantagruelism, parallelism,
parasitism, pastoralism,
paternalism, patriotism,
Peeping Tomism,
perfectionism, personalism,
pharisaism, physicalism,
plebeianism, poeticism,
polyglotism, polytheism,
positivism, postmodernism,
pragmaticism, primitivism,
probabilism, progressivism,
proselytism, protectionism,
Protestantism, provincialism,
pseudomorphism,
psychologism, puritanism,
radicalism, rationalism,
recidivism, reductionism,

refugeeism, regionalism, relativism, restrictionism, revisionism, revivalism, ritualism, romanticism, ruffianism, Sadduceeism, salvationism, sansculottism, sardonicism, scholasticism, secessionism, sectarianism, sectionalism, secularism, sensualism, separatism, serialism, Slavophilism, solidarism, somnambulism, sovietism, Stakhanovism, structuralism, subjectivism, suprematism, surrealism, Sybaritism, sycophantism, systematism, Tammanyism, teetotalism, theocentrism, triumphalism, Uncle Tomism, vagabondism, ventriloquism, vigilantism, voluntarism, volunteerism, Wesleyanism, workaholism, Zwinglianism, abolitionism, academicism, agrarianism, Americanism, analphabetism, anthropomorphism, anthropopathism, anti-Semitism, Arminianism, autoerotism, barbarianism, bibliophilism, bicameralism, biculturalism, biloquialism, bipartisanism, bohemianism, colloquialism, colonialism, conceptualism, confessionalism, constitutionalism, conventionalism, corporativism, cosmopolitism, deviationism, ecumenicism, emotionalism, esotericism, Europocentrism,

evolutionism, exhibitionism, existentialism, expatriatism, fundamentalism, governmentalism, Hegelianism, hermaphroditism, hypercriticism, hyperrealism, hyperurbanism, imperialism, incendiarism, incrementalism, indeterminism, industrialism, instrumentalism, interventionism, introspectionism, irrationalism, isolationism, Malthusianism, Manichaeanism, manorialism, materialism, millennialism, Monarchianism, mongolianism, Monophysitism, Muhammadanism, multilingualism, neoclassicism, Neoplatonism, neorealism, Nestorianism, Occidentalism, operationism, orientalism, Palladianism, parajournalism, parochialism, particularism, pedestrianism, Pelagianism, Pentecostalism, phenomenalism, photojournalism, pictorialism, pococurantism, Postimpressionism, professionalism, pseudoclassicism, reconstructionism, republicanism, Rosicrucianism, sacerdotalism, sacramentalism, self-determinism, sadomasochism, sectarianism, sensationalism, sentimentalism, socinianism, spiritualism, theatricalism, Tractarianism, traditionalism, transcendentalism, transsexualism, trilateralism, ultramontanism, universalism, utopianism, vernacularism, Victorianism, vocationalism, voluntaryism, Albigensianism, anticlericalism, antiquarianism, apocalypticism, assimilationism, associationism, Augustinianism, autoeroticism, ceremonialism, collaborationism, congregationalism, cosmopolitanism, ecclesiasticism, ecumenicalism, environmentalism, Evangelicalism, Hamiltonianism, homoeroticism, epicureanism, experimentalism, immaterialism, individualism, institutionalism, intellectualism, internationalism, libertarianism, middle-of-the-roadism, millenarianism, neo-conservatism, neo-impressionism, operationalism, Pan-Americanism, Peripateticism, photoperiodism, Pre-Raphaelitism, Presbyterianism, Pythegoreanism, Rastafarianism, reactionaryism, Sabbatarianism, supernaturalism, Swedenborgianism, territorialism, Trinitarianism, unitarianism, vegetarianism, Zoroastrianism, Aristotelianism, authoritarianism, egalitarianism, Episcopalianism, humanitarianism, Machiavellianism, neocolonialism, neo-Expressionism, predestinarianism, representationalism, utilitarianism, establishmentarianism, latitudinarianism

isma \iz-mə\ charisma, melisma

ismal \iz-məl\ see YSMAL

¹isme \īm\ see ¹IME

²isme \iz²m\ see ISM

ismo \ēz-mō\ machismo, verismo, caudillismo

iso \ē-sō\ miso, piso

isom \iz-əm\ see ISM

¹ison \īs-ᵊn\ bison, hyson, Meissen, streptomycin, Aureomycin, erythromycin

²ison \iz-ᵊn\ dizen, mizzen, prison, risen, weasand, wizen, arisen, imprison, Tok Pisin, uprisen

isor \ī-zər\ see IZER

isored \ī-zərd\ guisard, visored

isory \īz-rē\ advisory, provisory, revisory, supervisory

isp \isp\ crisp, lisp, LISP, wisp, will-o-the-wisp

isper \is-pər\ crisper, lisper, whisper

ispy \is-pē\ crispy, wispy

isque \isk\ see ISK

iss \is\ bis, bliss, cis, Chris, cuisse, Dis, hiss, kiss, miss, sis, Swiss, this, vis, wis, abyss, amiss, coulisse, dehisce, dismiss, iwis, koumiss, remiss, submiss, ambergris, hit-and-miss, hit-or-miss, reminisce, verdigris

issa \is-ə\ abscissa, mantissa, Melissa, Orissa, vibrissa

issable \is-ə-bəl\ see ISSIBLE

issal \is-əl\ see ISTLE

issance \is-ᵊns\ see ISCENCE

issant \is-ᵊnt\ see ISCENT

¹**isse** \is\ see ISS

²**isse** \ēs\ see IECE

issed \ist\ see ²IST

issel \is-əl\ see ISTLE

isser \is-ər\ hisser, kisser

issible \is-ə-bəl\ kissable, miscible, admissible, immiscible, municipal, omissible, permissible, remissible, transmissible, impermissible, inadmissible

issile \is-əl\ see ISTLE

¹**ission** \ish-ən\ see ITION

²**ission** \izh-ən\ see ISION

issionable \ish-nə-bəl\ fissionable, conditionable

issioner \ish-nər\ see ITIONER

issive \is-iv\ missive, admissive, derisive, dismissive, emissive, permissive, submissive, transmissive

issome \is-əm\ lissome, alyssum

issor \iz-ər\ scissor, whizzer

¹**issue** \ish-ü\ fichu, issue, tissue, reissue, Mogadishu, overissue

²**issue** \ish-ə\ see ITIA

issure \ish-ər\ see ISHER

issus \is-əs\ byssus, missus, Mrs., narcissus, Narcissus

issy \is-ē\ hissy, missy, prissy, sissy

¹**ist** \īst\ Christ, feist, heist, hist, tryst, zeitgeist, Antichrist, black-a-vised, poltergeist—*also pasts of verbs listed at* ¹ICE

²**ist** \ist\ cist, cyst, fist, gist, grist, kist, list, Liszt, mist, schist, tryst, twist, whist, wist, wrist, assist, backlist, blacklist, checklist, consist, delist, desist, encyst, enlist, entwist, exist, handlist, insist, persist, playlist, protist, Rehnquist, resist, shortlist, subsist, untwist, catechist, coexist, dadaist, exorcist, intertwist, preexist, love-in-a-mist—*also pasts of verbs listed at* ISS

³**ist** \ēst\ see ¹EAST

¹**ista** \ē-stə\ turista, camorrista, Fidelista

²**ista** \is-tə\ crista, vista, arista, ballista, sacahuiste

istaed \is-təd\ see ISTED

istal \is-tᵊl\ Bristol, crystal, Crystal, distal, listel, pistil, pistol

istan \is-tən\ see ISTON

istance \is-təns\ see ISTENCE

istant \is-tənt\ see ISTENT

¹**iste** \is-tē\ see ²ICITY

²**iste** \ēst\ see ¹EAST

³**iste** \is-tə\ see ²ISTA

isted \is-təd\ twisted, vistaed, closefisted, enlisted, hamfisted, hardfisted, limpwristed, tightfisted, two-fisted, unlisted, untwisted, whitelisted, ironfisted, unassisted—*also pasts of verbs listed at* ²IST

istel \is-t³l\ see ISTAL

isten \is-³n\ christen, glisten, listen, Nisan

istenable \is-nə-bəl\ listenable, medicinable

istence \is-təns\ distance, assistance, consistence, existence, insistence, outdistance, persistence, resistance, subsistence, coexistence, inconsistence, inexistence, nonexistence, nonresistance, preexistence

istency \is-tən-sē\ consistency, insistency, persistency, inconsistency

istent \is-tənt\ distant, assistant, consistent, existent, insistent, persistent, resistant, subsistent, coexistent, equidistant, inconsistent, inexistent, nonexistent, nonpersistent, nonresistant, preexistent

ister \is-tər\ bister, blister, clyster, glister, klister, lister, Lister, mister, sister, twister, resister, resistor, solicitor, stepsister, transistor

istery \is-trē\ see ISTORY

istful \ist-fəl\ tristful, wistful

isthmus \is-məs\ see ISTMAS

isti \is-tē\ see ²ICITY

istic \is-tik\ cystic, distich, fistic, mystic, artistic, autistic, ballistic, cladistic, cubistic, eristic, fascistic, faunistic, floristic, heuristic, holistic, hubristic, juristic, linguistic, logistic, meristic, monistic, patristic, phlogistic, puristic, sadistic, simplistic, sophistic, statistic, stylistic, Taoistic, theistic, Thomistic, touristic, truistic, veristic, wholistic, Yahwistic, activistic, agonistic, alchemistic, altruistic, amoristic, anarchistic, animistic, aphoristic, archaistic, atavistic, atheistic, atomistic, belletristic, cabalistic, Calvinistic, casuistic, catechistic, Catharistic, centralistic, chauvinistic, communistic, crosslinguistic, dadaistic, dualistic, dyslogistic, egoistic, egotistic, essayistic, eucharistic, eulogistic, euphemistic, euphuistic, exorcistic, fabulistic, familistic, fatalistic, feministic, fetishistic, feudalistic, fideistic, formalistic, futuristic, gongoristic, haggadistic, Hebraistic, hedonistic, Hellenistic, humanistic, humoristic, idealistic, imagistic, inartistic, Jansenistic, jingoistic, journalistic, Judaistic, Lamaistic, legalistic, masochistic, mechanistic, melanistic, mentalistic,

methodistic, modernistic,
moralistic, narcissistic,
nationalistic, nativistic,
nepotistic, nihilistic,
novelistic, onanistic,
optimistic, pantheistic,
pessimistic, pianistic, pietistic,
plagiaristic, Platonistic,
pluralistic, pointillistic,
populistic, pugilistic,
quietistic, realistic,
Romanistic, sciolistic,
shamanistic, shintoistic,
socialistic, solecistic,
solipsistic, specialistic,
surrealistic, syllogistic,
symbolistic, synchronistic,
syncretistic, synergistic,
terroristic, totalistic,
totemistic, ultraistic,
unrealistic, urbanistic,
utopistic, vandalistic,
verbalistic, vitalistic,
voodooistic, voyeuristic,
Zionistic, absolutistic,
adventuristic, anachronistic,
animalistic, anomalistic,
antagonistic, behavioristic,
cannibalistic, capitalistic,
characteristic, collectivistic,
contortionistic, deterministic,
evangelistic, eudaemonistic,
euhemeristic, expansionistic,
expressionistic,
extralinguistic, functionalistic,
Hinayanistic, hypocoristic,
immanentistic,
impressionistic, liberalistic,
literalistic, Mahayanistic,
melioristic, mercantilistic,
militaristic, mediumistic,
metalinguistic, misogynistic,

monopolistic, monotheistic,
naturalistic, negativistic,
neologistic, opportunistic,
paternalistic, physicalistic,
polytheistic, probabilistic,
propagandistic,
psycholinguistic, rationalistic,
recidivistic, reductionistic,
relativistic, revivalistic,
ritualistic, secularistic,
sensualistic, separatistic,
sociolinguistic,
somnambulistic,
ventriloquistic, violinistic,
voluntaristic, colonialistic,
commercialistic,
Deuteronomistic,
emotionalistic, exhibitionistic,
fundamentalistic,
existentalistic, imperialistic,
indeterministic,
introspectionistic,
irrationalistic, materialistic,
oligopolistic,
Postimpressionistic,
sadomasochistic,
sensationalistic,
sociolinguistic, spiritualistic,
traditionalistic, individualistic
istical \is-ti-kəl\ mystical,
deistical, eristical, linguistical,
logistical, monistical,
patristical, sophistical,
statistical, theistical,
alchemistical, atheistical,
casuistical, egoistical,
egotistical, exorcistical,
pantheistical, anomalistical,
hypocoristical, monotheistical,
polytheistical
istich \is-tik\ see ISTIC
istics \is-tiks\ ballistics, ekistics,

linguistics, logistics,
patristics, statistics, stylistics,
futuristics, criminalistics—
*also plurals and possessives
of nouns listed at* ISTIC
istie \is-tē\ see ²ICITY
istil \is-tᵊl\ see ISTAL
istin \is-tən\ see ISTON
istine \is-tən\ see ISTON
istle \is-əl\ bristle, fissile,
gristle, missal, missile,
scissile, thistle, whistle,
abyssal, dickcissel, dismissal,
epistle, pennywhistle
istler \is-lər\ whistler, Whistler,
epistler
istless \ist-ləs\ listless, resistless
istly \is-lē\ bristly, gristly,
thistly, sweet cicely
istmas \is-məs\ Christmas,
isthmus, Kiritimati
isto \is-tō\ aristo, Callisto
istol \is-tᵊl\ see ISTAL
iston \is-tən\ Kristin, piston,
Tristan, Philistine, phlogiston,
amethystine
istor \is-tər\ see ISTER
istory \is-trē\ blistery, history,
mystery, consistory,
prehistory
istral \is-trəl\ mistral, sinistral
istress \is-trəs\ mistress,
headmistress, postmistress,
schoolmistress, sinistrous,
taskmistress, toastmistress
istrophe \is-trə-fē\ antistrophe,
epistrophe
istrous \is-trəs\ see ISTRESS
isty \is-tē\ see ²ICITY
isus \ī-səs\ see ISIS
iszt \ist\ see ²IST
¹it \it\ bit, bitt, brit, Brit, chit,

dit, fit, flit, frit, git, grit, hit,
it, kit, knit, lit, mitt, nit, pit,
Pitt, quit, sit, skit, slit, snit,
spit, split, Split, sprit, teat, tit,
twit, whit, wit, writ, zit,
acquit, admit, armpit, backbit,
backfit, befit, bowsprit,
Brigitte, bushtit, cesspit,
close-knit, cockpit, commit,
culprit, demit, Dewitt, dimwit,
emit, fleapit, gaslit, godwit,
half-wit, henbit, house-sit,
legit, lit crit, misfit, mishit,
moonlit, nitwit, obit, omit,
outfit, outwit, peewit, permit,
pinch-hit, Prakrit, pulpit, refit,
remit, sandpit, Sanskrit,
snakebit, starlit, submit, sunlit,
switch-hit, tidbit, tight-knit,
titbit, tomtit, transmit,
turnspit,twilit, two-bit, unfit,
unknit,well-knit, baby-sit,
benefit,candlelit, counterfeit,
hypocrite, intermit, intromit,
manumit, megahit, recommit,
retrofit, cost-benefit, lickety-
split, overcommit, jack-in-the-
pulpit
²it \ē\ see ¹EE
³it \ēt\ see ¹EAT
¹ita \īt-ə\ vita, baryta, amanita
²ita \ēt-ə\ cheetah, eta, Greta,
Nita, pita, Rita, theta, vita,
zeta, Akita, Anita, Bonita,
bonito, casita, excreta,
Granita, Juanita, Lolita,
mosquito, partita, Suita,
amanita, arboreta, feterita,
incognita, manzanita,
margarita, senhorita, senorita,
Bhagavad Gita
¹itable \īt-ə-bəl\ citable,

writable, excitable, indictable,
copyrightable, extraditable
²**itable** \it-ə-bəl\ see ITTABLE
itae \īt-ē\ see ²ITE
itain \it-n\ see ITTEN
¹**ital** \īt-ᵊl\ title, vital, detrital,
entitle, nontitle, recital,
requital, subtitle, disentitle,
intravital, supravital
²**ital** \it-ᵊl\ see ITTLE
italer \it-ᵊl-ər\ whittler,
victualler, belittler, Hospitaler
italist \īt-ᵊl-əst\ titlist, vitalist,
recitalist
itan \īt-ᵊn\ see IGHTEN
itant \īt-ᵊnt\ mightn't, excitant,
incitant, renitent
itany \it-ᵊn-ē\ Brittany, dittany,
litany
itch \ich\ ditch, fitch, flitch,
glitch, hitch, itch, kitsch,
niche, pitch, quitch, rich,
snitch, stitch, such, switch,
twitch, which, witch,
backstitch, bewitch, cross-
stitch, enrich, fast-twitch,
hemstitch, lockstitch, slow-
pitch, slow-twitch, topstitch,
unhitch, whipstitch,
czarevitch, featherstitch,
microswitch
itchen \ich-ən\ kitchen, richen
itchener \ich-nər\ Kitchener,
Michener
itcher \ich-ər\ hitcher, pitcher,
richer, snitcher, stitcher,
switcher, enricher,
hemstitcher, Lubavitcher,
water witcher
itchery \ich-ə-rē\ bitchery,
obituary, stitchery, witchery,
bewitchery

itches \ich-əz\ britches, riches,
Dutchman's-breeches—*also
plurals and possessives of
nouns and third person
singular presents of verbs
listed at* ITCH
itchman \ich-mən\ pitchman,
switchman
itchment \ich-mənt\
bewitchment, enrichment
itchy \ich-ē\ bitchy, itchy,
kitschy, pitchy, twitchy, witchy
it'd \it-əd\ see ITTED
¹**ite** \īt\ bight, bite, blight,
bright, byte, cite, dight, dite,
Dwight, fight, flight, fright,
height, hight, kite, knight,
krait, kyte, light, lite, might,
mite, night, plight, quite,
right, rite, sight, site, sleight,
slight, smite, spite, sprite,
tight, trite, white, White,
wight, Wight, wite, wright,
Wright, write, affright,
airtight, albite, alight, all
right, all-night, aright,
backbite, backlight, bedight,
Birchite, birthright, bobwhite,
bombsight, bullfight,
campsite, cockfight, contrite,
Cushite, daylight, deadlight,
delight, despite, dogfight,
downright, droplight,
earthlight, excite, eyebright,
eyesight, fanlight, finite,
firefight, firelight, fistfight,
flashlight, fleabite, floodlight,
foresight, forthright, fortnight,
frostbite, Gadite, gaslight,
gastight, ghostwrite, graphite,
gunfight, Gunite, half-light,
Hamite, handwrite, headlight,

highlight, hindsight, Hittite,
homesite, hoplite, Hussite,
ignite, illite, infight, in-flight,
incite, indict, indite, insight,
invite, jacklight, jadeite,
lamplight, Levite, lighttight,
lignite, limelight, lintwhite,
lowlight, Lucite, Luddite,
lyddite, Melchite, midnight,
millwright, miswrite,
moonlight, night-light, off-
site, off-white, on-site,
outright, outsight, partite,
penlight, playwright, polite,
prizefight, pyrite, recite,
requite, respite, rushlight,
safelight, searchlight, Semite,
Servite, Shemite, Shiite,
shipwright, sidelight,
skintight, skylight, skywrite,
smectite, snakebite, snow-
white, spaceflight, speedlight,
spotlight, starlight, sticktight,
stoplight, streetlight, sunlight,
Sunnite, taillight, termite,
tonight, torchlight, trothplight,
twilight, twi-night, typewrite,
unite, unsight, upright,
uptight, wainwright,
weeknight, wheelwright,
acolyte, aconite, Ammonite,
Amorite, amosite, anchorite,
anthracite, antiwhite,
apartheid, appetite, Bakelite,
Benthamite, bipartite, black-
and-white, blatherskite,
bleacherite, chalcocite,
Canaanite, Carmelite,
castroite, catamite, cellulite,
copyright, disinvite, disunite,
dynamite, erudite, expedite,
extradite, Fahrenheit,

featherlight, fly-by-night,
gelignite, gesundheit,
gigabyte, Hashemite,
Hepplewhite, Himyarite,
Hitlerite, hug-me-tight,
impolite, Ishmaelite, Israelite,
Jacobite, Josephite,
Kimberlite, laborite, Leninite,
leukocyte, lily-white, localite,
malachite, manganite,
Marcionite, Masonite,
Mennonite, Minorite,
Moabite, muscovite, Nazirite,
out-of-sight, overbite,
overflight, overnight,
oversight, overwrite, parasite,
perovskite, plebiscite,
proselyte, Puseyite, pyrrhotite,
recondite, reunite, satellite,
shergottite, socialite, sodalite,
sodomite, Stagirite, stalactite,
stalagmite, Sybarite, time-of-
flight, transfinite, transvestite,
tripartite, troglodyte,
Trotskyite, ultralight,
underwrite, urbanite,
Wahhabite, watertight,
Wycliffite, yesternight,
adipocyte, anthophyllite,
cosmopolite, exurbanite,
gemütlichkeit, hermaphrodite,
Indo-Hittite, McCarthyite,
multipartite, quadripartite,
suburbanite, theodolite,
Areopagite, Pre-Raphaelite,
Great Australian Bight
²ite \īt-ē\ flighty, mighty,
nightie, righty, whitey, whity,
almighty, Almighty, Venite,
Aphrodite, aqua vitae,
arborvitae, lignum vitae
³ite \it\ see ¹IT

⁴ite \ēt\ see ¹EAT

ited \īt-əd\ see IGHTED

iteful \īt-fəl\ see IGHTFUL

itely \īt-lē\ see IGHTLY

item \īt-əm\ item, ad infinitum

itement \īt-mənt\ alightment, excitement, incitement, indictment

iten \īt-ᵊn\ see IGHTEN

itener \īt-nər\ see IGHTENER

itent \īt-ᵊnt\ see ITANT

iteor \ēt-ē-ər\ see ETEOR

¹iter \īt-ər\ blighter, fighter, lighter, miter, niter, titer, writer, all-nighter, braillewriter, exciter, first-nighter, lamplighter, nail-biter, one-nighter, prizefighter, screenwriter, scriptwriter, songwriter, speechwriter, sportswriter, states righter, typewriter, copywriter, expediter, fly-by-nighter, Gastarbeiter, underwriter, teletypewriter—*also nouns and comparatives of adjectives formed by adding -er to verbs listed at* ¹ITE

²iter \it-ər\ see ITTER

³iter \ēt-ər\ see ¹EATER

iteral \it-ə-rəl\ clitoral, literal, littoral, sublittoral, triliteral

iterally \it-ər-lē\ see ITTERLY

iterate \it-ə-rət\ literate, illiterate, nonliterate, postliterate, preliterate, presbyterate, subliterate, semiliterate

¹ites \īt-ēz\ barytes, sorites, Thersites—*also plurals and possessives of nouns listed at* ²ITE

²ites \īts\ see IGHTS

itey \īt-ē\ see ²ITE

ith \ith\ fifth, frith, grith, kith, myth, pith, sith, smith, Smith, swith, with, withe, blacksmith, forthwith, goldsmith, Goldsmith, gunsmith, herewith, locksmith, songsmith, therewith, tinsmith, tunesmith, wherewith, whitesmith, wordsmith, coppersmith, eolith, Granny Smith, Hammersmith, megalith, metalsmith, microlith, monolith, neolith, silversmith, paleolith

³ith \ēt\ see ¹EAT

⁴ith \ēth\ see ¹EATH

¹ithe \ī<u>th</u>\ blithe, kithe, lithe, scythe, tithe, withe, writhe

²ithe \ith\ see ²ITH

³ithe \i<u>th</u>\ see ¹ITH

¹ithee \ith-ē\ see ²ITHY

²ithee \i<u>th</u>-ē\ see ¹ITHY

ither \i<u>th</u>-ər\ blither, cither, dither, hither, slither, swither, thither, whither, wither, zither, come-hither, nowhither, somewhither

itherward \i<u>th</u>-ər-wərd\ thitherward, whitherward

ithesome \ī<u>th</u>-səm\ blithesome, lithesome

ithia \ith-ē-ə\ see YTHIA

ithic \ith-ik\ lithic, ornithic, batholithic, Eolithic, granolithic, megalithic, Mesolithic, monolithic, neolithic, Paleolithic

ithing \ī-<u>th</u>iŋ\ tithing, trithing

ithmic \ith-mik\ see YTHMIC

¹ithy \i<u>th</u>-ē\ prithee, withy

²ithy \ith-ē\ mythy, pithy, prithee, smithy, withy

iti \ēt-ē\ see EATY

¹itia \ish-ə\ Lycia, Mysia, wisha, Alicia, Cilicia, comitia, episcia, Galicia, indicia, Letitia, militia, Patricia, Phoenicia, Dionysia

²itia \ē-shə\ see ¹ESIA

itial \ish-əl\ see ICIAL

¹itian \ish-ən\ see ITION

²itian \ē-shən\ see ¹ETION

itiate \ish-ət\ initiate, novitiate, uninitiate

itic \it-ik\ clitic, critic, arthritic, bronchitic, dendritic, enclitic, granitic, graphitic, Hamitic, jaditic, mephitic, proclitic, pruritic, rachitic, Sanskritic, Semitic, Shemitic, Sinitic, anaclitic, analytic, anchoritic, catalytic, cenobitic, copralitic, crystallitic, diacritic, dialytic, dynamitic, eremitic, Himyaritic, hypercritic, jesuitic, paralytic, parasitic, sodomitic, stalactitic, stalagmitic, sybaritic, thallophytic, thrombolytic, troglodytic, cryptanalytic, electrolytic, hermaphroditic, meteoritic, Monophysitic, psychoanalytic

itical \it-i-kəl\ critical, Levitical, political, analytical, apolitical, cenobitical, diacritical, eremitical, hypercritical, hypocritical, impolitical, Jacobitical, jesuitical,

parasitical, sodomitical, supercritical, geopolitical, meteoritical, sociopolitical

itics \it-iks\ Semitics, analytics, meteoritics—*also plurals and possessives of nouns listed at* ITIC

itid \it-əd\ see ITTED

itimati \is-məs\ see ISTMAS

itin \īt-ᵊn\ see IGHTEN

iting \īt-iŋ\ biting, flyting, lighting, whiting, writing, backbiting, bullfighting, cockfighting, daylighting, exciting, freewriting, frostbiting, handwriting, infighting, inviting, newswriting, prewriting, prizefighting, skywriting, songwriting, sportswriting, typewriting

ition \ish-ən\ fission, hycian, mission, titian, Titian, addition, admission, ambition, attrition, audition, beautician, clinician, cognition, coition, commission, condition, contrition, demission, dentition, dismission, Domitian, edition, emission, ethician, fruition, ignition, lenition, logician, magician, monition, mortician, munition, musician, nutrition, omission, optician, partition, patrician, perdition, permission, petition, Phoenician, physician, position, punition, remission, rendition, sedition, submission, suspicion, tactician, technician, tradition,

transition, transmission,
tuition, volition, abolition,
acquisition, admonition,
aesthetician, air-condition,
ammunition, apparition,
apposition, coalition,
competition, composition,
cosmetician, decommission,
decondition, definition,
demolition, deposition,
dietitian, Dionysian,
disposition, disquisition,
electrician, erudition,
exhibition, expedition,
exposition, extradition,
imposition, inhibition,
inquisition, intermission,
intromission, intuition,
linguistician, logistician,
malnutrition, malposition,
manumission, mathematician,
mechanician, micturition,
obstetrician, opposition,
Ordovician, parturition,
phonetician, politician,
precognition, precondition,
premonition, preposition,
prohibition, proposition,
recognition, recondition,
repetition, requisition,
rhetorician, statistician,
submunition, superstition,
supposition, transposition,
academician, arithmetician,
decomposition, diagnostician,
dialectician, disinhibition,
geometrician, geriatrician,
indisposition, interposition,
juxtaposition, metaphysician,
onomastician, pediatrician,
presupposition, redefinition,

semiotician, theoretician,
superimposition

itionable \ish-nə-bəl\ see
ISSIONABLE

itional \ish-ə-nəl\ additional,
attritional, cognitional,
coitional, conditional,
nutritional, positional,
traditional, transitional,
tuitional, volitional,
apparitional, appositional,
compositional, definitional,
depositional, expositional,
inquisitional, oppositional,
prepositional, propositional,
repetitional, suppositional,
transpositional, unconditional,
juxtapositional,
presuppositional

itioner \i-shə-nər\ missioner,
commissioner, conditioner,
parishioner, partitioner,
petitioner, practitioner,
exhibitioner, malpractitioner,
nurse-practitioner

itionist \i-shə-nəst\ nutritionist,
partitionist, abolitionist,
coalitionist, demolitionist,
exhibitionist, intuitionist,
oppositionist, prohibitionist

itious \ish-əs\ see ¹ICIOUS

itis \īt-əs\ situs, Titus, arthritis,
botrytis, bronchitis, bursitis,
colitis, cystitis, detritus,
gastritis, iritis, mastitis,
nephritis, neuritis, phlebitis,
dermatitis, enteritis, gingivitis,
hepatitis, Heracleitus, ileitis,
laryngitis, meningitis,
pharyngitis, pneumonitis,
prostatitis, retinitis, sinusitis,
tonsillitis, spondylitis,

tendinitis, urethritis, vaginitis, appendicitis, conjunctivitis, encephalitis, endocarditis, endometritus, folliculitis, Hermaphroditus, peritonitis, analysis situs, diverticulitis, gastroenteritis, poliomyelitis

itish \it-ish\ British, skittish

itius \ish-əs\ see ICIOUS

itle \īt-ᵊl\ see ¹ITAL

it'll \it-ᵊl\ see ITTLE

itment \it-mənt\ fitment, commitment, remitment, recommitment, overcommitment

itness \it-nəs\ fitness, witness, earwitness, eyewitness, unfitness

itney \it-nē\ jitney, Whitney, Mount Whitney

¹ito \ēt-ō\ keto, Leto, Quito, Tito, veto, bonito, burrito, graffito, magneto, Miskito, mosquito, Negrito, Hirohito, incognito, sanbenito

²ito \ēt-ə\ see ²ITA

¹iton \it-ᵊn\ see ITTEN

²iton \īt-ᵊn\ see IGHTEN

itoral \it-ə-rəl\ see ITERAL

itra \ē-trə\ see ²ETRA

itral \ī-trəl\ mitral, nitrile

itrile \ī-trəl\ see ITRAL

it's \its\ see ITS

its \its\ blitz, ditz, Fritz, glitz, grits, it's, its, quits, spitz, Chemnitz, Saint Kitts, slivovitz—*also plurals and possessives of nouns and third person singular presents of verbs listed at* ¹IT

itsail \it-səl\ see ITZEL

itsch \ich\ see ITCH

itschy \ich-ē\ see ITCHY

itsy \it-sē\ see ITZY

itt \it\ see ¹IT

itta \it-ə\ shittah, vitta

ittable \it-ə-bəl\ committable, habitable, hospitable, remittable, transmittable, inhospitable

ittah \it-ə\ see ITTA

ittal \it-ᵊl\ see ITTLE

ittance \it-ᵊns\ pittance, quittance, acquittance, admittance, emittance, immittance, remittance, transmittance, intermittence

ittany \it-ᵊn-ē\ see ITANY

itte \it\ see ¹IT

itted \it-əd\ fitted, it'd, nitid, pitted, teated, witted, committed, dim-witted, half-witted, quick-witted, sharp-witted, slow-witted, thick-witted, unbitted, unfitted, uncommitted—*also pasts of verbs listed at* ¹IT

ittee \it-ē\ see ITTY

itten \it-ᵊn\ bitten, Britain, Briton, Britten, kitten, litten, Lytton, mitten, smitten, witting, written, backbitten, flea-bitten, Great Britain, hard-bitten, New Britain, rewritten, snakebitten, unwritten

ittence \it-ᵊns\ see ITTANCE

ittent \it-ᵊnt\ remittent, intermittent, intromittent

itter \it-ər\ bitter, chitter, critter, fitter, flitter, fritter, glitter, hitter, jitter, knitter, litter, quitter, quittor, sitter, skitter, slitter, spitter, titter, twitter, aglitter, atwitter, bed-sitter, embitter, emitter, hairsplitter, no-hitter, outfitter, rail-splitter, remitter, shipfitter, steamfitter, switch-hitter, transmitter, benefiter, counterfeiter, intromitter

itterer \it-ər-ər\ fritterer, litterer, twitterer

itterly \it-ər-lē\ bitterly, literally

ittern \it-ərn\ bittern, cittern, gittern

ittery \it-ə-rē\ glittery, jittery, littery, skittery, twittery

ittie \it-ē\ see ITTY

ittier \it-ē-ər\ grittier, prettier, Whittier, wittier

ittiness \it-ē-nəs\ grittiness, prettiness, wittiness

¹itting \it-iŋ\ fitting, sitting, splitting, witting, befitting, earsplitting, fence-sitting, formfitting, hairsplitting, hard-hitting, house-sitting, resitting, sidesplitting, unfitting, unwitting, unremitting

²itting \it-ᵊn\ see ITTEN

ittish \it-ish\ see ITISH

ittle \it-ᵊl\ brittle, it'll, kittle, little, skittle, spital, spittle, tittle, victual, whittle, wittol, acquittal, belittle, committal, embrittle, hospital, lickspittle, remittal, transmittal, noncommittal, recommittal

ittler \it-ᵊl-ər\ see ITALER

ittol \it-ᵊl\ see ITTLE

ittor \it-ər\ see ITTER

ittoral \it-ə-rəl\ see ITERAL

itts \its\ see ITS

itty \it-ē\ bitty, city, ditty,

gritty, kitty, Kitty, pity, pretty, tittie, witty, committee, self-pity, itty-bitty, Kansas City, megacity, nitty-gritty, Salt Lake City, subcommittee, supercity, Walter Mitty, Ho Chi Minh City

itual \ich-ə-wəl\ ritual, habitual

ituary \ich-ə-rē\ see ¹ITCHERY

itum \īt-əm\ see ITEM

itus \īt-əs\ see ITIS

¹ity \it-ē\ see ITTY

²ity \īt-ē\ see ²ITE

itz \its\ see ITS

¹itza \ēt-sə\ pizza, czaritza, Chichén Itza, Katowice

²itza \it-sə\ czaritza, tamburitza

itzel \it-səl\ schnitzel, spritsail, Wiener schnitzel

itzi \it-sē\ see ITZY

itzy \it-sē\ bitsy, glitzy, Mitzi, ritzy, schizy

iu \ü\ see ¹EW

¹ius \ē-əs\ see ¹EUS

²ius \ī-əs\ see ¹IAS

¹iv \iv\ see ²IVE

²iv \ēf\ see ¹IEF

³iv \if\ see IFF

⁴iv \ēv\ see EAVE

¹iva \ī-və\ Saiva, gingiva, Godiva, saliva

²iva \ē-və\ diva, Eva, kiva, Shiva, siva, Siva, viva, geneva, Geneva, yeshiva

³iva \iv-ə\ Shiva, Siva

¹ivable \ī-və-bəl\ drivable, derivable, revivable, survivable

²ivable \iv-ə-bəl\ livable, forgivable

ival \ī-vəl\ rival, archival, arrival, revival, survival, adjectival, conjunctival, genitival, substantival, infinitival

ivalent \iv-ə-lənt\ ambivalent, equivalent, unambivalent

ivan \iv-ən\ see IVEN

ivance \ī-vəns\ connivance, contrivance, survivance

ivative \iv-ət-iv\ privative, derivative

¹**ive** \īv\ chive, dive, drive, five, gyve, hive, I've, jive, live, rive, shrive, skive, strive, thrive, wive, alive, archive, Argive, arrive, beehive, connive, contrive, deprive, derive, endive, nosedive, ogive, revive, self-drive, skin-dive, survive, test-drive, forty-five, overdrive, power-dive

²**ive** \iv\ give, live, sheave, shiv, sieve, spiv, forgive, misgive, outlive, relive, unlive, underactive

³**ive** \ēv\ see ¹EAVE

ivel \iv-əl\ civil, drivel, frivol, shrivel, snivel, swivel

iven \iv-ən\ driven, given, riven, Sivan, striven, thriven, forgiven, menu-driven

¹**iver** \ī-vər\ diver, driver, fiver, arriver, cabdriver, conniver, contriver, deriver, reviver, screwdriver, survivor

²**iver** \iv-ər\ flivver, giver, liver, quiver, river, shiver, sliver, almsgiver, aquiver, deliver, downriver, forgiver, lawgiver, quicksilver, upriver, Guadalquivir

¹**ivers** \ī-vərz\ divers, vivers—

also plurals and possessives of nouns listed at ¹IVER

²**ivers** \ē-vərz\ see EAVERS

ivery \iv-rē\ livery, shivery, delivery

ives \īvz\ fives, hives, Ives—*also plurals and possessives of nouns and third person singular presents of verbs listed at* ¹IVE

ivet \iv-ət\ civet, divot, pivot, privet, rivet, swivet, trivet

¹**ivi** \iv-ē\ see IVVY

²**ivi** \ē-vē\ see EAVEY

ivia \iv-ē-ə\ Bolivia, Olivia

ivial \iv-ē-əl\ trivial, convivial, quadrivial

ivid \iv-əd\ livid, vivid

ivil \iv-əl\ see IVEL

ivilly \iv-ə-lē\ civilly, privily, uncivilly

ivily \iv-ə-lē\ see IVILLY

iving \iv-iŋ\ giving, living, almsgiving, forgiving, free-living, misgiving, thanksgiving

ivion \iv-ē-ən\ Vivian, oblivion

ivious \iv-ē-əs\ lascivious, oblivious

ivir \iv-ər\ see ²IVER

ivity \iv-ət-ē\ privity, acclivity, activity, captivity, declivity, festivity, motivity, nativity, proclivity, absorptivity, adaptivity, additivity, affectivity, aggressivity, coercivity, cognitivity, collectivity, compulsivity, conductivity, connectivity, creativity, destructivity, diffusivity, directivity, effectivity, emissivity, emotivity, exclusivity, exhaustivity, expansivity, expressivity, impassivity, inactivity, infectivity, negativity, perceptivity, perfectivity, permittivity, positivity, primitivity, productivity, progressivity, reactivity, receptivity, reflexivity, relativity, resistivity, retentivity, selectivity, sensitivity, subjectivity, susceptivity, transitivity, distributivity, hyperactivity, insensitivity, overactivity, retroactivity, radioactivity, hypersensitivity

ivium \iv-ē-əm\ trivium, quadrivium

iviut \ē-vē-ət\ see EVIATE

ivo \ē-vō\ see EVO

ivocal \iv-ə-kəl\ equivocal, univocal, unequivocal

ivol \iv-əl\ see IVEL

ivor \ī-vər\ see ¹IVER

ivorous \iv-rəs\ carnivorous, granivorous, omnivorous, insectivorous

ivot \iv-ət\ see IVET

ivus \ē-vəs\ see EVOUS

ivver \iv-ər\ see ²IVER

ivvy \iv-ē\ chivy, civvy, divvy, Livy, privy, skivvy, tantivy, divi-divi

ivy \iv-ē\ see IVVY

iw \ef\ see ¹EF

iwi \ē-wē\ see EEWEE

¹ix \iks\ Brix, Dix, fix, mix, nix, pyx, six, Styx, admix, affix, blanc fixe, commix, deep-six, immix, infix, postfix, prefix, premix, prix fixe, prolix, subfix, suffix, transfix, unfix, antefix, cicatrix, crucifix, eighty-six, intermix, politics, six-o-six, superfix, geopolitics, RU 486—*also plurals and possessives of nouns and third person singular presents of verbs listed at* ICK

²ix \ē\ see ¹EE

ixal \ik-səl\ pixel, affixal, prefixal, suffixal

¹ixe \ēks\ breeks, prix fixe, idée fixe, Macgillicuddy's Reeks—*also plurals and possessives of nouns and third person singular presents of verbs listed at* ¹EAK

²ixe \iks\ see ¹IX

³ixe \ēsh\ see ²ICHE

ixed \ikst\ fixed, mixed, twixt, betwixt, well-fixed—*also pasts of verbs listed at* ¹IX

ixel \ik-səl\ see IXAL

ixen \ik-sən\ vixen, Nixon, Mason-Dixon

ixer \ik-sər\ fixer, mixer, elixir

ixia \ik-sē-ə\ asphyxia, panmixia

ixie \ik-sē\ Dixie, nixie, Nixie, pixie, pyxie, tricksy

ixion \ik-shən\ see ICTION

ixir \ik-sər\ see IXER

ixit \ik-sət\ quixote, ipse dixit

ixon \ik-sən\ see IXEN

ixote \ik-sət\ see IXIT

ixt \ikst\ see IXED

ixture \iks-chər\ fixture, mixture, admixture, commixture, intermixture

iya \ē-ə\ see ¹IA

iyeh \ē-ə\ see ¹IA

¹**iz** \iz\ biz, fizz, frizz, his, is,
Ms., phiz, quiz, 'tis, whiz,
wiz, gee-whiz, show biz

²**iz** \ēz\ see EZE

¹**iza** \ē-zə\ see EZA

²**iza** \ē-thə\ see ETHA

izabeth \iz-ə-bəth\ Elisabeth,
Elizabeth, Port Elizabeth

izable \ī-zə-bəl\ sizable,
advisable, cognizable,
devisable, excisable,
amortizable, analyzable,
criticizable, dramatizable,
exercisable, fertilizable,
hypnotizable, inadvisable,
localizable, magnetizable,
mechanizable, memorizable,
pulverizable, recognizable,
vaporizable, computerizable,
generalizable,
uncompromisable

izar \ī-zər\ see IZER

izard \iz-ərd\ blizzard, gizzard,
izzard, lizard, vizard, wizard

¹**ize** \īz\ guise, prise, prize, rise,
size, wise, abscise, advise,
apprise, apprize, arise, assize,
baptize, breadthwise, capsize,
chastise, clockwise, cognize,
comprise, crabwise,
crosswise, demise, despise,
devise, disguise, disprize,
downsize, earthrise, edgewise,
emprise, endwise, excise,
fanwise, franchise, full-size,
grecize, high-rise, incise,
king-size, leastwise,
lengthwise, Levi's, life-size,
likewise, low-rise, man-size,
midsize, misprize, moonrise,
nowise, outsize, piecewise,
pint-size, premise, quantize,

remise, reprise, revise,
slantwise, streetwise, stylize,
suffice, sunrise, surmise,
surprise, twin-size, uprise,
advertise, aggrandize,
agonize, alchemize, amortize,
analyze, anglicize, anywise,
aphorize, arabize, atomize,
authorize, autolyze, balkanize,
barbarize, bastardize,
bestialize, bolshevize,
botanize, bowdlerize,
brutalize, burglarize, canalize,
canonize, capsulize,
caramelize, carbonize,
cartelize, catalyze, catechize,
cauterize, centralize,
channelize, Christianize,
cicatrize, circumcise, civilize,
classicize, colonize,
communize, compromise,
concertize, concretize,
creolize, criticize, crystalize,
customize, demonize,
deputize, dialyze, digitize,
disfranchise, dogmatize,
dramatize, elegize, empathize,
emphasize, energize,
enfranchise, enterprise,
equalize, erotize, eternize,
etherize, eulogize, euphemize,
exercise, exorcise, factorize,
fantasize, fascistize, feminize,
fertilize, feudalize, fictionize,
finalize, formalize, formulize,
fossilize, fragmentize,
fraternize, gallicize, galvanize,
germanize, ghettoize,
glamorize, globalize,
gormandize, gothicize,
gourmandize, grecianize,
harmonize, heathenize,

hebraize, hellenize,
hierarchize, humanize,
hybridize, hypnotize, idolize,
immunize, improvise, ionize,
ironize, Islamize, itemize,
jeopardize, journalize,
Judaize, laicize, latinize,
legalize, lionize, liquidize,
localize, magnetize,
marbleize, martyrize,
maximize, mechanize,
melanize, melodize,
memorize, merchandise,
mesmerize, methodize,
metricize, minimize, mobilize,
modernize, moisturize,
monetize, mongrelize,
moralize, motorize, mythicize,
narcotize, nasalize, neutralize,
normalize, notarize, novelize,
obelize, odorize, optimize,
organize, ostracize, otherwise,
oversize, oxidize, paganize,
paradise, paralyze, pasteurize,
patronize, pauperize, penalize,
penny-wise, pidginize,
plagiarize, plasticize,
Platonize, pluralize, pocket-
size, poetize, polarize,
polemize, pressurize,
privatize, prussianize,
publicize, pulverize,
randomize, realize, recognize,
rhapsodize, robotize,
romanize, rubberize, sanitize,
satirize, scandalize,
schematize, schismatize,
scrutinize, sensitize,
sermonize, signalize,
simonize, sinicize, slenderize,
sloganize, socialize,
sodomize, solarize, sonnetize,

specialize, stabilize, Stalinize,
standardize, sterilize,
stigmatize, strategize,
subsidize, summarize,
supervise, syllogize,
symbolize, sympathize,
synchronize, syncretize,
synopsize, synthesize,
systemize, tantalize, televise,
temporize, tenderize, terrorize,
tetanize, teutonize, texturize,
theorize, thermalize, totalize,
tranquilize, traumatize,
tyrannize, unionize, unitize,
urbanize, utilize, valorize,
vandalize, vaporize, verbalize,
vernalize, victimize, vitalize,
vocalize, vulcanize, vulgarize,
weather-wise, weatherize,
westernize, winterize,
womanize, worldly-wise,
accessorize, acclimatize,
actualize, allegorize,
alphabetize, analogize,
anatomize, anesthetize,
animalize, annualize,
antagonize, anthologize,
anticlockwise, apologize,
apostatize, apostrophize,
arabicize, aromatize, baby
blue-eyes, bureaucratize,
cannibalize, capitalize,
categorize, catholicize,
characterize, commercialize,
communalize, computerize,
conservatize, containerize,
contrariwise, conveyorize,
cosmeticize,
counterclockwise, criminalize,
cryptanalize, decentralize,
decolonize, de-emphasize,
de-energize, dehumanize,

deionize, demagnetize, demobilize, democratize, demoralize, deodorize, depersonalize, depolarize, desalinize, desensitize, destabilize, digitalize, disenfranchise, disorganize, economize, emotionalize, epitomize, epoxidize, eroticize, eternalize, euthanatize, evangelize, extemporize, externalize, familiarize, fanaticize, federalize, fictionalize, formularize, gelatinize, generalize, geologize, Hispanicize, homogenize, hospitalize, hypothesize, idealize, illegalize, immobilize, immortalize, impersonalize, Indianize, indigenize, initialize, internalize, italicize, legitimize, liberalize, literalize, lobotomize, lysogenize, macadamize, metabolize, metastasize, militarize, mineralize, monopolize, mythologize, nationalize, naturalize, parenthesize, philosophize, politicize, popularize, proselytize, regularize, reorganize, revitalize, romanticize, secularize, sexualize, sovietize, subjectivize, suburbanize, subvocalize, systematize, temporalize, theologize, traditionalize, transistorize, trivialize, ventriloquize, visualize, Americanize, apotheosize, colonialize, compartmentalize, conceptualize, contextualize, decriminalize, demilitarize, denaturalize, departmentalize, depoliticize, desexualize, Europeanize, exteriorize, ideologize, immaterialize, individualize, industrialize, internationalize, legitimatize, materialize, miniaturize, particularize, politicalize, phychoanalyze, self-actualize, sentimentalize, spiritualize, underutilize, universalize, constitutionalize, dematerialize, editorialize, intellectualize, deinstitutionalize—*also plurals and possessives of nouns and third person singular presents of verbs listed at* ¹�

²**ize** \ēz\ see EZE

ized \īzd\ sized, advised, outsized, ergotized, ill-advised, pearlized, Sanforized, unadvised, undersized, varisized, well-advised, elasticized, modularized, unexercised, immunocompromised—*also pasts of verbs listed at* IZE

¹**izen** \īz-ᵊn\ bison, dizen, greisen, bedizen, horizon, spiegeleisen

²**izen** \iz-ᵊn\ see ²ISON

izer \ī-zər\ Dreiser, geyser, kaiser, miser, prizer, riser, sizar, visor, wiser, adviser, divisor, incisor, appetizer, atomizer, energizer,

enterpriser, equalizer,
exerciser, fertilizer, organizer,
oxidizer, stabilizer,
supervisor, synthesizer,
totalizer, tranquilizer,
tyrannizer, vaporizer,
complementizer, deodorizer—
also nouns formed by adding
-er *to verbs listed at* IZE

izing \ī-ziŋ\ rising, sizing,
uprising, appetizing,
enterprising, merchandising,
self-sufficing, unsurprising,
self-sacrificing,
uncompromising

¹izo \ē-zō\ sleazo, chorizo,
mestizo

²izo \ē-sō\ see ISO

izon \īz-ᵊn\ see ¹IZEN

izy \it-sē\ see ITZY

izz \iz\ see ¹IZ

izza \ēt-sə\ see ¹ITZA

izzard \iz-ərd\ see IZARD

izzen \iz-ᵊn\ see ²ISON

izzer \iz-ər\ see ISSOR

izzical \iz-i-kəl\ see YSICAL

izzie \i-zē\ see IZZY

izzle \iz-əl\ chisel, drizzle,
fizzle, frizzle, grizzle, mizzle,
pizzle, sizzle, swizzle

izzled \iz-əld\ chiseled,
grizzled—*also pasts of verbs
listed at* IZZLE

izzler \iz-lər\ chiseler, sizzler,
swizzler

izzly \iz-lē\ drizzly, grisly,
grizzly, mizzly

izzy \iz-ē\ busy, dizzy, fizzy,
frizzy, tizzy, tin lizzie

O

¹**o** \ü\ see ¹EW

²**o** \ō\ see ¹OW

³**o** \ər\ see ¹EUR

¹**oa** \ō-ə\ boa, Goa, koa, moa,
Noah, proa, stoa, aloha,
balboa, Balboa, jerboa,
Samoa, Krakatoa, Mauna Loa,
Shenandoah, Sinaloa,
Guanabacoa, João Pessoa

²**oa** \ō\ see ¹OW

oable \ü-ə-bəl\ see UABLE

oach \ōch\ broach, brooch,
coach, loach, poach, roach,
abroach, approach, caroche,
cockroach, encroach,
reproach, stagecoach

oachable \ō-chə-bəl\ coachable,
approachable, inapproachable,
irreproachable,
unapproachable

oacher \ō-chər\ broacher,
coacher, cloture, poacher,
encroacher

¹**oad** \ōd\ see ODE

²**oad** \òd\ see ¹AUD

oader \ōd-ər\ see ODER

oadie \ōd-ē\ see ²ODY

oady \ōd-ē\ see ²ODY

oaf \ōf\ loaf, oaf, qoph,
meatloaf, witloof, sugarloaf

oafer \ō-fər\ see OFER

oagie \ō-gē\ see OGIE

oah \ō-ə\ see ¹OA

oak \ōk\ see OKE

oaken \ō-kən\ see OKEN

oaker \ō-kər\ see OKER

oakum \ō-kəm\ see OKUM

oaky \ō-kē\ see OKY

oal \ōl\ see ¹OLE

oalie \ō-lē\ see ¹OLY

¹**oam** \ō-əm\ see ¹OEM

²**oam** \ōm\ see ¹OME

oamer \ō-mər\ see ¹OMER

oaming \ō-miŋ\ coaming,
combing, gloaming,
Wyoming—*also present
participles of verbs listed at*
¹OME

oamy \ō-mē\ foamy, homey,
loamy, show-me, Suomi,
Dahomey, Naomi, Salome

¹**oan** \ō-ən\ Owen, roan, rowan,
Minoan, Samoan, waygoing,
Eskimoan, protozoan

²**oan** \ōn\ see ¹ONE

oaner \ō-nər\ see ¹ONER

oaning \ō-niŋ\ see ²ONING

oap \ōp\ see OPE

oaper \ō-pər\ see OPER

oapy \ō-pē\ see OPI

oar \òr\ see ¹OR

oard \òrd\ board, bored, chord,
cord, cored, floored, ford,
Ford, gourd, hoard, horde,
lord, Lord, oared, pored,
poured, sward, sword, toward,
ward, Ward, aboard, accord,
afford, award, backboard,
backsword, baseboard,
billboard, blackboard,
breadboard, broadsword,
buckboard, cardboard,

chalkboard, chessboard, chipboard, clapboard, clipboard, concord, corkboard, dashboard, discord, duckboard, fjord, flashboard, floorboard, footboard, freeboard, garbord, Gaylord, greensward, hardboard, headboard, inboard, keyboard, kickboard, landlord, lapboard, leeboard, longsword, matchboard, moldboard, onboard, outboard, packboard, pasteboard, patchboard, pegboard, pressboard, punchboard, rearward, record, reward, sailboard, scoreboard, seaboard, shipboard, sideboard, signboard, skateboard, slumlord, smallsword, snowboard, soundboard, splashboard, springboard, surfboard, switchboard, tailboard, untoward, wallboard, washboard, word-hoard, warlord, whipcord, aboveboard, bungee cord, centerboard, checkerboard, clavichord, disaccord, fiberboard, fingerboard, harpsichord, mortarbord, motherboard, overboard, overlord, paddleboard, paperboard, pinafored, plasterboard, pompadoured, shuffleboard, smorgasbord, storyboard, teeterboard, tetrachord, untoward, weatherboard, misericord,

particleboard—*also pasts of verbs listed at* ¹OR

oarder \ōrd-ər\ boarder, hoarder, keyboarder, skateboarder, surfboarder

oarding \ōrd-iŋ\ boarding, hoarding, skateboarding, weatherboarding

oared \ōrd\ see OARD

¹oarer \ōr-ər\ see ¹ORER

²oarer \or-ər\ see ¹ORRER

oaring \or-iŋ\ see ORING

oarious \or-ē-əs\ see ORIOUS

oarish \or-ish\ see ¹ORISH

¹oarse \ōrs\ see ¹OURSE

²oarse \ors\ see ¹ORSE

oarsen \ōrs-ᵊn\ coarsen, hoarsen, whoreson

oarsman \ōrz-mən\ oarsman, outdoorsman

oart \ort\ see ¹ORT

oary \ōr-ē\ see ORY

oast \ōst\ see ²OST

oastal \ōs-tᵊl\ see ¹OSTAL

oaster \ō-stər\ coaster, poster, roaster, throwster, toaster, billposter, four-poster, roller-coaster, roller coaster

oasty \ō-stē\ see OSTY

oat \ōt\ bloat, boat, coat, cote, dote, float, gloat, goat, groat, haute, moat, mote, note, oat, phot, quote, rote, shoat, smote, stoat, throat, tote, vote, wrote, afloat, airboat, bareboat, bluecoat, bumboat, capote, catboat, compote, connote, coyote, cutthroat, demote, denote, devote, dovecote, eighth note, emote, endnote, fireboat, fistnote, flatboat, footnote, greatcoat, gunboat, half note, headnote, Hohhot, houseboat, housecoat, iceboat, keelboat, keynote, lifeboat, longboat, one-note, pigboat, promote, Q-boat, quarter note, raincoat, Rajkot, redcoat, remote, rewrote, rowboat, sailboat, scapegoat, sheepcote, showboat, speedboat, steamboat, stoneboat, Sukkot, Sukkoth, surfboat, tailcoat, topcoat, towboat, tugboat, turncoat, U-boat, unquote, wainscot, whaleboat, whitethroat, whole note, woodnote, workboat, anecdote, antidote, asymptote, creosote, entrecote, ferryboat, Huhehot, motorboat, overcoat, paddleboat, papillote, petticoat, powerboat, redingote, riverboat, rubythroat, Shabuoth, Sialkot, sugarcoat, symbiote, table d'hôte, sixteenth note, undercoat, yellowthroat, thirty-second note

oate \ō-ət\ see ¹OET

oated \ōt-əd\ coated, noted, throated, devoted, tailcoated, petticoated—*also pasts of verbs listed at* OAT

oaten \ōt-ᵊn\ see OTON

oater \ōt-ər\ bloater, boater, coater, doter, floater, gloater, motor, noter, oater, rotor, scoter, toter, voter, houseboater, iceboater, keynoter, promoter, pulmotor, sailboater, tilt-rotor, trimotor, locomotor, motorboater

oath \ōth\ see OWTH

oathe \ō<u>th</u>\ see OTHE

oathing \ō-<u>thi</u>ŋ\ see OTHING

oating \ōt-iŋ\ boating, coating, floating, free floating, sailboating, scapegoating, speedboating, wainscoting, motorboating, undercoating— *also present participles of verbs listed at* OAT

oatswain \ōs-ᵊn\ see OSIN

oaty \ōt-ē\ see ¹OTE

oax \ōks\ coax, hoax—*also plurals and possessives of nouns and third person singular presents of verbs listed at* OKE

¹ob \äb\ Ab, blob, bob, Bob, cob, daub, fob, glob, gob, hob, job, knob, lob, mob, nob, Ob, rob, slob, snob, sob, squab, stob, swab, throb, yob, bedaub, corncob, demob, doorknob, heartthrob, hobnob, kabob, macabre, nabob, nawab, Punjab, skibob, memsahib, shish kebab, thingamabob

²ob \ōb\ see ¹OBE

oba \ō-bə\ arroba, jojoba, algaroba, Manitoba

obably \äb-lē\ see OBBLY

obal \ō-bəl\ see OBLE

obally \ō-bə-lē\ globally, primum mobile

obar \ō-bər\ see OBER

obber \äb-ər\ bobber, caber, clobber, cobber, jobber, robber, slobber, swabber, throbber, hobnobber, Micawber, Skibobber, stockjobber

obbery \äb-rē\ bobbery, jobbery, robbery, slobbery, snobbery, corroboree

obbes \äbz\ Hobbes—*also possessives and plurals of nouns and third person singular presents of verbs listed at* OB

obbet \äb-ət\ gobbet, probit

obbie \äb-ē\ see OBBY

obbin \äb-ən\ see OBIN

obbish \äb-ish\ slobbish, snobbish

obble \äb-əl\ see ¹ABBLE

obbler \äb-lər\ cobbler, gobbler, hobbler, nobbler, squabbler, wobbler

obbly \äb-lē\ knobbly, probably, wobbly, Wobbly

obby \äb-ē\ Bobbie, bobby, Bobby, cobby, dobby, globby, hobby, knobby, lobby, nobby, snobby, swabbie, Mesabi, Punjabi, Wahhabi, Abu Dhabi, Hammurabi

¹obe \ōb\ daube, globe, Job, lobe, probe, robe, strobe, bathrobe, conglobe, disrobe, earlobe, enrobe, microbe, wardrobe, Anglophobe, claustrophobe, Francophobe, homophobe, negrophobe, xenophobe, ailurophobe, computerphobe

²obe \ō-bē\ see OBY

obeah \ō-bē-ə\ see OBIA

obee \ō-bē\ see OBY

obelus \äb-ə-ləs\ see ABILIS

ober \ō-bər\ lobar, sober, October

obi \ō-bē\ see OBY

obia \ō-bē-ə\ cobia, obeah, phobia, acrophobia, algophobia, Anglophobia, claustrophobia, homophobia, hydrophobia, negrophobia, photophobia, technophobia, xenophobia, agoraphobia, triskaidekaphobia

obic \ō-bik\ phobic, aerobic, anaerobic, claustrophobic, homophobic, hydrophobic, photophobic, xenophobic

¹obile \ō-bə-lē\ see OBALLY

²obile \ō-bəl\ see OBLE

obin \äb-ən\ bobbin, dobbin, graben, robin, Robin, Robyn, round-robin

¹obit \ō-bət\ obit, Tobit, post-obit

²obit \äb-ət\ see OBBET

oble \ō-bəl\ coble, global, mobile, noble, airmobile, ennoble, Grenoble, ignoble, immobile, San Cristóbal

obo \ō-bō\ gobo, hobo, kobo, lobo, oboe, adobo

oboe \ō-bō\ see OBO

obol \äb-əl\ see ¹ABBLE

oboree \äb-ə-rē\ see OBBERY

obot \ō-bət\ see ¹OBIT

obra \ō-brə\ cobra, dobra

obster \äb-stər\ lobster, mobster

obular \äb-yə-lər\ globular, lobular

obule \äb-yül\ globule, lobule

oby \ō-bē\ Gobi, goby, Kobe, obi, Obie, toby, Toby, adobe, Nairobi, Okeechobee

obyn \äb-ən\ see OBIN

¹oc \ōk\ see OKE

²oc \äk\ see ¹OCK

³oc \ok\ see ALK

oca \ō-kə\ coca, mocha, oca,

Asoka, carioca, Fukuoka, mandioca, Shizuoka, tapioca

ocable \ō-kə-bəl\ smokable, vocable, evocable

ocage \äk-ij\ see OCKAGE

ocal \ō-kəl\ focal, local, socle, vocal, yokel, bifocal, subvocal, trifocal, unvocal

ocally \ō-kə-lē\ locally, vocally

ocative \äk-ət-iv\ locative, vocative, evocative, provocative

occa \äk-ə\ see ¹AKA

occer \äk-ər\ see OCKER

occie \äch-ē\ see OTCHY

occhi \ȯ-kē\ see ALKIE

occo \äk-ō\ socko, taco, cheechako, guanaco, morocco, Morocco, scirocco, sirocco

occule \äk-yül\ floccule, locule

occulent \äk-yə-lənt\ flocculent, inoculant

occulus \äk-yə-ləs\ flocculus, loculus, oculus

oce \ō-chē\ see ¹OCHE

ocean \ō-shən\ see OTION

ocent \ōs-ᵊnt\ docent, nocent

ocess \äs-əs\ Knossos, process, colossus, proboscis

¹och \ōk\ see OKE

²och \äk\ see ¹OCK

³och \ȯsh\ see ²ASH

⁴och \ȯk\ see ALK

ocha \ō-kə\ see OCA

ochal \äk-əl\ see OCKLE

ochan \ä-ḵən\ see ACHEN

¹oche \ō-chē\ Kochi, Sochi, penoche, sotto voce, veloce, mezza voce

²oche \ōsh\ cloche, gauche,

skosh, brioche, caroche, guilloche

³oche \ō-kē\ see OKY

⁴oche \ōch\ see OACH

⁵oche \ȯsh\ see ²ASH

ochee \ō-kē\ see OKY

ocher \ō-kər\ see OKER

ochi \ō-chē\ see ¹OCHE

ochle \ək-əl\ see UCKLE

ochs \äks\ see OX

ochum \ō-kəm\ see OKUM

ocia \ō-shə\ see ¹OTIA

ociable \ō-shə-bəl\ sociable, associable, dissociable, insociable, negotiable, unsociable, indissociable, renegotiable

ocial \ō-shəl\ social, asocial, dissocial, precocial, unsocial, antisocial

ocile \äs-əl\ see OSSAL

ocious \ō-shəs\ atrocious, ferocious, precocious, Theodosius

¹ock \äk\ Bach, bloc, block, bock, brock, chock, clock, cock, croc, crock, doc, dock, floc, flock, frock, hock, Jacque, Jacques, jock, knock, lakh, loch, lock, Locke, lough, Mach, moc, mock, nock, pock, roc, rock, schlock, shock, smock, sock, stock, wok, yak, yock, acock, ad hoc, aftershock, amok, Arak, backblock, Balzac, bangkok, Bangkok, baroque, Bartok, bawcock, bedrock, bemock, bibcock, bitstock, blackcock, blesbok, bloodstock, bois d'arc, Brecknock, breechblock, burdock, buttstock, caprock, coldcock, Comstock, deadlock, debacle, defrock, dry dock, duroc, Dvořák, earlock, en bloc, epoch, fatstock, feedstock, fetlock, firelock, flintlock, forelock, foreshock, gamecock, gemsbok, gridlock, gunlock, Hancock, havelock, haycock, headlock, headstock, hemlock, Hickock, Iraq, jazz-rock, Kanak, Kazak, Kazakh, kapok, kneesock, Langnedoc, livestock, lovelock, matchlock, Mohock, Nisroch, nostoc, o'clock, oarlock, padlock, peacock, penstock, petcock, pibroch, picklock, pinchcock, Polack, post doc, post hoc, rhebok, rimrock, roadblock, rootstock, Rorschach, Rostock, rowlock, shamrock, Sheetrock, sherlock, shylock, Sirach, slick rock, Slovak, springbok, steenbok, stopcock, Tarlak, tarok, ticktock, traprock, van Gogh, warlock, wedlock, woodcock, wristlock, zwieback, alpenstock, Anahuac, antiknock, antilock, Antioch, Arawak, Ayers Rock, billycock, chockablock, hammerlock, hollyhock, interlock, John Hancock, lady's-smock, laughingstock, Little Rock, manioc, mantlerock, monadnock, Offenbach, Otomac, poppycock, Ragnarok, Sarawak, shuttlecock, spatterdock, turkey-cock, weathercock, Czechoslovak, Bialystok, electroshock, Inupiaq, Pontianak, Vladivostok

²ock \ók\ see ALK

ockage \äk-ij\ blockage, brockage, dockage, lockage, socage

ocke \äk\ see ¹OCK

ocked \äkt\ blocked, crocked, concoct, decoct, entr'acte, half-cocked, landlocked, periproct, entoproct—*also pasts of verbs listed at* ¹OCK

ocker \äk-ər\ blocker, clocker, cocker, docker, hocker, knocker, locker, makar, mocker, rocker, shocker, soccer, stocker, footlocker, appleknocker, beta-blocker, knickerbocker

ockery \äk-rē\ crockery, mockery, rockery

ocket \äk-ət\ brocket, crocket, Crockett, docket, locket, pocket, rocket, socket, sprocket, pickpocket, skyrocket, out-of-pocket, retro-rocket

ockett \äk-ət\ see OCKET

ockey \äk-ē\ see OCKY

ockian \äk-ē-ən\ Comstockian, Slovakian, Czechoslovakian

ockiness \äk-ē-nəs\ cockiness, rockiness, stockiness

ocking \äk-iŋ\ flocking, shocking, smocking, stocking, bluestocking, silk-stocking

ockish \äk-ish\ blockish, stockish

ockle \äk-əl\ coccal, cockle, socle, debacle, epochal

ockney \äk-nē\ cockney, Procne

ocko \äk-ō\ see OCCO

ocks \äks\ see OX

ocky \äk-ē\ blocky, cocky, hockey, jockey, pocky, rocky, Rocky, sake, schlocky, stocky, Yaqui, Abnaki, Iraqi, Ontake, pea cocky, rumaki, jabberwocky, Kawasaki, Miyazaki, Nagasaki, Okazaki, sukiyaki, teriyaki, Amagasaki, enokidake

ocle \ō-kəl\ see OCAL

ocne \äk-nē\ see OCKNEY

oco \ō-kō\ coco, cocoa, loco, poco, Bioko, iroko, rococo, crème de cacao, locofoco, Orinoco, poco a poco

ocoa \ō-kō\ see OCO

ocracy \äk-rə-sē\ autocracy, bureaucracy, democracy, hypocrisy, mobocracy, plutocracy, slavocracy, technocracy, theocracy, aristocracy, gerontocracy, gynecocracy, meritocracy, thalassocracy

ocre \ō-kər\ see OKER

ocrisy \äk-rə-sē\ see OCRACY

ocsin \äk-sən\ see OXIN

oct \äkt\ see OCKED

oction \äk-shən\ concoction, decoction

octor \äk-tər\ doctor, proctor, concocter

oculant \äk-yə-lənt\ see OCCULENT

ocular \äk-yə-lər\ jocular, locular, ocular, binocular, monocular, intraocular

ocule \äk-yül\ see OCCULE

oculus \äk-yə-ləs\ see OCCULUS

ocum \ō-kəm\ see OKUM

ocus \ō-kəs\ crocus, focus, hocus, locus, prefocus, refocus, soft-focus, hocus-pocus

ocused \ō-kəst\ see OCUST

ocust \ō-kəst\ locust, unfocused

ocutor \äk-yət-ər\ prolocutor, interlocutor

¹od \äd\ bod, clod, cod, fade, Fahd, gaud, god, hod, mod, nod, od, odd, plod, pod, prod, quad, quod, rod, scrod, shod, sod, squad, tod, trod, wad, Akkad, amphipod, Arad, aubade, ballade, Belgrade, Beograde, bipod, Cape Cod, couvade, croustade, dry-shod, ephod, facade, fantod, glissade, hot-rod, jihad, lingcod, Nimrod, oeillade, pomade, peasecod, ramrod, Riyadh, roughshod, roulade, saccade, scalade, seedpod, slipshod, synod, tie-rod, tightwad, tomcod, torsade, tripod, accolade, arthropod, Ashkhabad, Bacolod, bigarade, carbonnade, chiffonade, defilade, demigod, enfilade, esculade, esplanade, fulsillade, gallopade, gastropod, goldenrod, hexapod, lycopod, monkeypod, Novgorod, Novi Sad, octopod, promenade, pseudopod, Ahmadabad, Allahabad, cephalopod, Faisalabad, Islamabad, ornithopod, prosauropod, rodomontade, dégringolade, fanfaronade, Upanishad, Scheherazade, Nizhni Novgorod

²**od** \ō\ see ¹OW

³**od** \ōd\ see ODE

⁴**od** \ud\ see ¹OOD

⁵**od** \od\ see ¹AUD

o'd \üd\ see UDE

oda \ōd-ə\ coda, Rhoda, soda, Baroda, pagoda, sal soda

odal \ōd-ᵊl\ Godel, modal, nodal, yodel, cathodal, intermodal

odden \äd-ᵊn\ sodden, trodden, downtrodden, Ibadan

odder \äd-ər\ dodder, fodder, khaddar, modder, nodder, odder, plodder, prodder, solder, wadder, glissader, hot-rodder—*also comparatives of adjectives listed at* ¹OD

oddery \äd-rē\ see AWDRY

oddess \äd-əs\ bodice, goddess, demigoddess

oddish \äd-ish\ cloddish, kaddish

oddle \äd-ᵊl\ coddle, model, noddle, swaddle, toddle, twaddle, waddle, remodel, mollycoddle

oddler \äd-lər\ coddler, modeler, toddler, twaddler, waddler, mollycoddler

oddly \äd-lē\ see ODLY

oddy \äd-ē\ see ¹ODY

ode \ōd\ bode, bowed, code, goad, load, lode, mode, node, ode, road, rode, Spode, strode, toad, toed, woad, wood, abode, bestrode, boatload, busload, byroad, carload, cartload, caseload, commode, corrode, crossroad, decode, displode, embowed, encode, epode, erode, explode, forebode, freeload, geode, highroad, implode, inroad, no-load, off-load, outmode, payload, planeload, postcode, railroad, rhapsode, sarod, shipload, square-toed, threnode, trainload, truckload, two-toed, unload, upload, à la mode, antipode, Comstock Lode, discommode, eigenmode, electrode, episode, impastoed, incommode, Kozhikode, Nesselrode, overrode, palinode, pigeon-toed—*also pasts of verbs listed at* ¹OW

odeine \ōd-ē-ən\ see ODIAN

odel \ōd-ᵊl\ see ODAL

odeler \äd-lər\ see ODDLER

oden \ōd-ᵊn\ loden, Odin, Woden

odeon \ōd-ē-ən\ see ODIAN

oder \ōd-ər\ coder, loader, Oder, odor, breechloader, decoder, freeloader, malodor, railroader, unloader, middle-of-the-roader

oderate \äd-rət\ quadrate, moderate, immoderate

odes \ōdz\ Rhodes—*possessives and plurals of nouns and third person singular presents of verbs listed at* ODE

odest \äd-əst\ Mahdist, modest, haggadist, immodest—*also superlatives of adjectives listed at* ¹OD

odesy \äd-ə-sē\ odyssey, geodesy, theodicy

odeum \ōd-ē-əm\ see ODIUM

odge \äj\ see ¹AGE

odger \äj-ər\ codger, dodger, lodger, roger, Roger, Jolly Roger, stinking roger

odgy \äj-ē\ dodgy, podgy, stodgy, mistagogy, pedagogy

odian \ōd-ē-ən\ Cambodian, custodian, melodeon, nickelodeon

odic \äd-ik\ zaddik, cathodic, ergodic, melodic, methodic, monodic, periodic, prosodic, rhapsodic, spasmodic, synodic, threnodic, episodic, periodic, antismasmodic, aperiodic, upanishadic, quasiperiodic

odical \äd-i-kəl\ methodical, monodical, prosodical, synodical, episodical, immethodical, periodical

odice \äd-əs\ see ODDESS

odicy \äd-ə-sē\ see ODESY

odie \ō-dē\ see ²ODY

odin \ōd-ᵊn\ see ODEN

odious \ōd-ē-əs\ odious, commodious, melodious, Methodius, incommodious

odity \äd-ət-ē\ oddity, commodity, incommodity

odium \ōd-ē-əm\ odeum, odium, podium, rhodium, sodium

odius \ō-dē-əs\ see ODIOUS

odless \äd-ləs\ godless, rodless

odling \äd-liŋ\ codling, godling

odly \äd-lē\ godly, oddly, ungodly

odo \ōd-ō\ dodo, Komodo, Quasimodo

odom \äd-əm\ shahdom, Sodom

odor \ōd-ər\ see ODER

odsk \ätsk\ see ATSK

odular \äj-ə-lər\ modular, nodular

odule \äj-ül\ module, nodule

¹ody \äd-ē\ body, cloddy, gaudy, Mahdi, noddy, sadhe, shoddy, toddy, waddy, wadi, anybody, blackbody, dogsbody, embody, homebody, nobody, somebody, wide-body, antibody, busybody, disembody, everybody, Irrawaddy, underbody

²ody \ōd-ē\ Cody, Jodie, Jody, roadie, toady, polypody

odyssey \äd-ə-sē\ see ODESY

odz \üj\ see ¹UGE

¹oe \ō\ see ¹OW

²oe \ō-ē\ see OWY

³oe \ē\ see ¹EE

⁴oe \öï\ see OY

¹oea \öi-ə\ see OIA

²oea \ē-ə\ see ¹IA

oeba \ē-bə\ see EBA

oebe \ē-bē\ see ¹EBE

oebel \ā-bəl\ see ABLE

oebus \ē-bəs\ see EBUS

oed \ōd\ see ODE

oehn \ən\ see UN

oeia \ē-ə\ see ¹IA

oeic \ē-ik\ see EIC

oek \úk\ see ¹OOK

oel \ō-əl\ Joel, Lowell, Noel, bestowal, Baden-Powell, protozoal

¹oeless \ō-ləs\ see OLUS

²oeless \ü-ləs\ see EWLESS

¹**oem** \ō-əm\ poem, proem, jeroboam

²**oem** \ōm\ see ¹OME

³**oem** \óm\ see ¹AUM

oeman \ō-mən\ see OMAN

oena \ē-nə\ see ²INA

¹**oentgen** \en-chən\ see ENSION

²**oentgen** \ən-chən\ see UNCHEON

oepha \ē-fə\ see EPHA

¹**o'er** \ōr\ see ¹ORE

²**o'er** \ór\ see ¹OR

¹**oer** \ōr\ see ¹OR

²**oer** \ü-ər\ see ¹EWER

³**oer** \úr\ see ¹URE

⁴**oer** \ō-ər\ blower, knower, lower, mower, sewer, shower, sower, beachgoer, churchgoer, flamethrower, filmgoer, foregoer, forgoer, mindblower, snowblower, snowthrower, winegrower, concertgoer, moviegoer, cinemagoer, operagoer, theatergoer, whistleblower

¹**oes** \əz\ see ¹EUSE

²**oes** \ōz\ see ²OSE

³**oes** \üz\ see ²USE

oesia \ē-shə\ see ¹ESIA

oesn't \əz-ⁿnt\ see ASN'T

oest \ü-əst\ see OOIST

oesus \ē-səs\ see ESIS

¹**oet** \ō-ət\ poet, inchoate, introit

²**oet** \óit\ see ¹OIT

oetess \ō-ət-əs\ coitus, poetess

oeuf \əf\ see UFF

oeur \ər\ see ¹EUR

oeuvre \ərv\ see ERVE

oey \ō-ē\ see OWY

¹**of** \äv\ see ²OLVE

²**of** \əv\ see ¹OVE

³**of** \óf\ see ²OFF

ofar \ō-fər\ see OFER

ofer \ō-fər\ chauffeur, gofer, gopher, loafer, Ophir, shofar

¹**off** \äf\ boff, coif, doff, goif, kaph, prof, quaff, scoff, shroff, taw, toff, carafe, cook-off, pilaf, Romanov

²**off** \óf\ cough, doff, off, scoff, taw, trough, Azov, beg off, blast-off, brush-off, cast-off, castoff, checkoff, Chekhov, cook-off, cutoff, die-off, drop-off, face-off, falloff, far-off, goof-off, hands-off, jump-off, Khartov, kickoff, Kirov, knockoff, Khruschev, layoff, leadoff, lift-off, Lvov, one-off, Pavlov, payoff, pick-off, pickoff, play-off, rake-off, rip-off, roll-off, runoff, Salchow, sawed-off, sell-off, send-off, setoff, show-off, shutoff, spin-off, standoff, takeoff, Tambov, tap-off, tip-off, trade-off, turnoff, well-off, Wolof, write-off, Wroclaw, better-off, cooling-off, damping-off, Gorbachev, Molotov, Nabokov, philosophe, Pribilof, Rostov, beef Stroganoff, Rachmaninoff, Rimsky-Korsakov

¹**offal** \äf-əl\ see AFEL

²**offal** \ó-fəl\ see AWFUL

offaly \óf-ə-lē\ see AWFULLY

offee \ó-fē\ coffee, toffee

¹**offer** \äf-ər\ coffer, gauffer, goffer, offer, proffer, quaffer, scoffer, troffer, reoffer

²**offer** \óf-ər\ goffer, offer, troffer, reoffer

offin \ȯ-fən\ coffin, dauphin, soften, uncoffin

offit \äf-ət\ see OFIT

offle \ȯ-fəl\ see AWFUL

ofit \äf-ət\ profit, prophet, soffit, nonprofit, not-for-profit

ofle \ü-fəl\ see UEFUL

¹oft \ȯft\ croft, loft, oft, soft, toft, aloft, hayloft, undercroft—*also pasts of verbs listed at* ²OFF

²oft \äft\ see ¹AFT

often \ȯ-fən\ see OFFIN

ofty \ȯf-tē\ lofty, softy, toplofty

¹og \äg\ bog, clog, cog, flog, fog, frog, grog, hog, jog, log, nog, Prague, prog, quag, shog, slog, smog, tog, wog, agog, backlog, bullfrog, defog, eclogue, eggnog, footslog, groundhog, gulag, photog, prologue, putlog, quahog, Rolvaag, sandhog, stalag, warthog, analog, analogue, antilog, apalogue, catalog, decalogue, demagogue, dialogue, golliwog, monologue, mummichog, mystagogue, nouvelle vague, pedagogue, pollywog, semilog, sinologue, synagogue, Taganrog, theologue, waterlog

²og \ȯg\ bog, clog, dog, fog, frog, hog, jog, log, smog, wog, backlog, bandog, befog, bird-dog, bulldog, bullfrog, coydog, defog, eclogue, firedog, groundhog, hangdog, hedgehog, hotdog, lapdog, leapfrog, prologue, quahog, sandhog, seadog, sheepdog, warthog, watchdog, analog, analogue, apologue, catalog, decalogue, dialogue, dog-eat-dog, duologue, epilogue, homologue, monologue, mummichog, overdog, pettifog, pollywog, sinologue, theologue, Tagalog, travelogue, underdog, waterlog, yellow-dog, ideologue

³og \ōg\ see ¹OGUE

oga \ō-gə\ toga, yoga, Conestoga

ogamous \äg-ə-məs\ endogamous, exogamous, monogamous, heterogamous

ogamy \äg-ə-mē\ endogamy, exogamy, homogamy, misogamy, monogamy

ogan \ō-gən\ brogan, Mount Logan, shogun, slogan

ogany \äg-ə-nē\ see OGONY

ogative \äg-ət-iv\ derogative, prerogative, interrogative

¹oge \ōj\ doge, gamboge, horologe

²oge \ōzh\ loge, Limoges

³oge \ō-jē\ see OJI

⁴oge \üzh\ see ²UGE

ogel \ō-gəl\ see ¹OGLE

ogenous \äj-ə-nəs\ androgynous, erogenous, homogenous, monogynous, heterogenous

ogeny \äj-ə-nē\ progeny, androgeny, autogeny, homogeny, misogyny, monogyny, ontogeny, phylogeny, heterogeny

¹oger \äj-ər\ see ODGER

²oger \ȯg-ər\ see ²OGGER

oges \ōzh\ see ²OGE

¹**ogey** \ō-gē\ see OGIE

²**ogey** \ùg-ē\ see OOGIE

oggan \äg-ən\ see OGGIN

oggar \äg-ər\ see ¹OGGER

¹**ogger** \äg-ər\ agar, clogger, flogger, Hoggar, jogger, laager, lager, logger, slogger, Ahaggar, defogger, footslogger, agar-agar, cataloger, pettifogger

²**ogger** \óg-ər\ auger, augur, clogger, jogger, logger, maugre, sauger, defogger, hotdogger, cataloger, pettifogger

¹**oggery** \äg-rē\ toggery, demagoguery

²**oggery** \ó-gə-rē\ augury, doggery

oggin \äg-ən\ noggin, toboggan, Copenhagen

oggle \äg-əl\ boggle, goggle, joggle, ogle, toggle, boondoggle, hornswoggle, synagogal

¹**oggy** \äg-ē\ boggy, foggy, groggy, moggy, quaggy, smoggy, soggy, yagi, demagogy

²**oggy** \óg-ē\ foggy, soggy

¹**ogh** \ōg\ see ¹OGUE

²**ogh** \ōk\ see OKE

³**ogh** \äk\ see ¹OCK

⁴**ogh** \ō\ see OW

ogi \ō-gē\ see OGIE

ogian \ō-jən\ see OJAN

ogic \äj-ik\ logic, choplogic, illogic, anagogic, analogic, biologic, chronologic, cryptologic, cytologic, demagogic, dendrologic,

dialogic, ecologic, ethnologic, geologic, histologic, horologic, hydrologic, mythologic, neurologic, nosologic, oncologic, pathologic, pedagogic, pedologic, petrologic, phonologic, proctologic, psychologic, serologic, technologic, theologic, virologic, zoologic, dermatologic, etiologic, gerontologic, gynecologic, hagiologic, hematologic, ideologic, immunologic, ophthalmologic, ornithologic, pharmacologic, physiologic, roentgenologic, sociologic, teleologic, teratologic, toxicologic, volcanologic, bacteriologic, endocrinologic, meteorologic, paleontologic, parasitologic, sedimentologic, symptomologic, epidemiologic

ogical \äj-i-kəl\ logical, alogical, illogical, anagogical, analogical, biological, Christological, chronological, cosmological, cryptological, cytological, dendrological, ecological, enological, ethnological, ethological, extralogical, gemological, geological, graphological, histological, horological, hydrological, limnological, morphological, mycological, mythological, necrological, neurological, nomological, oncological, pathological, pedagogical, pedological,

penological, petrological,
philological, phonological,
phrenological, phycological,
proctological, psephological,
psychological, scatological,
seismological, serological,
sinological, tautological,
technological, theological,
topological, typological,
ufological, virological,
zoological, abiological,
anthropological,
archaeological, cardiological,
climatological, criminological,
demonological,
dermatological,
embryological, entomological,
eschatological, etiological,
etymological, futurological,
genealogical, gerontological,
gynecological, hagiological,
hematological, herpetological,
ichthyological, iconological,
ideological, immunological,
Mariological, methodological,
mineralogical, musicological,
numerological,
ophthalmological,
ornithological,
pharmacological,
phraseological, physiological,
primatological,
roentgenological,
selenological, semiological,
sociological, teleological,
teratological, terminological,
thanatological, toxicological,
volcanological,
bacteriological,
characterological,
dialectological,
ecclesiological,

endocrinological,
epistemological,
geomorphological,
meteorological,
paleontological,
parasitological,
phenomenological,
sedimentological,
symptomatological,
epidemiological,
gastroenterological

ogie \ō-gē\ bogey, bogie, dogie,
fogy, hoagie, logy, pogy,
stogie, vogie, yogi, pirogi

¹ogle \ō-gəl\ Gogel, ogle

²ogle \äg-əl\ see OGGLE

oglio \ōl-yō\ see ¹OLLO

¹ogna \ō-nə\ see ONA

²ogna \ō-nē\ see ¹ONY

³ogna \ōn-yə\ see ²ONIA

ogne \ōn\ see ¹ONE

ogned \ōnd\ see ¹ONED

ogo \ō-gō\ go-go, logo, Logo,
Togo, a-go-go

ogony \äg-ə-nē\ cosmogony,
mahogany, theogony

ographer \äg-rə-fər\
biographer, cartographer,
chorographer, cryptographer,
demographer, discographer,
ethnographer, geographer,
lithographer, mythographer,
phonographer, photographer,
pornographer, stenographer,
typographer, bibliographer,
choreographer, hagiographer,
heliographer, iconographer,
lexicographer, oceanographer,
paleographer, autobiographer,
biogeographer,
chromatographer,

cinematographer,
historiographer

ography \äg-rə-fē\ aerography,
autography, biography,
cacography, cartography,
chorography, chronography,
cosmography, cryptography,
demography, discography,
ethnography, filmography,
geography, holography,
hydrography, hypsography,
lithography, lymphography,
mammography, mythography,
nomography, orthography,
phonography, photography,
pictography, planography,
pornography, reprography,
sonography, stenography,
thermography, tomography,
topography, typography,
venography, xerography,
xylography, angiography,
aortography, bibliography,
cardiography, choreography,
chromatography,
crystallography, hagiography,
heliography, iconography,
lexicography, metallography,
oceanography, paleography,
physiography, radiography,
roentgenography,
videography, arteriography,
autobiography,
cinematography,
encephalography,
historiography,
psychobiography,
electroencephalography

ogress \ō-grəs\ ogress, progress

ogrom \äg-rəm\ grogram,
pogrom

¹ogue \ōg\ brogue, drogue,
rogue, togue, vogue, yogh,
collogue, crannog, pirogue,
prorogue, Krivoy Rog,
disembogue

²ogue \äg\ see ¹OG

³ogue \óg\ see ²OG

oguery \äg-rē\ see ¹OGGERY

oguish \ō-gish\ roguish,
voguish

ogun \ō-gən\ see OGAN

ogynous \äj-ə-nəs\ see
OGENOUS

ogyny \äj-ə-nē\ see OGENY

oh \ō\ see ¹OW

oha \ō-ə\ see ¹OA

ohl \ōl\ see ¹OLE

ohm \ōm\ see ¹OME

ohn \än\ see ¹ON

ohns \änz\ see ONZE

ohn's \onz\ see ONZE

ohnson \än-sən\ Johnson,
Jonson, Wisconsin

ohr \ōr\ see ¹OR

¹oi \ä\ see ¹A

²oi \ói\ see OY

oia \ói-ə\ cholla, Goya, Hoya,
olla, toea, Nagoya, sequoia,
Sequoya, atemoya,
cherimoya, paranoia

oian \ói-ən\ see OYEN

oic \ō-ik\ stoic, azoic, bistroic,
echoic, heroic, anechoic,
Cenozoic, Mesozoic, mock-
heroic, vetinoic, antiheroic,
Paleozoic

oice \óis\ choice, Joyce, Royce,
voice, devoice, Du Bois,
invoice, pro-choice, rejoice,
unvoice, sailor's-choice

oiced \óist\ see OIST

oicer \ói-sər\ choicer, voicer,
pro-choicer, rejoicer

¹oid \ȯid\ Boyd, Floyd, Freud, void, android, avoid, chancroid, colloid, conoid, cuboid, cycloid, deltoid, dendroid, devoid, discoid, factoid, fungoid, globoid, hydroid, hypnoid, keloid, mucoid, Negroid, ovoid, percoid, prismoid, pygmoid, rhizoid, rhomboid, schizoid, scombroid, sigmoid, spheroid, steroid, styloid, tabloid, thalloid, thyroid, toroid, toxoid, trochoid, typhoid, Veddoid, viroid, adenoid, alkaloid, amoeboid, aneroid, anthropoid, arachnoid, asteroid, Australoid, carcinoid, Caucasoid, celluloid, crystalloid, ellipsoid, embryoid, eunuchoid, helicoid, hemorrhoid, hominoid, humanoid, hysteroid, metalloid, Mongoloid, myeloid, nautiloid, nucleoid, obovoid, opioid, osteoid, overjoyed, paranoid, philanthropoid, planetoid, Polaroid, retinoid, rheumatoid, solenoid, Stalinoid, trapezoid, unalloyed, unemployed, cannabinoid, carotenoid, eicosanoid, meteoroid, tuberculoid, underemployed, Neanderthaloid—*also pasts of verbs listed at* OY

²oid \ä\ see ¹A

oidal \ȯid-ᵊl\ chancroidal, choroidal, colloidal, conchoidal, cuboidal, cycloidal, discoidal, spheroidal, toroidal, adenoidal, asteroidal, ellipsoidal, emulsoidal, hemorrhoidal, metalloidal, planetoidal, saccharoidal, trapezoidal, paraboloidal

oider \ȯid-ər\ broider, voider, avoider, embroider, reembroider

oie \ä\ see ¹A

oif \äf\ see ¹OFF

oign \ȯin\ see ¹OIN

oil \ȯil\ boil, Boyle, broil, coil, Doyle, foil, hoyle, moil, loyal, noil, oil, roil, royal, Royal, soil, spoil, toil, voile, aboil, airfoil, assoil, charbroil, cinquefoil, despoil, embroil, entoil, garboil, gargoyle, gumboil, hard-boil, Isle Royal, langue d'oïl, milfoil, non-oil, parboil, recoil, subsoil, supercoil, tinfoil, topsoil, trefoil, turmoil, counterfoil, disloyal, hydrofoil, quatrefoil, rhyme royal, surroyal, pennyroyal

oilage \ȯi-lij\ soilage, spoilage

¹oile \äl\ see ¹AL

²oile \ȯil\ see OIL

oiled \ȯild\ foiled, oiled, hard-boiled, soft-boiled, uncoiled, well-oiled—*also pasts of verbs listed at* OIL

oiler \ȯi-lər\ boiler, broiler, moiler, oiler, spoiler, toiler, charbroiler, despoiler, Free-Soiler, subsoiler, potboiler

oiling \ȯi-liŋ\ boiling, moiling

oilless \ȯil-ləs\ soilless, recoilless

oilsman \óilz-mən\ foilsman, spoilsman

oilus \ói-ləs\ see OYLESS

oily \ói-lē\ doily, oily, roily

¹oin \óin\ coin, foin, groin, groyne, join, loin, quoin, adjoin, Burgoyne, conjoin, Des Moines, disjoin, eloign, enjoin, essoin, purloin, recoin, rejoin, sainfoin, sirloin, subjoin, tenderloin, Assiniboin

²oin \aⁿ\ see ⁴IN

oine \än\ see ¹ON

oined \óind\ conjoined, uncoined—*also pasts of verbs listed at* ¹OIN

oiner \ói-nər\ coiner, joiner

oines \óin\ see ¹OIN

o-ing \ō-iŋ\ see ¹OING

¹oing \ō-iŋ\ bowing, going, knowing, rowing, sewing, showing, churchgoing, deep-going, foregoing, free-flowing, glassblowing, ingrowing, mind-blowing, ongoing, outgoing, seagoing, waygoing, concertgoing, easygoing, moviegoing, oceangoing, operagoing, theatergoing, thoroughgoing, whistle-blowing, to-ing and fro-ing—*also present participles of verbs listed at* ¹OW

²oing \ü-iŋ\ bluing, doing, Ewing, misdoing, undoing, wrongdoing, evildoing—*also present participles of verbs listed at* ¹EW

³oing \ō-ən\ see ¹OAN

oings \ō-iŋz\ outgoings—*also possessives and plurals of nouns and third person singular presents of verbs listed at* ¹OING

¹oint \óint\ joint, point, adjoint, anoint, appoint, aroint, ballpoint, bluepoint, checkpoint, conjoint, disjoint, drypoint, eyepoint, gunpoint, knifepoint, midpoint, nonpoint, outpoint, pinpoint, pourpoint, standpoint, tuck-point, viewpoint, counterpoint, disappoint, needlepoint, petit point, silverpoint

²oint \ant\ see ⁵ANT

ointe \ant\ see ⁵ANT

ointed \óint-əd\ jointed, pointed, lap-jointed, loose-jointed, double-jointed, well-appointed —*also pasts of verbs listed at* ¹OINT

ointer \óint-ər\ jointer, pointer, anointer

ointing \óin-tiŋ\ finger-pointing—*present participles of verbs listed at* ¹OINT

ointment \óint-mənt\ ointment, anointment, appointment, disappointment

¹oir \īr\ see ¹IRE

²oir \är\ see ³AR

³oir \óir\ see OYER

⁴oir \ór\ see ¹OR

¹oire \är\ see ³AR

²oire \óir\ see OYER

³oire \ór\ see ¹OR

¹ois \ä\ see ¹A

²ois \ói\ see OY

³ois \ō-əs\ Lois, Powys

⁴ois \óis\ see OICE

¹oise \äz\ poise, 'twas, vase, was, Ahwaz, bourgeoise, Lamaze, Shiraz, vichyssoise, The Afars and the Isas—*also plurals and possessives of nouns and third person singular presents of verbs listed at* ¹A

²oise \óiz\ hoise, noise, Noyes, poise, turquoise, counterpoise, equipoise, avoirdupois—*also plurals and possessives of nouns and third person singular presents of verbs listed at* OY

³oise \oi-zē\ see OISY

oison \óiz-ᵊn\ foison, poison, empoison

oist \óist\ foist, hoist, joist, moist, voiced, unvoiced, semimoist—*also pasts of verbs listed at* OICE

oister \ói-stər\ cloister, moister, oyster, roister

oisterous \ói-strəs\ see OISTRESS

oistral \ói-strəl\ cloistral, coistrel

oistrel \ói-strəl\ see OISTRAL

oistress \ói-strəs\ cloistress, boisterous, roisterous

oisy \ói-zē\ Boise, noisy, cramoisie

¹oit \óit\ doit, droit, poet, quoit, adroit, Detroit, exploit, maladroit, Massasoit

²oit \āt\ see ¹ATE

³oit \ō-ət\ see ¹OET

⁴oit \ä\ see ¹A

oite \ät\ see ¹OT

oiter \óit-ər\ goiter, loiter, exploiter, reconnoiter

oitus \ō-ət-əs\ see OETESS

oivre \äv\ see ¹OLVE

¹oix \ä\ see ¹A

²oix \ói\ see OY

oiz \óis\ see ²OISE

ojan \ō-jən\ Trojan, theologian

oje \ō-jē\ see OJI

oji \ō-jē\ Moji, shoji, anagoge, Hachioje

¹ok \äk\ see ¹OCK

²ok \ək\ see UCK

³ok \ók\ see ALK

oka \ō-kə\ see OCA

okable \ō-kə-bəl\ see OCABLE

¹oke \ōk\ bloke, broke, choke, cloak, coke, Coke, croak, folk, hoke, joke, moke, oak, oke, poke, Polk, roque, smoke, soak, soke, spoke, stoke, stroke, toke, toque, woke, yogh, yoke, yolk, ad hoc, awoke, backstroke, baroque, bespoke, breaststroke, chain-smoke, convoke, cowpoke, downstroke, evoke, heatstroke, housebroke, in-joke, invoke, keystroke, kinfolk, kinsfolk, menfolk, Nisroch, outspoke, presoak, provoke, revoke, she-oak, sidestroke, slowpoke, sunchoke, sunstroke, townsfolk, uncloak, unyoke, upstroke, workfolk, artichoke, equivoque, fisherfolk, gentlefolk, herrenvolk, masterstroke, okeydoke, Roanoke, thunderstroke, womenfolk, Mount Revelstoke

²oke \ō-kē\ see OKY

³oke \ō\ see ¹OW

⁴oke \ùk\ see ¹OOK

oked \ōkt\ stoked, yolked

okee \ō-kē\ see OKY

okel \ō-kəl\ see OCAL

oken \ō-kən\ broken, oaken,
spoken, token, woken,
awoken, bespoken, betoken,
fair-spoken, foretoken, free-
spoken, heartbroken,
housebroken, outspoken,
plainspoken, short-spoken,
soft-spoken, unbroken, well-
spoken, wind-broken

oker \ō-kər\ broker, choker,
croaker, joker, ocher, poker,
soaker, smoker, stoker,
stroker, chain-smoker,
invoker, pawnbroker,
provoker, revoker,
stockbroker, mediocre

okey \ō-kē\ see OKY

oki \ō-kē\ see OKY

okie \ō-kē\ see OKY

oking \ō-kiŋ\ broking, choking

oko \ō-kō\ see OCO

okum \ō-kəm\ Bochum,
hokum, locum, oakum

oky \ō-kē\ choky, croaky,
folkie, hokey, Loki, Okie,
pokey, poky, smoky, troche,
trochee, yolky, enoki, Great
Smoky, hokeypokey, karaoke,
Okefenokee

¹ol \ōl\ see ¹OLE

²ol \äl\ see ¹AL

³ol \ól\ see ALL

ola \ō-lə\ bola, cola, Kola, Lola,
tola, Zola, Angola, boffola,
Canola, gondola, granola,
mandola, payola, pergola,
plugola, scagliola, Savanarola,
viola, Viola, acerola,
ayatollah, braciola, Española,
gladiola, Gorgonzola,
hemiola, Hispaniola, moviola,
Osceola, roseola, Victrola

olable \ō-lə-bəl\ see OLLABLE

olace \äl-əs\ see OLIS

olan \ō-lən\ see OLON

oland \ō-lənd\ see OWLAND

olander \əl-ən-dər\ colander,
Julunder

¹olar \ō-lər\ see OLLER

²olar \äl-ər\ see OLLAR

olas \ō-ləs\ see OLUS

olater \äl-ət-ər\ bardolater,
idolater, bibliolater,
Mariolater

olatrous \äl-ə-trəs\ idolatrous,
bibliolatrous, heliolatrous

olatry \äl-ə-trē\ bardolatry,
idolatry, statolatry, zoolatry,
bibliolatry, heliolatry,
iconolatry, Mariolatry

¹old \ōld\ bold, bowled, cold,
fold, gold, hold, mold, mould,
old, polled, scold, sold, soled,
souled, told, wold, acold, age-
old, ahold, behold, billfold,
blindfold, controlled,
Cotswold, cuckold, enfold,
fanfold, foothold, foretold,
freehold, gatefold, handhold,
household, ice-cold, infold,
leasehold, pinfold, potholed,
roothold, scaffold, sheepfold,
stone-cold, stronghold,
threshold, toehold, twice-told,
unfold, unmold, untold,
uphold, whole-souled,
withhold, centerfold,
copyhold, fingerhold,
manifold, manyfold,

marigold, multifold, oversold,
petioled, severalfold,
stranglehold, throttlehold—
also pasts of verbs listed at
¹OLE

²**old** \old\ see ALD

oldan \ōl-dən\ see OLDEN

olden \ōl-dən\ golden, holden,
olden, soldan, beholden,
embolden

¹**older** \ōl-dər\ boulder, folder,
holder, molder, polder,
shoulder, smolder,
bondholder, cardholder,
householder, jobholder,
landholder, placeholder,
shareholder, slaveholder,
stadtholder, stakeholder,
stallholder, stockholder,
toolholder, officeholder,
titleholder, policyholder—
*also comparatives of
adjectives listed at* ¹OLD

²**older** \äd-ər\ see ODDER

oldi \ol-dē\ see ALDI

oldie \ōl-dē\ see OLDY

olding \ōl-diŋ\ folding, holding,
molding, hand-holding,
inholding, landholding,
slaveholding

oldster \ōl-stər\ see OLSTER

oldt \ōlt\ ¹OLT

oldy \ōl-dē\ moldy, oldie

¹**ole** \ōl\ bole, boll, bowl, coal,
cole, Cole, dhole, dole, droll,
foal, goal, hole, knoll, kohl,
Kohl, mole, ole, pole, Pole,
poll, prole, role, roll, scroll,
Seoul, shoal, skoal, sol, sole,
soul, stole, stroll, thole, tole,
toll, troll, vole, whole,
armhole, atoll, bankroll,
beanpole, bedroll, blowhole,
bolthole, borehole, bunghole,
cajole, catchpole, charcoal,
chuckhole, condole, console,
control, creole, Creole,
drumroll, enroll, ensoul, extol,
eyehole, fishbowl, flagpole,
foxhole, frijol, hellhole,
Huichol, inscroll, insole,
keyhole, kneehole, knothole,
logroll, loophole, manhole,
maypole, midsole, Mongol,
Nicole, outsole, parole, patrol,
payroll, peephole, pesthole,
pinhole, pistole, pitchpole,
porthole, posthole, pothole,
redpoll, resole, ridgepole,
Sheol, sinkhole, sotol,
stokehole, tadpole, taphole,
thumbhole, top-hole,
touchhole, turnsole, unroll,
Walpole, washbowl,
wormhole, amatol, aureole,
banderole, bannerol,
barcarole, buttonhole,
cabriole, camisole, capriole,
caracole, carmagnole,
casserole, croquignole,
cubbyhole, decontrol,
Demerol, escarole, farandole,
fumarole, girandole, grand
guignol, innersole, methanol,
oriole, oversoul, petiole, pick-
and-roll, pigeonhole, protocol,
rigmarole, Seminole,
cholesterol, Costa del Sol

²**ole** \ō-lē\ see ¹OLY

³**ole** \ol\ see ALL

olean \ō-lē-ən\ see ¹OLIAN

oled \ōld\ see ¹OLD

oleful \ōl-fəl\ doleful, soulful

olely \ō-lē\ see ¹OLY

¹**olem** \ō-ləm\ golem, solum

²**olem** \ā-ləm\ see ALAAM

olemn \äl-əm\ see OLUMN

¹**oleon** \ō-lē-ən\ see ¹OLIAN

²**oleon** \ōl-yən\ see ²OLIAN

¹**oler** \ō-lər\ see OLLER

²**oler** \äl-ər\ see OLLAR

olery \ōl-rē\ see OLLERY

olesome \ōl-səm\ dolesome, Folsom, wholesome

oless \ō-ləs\ see OLUS

oleum \ō-lē-əm\ see OLIUM

oleus \ō-lē-əs\ coleus, soleus

oley \ō-lē\ see ¹OLY

¹**olf** \älf\ golf, Rolf, Adolph, Randolph, Rudolph, Lake Rudolf

²**olf** \əlf\ see ULF

olfing \óf-iŋ\ see OFFING

olga \äl-gə\ Olga, Volga

oli \ō-lē\ see ¹OLY

olia \ō-lē-ə\ Mongolia, pignolia, Anatolia, melancholia, Inner Mongolia, Outer Mongolia

olian \ō-lē-ən\ aeolian, Aeolian, eolian, Mongolian, napoleon, Napoleon, simoleon, Tyrolean, Anatolian

¹**olic** \äl-ik\ colic, frolic, Gaelic, rollick, Aeolic, bucolic, carbolic, embolic, Mongolic, symbolic, systolic, alcoholic, anabolic, apostolic, catabolic, diabolic, hyperbolic, melancholic, metabolic, parabolic, vitriolic, workaholic

²**olic** \ō-lik\ colic, fumarolic, bibliopolic

olicking \ä-lik-iŋ\ frolicking, rollicking

olicy \äl-ə-sē\ policy, Wallasey

olid \äl-əd\ solid, squalid, stolid—*also pasts of verbs listed at* ²ALA

¹**olin** \äl-ən\ see ⁵OLLEN

²**olin** \ō-lən\ see OLON

olis \äl-əs\ braless, Hollis, polis, solace, tallith, Wallace, Wallis, Cornwallis, Manizales, torticollis

olish \äl-ish\ polish, abolish, demolish, apple-polish

olitan \äl-ət-ᵊn\ cosmopolitan, megapolitan, metropolitan, Neapolitan, megalopolitan

olity \äl-ət-ē\ see ¹ALITY

olium \ō-lē-əm\ scholium, linoleum, petroleum, trifolium

olivar \äl-ə-vər\ see OLIVER

¹**olk** \elk\ see ¹ELK

²**olk** \ōk\ see OKE

³**olk** \əlk\ see ULK

⁴**olk** \ók\ see ALK

olked \ōkt\ see OKED

olkie \ō-kē\ see OKY

olky \ō-kē\ see OKY

¹**oll** \ōl\ see ¹OLE

²**oll** \äl\ see ¹AL

³**oll** \ól\ see ALL

¹**olla** \äl-ə\ see ²ALA

²**olla** \ói-ə\ see OIA

ollable \ō-lə-bəl\ controllable, inconsolable, uncontrollable

ollack \äl-ək\ see OLOCH

¹**ollah** \ō-lə\ see OLA

²**ollah** \äl-ə\ see ²ALA

³**ollah** \əl-ə\ see ¹ULLAH

ollands \äl-ənz\ see OLLINS

ollar \äl-ər\ choler, collar, dollar, dolor, haler, holler, Mahler, scholar, squalor, taler, thaler, blue-collar, brass-collar, half-dollar,

white-collar, Emmentaler,
Eurodollar, petrodollar

ollard \äl-ərd\ bollard, collard,
collered, hollered, Lollard,
pollard

olled \ōld\ see ¹OLD

ollee \ō-lē\ see ¹OLY

ollege \äl-ij\ see OWLEDGE

¹**ollen** \ō-lən\ see OLON

²**ollen** \əl-ə\ see ¹ULLAH

³**ollen** \əl-ən\ see ULLEN

⁴**ollen** \ȯ-lən\ see ALLEN

⁵**ollen** \äl-ən\ Colin, pollen,
Rollin, Nordrhein-Westfalen

oller \ō-lər\ bowler, choler,
dolor, droller, molar, polar,
poler, poller, roller, solar,
stroller, troller, bankroller,
cajoler, comptroller,
controller, extoller, patroller,
premolar, steamroller,
antisolar, buttonholer,
logroller, Maryknoller,
pigeonholer

ollery \ōl-rē\ drollery, cajolery

ollet \äl-ət\ collet, Smollett,
tallith, wallet,
whatchamacallit

ollett \äl-ət\ see OLLET

olley \äl-ē\ see ¹OLLY

ollick \äl-ik\ see ¹OLIC

ollicking \ä-lik-iŋ\ see
OLICKING

ollie \äl-ē\ see ¹OLLY

ollin \äl-ən\ see ⁵OLLEN

olling \ō-liŋ\ bowling,
logrolling—*also present
participles of verbs listed at*
¹OLE

ollins \äl-ənz\ collins, Hollands,
Tom Collins

ollis \äl-əs\ see OLIS

ollity \äl-ət-ē\ see ¹ALITY

¹**ollo** \ōl-yō\ imbroglio, arroz
con pollo

²**ollo** \ō-yō\ yo-yo, criollo

³**ollo** \äl-ō\ see ¹OLLOW

ollop \äl-əp\ collop, dollop,
lollop, polyp, scallop, scollop,
trollop, wallop, codswallop,
escallop

¹**ollow** \äl-ō\ follow, hollo,
hollow, swallow, wallow,
Apollo, robalo, Leoncavallo

²**ollow** \äl-ə\ see ²ALA

ollower \äl-ə-wər\ follower,
swallower, wallower

ollster \ōl-stər\ see OLSTER

¹**olly** \äl-ē\ Bali, Cali, brolly,
collie, colly, dolly, folly,
golly, Halle, holly, Holly,
jolly, Lally, lolly, Mali,
Mollie, molly, Molly, Ollie,
Pali, poly, Polly, quale,
Raleigh, trolley, volley,
Denali, finale, Kigali,
loblolly, Nepali, petrale,
Somali, Svengali, tamale,
melancholy, pastorale, teocalli

²**olly** \ȯ-lē\ see AWLY

olm \ōm\ see ¹OME

olman \ōl-mən\ dolman,
dolmen, patrolman

olmen \ōl-mən\ see OLMAN

olmes \ōmz\ Holmes—*also
possessives and plurals of
nouns and third person
singular presents of verbs
listed at* ¹OME

olo \ō-lō\ bolo, kolo, nolo, polo,
solo, Barolo, Marco Polo

oloch \äl-ək\ Moloch, pollack,
rowlock

ologer \äl-ə-jər\ astrologer,

chronologer, horologer,
mythologer

ologist \äl-ə-jəst\ anthologist,
biologist, cetologist,
conchologist, cosmologist,
cryptologist, cytologist,
dendrologist, ecologist,
enologist, ethnologist,
ethologist, fetologist,
gemologist, geologist,
graphologist, histologist,
horologist, hydrologist,
Indologist, limnologist,
mixologist, morphologist,
mycologist, mythologist,
necrologist, nephrologist,
neurologist, oncologist,
ontologist, oologist,
pathologist, pedologist,
penologist, petrologist,
philologist, phonologist,
phrenologist, phycologist,
psychologist, seismologist,
serologist, sexologist,
sinologist, technologist,
topologist, typologist,
ufologist, virologist,
zoologist, anthropologist,
archaeologist, audiologist,
cardiologist, climatologist,
cosmetologist, criminologist,
dermatologist, Egyptologist,
embryologist, entomologist,
enzymologist, escapologist,
etymologist, futurologist,
genealogist, gerontologist,
gynecologist, hematologist,
herpetologist, ichthyologist,
ideologist, immunologist,
kremlinologist, lexicologist,
martyrologist, methodologist,
mineralogist, musicologist,
nematalogist, numerologist,
oceanologist, ophthalmologist,
ornithologist, osteologist,
papyrologist, pharmacologist,
phraseologist, physiologist,
planetologist, primatologist,
rheumatologist,
roentgenologist, semiologist,
sociologist, speleologist,
teleologist, teratologist,
thanatologist, toxicologist,
urbanologist, volcanologist,
bacteriologist, diabetologist,
dialectologist,
endocrinologist,
epistemologist, liturgiologist,
meteorologist, neonatologist,
paleontologist, parasitologist,
phenomenologist,
sedimentologist,
anesthesiologist,
epidemiologist,
gastroenterologist,
otolaryngologist

ologous \äl-ə-gəs\ heterologous,
homologous, tautologous

ology \äl-ə-jē\ anthology,
apology, astrology, biology,
bryology, cetology,
Christology, chronology,
conchology, cosmology,
cryptology, cytology,
dendrology, doxology,
ecology, enology, ethnology,
ethology, fetology, gemology,
geology, graphology,
haplology, histology,
homology, horology,
hydrology, hymnology,
Indology, limnology,
lithology, mixology,
morphology, mycology,

myology, mythology, necrology, nephrology, neurology, nosology, oncology, ontology, oology, pathology, pedology, penology, petrology, philology, phlebology, phonology, phrenology, phycology, proctology, psychology, scatology, seismology, serology, sexology, sinology, symbology, tautology, technology, tetralogy, theology, topology, trichology, typology, ufology, urology, virology, zoology, angelology, anthropology, archaeology, audiology, axiology, cardiology, climatology, codicology, cohomology, cosmetology, craniology, criminology, dactylology, demonology, deontology, dermatology, Egyptology, embryology, entomology, enzymology, escapology, eschatology, etiology, etymology, futurology, genealogy, gerontology, gynecology, hematology, herpetology, ichthyology, iconology, ideology, immunology, kremlinology, laryngology, lexicology, lichenology, Mariology, martyrology, methodology, mineralogy, museology, musicology, narratology, nematology, numerology, oceanology, opthalmology, ornithology, osteology, pharmacology, phraseology, physiology, planetology, primatology, radiology, reflexology, rheumatology, roentgenology, semiology, sociology, speleology, sumerology, teleology, teratology, terminology, thanatology, toxicology, urbanology, volcanology, vulcanology, bacteriology, chronobiology, cryptozoology, dialectology, ecclesiology, endocrinology, epistemology, liturgiology, metapsychology, meteorology, microbiology, micromorphology, neonatology, onomatology, paleontology, parapsychology, parasitology, phenomenology, sedimentology, symptomatology, anesthesiology, epidemiology, ethnomusicology, gastroenterology, otolaryngology, paleobiology, paleopathology, periodontology, otorhinolaryngology

olon \ō-lən\ bowline, Colin, colon, Nolan, solon, stolen, stollen, stolon, swollen, eidolon, semicolon

olonel \ərn-ᵊl\ see ERNAL

olonist \äl-ə-nəst\ colonist, Stalinist

¹olor \əl-ər\ color, cruller, ˌ culler, muller, sculler, bicolor, discolor, off-color, three-color, tricolor, Technicolor, watercolor

²**olor** \ō-lər\ see OLLER

³**olor** \äl-ər\ see OLLAR

olored \əl-ərd\ colored, dullard, bicolored, rose-colored, varicolored

olp \ōp\ see OPE

olpen \ō-pən\ see OPEN

olph \älf\ see OLF

ols \älz\ hols, Casals

olsom \ōl-səm\ see OLESOME

olster \ōl-stər\ bolster, holster, oldster, pollster, upholster

¹**olt** \ōlt\ bolt, colt, dolt, holt, jolt, molt, poult, smolt, volt, eyebolt, Humboldt, kingbolt, revolt, ringbolt, unbolt, thunderbolt

²**olt** \ȯlt\ see ALT

olta \äl-tə\ see ALTA

olter \ōl-tər\ bolter, coulter

oltish \ōl-tish\ coltish, doltish

oluble \äl-yə-bəl\ soluble, voluble, dissoluble, insoluble, irresoluble, resoluble, indissoluble

olum \ō-ləm\ see OLEM

olumn \äl-əm\ column, slalom, solemn, Malayalam

olus \ō-ləs\ bolas, bolus, solus, snowless, toeless, Coriolus, electroless, gladiolus, holus-bolus

olvable \äl-və-bəl\ solvable, dissolvable, evolvable, insolvable, resolvable, revolvable, irresolvable

¹**olve** \älv\ salve, solve, absolve, au poivre, convolve, devolve, dissolve, evolve, involve, resolve, revolve, coevolve

²**olve** \äv\ grave, of, salve, Slav, suave, taw, waw, moshav,

thereof, whereof, Zouave, Tishah-b'Ab, unheard-of, well-thought-of

olvement \älv-mənt\ evolvement, involvement, noninvolvement

olvent \äl-vənt\ solvent, dissolvent

olver \äl-vər\ solver, absolver, dissolver, involver, revolver

¹**oly** \ō-lē\ goalie, holey, holy, lowly, mole, moly, pollee, slowly, solely, aioli, amole, anole, cannoli, frijole, pinole, unholy, guacamole, ravioli, roly-poly

²**oly** \äl-ē\ see ¹OLLY

olyp \äl-əp\ see OLLOP

¹**om** \äm\ balm, bomb, bombe, calm, from, gaum, Guam, glom, malm, mom, palm, Pom, pram, prom, psalm, qualm, rhomb, ROM, tom, A-bomb, aplomb, ashram, becalm, Ceram, cheongsam, coulomb, Coulomb, dive-bomb, embalm, EPROM, firebomb, grande dame, H-bomb, imam, Islam, Long Tom, napalm, nizam, noncom, phenom, pogrom, pom-pom, reclame, rhabdom, salaam, seram, sitcom, Songnam, tam-tam, therefrom, tom-tom, wherefrom, wigwam, cardamom, diatom, intercom, Peeping Tom, Uncle Tom, Vietnam, Dar es Salaam, Omar Kayyam

²**om** \ōm\ see ¹OME

³**om** \üm\ see ¹OOM

⁴**om** \əm\ see ¹UM
⁵**om** \úm\ see ²UM
⁶**om** \ȯm\ see ¹AUM
oma \ō-mə\ chroma, coma, Roma, soma, aroma, diploma, glaucoma, sarcoma, Tacoma, carcinoma, granuloma, melanoma, Oklahoma, glioblastoma, neurofibroma
omac \ō-mik\ see ²OMIC
¹**omace** \äm-əs\ see OMISE
²**omace** \əm-əs\ see UMMOUS
omach \əm-ək\ see UMMOCK
omache \äm-ə-kē\ see OMACHY
omachy \äm-ə-kē\ Andromache, logomachy
omal \ō-məl\ domal, stomal, prodromal, chromosomal
omaly \äm-ə-lē\ balmily, homily, anomaly
oman \ō-mən\ bowman, foeman, gnomon, nomen, omen, Roman, showman, snowman, yeoman, agnomen, cognomen, crossbowman, longbowman, praenomen, Sertoman
omany \äm-ə-nē\ see OMINY
omas \äm-əs\ see OMISE
omathy \äm-ə-thē\ chrestomathy, stichomythy
¹**omb** \ōm\ see ¹OME
²**omb** \üm\ see ¹OOM
³**omb** \äm\ see ¹OM
⁴**omb** \əm\ see ¹UM
omba \äm-bə\ see AMBA
¹**ombe** \ōm\ see ¹OME
²**ombe** \üm\ see ¹OOM
³**ombe** \äm\ see ¹OM
ombed \ümd\ see OOMED
¹**omber** \äm-ər\ bomber, calmer, palmar, palmer, Palmer, dive-bomber, embalmer, fighter-bomber
²**omber** \äm-bər\ ombre, sambar, somber
³**omber** \ō-mər\ see ¹OMER
ombic \ō-mik\ see ²OMIC
ombical \ō-mi-kəl\ see ²OMICAL
ombie \äm-bē\ zombie, Abercrombie
ombing \ō-miŋ\ see OAMING
¹**ombo** \äm-bō\ combo, mambo, sambo
²**ombo** \əm-bō\ see UMBO
¹**ombre** \äm-brē\ hombre, ombre
²**ombre** \äm-bər\ see ²OMBER
³**ombre** \əm-brē\ see UMBERY
ombus \äm-bəs\ rhombus, thrombus
¹**ome** \ōm\ brougham, chrome, comb, combe, dome, foam, gloam, gnome, holm, home, loam, mome, nome, ohm, om, poem, pome, roam, Rom, Rome, tome, airdrome, at-home, bichrome, cockscomb, coulomb, coxcomb, defoam, down-home, Jerome, Nichrome, ogham, seadrome, shalom, sholom, Stockholm, syndrome, aerodrome, astrodome, catacomb, chromosome, currycomb, double-dome, gastronome, halidrome, hecatomb, hippodrome, honeycomb, metronome, monochrome, motordrome, palindrome, ribosome, stay-at-home, Styrofoam
²**ome** \ō-mē\ see OAMY
³**ome** \əm\ see ¹UM

omedy \äm-əd-ē\ comedy,
psalmody, tragicomedy
omely \əm-lē\ see ²UMBLY
omen \ō-mən\ see OMAN
omenal \äm-ən-ᵊl\ see OMINAL
omene \äm-ə-nē\ see OMINY
¹omer \ō-mər\ comber, foamer,
homer, Homer, omer, roamer,
vomer, beachcomber,
Reaumur, Lag b'Omer,
misnomer
²omer \əm-ər\ see UMMER
omery \əm-ə-rē\ see UMMERY
omet \äm-ət\ comet, grommet,
vomit
ometer \äm-ət-ər\ barometer,
chronometer, cyclometer,
drunkometer, ergometer,
gasometer, geometer,
hydrometer, hygrometer,
kilometer, manometer,
micrometer, odometer,
pedometer, photometer,
pulsometer, pyrometer,
rheometer, seismometer,
spectrometer, speedometer,
tachometer, thermometer,
anemometer, audiometer,
diffractometer, electrometer,
magnetometer, alcoholometer
ometry \äm-ə-trē\ astrometry,
barometry, chronometry,
cytometry, geometry,
isometry, micrometry,
optometry, photometry,
psychometry, seismometry,
thermometry, craniometry,
sociometry, trigonometry
omey \ō-mē\ see OAMY
omi \ō-mē\ see OAMY
omia \ō-mē-ä\ peperomia,
Utsunomia

¹omic \äm-ik\ comic, anomic,
atomic, coelomic, Islamic,
tsunamic, agronomic,
anatomic, antinomic,
autonomic, economic,
ergonomic, gastronomic,
metronomic, subatomic,
taxonomic, tragicomic,
Deuteronomic, heroicomic,
physiognomic, polyatomic,
seriocomic, macroeconomic,
microeconomic,
socioeconomic
²omic \ō-mik\ gnomic,
oghamic, Potomac, rhizomic,
catacombic, monochromic,
palindromic
¹omical \äm-i-kəl\ comical,
domical, agronomical,
anatomical, astronomical,
economical, gastronomical,
metronomical, tragicomical,
heroicomical, physiognomical
²omical \ō-mi-kəl\ domical,
coxcombical
omics \äm-iks\ atomics,
Islamics, tectonics,
bionomics, economics,
ergonomics, macroeconomics,
microeconomics—*also
plurals and possessives of
nouns listed at* ¹OMIC
omily \äm-ə-lē\ see OMALY
ominal \äm-ən-ᵊl\ nominal,
abdominal, cognominal,
phenomenal, epiphenomenal
ominance \äm-nəns\
dominance, prominence,
predominance
ominant \äm-nənt\ dominant,
prominent, predominant,

semidominant, subdominant, superdominant

ominate \äm-ə-nət\ innominate, prenominate

omine \äm-ə-nē\ see OMINY

ominence \äm-nəns\ see OMINANCE

ominent \äm-nənt\ see OMINANT

¹**oming** \əm-iŋ\ coming, plumbing, becoming, forthcoming, homecoming, incoming, oncoming, shortcoming, upcoming, unbecoming, up-and-coming—*also present participles of verbs listed at* ¹UM

²**oming** \ō-miŋ\ see OAMING

omini \äm-ə-nē\ see OMINY

ominous \äm-ə-nəs\ ominous, prolegomenous

ominy \äm-ə-nē\ hominy, Romany, Melpomene, anno Domini, eo nomine

omise \äm-əs\ pomace, promise, shammes, shamus, Thomas, Saint Thomas, doubting Thomas

omish \ō-mish\ gnomish, Romish

omit \äm-ət\ see OMET

omium \ō-mē-əm\ chromium, holmium, encomium, prostomium

¹**omma** \äm-ə\ see ²AMA

²**omma** \əm-ə\ see UMMA

¹**ommel** \äm-əl\ pommel, Jamil, Rommel, trommel

²**ommel** \əm-əl\ pommel, pummel, Beau Brummell

ommet \äm-ət\ see OMET

ommie \äm-ē\ see ¹AMI

ommon \äm-ən\ Amon, Brahman, common, shaman, yamen, Roscommon, Tutankhamen

ommoner \äm-ə-nər\ almoner, commoner, gewürztraminer

¹**ommy** \äm-ē\ see ¹AMI

²**ommy** \əm-ē\ see UMMY

omo \ō-mō\ bromo, Como, homo, Pomo, promo, Oromo, majordomo

omon \ō-mən\ see OMAN

¹**omp** \ämp\ champ, chomp, clomp, comp, pomp, romp, stamp, stomp, swamp, tramp, tromp, whomp

²**omp** \əmp\ see UMP

ompany \əmp-nē\ company, accompany, intracompany

ompass \əm-pəs\ compass, rumpus, encompass, gyrocompass

omper \äm-pər\ romper, stamper, stomper, swamper, wafflestomper

ompers \äm-pərz\ Gompers—*also possessives and plurals of nouns listed at* OMPER

ompey \äm-pē\ see OMPY

omplement \äm-plə-mənt\ complement, compliment

ompliment \äm-plə-mənt\ see OMPLEMENT

ompo \äm-pō\ campo, compo

ompous \äm-pəs\ see ¹OMPASS

ompson \äm-sən\ see AMSUN

ompt \aùnt\ see ²OUNT

ompy \äm-pē\ Pompey, swampy

omythy \äm-ə-thē\ see OMATHY

¹**on** \än\ ban, Bonn, chon, con,

conn, dawn, don, Don, Donn, drawn, Fan, faun, fawn, gone, guan, Han, John, Jon, khan, maun, mon, on, pan, pawn, phon, prawn, Ron, Shan, spawn, swan, Vaughn, wan, yawn, yon, yuan, aeon, add-on, agon, agone, Akan, alençon, Amman, ancon, anon, Anshan, Anton, archon, argon, Argonne, Aswan, atman, Avon, axon, barchan, baton, blouson, bon ton, bonbon, boron, boson, bouillon, Brython, bygone, caisson, Calgon, canton, capon, Ceylon, chaconne, chiffon, chignon, Chiron, chiton, chrismon, cistron, clip-on, codon, come-on, cordon, coupon, crampon, crayon, crepon, cretonne, crouton, Dacron, dead-on, Dear John, dewan, doggone, doggoned, Dogon, Don Juan, eon, exon, far-gone, flacon, foregone, Freon, fronton, Fujian, Garonne, Gibran, gluon, gnomon, Golan, Gosplan, guidon, hadron, Hainan, hazan, Henan, hogan, Huainan, Hunan, icon, Inchon, intron, Ivan, Jinan, Kanban, kaon, Kashan, Kazan, Kerman, Khoisan, Kirman, koan, krypton, kurgan, Kurgan, lauan, Leon, lepton, liman, log on, Luzon, macron, Massan, Medan, Memnon, meson, micron, Milan, mod con, moron, mouton, Multan, muon,

natron, neon, nephron, neuron, neutron, ninon, nylon, odds-on, Oman, Oran, Orlon, outgone, pacon, parton, Pathan, pavane, pecan, peon, Phaethon, photon, phyton, pion, pinon, piton, plankton, pluton, pompon, prion, proton, Pusan, put-on, pylon, python, Qur'an, radon, rayon, recon, rhyton, run-on, Saint John, Saipan, salon, San Juan, Schumann, Shaban, shaman, shaitan, Shingon, Simplon, Sjoelland, slip-on, snap-on, solon, soupçon, soutane, Stefan, stolon, Suwon, Szechuan, Szechwan, Tainan, Taiwan, taipan, tampon, taxon, Teflon, teston, Tétouan, Tetuán, thereon, tisane, torchon, toucan, toyon, trigon, Tristan, triton, trogon, Tucson, Typhon, tzigane, uhlan, Ulsan, upon, walk-on, witan, whereon, Wonsan, wonton, Wuhan, xenon, Xi'an, yaupon, Yukon, Yunnan, Yvonne, zircon, Abadan, Abijan, Acheron, Ahriman, aileron, amazon, Amazon, amnion, Aragon, autobahn, Avalon, Babylon, Bakhtaran, Balaton, balmacaan, Bantustan, Barbizon, baryon, Basilan, betatron, biathlon, cabochon, calutron, carillon, carryon, celadon, chorion, colophon, Culiacàn, cyclotron, decagon, decathlon, demijohn, deuteron, dipteron, echelon, electron, elevon, epsilon, etymon, fermion, follow-on, Fujisan, Genghis Khan, goings-on, gonfalon, Grand Teton, graviton, harijan, helicon, heptagon, hexagon, hopping John, Huascaràn, Ilion, Irian, Isfahan, Kazakhstan, Kublai Khan, Kyrgyzstan, Lake Huron, Lebanon, leprechaun, lexicon, liaison, Lipizzan, logion, macédoine, marathon, Marathon, marzipan, mastodon, Mazatlàn, Mbabane, Mellotron, Miquelon, morion, myrmidon, negatron, nonagon, noumenon, nucleon, Oberon, octagon, omicron, Oregon, organon, ostracon, Pakistan, Palawan, pantheon, paragon, Parmesan, parmigiana, Parthenon, pentagon, Percheron, Phaethon, Phlegethon, polygon, positron, Procyon, put-upon, Rajasthan, Ramadan, Rubicon, silicon, Suleiman, tachyon, Taiyuan, talkathon, Teheran, telamon, telethon, thereupon, Tian Shan, Tucuman, undergone, upsilon, virion, walkathon, whereupon, woebegone, Yerevan, Zahedan, abutilon, Agamemnon, archenteron, arrière-ban, asyndeton, automaton, Azerbaijan, Bellerophon, bildungsroman, carrying-on, Diazenon, dimetrodon, dodecagon, encephalon, ephemeron, himation, interferon, kakiemon, Laocoön, mesenteron, Michoacàn, millimicron, oxymoron, phenomenon, protozoon, Saskatchewan, septentrion, sine qua non, t'ai chi ch'uan, Taklimakan, Vientiane, West Irian, Xiangtan, anacoluthon, diencephalon, ferrosilicon, mesencephalon, metencephalon, prolegomenon, prothalamion, prosencephalon, pteranodon, spermatozoon, telencephalon, ultramarathon, epiphenomenon, myelencephalon, kyrie eleison, San Miguel de Tucumàn

²**on** \ōⁿ\ fond, ton, ballon, baton, bouillon, Dijon, flacon, fourgon, frisson, Gabon, garçon, lorgnon, Lyons, maçon, marron, Marron, mouflon, soupçon, Toulon, Villon, Aubusson, bourguignon, feuilleton, Ganelon, gueridon, limaçon, papillon, filet mignon, Saint Emilion

³**on** \òn\ awn, Bonn, bonne, brawn, dawn, Dawn, drawn, faun, fawn, gone, lawn, maun, on, pawn, prawn, Sean, spawn, Vaughn, won, yawn, add-on, agon, agone, begone, bygone, chaconne, clip-on, come-on, dead-on, doggone, far-gone, foregone, hands-on, hard-on, head-on, hereon,

impawn, indrawn, Kherson, odds-on, outgone, Puchon, put-on, Quezon, run-on, slip-on, snap-on, Taejon, thereon, turned-on, upon, walk-on, whereon, wiredrawn, withdrawn, bourguignonne, carryon, follow-on, goings-on, hanger-on, hereupon, looker-on, put-upon, thereupon, undergone, whereupon, woebegone, carrying-on

⁴on \ōn\ see ¹ONE

⁵on \ən\ see UN

¹ona \ō-nə\ dona, Dona, Jonah, krone, Mona, Nona, Rhona, Rona, Shona, trona, Ancona, Bellona, bologna, Bologna, cinchona, corona, kimono, Leona, madrona, Pamplona, persona, Ramona, Verona, Arizona, Barcelona, Desdemona, in propria persona

²ona \än-ə\ see ¹ANA

oña \ōn-yə\ see ³ONIA

onachal \än-i-kəl\ see ONICAL

onae \ō-nē\ see ¹ONY

onah \ō-nə\ see ONA

¹onal \ōn-ᵊl\ clonal, tonal, zonal, atonal, coronal, hormonal, baritonal, microtonal, polyclonal, polytonal, semitonal

²onal \än-ᵊl\ Donal, Ronal

onald \än-ᵊld\ Donald, Ronald, MacDonald

onant \ō-nənt\ see ONENT

onas \ō-nəs\ see ²ONUS

onative \ō-nət-iv\ conative, donative

onc \äŋk\ see ¹ONK

¹once \äns\ see ²ANCE

²once \əns\ see UNCE

¹onch \äŋk\ see ¹ONK

²onch \änch\ see ¹AUNCH

oncha \äŋ-kə\ see ANKA

oncho \än-chō\ honcho, poncho, rancho

onchus \äŋ-kəs\ bronchus, rhonchus

onco \äŋ-kō\ bronco, Franco

¹ond \änd\ blond, bond, fond, frond, Gond, pond, rand, sonde, wand, yond, abscond, Armand, beau monde, beyond, despond, fishpond, Gironde, gourmand, haut monde, millpond, neoned, pair-bond, respond, allemande, towmond, correspond, demimonde, Eurobond, Trebizond, Trobriand, vagabond, radiosonde, slough of despond—*also pasts of verbs listed at* ¹ON

²ond \ōⁿ\ see ²ON

³ond \ònt\ see ¹AUNT

onda \än-də\ Lahnda, Rhonda, Rhondda, Ronda, Wanda, Golconda, Luganda, Ruanda, Rwanda, Uganda, anaconda, Campo Grande

ondam \än-dəm\ see ¹ONDOM

ondant \än-dənt\ see ONDENT

onday \ən-dē\ see UNDI

ondays \ən-dēz\ see UNDAYS

ondda \än-də\ see ONDA

onde \änd\ see ¹OND

ondeau \än-dō\ see ONDO

ondel \än-dᵊl\ condyle, fondle, rondel

ondence \än-dəns\
  correspondence, despondence
ondency \än-dən-sē\
  despondency, correspondency
ondent \än-dənt\ fondant,
  despondent, respondent,
  corespondent, correspondent
¹onder \än-dər\ bonder, condor,
  maunder, ponder, squander,
  wander, yonder, zander,
  absconder, responder,
  transponder—*also
  comparatives of adjectives
  listed at* ¹OND
²onder \ən-dər\ see UNDER
ondly \än-lē\ see ¹ANLY
ondness \än-nəs\ see ANNESS
ondo \än-dō\ condo, Hondo,
  rondeau, rondo, secondo,
  tondo, forzando, glissando,
  lentando, parlando,
  scherzando, sforzando,
  allargando, rallentando,
  ritardando, accelerando
¹ondom \än-dəm\ condom,
  quondam
²ondom \ən-dəm\ see UNDUM
ondor \än-dər\ see ¹ONDER
ondrous \ən-drəs\ see
  UNDEROUS
ondyle \än-dᵊl\ see ONDEL
¹one \ōn\ blown, bone, clone,
  cone, crone, drone, flown,
  groan, grown, hone, Joan,
  known, loan, lone, moan,
  Mon, mown, none, own,
  phone, pone, prone, Rhone,
  roan, Saône, scone, sewn,
  shone, shoon, shown, sone,
  sown, stone, throne, thrown,
  tone, trone, won, zone, agon,
  aitchbone, alone, atone,

backbone, bemoan, birthstone,
Blackstone, breastbone,
brimstone, brownstone,
capstone, cheekbone,
chinbone, cogon, cologne,
Cologne, colon, Coloón,
condone, curbstone, cyclone,
daimon, debone, depone,
dethrone, disown, drystone,
earphone, enthrone,
fieldstone, flagstone,
flyblown, freestone, full-
blown, gallstone, gemstone,
Gijón, Gladstone, gravestone,
grindstone, hailstone,
halftone, handblown, high-
flown, hipbone, homegrown,
hormone, impone, ingrown,
inkstone, intone, jawbone,
keystone, León, leone,
limestone, lodestone, Mount
Mayon, milestone, millstone,
misknown, moonstone,
oilstone, outgrown, outshown,
ozone, peon, pinbone,
pinecone, pinon, pinyon,
postpone, propone, Ramon,
rezone, rhinestone, sandstone,
shade-grown, shinbone,
Shoshone, soapstone, T-bone,
tailbone, thighbone,
tombstone, touchstone,
Touch-Tone, tritone,
trombone, turnstone, twelve-
tone, two-tone, Tyrone,
unknown, unthrone, well-
known, whalebone, wheel-
thrown, whetstone,
windblown, wishbone,
Yangon, allophone,
anglophone, anklebone,

barbitone, Barbizon, barytone, Bayamon, bombardon, Canal Zone, chaperon, cherrystone, cobblestone, collarbone, cornerstone, cortisone, cuttlebone, diaphone, Dictaphone, epigone, francophone, free-fire zone, Gaborone, gramophone, herringbone, homophone, ironstone, knucklebone, marrowbone, megaphone, mellophone, methadone, microphone, microtone, minestrone, monotone, overblown, overflown, overgrown, overthrown, overtone, Picturephone, polyphone, rottenstone, sacaton, saxophone, semitone, shacklebone, silicone, sousaphone, speakerphone, stepping-stone, telephone, Toreón, undertone, vibraphone, xylophone, Yellowstone, anticyclone, Asunción, bred-in-the-bone, Concepción, eau de cologne, mesocyclone, norethindrone, Nuevo Leon, radiophone, sine qua non, testosterone, videophone, Darby and Joan, Ponce de Leon, Sierra Leone, radiotelephone

²one \ō-nē\ see ¹ONY

³one \än\ see ¹ON

⁴one \ən\ see UN

⁵one \ȯn\ see ³ON

onean \ō-nē-ən\ see ¹ONIAN

¹oned \ōnd\ boned, stoned, toned, cologned, high-toned, pre-owned, rawboned, rhinestoned, two-toned, cobblestoned—*also pasts of verbs listed at* ¹ONE

²oned \än\ see ¹ON

oneless \ōn-ləs\ boneless, toneless

onely \ōn-lē\ lonely, only, pronely

onement \ōn-mənt\ atonement, cantonment, dethronement, disownment, enthronement

oneness \ən-nəs\ dunness, doneness, oneness, rotundness

onent \ō-nənt\ sonant, component, deponent, exponent, opponent, proponent, bicomponent

oneous \ō-nē-əs\ see ONIOUS

¹oner \ō-nər\ boner, donor, droner, groaner, honer, loaner, loner, stoner, toner, zoner, condoner, dethroner, intoner, landowner, shipowner, telephoner

²oner \ȯn-ər\ see ¹AWNER

onerous \än-ə-rəs\ onerous, sonorous

ones \ōnz\ Jones, nones, sawbones, Davy Jones, lazybones, skull and crossbones—*also plurals and possessives of nouns and third person singular presents of verbs listed at* ¹ONE

onest \än-əst\ honest, dishonest, Hinayanist, Mahayanist

¹oney \ō-nē\ see ¹ONY

²oney \ən-ē\ see UNNY

³oney \ü-nē\ see OONY

¹ong \äŋ\ Chang, Fang, gong, hong, Huang, prong, Shang, Tang, tong, yang, Anyang, barong, biltong, Da Nang, dugong, Guiyang, Hanyang, Heng-yang, Hong Kong, kiang, liang, Mah-Jongg, Malang, Padang, satang, Wuchang, Zhejiang, Zhenjiang, billabong, Chittagong, Liaoyang, Pyong-yang, Semarang, scuppernong, Shenyang, Sturm und Drang, Vietcong, Shijiazhuang, Ujung Pandang, Wollongong, ylang-ylang, Heilongjiang

²ong \óŋ\ bong, dong, gong, long, prong, song, strong, thong, throng, tong, wrong, agelong, along, Armstrong, barong, belong, biltong, birdsong, chaise longue, daylong, dingdong, diphthong, dugong, endlong, erelong, furlong, Geelong, Haiphong, headlong, headstrong, Kaesong, kampong, lifelong, livelong, Mekong, monthlong, Nanchang, nightlong, oblong, oolong, part-song, ping-pong, Ping-Pong, plainsong, prolong, sarong, Shandong, sidelong, singsong, so long, souchong, weeklong, yard-long, billabong, Chittagong, cradlesong, evensong, Palembang, scuppernong, sing-along, summerlong, tagalong, Vietcong

³ong \əŋ\ see ¹UNG
⁴ong \ùng\ see ²UNG
onga \äŋ-gə\ conga, panga,

tonga, Tonga, Kananga, mridanga, Alba Longa, Zamboanga, Bucaramanga
onge \ənj\ see UNGE
onged \óŋd\ pronged, thonged, multipronged—*also pasts of verbs listed at* ²ONG
¹onger \əŋ-gər\ hunger, monger, younger, fellmonger, fishmonger, ironmonger, newsmonger, phrasemonger, scaremonger, warmonger, whoremonger, wordmonger, costermonger, fashionmonger, gossipmonger, rumormonger, scandalmonger
²onger \ən-jər\ see ¹UNGER
ongery \əŋ-grē\ hungry, fellmongery, ironmongery
ongful \óŋ-fəl\ wrongful, songful
ongin \ən-jən\ see UNGEON
ongish \óŋ-ish\ longish, strongish
ongo \äŋ-gō\ bongo, Congo, congou, Kongo, mongo, Niger-Congo, Pago Pago
ongous \əŋ-gəs\ see UNGOUS
¹ongue \əŋ\ see ¹UNG
²ongue \óŋ\ see ²ONG
ongued \əŋd\ lunged, tongued
ongy \ən-jē\ see UNGY
onhomous \än-ə-məs\ see ONYMOUS
oni \ō-nē\ see ¹ONY
¹onia \ō-nē-ə\ bignonia, clintonia, Estonia, Laconia, Livonia, mahonia, paulownia, Polonia, Slavonia, Snowdonia, tithonia, valonia, zirconia, Amazonia,

Caledonia, Catalonia,
Macedonia

²**onia** \ō-nyə\ Konya, Sonia,
Sonja, Sonya, ammonia,
Bologna, pneumonia, Polonia,
tithonia, valonia, anhedonia,
Caledonia, Macedonia, New
Caledonia, Patagonia

³**onia** \ōn-yə\ doña, begonia

onial \ō-nē-əl\ baronial,
colonial, ceremonial,
matrimonial, testimonial

¹**onian** \ō-nē-ən\ chthonian,
aeonian, Antonian, Baconian,
Clactonian, demonian,
Devonian, draconian,
Estonian, Etonian, favonian,
gorgonian, Ionian, Jacksonian,
Oxonian, plutonian,
Samsonian, Shoshonean,
Slavonian, Amazonian,
Apollonian, Arizonian,
Babylonian, calypsonian,
Chalcedonian, Hamiltonian,
parkinsonian

²**onian** \ō-nyən\ Zonian,
Amazonian, Babylonian,
Estonian, Macedonian

onic \än-ik\ chronic, chthonic,
conic, dornick, phonic, sonic,
tonic, Aaronic, agonic, atonic,
benthonic, bionic, Brittonic,
Brythonic, bubonic, Byronic,
canonic, carbonic, cryonic,
cyclonic, daimonic, demonic,
draconic, euphonic,
gnomonic, harmonic, hedonic,
ionic, Ionic, ironic, laconic,
Masonic, mnemonic,
planktonic, platonic, plutonic,
pneumonic, Puranic,
Pythonic, sardonic, Saronic,

sermonic, Slavonic,
symphonic, synchronic,
tectonic, Teutonic, ultrasonic,
zirconic, catatonic,
diachronic, diatonic,
disharmonic, electronic,
embryonic, hegemonic,
histrionic, homophonic,
hydroponic, inharmonic,
isotonic, macaronic,
megaphonic, microphonic,
monophonic, monotonic,
nonionic, pharaonic,
Philharmonic, polyphonic,
quadraphonic, semitonic,
Solomonic, supersonic,
supertonic, telephonic,
thermionic, architectonic,
chameleonic, cardiotonic,
electrotonic, geotectonic,
Neoplatonic, stereophonic,
extraembryonic

onica \än-i-kə\ Monica,
harmonica, japonica,
Salonika, veronica, Veronica,
Thessalonica

onical \än-i-kəl\ chronicle,
conical, monachal, monocle,
canonical, demonical,
ironical, deuterocanonical

onicals \än-i-kəlz\ Chronicles,
canonicals

onicker \ä-ni-kər\ see
ONNICKER

onicle \än-i-kəl\ see ONICAL

onicles \än-i-kəlz\ see ONICALS

onics \än-iks\ onyx, phonics,
bionics, cryonics, mnemonics,
Ovonics, photonics, sardonyx,
tectonics, avionics,
electronics, histrionics,
hydroponics, microphonics,

nucleonics, quadriphonics,
radionics, supersonics,
thermionics, architectonics—
*also plurals and possessives
of nouns listed at* ONIC
onika \än-i-kə\ see ONICA
oniker \ä-ni-kər\ see ONNICKER
¹oning \än-iŋ\ awning,
couponing
²oning \ō-niŋ\ loaning,
jawboning, landowning
onion \ən-yən\ see UNION
onious \ō-nē-əs\ erroneous,
euphonious, felonious,
harmonious, Polonius,
Suetonius, symphonious,
acrimonious, ceremonious,
disharmonious, inharmonious,
parsimonious, sanctimonious,
Marcus Antonius,
unceremonious
¹onis \ō-nəs\ see ²ONUS
²onis \än-əs\ see ¹ONUS
onish \än-ish\ donnish, monish,
admonish, astonish,
premonish, leprechaunish
onishment \än-ish-mənt\
admonishment, astonishment
onium \ō-nē-əm\ euphonium,
harmonium, plutonium,
pandemonium, Pandemonium
onius \ō-nē-əs\ see ONIOUS
onja \ō-nyə\ see ²ONIA
onjon \ən-jən\ see UNGEON
onjure \än-jər\ conjure, rondure
¹onk \äŋk\ ankh, bronc, clonk,
conch, conk, Franck, honk,
Planck, plonk, zonk,
honkytonk
²onk \əŋk\ see UNK
onker \äŋ-kər\ conker, conquer,
honker

¹onkey \äŋ-kē\ see ONKY
²onkey \əŋ-kē\ see UNKY
onkian \äŋ-kē-ən\ conquian,
Algonkian
onky \äŋ-kē\ conkey, donkey,
honkie, wonky, yanqui
onless \ən-ləs\ see UNLESS
only \ōn-lē\ see ONELY
onment \ōn-mənt\ see
ONEMENT
¹onn \än\ see ¹ON
²onn \ȯn\ see ³ON
¹onna \ȯn-ə\ donna, Donna,
fauna, prima donna,
megafauna
²onna \än-ə\ see ¹ANA
onnage \ən-ij\ see UNNAGE
¹onne \än\ see ¹ON
²onne \ən\ see UN
³onne \ȯn\ see ³ON
onner \än-ər\ see ¹ONOR
onnet \än-ət\ bonnet, sonnet,
bluebonnet, sunbonnet,
warbonnet
onnicker \ä-ni-kər\ donnicker,
doniker, monicker, moniker
onnie \än-ē\ see ¹ANI
onnish \än-ish\ see ONISH
onnor \än-ər\ see ¹ONOR
¹onny \än-ē\ see ¹ANI
²onny \ən-ē\ see UNNY
¹ono \ō-nō\ phono, cui bono,
kimono, pro bono, kakemono,
makimono
²ono \ō-nə\ see ONA
³ono \än-ō\ see ¹ANO
onocle \än-i-kəl\ see ONICAL
onomer \än-ə-mər\ monomer,
astronomer, comonomer
onomist \än-ə-məst\
agronomist, autonomist,
economist, ergonomist,

gastronomist, synonymist,
taxonomist, Deuteronomist

onomous \än-ə-məs\ see
ONYMOUS

onomy \än-ə-mē\ agronomy,
antonymy, astronomy,
autonomy, economy,
eponymy, gastronomy,
homonomy, metonymy,
synonymy, taphonomy,
taxonomy, toponymy,
Deuteronomy, diseconomy,
heteronomy, teleonomy

¹onor \än-ər\ Bonner, fawner,
goner, honor, dishonor,
O'Connor, Lipizzaner,
marathoner, Afrikaner,
weimaraner

²onor \ō-nər\ see ¹ONER

onorous \än-ə-rəs\ see
ONEROUS

onquer \äŋ-kər\ see ONKER

onquian \äŋ-kē-ən\ see ONKIAN

¹ons \änz\ see ONZE

²ons \ōⁿ\ see ²ON

onsil \än-səl\ see ONSUL

onsin \än-sən\ see OHNSON

onson \än-sən\ see OHNSON

onsor \än-sər\ panzer, sponsor

onsul \än-səl\ consul, tonsil

on't \ōnt\ don't, won't

¹ont \ənt\ blunt, brunt, bunt,
front, grunt, hunt, lunt, punt,
runt, shunt, strunt, stunt,
want, wont, affront,
beachfront, bowfront,
breakfront, confront,
forefront, housefront,
lakefront, manhunt, out-front,
seafront, shirtfront,
shorefront, storefront, swell-
front, up-front, witch-hunt,

battlefront, oceanfront,
riverfront, waterfront

²ont \änt\ see ²ANT

³ont \ónt\ see ¹AUNT

¹ontal \änt-ᵊl\ pontil, fontal,
quantal, horizontal,
periodontal

²ontal \ənt-ᵊl\ see UNTLE

ontan \änt-ⁿ\ see ONTON

ontas \änt-əs\ see ONTUS

¹onte \änt-ē\ see ¹ANTI

²onte \än-tā\ see ¹ANTE

onted \ónt-əd\ vaunted, wonted,
undaunted—*also pasts of
verbs listed at* ¹AUNT

onter \ənt-ər\ see UNTER

onth \ənth\ month, billionth,
millionth, trillionth,
twelvemonth

ontian \änt-ē-ən\ Zontian, post-
Kantian

ontic \änt-ik\ ontic, deontic,
Vedantic, orthodontic,
anacreontic

ontil \änt-ᵊl\ see ¹ONTAL

ontinent \änt-ᵊn-ənt\ continent,
incontinent, subcontinent,
supercontinent

ontis \än-təs\ see ²ANTOS

ontist \änt-əst\ Vedantist,
orthodontist, prosthodontist

onto \än-tō\ see ¹ANTO

onton \änt-ᵊn\ ponton, wanton,
Lahontan

ontra \än-trə\ contra, mantra,
tantra, per contra

ontre \änt-ər\ see ¹AUNTER

ontus \änt-əs\ Pontus,
Pocahontas

onty \änt-ē\ see ¹ANTI

¹onus \än-əs\ Cronus, Faunus,
Adonis

²**onus** \ō-nəs\ bonus, Cronus, Jonas, onus, slowness, Adonis, colonus

¹**ony** \ō-nē\ bony, coney, crony, phony, pony, stony, Toni, tony, Tony, yoni, baloney, Benoni, bologna, canzone, Marconi, Moroni, Oenone, padrone, spumoni, tortoni, abalone, acrimony, agrimony, alimony, antimony, cannelloni, ceremony, chalcedony, colophony, macaroni, mascarpone, matrimony, minestrone, palimony, parsimony, patrimony, pepperoni, provolone, rigatoni, sanctimony, telephony, testimony, zabaglione, con espressione, conversazione, dramatis personae

²**ony** \än-ē\ see ¹ANI

onya \ō-nyə\ see ²ONIA

onymist \än-ə-məst\ see ONOMIST

onymous \än-ə-məs\ bonhomous, anonymous, antonymous, autonomous, eponymous, homonymous, pseudonymous, synonymous, heteronomous

onymy \än-ə-mē\ see ONOMY

¹**onyon** \än-yən\ ronyon, wanion

²**onyon** \ən-yən\ see UNION

onyx \än-iks\ see ONICS

onze \änz\ bonze, bronze, pons, long johns, Saint John's, Afrikaans, solitons, islet of Langerhans—*also plurals and possessives of nouns and third person singular presents of verbs listed at* ¹ON

onzi \än-zē\ see ONZY

onzy \än-zē\ bronzy, Ponzi

¹**oo** \ü\ see ¹EW

²**oo** \ō\ see ¹OW

oob \üb\ see UBE

oober \ü-bər\ see UBER

ooby \ü-bē\ booby, looby, ruby, Ruby

¹**ooch** \üch\ brooch, hooch, mooch, pooch, smooch, capuche, scaramouch

²**ooch** \ōch\ see OACH

oocher \ü-chər\ see UTURE

oochy \ü-chē\ smoochy, Baluchi, penuche, Vespucci, Kawaguchi

¹**ood** \u̇d\ good, hood, pud, rudd, should, stood, wood, would, yod, basswood, bentwood, blackwood, boxwood, brushwood, childhood, cordwood, deadwood, do-good, dogwood, driftwood, Ellwood, Elwood, falsehood, fatwood, feel-good, firewood, fruitwood, girlhood, godhood, greasewood, greenwood, groundwood, gumwood, hardwood, ironwood, kingwood, knighthood, maidhood, manhood, monkhood, monkshood, Mount Hood, no-good, pinewood, plywood, priesthood, pulpwood, redwood, rosewood, sainthood, selfhood, Sherwood, softwood, sonhood, statehood,

stinkwood, Talmud,
teakwood, unhood,
Wedgwood, wifehood,
withstood, wormwood,
arrowwood, bachelorhood,
brotherhood, buttonwood,
candlewood, cedarwood,
cottonwood, fatherhood,
hardihood, Hollywood,
likelihood, livelihood,
maidenhood, motherhood,
nationhood, neighborhood,
parenthood, peckerwood,
personhood, Robin Hood,
sandalwood, scattergood,
servanthood, sisterhood,
spinsterhood, toddlerhood,
tulipwood, understood,
widowhood, womanhood,
misunderstood, unlikelihood,
widowerhood
²**ood** \ōd\ see ODE
³**ood** \üd\ see UDE
⁴**ood** \əd\ see ¹UD
¹**ooded** \əd-əd\ blooded, cold-
blooded, full-blooded, half-
blooded, hot-blooded, pure-
blooded, red-blooded,
star-studded, warm-blooded—
also pasts of verbs listed at
¹UD
²**ooded** \ud-əd\ hooded,
wooded, hard-wooded, soft-
wooded
¹**ooder** \üd-ər\ see UDER
²**ooder** \əd-ər\ see UDDER
ooding \ud-iŋ\ pudding, do-
gooding
oodle \üd-ᵊl\ boodle, doodle,
feudal, noodle, poodle,
strudel, caboodle, flapdoodle,
paludal, Yankee-Doodle

oodman \ud-mən\ goodman,
woodman
oodoo \üd-ü\ doo-doo, hoodoo,
kudu, voodoo
oods \udz\ backwoods, dry
goods, piney woods—*also
plurals and possessives of
nouns and third person
singular presents of verbs
listed at* ¹OOD
oodsman \udz-mən\ woodsman,
backwoodsman, ombudsman
¹**oody** \üd-ē\ broody, Judi,
Judie, Judy, moody, Rudy,
Trudy
²**oody** \ud-ē\ cuddy, goody,
hoody, woody, goody-goody
³**oody** \əd-ē\ see ¹UDDY
ooer \ü-ər\ see ¹EWER
ooey \ü-ē\ see EWY
¹**oof** \üf\ goof, kloof, poof,
pouf, proof, roof, spoof,
woof, aloof, behoof, disproof,
fireproof, foolproof, forehoof,
rustproof, shadoof,
soundproof, sunroof, Tartuffe,
unroof, bulletproof, opera
bouffe, shatterproof,
waterproof, weatherproof
²**oof** \uf\ hoof, poof, roof, woof,
forehoof, Tartuffe
³**oof** \ōf\ see OAF
⁴**oof** \üv\ see ³OVE
oofah \ü-fə\ see UFA
¹**oofer** \ü-fər\ proofer, roofer,
twofer, waterproofer
²**oofer** \uf-ər\ hoofer, woofer
oofy \ü-fē\ goofy, spoofy, Sufi
ooga \ü-gə\ see UGA
ooge \üj\ see ¹UGE
ooger \ug-ər\ see UGUR

oogie \ùg-ē\ bogey, boogie, boogie-woogie

oo-goo \ü-gü\ see UGU

ooh \ü\ see ¹EW

ooh-pooh \ü-pü\ hoopoe, pooh-pooh

ooi \ü-ē\ see EWY

ooist \ü-əst\ doest, tattooist, voodooist—*also superlatives of adjectives listed at* ¹EW

¹ook \ùk\ book, brook, Brooke, chook, cook, Cook, crook, gook, hook, look, nook, rook, schnook, shook, snook, stook, took, bankbook, betook, billhook, caoutchouc, chapbook, checkbook, Chinook, cookbook, forsook, fishhook, guidebook, handbook, hornbook, hymnbook, Insbruck, Kobuk, logbook, matchbook, mistook, Mount Cook, notebook, outlook, partook, passbook, Pembroke, playbook, pothook, promptbook, psalmbook, retook, schoolbook, scrapbook, sketchbook, skyhook, songbook, studbook, textbook, unhook, Windhoek, workbook, yearbook, buttonhook, copybook, donnybrook, gerenuk, inglenook, Leeuwenhoek, overbook, overlook, overtook, pocketbook, storybook, tenterhook, undertook, Volapuk, gobbledygook

²ook \ük\ see UKE

ooka \ü-kə\ yuca, bazooka, felucca, palooka, Toluca, verruca, Juan de Fuca

ookah \ùk-ə\ hookah, sukkah

ooke \ùk\ see ¹OOK

ooker \ùk-ər\ booker, cooker, hooker, Hooker, looker, snooker, good-looker, onlooker

ookery \ùk-ə-rē\ crookery, rookery

ookie \ùk-ē\ bookie, brookie, cookie, cooky, hooky, nooky, rookie, rooky, Takatsuki, walkie-lookie

ooking \ùk-iŋ\ booking, cooking, good-looking, onlooking

ooklet \ùk-lət\ booklet, brooklet, hooklet

¹ooks \üks\ deluxe, gadzooks—*also plurals and possessives of nouns and third person singular presents of verbs listed at* UKE

²ooks \ùks\ Brooks, crux, luxe, zooks, deluxe, gadzooks—*also plurals and possessives of nouns and third person singular presents of verbs listed at* ¹OOK

¹ooky \ü-kē\ kooky, spooky, bouzouki, Kabuki, saluki, tanuki

²ooky \ùk-ē\ see OOKIE

¹ool \ül\ boule, boulle, buhl, cool, drool, fool, fuel, ghoul, gul, joule, mewl, mule, pool, Poole, pul, pule, rule, school, spool, stool, tool, tulle, you'll, yule, air-cool, ampoule, babul, Banjul, befool, Blackpool, carpool, cesspool, curule, Elul, faldstool, footstool, hangul, Kabul, Kurnool, misrule, Mosul, preschool, retool, self-rule, synfuel, toadstool, tomfool, uncool, vanpool, whirlpool, Barnaul, fascicule, gallinule, graticule, groupuscule, Hartlepool, Istanbul, lenticule, Liverpool, majuscule, minuscule, molecule, monticule, overrule, reticule, ridicule, vestibule, water-cool, biomolecule

²ool \ul\ see ¹UL

oola \ü-lə\ see ULA

oole \ül\ see ¹OOL

oolean \ü-lē-ən\ see ULEAN

ooled \üld\ bejeweled, unschooled, vestibuled—*also pasts of verbs listed at* ¹OOL

ooler \ü-lər\ cooler, gular, puler, ruler, carpooler, grade-schooler, high schooler, preschooler, ridiculer, watercooler

oolie \ü-lē\ see ULY

oolish \ü-lish\ coolish, foolish, ghoulish, mulish, pound-foolish

¹oolly \ü-lē\ see ULY

²oolly \ul-ē\ see ²ULLY

¹oom \üm\ bloom, boom, broom, brougham, brume, combe, cwm, doom, flume, fume, gloom, glume, groom, Hume, khoum, loom, neume, plume, rheum, room, spume, tomb, toom, vroom, whom, womb, zoom, abloom, assume, backroom, ballroom, barroom, bathroom, bedroom, boardroom, bridegroom, broadloom, checkroom, classroom, cloakroom, coatroom, consume, costume, courtroom, darkroom, dayroom, entomb, enwomb, exhume, foredoom, greenroom, guardroom, headroom, heirloom, homeroom, houseroom, illume, inhume, jibboom, Khartoum, legroom, legume, lunchroom, mudroom, mushroom, newsroom, perfume, playroom, poolroom, pressroom, presume, proofroom, relume, resume, salesroom, schoolroom, showroom, sickroom, simoom, stateroom, stockroom, storeroom, subsume, taproom, Targum, tearoom, toolroom, wardroom, washroom, workroom, anteroom, checkerbloom, dyer's broom, elbowroom, impostume, locker-room, miniboom, nom de plume, smoke-filled room, witches'-broom

²oom \um\ see ²UM

oomed \ümd\ groomed, plumed, wombed, well-groomed—*also pasts of verbs listed at* ¹OOM

oomer \ü-mər\ see UMER

oomily \ü-mə-lē\ gloomily, contumely

¹ooming \ü-mən\ see UMAN

²ooming \ü-miŋ\ see UMING

oomlet \üm-lət\ boomlet, plumelet

oomy \ü-mē\ bloomy, boomy,

doomy, fumy, gloomy,
plumy, rheumy, roomy,
spumy, costumey

¹oon \ün\ boon, Boone, coon,
croon, dune, goon, hewn,
June, loon, lune, moon, noon,
prune, rune, shoon, soon,
spoon, swoon, strewn, toon,
tune, aswoon, attune, baboon,
balloon, bassoon, buffoon,
Calhoun, cardoon, cartoon,
cocoon, commune, doubloon,
dragoon, festoon, fine-tune,
forenoon, gaboon, gadroon,
galloon, Gudrun, half-moon,
harpoon, immune, impugn,
jargoon, jejune, Kowloon,
Kunlun, lagoon, lampoon,
lardoon, maroon, monsoon,
Neptune, oppugn, Pashtun,
patroon, platoon, poltroon,
pontoon, premune, puccoon,
quadroon, raccoon, ratoon,
repugn, rockoon, rough-hewn,
saloon, shalloon, soupspoon,
spittoon, spontoon, teaspoon,
Torun, tribune, triune, tuchun,
tycoon, typhoon, untune,
Walloon, afternoon,
barracoon, Brigadoon,
Cameroon, demilune,
dessertspoon, honeymoon,
importune, macaroon,
octoroon, opportune,
pantaloon, picaroon,
picayune, rigadoon,
saskatoon, Saskatoon,
tablespoon, contrabassoon,
inopportune

²oon \ōn\ see ¹ONE

oona \ü-nə\ see UNA

oonal \ün-ᵊl\ see UNAL

oone \ün\ see ¹OON

ooner \ü-nər\ crooner, crowner,
lunar, pruner, schooner,
sooner, swooner, tuner,
harpooner, lacunar,
lampooner, oppugner,
honeymooner, semilunar

¹oonery \ün-rē\ buffoonery,
lampoonery, poltroonery

²oonery \ü-nə-rē\ see UNARY

ooney \ü-nē\ see OONY

oonie \ü-nē\ see OONY

ooning \ü-niŋ\ nooning,
ballooning, cartooning,
gadrooning

oonish \ü-nish\ moonish,
buffoonish, cartoonish,
picayunish

oonless \ün-ləs\ moonless,
tuneless, woundless

oons \ünz\ lunes, zounds,
eftsoons, afternoons—*also
plurals and possessives of
nouns and third person
singular presents of verbs
listed at* ¹OON

oony \ü-nē\ gooney, loony,
luny, Moonie, moony, muni,
puisne, puny, spoony, Zuni,
Mulroney

o-op \üp\ see ¹OOP

oop \üp\ bloop, coop, croup,
droop, drupe, dupe, goop,
group, hoop, loop, loupe,
poop, roup, scoop, sloop,
snoop, soup, stoop, stoup,
stupe, swoop, troop, troupe,
whoop, age-group, in-group,
out-group, recoup, regroup,
subgroup, T-group, alley-oop,
cock-a-hoop, Guadalupe,

Guadeloupe, nincompoop, paratroop, supergroup

ooped \üpd\ looped—*pasts of verbs listed at* OOP

oopee \ü-pē\ see OOPY

ooper \ü-pər\ blooper, cooper, Cooper, Cowper, duper, grouper, looper, scooper, snooper, stupor, swooper, super, trooper, trouper, party pooper, paratrooper, pooper-scooper, super-duper

ooping \ü-piŋ\ grouping, trooping, trouping

oopoe \ü-pü\ see OOH-POOH

oops \ùps\ hoops, oops, whoops, woops

oopy \ü-pē\ croupy, droopy, groupie, Kewpie, loopy, snoopy, soupy, Tupi, whoopee

¹oor \ōr\ see ¹OR

²oor \ùr\ see ¹URE

¹oorage \ùr-ij\ moorage, sewerage

²oorage \ōr-ij\ see ²ORAGE

³oorage \ȯr-ij\ see ³ORAGE

¹oore \ōr\ see ¹ORE

²oore \ùr\ see ¹URE

oored \ōrd\ see OARD

oorer \ōr-ər\ see ¹ORER

oori \ùr-ē\ see ¹URY

¹ooring \ōr-iŋ\ see ¹ORING

²ooring \ùr-iŋ\ see URING

¹oorish \ùr-ish\ boorish, Moorish, poorish

²oorish \ȯr-ish\ see ¹ORISH

oorly \ùr-lē\ see URELY

oorman \ōr-mən\ see OREMAN

oors \ōrz\ Bors, yours, drawers, indoors, outdoors, underdrawers, withindoors,

withoutdoors, Louis Quatorze—*also plurals and possessives of nouns and third person singular presents of verbs listed at* ¹ORE

oorsman \ōrz-mən\ see OARSMAN

oort \ȯrt\ see ¹ORT

oosa \ü-sə\ see ¹USA

¹oose \üs\ see ¹USE

²oose \üz\ see ²USE

¹ooser \ü-sər\ see UCER

²ooser \ü-zər\ see USER

oosey \ü-sē\ see UICY

¹oosh \üsh\ see OUCHE

²oosh \ùsh\ see ²USH

oost \üst\ boost, juiced, Proust, roost, langouste, produced, self-induced, Zlatoust—*also pasts of verbs listed at* ¹USE

oosy \ü-zē\ see OOZY

¹oot \ùt\ foot, put, root, Root, soot, afoot, barefoot, bigfoot, bird's-foot, Blackfoot, clubfoot, crow's-foot, enroot, flatfoot, forefoot, hotfoot, input, kaput, outfoot, output, Rajput, snakeroot, splayfoot, taproot, throughput, uproot, acre-foot, arrowroot, bitterroot, cajeput, candle-foot, gingerroot, orrisroot, pussyfoot, tenderfoot, underfoot

²oot \üt\ see UTE

³oot \ət\ see ¹UT

¹ootage \üt-ij\ fruitage, rootage, scutage

²ootage \ùt-ij\ footage, rootage

¹ooted \üt-əd\ booted, fruited, muted, suited, abluted, deep-rooted, jackbooted, pantsuited, voluted—*also pasts of verbs listed at* UTE

²**ooted** \ut-əd\ footed, barefooted, clubfooted, deep-rooted, duckfooted, fleet-footed, four-footed, light-footed, slow-footed, splayfooted, surefooted, web-footed, wing-footed, cloven-footed—*also pasts of verbs listed at* ¹OOT

¹**ooter** \ut-ər\ footer, putter, shot-putter, pussyfooter

²**ooter** \üt-ər\ see UTER

¹**ooth** \ü<u>th</u>\ smooth, soothe, tooth

²**ooth** \üth\ booth, Booth, couth, crwth, routh, ruth, Ruth, scouth, sleuth, sooth, tooth, truth, Truth, youth, bucktooth, Duluth, eyetooth, forsooth, half-truth, sawtooth, selcouth, tollbooth, uncouth, untruth, vermouth, snaggletooth

oothe \ü<u>th</u>\ see ¹OOTH

oothed \ütht\ toothed, gap-toothed, snaggletoothed

oothless \üth-ləs\ see UTHLESS

oothly \üth-lē\ soothly, uncouthly

oothy \ü-thē\ couthie, toothy

ootie \üt-ē\ see ¹OOTY

¹**ooting** \ut-iŋ\ footing, off-putting

²**ooting** \üt-iŋ\ see UTING

ootle \üt-ᵊl\ see UTILE

ootless \üt-ləs\ bootless, fruitless

ootlet \üt-lət\ fruitlet, rootlet

oots \üts\ boots, firstfruits, grassroots, slyboots, Vaduz, shoot-the-chutes—*also plurals and possessives of nouns and third person singular presents of verbs listed at* UTE

ootsie \ut-sē\ footsie, tootsie

¹**ooty** \üt-ē\ beauty, booty, Clootie, cootie, cutie, duty, footy, fluty, fruity, hooty, rooty, snooty, sooty, tutti, zooty, agouti, Djibouti, Funafuti, heavy-duty, persecutee, tutti-frutti

²**ooty** \ut-ē\ rooty, sooty, tutti

³**ooty** \ət-ē\ see UTTY

oove \üv\ see ³OVE

oover \ü-vər\ see ³OVER

oovy \ü-vē\ groovy, movie

ooze \üz\ see ²USE

oozer \ü-zər\ see USER

oozle \ü-zəl\ see ²USAL

oozy \ü-zē\ bluesy, boozy, choosy, floozy, newsy, oozy, Susie, woozy, Jacuzzi

¹**op** \äp\ bop, chap, chop, clop, cop, crop, drop, flop, fop, glop, hop, knop, lop, mop, op, plop, pop, prop, scop, shop, slop, sop, stop, strop, swap, top, whop, wop, Aesop, airdrop, atop, backdrop, backstop, bakeshop, barhop, bebop, bellhop, blacktop, bookshop, carhop, cartop, chop-chop, clip-clop, clop-clop, coin-op, cooktop, co-op, desktop, dewdrop, doorstop, dramshop, Dunlop, eardrop, eavesdrop, ESOP, estop, f-stop, fire-stop, flattop, flip-flop, foretop, grogshop, gumdrop, hardtop, hedgehop, high-top, hilltop, hip-hop,

hockshop, housetop, joypop, maintop, milksop, nonstop, one-stop, outcrop, pawnshop, pop-top, ragtop, raindrop, redtop, ripstop, rooftop, sharecrop, shortstop, skin-pop, slipslop, snowdrop, soursop, stonecrop, sweatshop, sweetshop, teardrop, tip-top, treetop, unstop, workshop, agitprop, barbershop, carrottop, countertop, double-crop, double-stop, Ethiop, island-hop, lollipop, malaprop, mom-and-pop, mountaintop, overtop, table-hop, tabletop, techno-pop, teenybop, turboprop, whistle-stop, window-shop, Babelthuap

²op \ō\ see ¹OW

opa \ō-pə\ opa, opah, Europa

opah \ō-pə\ see OPA

opal \ō-pəl\ copal, nopal, opal, Opal, Simferopol, Constantinople

ope \ōp\ cope, coup, dope, grope, holp, hope, Hope, lope, mope, nope, ope, pope, Pope, rope, scop, scope, slope, soap, stope, taupe, tope, trope, aslope, borescope, downslope, elope, gantlope, gantelope, Good Hope, myope, nightscope, pyrope, sandsoap, soft-soap, tightrope, towrope, antelope, antipope, calliope, cantaloupe, chronoscope, envelope, epitope, Ethiope, gyroscope, horoscope, interlope, isotope, kinescope, microscope, misanthrope,

periscope, phalarope, radarscope, sniperscope, snooperscope, stethoscope, telescope, heliotrope, kaleidoscope, stereoscope

opean \ō-pē-ən\ see OPIAN

opee \ō-pē\ see OPI

open \ō-pən\ holpen, open, reopen, wide-open

opence \əp-əns\ see UPPANCE

openny \əp-nē\ threepenny, twopenny

oper \ō-pər\ coper, doper, groper, loper, moper, roper, soaper, toper, eloper, no-hoper, soft-soaper, interloper

opera \äp-rə\ see OPRA

opery \ō-prē\ popery, ropery

opey \ō-pē\ see OPI

oph \ōf\ see OAF

ophagous \äf-ə-gəs\ coprophagous, esophagus, necrophagous, sarcophagus, zoophagous, anthropophagous

ophagy \äf-ə-jē\ geophagy, coprophagy, anthropophagy

¹ophe \ō-fē\ see OPHY

²ophe \ōf\ see ²OFF

opher \ō-fər\ see OFER

ophet \äf-ət\ see OFIT

¹ophic \äf-ik\ strophic, antistrophic, apostrophic, catastrophic

²ophic \ō-fik\ strophic, trophic, atrophic

ophical \äf-i-kəl\ philosophical, theosophical

ophie \ō-fē\ see OPHY

ophir \ō-fər\ see OFER

ophonous \äf-ə-nəs\ cacophonous, homophonous

ophony \äf-ə-nē\ cacophony,

colophony, homophony, monophony, theophany, heterophony, stereophony

ophy \ō-fē\ Sophie, sophy, strophe, trophy

opi \ō-pē\ dopey, Hopi, mopey, ropy, soapy, topee, topi

opia \ō-pē-ə\ dystopia, myopia, sinopia, utopia, cornucopia, Ethiopia

opian \ō-pē-ən\ Aesopian, cyclopean, dystopian, utopian, Ethiopian, cornucopian

¹opic \äp-ik\ topic, tropic, Aesopic, anthropic, ectopic, Ethiopic, subtropic, gyroscopic, hygroscopic, macroscopic, microscopic, misanthropic, periscopic, philanthropic, semitropic, stethoscopic, telescopic, kaleidoscopic, stereoscopic

²opic \ō-pik\ tropic, myopic, Ethiopic, psychotropic

opical \äp-i-kəl\ topical, tropical, anthropical, subtropical, microscopical, philanthropical, semitropical, Neotropical

oplar \äp-lər\ see OPPLER

ople \ō-pəl\ see OPAL

opol \ō-pəl\ see OPAL

¹opolis \äp-ə-ləs\ propolis, acropolis, cosmopolis, necropolis, Heliopolis, megalopolis, metropolis, Florianopolis

²opolis \äp-ləs\ see OPLESS

opolist \äp-ə-ləst\ monopolist, bibliopolist

opoly \äp-ə-lē\ choppily, floppily, sloppily, duopoly, monopoly, vox populi, oligopoly, Tiruchchirappalli

oppa \äp-ə\ see ¹APA

opped \äpt\ see OPT

oppel \äp-əl\ see OPPLE

opper \äp-ər\ bopper, chopper, copper, cropper, dropper, flopper, hopper, lopper, mopper, popper, proper, shopper, stopper, swapper, topper, whopper, yapper, clodhopper, eavesdropper, eyedropper, eyepopper, grasshopper, hedgehopper, improper, job-hopper, joypopper, leafhopper, namedropper, rockhopper, sharecropper, showstopper, skin-popper, table-hopper, teenybopper, treehopper, woodchopper, window-shopper

oppery \äp-rē\ coppery, foppery

oppet \äp-ət\ moppet, poppet

oppily \äp-ə-lē\ see OPOLY

oppiness \äp-ē-nəs\ choppiness, floppiness, sloppiness

opping \äp-iŋ\ hopping, sopping, topping, whopping, clodhopping, eye-popping, job-hopping, name-dropping, outcropping

opple \äp-əl\ popple, stopple, topple, estoppel

oppler \äp-lər\ Doppler, poplar

oppy \äp-ē\ choppy, copy, crappie, floppy, gloppy, hoppy, kopje, poppy, sloppy, soppy, stroppy, jalopy, okapi, serape, microcopy, Nahuel Huapi, photocopy

opra \äp-rə\ copra, opera

ops \äps\ chops, copse, Ops, tops, beechdrops, cyclops, eyedrops, Pelops, pinedrops, sundrops, muttonchops, triceratops—*also plurals and possessives of nouns and third person singular presents of verbs listed at* ¹OP

opse \äps\ see OPS

opsy \äp-sē\ dropsy, autopsy, biopsy, necropsy

opt \äpt\ Copt, knopped, opt, topped, adopt, close-cropped, co-opt, end-stopped—*also pasts of verbs listed at* ¹OP

opter \äp-tər\ copter, adopter, helicopter, ornithopter

optic \äp-tik\ Coptic, optic, panoptic, synoptic, electro-optic

optimist \äp-tə-məst\ optimist, Optimist, Soroptimist

option \äp-shən\ option, adoption, co-option

optric \äp-trik\ catoptric, dioptric

opula \äp-yə-lə\ copula, scopula

opulace \äp-yə-ləs\ populace, populous

opulate \äp-yə-lāt\ copulate, populate, over-populate

opuli \äp-ə-lē\ see OPOLY

opulous \äp-yə-ləs\ see OPULACE

opus \ō-pəs\ opus, Canopus, magnum opus, pithecanthropus

¹opy \ō-pē\ see OPI

²opy \äp-ē\ see OPPY

¹oque \ōk\ see OKE

²oque \äk\ see ¹OCK

³oque \ȯk\ see ALK

oquial \ō-kwē-əl\ colloquial, ventriloquial

¹or \ȯr\ boar, Boer, Bohr, bore, chore, core, corps, crore, door, drawer, floor, for, fore, four, frore, gore, Gore, hoar, hoer, kor, lore, Moore, mor, more, More, nor, o'er, oar, or, ore, poor, pore, pour, roar, score, shore, snore, soar, sore, splore, spoor, spore, store, swore, Thor, tor, tore, torr, war, whore, wore, yore, your, you're, abhor, actor, adore, afore, and/or, ashore, backdoor, bailor, bandore, Beardmore, bedsore, before, bezoar, bookstore, candor, captor, centaur, claymore, closed-door, condor, decor, deplore, dime-store, donor, downpour, drugstore, encore, ephor, explore, Exmoor, eyesore, feoffor, fetor, Fillmore, folklore, footsore, forebore, forswore, forscore, galore, hardcore, ichor, ignore, implore, Indore, indoor, inpour, inshore, Lahore, lakeshore, Lenore, lessor, memoir, mentor, Mysore, nearshore, Nestor, offshore, onshore, outdoor, outpour, outsoar, outwore, pastor, psywar, rancor, rapport, raptor, Realtor, restore, rhetor, savior, seafloor, seashore, sector, seignior, senhor, señor, sensor, settlor, Seymour, signor, smoothbore, sophomore, stentor, stertor, stressor, stridor, subfloor, temblor, tensor, therefor, therefore, threescore, Timor, trapdoor, turgor, uproar, vendor, wherefore, woodlore, albacore, alongshore, anaphor, anymore, archosaur, Baltimore, Bangalore, Barrymore, brontosaur, carnivore, CD4, Coimbatore, commodore, comprador, confessor, consignor, corridor, cuspidor, devisor, dinosaur, door-to-door, Ecuador, either-or, Eleanor, Eleanore, elector, Elinor, en rapport, evermore, franchisor, furthermore, guarantor, Gwalior, hackamore, hadrosaur, hellebore, herbivore, heretofore, humidor, Labrador, louis d'or, man-of-war, manticore, matador, metaphor, meteor, millepore, Minotaur, mirador, Mount Rushmore, nevermore, omnivore, out-of-door, petit four, picador, pinafore, pompadour, predator, promisor, pterosaur, reservoir, sagamore, Salvador, Salvatore, semaphore, Singapore, stegosaur, stevedore, superstore, sycamore, Theodore, theretofore, troubador, tug-of-war, two-by-four, uncalled-for, underscore, vavasor, warrantor, alienor, ambassador, ankylosaur, conquistador, conservator,

Corregidor, de Pompadour, El Salvador, esprit de corps, forevermore, hereinbefore, ichthyosaur, insectivore, legislator, plesiosaur, San Salvadore, toreador, tyrannosaur, Ulan Bator, administrator, lobster thermidor, Talleyrand-Perigord

²or \ər\ see ¹EUR

ora \ōr-ə\ aura, bora, Cora, Dora, flora, Flora, hora, Laura, Lora, mora, Nora, sora, Torah, Andorra, angora, aurora, Aurora, begorra, camorra, fedora, gemara, Gomorrah, Lenora, Masora, menorah, pandora, Pandora, remora, senhora, señora, signora, Sonora, grandiflora, Juiz de Fora, Leonora, Simchas Torah, Tuscarora, Lomas de Zamora

orable \ōr-ə-bəl\ horrible, pourable, storable, adorable, deplorable, restorable

orace \òr-əs\ see AURUS

oracle \òr-ə-kəl\ coracle, oracle

orage \ōr-ij\ borage, floorage, forage, porridge, storage

orah \ōr-ə\ see ORA

¹oral \ōr-əl\ aural, choral, coral, Coral, floral, laurel, Laurel, moral, oral, quarrel, sorrel, aboral, amoral, auroral, balmoral, binaural, immoral, monaural, peroral, restoral, sororal

²oral \òrl\ schorl, whorl, ceorl

oram \ōr-əm\ see ORUM

orate \ōr-ət\ see ORET

orative \ōr-ət-iv\ explorative, pejorative, restorative

oray \ə-rē\ see URRY

orb \ȯrb\ forb, orb, sorb, Sorb, absorb, adsorb, desorb, resorb

orbate \ȯr-bət\ see ORBIT

orbeil \ȯr-bəl\ see ORBEL

orbel \ȯr-bəl\ corbeil, corbel, warble

orbent \ȯr-bənt\ absorbent, immunosorbent

orbet \ȯr-bət\ see ORBIT

orbit \ȯr-bət\ orbit, sorbet, adsorbate

orc \ȯrk\ see ²ORK

orca \ȯr-kə\ orca, Majorca, Minorca, Palma de Mallorca

orcas \ȯr-kəs\ Dorcas, orchis

orce \ȯrs\ see ¹OURSE

orced \ȯrst\ see ¹ORST

¹orceful \ōrs-fəl\ forceful, resourceful

²orceful \ȯrs-fəl\ see ORSEFUL

¹orcement \ōr-smənt\ deforcement, divorcement, enforcement, reinforcement

²orcement \ȯr-smənt\ see ORSEMENT

orcer \ōr-sər\ courser, enforcer, reinforcer—*also comparatives of adjectives listed at* ¹OURSE

orch \ȯrch\ porch, scorch, torch, blowtorch, sunporch

orcher \ȯr-chər\ scorcher, torture

orchid \ȯr-kəd\ forked, orchid, cryptorchid, monorchid

orchis \ȯr-kəs\ see ORCAS

¹ord \ōrd\ see OARD

²ord \ərd\ see IRD

³ord \ȯr\ see ¹OR

ordan \ȯrd-ᵊn\ see ²ARDEN

ordancy \ȯrd-ᵊn-sē\ mordancy, discordancy

ordant \ȯrd-ᵊnt\ mordant, mordent, accordant, concordant, discordant

orde \ōrd\ see OARD

orded \ȯrd-əd\ see ²ARDED

ordent \ȯrd-ᵊnt\ see ORDANT

order \ȯrd-ər\ boarder, border, corder, order, warder, awarder, disorder, recorder, reorder, rewarder, made-to-order

ordered \ȯrd-ərd\ bordered, ordered—*also pasts of verbs listed at* ORDER

orders \ȯrd-ərz\ Borders—*also possessives and plurals of nouns and third person singular presents of verbs listed at* ORDER

ordial \ȯrd-ē-əl\ exordial, primordial

ordid \ȯrd-əd\ see ²ARDED

¹ording \ȯrd-iŋ\ lording, recording, rewarding—*also present participles of verbs listed at* ²OARD

²ording \ərd-iŋ\ see ERDING

ordingly \ȯrd-iŋ-lē\ accordingly, rewardingly

ordion \ȯrd-ē-ən\ accordion, Edwardian

ordist \ȯrd-əst\ recordist, clavichordist, harpsichordist

ordon \ȯrd-ᵊn\ see ²ARDEN

ordure \ȯr-jər\ see ORGER

¹ordy \ȯrd-ē\ Geordie, Lordy, awardee

²ordy \ərd-ē\ see URDY

¹ore \ōr-ē\ see ORY

²ore \u̇r\ see ¹URE

³**ore** \ər-ə\ see ¹OROUGH

⁴**ore** \ōr\ see ¹OR

oreal \ōr-ē-əl\ see ORIAL

orean \ōr-ē-ən\ see ORIAN

oreas \ōr-ē-əs\ see ORIOUS

ored \ōrd\ see OARD

oredom \ōrd-əm\ boredom, whoredom

orehead \ór-əd\ see ORRID

¹**oreign** \är-ən\ see ¹ORIN

²**oreign** \ór-ən\ see ²ORIN

oreigner \ór-ə-nər\ see ORONER

orem \ōr-əm\ see ORUM

oreman \ōr-mən\ corpsman, doorman, foreman, longshoreman

orence \ór-ən(t)s\ see AWRENCE

oreous \ōr-ē-əs\ see ORIOUS

orer \ōr-ər\ borer, corer, floorer, pourer, roarer, scorer, schnorrer, snorer, soarer, adorer, deplorer, explorer— *also comparatives of adjectives listed at* ¹ORE

¹**ores** \ōr-əs\ see ¹ORUS

²**ores** \ōrz\ Azores, indoors, outdoors—*also possessives and plurals of nouns and third person singular presents of verbs listed at* ¹ORE

³**ores** \ór-əs\ see AURUS

oreson \órs-ⁿn\ see OARSEN

orest \ór-əst\ see ¹ORIST

orester \ór-ə-stər\ see ORISTER

oret \ōr-ət\ floret, sororate

oreum \ōr-ē-əm\ see ORIUM

oreward \ōr-wərd\ see OREWORD

oreword \ōr-wərd\ foreword, shoreward

orey \ór-ē\ see ORY

orf \órf\ see ORPH

¹**org** \órg\ morgue, cyborg

²**org** \ór-ē\ see ORY

organ \ór-gən\ gorgon, morgan, Morgan, organ, Glamorgan, Demogorgon, Mid Glamorgan, South Glamorgan, West Glamorgan

orge \órj\ forge, George, gorge, scourge, disgorge, drop-forge, engorge, Lloyd George, reforge, Olduvai Gorge

orger \ór-jər\ bordure, forger, gorger, ordure

orgi \ór-gē\ see ORGY

orgia \ór-jə\ Borgia, Georgia, Strait of Georgia

orgian \ór-jən\ Georgian, Swedenborgian

orgon \ór-gən\ see ORGAN

orgue \órg\ see ORG

orgy \ór-gē\ corgi, porgy

ori \ór-ē\ see ORY

oria \ór-ē-ə\ gloria, Gloria, noria, scoria, centaurea, euphoria, Peoria, Pretoria, victoria, Victoria, Vitoria, phantasmagoria

orial \ōr-ē-əl\ boreal, oriel, oriole, arboreal, armorial, auctorial, authorial, cantorial, censorial, corporeal, cursorial, factorial, fossorial, manorial, marmoreal, memorial, pictorial, praetorial, proctorial, raptorial, rectorial, sartorial, seignorial, sensorial, sponsorial, tonsorial, tutorial, uxorial, vectorial, conductorial, consistorial, curatorial, dictatorial, directorial, editorial, equatorial, immemorial,

incorporeal, janitorial,
monitorial, monsignorial,
natatorial, piscatorial,
preceptorial, professorial,
purgatorial, reportorial,
senatorial, territorial,
ambassadorial, conservatorial,
combinatorial, conspiratorial,
extracorporeal, gladiatorial,
gubernatorial, imperatorial,
inquisitorial, legislatorial,
procuratorial, propriatorial,
prosecutorial, extraterritorial,
improvisatorial

oriam \ōr-ē-əm\ see ORIUM

orian \ȯr-ē-ən\ Dorian, saurian,
Taurean, aurorean, Gregorian,
historian, Nestorian,
praetorian, stentorian,
victorian, dinosaurian,
hyperborean, Oratorian,
prehistorian, senatorian,
terpsichorean, salutatorian,
valedictorian

oriant \ōr-ē-ənt\ see ORIENT

oriat \ȯr-ē-ət\ see ²AUREATE

oric \ȯr-ik\ auric, choric, Doric,
toric, Armoric, caloric,
clitoric, dysphoric, euphoric,
folkloric, historic, phosphoric,
plethoric, pyloric, anaphoric,
cataphoric, metaphoric,
meteoric, paregoric,
prehistoric, sophomoric,
aleatoric, phantasmagoric

orical \ȯr-i-kəl\ auricle,
historical, rhetorical,
ahistorical, allegorical,
categorical, metaphorical,
oratorical, transhistorical,
sociohistorical

orics \ȯr-iks\ see ORYX

orid \ȯr-əd\ see ORRID

oriel \ōr-ē-əl\ see ORIAL

orient \ōr-ē-ənt\ orient, Orient,
euphoriant

¹orin \ȯr-ən\ florin, foreign,
Lauren, Orrin, sarin, sporran,
warren, Warren, Gagarin,
cyclosporine

²orin \ōr-ən\ see ¹ORINE

¹orine \ōr-ən\ chlorine, florin,
cephalosporin

²orine \ȯr-ən\ see ¹ORIN

oring \ōr-iŋ\ boring, flooring,
roaring, shoring, inpouring,
longshoring, outpouring, rip-
roaring—*also present
participles of verbs listed at*
¹OR

öring \ər-iŋ\ see URRING

oriole \ōr-ē-əl\ see ORIAL

orious \ȯr-ē-əs\ aureus, Boreas,
glorious, arboreous,
censorious, inglorious,
laborious, notorious, sartorius,
uproarious, uxorious,
vainglorious, victorious,
meritorious

¹oris \ōr-əs\ see ¹ORUS

²oris \ȯr-əs\ see AURUS

¹orish \ȯr-ish\ boarish, poorish,
whorish, folklorish

²orish \ür-ish\ see ¹OORISH

orist \ȯr-əst\ florist, forest,
Forrest, sorest, afforest, Black
Forest, deforest, folklorist,
reforest, allegorist, Petrified
Forest—*also superlatives of
adjectives listed at* ¹OR

orister \ȯr-ə-stər\ chorister,
forester

ority \ȯr-ət-ē\ authority,
majority, minority, priority,

seniority, sonority, apriority, exteriority, inferiority, interiority, posteriority, superiority

orium \ōr-ē-əm\ castoreum, ciborium, emporium, pastorium, scriptorium, sensorium, auditorium, crematorium, in memoriam, moratorium, natatorium, sanitorium, sudatorium

¹**ork** \ərk\ burke, Burke, chirk, cirque, clerk, dirk, Dirk, irk, jerk, kirk, Kirk, lurk, murk, perk, quirk, shirk, smirk, stirk, Turk, work, yerk, zerk, artwork, berserk, breastwork, brickwork, bridgework, brightwork, brushwork, capework, casework, clockwork, coachwork, de Klerk, ductwork, Dunkirk, earthwork, falsework, fieldwork, firework, flatwork, footwork, formwork, framework, goldwork, groundwork, guesswork, hackwork, handwork, headwork, homework, housework, ironwork, knee-jerk, legwork, lifework, make-work, meshwork, millwork, network, outwork, paintwork, patchwork, piecework, presswork, quillwork, rework, roadwork, salesclerk, schoolwork, Selkirk, Southwark, spadework, steelwork, stickwork, stonework, teamwork, timework, topwork, waxwork, webwork, woodwork,

basketwork, busywork, crewelwork, donkeywork, fancywork, handiwork, journeywork, laquerwork, masterwork, needlework, openwork, overwork, paperwork, plasterwork, soda jerk, wonderwork, cabinetwork

²**ork** \órk\ cork, Cork, dork, fork, pork, quark, stork, torque, York, bulwark, Cape York, futhorc, hayfork, New York, North York, pitchfork, uncork

¹**orked** \órkt\ corked, forked, uncorked

²**orked** \ór-kəd\ see ORCHID

¹**orker** \ər-kər\ jerker, lurker, shirker, worker, berserker, caseworker, dockworker, fieldworker, handworker, ironworker, outworker, pieceworker, steelworker, tearjerker, wageworker, woodworker, autoworker, metalworker, needleworker, wonderworker

²**orker** \ór-kər\ corker, forker, porker, torquer

orkie \ór-kē\ see ORKY

orking \ər-kiŋ\ hardworking, tear-jerking, woodworking, wonder-working

orky \ór-kē\ corky, dorky, forky, Gorky, porky, Yorkie

¹**orl** \ərl\ see ¹IRL

²**orl** \órl\ see ³ORAL

orld \ərld\ burled, knurled, whorled, world, dreamworld, New World, old-world, demiworld, microworld, netherworld, otherworld, underworld—*also pasts of verbs listed at* ¹IRL

orled \ərld\ *see* ORLD

¹**orm** \ərm\ berm, firm, germ, herm, perm, Perm, sperm, squirm, term, therm, worm, affirm, bookworm, budworm, confirm, cutworm, deperm, deworm, earthworm, flatworm, glowworm, heartworm, hookworm, hornworm, inchworm, infirm, long-term, lugworm, lungworm, midterm, pinworm, ringworm, roundworm, sandworm, screwworm, short-term, silkworm, tapeworm, woodworm, angleworm, armyworm, caddis worm, disaffirm, disconfirm, gymnosperm, pachyderm, reconfirm, angiosperm, echinoderm

²**orm** \órm\ corm, dorm, form, norm, storm, swarm, warm, aswarm, barnstorm, brainstorm, conform, deform, Delorme, firestorm, free-form, hailstorm, inform, L-form, landform, life-form, lukewarm, perform, planform, platform, postform, preform, rainstorm, re-form, reform, sandstorm, snowstorm, transform, triform, windstorm, chloroform, cruciform, dendriform, dentiform, disciform, fungiform, fusiform, letterform, microform, multiform, nonconform, thunderstorm, uniform, vermiform

ormable \ór-mə-bəl\ formable, conformable, performable, transformable

ormal \ór-məl\ formal, normal, abnormal, conformal, informal, subnormal, paranormal, semiformal, supernormal

ormally \ór-mə-lē\ formally, formerly, normally, stormily, abnormally, informally, subnormally, paranormally, supernormally

orman \ór-mən\ corpsman, Mormon, Norman, Anglo-Norman

ormance \ór-məns\ conformance, performance, nonconformance

ormant \ór-mənt\ dormant, formant, informant

ormative \ór-mət-iv\ formative, normative, informative, performative, reformative, transformative

orme \órm\ *see* ²ORM

ormed \órmd\ formed, normed, informed, malformed, unformed—*also pasts of verbs listed at* ²ORM

¹**ormer** \ór-mər\ dormer, former, swarmer, warmer, barnstormer, benchwarmer, brainstormer, conformer, heart-warmer, informer, performer, reformer, transformer

²**ormer** \ər-mər\ *see* URMUR

ormerly \ȯr-mə-lē\ see
  ORMALLY
ormie \ȯr-mē\ see ¹ORMY
ormily \ȯr-mə-lē\ see ORMALLY
orming \ȯr-miŋ\ brainstorming,
  heartwarming, housewarming,
  habit-forming, nonperforming
ormist \ȯr-məst\ warmest,
  conformist, reformist,
  nonconformist
ormity \ȯr-mət-ē\ conformity,
  deformity, enormity,
  nonconformity, uniformity
ormless \ȯrm-ləs\ formless,
  gormless
ormon \ȯr-mən\ see ORMAN
¹**ormy** \ȯr-mē\ stormy, dormie
²**ormy** \ər-mē\ see ERMY
¹**orn** \ȯrn\ born, borne, bourn,
  corn, horn, lorn, morn,
  mourn, Norn, porn, scorn,
  shorn, sworn, thorn, torn,
  warn, worn, acorn, adorn,
  airborne, alphorn, althorn,
  baseborn, bicorne, bighorn,
  blackthorn, boxthorn,
  broomcorn, buckthorn,
  bullhorn, Cape Horn,
  careworn, Christ's-thorn,
  Dearborn, dehorn, earthborn,
  einkorn, firethorn, firstborn,
  foghorn, foreborn, foresworn,
  forewarn, forlorn, forworn,
  freeborn, greenhorn,
  hartshorn, hawthorn,
  Hawthorne, highborn, inborn,
  inkhorn, krummhorn, leghorn,
  longhorn, lovelorn, lowborn,
  newborn, outworn, popcorn,
  pronghorn, reborn, seaborne,
  shipborne, shoehorn,
  shopworn, shorthorn,

skyborne, soilborne, staghorn,
stillborn, stinkhorn, suborn,
timeworn, tinhorn, tricorne,
trueborn, twice-born, unborn,
unworn, wayworn, wellborn,
well-worn, wind-borne,
alpenhorn, barleycorn,
Capricorn, flügelhorn,
foreign-born, Golden Horn,
Matterhorn, peppercorn,
unicorn, waterborne,
waterworn, weatherworn,
winterbourne
²**orn** \ərn\ see URN
ornament \ȯr-nə-mənt\
  ornament, tournament
¹**orne** \ōrn\ see ¹ORN
²**orne** \ȯrn\ see ²ORN
orned \ȯrnd\ horned, thorned,
  unadorned—*also pasts of
  verbs listed at* ²ORN
orner \ȯr-nər\ warner, Warner,
  Cape Horner, dehorner,
  suborner
ornery \än-rē\ see ¹ANNERY
orney \ər-nē\ see ¹OURNEY
ornful \ȯrn-fəl\ mournful,
  scornful
ornice \ȯr-nəs\ cornice, ornice,
  notornis
orning \ȯr-niŋ\ morning,
  mourning, warning, aborning
ornis \ȯr-nəs\ see ORNICE
ornment \ərn-mənt\ see
  ERNMENT
orny \ȯr-nē\ corny, horny,
  porny, thorny, tourney
¹**oro** \ər-ə\ see ¹OROUGH
²**oro** \ō-rō\ Chamorro, Mindoro,
  Rio de Oro
oroner \ȯr-ə-nər\ coroner,
  foreigner, warrener

¹orough \ər-ə\ borough, burgh, burro, burrow, curragh, furrow, ore, thorough, Gainsborough, Greensboro, Roxborough, Scarborough, Yarborough, Edinburgh, kookaburra, Peterborough, Soke of Peterborough, Huntingdon and Peterborough

²orough \ər-ō\ see ¹URROW

¹orous \ōr-əs\ see ¹ORUS

²orous \ȯr-əs\ see AURUS

orp \ȯrp\ dorp, gorp, thorp, warp, Australorp, Krugersdorp, octothorp, Oglethorpe

orpe \ȯrp\ see ORP

orper \ȯr-pər\ dorper, torpor

orph \ȯrf\ corf, dwarf, morph, Düsseldorf, anthropomorph

orphan \ȯr-fən\ orphan, endorphin, beta-endorphin

orpheus \ȯr-fē-əs\ Morpheus, Orpheus

orphic \ȯr-fik\ orphic, ectomorphic, endomorphic, mesomorphic, pseudomorphic, metamorphic, anthropomorphic

orphin \ȯr-fən\ see ORPHAN

orphous \ȯr-fəs\ amorphous, isomorphous

orphrey \ȯr-frē\ orphrey, porphyry

orphyrin \ȯr-fə-rən\ see ARFARIN

orphyry \ȯr-frē\ see ORPHREY

orpoise \ȯr-pəs\ see ORPUS

orpor \ȯr-pər\ see ORPER

orps \ōr\ see ¹OR

¹orpsman \ōr-mən\ see OREMAN

²orpsman \ȯr-mən\ see ORMAN

orpus \ȯr-pəs\ corpus, porpoise, habeas corpus

orque \ȯrk\ see ²ORK

orquer \ȯr-kər\ see ²ORKER

¹orra \är-ə\ see ¹ARA

²orra \ȯr-ə\ see ²ORA

³orra \ō-rə\ see ¹ORA

orrader \är-əd-ər\ see ORRIDOR

¹orrah \ōr-ə\ see ORA

²orrah \är-ə\ see ¹ARA

¹orran \är-ən\ see ¹ORIN

²orran \ȯr-ən\ see ²ORIN

orrence \ȯr-əns\ see AWRENCE

orrel \ȯr-əl\ see ²ORAL

orrent \ȯr-ənt\ horrent, torrent, warrant, abhorrent

¹orrer \ȯr-ər\ borer, horror, roarer, schnorrer, sorer, abhorrer, explorer

²orrer \ōr-ər\ see ¹ORER

orres \ȯr-əs\ see AURUS

orrest \ȯr-əst\ see ¹ORIST

orrible \ȯr-ə-bəl\ see ²ORABLE

orrid \ȯr-əd\ florid, horrid, torrid

¹orridge \är-ij\ see ¹ORAGE

²orridge \ȯr-ij\ see ³ORAGE

orridor \är-əd-ər\ corridor, forrader

¹orrie \är-ē\ see ¹ARI

²orrie \ȯr-ē\ see ORY

orrier \ȯr-ē-ər\ see ARRIOR

orrin \ȯr-ən\ see ²ORIN

¹orris \är-əs\ charas, Juárez, Maurice, morris, Morris, Norris, orris, Banaras, Benares, Polaris, Ciudad Juárez

²orris \ōr-əs\ see ¹ORUS

³orris \ȯr-əs\ see AURUS

orro \ō-rō\ see ²ORO

orror \ór-ər\ see ¹ORRER

¹**orrow** \är-ō\ borrow, claro, morrow, sorrow, taro, Pizarro, saguaro, tomorrow, Catanzaro, Kilimanjaro, Mohenjo-Daro

²**orrow** \är-ə\ see ¹ARA

¹**orry** \är-ē\ see ¹ARI

²**orry** \ər-ē\ see URRY

ors \ōrz\ see OORS

orsal \ór-səl\ see ORSEL

¹**orse** \órs\ coarse, corse, course, force, gorse, hoarse, horse, Morse, Norse, source, clotheshorse, concourse, deforce, discourse, divorce, endorse, enforce, extrorse, introrse, midcourse, packhorse, perforce, post-horse, racecourse, racehorse, recourse, remorse, retrorse, sawhorse, stringcourse, unhorse, war-horse, Whitehorse, workhorse, charley horse, Crazy Horse, hobbyhorse, nonrecourse, stalking-horse, reinforce, watercourse

²**orse** \ərs\ see ERSE

orseful \órs-fəl\ forceful, remorseful, resourceful

orsel \ór-səl\ dorsal, morsel

orseman \ór-smən\ horseman, Norseman

orsement \ór-smənt\ endorsement, reinforcement

orsen \ərs-ᵊn\ see ERSON

orser \ər-sər\ see URSOR

orset \ór-sət\ corset, Dorset

orsey \ór-sē\ see ORSY

orsion \ór-shən\ see ²ORTION

¹**orst** \órst\ forced, horst—*also pasts of verbs listed at* ¹ORSE

²**orst** \ərst\ see URST

orsted \ər-stəd\ see ERSTED

orsum \ór-səm\ dorsum, foursome

orsy \ór-sē\ gorsy, horsey

¹**ort** \órt\ boart, bort, court, fort, forte, mort, Oort, ort, port, Porte, quart, short, snort, sort, sport, swart, thwart, tort, torte, wart, wort, abort, airport, amort, aport, assort, athwart, backcourt, bellwort, birthwort, bistort, Bridgeport, cavort, cohort, colewort, comport, consort, contort, crosscourt, deport, disport, distort, downcourt, effort, escort, exhort, export, extort, forecourt, frontcourt, glasswort, gosport, half-court, homeport, milkwort, Newport, outport, passport, presort, purport, ragwort, report, re-sort, resort, retort, seaport, Shreveport, spaceport, spoilsport, Stockport, support, transport, bladderwort, davenport, life-support, nonsupport, pennywort, Saint-John's wort, teleport, ultrashort, worrywart, pianoforte, underreport

²**ort** \ōr\ see ¹OR

³**ort** \ərt\ see ¹ERT

ortable \órt-ə-bəl\ portable, deportable, exportable, importable, reportable, supportable, transportable, insupportable

ortage \ort-ij\ portage, shortage, colportage

ortal \ort-ᵊl\ chortle, mortal, portal, quartile, immortal

ortar \ort-ər\ see ORTER

ortative \ort-ət-iv\ hortative, portative, assortative, exhortative

¹orte \ort\ see ¹ORT

²orte \ort-ē\ see ORTY

orted \ort-əd\ warted, assorted, ill-sorted—*also pasts of verbs listed at* ¹ORT

ortedly \ort-əd-lē\ purportedly, reportedly

orten \ort-ᵊn\ quartan, shorten, foreshorten

orter \ort-ər\ mortar, porter, Porter, quarter, snorter, sorter, colporteur, distorter, exhorter, exporter, extorter, headquarter, importer, lambs-quarter, reporter, resorter, ripsnorter, transporter—*also comparatives of adjectives listed at* ¹ORT

orteur \ort-ər\ see ORTER

¹orth \orth\ forth, Forth, fourth, north, North, thenceforth, Firth of Forth

²orth \ərth\ see IRTH

orthful \ərth-fəl\ see IRTHFUL

orthless \ərth-ləs\ see IRTHLESS

orthy \ər-thē\ earthy, worthy, airworthy, blameworthy, Galsworthy, newsworthy, noteworthy, praiseworthy, seaworthy, trustworthy, creditworthy

ortic \ort-ik\ see ²ARTIC

ortical \ort-i-kəl\ cortical, vortical

ortie \ort-ē\ see ORTY

orting \ort-iŋ\ sporting, self-supporting

ortion \or-shən\ portion, torsion, abortion, apportion, contortion, distortion, extorsion, extortion, proportion, retortion, disproportion, proabortion, reapportion, antiabortion

ortionate \or-shnət\ extortionate, proportionate, disproportionate

ortionist \or-shnəst\ abortionist, contortionist, extortionist

ortis \ort-əs\ fortis, mortise, tortoise, aquafortis, rigor mortis

ortise \ort-əs\ see ORTIS

ortive \ort-iv\ sportive, abortive, contortive, extortive

ortle \ort-ᵊl\ see ORTAL

ortly \ort-lē\ courtly, portly, shortly, thwartly

ortment \ort-mənt\ assortment, comportment, deportment, disportment

ortoise \ort-əs\ see ORTIS

orton \ort-ᵊn\ Morton, Norton, Wharton

orts \orts\ quartz, shorts, sports, undershorts—*also plurals and possessives of nouns and third person singular presents of verbs listed at* ¹ORT

ortunate \orch-nət\ fortunate, importunate, unfortunate

orture \or-chər\ see ORCHER

orty \ort-ē\ forty, shorty, sortie, sporty, warty, mezzo forte, pianoforte

orum \ōr-əm\ foram, forum,

jorum, quorum, decorum,
Mizoram, ad valorem,
cockalorum, indecorum,
Karakoram, variorum, pons
asinorum, sanctum sanctorum,
schola cantorum

¹orus \ōr-əs\ Boris, chorus,
Doris, Horus, loris, porous,
sorus, torus, canorous,
decorous, Delores, Dolores,
pelorus, phosphorus,
sonorous, deoch an doris,
doch-an-dorris

²orus \òr-əs\ see AURUS

orward \òr-wərd\ forward,
shoreward, flash-forward,
henceforward, carryforward

ory \òr-ē\ Corey, corrie, dory,
glory, gory, hoary, Laurie,
Lori, lorry, lory, nori, quarry,
saury, sorry, story, Tory, zori,
centaury, clerestory, John
Dory, outlawry, satori,
vainglory, a priori, allegory,
amatory, auditory, cacciatore,
castratory, category, con
amore, crematory, damnatory,
decretory, desultory, dilatory,
dormitory, expletory,
feudatory, fumitory,
Goteborg, gustatory, gyratory,
hortatory, hunky-dory,
inventory, laudatory, lavatory,
mandatory, migratory,
minatory, monitory,
Montessori, nugatory,
offertory, oratory, overstory,
predatory, prefatory,
probatory, promissory,
promontory, purgatory,
repertory, Ruwenzori,
signatory, statutory, sudatory,

territory, transitory,
understory, vibratory,
vomitory, yakitori,
accusatory, admonitory,
adulatory, a fortiori, aleatory,
ambulatory, amendatory,
applicatory, approbatory,
celebratory, circulatory,
combinatory, commendatory,
compensatory, condemnatory,
confirmatory, confiscatory,
conservatory, consolatory,
contributory, copulatory,
cosignatory, declamatory,
declaratory, dedicatory,
defamatory, denigratory,
depilatory, depository,
derogatory, designatory,
dispensatory, divinatory,
escalatory, excitatory,
exclamatory, exculpatory,
excusatory, exhibitory,
exhortatory, expiatory,
expiratory, explanatory,
explicatory, exploratory,
expository, expurgatory,
incantatory, incubatory,
indicatory, inflammatory,
informatory, innovatory,
inspiratory, inundatory,
invitatory, judicatory,
laboratory, Lake Maggiore,
masticatory, masturbatory,
memento mori, millefiori,
modulatory, obfuscatory,
obligatory, observatory,
performatory, persecutory,
predicatory, premonitory,
preparatory, prohibitory,
reformatory, regulatory,
repository, retributory,
revelatory, respiratory,

salutatory, stipulatory,
supplicatory, transmigratory,
undulatory, adjudicatory, a
posteriori, annihilatory,
annunciatory, anticipatory,
appreciatory, assimilatory,
circumlocutory, classificatory,
concilliatory, confabulatory,
congratulatory, de-escalatory,
denunciatory, depreciatory,
discriminatory, ejaculatory,
hallucinatory, improvisatore,
improvisatory, interrogatory,
intimidatory, investigatory,
participatory, propitiatory,
recommendatory,
recriminatory, renunciatory,
reverberatory, viola d'amore,
ameliticatory,
overcompensatory,
reconciliatory, supererogatory,
immunoregulatory

oryx \ór-iks\ oryx, Armorics,
combinatorics

orze \ōrz\ see OORS

¹os \äs\ boss, doss, dross, floss,
fosse, gloss, joss, Maas, os,
pross, stoss, toss, Argos,
bathos, benthos, bugloss,
chaos, Chios, cosmos, Delos,
demos, Ellás, emboss, Eos,
epos, Eros, ethos, Hyksos,
kaross, kudos, kvass, Lagos,
Laplace, Lemnos, Lesbos,
Logos, Madras, Melos,
mythos, nol-pros, nonpros,
Paros, pathos, peplos, pharos,
ringtoss, Samos, telos, topos,
tripos, coup de grace,
demitasse, extrados, gravitas,
intrados, isogloss, omphalos,

reredos, semigloss, Thanatos,
underboss, volte-face

²os \ō\ see ¹OW

³os \ōs\ see ¹OSE

⁴os \ós\ see ¹OSS

¹osa \ō-sə\ Xhosa, Formosa,
mimosa, Reynosa, curiosa,
virtuosa, anorexia nervosa

²osa \ō-zə\ mimosa, mucosa,
serosa, Spinoza, sub rosa,
curiosa, virtuosa, Zaragoza

¹osable \ō-zə-bəl\ closable,
disposable, erosible,
explosible, opposable,
reclosable, supposable,
decomposable, superposable,
indecomposable,
superimposable

²osable \ü-zə-bəl\ see USABLE

osal \ō-zəl\ hosel, losel,
deposal, disposal, proposal,
reposal, supposal

osan \ōs-ᵊn\ see OSIN

osch \äsh\ see ²ASH

¹oschen \ō-shən\ see OTION

²oschen \ó-shən\ see AUTION

oscible \äs-ə-bəl\ see OSSIBLE

osco \äs-kō\ see OSCOE

oscoe \äs-kō\ Bosco, roscoe,
Roscoe, fiasco

oscopy \äs-kə-pē\ arthroscopy,
microscopy, spectroscopy,
sigmoidoscopy

¹ose \ōs\ close, dose, gross, os,
arkose, Carlos, cosmos,
crustose, cymose, dextrose,
engross, erose, fructose,
globose, glucose, jocose,
lactose, maltose, mannose,
megadose, morose, mythos,
nodose, pappose, pathos,
pentose, pilose, plumose,

ramose, rhamnose, ribose, rugose, scapose, schistose, setose, spinose, strigose, sucrose, Sukkoth, triose, vadose, ventricose, verbose, viscose, adios, adipose, bellicose, calvados, cellulose, comatose, diagnose, grandiose, granulose, Helios, lachrymose, otiose, overdose, racemose, Shabuoth, tuberose, varicose, inter alios, inter vivos, metamorphose, religiose

²ose \ōz\ brose, Broz, chose, close, clothes, cloze, doze, froze, gloze, hose, nose, pose, prose, rose, Rose, Ambrose, appose, aros, bedclothes, bluenose, brownnose, bulldoze, Burroughs, compose, depose, dextrose, disclose, dispose, enclose, expose, foreclose, fructose, glucose, hardnose, impose, nightclothes, oppose, plainclothes, primrose, propose, quickfroze, repose, rockrose, suppose, transpose, tuberose, unclose, uprose, viscose, wind rose, Berlioz, counterpose, decompose, diagnose, discompose, indispose, interpose, juxtapose, letters close, pettitoes, predispose, presuppose, pussytoes, recompose, shovelnose, superpose, underclothes, anastomose, metamorphose, overexpose, superimpose, underexpose—*also plurals*

and possessives of nouns and third person singular presents of verbs listed at ¹OW

³ose \üz\ see ²USE

osed \ōzd\ closed, nosed, composed, exposed, hard-nosed, opposed, pug-nosed, snub-nosed, stenosed, supposed, unclosed, indisposed, shovel-nosed, toffee-nosed, well-disposed—*also pasts of verbs listed at* ²OSE

osee \ō-zē\ see OSY

osel \ō-zəl\ see OSAL

osen \ōz-ᵊn\ chosen, frozen, quickfrozen, lederhosen

¹oser \ō-zər\ closer, dozer, poser, proser, brownnoser, bulldozer, composer, discloser, disposer, exposer, imposer, opposer, proposer, decomposer, interposer, photocomposer

²oser \ü-zər\ see USER

¹oset \ō-zət\ see ²OSIT

²oset \äz-ət\ see ¹OSIT

³oset \äs-ət\ see OSSET

osey \ō-zē\ see OSY

¹osh \òsh\ see ²ASH

²osh \ōsh\ see ²OCHE

¹oshed \äsht\ sloshed, galoshed—*also pasts of verbs listed at* ¹ASH

²oshed \òsht\ see ¹ASHED

oshen \ō-shən\ see OTION

osher \äsh-ər\ see ¹ASHER

osia \ō-shə\ see ¹OTIA

osible \ō-zə-bəl\ see ¹OSABLE

osier \ō-zhər\ see OSURE

osily \ō-zə-lē\ cozily, nosily, rosily

osin \ōs-ᵊn\ boatswain, Mosan, pocosin

osing \ō-ziŋ\ closing, nosing, disclosing, imposing, supposing

osion \ō-zhən\ plosion, corrosion, displosion, erosion, explosion, implosion

osis \ō-səs\ gnosis, hypnosis, narcosis, necrosis, neurosis, orthosis, osmosis, prognosis, psychosis, sclerosis, thrombosis, brucellosis, cyanosis, dermatosis, diagnosis, halitosis, heterosis, psittacosis, scoliosis, silicosis, symbiosis, anaplasmosis, autohypnosis, coccidiosis, hyperhidrosis, pediculosis, psychoneurosis, tuberculosis, mononucleosis, immunodiagnosis, neurofibromatosis

¹osit \äz-ət\ closet, posit, composite, deposit, exposit

²osit \ō-zət\ prosit, roset

osite \äz-ət\ see ¹OSIT

ositive \äz-ət-iv\ positive, appositive, seropositive

ositor \äz-ət-ər\ compositor, depositor, expositor

osius \ō-shəs\ see OCIOUS

osive \ō-siv\ plosive, corrosive, erosive, explosive, implosive, purposive

osk \äsk\ mosque, kiosk, abelmosk

¹oso \ō-sō\ proso, maestoso, rebozo, arioso, furioso, grazioso, grandioso, mafioso, Mato Grosso, oloroso, spiritoso, vigoroso, virtuoso, concerto grosso

²oso \ō-zō\ bozo, rebozo, furioso, gracioso, grandioso, spiritoso, vigoroso

³oso \ü-sō\ see USOE

osophy \äs-ə-fē\ philosophy, theosophy, anthroposophy

osque \äsk\ see OSK

¹oss \ós\ boss, cross, crosse, floss, gloss, loss, moss, Ross, sauce, toss, across, bugloss, crisscross, emboss, Kinross, kouros, lacrosse, outcross, pathos, ringtoss, topcross, uncross, albatross, applesauce, autocross, double-cross, intercross, motocross, semigloss

²oss \ōs\ see ¹OSE

³oss \äs\ see ¹OS

ossa \äs-ə\ see ¹ASA

ossable \äs-ə-bəl\ see OSSIBLE

ossal \äs-əl\ docile, dossal, fossil, glossal, jostle, tassel, throstle, warsle, wassail, apostle, colossal, indocile, isoglossal

¹osse \äs\ see ¹OS

²osse \äs-ē\ see ¹OSSY

³osse \ós\ see ¹OSS

ossed \óst\ see ³OST

osser \ó-sər\ Chaucer, crosser, saucer, double-crosser

osset \äs-ət\ cosset, faucet, Osset, posset, Samoset

ossible \äs-ə-bəl\ possible, cognoscible, embossable, impossible

ossic \äs-ik\ see OSSICK

ossick \äs-ik\ fossick, isoglossic

ossil \äs-əl\ see OSSAL

ossity \äs-ət-ē\ adiposity, atrocity, callosity, ferocity, gibbosity, monstrosity, pomposity, porosity, precocity, velocity, viscosity, zygosity, animosity, bellicosity, curiosity, generosity, grandiosity, hideosity, luminosity, nebulosity, preciosity, reciprocity, scrupulosity, sensuosity, sinuosity, strenuosity, tortuosity, tuberosity, varicosity, virtuosity, impetuosity, religiosity, voluminosity, impecuniosity

ossly \òs-lē\ costly, crossly

osso \ō-sō\ see ¹OSO

ossos \äs-əs\ see OCESS

ossular \äs-ə-lər\ grossular, wassailer

ossum \äs-əm\ blossom, passim, possum, opossum

ossus \äs-əs\ see OCESS

¹ossy \äs-ē\ Aussie, bossy, dassie, drossy, flossy, glossy, posse, quasi, dalasi, Kumasi, Likasi, sannyasi

²ossy \ò-sē\ Aussie, bossy, lossy, mossy

¹ost \äst\ sol-faist, Pentecost, teleost—*also pasts of verbs listed at* ¹OS

²ost \ōst\ boast, coast, ghost, host, most, oast, post, roast, toast, almost, bedpost, compost, doorpost, endmost, foremost, gatepost, goalpost, Gold Coast, guidepost, headmost, hindmost, impost, inmost, midmost, milepost, Milquetoast, outmost, outpost, provost, rearmost, riposte, seacoast, signpost, sternmost, sternpost, topmost, upcoast, upmost, utmost, aftermost, ante-post, bottommost, coast-to-coast, easternmost, farthermost, fingerpost, furthermost, headforemost, hithermost, innermost, Ivory Coast, lowermost, nethermost, northernmost, outermost, rudderpost, southernmost, sternforemost, undermost, uppermost, uttermost, westernmost

³ost \òst\ cost, frost, lost, accost, defrost, exhaust, hoarfrost, star-crossed, holocaust, Pentecost, permafrost—*also pasts of verbs listed at* ¹OSS

⁴ost \əst\ see ¹UST

osta \äs-tə\ costa, pasta

¹ostal \ōs-t°l\ coastal, postal, bicoastal, intercostal

²ostal \äs-t°l\ see OSTEL

ostasy \äs-tə-sē\ apostasy, isostasy

oste \ōst\ see ²OST

ostel \äs-t°l\ hostel, hostile, Pentecostal

¹oster \äs-tər\ coster, foster, Foster, roster, impostor, piaster, Double Gloucester, paternoster, snollygoster

²oster \òs-tər\ foster, Foster, roster, Double Gloucester

³oster \ō-stər\ see OASTER

ostic \äs-tik\ Gnostic, acrostic, agnostic, prognostic, diagnostic ostile \äs-tᵊl\ see OSTEL

ostle \äs-əl\ see OSSAL

¹ostly \ōst-lē\ ghostly, hostly, mostly

²ostly \ós-lē\ see OSSLY

ostomy \äs-tə-mē\ ostomy, colostomy, enterostomy

oston \ós-tən\ Austin, Boston, Godwin Austen

ostor \äs-tər\ see ¹OSTER

¹ostral \ós-trəl\ austral, rostral

²ostral \äs-trəl\ see OSTREL

ostrel \äs-trəl\ austral, costrel, nostril, rostral, wastrel, colostral

ostril \äs-trəl\ see OSTREL

ostrum \äs-trəm\ nostrum, rostrum, colostrum

osty \ō-stē\ ghosty, toasty

osure \ō-zhər\ closure, crosier, osier, composure, disclosure, disposure, enclosure, exclosure, exposure, foreclosure, discomposure, overexposure, underexposure

osy \ō-zē\ cozy, dozy, mosey, nosy, Osee, posy, prosy, rosy, ring-around-a-rosy

osyne \äs-ᵊn-ē\ Euphrosyne, Mnemosyne

osz \ósh\ see ²ASH

oszcz \ósh\ see ²ASH

¹ot \ät\ aught, baht, blot, boite, bot, chott, clot, cot, dot, ghat, got, grot, hot, jat, jot, khat, knot, kyat, lot, Lot, lotte, motte, naught, not, plot, pot, rot, scot, Scot, Scott, shot, skat, slot, snot, sot, spot, squat, swat, swot, tot, trot, watt, Watt, what, wot, yacht, allot, ascot, begot, besot, big

shot, bloodshot, bowknot, boycott, buckshot, bullshot, cachepot, calotte, cannot, Connacht, crackpot, Crockpot, culotte, dashpot, despot, dreadnought, earshot, ergot, escot, eyeshot, eyespot, feedlot, fiat, firepot, fleshpot, forgot, fox-trot, fusspot, fylfot, garrote, gavotte, grapeshot, gunshot, half-knot, have-not, highspot, hotchpot, hotshot, ikat, jackpot, Korat, kumquat, long shot, loquat, marplot, mascot, motmot, nightspot, one-shot, Pequot, potshot, Rabat, red-hot, robot, Sadat, sandlot, sexpot, Shabbat, shallot, Shebat, sheepcote, slingshot, slipknot, slungshot, snapshot, somewhat, stinkpot, stockpot, subplot, sunspot, teapot, tin-pot, topknot, tosspot, try-pot, upshot, wainscot, whatnot, white-hot, woodlot, aeronaut, aliquot, apparat, apricot, aquanaut, argonaut, astronaut, bergamot, cachalot, Camelot, caveat, carry-cot, coffeepot, cosmonaut, counterplot, diddley-squat, doodley-squat, flowerpot, gallipot, guillemot, Gujarat, Hottentot, Huguenot, kilowatt, Lancelot, megawatt, microdot, Nouakchott, ocelot, overshot, paraquat, patriot, Penobscot, peridot, polka dot, polyglot, samizdat, sansculotte, scattershot, terawatt, tommyrot, touch-me-not, underplot, undershot,

Willemstadt, Wyandot, wyandotte, compatriot, forget-me-not, immunoblot, Inupiat, requiescat, Johnny-on-the-spot

²ot \ō\ see ¹OW

³ot \ōt\ see OAT

⁴ot \ȯt\ see ¹OUGHT

ôt \ō\ see ¹OW

ota \ōt-ə\ bota, flota, lota, quota, rota, biota, Dakota, iota, Lakota, pelota, Toyota, Minnesota, North Dakota, South Dakota

otable \ōt-ə-bəl\ notable, potable, quotable

otage \ōt-ij\ dotage, flotage, anecdotage

otal \ōt-ᵊl\ dotal, motile, scrotal, total, immotile, subtotal, teetotal, anecdotal, antidotal, sacerdotal

otalist \ōt-ᵊl-əst\ teetotalist, anecdotalist, sacerdotalist

otamus \ät-ə-məs\ see OTOMOUS

otany \ät-ᵊn-ē\ botany, cottony, monotony

otarist \ōt-ə-rəst\ motorist, votarist

otary \ōt-ə-rē\ coterie, rotary, votary, locomotory, prothonotary

otas \ō-təs\ see OTUS

otch \äch\ blotch, botch, crotch, hotch, notch, scotch, Scotch, splotch, swatch, watch, bird-watch, deathwatch, debauch, dogwatch, hopscotch, hotchpotch, Sasquatch, stopwatch, top-notch, wristwatch, butterscotch

otchet \äch-ət\ crotchet, rochet

otchman \äch-mən\ Scotchman, watchman

otchy \äch-ē\ blotchy, boccie, botchy, splotchy, hibachi, huarache, huisache, Karachi, vivace, mariachi

¹ote \ōt-ē\ dhoti, floaty, loti, roti, throaty, cenote, coyote, chayote, peyote, quixote

²ote \ōt\ see OAT

³ote \ät\ see ¹OT

otea \ōt-ē-ə\ protea, scotia

oted \ōt-əd\ see OATED

otem \ōt-əm\ see OTUM

oten \ōt-ᵊn\ see OTON

oter \ōt-ər\ see OATER

oterie \ōt-ə-rē\ see OTARY

¹oth \äth\ broth, cloth, froth, Goth, moth, sloth, swath, troth, wroth, betroth, breechcloth, broadcloth, cheesecloth, dishcloth, facecloth, floorcloth, loincloth, Naboth, oilcloth, sackcloth, sailcloth, washcloth, Alioth, behemoth, tablecloth, Ustrogoth, Visigoth

²oth \ōs\ see ¹OSE

³oth \ōt\ see OAT

⁴oth \ōth\ see OWTH

othal \ȯth-əl\ see OTHEL

othe \ōth\ clothe, loathe, betroth, unclothe

othel \ȯth-əl\ brothel, betrothal

¹other \əth-ər\ brother, mother, nother, other, rather, smother, tother, another, foremother, godmother, grandmother, housemother, stepbrother, stepmother

²other \äth-ər\ see ¹ATHER

otherly \ə<u>th</u>-ər-lē\ brotherly, motherly, southerly, grandmotherly

othes \ōz\ see ²OSE

othesis \äth-ə-səs\ prothesis, hypothesis

othic \äth-ik\ gothic, neo-Gothic, Ostrogothic, Visigothic

othing \ō-<u>th</u>iŋ\ clothing, loathing, underclothing

otho \ō-tō\ see ¹OTO

¹**oti** \ōt-ē\ see ¹OTE

²**oti** \ót-ē\ see AUGHTY

¹**otia** \ō-shə\ scotia, Scotia, agnosia, dystocia, Cappadocia, Nova Scotia

²**otia** \ōt-ē-ə\ see OTEA

otiable \ō-shə-bəl\ see OCIABLE

otiant \ō-shənt\ see OTIENT

¹**otic** \ät-ik\ Scotic, aquatic, biotic, chaotic, demotic, despotic, erotic, exotic, hypnotic, narcotic, necrotic, neurotic, Nilotic, osmotic, psychotic, quixotic, robotic, sclerotic, semiotic, abiotic, anecdotic, asymptotic, bibliotic, embryotic, epiglottic, homeotic, Huguenotic, idiotic, macrobiotic, melanotic, patriotic, posthypnotic, sansculottic, symbiotic, antibiotic, autoerotic, compatriotic, homoerotic

²**otic** \ōt-ik\ lotic, photic, aphotic, aprotic, dichotic, robotic

³**otic** \ót-ik\ see AUTIC

otica \ät-i-kə\ erotica, exotica

otice \ōt-əs\ see OTUS

otics \ät-iks\ robotics, astronautics, bibliotics—*also plurals and possessives of nouns listed at* ¹OTIC

otid \ät-əd\ see OTTED

otient \ō-shənt\ quotient, negotiant

otile \ōt-ᵊl\ see OTAL

¹**oting** \ōt-iŋ\ see OATING

²**oting** \ät-iŋ\ see OTTING

¹**otinous** \ät-nəs\ see OTNESS

²**otinous** \ät-ᵊn-əs\ see ¹OTONOUS

otion \ō-shən\ Goshen, groschen, lotion, motion, notion, ocean, potion, commotion, demotion, devotion, emotion, Laotian, promotion, slow-motion, locomotion

otional \ō-shnəl\ motional, notional, devotional, emotional, promotional, unemotional

otis \ōt-əs\ see OTUS

otist \ōt-əst\ protist, Scotist, anecdotist

otive \ōt-iv\ motive, votive, emotive, promotive, automotive, locomotive

otl \ät-ᵊl\ see OTTLE

otle \ät-ᵊl\ see OTTLE

otley \ät-lē\ see OTLY

otly \ät-lē\ Atli, hotly, motley

otment \ät-mənt\ allotment, ballottement

otness \ät-nəs\ hotness, squatness

oto \ō-tō\ koto, photo, roto, Sotho, Basotho, con moto, de Soto, ex-voto, in toto, Kyoto,

Lesotho, Mosotho, Sesotho, Kumamoto, telephoto

otomous \ät-ə-məs\ dichotomous, hippopotamus

otomy \ät-ə-mē\ dichotomy, lobotomy, tracheotomy, episiotomy

oton \ōt-ᵊn\ croton, Jotun, oaten, Lofoten, verboten

¹otonous \ät-ᵊn-əs\ rottenness, monotonous, serotinous

²otonous \ät-nəs\ see OTNESS

otor \ōt-ər\ see OATER

otorist \ōt-ə-rəst\ see OTARIST

otory \ōt-ə-rē\ see OTARY

ots \äts\ Graz, hots, lots, Scots, Spaatz, swats, ersatz, Galati—*also plurals and possessives of nouns and third person singular presents of verbs listed at* ¹OT

otsk \ätsk\ see ATSK

otsman \ät-smən\ Scotsman, yachtsman

ott \ät\ see ¹OT

otta \ät-ə\ see ¹ATA

ottage \ät-ij\ cottage, plottage, pottage, wattage

ottal \ät-ᵊl\ see OTTLE

¹otte \ät\ see ¹OT

²otte \ȯt\ see ¹OUGHT

otted \ät-əd\ knotted, potted, spotted, carotid, proglottid, polka-dotted—*also pasts of verbs listed at* ¹OT

ottement \ät-mənt\ see OTMENT

otten \ät-ᵊn\ cotton, gotten, gratin, ratton, rotten, shotten, au gratin, begotten, forgotten, guncotton, ill-gotten, misbegotten, sauerbraten

ottenness \ät-ᵊn-əs\ see ¹OTONOUS

otter \ät-ər\ blotter, cotter, dotter, knotter, otter, plotter, potter, Potter, Qatar, rotter, spotter, squatter, swatter, Tatar, totter, trotter, water, alotter, boycotter, flyswatter, garroter, globe-trotter, pinspotter, sandlotter, alma mater, imperator, teeter-totter—*also comparatives of adjectives listed at* ¹OT *and words ending in* -water *listed at* ¹ATER

ottery \ät-ə-rē\ lottery, pottery, Tatary, tottery, watery

ottic \ät-ik\ see ¹OTIC

ottid \ät-əd\ see OTTED

ottie \ät-ē\ see ATI

otting \ät-iŋ\ jotting, wainscoting

ottis \ät-əs\ glottis, clematis, epiglottis, literatus

ottische \ät-ish\ see OTTISH

ottish \ät-ish\ hottish, schottische, Scottish, sottish, sanculottish

ottle \ät-ᵊl\ bottle, dottle, glottal, mottle, pottle, ratel, rotl, throttle, wattle, atlatl, bluebottle, Aristotle, monocotyl, Nahuatl, epiglottal, Quetzalcoatl

¹otto \ät-ō\ see ¹ATO

²otto \ȯt-ō\ see ¹AUTO

ottom \ät-əm\ see ¹ATUM

otty \ät-ē\ see ATI

otum \ōt-əm\ notum, scrotum, totem, factotum, teetotum

otun \ōt-ᵊn\ see OTON

oture \ō-chər\ see OACHER

otus \ōt-əs\ lotus, notice, Otis, denotice, Pelotas

oty \ȯt-ē\ see ¹AUGHTY

otyl \ät-ᵊl\ see OTTLE

¹**ou** \ō\ see ¹OW

²**ou** \ü\ see ¹EW

³**ou** \au̇\ see ²OW

oubled \ə-bəld\ see UBBLED

ouble \əb-əl\ see UBBLE

oubler \əb-lər\ doubler, bubbler, troubler

oubly \əb-lē\ see UBBLY

oubt \au̇t\ see ³OUT

oubted \au̇t-əd\ see OUTED

oubter \au̇t-ər\ see ²OUTER

¹**ouc** \ü\ see ¹EW

²**ouc** \ük\ see UKE

³**ouc** \u̇k\ see ¹OOK

ouce \üs\ see ¹USE

¹**oucester** \äs-tər\ see ¹OSTER

²**oucester** \ȯs-tər\ see ²OSTER

¹**ouch** \üch\ see ¹OOCH

²**ouch** \üsh\ see OUCHE

³**ouch** \əch\ see ¹UTCH

⁴**ouch** \au̇ch\ couch, crouch, grouch, ouch, pouch, slouch, vouch, avouch, debouch, scaramouch, retort pouch

ouche \üsh\ douche, louche, ruche, squoosh, swoosh, whoosh, barouche, capuche, cartouche, debouch, farouche, kurus, tarboosh, scaramouch

¹**ouchy** \əch-ē\ see UCHY

²**ouchy** \au̇-chē\ grouchy, pouchy, slouchy

ou'd \üd\ see UDE

¹**oud** \üd\ see UDE

²**oud** \au̇d\ boughed, bowed, cloud, crowd, loud, proud, shroud, stroud, aloud, becloud, enshroud, highbrowed, house-proud, purse-proud, Red Cloud, unbowed, overcrowd, thundercloud—*also pasts of verbs listed at* ²OW

ouda \üd-ə\ see UDA

oudy \au̇d-ē\ see OWDY

oue \ü\ see ¹EW

ouf \üf\ see ¹OOF

ouffe \üf\ see ¹OOF

oug \əg\ see UG

¹**ouge** \üj\ see ¹UGE

²**ouge** \üzh\ see ²UGE

³**ouge** \au̇j\ gouge, scrouge

¹**ough** \ō\ see ¹OW

²**ough** \ü\ see ¹EW

³**ough** \au̇\ see ²OW

⁴**ough** \äk\ see ¹OCK

⁵**ough** \əf\ see UFF

⁶**ough** \ȯf\ see ²OFF

¹**ougham** \ōm\ see ¹OME

²**ougham** \üm\ see ¹OOM

oughed \au̇d\ see ²OUD

oughen \əf-ən\ see UFFIN

ougher \əf-ər\ see UFFER

oughie \əf-ē\ see UFFY

oughish \əf-ish\ see UFFISH

oughly \əf-lē\ see UFFLY

oughs \ōz\ see ²OSE

¹**ought** \ȯt\ aught, bought, brought, caught, dot, fought, fraught, ghat, lotte, naught, nought, ought, sought, taught, taut, thought, wrought, besought, distraught, dreadnought, forethought, handwrought, high-wrought, onslaught, self-taught, store-bought, unthought, aeronaut, aforethought, afterthought, aquanaut, argonaut, astronaut,

cosmonaut, juggernaut, overbought, overwrought

²ought \aut\ see ³OUT

oughten \ȯt-ᵊn\ see AUTEN

oughty \aut-ē\ doughty, droughty, gouty, pouty, snouty, trouty

¹oughy \ō-ē\ see OWY

²oughy \ü-ē\ see EWY

ouie \ü-ē\ see EWY

ouille \ü-ē\ see EWY

¹ouis \ü-ē\ see EWY

²ouis \ü-əs\ see EWESS

ouk \ük\ see UKE

ouki \ü-kē\ see OOKY

¹oul \ōl\ see ¹OLE

²oul \ül\ see ¹OOL

³oul \aul\ see ²OWL

¹ould \ōld\ see ¹OLD

²ould \ud\ see ¹OOD

oulder \ōl-dər\ see ¹OLDER

ouldered \ōl-dərd\ bouldered, shouldered, round-shouldered, square-shouldered—*also pasts of verbs listed at* ¹OLDER

ouldest \ud-əst\ couldest, shouldest, wouldest, Talmudist

ouldn't \ud-ᵊnt\ shouldn't, wouldn't

¹oule \ü-lē\ see ULY

²oule \ül\ see ¹OOL

ouled \ōld\ see ¹OLD

oulee \ü-lē\ see ULY

¹ouleh \ü-lə\ see ULA

²ouleh \ü-lē\ see ULY

ouli \ü-lē\ see ULY

oulie \ü-lē\ see ULY

ouling \au-liŋ\ see ²OWLING

oulish \ü-lish\ see OOLISH

¹ou'll \ül\ see ¹OOL

²ou'll \ul\ see ¹UL

oulle \ül\ see ¹OOL

oulli \ü-lē\ see ULY

oully \au-lē\ see ²OWLY

oult \ōlt\ see ¹OLT

oulter \ōl-tər\ see OLTER

oum \üm\ see ¹OOM

oumenal \ü-mən-ᵊl\ see UMINAL

¹oun \aun\ see ²OWN

²oun \ün\ see ¹OON

ounce \auns\ bounce, flounce, jounce, ounce, pounce, trounce, announce, denounce, enounce, pronounce, renounce, mispronounce

ouncement \aun-smənt\ announcement, denouncement, pronouncement

ouncer \aun-sər\ bouncer, announcer

ouncil \aun-səl\ see OUNSEL

ouncy \aun-sē\ bouncy, flouncy, jouncy, viscountcy

¹ound \ünd\ stound, swound, wound—*also pasts of verbs listed at* ¹OON

²ound \aund\ bound, crowned, found, ground, hound, mound, pound, Pound, round, sound, stound, swound, wound, abound, aground, all-round, around, astound, background, black-crowned, bloodhound, campground, chowhound, compound, confound, coonhound, dachshund, deerhound, deskbound, earthbound, eastbound, elkhound, expound, fairground, fogbound, foot-pound, foreground, foxhound, go-round, greyhound, hardbound, hellhound, hidebound, homebound, horehound, housebound, icebound, impound, inbound, newfound, newshound, northbound, outbound, playground, pot-bound, profound, propound, rebound, redound, resound, rockbound, snowbound, softbound, southbound, spellbound, stone-ground, stormbound, strikebound, surround, unbound, well-found, westbound, white-crowned, wolfhound, year-round, aboveground, all-around, belowground, battleground, decompound, go-around, muscle-bound, outward-bound, paperbound, Puget Sound, runaround, turnaround, ultrasound, underground, weather-bound, wraparound, merry-go-round, superabound—*also pasts of verbs listed at* ²OWN

oundal \aun-d°l\ poundal, roundel

oundary \aun-drē\ see OUNDRY

ounded \aun-dəd\ drownded, rounded, confounded, unbounded, unfounded, well-founded, well-grounded

oundel \aun-d°l\ see OUNDAL

ounder \aun-dər\ bounder, flounder, founder, grounder, pounder, rounder, sounder, all-rounder, backgrounder, dumbfounder, tenpounder

ounding \aun-diŋ\ drownding, grounding, sounding, astounding, high-sounding, rockhounding

¹oundless \ün-ləs\ see OONLESS

²oundless \aun-ləs\ groundless, soundless

oundlet \aun-lət\ see OWNLET

oundling \aun-liŋ\ foundling, groundling

oundly \aund-lē\ roundly, soundly

oundness \aun-nəs\ roundness, unsoundness

oundry \aun-drē\ boundary, foundry

¹ounds \ünz\ see OONS

²ounds \aunz\ hounds, zounds, inbounds, Barren Grounds, out-of-bounds—*also plurals and possessives of nouns and third person singular presents of verbs listed at* ²OUND

oundsel \aun-səl\ see OUNSEL

oundsman \aunz-mən\ see OWNSMAN

ounge \aunj\ lounge, scrounge, chaise lounge

¹ounger \aun-jər\ lounger, scrounger

²ounger \əŋ-gər\ see ¹ONGER

ounker \əŋ-kər\ see UNKER

ounsel \aun-səl\ council, counsel, groundsel

¹ount \änt\ see ²ANT

²ount \aunt\ count, fount, mount, account, amount, demount, discount, dismount, high-count, miscount, recount, remount, seamount, surmount, viscount, catamount, paramount, rediscount, tantamount, undercount

ountable \aunt-ə-bəl\

countable, accountable, demountable, discountable, surmountable, insurmountable, unaccountable

ountain \aůnt-ᵊn\ fountain, mountain, transmountain, cat-a-mountain, Riding Mountain

ountcy \aůn-sē\ see OUNCY

ounter \aůnt-ər\ counter, discounter, encounter, recounter, rencounter

ountess \aůnt-əs\ countess, viscountess

ountie \aůnt-ē\ see OUNTY

ounting \aůnt-iŋ\ mounting, accounting

ounty \aůnt-ē\ bounty, county, Mountie, viscounty

¹**oup** \ōp\ see OPE

²**oup** \ü\ see ¹EW

³**oup** \üp\ see ¹OOP

¹**oupe** \ōp\ see OPE

²**oupe** \üp\ see ¹OOP

ouper \ü-pər\ see OOPER

oupie \ü-pē\ see OOPY

ouping \ü-piŋ\ see OOPING

ouple \əp-əl\ see ¹UPLE

ouplet \əp-lət\ see ¹UPLET

oupous \ü-pəs\ see UPUS

oupy \ü-pē\ see OOPY

¹**our** \ōr\ see ¹OR

²**our** \ůr\ see ¹URE

³**our** \aůr\ see ²OWER

⁴**our** \är\ see ³AR

⁵**our** \ər\ see ¹EUR

oura \ůr-ə\ see URA

ourable \ōr-ə-bəl\ see ¹ORABLE

ourage \ər-ij\ courage, demurrage, discourage, encourage

¹**ourbon** \ər-bən\ see ¹URBAN

²**ourbon** \ůr-bən\ see ²URBAN

¹**ource** \ōrs\ see ¹OURSE

²**ource** \ȯrs\ see ¹ORSE

¹**ourceful** \ōrs-fəl\ see ¹ORCEFUL

²**ourceful** \ȯrs-fəl\ see ORSEFUL

ourcing \ōr-siŋ\ outsourcing— *also present participles of verbs listed at* ¹OURSE

ourd \ōrd\ see OARD

ourde \ůrd\ see ¹URED

¹**ou're** \ōr\ see ¹OR

²**ou're** \ü-ər\ see ¹EWER

³**ou're** \ůr\ see URE

⁴**ou're** \ər\ see ¹EUR

oured \ōrd\ see OARD

¹**ourer** \ōr-ər\ see ¹ORER

²**ourer** \ůr-ər\ see ¹URER

³**ourer** \aůr-ər\ flowerer, scourer, deflowerer, devourer—*also comparatives of adjectives listed at* ²OWER

¹**ourg** \ůr\ see ¹URE

²**ourg** \ərg\ see ERG

¹**ourge** \ərj\ see URGE

²**ourge** \ȯrj\ see ORGE

ourger \ər-jər\ see ERGER

ouri \ůr-ē\ see ¹URY

¹**ourier** \ůr-ē-ər\ courier, couturier, couturiere, vaunt-courier

²**ourier** \ər-ē-ər\ see URRIER

¹**ouring** \ōr-iŋ\ see ORING

²**ouring** \ůr-iŋ\ see URING

ourish \ər-ish\ currish, flourish, nourish, amateurish

ourist \ůr-əst\ see URIST

ourly \aůr-lē\ dourly, hourly, sourly

¹**ourn** \ōrn\ see ¹ORN

²**ourn** \ərn\ see URN

³**ourn** \ȯrn\ see ²ORN

ournal \ərn-ᵊl\ see ERNAL

ournament \ȯr-nə-mənt\ see ORNAMENT

ourne \ȯrn\ see ¹ORN

¹ourney \ər-nē\ Bernie, Ernie, ferny, gurney, journey, tourney, attorney

²ourney \ȯr-nē\ see ORNY

ourneyer \ər-nē-ər\ journeyer, vernier

ournful \ȯrn-fəl\ see ORNFUL

ourning \ȯr-niŋ\ see ORNING

ournment \ərn-mənt\ see ERNMENT

¹ours \ōrz\ see ¹OORS

²ours \ärz\ see ARS

³ours \ȯrz\ see ²OORS

⁴ours \au̇rz\ ours, after-hours—*also plurals and possessives of nouns and third singular presents of verbs listed at* ²OWER

⁵ours \u̇r\ see ¹URE

¹ourse \ōrs\ coarse, course, force, hoarse, source, concourse, deforce, discourse, divorce, enforce, perforce, racecourse, recourse, resource, intercourse, reinforce, telecourse, tour de force, watercourse

²ourse \ȯrs\ see ¹ORSE

oursome \ȯr-səm\ see ORSUM

¹ourt \ȯrt\ see ¹ORT

²ourt \u̇rt\ see ¹URT

ourtesy \ərt-ə-sē\ courtesy, curtesy, discourtesy

ourth \ȯrth\ see ¹ORTH

ourtier \ȯr-chər\ see ORCHER

¹ourtly \ȯrt-lē\ see ¹ORTLY

²ourtly \ȯrt-lē\ see ²ORTLY

oury \au̇r-ē\ see OWERY

¹ous \ü\ see ¹EW

²ous \üs\ see ¹USE

¹ousa \ü-sə\ see ¹USA

²ousa \ü-zə\ see ²USA

ousal \au̇-zəl\ housel, spousal, tousle, arousal, carousal

ousand \au̇z-ᵊn\ see OWSON

¹ouse \üs\ see ¹USE

²ouse \au̇s\ blouse, chiaus, chouse, douse, Gauss, grouse, house, Klaus, Laos, louse, mouse, scouse, souse, spouse, Strauss, baghouse, bathhouse, Bauhaus, birdhouse, blockhouse, bughouse, bunkhouse, cathouse, chophouse, clubhouse, cookhouse, courthouse, deckhouse, degauss, delouse, doghouse, dollhouse, dormouse, espouse, farmhouse, firehouse, flophouse, gashouse, gatehouse, glasshouse, greenhouse, guardhouse, henhouse, hothouse, icehouse, in-house, jailhouse, lighthouse, lobscouse, longhouse, madhouse, Manaus, nuthouse, outhouse, penthouse, playhouse, poorhouse, roadhouse, roughhouse, roundhouse, schoolhouse, smokehouse, springhouse, statehouse, storehouse, teahouse, titmouse, tollhouse, warehouse, washhouse, wheelhouse, White House, whorehouse, workhouse, boardinghouse, clearinghouse, coffeehouse, countinghouse, customhouse, house-to-house, meetinghouse, Mickey Mouse, overblouse, pilothouse, porterhouse, powerhouse, slaughterhouse, sugarhouse, summerhouse, treasure-house, Westinghouse

³**ouse** \aüz\ blouse, bouse, bowse, browse, douse, dowse, drowse, house, mouse, rouse, spouse, touse, arouse, carouse, delouse, doss-house, espouse, rehouse, roughhouse, warehouse—*also plurals and possessives of nouns and third person singular presents of verbs listed at* ²OW

⁴**ouse** \üz\ see ²USE

ousel \aü-zəl\ see OUSAL

ouser \aü-zər\ dowser, houser, mouser, schnauzer, trouser, wowser, warehouser, rabble-rouser

ousin \əz-ᵊn\ see ¹OZEN

ousinage \əz-ᵊn-ij\ cousinage, cozenage

ousing \aü-ziŋ\ housing, rousing, rabble-rousing

¹**ousle** \ü-zəl\ see ²USAL

²**ousle** \aü-zəl\ see OUSAL

ousse \üs\ see ¹USE

ousseau \ü-sō\ see USOE

¹**oust** \aüst\ Faust, joust, oust, roust—*also pasts of verbs listed at* ²OUSE

²**oust** \üst\ see OOST

ouste \üst\ see OOST

¹**ousy** \aü-zē\ see OWSY

²**ousy** \aü-sē\ mousy, Firdawsi

¹**out** \ü\ see ¹EW

²**out** \üt\ see UTE

³**out** \aüt\ bout, clout, doubt, drought, flout, glout, gout, grout, knout, kraut, lout, out, pout, rout, route, scout, shout, snout, spout, sprout, stout, tout, trout, ablaut, about, all-out, bailout, blackout, blissed-out, blowout, breakout, breechclout, brownout, burned-out, burnout, checkout, clapped-out, closeout, cookout, cop-out, cutout, devout, dishclout, downspout, dropout, dugout, eelpout, fade-out, fallout, far-out, flameout, flat-out, foldout, force-out, freak-out, freeze out, full-out, gross-out, groundout, handout, hangout, hideout, holdout, ice-out, knockout, layout, lights-out, lockout, lookout, misdoubt, payout, phaseout, pitchout, printout, psych-out, pullout, punch-out, putout, rainspout, readout, redoubt, rollout, sellout, setout, shakeout, shoot-out, shutout, sick-out, sold-out, spaced-out, speak-out, spinout, stakeout, standout, straight-out, stressed-out, stretch-out, strikeout, takeout, thought-out, throughout, throw out, time-out, tryout, turnout, umlaut, veg out, walkout, washed-out, washout, way-out, whacked-out, whiteout, wigged-out, wipeout, without, workout, worn-out, zonked-out, all get-out, carryout, diner-out, down-and-out, falling-out, gadabout,

hereabout, knockabout,
layabout, out-and-out,
roundabout, rouseabout,
roustabout, runabout,
sauerkraut, stirabout,
thereabout, turnabout,
walkabout, waterspout

¹oute \üt\ see UTE

²oute \aut\ see ³OUT

outed \aut-əd\ snouted, spouted,
undoubted—*also pasts of
verbs listed at* ³OUT

¹outer \üt-ər\ see UTER

²outer \aut-ər\ doubter, flouter,
grouter, outer, pouter, router,
scouter, shouter, spouter,
touter, come-outer, down-and-
outer, out-and-outer

¹outh \üth\ see ²OOTH

²outh \auth\ mouth, routh,
scouth, south, bad-mouth,
goalmouth, loudmouth, poor-
mouth, blabbermouth,
cottonmouth, hand-to-mouth,
motormouth, word-of-mouth

outherly \ǝth-ər-lē\ see
OTHERLY

outhey \au-thē\ see OUTHY

outhful \üth-fəl\ see UTHFUL

outhie \u-thē\ see OOTHY

outhly \üth-lē\ see OOTHLY

outhy \au-thē\ mouthy, Southey

outi \üt-ē\ see ¹OOTY

outing \aut-iŋ\ outing, scouting

outish \aut-ish\ loutish, snoutish

outre \üt-ər\ see UTER

outrement \ü-trə-mənt\ see
UTRIMENT

outs \auts\ hereabouts, ins and
outs, thereabouts,
whereabouts

outy \aut-ē\ see OUGHTY

ou've \üv\ see ³OVE

ouver \ü-vər\ see ³OVER

oux \ü\ see ¹EW

ouy \ē\ see ¹EE

ouyhnhnm \in-əm\ see INIM

ouzel \ü-zəl\ see ²USAL

¹ov \äf\ see ¹OFF

²ov \óf\ see ²OFF

ova \ō-və\ nova, Cralova,
Jehovah, Moldova, bossa
nova, Casanova,
Czestochowa, Kemerovo,
supernova

ovable \ü-və-bəl\ movable,
provable, approvable,
disprovable, immovable,
improvable, removable,
irremovable

ovah \ō-və\ see OVA

oval \ü-vəl\ approval, removal,
disapproval

ovat \əv-ət\ see OVET

¹ove \əv\ dove, glove, love, of,
shove, above, foxglove,
hereof, kid-glove, ringdove,
thereof, truelove, whereof,
ladylove, light-o'-love,
roman-fleuve, turtledove,
unheard of, well-thought-of,
hereinabove

²ove \ōv\ clove, cove, dove,
drove, fauve, grove, hove,
Jove, mauve, rove, stove,
strove, throve, trove, wove,
alcove, behove, cookstove,
mangrove, woodstove, Garden
Grove, interwove, treasure
trove

³ove \üv\ groove, move, poof,
poove, prove, you've,
approve, behoove, commove,

disprove, improve, remove, reprove, disapprove

¹**ovel** \äv-əl\ grovel, novel, antinovel, Yaroslavl

²**ovel** \əv-əl\ grovel, hovel, shovel

ovement \üv-mənt\ movement, improvement

¹**oven** \əv-ən\ coven, oven, sloven

²**oven** \ō-vən\ cloven, coven, woven, Beethoven, handwoven, interwoven

¹**over** \əv-ər\ cover, glover, hover, lover, plover, bedcover, discover, dustcover, hardcover, re-cover, recover, slipcover, softcover, uncover, windhover, undercover

²**over** \ō-vər\ clover, Dover, drover, Grover, over, plover, rover, stover, trover, allover, changeover, crossover, cutover, flashover, flopover, flyover, hangover, Hannover, Hanover, holdover, layover, leftover, makeover, moreover, once-over, Passover, popover, pullover, pushover, rollover, runover, slipover, spillover, stopover, strikeover, takeover, turnover, voice-over, walkover, warmed-over, carryover, crossing-over, going-over, Strait of Dover

³**over** \ü-vər\ groover, Hoover, louver, mover, prover, earthmover, improver, maneuver, remover, reprover, Vancouver, disapprover

⁴**over** \äv-ər\ see ¹AVER

overable \əv-rə-bəl\

discoverable, recoverable, irrecoverable

overly \əv-ər-lē\ loverly, Sir Roger de Coverley

overt \ō-vərt\ covert, overt

overy \əv-rē\ discovery, recovery

ovet \əv-ət\ covet, lovat

ovey \ə-vē\ covey, lovey-dovey

ovian \ō-vē-ən\ Jovian, Markovian, Pavlovian, Varsovian

ovie \ü-vē\ see OOVY

ovo \ō-vō\ Provo, ab ovo, de novo, Porto Novo

ovost \äv-əst\ see AVIST

ovsk \ôfsk\ Dnepropetrovsk, Petropavlovsk

¹**ow** \ō\ beau, blow, bow, bro, Chou, crow, do, doe, dough, ewe, floe, flow, foe, fro, froe, frow, glow, go, grow, ho, hoe, jo, Jo, joe, Joe, know, lo, low, mho, mot, mow, no, No, O, oh, owe, Po, Poe, pow, pro, rho, roe, row, schmo, sew, shew, show, sloe, slow, snow, so, sow, stow, Stowe, strow, though, throe, throw, toe, tow, trow, whoa, woe, yo, aglow, ago, airflow, airglow, alow, although, backflow, backhoe, bandeau, Baotou, barlow, bateau, below, bestow, bon mot, Bordeaux, bravo, by-blow, cachepot, caló, Carlow, chapeau, chateau, Chi-Rho, cockcrow, cornrow, crossbow, Day-Glo, dayglow, Defoe, de trop, deathblow, deco, down-bow, elbow, escrow,

fencerow, flambeau, flyblow, fogbow, forego, foreknow, forgo, Fuzhou, galop, Gateau, genro, gigot, go-slow, Gounod, Guangzhou, gung ho, hallo, Hangzhou, Hankow, heave-ho, hedgerow, heigh-ho, hello, hollo, hullo, inflow, jabot, Jane Doe, jim crow, Jinzhou, John Doe, Hounslow, kayo, KO, Kwangchow, Lanzhou, longbow, low-low, macho, mahoe, maillot, manteau, Marlowe, matelot, merlot, Meursault, Miró, misknow, Moho, mojo, Monroe, morceau, Moscow, mucro, mudflow, nightglow, no-no, no-show, nouveau, outflow, outgo, outgrow, oxbow, Paot'ou, Pernod, picot, Pinot, plateau, pronto, Quanzhou, rainbow, reflow, regrow, repo, reseau, rondeau, rondo, Roseau, rouleau, Rousseau, sabot, salchow, scarecrow, self-sow, serow, shadblow, Shantou, sideshow, skid row, Soho, so-so, sourdough, sunbow, Suzhou, tableau, Taizhou, tiptoe, Thoreau, tonneau, trousseau, Trudeau, uh-oh, unsew, up-bow, upthrow, van Gogh, Watteau, windrow, windthrow, Xuzhou, Zhangzhou, Zhengzhou, Zhuzhon, Zibo, afterglow, aikido, alpenglow, Angelo, apropos, art deco, art nouveau, audio, Baguio, Bamako, barrio, Bergamo,

bibelot, Bilbao, bordereau, Borneo, buffalo, Buffalo, bungalow, Bushido, buteo, calico, cameo, cachalot, cembalo, centimo, CEO, chassepot, cheerio, Cicero, Clemenceau, cogito, comedo, comme il faut, Comoro, counterflow, curaçao, Curaçao, curassow, curio, daimyo, danio, dataflow, Delano, Diderot, do-si-do, domino, dynamo, embryo, entrepôt, Erato, escargot, Eskimo, extrados, fabliau, folio, fricandeau, furbelow, gigolo, go-no-go, guacharo, hammertoe, haricot, heel-and-toe, hetero, HMO, Holy Joe, Idaho, indigo, Jericho, kakapo, Kosciuszko, latigo, long-ago, Maceió, Manchukuo, Mario, massicot, medico, Mexico, mistletoe, modulo, Monaco, Navaho, Navajo, NCO, nuncio, oleo, olio, overflow, overgrow, overthrow, ovolo, Pamlico, Papago, patio, peridot, picaro, piccolo, Pierrot, polio, pomelo, pompano, portico, PPO, Prospero, proximo, quid pro quo, radio, raree-show, ratio, Richard Roe, Rochambeau, rococo, rodeo, Romeo, saddlebow, Sapporo, sapsago, Scorpio, semipro, sloppy joe, so-and-so, SRO, standing O, status quo, stereo, stop-and-go, studio, subito, tallyho, tangelo, Taranto, ticktacktoe, tic-tac-toe, tit-tat-toe, TKO, to-and-fro, Tokyo, tombolo, touch-and-go, touraco, tournedos, tremolo, tuckahoe, tupelo, UFO, ultimo, undergo, undertow, Veneto, vertigo, vibrio, virago, vireo, zydeco, Antonio, Arapaho, centesimo, con spirito, continuo, DMSO, Etobicoke, ex nihilo, fantastico, fellatio, Fernando Póo, fortissimo, Geronimo, get-up-and-go, Guantanamo, hereinbelow, in utero, in vacuo, La Rochfoucauld, lentissimo, lothario, magnifico, malapropos, milesimo, New Mexico, oregano, politico, portfolio, presidio, prestissimo, punctilio, Querétaro, Quintana Roo, Rosario, quo warranto, Sarajevo, scenario, simpatico, Zhangjiakou, ab initio, archipelago, braggadocio, duodecimo, ex officio, generalissimo, impresario, internuncio, oratorio, Paramaribo, pianissimo, rose of Jericho

²ow \aủ\ bough, bow, brow, chiao, chow, ciao, cow, dhow, Dou, dow, Dow, Frau, hao, how, howe, Howe, jow, Lao, mow, now, ow, plow, pow, prau, prow, row, scow, slough, sough, sow, Tao, tau, thou, vow, wow, Yao, allow, avow, Belau, Bissau, bowwow, cacao, cahow, Callao, Davao, chowchow, chow chow, Cracow, Donau,

endow, enow, erenow, eyebrow, gangplow, Haikou, Hankow, hausfrau, haymow, highbrow, hoosegow, Jungfrau, know-how, kowtow, Krakow, landau, lowbrow, luau, Lucknow, Macao, meow, miaow, Moscow, Niihau, nohow, Pelau, powwow, Qing-dao, snowplow, somehow, Zwickau, anyhow, curaçao, Curaçao, disallow, disavow, disendow, middlebrow, Guinea-Bissau, Marianao, Mindanao, holier-than-thou

³ow \óv\ see ²OFF

owa \ō-v³\ see OVA

¹owable \ō-ə-bəl\ knowable, sewable, unknowable

²owable \aủ-ə-bəl\ plowable, allowable, disavowable

owage \ō-ij\ flowage, stowage, towage

¹owal \ō-əl\ see OEL

²owal \aủl\ see ²OWL

¹owan \ō-ən\ see ¹OAN

²owan \aủ-ən\ Gawain, gowan, rowan, rowen, Bandar Seri Begawan

¹oward \ōrd\ see OARD

²oward \aủrd\ see OWERED

¹owd \üd\ see UDE

²owd \aủd\ see ²OUD

owdah \aủd-ə\ see ³AUDE

owder \aủd-ər\ chowder, powder, gunpowder, five-spice powder—*also comparatives of adjectives listed at* ²OUD

owdown \ō-daủn\ blowdown,

lowdown, showdown, slowdown

owdy \aúd-ē\ cloudy, dowdy, howdy, rowdy, cum laude, pandowdy, magna cum laude, summa cum laude

owe \ō\ see ¹OW

¹owed \ōd\ see ODE

²owed \aúd\ see ²OUD

owedly \aú-əd-lē\ allowedly, avowedly

owel \aúl\ see ²OWL

oweling \aú-liŋ\ see ²OWLING

¹owell \aúl\ see ²OWL

²owell \ō-əl\ see OEL

¹owen \ō-ən\ see ²OWAN

²owen \ō-ən\ see ¹OAN

¹ower \ōr\ see ¹OR

²ower \aúr\ bower, cower, dour, dower, flour, flower, gaur, giaour, glower, hour, lower, our, plower, power, scour, shower, sour, tour, tower, vower, avower, cornflower, deflower, devour, embower, empower, firepower, high-power, man-hour, mayflower, moonflower, off-hour, pasqueflower, Peshawar, repower, safflower, sunflower, wallflower, watchtower, wildflower, willpower, candlepower, cauliflower, disendower, Eisenhower, overpower, passionflower, person-hour, Schopenhauer, superpower, sweet-and-sour, thundershower, waterpower, womanpower

³ower \ō-ər\ see ⁵OER

owered \aúrd\ coward, flowered, powered, towered,

high-powered, ivory-towered, superpowered, underpowered—*also pasts of verbs listed at* ²OWER

owerer \aúr-ər\ see ³OURER

owerful \aúr-fəl\ flowerful, powerful

owering \aú-riŋ\ lowering, nonflowering

owery \aúr-ē\ bowery, cauri, dowry, floury, flowery, kauri, Maori, showery

owff \aúf\ howff, langlauf

owhee \ō-ē\ see OWY

owie \aú-ē\ Maui, zowie

owing \ō-iŋ\ see ¹OING

¹owl \ōl\ see ¹OLE

²owl \aúl\ bowel, cowl, dowel, foul, fowl, growl, Howell, howl, jowl, owl, prowl, rowel, scowl, towel, trowel, vowel, yowl, avowal, batfowl, befoul, embowel, peafowl, seafowl, wildfowl, disavowal, disembowel, waterfowl

owland \ō-lənd\ lowland, Poland, Roland

owledge \äl-ij\ college, knowledge, acknowledge, foreknowledge

¹owler \ō-lər\ see OLLER

²owler \aú-lər\ growler, howler, waterfowler

owless \ō-ləs\ see OLUS

owline \ō-lən\ see OLON

¹owling \ō-liŋ\ see OLLING

²owling \aú-liŋ\ cowling, growling, howling, toweling, antifouling, biofouling, waterfowling

owlock \äl-ək\ see OLOCH

¹owly \ō-lē\ see ¹OLY

²**owly** \au̇-lē\ foully, growly, haole, jowly

¹**owman** \ō-mən\ see OMAN

²**owman** \au̇-mən\ bowman, cowman, plowman

ow-me \ō-mē\ see OAMY

¹**own** \ōn\ see ¹ONE

²**own** \au̇n\ brown, Brown, clown, crown, down, Down, drown, frown, gown, lown, noun, town, blowdown, boomtown, breakdown, Bridgetown, bringdown, Capetown, clampdown, closedown, comedown, cooldown, countdown, crackdown, crosstown, downtown, drawdown, embrown, facedown, Freetown, Georgetown, George Town, godown, hoedown, hometown, Jamestown, knockdown, letdown, lockdown, lookdown, lowdown, markdown, meltdown, nightgown, pastedown, phasedown, pronoun, pushdown, put-down, renown, rubdown, rundown, scaledown, shakedown, showdown, shutdown, sitdown, slowdown, Southdown, splashdown, stand-down, step-down, stripped-down, sundown, thumbs-down, tiedown, top-down, touchdown, turndown, uncrown, uptown, Von Braun, write-down, Youngstown, Allentown, broken-down, buttondown, Charlottetown, Chinatown, dressing-down, eiderdown, Germantown, hand-me-down, reach-me-down, shantytown, tumbledown, upside down, watered-down, man-about-town

owndead \au̇n-dəd\ see OUNDED

ownding \au̇n-diŋ\ see OUNDING

¹**owned** \ōnd\ see ¹ONED

²**owned** \au̇nd\ see ²OUND

¹**owner** \ō-nər\ see ¹ONER

²**owner** \ü-nər\ see OONER

³**owner** \au̇-nər\ browner, crowner, downer, sundowner

owness \ō-nəs\ see ²ONUS

ownia \ō-nē-ə\ see ¹ONIA

ownie \au̇-nē\ see OWNY

¹**owning** \ō-niŋ\ see ²ONING

²**owning** \au̇-niŋ\ Browning— *also present participles of verbs listed at* ²OWN

ownish \au̇-nish\ brownish, clownish

ownlet \au̇n-lət\ roundlet, townlet

ownsman \au̇nz-mən\ gownsman, groundsman, roundsman, townsman

owny \au̇-nē\ brownie, browny, downy, townie

owper \ü-pər\ see OOPER

owry \au̇r-ē\ see OWERY

owse \au̇z\ see ²OUSE

owser \au̇-zər\ see OUSER

owson \au̇z-ᵊn\ thousand, advowson

owster \ō-stər\ see OASTER

owsy \au̇-zē\ blousy, blowsy, drowsy, lousy

owth \ōth\ both, growth, loath, loth, oath, quoth, sloth, troth,

wroth, betroth, outgrowth,
upgrowth, Alioth,
intergrowth, overgrowth,
undergrowth

owy \ō-ē\ blowy, Chloe,
doughy, joey, Joey, showy,
snowy, towhee, echoey,
kalanchoe

owys \ō-əs\ see ³OIS

ox \äks\ box, cox, fox, Fox,
gox, Knox, lox, ox, pax,
phlox, pox, aurochs, bandbox,
boondocks, cowpox, detox,
dreadlocks, firebox, Fort
Knox, gearbox, gravlax,
hatbox, hotbox, icebox,
jukebox, lockbox, mailbox,
matchbox, musk-ox, outfox,
pillbox, postbox, redox,
saltbox, sandbox, skybox,
smallpox, snuffbox, soapbox,
strongbox, sweatbox, toolbox,
unbox, volvox, witness-box,
workbox, Xerox, chatterbox,
equinox, orthodox, Orthodox,
paradox, pillar-box,
shadowbox, Skinner box,
tinderbox, econobox, Greek
Orthodox, heterodox,
homeobox, jack-in-the-box,
unorthodox, neoorthodox,
dementia praecox—*also
plurals and possessives of
nouns and third person
singular presents of verbs
listed at* ¹OCK

oxen \äk-sən\ oxen,
Niedersachsen

oxer \äk-sər\ boxer, Boxer,
bobby-soxer

oxie \äk-sē\ see OXY

oxin \äk-sən\ coxswain, tocsin,

toxin, dioxin, aflatoxin,
mycotoxin

oxswain \äk-sən\ see OXIN

oxy \äk-sē\ boxy, doxy, foxy,
moxie, oxy, proxy, epoxy,
orthodoxy, Orthodoxy,
heterodoxy, neoorthodoxy

oy \ȯi\ boy, buoy, cloy, coy,
foy, goy, hoy, joy, Joy, koi,
ploy, poi, Roy, soy, strawy,
toy, troy, Troy, ahoy, alloy,
Amoy, annoy, batboy,
bellboy, bok choy, borzoi,
busboy, callboy, carboy,
charpoy, choirboy, convoy,
cowboy, decoy, deploy,
destroy, doughboy, employ,
enjoy, envoy, fly-boy,
footboy, Hanoi, hautbois,
highboy, houseboy, killjoy,
Khoikhoi, Leroy, linkboy,
lowboy, McCoy, newsboy,
pak choi, playboy,plowboy,
po'boy, postboy, potboy,
Quemoy, Rob Roy, Saint
Croix, Savoy, schoolboy,
sepoy, tallboy, teapoy,
Tolstoy, tomboy, travois,
viceroy, Adonai, attaboy,
bullyboy, copyboy, corduroy,
hoi polloi, Illinois, Iroquois,
Kawagoe, maccaboy, Niterói,
overjoy, paperboy, redeploy,
reemploy, Tinkertoy, Helen of
Troy

oya \ȯi-ə\ see OIA

oyable \ȯi-ə-bəl\ deployable,
employable

¹oyal \īl\ see ¹ILE

²oyal \ȯil\ see OIL

oyalist \ȯi-ə-ləst\ loyalist,
royalist

oyalty \ȯil-tē\ loyalty, royalty, disloyalty, viceroyalty

oyance \ȯi-əns\ buoyance, joyance, annoyance, chatoyance, clairvoyance, flamboyance

oyancy \ȯi-ən-sē\ buoyancy, chatoyancy, flamboyancy

oyant \ȯi-ənt\ buoyant, chatoyant, clairvoyant, flamboyant

oyce \ȯis\ see OICE

oyd \ȯid\ see ¹OID

oyden \ȯi-dᵊn\ Croydon, hoyden

oydon \ȯi-dᵊn\ see OYDEN

oyed \ȯid\ see ¹OID

oyen \ȯi-ən\ doyen, Goyen, Iroquoian

oyer \ȯir\ coir, foyer, moire, caloyer, destroyer

oyes \ȯiz\ see ²OISE

oying \ȯiŋ\ see AWING

oyle \ȯil\ see OIL

oyless \ȯi-ləs\ joyless, Troilus

oyment \ȯi-mənt\ deployment, employment, enjoyment, unemployment

oyne \ȯin\ see ¹OIN

¹oyo \ȯi-ō\ boyo, arroyo

²oyo \ȯi-ə\ see OIA

o-yo \ō-yō\ see ²OLLO

oyster \ȯi-stər\ see OISTER

¹oz \əz\ see ¹EUSE

²oz \óz\ see ¹AUSE

³oz \ōz\ see ²OSE

oza \ō-zə\ see ²OSA

oze \ōz\ see ²OSE

¹ozen \əz-ᵊn\ cousin, cozen, dozen, cater-cousin

²ozen \ōz-ᵊn\ see OSEN

ozenage \əz-ᵊn-ij\ see OUSINAGE

ozer \ō-zər\ see ¹OSER

ozily \ō-zə-lē\ see OSILY

¹ozo \ō-sō\ see ¹OSO

²ozo \ō-zō\ see ²OSO

ozy \ō-zē\ see OSY

ozzer \äz-ər\ rozzer, alcazar

ozzle \äz-əl\ Basel, Basil, nozzle, schnozzle

u

¹u \ü\ see ¹EW

²u \ə\ Chang-de, hao-tzu

¹ua \ü-ə\ skua, Karlsruhe, lehua, Quechua, Timucua

²ua \ä\ see ¹A

uable \ü-ə-bəl\ chewable, doable, suable, viewable, accruable, construable, renewable

ual \ü-əl\ see ¹UEL

uan \ü-ən\ bruin, ruin, Siouan, yuan

uancy \ü-ən-sē\ see UENCY

uant \ü-ənt\ see UENT

uart \ùrt\ see ¹URT

ub \əb\ blub, chub, club, cub, drub, dub, flub, grub, hub, nub, pub, rub, scrub, shrub, slub, snub, stub, sub, tub, bathtub, flubdub, hubbub, nightclub, washtub, overdub, Beelzebub

uba \ü-bə\ Cuba, juba, scuba, tuba, Aruba, Santiago de Cuba

ubal \ü-bəl\ Jubal, nubile, ruble, tubal

uban \ü-bən\ see EUBEN

ubbard \əb-ərd\ cupboard, Mother Hubbard

ubber \əb-ər\ blubber, clubber, drubber, dubber, grubber, lubber, rubber, scrubber, slubber, snubber, tubber, landlubber, nightclubber, money-grubber

ubbery \əb-rē\ blubbery, rubbery, shrubbery

ubbily \əb-ə-lē\ bubbly, chubbily, grubbily

ubbin \əb-ən\ dubbin, nubbin

ubbing \əb-iŋ\ drubbing, rubbing, slubbing, landlubbing

ubble \əb-əl\ bubble, double, nubble, rubble, stubble, trouble, abubble, redouble, undouble, hubble-bubble

ubbled \ə-bəld\ bubbled, doubled, troubled, redoubled

ubbler \əb-lər\ see OUBLER

¹ubbly \əb-lē\ bubbly, doubly, nubbly, stubbly

²ubbly \əb-ə-lē\ see UBBILY

ubby \əb-ē\ chubby, clubby, cubby, grubby, hubby, nubby, Rabi, scrubby, shrubby, snubby, stubby, tubby

ube \üb\ boob, cube, lube, rube, tube, blowtube, Danube, flashcube, haboob, jujube, hypercube

uben \ü-bən\ see EUBEN

ubens \ü-bənz\ Rubens—*also possessives and plurals of nouns listed at* EUBEN

uber \ü-bər\ Buber, cuber, goober, tuber

uberance \ü-brəns\ exuberance, protuberance

uberant \ü-brənt\ exuberant, protuberant

uberous \ü-brəs\ see UBRIS

ubic \ü-bik\ cubic, pubic, cherubic

ubile \ü-bəl\ see UBAL

ubious \ü-bē-əs\ dubious, rubious

ubis \ü-bəs\ pubis, rubus, Anubis

uble \ü-bəl\ see UBAL

ublic \əb-lik\ public, republic

ublican \əb-li-kən\ publican, republican

ubman \əb-mən\ clubman, Tubman

ubric \ü-brik\ lubric, rubric

ubrious \ü-brē-əs\ lugubrious, salubrious, insalubrious

ubris \ü-brəs\ hubris, tuberous

ubtile \ət-ᵊl\ see UTTLE

ubus \ü-bəs\ see UBIS

uby \ü-bē\ see OOBY

uca \ü-kə\ see OOKA

ucal \ü-kəl\ ducal, nuchal, archducal

ucan \ü-kən\ glucan, kuchen, Lucan, interleukin

ucat \ək-ət\ see UCKET

¹ucca \ü-kə\ see OOKA

²ucca \ək-ə\ see UKKA

uccal \ək-əl\ see UCKLE

ucci \ü-chē\ see OOCHY

ucco \ək-ō\ see UCKO

uccor \ək-ər\ see UCKER

uccory \ək-rē\ see UCKERY

ucculence \ək-yə-ləns\ see UCULENCE

uce \üs\ see ¹USE

uced \üst\ see OOST

ucement \ü-smənt\ inducement, seducement

ucence \üs-ᵊns\ nuisance, translucence

ucer \ü-sər\ juicer, looser, adducer, Bull Mooser, inducer, lime-juicer, producer, transducer, introducer, reproducer

¹uch \ich\ see ITCH

²uch \ük\ see UKE

³uch \əch\ see ¹UTCH

uchal \ü-kəl\ see UCAL

¹uche \ü-chē\ see OOCHY

²uche \üch\ see ¹OOCH

³uche \üsh\ see OUCHE

uchen \ü-kən\ see UCAN

ucher \ü-chər\ see UTURE

uchin \ü-shən\ see UTION

uchsia \ü-shə\ see UTIA

uchy \əch-ē\ duchy, smutchy, touchy, archduchy

ucia \ü-shə\ see UTIA

ucial \ü-shəl\ crucial, fiducial

ucian \ü-shən\ see UTION

ucible \ü-sə-bəl\ crucible, deducible, educible, inducible, producible, protrusible, irreducible, reproducible, irreproducible

ucid \ü-səd\ deuced, lucid, pellucid, Seleucid

ucifer \ü-sə-fər\ crucifer, Lucifer

ucity \ü-sət-ē\ abstrusity, caducity

ucive \ü-siv\ see USIVE

¹uck \ək\ buck, Buck, chuck, cluck, cruck, duck, guck, huck, luck, muck, pluck, puck, Puck, ruck, schmuck, shuck, snuck, struck, stuck, suck, truck, Truk, tuck, yech, yuck, amok, awestruck, bushbuck, Canuck, dumbstruck, Kalmuck, lame-duck, light-struck, moonstruck, mukluk, muktuk, potluck, reedbuck, roebuck, sawbuck, shelduck, stagestruck, starstruck, sunstruck, unstuck, upchuck, woodchuck, geoduck, Keokuk, Habakkuk, megabuck, muckamuck, nip and tuck, high-muck-a-muck

²uck \ùk\ see ¹OOK

ukar \ək-ər\ see UCKER

ucker \ək-ər\ bucker, chukar, chukker, ducker, mucker, plucker, pucker, shucker, succor, sucker, trucker, tucker, bloodsucker, sapsucker, seersucker

uckery \ək-rē\ puckery, succory

ucket \ək-ət\ bucket, ducat, tucket, gutbucket, Nantucket

uckle \ək-əl\ buccal, buckle, chuckle, knuckle, suckle, truckle, Arbuckle, bare-knuckle, parbuckle, pinochle, swashbuckle, turnbuckle, unbuckle, honeysuckle

uckled \ək-əld\ cuckold, knuckled, bare-knuckled—*also pasts of verbs listed at* UCKLE

uckler \ək-lər\ buckler, knuckler, swashbuckler

uckling \ək-liŋ\ duckling, suckling, swashbuckling

ucko \ək-ō\ bucko, stucco

uckold \ək-əld\ see UCKLED

uckoo \ü-kü\ cuckoo, Maluku

ucks \əks\ see ¹UX

uckus \ùk-əs\ ruckus, Sukkoth

ucky \ək-ē\ ducky, lucky, mucky, plucky, yucky, Kentucky, unlucky, happy-go-lucky

uco \ü-kō\ pachuco, osso buco

ucre \ü-kər\ euchre, lucre

uct \əkt\ duct, abduct, adduct, conduct, construct, deduct, destruct, eruct, induct, instruct, obstruct, aqueduct, deconstruct, reconstruct, usufruct, viaduct—*also pasts of verbs listed at* UCK

uctable \ək-tə-bəl\ see UCTIBLE

uctal \ək-t³l\ ductal, ductile

uctance \ək-təns\ conductance, inductance, reluctance

uctible \ək-tə-bəl\ conductible, constructible, deductible, destructible, indestructible, ineluctable, reconstructible

uctile \ək-t³l\ see UCTAL

ucting \ək-tiŋ\ ducting, semiconducting

uction \ək-shən\ fluxion, ruction, suction, abduction, adduction, conduction, construction, deduction, destruction, eduction, effluxion, induction, instruction, obstruction, production, reduction, seduction, deconstruction, introduction, reconstruction, reproduction, photoreproduction

uctive \ək-tiv\ adductive, conductive, constructive, deductive, destructive, inductive, instructive, productive, reductive, seductive, reconstructive, reproductive, self-destructive, counterproductive

uctor \ək-tər\ abductor, adductor, conductor, constructor, destructor, eductor, inductor, instructor, reconstructor, semiconductor

uctress \ək-trəs\ conductress, instructress, seductress

uculence \ək-yə-ləns\ succulence, truculence

ucy \ü-sē\ see UICY

¹ud \əd\ blood, bud, crud, cud, dud, flood, fud, Judd, mud, rudd, scud, spud, stud, sudd, thud, coldblood, disbud, full-blood, half-blood, hotblood, lifeblood, oxblood, redbud, rosebud, warmblood, stick-in-the-mud

²ud \üd\ see UDE

³ud \ud\ see ¹OOD

uda \üd-ə\ Buddha, Gouda, Judah, Barbuda, Bermuda, remuda, barracuda, Buxtehude, Gautama Buddha

udable \üd-ə-bəl\ excludable, extrudable, includable, ineludible

udah \üd-ə\ see UDA

udal \üd-ᵊl\ see OODLE

udas \üd-əs\ Judas, Santa Gertrudis

¹udd \ud\ see ¹OOD

²udd \əd\ see ¹UD

udded \əd-əd\ see ¹OODED

udder \əd-ər\ budder, flooder, judder, rudder, shudder, udder

uddha \üd-ə\ see UDA

uddhist \üd-əst\ see ¹UDIST

uddie \əd-ē\ see ¹UDDY

¹udding \əd-iŋ\ budding, studding

²udding \ud-iŋ\ see OODING

uddle \əd-ᵊl\ buddle, cuddle, fuddle, huddle, muddle, puddle, ruddle, befuddle

uddly \əd-lē\ cuddly, Dudley, muddly, studly

¹uddy \əd-ē\ bloody, buddy, Buddy, cruddy, cuddy, duddie, muddy, ruddy, study, fuddy-duddy, understudy

²uddy \ud-ē\ see ²OODY

¹ude \üd\ brood, crowd, crude, dude, feud, food, hued, Jude, lewd, mood, nude, oud, pood, prude, pseud, rood, rude, shrewd, snood, stewed, who'd, wood, wud, you'd, allude, collude, conclude, delude, denude, elude, etude, exclude, extrude, exude, fast-food, Gertrude, include, intrude, obtrude, occlude, postlude, preclude, prelude, protrude, quaalude, Quaalude, seafood, seclude, subdued, transude, unglued, altitude, amplitude, aptitude, attitude, certitude, consuetude, crassitude, desuetude, finitude, fortitude, gratitude, habitude, hebetude, interlude, lassitude, latitude, longitude, magnitude, mansuetude, multitude, negritude, platitude, plenitude, plentitude, promptitude, pulchritude, quietude, rectitude, seminude, servitude, solitude, turpitude, vastitude, beatitude, correctitude, decrepitude, exactitude, inaptitude, incertitude, ineptitude, infinitude,

ingratitude, inquietude,
similitude, solicitude,
vicissitude, dissimilitude,
inexactitude, verisimilitude

²ude \üd-ə\ see UDA

udel \üd-ᵊl\ see OODLE

udence \ü-dᵊn(t)s\ Prudence,
students, imprudence,
jurisprudence

udeness \üd-nəs\ see UDINOUS

udent \üd-ᵊnt\ prudent,
imprudent, student,
jurisprudent

udents \ü-dᵊn(t)s\ see UDENCE

uder \üd-ər\ brooder, Tudor,
concluder, deluder, excluder,
extruder, intruder, obtruder,
preluder—*also comparatives
of adjectives listed at* UDE

¹udge \əj\ budge, drudge,
fudge, grudge, judge, nudge,
sludge, smudge, trudge,
adjudge, begrudge, forejudge,
misjudge, prejudge

²udge \üj\ see ¹UGE

udgeon \əj-ən\ bludgeon,
dudgeon, gudgeon,
curmudgeon

udget \əj-ət\ budget, fussbudget

udgie \əj-ē\ see UDGY

udging \əj-iŋ\ drudging,
grudging

udgy \əj-ē\ budgie, pudgy,
sludgy, smudgy

udible \üd-ə-bəl\ see UDABLE

udi \ü-dē\ see ¹OODY

udie \ü-dē\ see ¹OODY

udinal \üd-nəl\ altitudinal,
aptitudinal, attitudinal,
latitudinal, longitudinal,
platitudinal

udinous \üd-nəs\ crudeness,
lewdness, rudeness,
shrewdness, altitudinous,
multitudinous, platitudinous,
plenitudinous, pulchritudinous

udis \üd-əs\ see UDAS

udish \üd-ish\ dudish, prudish

¹udist \üd-əst\ Buddhist,
feudist, nudist—*also
superlatives of adjectives
listed at* UDE

²udist \ud-əst\ see OULDEST

udity \üd-ət-ē\ crudity, nudity

udley \əd-lē\ see UDDLY

udly \əd-lē\ see UDDLY

udo \üd-ō\ judo, kudo, pseudo,
scudo, escudo, Matsudo,
testudo

udor \üd-ər\ see UDER

udsman \udz-mən\ see
OODSMAN

udson \əd-sən\ Hudson, Judson

udu \üd-ü\ see OODOO

¹udy \ü-dē\ see ¹OODY

²udy \əd-ē\ see ¹UDDY

¹ue \ü\ see EW

²ue \ā\ see AY

ued \üd\ see UDE

ueful \ü-fəl\ rueful, pantofle

ueghel \ü-gəl\ see UGAL

ueil \əi\ Arauil, Argentueil

¹uel \ü-əl\ crewel, cruel, dual,
duel, gruel, jewel, Jewel,
Jewell, newel, Newell,
accrual, eschewal, refuel,
renewal, Pantagruel

²uel \ül\ see ¹OOL

uely \ü-lē\ see ULY

uement \ü-mənt\ see EWMENT

uence \ü-əns\ affluence,
confluence, congruence,

effluence, influence,
pursuance, refluence,
incongruence
uency \ü-ən-sē\ fluency,
truancy, affluency,
congruency, nonfluency
ueness \ü-nəs\ see EWNESS
uenster \ən-stər\ see UNSTER
uent \ü-ənt\ fluent, suint, truant,
affluent, confluent, congruent,
effluent, influent, incongruent
uer \ü-ər\ see [1]EWER
uerdon \ərd-ᵊn\ see URDEN
uerile \ur-əl\ see URAL
ues \üz\ see [2]USE
uesman \üz-mən\ see EWSMAN
uesome \ü-səm\ gruesome,
twosome
uesy \ü-zē\ see OOZY
uet \ü-ət\ bluet, cruet, peewit,
suet, conduit, intuit
uette \et\ see [1]ET
uey \ü-ē\ see EWY
ufa \ü-fə\ loofah, tufa, opera
buffa
uff \əf\ bluff, buff, chough,
chuff, cuff, duff, fluff, gruff,
guff, huff, luff, muff, puff,
rough, ruff, scruff, scuff,
slough, snuff, sough, stuff,
tough, tuff, dyestuff, earmuff,
enough, foodstuff, handcuff,
rebuff, oeil-de-boeuf,
overstuff
uffa \ü-fə\ see UFA
[1]uffe \üf\ see [1]OOF
[2]uffe \uf\ see [2]OOF
uffed \əft\ chuffed, ruffed, tuft,
candytuft—*also pasts of verbs
listed at* UFF
uffel \əf-əl\ see [1]UFFLE

uffer \əf-ər\ bluffer, buffer,
duffer, puffer, rougher,
snuffer, stuffer, suffer,
candlesnuffer—*also
comparatives of adjectives
listed at* UFF
uffet \əf-ət\ buffet, tuffet
uffin \əf-ən\ muffin, puffin,
roughen, toughen, ragamuffin
uffish \əf-ish\ huffish, roughish
[1]uffle \əf-əl\ duffel, muffle,
ruffle, scuffle, shuffle, snuffle,
truffle, kerfuffle, reshuffle,
unmuffle
[2]uffle \ü-fəl\ see UEFUL
uffled \əf-əld\ truffled,
unruffled—*also pasts of verbs
listed at* UFFLE
uffler \əf-lər\ muffler, shuffler,
snuffler
uffly \əf-lē\ bluffly, gruffly,
roughly, ruffly
uffy \əf-ē\ chuffy, fluffy, huffy,
puffy, scruffy, snuffy, stuffy,
toughie
ufi \ü-fē\ see OOFY
ufous \ü-fəs\ rufous, Rufus
uft \əft\ see UFFED
ufti \əf-tē\ mufti, tufty
ufty \əf-tē\ see UFTI
ufus \ü-fəs\ see UFOUS
ug \əg\ bug, chug, Doug, drug,
dug, fug, hug, jug, lug, mug,
plug, pug, rug, shrug, slug,
smug, snug, thug, trug, tug,
ugh, vug, bedbug, billbug,
debug, earplug, firebug,
fireplug, goldbug, humbug,
lovebug, stinkbug, unplug,
antidrug, chugalug,
doodlebug, jitterbug, ladybug,

litterbug, mealybug, shutterbug

uga \ü-gə\ beluga, Cayuga, Kaluga, Sevruga, Tortuga, Chattanooga

ugal \ü-gəl\ Brueghel, bugle, frugal, fugal, fugle, kugel, conjugal

ugar \úg-ər\ see UGUR

¹uge \üj\ huge, kludge, Lodz, scrooge, scrouge, stooge, deluge, centrifuge, subterfuge

²uge \üzh\ Bruges, luge, rouge, deluge, gamboge, refuge, Baton Rouge

ugel \ü-gəl\ see UGAL

uges \üzh\ see ²UGE

uggaree \əg-rē\ see ¹UGGERY

¹ugger \əg-ər\ bugger, chugger, lugger, mugger, plugger, rugger, slugger, Bavagar, Jamnagar, Srinagar, hugger-mugger, Navanagar

²ugger \úg-ər\ see UGUR

¹uggery \əg-rē\ buggery, puggaree, snuggery, thuggery, skulduggery

²uggery \úg-rē\ see UGARY

ugget \əg-ət\ drugget, nugget

uggie \əg-ē\ see UGGY

uggish \əg-ish\ sluggish, thuggish

uggle \əg-əl\ guggle, juggle, smuggle, snuggle, struggle

uggler \əg-lər\ juggler, smuggler, struggler

uggy \əg-ē\ buggy, druggie, druggy, fuggy, luggie, muggy

¹ugh \əg\ see UG

²ugh \ü\ see ¹EW

ughes \üz\ see ²USE

ugle \ü-gəl\ see UGAL

ugli \ə-glē\ see UGLY

uglia \ûl-yə\ see ULIA

ugly \əg-lē\ smugly, Ugli, ugly, plug-ugly

ugn \ün\ see ¹OON

ugner \ü-nər\ see OONER

ugric \ü-grik\ tugrik, Ugric, Finno-Ugric

ugrik \ü-grik\ see UGRIC

ugu \ü-gü\ fugu, goo-goo

ugur \úg-ər\ booger, bugger, sugar

uhe \ü-ə\ see UA

uhl \ül\ see ¹OOL

¹uhr \ər\ see ¹EUR

²uhr \úr\ see ¹URE

ührer \úr-ər\ see ¹URER

¹ui \ā\ see ¹AY

²ui \ē\ see ¹EE

uice \üs\ see ¹USE

uiced \üst\ see OOST

uiceless \ü-sləs\ see USELESS

uicer \ü-sər\ see UCER

uicy \ü-sē\ goosey, juicy, Lucy, sluicy, sprucy, Brancusi, Watsui, acey-deucey, Arginusae, loosey-goosey

uid \ü-id\ Clwyd, druid, fluid

uidable \īd-ə-bəl\ see ¹IDABLE

uidance \īd-ᵊns\ see IDANCE

uide \īd\ see ¹IDE

uided \īd-əd\ see IDED

uider \īd-ər\ see ¹IDER

uidon \īd-ᵊn\ see IDEN

uiker \ī-kər\ see IKER

uild \ild\ see ILLED

uilder \il-dər\ see ILDER

uilding \il-diŋ\ see ILDING

uile \īl\ see ¹ILE

uileless \īl-ləs\ see ILELESS

uiler \ī-lər\ see ILAR

uilleann \i-lən\ see ILLON

uilt \ilt\ see ILT
uimpe \amp\ see ³AMP
¹uin \ü-ən\ see UAN
²uin \ən\ see UN
³uin \aⁿ\ see ⁴IN
uing \ü-iŋ\ see ²OING
uint \ü-ənt\ see UENT
uir \ὺr\ see ¹URE
uirdly \ὺr-lē\ see URELY
uis \ü-əs\ see EWESS
uisance \üs-ᵊns\ see UCENCE
uisard \ī-zərd\ see ISORED
¹uise \üz\ see ²USE
²uise \ῑz\ see IZE
uiser \ü-zər\ see USER
uish \ü-ish\ see EWISH
uisne \ü-nē\ see OONY
uiste \is-tē\ see ²ICITY
¹uit \ü-ət\ see UET
²uit \üt\ see UTE
uitable \üt-ə-bəl\ see UTABLE
uitage \üt-ij\ see ¹OOTAGE
uite \üt\ see UTE
uited \üt-əd\ see ¹OOTED
uiter \üt-ər\ see UTER
uiterer \üt-ər-ər\ fruiterer,
  pewterer
uiting \üt-iŋ\ see UTING
uitless \üt-ləs\ see OOTLESS
uitlet \üt-lət\ see OOTLET
uitor \üt-ər\ see UTER
uitous \ü-ət-əs\ circuitous,
  fortuitous, gratuitous
uits \üts\ see OOTS
¹uittle \üt-ᵊl\ see UTILE
²uittle \ət-ᵊl\ see UTTLE
¹uity \ü-ət-ē\ acuity, annuity,
  circuity, congruity, fatuity,
  fortuity, gratuity, vacuity,
  ambiguity, assiduity,
  conspicuity, contiguity,
  continuity, incongruity,

ingenuity, perpetuity,
promiscuity, superfluity,
discontinuity
²uity \üt-ē\ see ¹OOTY
¹uk \ük\ see UKE
²uk \ůk\ see ¹OOK
³uk \ək\ see UCK
ukar \ə-kər\ see UCKER
uke \ük\ cuke, duke, fluke,
  gook, juke, kook, Luke, nuke,
  puke, snook, souk, spook,
  suq, tuque, uke, yeuk,
  archduke, Baruch,
  caoutchouc, Chinook, Kirkuk,
  Mamluk, rebuke, Heptateuch,
  Hexateuch, Pentateuch
¹uki \ü-kē\ see ¹OOKY
²uki \ů-kē\ see OOKIE
ukka \ək-ə\ chukka, pukka,
  yucca, felucca
ukkah \ůk-ə\ OOKAH
ukker \ək-ər\ see UCKER
ukkoth \ůk-əs\ see UCKUS
uku \ü-kü\ see UCKOO
¹ul \ůl\ bull, Bull, full, pull,
  shul, wool, you'll, armful,
  bagful, bellpull, brimful,
  bulbul, canful, capful, carful,
  cheekful, chestful, chock-full,
  cupful, drawerful, earful,
  eyeful, fistful, forkful,
  glassful, handful, houseful,
  jarful, John Bull, jugful, leg-
  pull, mouthful, outpull,
  pailful, panful, pipeful,
  plateful, potful, push-pull,
  rackful, roomful, sackful,
  scoopful, shelfful, skinful,
  spoonful, stickful, tankful,
  tinful, topful, trainful, trayful,
  trunkful, tubful, barrelful,
  basketful, bellyful,

teaspoonful, dyed-in-the-wool, tablespoonful

²**ul** \ül\ see ¹OOL

³**ul** \əl\ see ¹ULL

ula \ü-lə\ Beulah, Fula, hula, moola, pula, Tula, ampulla, tabbouleh, Ashtabula, San Pedro Sula

ular \ü-lər\ see OOLER

ulcent \əl-sənt\ see ULSANT

ulcer \əl-sər\ see ULSER

ulch \əlch\ cultch, gulch, mulch

¹**ule** \ü-lē\ see ULY

²**ule** \ül\ see ¹OOL

ulean \ü-lē-ən\ Boolean, Acheulean, cerulean

uled \üld\ see OOLED

ulep \ü-ləp\ see ULIP

uler \ü-lər\ see OOLER

ules \ülz\ Jules—*also possessives and plurals of nouns and third person singular presents of verbs listed at* ¹OOL

ulet \əl-ət\ see ¹ULLET

¹**uley** \ü-lē\ see ULY

²**uley** \ül-ē\ see ²ULLY

ulf \əlf\ golf, gulf, Gulf, engulf, Beowulf, Saronic Gulf

ulgar \əl-gər\ see ULGUR

ulge \əlj\ bulge, divulge, indulge, overindulge

¹**ulgence** \əl-jəns\ divulgence, indulgence, refulgence

²**ulgence** \ùl-jəns\ effulgence, refulgence

ulgent \əl-jənt\ fulgent, indulgent

ulgur \əl-gər\ bulgur, vulgar

ulhas \əl-əs\ see ULLUS

uli \ùl-ē\ see ²ULLY

ulia \ül-yə\ Julia, Puglia, Apulia, Friuli-Venezia Guilia

ulie \ü-lē\ see ULY

ulip \ü-ləp\ julep, tulip

ulish \ü-lish\ see OOLISH

ulity \ü-lət-ē\ credulity, garrulity, sedulity, incredulity

ulk \əlk\ bulk, hulk, skulk, sulk, yolk

ulky \əl-kē\ bulky, sulky

¹**ull** \əl\ cull, dull, gull, hull, Hull, lull, mull, null, scull, skull, stull, trull, annul, Choiseul, mogul, numskull, pas seul, monohull, multihull, Sitting Bull, Solihull, Kingston upon Hull

²**ull** \ùl\ see ¹UL

¹**ulla** \ùl-ə\ bulla, mullah, Sulla, ampulla

²**ulla** \ü-lə\ see ULA

³**ulla** \əl-ə\ see ¹ULLAH

ullage \əl-ij\ sullage, ullage

¹**ullah** \əl-ə\ Gullah, mullah, nullah, stollen, medulla, ayatollah

²**ullah** \ùl-ə\ see ¹ULLA

ullan \əl-ən\ see ULLEN

ullard \əl-ərd\ see OLORED

ullate \əl-ət\ see ¹ULLET

ulle \ül\ see ¹OOL

ullein \əl-ən\ see ULLEN

ullen \əl-ən\ mullein, stollen, sullen, Lucullan

¹**uller** \ùl-ər\ fuller, puller

²**uller** \əl-ər\ see ¹OLOR

ulles \əl-əs\ see ULLUS

¹**ullet** \əl-ət\ culet, cullet, gullet, mullet, cucullate

²**ullet** \ùl-ət\ bullet, Bullitt, pullet

ulley \úl-ē\ see ²ULLY

ullion \əl-yən\ cullion, mullion, scullion, slumgullion

ullis \əl-əs\ see ULLUS

ullitt \úl-ət\ see ²ULLET

ullman \úl-mən\ fulmine, Pullman

ullus \əl-əs\ Dulles, Agulhas, Catullus, portcullis, Cape Agulhas

¹ully \əl-ē\ cully, dully, gully, sully

²ully \úl-ē\ bully, fully, gully, muley, puli, pulley, woolly

ulmine \úl-mən\ see ULLMAN

ulp \əlp\ gulp, pulp, insculp

ulsant \əl-sənt\ pulsant, convulsant, demulcent

ulse \əls\ dulse, pulse, avulse, convulse, expulse, impulse, repulse

ulser \əl-sər\ pulser, ulcer

ulsion \əl-shən\ pulsion, avulsion, compulsion, convulsion, emulsion, evulsion, expulsion, impulsion, propulsion, repulsion, revulsion

ulsive \əl-siv\ compulsive, convulsive, emulsive, expulsive, impulsive, propulsive, repulsive

ult \əlt\ cult, adult, consult, exult, incult, indult, insult, occult, penult, result, tumult, catapult, antepenult

ultancy \əlt-ᵊn-sē\ consultancy, exultancy

ultant \əlt-ᵊnt\ consultant, exultant, resultant

ultch \əlch\ see ULCH

ulter \əl-tər\ consultor, insulter, occulter

ultery \əl-trē\ see ULTRY

ultor \əl-tər\ see ULTER

ultry \əl-trē\ sultry, adultery

ulture \əl-chər\ culture, multure, vulture, subculture, agriculture, apiculture, aquaculture, aviculture, counterculture, floriculture, horticulture, mariculture, monoculture, silviculture, viniculture, arboriculture

ulty \əl-tē\ see ¹ALTI

ulu \ü-lü\ lulu, Sulu, Zulu, Bangweulu, Honolulu

ulunder \əl-ən-dər\ see OLANDER

ulva \əl-və\ ulva, vulva

ulvar \əl-vər\ see ULVER

ulver \əl-vər\ culver, vulvar

uly \ü-lē\ bluely, boule, coolie, coolly, coulee, duly, ghoulie, Julie, muley, newly, puli, ruly, stoolie, Thule, truly, tule, Bernoulli, guayule, patchouli, tabbouleh, unduly, unruly, ultima Thule

¹um \əm\ bum, chum, come, crumb, cum, drum, dumb, from, glum, gum, hum, lum, mum, numb, plum, plumb, rhumb, rum, scrum, scum, slum, some, strum, sum, swum, them, thrum, thumb, alum, aplomb, become, benumb, degum, dim sum, dumdum, eardrum, ho-hum, humdrum, income, outcome, subgum, succumb, therefrom, Tom Thumb, tom-tom, wherefrom, yum-yum, bubblegum, kettledrum, overcome, sugarplum, hop-o'-my-thumb

²um \ŭm\ cum, groom, Qom, Targum, mare librum

³um \üm\ see ¹OOM

uma \ü-mə\ duma, pneuma, puma, satsuma, Ancohuma, Montezuma

umable \ü-mə-bəl\ assumable, consumable, presumable, subsumable, inconsumable

umage \əm-ij\ see UMMAGE

uman \ü-mən\ blooming, crewman, human, lumen, Newman, numen, Truman, Yuman, acumen, albumen, albumin, bitumen, ichneumon, illumine, inhuman, panhuman, subhuman, antihuman, catechumen, protohuman, superhuman

umanist \ü-mə-nəst\ see UMENIST

umanous \ü-mə-nəs\ see UMINOUS

umb \əm\ see ¹UM

umbar \əm-bər\ see ¹UMBER

umbed \əmd\ green-thumbed, unplumbed

umbel \əm-bəl\ see UMBLE

umbency \əm-bən-sē\ incumbency, recumbency

umbent \əm-bənt\ decumbent, incumbent, procumbent, recumbent, superincumbent

¹umber \əm-bər\ cumber, Humber, lumbar, lumber, number, slumber, umber, cucumber, encumber, outnumber, renumber,

disencumber, Reynolds number, Avogadro's number

²umber \əm-ər\ see UMMER

umbered \əm-bərd\ unnumbered, unencumbered—*also pasts of verbs listed at* ¹UMBER

umberland \əm-bər-lənd\ Cumberland, Northumberland

umberous \əm-brəs\ see UMBROUS

umbery \əm-brē\ ombre, slumbery

umbing \əm-iŋ\ see OMING

umble \əm-bəl\ bumble, crumble, fumble, grumble, humble, jumble, mumble, rumble, scumble, stumble, tumble, umbel, rough-and-tumble

umbler \əm-blər\ bumbler, fumbler, grumbler, mumbler, rumbler, stumbler, tumbler

umbling \əm-bliŋ\ rumbling, tumbling

¹umbly \əm-blē\ crumbly, grumbly, humbly, mumbly, rumbly

²umbly \əm-lē\ comely, dumbly, dumly, numbly

umbness \əm-nəs\ dumbness, glumness, numbness, alumnus

umbo \əm-bō\ gumbo, jumbo, umbo, Colombo, mumbo jumbo

umbra \əm-brə\ umbra, penumbra

umbral \əm-brəl\ see UMBRIL

umbria \əm-brē-ə\ Cumbria, Umbria, Northumbria

umbril \əm-brəl\ tumbril, umbral, penumbral

umbrous \əm-brəs\ cumbrous, slumberous

ume \üm\ see ¹OOM

umed \ümd\ see OOMED

umedly \ü-məd-lē\ consumedly, presumedly

umelet \üm-lət\ see OOMLET

umely \ü-mə-lē\ see OOMILY

umen \ü-mən\ see UMAN

umenist \ü-mə-nəst\ humanist, luminist, ecumenist, illuminist, phillumenist

umer \ü-mər\ bloomer, Bloomer, groomer, humor, roomer, rumor, Sumer, tumor, consumer, costumer, exhumer, perfumer, presumer, schussboomer

umeral \üm-rəl\ humeral, humoral, numeral

umerous \üm-rəs\ see UMOROUS

umerus \üm-rəs\ see UMOROUS

umey \ü-mē\ see OOMY

umf \əmf\ see UMPH

umi \ü-mē\ see OOMY

umice \əm-əs\ see UMMOUS

umid \ü-məd\ humid, tumid

¹umin \əm-ən\ cumin, summon

²umin \ü-mən\ see UMAN

uminal \ü-mən-°l\ luminal, noumenal

uminate \ü-mə-nət\ acuminate, illuminate

umine \ü-mən\ see UMAN

uming \ü-miŋ\ blooming, consuming, everblooming, time-consuming, unassuming—*also present participles of verbs listed at* ¹OOM

uminist \ü-mə-nəst\ see UMENIST

uminous \ü-mə-nəs\ luminous, numinous, albuminous, aluminous, bituminous, leguminous, quadrumanous, voluminous

umma \əm-ə\ gumma, momma, summa

ummage \əm-ij\ rummage, West Brumage

¹ummary \əm-rē\ see ²UMMERY

²ummary \əm-ə-rē\ see ¹UMMERY

ummate \əm-ət\ see UMMET

ummel \əm-əl\ see ²OMMEL

ummell \əm-əl\ see ²OMMEL

ummer \əm-ər\ bummer, comer, drummer, gummer, hummer, mummer, plumber, rummer, slummer, strummer, summer, latecomer, midsummer, newcomer, overcomer, up-and-comer— *also comparatives of adjectives listed at* ¹UM

ummery \əm-ə-rē\ flummery, mummery, summary, summery, Montgomery

ummet \əm-ət\ grummet, plummet, summit, consummate

ummie \əm-ē\ see UMMY

ummit \əm-ət\ see UMMET

ummock \əm-ək\ hummock, stomach

ummon \əm-ən\ see ¹UMIN

ummoner \əm-nər\ see UMNAR

ummous \əm-əs\ gummous, hummus, pomace, pumice

ummox \əm-əks\ flummox,

hummocks, lummox, stomachs

ummus \əm-əs\ see UMMOUS

ummy \əm-ē\ chummy, crummie, crummy, dummy, gummy, mommy, mummy, plummy, rummy, scummy, slummy, tummy, yummy

umnar \əm-nər\ summoner, Sumner, columnar

umner \əm-nər\ see UMNAR

umness \əm-nəs\ see UMBNESS

umnus \əm-nəs\ see UMBNESS

umor \ü-mər\ see UMER

umoral \üm-rəl\ see UMERAL

umorous \üm-rəs\ humerus, humorous, numerous, tumorous, innumerous

umous \ü-məs\ brumous, humus, spumous, posthumous

ump \əmp\ bump, chump, clomp, clump, comp, crump, dump, flump, frump, grump, hump, jump, lump, mump, plump, pump, rump, slump, stump, sump, thump, trump, tump, ump, whump, mugwump, no-trump, tub-thump, callithump, overtrump

umper \əm-pər\ bumper, dumper, jumper, lumper, plumper, pumper, stumper, thumper, tub-thumper, Bible-thumper

umph \əmf\ bumf, humph, galumph, harrumph

umpish \əm-pish\ dumpish, frumpish, lumpish, plumpish

umpkin \əŋ-kən\ see UNKEN

umple \əm-pəl\ crumple, rumple

umply \əm-plē\ crumply, plumply, rumply

umps \əms\ dumps, mumps— *also plurals and possessives of nouns and third person singular presents of verbs listed at* UMP

umption \əm-shən\ gumption, assumption, consumption, presumption, resumption, subsumption

umptious \əm-shəs\ bumptious, scrumptious, presumptuous

umptive \əm-tiv\ assumptive, consumptive, presumptive

¹umptuous \əm-chəs\ sumptuous, presumptuous

²umptuous \əm-shəs\ see UMPTIOUS

umpus \əm-pəs\ see ²OMPASS

umpy \əm-pē\ bumpy, clumpy, dumpy, frumpy, grumpy, humpy, jumpy, lumpy, stumpy

umulous \ü-myə-ləs\ see UMULUS

umulus \ü-myə-ləs\ cumulous, cumulus, tumulus

umus \ü-məs\ see UMOUS

umy \ü-mē\ see OOMY

¹un \ən\ bun, done, Donne, dun, fen, foehn, fun, gun, hon, Hun, jun, maun, none, nun, one, pun, run, shun, son, spun, stun, sun, sunn, ton, tonne, tun, won, A-1, begun, blowgun, chaconne, Chang-chun, Chaplin, finespun, first-run, flashgun, forerun, godson, grandson, handgun, hard-won, homespun, long run, outdone, outgun, outrun, popgun, pressrun, rerun, searun, shotgun, six-gun, stepson, undone, V-1, welldone, Acheron, Algonquin, allemande, all-or-none, Balzacian, hit-and-run, kiloton, machine-gun, megaton, one-on-one, one-to-one, overdone, overrun, PL/1, Sally Lunn, scattergun, tommy gun, twenty-one, underdone, underrun, Xiamen, alexandrine

²**un** \ün\ see ¹OON

³**un** \ün\ Fushun, Lushun, tabun

una \ü-nə\ Buna, Cunha, Luna, Poona, puna, tuna, Altoona, kahuna, lacuna, laguna, vicuña, Tristan da Cunha

¹**uña** \ü-nə\ see UNA

²**uña** \ün-yə\ see UNIA

unal \ün-ᵊl\ communal, jejunal, lagoonal, monsoonal, tribunal

unar \ü-nər\ see OONER

unary \ü-nə-rē\ unary, festoonery, sublunary, superlunary

unate \ü-nət\ unit, lacunate, tribunate

unc \əŋk\ see UNK

uncan \əŋ-kən\ see UNKEN

unce \əns\ dunce, once—*also plurals and possessives of nouns and third person singular presents of verbs listed at* ¹ONT

unch \ənch\ brunch, bunch, Bunche, crunch, hunch, lunch, munch, punch, scrunch, keypunch, ploughman's lunch

unche \ənch\ see UNCH

uncheon \ən-chən\ luncheon, puncheon, truncheon

uncher \ən-chər\ cruncher, luncher, muncher, cowpuncher, keypuncher, counterpuncher

unchy \ən-chē\ bunchy, crunchy, punchy

uncial \ən-sē-əl\ uncial, internuncial

uncle \əŋ-kəl\ nuncle, uncle, carbuncle, caruncle, furuncle, granduncle, peduncle

¹**unco** \əŋ-kō\ bunco, junco, unco

²**unco** \əŋ-kə\ see UNKAH

unct \əŋt\ trunked, adjunct, conjunct, defunct, disjunct—*also pasts of verbs listed at* UNK

unction \əŋ-shən\ function, junction, unction, compunction, conjunction, disjunction, dysfunction, injunction, malfunction, extreme unction

unctional \əŋ-shnəl\ functional, junctional, dysfunctional

unctious \əŋ-shəs\ compunctious, rambunctious

unctory \əŋ-trē\ emunctory, perfunctory

uncture \əŋ-chər\ juncture, puncture, acupuncture, conjuncture, disjuncture

uncular \əŋ-kyə-lər\ avuncular, carbuncular, peduncular

unculus \əŋ-kyə-ləs\ homunculus, ranunculus

¹**und** \ənd\ bund, fund, gunned,

defund, obtund, refund,
rotund, secund, cummerbund,
orotund, pudibund, rubicund,
underfund—*also pasts of
verbs listed at* UN

²**und** \ùnd\ bund, dachshund

³**und** \ùnt\ see ¹UNT

⁴**und** \aùnd\ see ²OUND

unda \ən-də\ Munda, Sunda,
osmunda, rotunda,
barramunda, floribunda

undae \ən-dē\ see UNDI

undant \ən-dənt\ abundant,
redundant, superabundant

unday \ən-dē\ see UNDI

undays \ən-dēz\ Mondays,
Sundays, undies—*also
plurals and possessives of
nouns listed at* UNDI

undem \ən-dəm\ see UNDUM

under \ən-dər\ Bandar, blunder,
plunder, sunder, thunder,
under, wonder, asunder,
hereunder, thereunder

underous \ən-drəs\ plunderous,
wondrous, thunderous

¹**undi** \ən-dē\ Monday, sundae,
Sunday, Whitmonday,
Whitsunday, barramundi, Bay
of Fundy, jaguarundi, Mrs.
Grundy, salmagundi,
coatimundi

²**undi** \ün-dē\ Burundi, Ruanda-
Urundi

undies \ən-dēz\ see UNDAYS

undity \ən-dət-ē\ fecundity,
profundity, rotundity,
moribundity, orotundity,
rubicundity

undle \ən-dᵊl\ bundle, rundle,
trundle, unbundle

undness \ən-nəs\ see ONENESS

undum \ən-dəm\ corundum, ad
eundem, Carborundum

undy \ən-dē\ see UNDI

une \ün\ see ¹OON

uneau \ü-nō\ see UNO

uneless \ün-ləs\ see OONLESS

uner \ü-nər\ see OONER

unes \ünz\ see OONS

¹**ung** \əŋ\ bung, clung, dung,
flung, hung, lung, pung, rung,
slung, sprung, strung, stung,
sung, swung, tongue, tung,
wrung, young, Young,
among, bee-stung, far-flung,
high-strung, Kaifeng, low-
slung, unstrung, unsung, well-
hung, adder's-tongue,
double-hung, double-tongue,
triple-tongue, overhung,
overstrung, underslung

²**ung** \ùŋ\ Jung, Kung, Sung,
Antung, Bandung, Dandong,
Dadong, Hamhung, Tatung,
Kaohsiung, Zigong, Nibelung,
geländesprung,
Götterdämmerung

ungal \əŋ-gəl\ see UNGLE

unge \ənj\ lunge, plunge,
sponge, expunge

unged \ənjd\ see ONGUED

ungeon \ən-jən\ donjon,
dungeon, spongin

¹**unger** \ən-jər\ lunger, plunger,
sponger, expunger

²**unger** \əŋ-gər\ see ¹ONGER

ungible \ən-jə-bəl\ fungible,
inexpungible

ungle \əŋ-gəl\ bungle, fungal,
jungle, pungle

ungo \əŋ-gō\ fungo, mungo

ungous \əŋ-gəs\ fungous,
fungus, humongous

ungry \ən-grē\ see ONGERY

ungus \əŋ-gəs\ see UNGOUS

ungy \ən-jē\ grungy, spongy

unha \ü-nə\ see UNA

uni \ü-nē\ see OONY

unia \ün-yə\ petunia, vicuña

unic \ü-nik\ eunuch, Munich, Punic, runic, tunic

unicate \ü-ni-kət\ tunicate, excommunicate

unich \ü-nik\ see UNIC

union \ən-yən\ bunion, grunion, onion, ronyon, trunnion, Paul Bunyan

unis \ü-nəs\ see EWNESS

¹unish \ən-ish\ Hunnish, punish

²unish \ü-nish\ see OONISH

unit \ü-nət\ see UNATE

unitive \ü-nət-iv\ punitive, unitive

unity \ü-nət-ē\ unity, community, disunity, immunity, impunity, importunity, opportunity, European Community

unk \əŋk\ bunk, chunk, clunk, drunk, dunk, flunk, funk, gunk, hunk, junk, monk, plunk, punk, shrunk, skunk, slunk, spunk, stunk, sunk, thunk, trunk, bohunk, chipmunk, debunk, Podunk, punch-drunk, quidnunc

unkah \əŋ-kə\ punkah, unco

unkard \əŋ-kərd\ bunkered, drunkard, Dunkard, hunkered

unked \əŋt\ see UNCT

unken \əŋ-kən\ Duncan, drunken, pumpkin, shrunken, sunken

unker \əŋ-kər\ bunker, Bunker, clunker, Dunker, flunker,

hunker, junker, lunker, plunker, punker, younker, debunker, spelunker

unkie \əŋ-kē\ see UNKY

unkin \əŋ-kəm\ see UNCAN

unks \əŋs\ hunks, quincunx— *also plurals and possessives of nouns and third singular presents of verbs listed at* UNK

unky \əŋ-kē\ chunky, clunky, donkey, flunky, funky, gunky, hunky, Hunky, junkie, junky, monkey, punkie, punky, spunkie, spunky

unless \ən-ləs\ runless, sonless, sunless

unn \ən\ see UN

unnage \ən-ij\ dunnage, tonnage, megatonnage

unned \ənd\ see ¹UND

unnel \ən-ᵊl\ funnel, gunnel, gunwale, runnel, trunnel, tunnel

unner \ən-ər\ cunner, gunner, runner, scunner, stunner, tonner, forerunner, front-runner, gunrunner, roadrunner, rumrunner

unnery \ən-rē\ gunnery, nunnery

unness \ən-nəs\ see ONENESS

unning \ən-iŋ\ cunning, running, stunning

unnion \ən-yən\ see UNION

unnish \ən-ish\ see ¹UNISH

unny \ən-ē\ bunny, funny, gunny, honey, money, runny, sonny, sunny, tunny, Ballymoney

uno \ü-nō\ Bruno, Juneau, Juno, numero uno

unster \ən-stər\ Meunster, punster

¹unt \únt\ dachshund, Dortmund, exeunt

²unt \ənt\ see ¹ONT

untal \ənt-ᵊl\ see UNTLE

unter \ənt-ər\ blunter, bunter, chunter, grunter, hunter, punter, shunter, confronter, foxhunter, headhunter, pothunter, witch-hunter

unting \ənt-iŋ\ bunting, foxhunting, head-hunting, witch-hunting—*also present participles of verbs listed at* ¹ONT

untle \ənt-ᵊl\ frontal, gruntle, confrontal, disgruntle, contrapuntal

unty \ənt-ē\ punty, runty

unwale \ən-ᵊl\ see UNNEL

unx \əŋs\ see UNKS

uny \ü-nē\ see OONY

unyan \ən-yən\ see UNION

uoth \ü-əs\ see EWESS

¹uoy \ü-ē\ see EWY

²uoy \ói\ see OY

uoyance \ü-əns\ see OYANCE

uoyancy \ói-ən-sē\ see OYANCY

uoyant \ói-ənt\ see OYANT

up \əp\ cup, dup, hup, pup, scup, sup, tup, up, yup, backup, balls-up, bang-up, beat-up, blowup, breakup, brush up, buildup, built-up, call-up, catch-up, change-up, checkup, chin-up, cleanup, close-up, cock-up, crack-up, cutup, dried-up, dustup, eggcup, eyecup, faceup, fill-up, flare-up, foul-up, frame-up, fry-up, getup, giddap, grown-up, hang-up, heads-up, hepped up, het up, holdup, hookup, hopped-up, jack-up, jam-up, kickup, kingcup, lash-up, lay-up, lead-up, letup, line up, linkup, lockup, lookup, louse up, made-up, makeup, markup, matchup, mix-up, mixed-up, mock-up, mop-up, mug up, nip-up, one-up, pasteup, pickup, pileup, pinup, pop-up, pull-up, punch-up, push-up, put-up, re-up, roundup, run-up, scaleup, screwup, send-up, setup, shack up, shake-up, shape-up, shook-up, shoot up, sign up, sit-up, slap-up, slipup, smashup, speedup, stand-up, start-up, step up, stepped-up, stickup, stuck-up, sum-up, sunup, take-up, teacup, thumbs-up, tie-up, toss-up, touch-up, trumped-up, tune-up, turnup, walk-up, warm-up, washed-up, washup, windup, wised-up, workup, wrap-up, write-up, belly up, buttercup, button-up, cover-up, dial-up, follow-up, higher-up, hurry-up, pick-me-up, pony up, runner-up, seven-up, shoot-em-up, summing-up, up-and-up, wickiup, winding-up, Johnny-jump-up, sunny-side up

upa \ü-pə\ pupa, stupa

upas \ü-pəs\ see UPUS

upboard \əb-ərd\ see UBBARD

upe \üp\ see ¹OOP

upel \ü-pəl\ see ²UPLE

upelet \ü-plət\ see ²UPLET

uper \ü-pər\ see OOPER

upi \ü-pē\ see OOPY

upid \ü-pəd\ Cupid, stupid

upil \ü-pəl\ see ²UPLE

¹uple \əp-əl\ couple, supple, decouple

²uple \ü-pəl\ cupel, duple, pupil, scruple, quadruple, quintuple, sextuple

³uple \üp-ᵊl\ supple, quadruple, quintuple, sextuple

¹uplet \əp-lət\ couplet, gradruplet, quintuplet, sextuplet

²uplet \ü-plət\ drupelet, quadruplet

uplicate \ü-pli-kət\ duplicate, quadruplicate, quintuplicate, sextuplicate

upor \ü-pər\ see OOPER

uppance \əp-əns\ threepence, twopence, comeuppance

upper \əp-ər\ crupper, scupper, supper, upper, stand-upper

uppie \əp-ē\ see UPPY

¹upple \üp-əl\ see ³UPLE

²upple \əp-əl\ see ¹UPLE

uppy \əp-ē\ cuppy, guppy, puppy, yuppie

upt \əpt\ abrupt, corrupt, disrupt, erupt, irrupt, developed, incorrupt, interrupt—*also pasts of verbs listed at* UP

upter \əp-tər\ corrupter, disrupter, interrupter

uptible \əp-tə-bəl\ corruptible, eruptible, irruptible, incorruptible, interruptible

uption \əp-shən\ abruption, corruption, disruption, eruption, irruption, interruption

uptive \əp-tiv\ corruptive, disruptive, eruptive, irruptive, interruptive

upus \ü-pəs\ croupous, lupus, upas

uq \ük\ see UKE

uque \ük\ see UKE

¹ur \ōr\ see ¹ORE

²ur \u̇r\ see ¹URE

³ur \ər\ see ¹EUR

ura \u̇r-ə\ dura, durra, Jura, sura, surah, Agoura, bravura, caesura, datura, Madura, tamboura, tempura, aqua pura, Arafura, Bujumbura, appoggiatura, Bonaventura, coloratura, Telanaipura, Anuradhapura, camera obscura

urable \u̇r-ə-bəl\ curable, durable, thurible, endurable, incurable, insurable, perdurable

uracy \u̇r-ə-sē\ curacy, obduracy

urae \u̇r-ē\ see ¹URY

urah \u̇r-ə\ see URA

ural \u̇r-əl\ crural, jural, mural, neural, plural, puerile, rural, Ural, caesural, commissural, extramural, intramural

uralist \u̇r-ə-ləst\ muralist, pluralist, ruralist

uran \ü-rən\ see ²URIN

urance \u̇r-əns\ durance, assurance, endurance, insurance, coinsurance, reassurance, reinsurance

urate \u̇r-ət\ curate, turret, obdurate, barbiturate

urative \ùr-ə-tiv\ curative, durative

urb \ərb\ see ERB

¹urban \ər-bən\ bourbon, Durban, rurban, turban, turbine, urban, Urban, exurban, suburban, interurban

²urban \ùr-bən\ bourbon, Bourbon, rurban

urber \ər-bər\ Berber, Ferber, Thurber, disturber

urbia \ər-bē-ə\ Serbia, exurbia, suburbia

urbid \ər-bəd\ turbid, verbid

urbine \ər-bən\ see ¹URBAN

urbit \ər-bət\ burbot, sherbet, turbit, turbot

urble \ər-bəl\ see ERBAL

urbot \ər-bət\ see URBIT

urcate \ər-kət\ see IRCUIT

urch \ərch\ birch, church, Church, curch, lurch, perch, search, smirch, besmirch, Christchurch, research, unchurch

urchin \ər-chən\ birchen, urchin

urchly \ərch-lē\ churchly, virtually

urcia \ər-shə\ see ERTIA

¹urd \ùrd\ see ¹URED

²urd \ərd\ see IRD

urdane \ərd-ᵊn\ see URDEN

urden \ərd-ᵊn\ burden, guerdon, lurdane, verdin, disburden, unburden, overburden

urder \ərd-ər\ see ERDER

urderer \ərd-ər-ər\ murderer, verderer

urdle \ərd-ᵊl\ curdle, girdle, hurdle, engirdle

urdu \ər-dü\ see ERDU

urdum \ərd-əm\ see IRDUM

urdy \ərd-ē\ birdie, sturdy, wordy, hurdy-gurdy, Mesa Verde, Monteverdi

¹ure \ùr\ Boer, boor, bourg, cure, dour, ewer, fewer, lure, moor, Moor, Moore, Muir, poor, pure, Ruhr, sewer, skewer, spoor, stour, sure, tour, Tours, your, you're, abjure, adjure, Adour, allure, amour, Ashur, assure, brochure, ceinture, cocksure, coiffure, conjure, contour, couture, demure, detour, dirt-poor, endure, ensure, Exmoor, faubourg, Fraktur, grandeur, gravure, guipure, hachure, immure, impure, insure, inure, kultur, land-poor, langur, ligure, manure, mature, mohur, obscure, parure, perdure, procure, secure, siddur, tambour, tandoor, tenure, Uighur, unmoor, velour, velure, amateur, aperture, armature, blackamoor, carrefour, carte du jour, coinsure, commissure, confiture, connoisseur, coverture, cubature, curvature, cynosure, debouchure, embouchure, epicure, filature, forfeiture, garniture, geniture, green-manure, haute couture, immature, insecure, ligature, manicure, overture, paramour, pedicure, plat du jour, portraiture, prelature, premature, quadrature, reassure, Reaumur, reinsure, saboteur, sepulture, sequitur, signature, simon-pure, sinecure, soup du jour, tablature, temperature, troubadour, white amur, vavasour, Yom Kippur, candidature, caricature, discomfiture, distemperature, divestiture, entablature, entrepreneur, expenditure, imprimatur, investiture, literature, miniature, musculature, nomenclature, nonsequitur, primogeniture, ultraminiature

²ure \úr-ē\ see ¹URY

urean \úr-ē-ən\ see URIAN

ureau \úr-ō\ see URO

¹ured \úrd\ gourde, Kurd, urd, assured, steward, underinsured—*also pasts of verbs listed at* ¹URE

²ured \ərd\ see IRD

urely \úr-lē\ buirdly, poorly, purely, surely, cocksurely, demurely, impurely, maturely, obscurely, immaturely, insecurely, prematurely

urement \úr-mənt\ allurement, immurement, inurement, procurement, securement

uren \úr-ən\ see ²URIN

ureous \úr-ē-əs\ see URIOUS

¹urer \úr-ər\ curer, führer, furor, furore, juror, lurer, tourer, abjurer, assurer, insurer, manurer, procurer, tambourer, coinsurer, reinsurer—*also comparatives of adjectives listed at* ¹URE

²urer \ər-ər\ see ERRER

¹urety \úr-ət-ē\ see URITY

²urety \úrt-ē\ see URTI

urey \ür-ē\ see ¹URY

urf \ərf\ kerf, scurf, serf, surf, turf, enserf, bodysurf

urfy \ər-fē\ Murphy, scurfy, turfy

urg \ərg\ see ERG

urgative \ər-gə-tiv\ see URGATIVE

urge \ərj\ dirge, merge, purge, scourge, serge, splurge, spurge, surge, urge, verge, converge, deterge, diverge, emerge, immerge, resurge, submerge, upsurge, dramaturge

urgence \ər-jəns\ see ERGENCE

urgency \ər-jən-sē\ see ERGENCY

urgent \ər-jənt\ urgent, assurgent, convergent, detergent, divergent, emergent, insurgent, resurgent, preemergent

urgeon \ər-jən\ burgeon, sturgeon, surgeon, virgin

¹urger \ər-gər\ burgher, turgor, cheeseburger, hamburger, Limburger

²urger \ər-jər\ see ERGER

urgery \ərj-rē\ see ERJURY

¹urgh \ər-ə\ see ¹OROUGH

²urgh \ər-ō\ see ¹URROW

³urgh \ərg\ see ERG

urgher \ər-gər\ see ¹URGER

urgic \ər-jik\ see ERGIC

urgical \ər-ji-kəl\ surgical, liturgical, theurgical, dramaturgical

urgid \ər-jəd\ turgid, synergid

urgle \ər-gəl\ burgle, gurgle

urgor \ər-gər\ see ¹URGER

urgy \ər-jē\ clergy, dramaturgy, metallurgy

uri \ur-ē\ see ¹URY

¹**urial** \ur-ē-əl\ curial, urial, Uriel, mercurial, seigneurial, tenurial, entrepreneurial

²**urial** \er-ē-əl\ see ARIAL

urian \ur-ē-ən\ durian, Hurrian, Arthurian, centurion, epicurean

uriance \ur-ē-əns\ see URIENCE

uriant \ur-ē-ənt\ see URIENT

¹**urible** \ur-ə-bəl\ see URABLE

²**urible** \er-ə-bəl\ see ERABLE

uric \ur-ik\ uric, mercuric, sulfuric

urid \ur-əd\ lurid, murid

urie \ur-ē\ see ¹URY

uriel \ur-ē-əl\ see ¹URIAL

urience \ur-ē-əns\ prurience, luxuriance

urient \ur-ē-ənt\ esurient, luxuriant, parturient

¹**urier** \er-ē-ər\ see ERRIER

²**urier** \ur-ē-ər\ see ¹OURIER

uriere \ur-ē-ər\ see ¹OURIER

¹**urin** \ər-ən\ burin, murrain

²**urin** \ur-ən\ burin, Huron, urine, Belgian Tervuren

urine \ur-ən\ see ²URIN

uring \ur-iŋ\ during, mooring, touring

urion \ur-ē-ən\ see URIAN

urious \ur-ē-əs\ curious, furious, spurious, incurious, injurious, luxurious, penurious, perjurious, sulfureous, usurious

uris \ur-əs\ see URUS

urist \ur-əst\ purist, tourist, manicurist, pedicurist, caricaturist, chiaroscurist, miniaturist—*also superlatives of adjectives listed at* ¹URE

urity \ur-ət-ē\ purity, surety, futurity, impurity, maturity, obscurity, security, immaturity, insecurity, prematurity

urk \ərk\ see ¹ORK

¹**urka** \ər-kə\ charka, circa, Gurkha, mazurka

²**urka** \ur-kə\ Gurkha, mazurka

urke \ərk\ see ¹ORK

urker \ər-kər\ see ¹ORKER

urkey \ər-kē\ see ERKY

¹**urkha** \ur-kə\ see ²URKA

²**urkha** \ər-kə\ see ¹URKA

urki \ər-kē\ see ERKY

urky \ər-kē\ see ERKY

url \ərl\ see ¹IRL

urled \ərld\ see ORLD

urlew \ərl-ü\ curlew, purlieu

urlieu \ərl-ü\ see URLEW

urlin \ər-lən\ see ERLIN

urling \ər-liŋ\ curling, hurling, sterling—*also present participles of verbs listed at* ¹IRL

urlish \ər-lish\ churlish, girlish

urly \ər-lē\ burley, burly, curly, early, girlie, hurly, knurly, pearly, squirrely, surly, swirly, twirly, whirly, hurly-burly

urman \ər-mən\ see ERMAN

urmity \ər-mət-ē\ see IRMITY

urmur \ər-mər\ firmer, infirmer, murmur, termer, wormer

urn \ərn\ burn, churn, curn, earn, erne, fern, kern, learn, pirn, quern, spurn, stern, tern, terne, turn, urn, yearn, adjourn, astern, attorn, casern, concern, discern, downturn, epergne, eterne, extern, heartburn, intern, lucerne, nocturn, nocturne, outturn, return, sauternes, secern, sojourn, sunburn, unlearn, upturn, U-turn, windburn, Comintern, overturn, taciturn, unconcern

urnable \ər-nə-bəl\ burnable, discernible, returnable, indiscernible

urnal \ərn-ᵊl\ see ERNAL

urne \ərn\ see URN

urned \ərnd\ burned, durned, concerned, unearned, unlearned, well-turned, windburned—*also pasts of verbs listed at* URN

urner \ər-nər\ burner, earner, turner, discerner, returner, afterburner

urnery \ər-nə-rē\ see ERNARY

urney \ər-nē\ see ¹OURNEY

urnian \ər-nē-ən\ see ERNIAN

urnish \ər-nish\ burnish, furnish

urnt \ərnt\ see EARNT

urnum \ər-nəm\ sternum, alburnum, laburnum, viburnum

uro \uṙ-ō\ bureau, duro, euro, enduro, maduro, politburo, chiaroscuro

uron \uṙ-ən\ see ²URIN

uror \uṙ-ər\ see ¹URER

urore \uṙ-ər\ see ¹URER

urous \uṙ-əs\ see URUS

urp \ərp\ burp, chirp, slurp, stirp, twerp, usurp

urphy \ər-fē\ see URFY

urple \ər-pəl\ purple, empurple

urplice \ər-pləs\ see URPLUS

urplus \ər-pləs\ surplice, surplus

urps \ərps\ see IRPS

urr \ər\ see ¹EUR

¹urra \uṙ-ə\ see URA

²urra \ər-ə\ see ¹OROUGH

urrage \ər-ij\ see OURAGE

urragh \ər-ə\ see ¹OROUGH

urrain \ər-ən\ see ¹URIN

urral \ər-əl\ see ERRAL

urrant \ər-ənt\ see URRENT

urray \ər-ē\ see URRY

urre \ər\ see ¹EUR

urred \ərd\ see IRD

urrence \ər-əns\ concurrence, conference, deterrence, incurrence, occurrence, transference, countertransference

urrent \ər-ənt\ currant, current, weren't, concurrent, crosscurrent, decurrent, deterrent, occurrent, recurrent, susurrant, countercurrent, undercurrent, supercurrent

urrer \ər-ər\ see ERRER

urret \uṙ-ət\ see URATE

urrey \ər-ē\ see URRY

urrian \uṙ-ē-ən\ see URIAN

urrie \ər-ē\ see URRY

urrier \ər-ē-ər\ courier, currier, furrier, hurrier, worrier—*also comparatives of adjectives listed at* URRY

urring \ər-iŋ\ furring, shirring, stirring, skiöring—*also present participles of verbs listed at* ¹EUR

urrish \ər-ish\ see OURISH

¹urro \ər-ə\ see ¹OROUGH

²**urro** \ər-ō\ see ¹URROW

¹**urrow** \ər-ō\ borough, burgh, burro, burrow, furrow, thorough

²**urrow** \ər-ə\ see ¹OROUGH

urry \ər-ē\ blurry, burry, curry, flurry, furry, dhurrie, gurry, hurry, Moray, Murray, murrey, scurry, slurry, spurrey, surrey, Surrey, whirry, worry, hurry-scurry

ursa \ər-sə\ see ERSA

ursal \ər-səl\ see ¹ERSAL

ursar \ər-sər\ see URSOR

ursary \ərs-rē\ bursary, cursory, mercery, nursery, anniversary

urse \ərs\ see ERSE

ursed \ərst\ see URST

ursement \ər-smənt\ see ERCEMENT

urser \ər-sər\ see URSOR

ursery \ərs-rē\ see URSARY

ursion \ər-zhən\ see ¹ERSION

ursionist \ərzh-nəst\ see ERSIONIST

ursive \ər-siv\ see ERSIVE

ursor \ər-sər\ bursar, cursor, mercer, nurser, purser, worser, disburser, disperser, precursor, rehearser, reverser, traverser

ursory \ərs-rē\ see URSARY

urst \ərst\ burst, cursed, durst, erst, first, Hearst, thirst, verst, worst, wurst, accursed, airburst, Amherst, athirst, cloudburst, downburst, emersed, feetfirst, groundburst, headfirst, outburst, sunburst, liverwurst, microburst—*also pasts of verbs listed at* ERSE

ursus \ər-səs\ see ERSUS

¹**ursy** \ər-sē\ see ERCY

²**ursy** \əs-ē\ see USSY

¹**urt** \urt\ yurt, Erfurt, Frankfurt, Betancourt

²**urt** \ərt\ see ¹ERT

urtain \ərt-ᵊn\ see ERTAIN

urtal \ərt-ᵊl\ see ERTILE

urtenance \ərt-ᵊn-əns\ see ERTINENCE

urtenant \ərt-nənt\ see IRTINENT

urter \ərt-ər\ see ERTER

urtesy \ərt-ə-sē\ see OURTESY

urthen \ər-thən\ burthen, earthen

urther \ər-thər\ further, murther

urti \urt-ē\ pretty, surety, Trimurti

urtium \ər-shəm\ nasturtium, sestertium

urtive \ərt-iv\ see ERTIVE

urtle \ərt-ᵊl\ see ERTILE

urton \ərt-ᵊn\ see ERTAIN

urture \ər-chər\ see IRCHER

uru \ur-ü\ guru, kuru, Nauru

urus \ur-əs\ urus, Arcturus, mercurous, sulfurous, Epicurus, sui juris, tinea cruris

urve \ərv\ see ERVE

urved \ərvd\ see ERVED

urviness \ər-vē-nəs\ see ERVINESS

urvy \ər-vē\ curvy, nervy, scurvy, topsy-turvy

¹**ury** \ur-ē\ curie, Curie, fleury, fury, houri, Jewry, jury, Kure, Urey, Bhojpuri, de jure, Missouri, tandoori, lusus naturae

²**ury** \er-ē\ see ¹ARY

urze \ərz\ see ERS

urzy \ər-zē\ see ERSEY

¹us \əs\ bus, buss, crus, cuss, fuss, Gus, Huss, muss, plus, pus, Russ, suss, thus, truss, us, airbus, concuss, cost-plus, discuss, nonplus, percuss, railbus, untruss, autobus, blunderbuss, microbus, minibus

²us \ü\ see ¹EW

³us \üs\ see ¹USE

⁴us \üsh\ see OUCHE

⁵us \üz\ see ²USE

¹usa \ü-sə\ Sousa, Azusa, Medusa, Appaloosa, Gebel Musa, Jebel Musa

²usa \ü-zə\ Sousa, Susa, Medusa, Arethusa

usable \ü-zə-bəl\ fusible, losable, usable, abusable, diffusible, excusable, infusible, reusable, transfusible, inexcusable, irrecusable

usae \ü-sē\ see UICY

¹usal \ü-səl\ streusel, occlusal

²usal \ü-zəl\ foozle, fusil, ouzel, snoozle, streusel, accusal, bamboozle, occlusal, perusal, refusal

usc \əsk\ see USK

uscan \əs-kən\ buskin, Ruskin, Tuscan, Etruscan, molluscan

uscat \əs-kət\ see USKET

uscle \əs-əl\ see USTLE

uscular \əs-kyə-lər\ muscular, corpuscular, crepuscular, majuscular

uscule \əs-kyül\ crepuscule, opuscule

¹use \üs\ Bruce, crouse, crus, cruse, deuce, douce, goose, juice, loose, moose, mousse, noose, nous, puce, rhus, ruse, Russ, schuss, sluice, spruce, truce, use, Zeus, Aarhus, abstruse, abuse, adduce, Arhus, Atreus, burnoose, caboose, Cayuse, Cepheus, ceruse, conduce, couscous, deduce, diffuse, disuse, educe, effuse, excuse, footloose, induce, Lanús, misuse, mongoose, Morpheus, negus, obtuse, Orpheus, papoose, Peleus, Perseus, prepuce, produce, profuse, Proteus, Purus, recluse, reduce, refuse, retuse, reuse, Sanctus, seduce, Tereus, Theseus, traduce, transduce, unloose, vamoose, Belarus, Betelgeuse, calaboose, charlotte russe, introduce, mass-produce, Odysseus, Prometheus, reproduce, self-abuse, Syracuse, Typhoeus, hypotenuse, Sancti Spiritus

²use \üz\ blues, booze, bruise, choose, cruise, cruse, Druze, flews, fuse, Hughes, lose, Meuse, muse, news, ooze, roose, ruse, schmooze, snooze, trews, use, whose, abuse, accuse, amuse, Andrews, bemuse, berceuse, chanteuse, chartreuse, coiffeuse, confuse, contuse, danseuse, defuse, diffuse, diseuse, disuse, effuse, Elbrus, enthuse, excuse, ill-use, infuse, masseuse, misuse, perfuse, peruse, recluse,

recuse, refuse, reuse, suffuse,
Toulouse, transfuse,
vendeuse, Betelgeuse,
disabuse, interfuse,
mitrailleuse, Newport News,
p's and q's, Santa Cruz, Vera
Cruz, Goody Two-shoes

used \üzd\ used, confused,
underused—*also pasts of
verbs listed at* ²USE

useless \ü-sləs\ juiceless,
useless

user \ü-zər\ boozer, bruiser,
chooser, cruiser, doozer, loser,
snoozer, user, abuser, accuser,
amuser, diffuser, excuser,
infuser, peruser, multiuser

¹**ush** \əsh\ blush, brush, crush,
flush, gush, hush, Cush, lush,
mush, plush, rush, shush,
slush, squush, thrush, tush,
airbrush, bulrush, bum's rush,
hairbrush, hush-hush, inrush,
nailbrush, onrush, paintbrush,
sagebrush, toothbrush, uprush,
bottlebrush, Hindu Kush,
underbrush

²**ush** \ush\ bush, Bush, mush,
push, shush, squoosh,
swoosh, tush, whoosh,
ambush, Hindu Kush,
rosebush, thornbush

ushabel \ə-shə-bəl\ crushable,
flushable

¹**usher** \əsh-ər\ blusher,
brusher, crusher, gusher,
musher, rusher, usher, four-
flusher, goldrusher—*also
comparatives of adjectives
listed at* ¹USH

²**usher** \ush-ər\ pusher,
ambusher

ushi \ush-ē\ see ²USHY

ushing \əsh-iŋ\ onrushing,
toothbrushing, unblushing—
*also present participles of
verbs listed at* ¹USH

ushu \ü-shü\ Kyushu,
Kitakyushu

¹**ushy** \əsh-ē\ brushy, gushy,
mushy, plushy, rushy, slushy

²**ushy** \ush-ē\ bushy, cushy,
mushy, pushy, sushi

usi \ü-sē\ see UICY

usian \ü-zhən\ see USION

¹**usible** \ü-sə-bəl\ see UCIBLE

²**usible** \ü-zə-bəl\ see USABLE

usic \ü-zik\ music, Tungusic

usie \ü-zē\ see OOZY

usil \ü-zəl\ see ²USAL

using \əs-iŋ\ busing, trussing,
antibusing

usion \ü-zhən\ fusion, affusion,
allusion, Carthusian,
collusion, conclusion,
confusion, contusion,
delusion, diffusion, effusion,
elusion, exclusion, extrusion,
illusion, inclusion, infusion,
intrusion, Malthusian,
obtrusion, occlusion,
perfusion, prelusion,
profusion, prolusion,
protrusion, reclusion,
seclusion, transfusion,
Venusian, Andalusian,
disillusion, malocclusion,
autotransfusion

usionist \üzh-nəst\ fusionist,
diffusionist, exclusionist,
illusionist, perfusionist

usity \ü-sət-ē\ see UCITY

usive \ü-siv\ abusive, allusive,
amusive, collusive,

conclusive, conducive, delusive, diffusive, effusive, elusive, exclusive, extrusive, illusive, inclusive, intrusive, obtrusive, occlusive, prelusive, protrusive, reclusive, inconclusive

usk \əsk\ brusque, cusk, dusk, husk, musk, rusk, tusk, subfusc

usker \əs-kər\ busker, husker, tusker

usket \əs-kət\ muscat, musket

uskie \əs-kē\ see USKY

uskin \əs-kən\ see USCAN

usky \əs-kē\ dusky, husky, muskie, musky

usly \əs-lē\ pussley, thusly

uso \ü-sō\ see USOE

usoe \ü-sō\ trousseau, whoso, Caruso, Robinson Crusoe

usory \üs-ə-rē\ delusory, prolusory, illusory

usque \əsk\ see USK

¹uss \ùs\ puss, Russ, schuss, chartreuse, sea puss, sourpuss, glamour-puss, octopus, platypus

²uss \üs\ see ¹USE

³uss \əs\ see ¹US

ussant \əs-ᵊnt\ mustn't, discussant

ussate \əs-ət\ see USSET

usse \üs\ see ¹USE

ussel \əs-əl\ see USTLE

ussell \əs-əl\ see USTLE

usset \əs-ət\ gusset, russet, decussate

ussia \əsh-ə\ Prussia, Russia, Belorussia

ussian \əsh-ən\ see USSION

ussing \əs-iŋ\ see USING

ussion \əsh-ən\ Prussian, Russian, concussion, discussion, percussion, Belorussian, repercussion

ussive \əs-iv\ jussive, tussive, concussive, percussive, repercussive

ussle \əs-əl\ see USTLE

ussley \əs-lē\ see USLY

ussy \əs-ē\ fussy, hussy, mussy, pursy, pussy

¹ust \əst\ bust, crust, dost, dust, gust, just, lust, must, musth, rust, thrust, trust, wast, adjust, adust, august, combust, degust, disgust, distrust, encrust, entrust, mistrust, moondust, piecrust, robust, stardust, upthrust, antitrust, dryasdust, unitrust, wanderlust—*also pasts of verbs listed at* ¹US

²ust \əs\ see ¹US

³ust \üst\ see OOST

ustable \əs-tə-bəl\ see USTIBLE

ustard \əs-tərd\ bustard, custard, mustard—*also pasts of verbs listed at* USTER

usted \əs-təd\ busted, disgusted, maladjusted, well-adjusted—*also pasts of verbs listed at* ¹UST

uster \əs-tər\ bluster, buster, cluster, Custer, duster, fluster, luster, muster, thruster, adjuster, blockbuster, combustor, deluster, gangbuster, lackluster, sodbuster, trustbuster, antitruster, filibuster

ustful \əst-fəl\ lustful, thrustful, trustful, distrustful

usth \əst\ see ¹UST

ustian \əs-chən\ see USTION

ustible \əs-tə-bəl\ adjustable, combustible, incombustible

ustin \əs-tən\ Justin, Augustine

ustine \əs-tən\ see USTIN

ustic \əs-tik\ fustic, rustic

ustion \əs-chən\ fustian, combustion

ustious \əs-chəs\ robustious, rumbustious

ustive \əs-tiv\ adjustive, combustive, maladjustive

ustle \əs-əl\ bustle, hustle, muscle, mussel, Russell, rustle, trestle, tussle, corpuscle, crepuscle, Jack Russell

ustn't \əs-ᵊnt\ see USSANT

ustom \əs-təm\ custom, frustum, accustom, disaccustom

ustor \əs-tər\ see USTER

ustrious \əs-trē-əs\ illustrious, industrious

ustrous \əs-trəs\ blustrous, lustrous

ustule \əs-chül\ frustule, pustule

ustum \əs-təm\ see USTOM

ustus \əs-təs\ Justus, Augustus

usty \əs-tē\ busty, crusty, dusty, fusty, gusty, lusty, musty, rusty, trusty

usy \iz-ē\ see IZZY

¹ut \ət\ but, butt, cut, glut, gut, hut, jut, mutt, nut, putt, rut, scut, shut, slut, smut, soot, strut, tut, ut, what, abut, beechnut, catgut, chestnut, clean-cut, clear-cut, cobnut, cockshut, crosscut, groundnut, haircut, locknut, offcut, peanut, pignut, rebut, recut, rotgut, shortcut, somewhat, tut-tut, uncut, walnut, woodcut, butternut, congregate, hazelnut, overcut, scuttlebutt, undercut, uppercut, open-and-shut

²ut \ü\ see ¹EW

³ut \üt\ see UTE

⁴ut \ut\ see ¹OOT

uta \üt-ə\ Baruta, likuta, valuta

utable \üt-ə-bəl\ mutable, scrutable, suitable, commutable, computable, disputable, immutable, inscrutable, permutable, statutable, executable, incommutable, incomputable, indisputable, irrefutable, prosecutable, substitutable

utage \üt-ij\ see ¹OOTAGE

utal \üt-ᵊl\ see UTILE

utan \üt-ᵊn\ cutin, gluten, Luton, mutine, Newton, Teuton, Laputan, rambutan, Rasputin, highfalutin

utant \üt-ᵊnt\ mutant, disputant, pollutant

utative \üt-ət-iv\ putative, commutative, imputative

¹utch \əch\ clutch, crutch, cutch, dutch, Dutch, grutch, hutch, much, scutch, smutch, such, touch, nonesuch, retouch, double-clutch, overmuch

²utch \uch\ butch, putsch

utcher \əch-ər\ scutcher, retoucher

utchy \əch-ē\ see UCHY

ute \üt\ boot, bruit, brut, brute, bute, Bute, butte, chute, cloot, coot, cute, flute, fruit, glout, hoot, jute, Jute, loot, lute, moot, mute, newt, pood, root, Root, rout, route, scoot, scute, shoot, snoot, soot, suit, suite, toot, tout, ut, Ute, acute, astute, Asyût, beetroot, Beirut, birthroot, bloodroot, breadfruit, butut, cahoot, Canute, cheroot, clubroot, commute, compute, confute, crapshoot, deaf-mute, depute, dilute, dispute, elute, en route, enroot, folkmoot, freeboot, galoot, grapefruit, hardboot, hirsute, imbrute, impute, jackboot, jackfruit, jumpsuit, kashruth, lawsuit, minute, nonsuit, offshoot, outshoot, Paiute, pantsuit, permute, playsuit, pollute, pursuit, recruit, refute, repute, salute, seaboot, snowsuit, solute, sunsuit, swimsuit, taproot, tracksuit, transmute, uproot, volute, absolute, Aleut, arrowroot, Asyût, attribute, autoroute, bandicoot, bitterroot, bodysuit, boilersuit, bumbershoot, constitute, convolute, Denver boot, destitute, disrepute, dissolute, evolute, execute, gingerroot, institute, involute, kiwifruit, malamute, overshoot, parachute, persecute, prosecute, prostitute, qiviut, resolute, restitute, revolute, subacute, substitute, troubleshoot, undershoot, electrocute, Hardecanute, Inuktitut, irresolute, reconstitute

uted \üt-əd\ see ¹OOTED

utee \üt-ē\ see ¹OOTY

utely \üt-lē\ cutely, mutely, accutely, astutely, minutely, absolutely, dissolutely, irresolutely

uten \üt-ᵊn\ see UTAN

uteness \üt-nəs\ cuteness, glutenous, glutinous, muteness, mutinous, acuteness, diluteness, hirsuteness, absoluteness, destituteness, dissoluteness, irresoluteness

utenist \üt-ᵊn-əst\ lutenist, Teutonist

utenous \üt-nəs\ see UTENESS

uteous \üt-ē-əs\ beauteous, duteous, gluteus, luteous

uter \üt-ər\ cooter, neuter, fluter, hooter, looter, pewter, rooter, router, scooter, shooter, souter, suiter, suitor, tooter, tutor, accoutre, commuter, computer, confuter, crapshooter, diluter, disputer, freebooter, peashooter, recruiter, saluter, sharpshooter, six-shooter, trapshooter, two-suiter, zoot-suiter, coadjutor, executor, instituter, persecutor, prosecutor, prostitutor, troubleshooter, microcomputer, minicomputer, superminicomputer—*also* *comparatives of adjectives listed at* UTE

utes \üts\ see OOTS

uteus \üt-ē-əs\ see UTEOUS

¹uth \üt\ see UTE

²uth \üth\ see ²OOTH

¹uther \ü-thər\ Luther, Uther

²uther \ə-ther\ see ¹OTHER

uthful \üth-fəl\ ruthful, truthful, youthful, untruthful

uthless \üth-ləs\ ruthless, toothless

uti \üt-ē\ see ¹OOTY

utia \ü-shə\ fuchsia, minutia, Saint Lucia

utian \ü-shən\ see UTION

utic \üt-ik\ maieutic, scorbutic, toreutic, hermeneutic, parachutic, propaedeutic, therapeutic

utical \üt-i-kəl\ cuticle, hermeneutical, pharmaceutical

uticle \üt-i-kəl\ see UTICAL

utie \üt-ē\ see ¹OOTY

utiful \üt-i-fəl\ beautiful, dutiful

utile \üt-ᵊl\ brutal, cuittle, footle, futile, tootle, utile, inutile, Kwakiutl

utin \üt-ᵊn\ see UTAN

utine \üt-ᵊn\ see UTAN

uting \üt-iŋ\ fluting, luting, suiting, hip-shooting, sharpshooting, trapshooting

¹utinous \üt-ᵊn-əs\ glutinous, mutinous

²utinous \üt-nəs\ see UTENESS

utiny \üt-ᵊn-ē\ mutiny, scrutiny

ution \ü-shən\ Lucian, ablution, Aleutian, capuchin, Confucian, dilution, elution, locution, pollution, solution, absolution, allocution, attribution, comminution, consecution, constitution, contribution, convolution, destitution, devolution, diminution, dissolution, distribution, elocution, evolution, execution, exsolution, institution, involution, lilliputian, persecution, prosecution, prostitution, resolution, restitution, retribution, revolution, Rosicrucian, substitution, antipollution, circumlocution, electrocution, irresolution, maldistribution, reconstitution, redistribution

utionary \ü-shə-ner-ē\ illocutionary, revolutionary

utionist \ü-shnəst\ devolutionist, elocutionist, evolutionist, revolutionist, redistributionist

utish \üt-ish\ brutish, Vutish

utist \üt-əst\ chutist, flutist, absolutist, parachutist, therapeutist—*also superlatives of adjectives listed at* UTE

utive \üt-iv\ dilutive, constitutive, persecutive, substitutive

utl \ü-tᵊl\ see UTILE

utland \ət-lənd\ Jutland, Rutland

utlass \ət-ləs\ cutlass, gutless

utler \ət-lər\ butler, Butler, cutler, sutler

utless \ət-ləs\ see UTLASS

utlet \ət-lət\ cutlet, nutlet

utment \ət-mənt\ hutment, abutment

utney \ət-nē\ chutney, gluttony, Ascutney

uto \üt-ō\ Bhutto, Pluto, putto, Basuto, cornuto, Maputo, tenuto, sostenuto

uton \üt-ⁿ\ see UTAN

utor \üt-ər\ see UTER

utriment \ü-trə-mənt\ nutriment, accoutrement

uts \əts\ see UTZ

utsch \uch\ see ²UTCH

utsi \üt-sē\ see ²UZZI

utsk \ütsk\ Irkutsk, Yakutsk

utsy \ət-sē\ gutsy, klutzy

utt \ət\ see ¹UT

uttack \ət-ək\ see UTTOCK

uttal \ət-ᵊl\ see UTTLE

utte \üt\ see UTE

uttee \ət-ē\ see UTTY

¹utter \ət-ər\ butter, clutter, cutter, flutter, gutter, mutter, nutter, putter, scutter, shutter, splutter, sputter, strutter, stutter, utter, abutter, aflutter, haircutter, price-cutter, rebutter, stonecutter, unclutter, woodcutter

²utter \ùt-ər\ see ¹OOTER

uttery \ət-ə-rē\ buttery, fluttery, spluttery

¹utti \üt-ē\ see ¹OOTY

²utti \ùt-ē\ see ²OOTY

utting \ùt-iŋ\ see ¹OOTING

uttish \ət-ish\ ruttish, sluttish

uttle \ət-ᵊl\ cuittle, scuttle, shuttle, subtile, subtle, rebuttal

utto \üt-ō\ see UTO

uttock \ət-ək\ buttock, Cuttack, futtock

utton \ət-ᵊn\ button, glutton, mutton, Sutton, keybutton, unbutton, leg-of-mutton

uttony \ət-nē\ see UTNEY

utty \ət-ē\ butty, gutty, jutty, nutty, puttee, putty, rutty, smutty

utum \üt-əm\ scutum, sputum

uture \ü-chər\ blucher, future, moocher, suture

uty \üt-ē\ see ¹OOTY

utz \əts\ futz, klutz, lutz, nuts, blood-and-guts—*also plurals and possessives of nouns and third person singular presents of verbs listed at* ¹UT

utzy \ət-sē\ see UTSY

uu \ü\ see ¹EW

uvial \ü-vē-əl\ fluvial, pluvial, alluvial, colluvial, diluvial, eluvial

uvian \ü-vē-ən\ alluvion, diluvian, Peruvian, vesuvian, Vesuvian, postdiluvian, antediluvian

uvion \ü-vē-ən\ see UVIAN

uvium \ü-vē-əm\ alluvium, colluvium, effluvium, eluvium

¹ux \əks\ crux, flux, lux, tux, afflux, aw-shucks, conflux, deluxe, efflux, influx, redux, reflux, Benelux—*also plurals and possessives of nouns and third person singular presents of verbs listed at* UCK

²ux \üks\ see ²OOKS

¹uxe \üks\ see ¹OOKS

²uxe \üks\ see ²OOKS

³uxe \əks\ see ¹UX

uxion \ək-shən\ see UCTION

uy \ī\ see ¹Y

uygur \ē-gər\ see EAGER

uyot \ē-ō\ see ²IO

uyp \īp\ see IPE

¹uz \üts\ see OOTS

²uz \úz\ see ²USE

uze \üz\ see ²USE

uzz \əz\ see ¹EUSE

¹uzzi \ü-zē\ see OOZY

²uzzi \üt-sē\ Tutsi, Abruzzi

uzzle \əz-əl\ guzzle, muzzle, nuzzle, puzzle

uzzler \əz-lər\ guzzler, puzzler, gas-guzzler

uzzy \əz-ē\ fuzzy, muzzy, scuzzy

y

¹**y** \ī\ ai, ay, aye, bi, buy, by, bye, chi, cry, die, dry, dye, eye, fie, fly, fry, guy, Guy, hi, hie, high, i, I, lie, lye, my, nigh, phi, pi, pie, ply, pry, psi, rye, scythe, sei, shy, sigh, sky, sly, spry, spy, sty, Tai, Thai, thigh, thy, tie, try, vie, why, wry, wye, xi, Y , aby, agley, air-dry, ally, Altai, anti, apply, assai, awry, aye-aye, Bacchae, Baha'i, banzai, barfly, Belgae, belie, bigeye, birds-eye, blackfly, blow-dry, blowby, blowfly, blue-sky, Bottai, bone-dry, bonsai, botfly, Brunei, buckeye, bugeye, bulls-eye, bye-bye, canaille, catchfly, cat's-eye, cockeye, cockshy, comply, cross-eye, deadeye, decry, deep-fry, deep-sky, deerfly, defy, Delphi, deny, descry, drip-dry, Dubai, elhi, Eli, espy, firefly, fish-eye, flyby, forby, freeze-dry, frogeye, gadfly, gallfly, GI, good-bye, greenfly, grisaille, gun-shy, Haggai, Hawkeye, hereby, hi-fi, hog-tie, horsefly, housefly, imply, jai alai, July, Katmai, Kaui, Kenai, knee-high, lanai, Lanai, lay-by, Levi, magpie, mao-tai, Masai, medfly, Moirai, mooneye, nearby, necktie, nisi, outbye, outcry, oxeye, Panay, panfry, Parcae, piece-dye, pigsty, pinkeye, Po Hai, pop eye, potpie, Qinghai, quasi, rabbi, re-try, red-eye, rely, reply, rocaille, rough-dry, Sakai, sci-fi, semi, Sendai, serai, shanghai, Shanghai, shoofly, shut-eye, Sinai, sky-high, small-fry, sockeye, stand by, standby, stir-fry, supply, swing-by, terai, test-fly, thereby, tie-dye, titi, tongue-tie, two-ply, untie, Versailles, walleye, watcheye, well-nigh, whereby, whitefly, wise guy, worms-eye, Adonai, alibi, alkali, amplify, apple-pie, argufy, basify, beautify, butterfly, by-and-by, calcify, certify, Chou En-lai, citify, clarify, classify, cockneyfy, codify, crucify, cut-and-dry, DIY, damnify, damselfly, dandify, deify, densify, dignify, dobsonfly, do-or-die, dragonfly, edify, falsify, fancify, fortify, frenchify, fructify, gasify, Gemini, gentrify, glorify, goggle-eye, goldeneye, gratify, Haggai, hexerei, horrify, Iceni, justify, lignify, liquefy, lithify, Lorelei, lullaby, Madurai, magnify, Malachi, Maracay, modify, mollify, Molokai, Mordecai, mortify, multi-ply,

multiply, mummify, mystify,
nazify, nitrify, notify, nullify,
occupy, Olduvai, ossify,
overbuy, overfly, overlie,
pacify, Paraguay, passerby,
peccavi, petrify, PPI,
preachify, prettify, prophesy,
purify, putrefy, qualify,
quantify, ramify, rarefy,
ratify, RBI, rectify, reify, res
gestae, resupply, Russify,
samurai, sanctify, satisfy,
scarify, semidry, signify,
simplify, sine die, specify,
speechify, stratify, stultify,
stupefy, Tenebrae, terrify,
testify, tigereye, typify,
uglify, ultrahigh, underlie,
unify, Uruguay, Veneti,
verify, versify, vilify, vinify,
vitrify, vivify, zombify,
acetify, acidify, a priori,
beatify, decertify, declassify,
demystify, denazify, detoxify,
Dioscuri, disqualify,
dissatisfy, diversify, electrify,
exemplify, facetiae, Helvetii,
humidify, identify, indemnify,
intensify, objectify, personify,
preoccupy, reliquiae, reunify,
revivify, rigidify, saponify,
solemnify, solidify, syllabify,
transmogrify, undersupply,
vox populi, a fortiori,
caravanserai, corpus delicti,
deacidify, dehumidify, ex
hypothesi, modus vivendi,
nolle prosequi, oversimplify,
amicus curiae, curriculum
vitae, modus operandi

²y \ē\ see ¹EE

ya \ē-ə\ see ¹IA

yable \ī-ə-bəl\ see ¹IABLE

yad \ī-əd\ dryad, dyad, naiad,
sayyid, triad, hamadryad,
jeremiad

yan \ī-ən\ see ¹ION

yant \ī-ənt\ see IANT

yatt \ī-ət\ see IET

ybe \īb\ see ¹IBE

ybele \ib-ə-lē\ Cybele,
ambiboly

yber \ī-bər\ see IBER

ybia \i-bē-ə\ see IBIA

ybris \ī-brəs\ see IBROUS

ycad \ī-kəd\ cycad, spiked

ycan \ī-kən\ see ¹ICHEN

yean \ī-cən\ see ¹ICHEN

yce \īs\ see ¹ICE

¹ych \ik\ see ICK

²ych \īk\ see ²IKE

yche \ī-kē\ see ¹IKE

ychnis \ik-nəs\ see ICKNESS

ycia \ish-ə\ see ¹ITIA

ycian \ish-ən\ see ITION

ycin \īs-ᵊn\ see ¹ISON

¹ycle \ī-kəl\ cycle, Michael,
recycle, Calvin cycle,
epicycle, Exercycle,
hemicycle, kilocycle,
motorcycle, unicycle, Wanne-
Eickel

²ycle \ik-əl\ see ICKLE

ycler \ik-lər\ see ICKLER

yd \ü-id\ see UID

yde \īd\ see ¹IDE

ydia \i-dē-ə\ see IDIA

ydian \id-ē-ən\ see IDIAN

ydice \id-ə-sē\ see IDICE

ydney \id-nē\ see IDNEY

ye \ī\ see ¹Y

yeable \ī-ə-bəl\ see ¹IABLE

yed \īd\ see ¹IDE

yer \īr\ see ¹IRE

yeth \ī-əth\ see ¹IATH

yfe \īf\ see IFE

yfed \ər-əd\ see OVED

yg \ig\ see IG

ygamous \ig-ə-məs\ see IGAMOUS

ygamy \ig-ə-mē\ see IGAMY

ygia \ī-jə\ see IJAH

ygian \ij-ən\ Phrygian, pidgin, pigeon, smidgen, stygian, wigeon, religion, Cantabrigian, irreligion, callipygian

ygiene \ī-jēn\ see AIJIN

ygma \ig-mə\ see IGMA

ygnet \ig-nət\ cygnet, signet

ygnus \ig-nəs\ see IGNESS

ygos \ī-gəs\ see YGOUS

ygous \ī-gəs\ gigas, azygos, callipygous, hemizygous, homozygous, steatopygous

ygrapher \ig-rə-fər\ see IGRAPHER

ygraphist \ig-rə-fəst\ see IGRAPHIST

ygyny \ij-ə-nē\ see IGINE

ying \ī-iŋ\ crying, flying, lying, trying, high-flying, low-lying, outlying, undying, nitrifying, terrifying, underlying

yke \īk\ see ²IKE

yked \īkt\ see ¹IKED

yl \ēl\ see ²EAL

ylan \il-ən\ see ILLON

ylar \ī-lər\ see ILAR

yle \īl\ see ¹ILE

ylem \ī-ləm\ see ILUM

yler \ī-lər\ see ILAR

ylet \ī-lət\ see ILOT

yley \ī-lē\ see YLY

yli \ē-lē\ see EELY

ylic \il-ik\ see ILIC

ylie \ī-lē\ see YLY

yling \ī-liŋ\ see ¹ILING

yll \īl\ see ¹ILE

ylla \il-ə\ see ²ILLA

yllable \il-ə-bəl\ see ILLABLE

yllary \il-ə-rē\ see ILLARY

yllic \il-ik\ see ILIC

yllis \il-əs\ see ILLUS

yllium \il-ē-əm\ see ILIUM

¹yllo \ē-lō\ see ²ILO

²yllo \ī-lō\ see ¹ILO

ylum \ī-ləm\ see ILUM

ylus \ī-ləs\ see ILUS

yly \ī-lē\ dryly, highly, maile, Philae, riley, shyly, slyly, smiley, Wiley, wily, Wyley, wryly, life of Riley

ym \im\ see ¹IM

yma \ī-mə\ Chaima, cyma

yman \ī-mən\ see IMEN

ymathy \im-ə-thē\ see IMOTHY

ymbal \im-bəl\ see IMBLE

ymbalist \im-bə-ləst\ cymbalist, symbolist

ymbol \im-bəl\ see IMBLE

ymbolist \im-bə-ləst\ see YMBALIST

yme \īm\ see ¹IME

ymeless \īm-ləs\ see IMELESS

ymen \ī-mən\ see IMEN

ymer \ī-mər\ see ¹IMER

¹ymic \ī-mik\ thymic, enzymic

²ymic \im-ik\ gimmick, mimic, bulimic, acronymic, antonymic, eponymic, homonymic, matronymic, metonymic, patronymic, synonymic, toponymic

ymical \im-i-kəl\ see IMICAL

ymie \ī-mē\ see IMY

ymion \im-ē-ən\ see IMIAN

ymity \im-ət-ē\ see IMITY

ymmetry \im-ə-trē\ see IMETRY

ymn \im\ see ¹IM

ymp \imp\ see IMP

ymph \imf\ lymph, nymph

ymric \im-rik\ Cymric, limerick

ymry \əm-rē\ see ²UMMERY

ymus \ī-məs\ see IMIS

ymy \ī-mē\ see IMY

yn \in\ see ¹IN

ynah \ī-nə\ see ¹INA

ynast \ī-nəst\ see ¹INIST

¹ynch \inch\ see INCH

²ynch \iŋk\ see INK

yncher \in-chər\ see INCHER

ynd \īnd\ see ¹IND

yndic \in-dik\ see INDIC

yne \īn\ see ¹INE

ynein \in-ē-ən\ see ¹INIAN

yness \ī-nəs\ see ¹INUS

ynia \in-ē-ə\ see INIA

ynic \in-ik\ see ²INIC

ynical \in-i-kəl\ see INICAL

ynn \in\ see ¹IN

ynne \in\ see ¹IN

ynth \inth\ see INTH

ynthia \in-thē-ə\ see INTHIA

ynx \iŋs\ see INX

yon \ī-ən\ see ¹ION

yone \ī-ə-nē\ see YONY

yony \ī-ə-nē\ bryony, Alcyone

yp \ip\ see IP

ypal \ī-pəl\ typal, disciple, archetypal, prototypal

ype \īp\ see IPE

yper \ī-pər\ see IPER

ypey \ī-pē\ see IPY

yph \if\ see IFF

yphen \ī-fən\ hyphen, siphon

yphic \if-ik\ see IFIC

yphony \if-ə-nē\ see IPHONY

ypic \ip-ik\ typic, philippic, genotypic, holotypic, stereotypic

yping \ī-piŋ\ see IPING

ypo \ī-pō\ hypo, typo

ypress \ī-prəs\ cypress, Cyprus, viperous

yprus \ī-prəs\ see YPRESS

ypse \ips\ see IPS

ypso \ip-sō\ see IPSO

ypsy \ip-sē\ gypsy, Gypsy, tipsy

ypt \ipt\ see IPT

yptian \ip-shən\ see IPTION

yptic \ip-tik\ cryptic, diptych, styptic, triptych, ecliptic, elliptic, apocalyptic

ypy \ī-pē\ see IPY

yr \ir\ see ²EER

yra \ī-rə\ Ira, Lyra, Myra, naira, bell-lyra, hegira, hetaira, palmyra, spirogyra

yral \ī-rəl\ see IRAL

yrant \ī-rənt\ see IRANT

yre \īr\ see ¹IRE

yreal \ir-ē-əl\ see ERIAL

yria \ir-ē-ə\ see ¹ERIA

yriad \ir-ē-əd\ see ERIOD

yrian \ir-ē-ən\ see ¹ERIAN

yric \ī-rik\ pyric, oneiric, panegyric, see ²ERIC

yrical \ir-i-kəl\ see ²ERICAL

¹yrie \ir-ē\ see EARY

²yrie \ī-rē\ see ¹IARY

yril \ir-əl\ see ¹ERAL

yrist \ir-əst\ see ¹ERIST

yrium \ir-ē-əm\ see ERIUM

yrna \ər-nə\ see ERNA

¹yro \ī-rō\ biro, Cairo, gyro, Gyro, tyro

²yro \ir-ō\ see ³ERO

yron \īr-ən\ see IREN

yros \ī-rəs\ see IRUS

yrrh \ər\ see ¹EUR
yrrha \ir-ə\ see ²ERA
yrrhic \ir-ik\ see ²ERIC
yrrhus \ir-əs\ see EROUS
yrse \ərs\ see ERSE
yrsus \ər-səs\ see ERSUS
yrtle \ərt-ᵊl\ see ERTILE
yrup \ər-əp\ see IRRUP
yrupy \ər-ə-pē\ see IRRUPY
yrus \ī-rəs\ see IRUS
ysail \ī-səl\ see ¹ISAL
ysch \ish\ see ¹ISH
yse \īs\ see ¹ICE
ysh \ish\ see ¹ISH
¹ysia \ish-ə\ see ITIA
²ysia \izh-ə\ see ISIA
¹ysian \is-ē-ən\ Piscean,
    Odyssean, Dionysian
²ysian \ish-ən\ see ITION
³ysian \izh-ən\ see ISION
⁴ysian \ī-sē-ən\ see ¹ISCEAN
ysical \iz-i-kəl\ physical,
    quizzical, metaphysical
ysis \ī-səs\ see ISIS
ysm \iz-əm\ see ISM
ysmal \iz-məl\ dismal, abysmal,
    baptismal, cataclysmal,
    catechismal
yson \īs-ᵊn\ see ¹ISON
yss \is\ see ¹ISS
yssal \is-əl\ see ISTLE
yssean \is-ē-ən\ see ¹YSIAN
ysseus \ish-əs\ see ¹ICIOUS
yssum \is-əm\ see ISSOME
yssus \is-əs\ see ISSUS

yst \ist\ see ²IST
ystal \is-tᵊl\ see ISTAL
¹yster \is-tər\ see ISTER
²yster \ī-stər\ see ¹EISTER
ystery \is-trē\ see ISTORY
ystic \is-tik\ see ISTIC
ystical \is-ti-kəl\ see ISTICAL
ystine \is-tən\ see ISTON
¹ysus \ē-səs\ see ESIS
²ysus \ī-səs\ see ISIS
yta \īt-ə\ see ¹ITA
yte \īt\ see ¹ITE
yterate \it-ə-rət\ see ITERATE
ytes \īt-ēz\ see ITES
¹ythe \ī\ see ¹Y
²ythe \īth̷\ see ¹ITHE
ythia \ith-ē-ə\ lithia, Scythia,
    forsythia, stichomythia
ythian \ith-ē-ən\ Pythian,
    Scythian
ythmic \ith̷-mik\ rhythmic,
    arrhythmic, eurythmic,
    logarithmic
ythy \i-thē\ see ITHY
ytic \it-ik\ see ITIC
ytical \it-i-kəl\ see ITICAL
ytics \it-iks\ see ITICS
yting \īt-iŋ\ see ITING
ytis \ī-təs\ see ITIS
ytton \it-ᵊn\ see ITTEN
yve \īv\ see ¹IVE
yx \iks\ see ¹IX
yxia \ik-sē-ə\ see IXIA
yxie \ik-sē\ see IXIE
yze \īz\ see IZE